64.00

D0555176

PATERNOSTER BIBLICAL MONOGRAPHS

Paul, Moses, and the History of Israel

The Letter/Spirit Contrast and the Argument from Scripture in 2 Corinthians 3

Series Preface

One of the major objectives of Paternoster is to serve biblical scholarship by providing a channel for the publication of theses and other monographs of high quality at affordable prices. Paternoster stands within the broad evangelical tradition of Christianity. Our authors would describe themselves as Christians who recognise the authority of the Bible, maintain the centrality of the gospel message and assent to the classical credal statements of Christian belief. There is diversity within this constituency; advances in scholarship are possible only if there is freedom for frank debate on controversial issues and for the publication of new and sometimes provocative proposals. What is offered in this series is the best of writing by committed Christians who are concerned to develop well-founded biblical scholarship in a spirit of loyalty to the historic faith.

Series Editors

I. Howard Marshall, Honorary Research Professor of New Testament, University of Aberdeen, Scotland, UK

Richard J. Bauckham, Professor of New Testament Studies and Bishop Wardlaw Professor, University of St Andrews, Scotland, UK

Craig Blomberg, Distinguished Professor of New Testament, Denver Seminary, Colorado, USA

Robert P. Gordon, Regius Professor of Hebrew, University of Cambridge, UK

Tremper Longman III, Robert H. Gundry Professor and Chair of the Department of Biblical Studies, Westmont College, Santa Barbara, California, USA

PATERNOSTER BIBLICAL MONOGRAPHS

Paul, Moses, and the History of Israel

**The Letter/Spirit Contrast
and the Argument from Scripture
in 2 Corinthians 3**

Scott J. Hafemann

WIPF & STOCK · Eugene, Oregon

Wipf and Stock Publishers
199 W 8th Ave, Suite 3
Eugene, OR 97401

Paul, Moses, and the History of Israel
The Letter/Spirit Contrast and the Argument from Scripture in 2 Corinthians 3
By Hafemann, Scott J.
Copyright©2005 Paternoster
ISBN 13: 978-1-59752-775-0
Publication date 6/10/2006
Previously published by Paternoster, 2005

This Edition reprinted by Wipf and Stock Publishers by arrangement with Paternoster

To
Prof. Dr. Peter Stulmacher,
Doktorvater

Acknowledgments

This book has had a long gestation period. The initial seeds were planted by my Doktorvater, Prof. Dr. Peter Stuhlmacher, who first suggested in 1980 that I write my dissertation on 2 Corinthians 3. Although I began to do so at that time, it soon became obvious that all I could hope to accomplish then was to complete the first part of the project. This initial work became my dissertation on 2 Cor. 2:14–3:3, the majority of which was first published under the title, *Suffering and the Spirit* (J.C.B. Mohr [Paul Siebeck], 1986), and then later released in an abridged form as *Suffering and Ministry in the Spirit* (Wm.B. Eerdmans, 1990). But the purpose of this earlier work was always to prepare to go on to the heart of the matter, as indicated by the fact that Chapter One of the present work is built upon an unpublished section of my dissertation. This goal would not have been accomplished had it not been for the continued support and encouragement of Prof. Stuhlmacher, under whose supervision and recommendation I enjoyed a year of post-graduate study at the University of Tübingen in the academic year 1989–1990. At that time he wisely insisted that I first bring this dormant seed to fruition before doing anything else, and it was this year of study that made it possible in the midst of the rigors of teaching and pastoring to bring this book to completion. Because Prof. Stuhlmacher's work on the eschatological framework of Paul's thought, together with his own willingness to rethink the age-old question of Paul and the Law, provided much of the impetus for my thinking, and because he has continued to be a model of what it means to be a Christian scholar in ways too many to recount here, I have dedicated this study to him with gratitude and admiration. From the very beginning he has continued to take a genuine interest in my work and life far beyond what any student deserves. His support has been invaluable, and those who are familiar with his contributions will detect his influence in the following pages in ways too subtle to footnote. In a very real way, this book bears the fruit of his labors, though he will no doubt not be pleased with all of my conclusions!

This study would not have been feasible without the generous support of the Alexander von Humboldt-Stiftung, Bonn, Germany, which provided a research fellowship to underwrite my year of study in Tübingen. Their commitment to research and support of their scholars provide a standard of excellence to be emulated. I am thankful to them and to Prof. Dr. Martin Hengel, without whose help and recommendation this fellowship would also not have been possible. I owe them a debt of gratitude I cannot repay. In addition, I wish to thank the The Association of Theological Schools in America and Canada, who granted me a Theological Scholarship and Research Award in 1989–1990 to meet the added expenses of living and studying in Germany. Without help from foundations and associations like these, serious scholarship would be much disadvantaged. In this regard I would like to express my appreciation to Profs. Hengel and Hofius for their willingness to accept this work in their series, and to the leadership and staff of J.C.B. Mohr (Paul Siebeck) for their publishing efforts and commitment to quality.

Many people have contributed to this project in different ways through the years, not the least of which are those scholars who have written serious works on 2 Cor. 3 in the last decade. This recent flurry of interest in 2 Cor. 3 has highlighted the significance of this passage for understanding Paul's thought and provided the contours for the current discussion. Although I often go my own way in the work which follows, testing my thesis against the recent works on 2 Cor. 3 of Belleville, Dumbrell, Hays, Hofius, Jones, Liebers, Prümm, Renwick, Stockhausen, Theobald, Vollenweider, and Wright has meant much more clarity in my conclusions. I am greatly indebted to their efforts. I am indebted as well to the trustees of Gordon-Conwell Theological Seminary who granted me a sabbatical in 1989–1990 and again in the fall of 1992, and to my colleagues for their genuine support and the value they place on research and writing. Among them, I am especially grateful to Greg Beale for his constant interest in the questions of exegesis and theology (rare in these days!), his own expertise in biblical theology, and for our ongoing discussions concerning the implications of inaugurated eschatology. I would also like to thank my teaching assistants Jeff Wisdom, who invested many hours in the bibliography, and David O'Brien, whose careful proof reading saved me from many errors. During his Th.M. studies Ed Keazirian read chapter three and made several helpful suggestions based on his own research concerning the golden calf backdrop to Romans 1:18 ff., for which I am thankful. Craig Torell provided helpful assistance in running searches on the TLG data base. I am also grateful to Jim Sweeney, who read the entire manuscript with his careful eye for detail. Special thanks go to my friend Paul House, whose interest in my work often kept it going in the midst of many other demands. Kathleen Stumcke gave freely of her time and editorial talent as an act of Christian charity. My sons John and Eric are to be thanked for their own recognition and acceptance of the place of "the book" in my life. And finally, this book, like all I do, came about in large measure because of my wife, Debara, who with her support took on this project as her own.

January 16, 1995   Scott Hafemann

Contents

Part Two

The Letter/Spirit Contrast within the Context of the
Second Giving of the Law

Introduction

The Current Debate Surrounding the Letter/Spirit Contrast and the Context for Solving It

In 2 Corinthians 3:6 Paul supports the assertion that his apostolic ministry is not "of the letter, but of the Spirit" with his now famous statement, "For the letter kills, but the Spirit makes alive".[1] This seemingly proverbial, thesis-like statement and the context within which it is found epitomize why Second Corinthians has come to be known as both "the paradise and the despair of the commentator."[2] Though theologically rich and suggestive, its apparent clarity and seemingly transparent significance for understanding Paul's thought are dangerously misleading. Embedded within an extended discussion concerning the nature and validity of Paul's apostolic office (2:14–3:6a and 4:1 ff.), and introduced just prior to an interpretation of the Old Testament tradition from Exodus 34:29 ff. (3:7–18), this contrast is one of the most difficult passages to understand within the Pauline corpus.[3] If "context is king" in exegetical study, the letter/Spirit contrast is protected by a very formidable monarch indeed.

1. The Modern Consensus Concerning the Meaning of the Letter/Spirit Contrast in 2 Cor. 3:6

The appeal of an exegetical and theological paradise often overshadows the perils of the passage, which, if not leading to despair, ought at least to create caution. Thus, in spite of the many interpretive and historical problems surrounding this text, there existed until recently a surprising degree of confidence that a consensus had already been reached regarding the meaning of the

---

[1] For the sake of uniformity, γράμμα will be translated literally as "letter" throughout this study. This should not be taken, however, as a prior indication of my own understanding of its actual meaning, since the precise denotation of this term in 2 Cor. 3:6 is once again a matter of dispute. See below, chapter two.

[2] Ralph P. Martin, *2 Corinthians, WBC Vol. 40*, 1986, p. x.

[3] The first part of this context was the subject of my earlier study, *Suffering and the Spirit, An Exegetical Study of II Cor. 2:14–3:3 within the Context of the Corinthian Correspondence, WUNT 2. Reihe 19*, 1986. But cf. already A. Jülicher, *Einleitung in das Neue Testament*, 1931[7], p. 85, who calls the "Lobpreis" in 3:1–4:6 the "rätselhaftesten unter den Paulusbriefen" (taken from I. Hermann, *Kyrios und Pneuma. Studien zur Christologie der paulinischen Hauptbriefe, SANT 2*, 1961, p. 20).

letter/Spirit antithesis. According to the prevailing opinion, γράμμα represented the Mosaic Law which "kills" because of its demand for an obedience impossible to render, and/or because it makes demands *per se* and thus produces, by its very nature, a legalistic works-righteousness. In contrast, πνεῦμα stood for the Gospel which, due to its promise of life and the power of the Spirit, "makes alive." Thus, with little serious regard for its own context, 2 Cor. 3:6 could simply and quickly be interpreted in line with Paul's other contrasts between the "works of the Law," the "Law," or simply "works" on the one hand, and "faith" or "grace" on the other (cf. Gal. 2:16; 3:2, 5, 10–12, 21–25; 5:4; ; Rom. 3:20–22, 28; 4:1–4; 6:14 f.; 9:30–32; 11:6). As such it was read as a distinction between two contrary principles of salvation or two theologically distinct dispensations.[4]

This consensus was even more surprising in view of the fact that for the 1200 years stretching from Origen to the Reformation there existed not one, but two competing interpretations of the letter/Spirit antithesis in 2 Cor. 3:6.[5] As G. Ebeling summarized it,

"In the ancient Church and in the Middle Ages the understanding of Spirit and letter gravitated into the interpretation of the antithesis as a *hermeneutical* principle (i.e. as the distinction between a literal and spiritual sense of Scripture) on the one hand, and as an *economy-of-salvation* contrast (i.e. as the distinction between the law and the Spirit, the OT and the NT) ... on the other."[6]

Ebeling's distinction between the "hermeneutical" and "economy-of-salvation" interpretations of the letter/Spirit antithesis was earlier proposed by B.

---

[4] This position received its classic formulation at the beginning of our century in Paul Feine's *Das gesetzfreie Evangelium des Paulus*, 1899, esp. pp. 159 f. and 195 f. on 2 Cor. 3:6 ff. For a more recent exposition of this view in relationship to 2 Cor. 3:6, see K. Prümm, *Theologie des Zweiten Korintherbriefes, Apostolat und christliche Wirklichkeit Band II/ Teil I, Diakonia Pneumatos. Der Zweite Korintherbrief als Zugang zur Apostolischen Botschaft*, 1960, pp. 176–188, 194–210. For the extension of the "killing" function of the Law to the nature of the Law *per se*, see R. Bultmann, *Theology of the New Testament, I*, 1951, pp. 240, 260–264, and his famous statement that *"man's effort to achieve salvation by keeping the Law* only leads him into sin, indeed this effort itself in the end *is already sin"* (p. 264, emphasis his).

[5] There is to date no comprehensive study of the history of the interpretation of the letter/ Spirit contrast available. Nevertheless, the basic lines of its development have already become clear through the initial works of K. Prümm, "Der Abschnitt über die Doxa des Apostolats, 2 Kor 3:1–4:6 in der Deutung des Hl. Johannes Chrysostomus, Eine Untersuchung zur Auslegungsgeschichte des paulinischen Pneuma," *Biblica* 30 (1949) 161–196 and 377–400; Beryl Smalley, *The Study of the Bible in the Middle Ages*, 1952; B. Schneider, "The Meaning of St. Paul's Antithesis 'The Letter and the Spirit'," *CBQ* 15 (1953) 163–207; R.M. Grant, *The Letter and the Spirit*, 1957; G. Ebeling, "Geist und Buchstabe," *RGG³*, Bd. 2, 1958, pp. 1290–1296; and Karl Froelich, "'Always to Keep the Literal Sense in Holy Scripture Means to Kill One's Soul': The State of Biblical Hermeneutics at the Beginning of the Fifteenth Century," in *Literary Uses of Typology from the Late Middle Ages to the Present*, ed. Earl Miner, 1977, pp. 20–48.

[6] "Geist," p. 1292 (translation given due to the abbreviated nature of the formulations in the original).

Schneider. But in Schneider's terminology, the distinction was between those who held to a "formalistic" interpretation and those who supported a "realistic" view. In the former, γϱάμμα referred to the material or literal sense of a document or norm over against its spiritual sense. In the latter, γϱάμμα represented the Mosaic law as a "cold, naked written law, lacking any internal force to give help towards its observance," while πνεῦμα referred to the Holy Spirit as the agent of the internal, active reality of grace, indwelling one as the "vivifying principle of Christian life."[7]

In the light of recent work on 2 Cor. 3:6 and the renewed debate concerning Paul's view of the Law and post-biblical Judaism, the clear-cut distinction which is made between these two competing interpretations is jarring. Equally striking are the stark negative connotations associated with the "letter" as the Mosaic law in the "realistic" ("economy-of-salvation") interpretation. We will return to these observations below. At this point in our discussion, however, the history of the interpretation of this passage has another important lesson to teach us. Those living in the current era of biblical interpretation must not overlook the fact that the consensus which existed in the modern period until recently is precisely the *opposite* of the predominant view in the Middle Ages. Scholars agree that Origen was the father of the "hermeneutical" or "formalistic" interpretation of the letter/Spirit contrast, and that his influence, as embodied in the Alexandrian school of exegesis,[8] soon became dominant, if not all-pervasive, until the Reformation.[9] What is significant for us to note is that 2 Cor. 3:6 became *the* biblical proof-text used to support the hermeneutical program of distinguishing between a literal or external and a spiritual or internal sense of Scripture and the allegorical method through which it was carried out, which together became determinative for the Middle Ages.[10]

---

[7] "Meaning," p. 164. Ebeling himself notes the correspondence between his view and Schneider's, cf. "Geist," p. 1292.

[8] The Fathers most often associated with the Alexandrian school are Origen (d. 254), Athanasius (d. 373), Gregory of Nazianzus (d. 389), Basil (d. 379), Gregory of Nyssa (d. 395), Cyril of Alexandria (d. 444), Eucherius of Lyons (d. 449), and Faustus of Riez (d. 490/500); cf. Schneider, "Meaning," pp. 164–184 and Ebeling, "Geist," p. 1292. The dates of their deaths are taken from *The New International Dictionary of the Christian Church*, ed. J.D. Douglas, 1974.

[9] Opinions vary as to the actual extent of the Alexandrian school's dominance. For example, Schneider gives the impression that the "realistic" approach was almost as important, whereas Grant and Smalley emphasize the pervasiveness of the "hermeneutical" approach. Smalley, *Bible*, p. 14, can even conclude that "To write a history of Origenist influence on the West would be tantamount to writing a history of western exegesis."

[10] For a vivid illustration of this from the writings of Claudius, Bishop of Turin (d. 827), cf. Smalley, *Bible*, p. 1. Origen's influence and the central role played by 2 Cor. 3:6 among the passages he used to justify his allegorical interpretations (i.e., Rom. 7:14; 1 Cor. 2:10, 12, 16; 9:9–10; 10:11; 2 Cor. 3:6; 3:15–16; Gal. 4:24) can be seen in the work of Gregory of Nyssa as outlined by Ronald E. Heine, "Gregory of Nyssa's Apology for Allegory," *Vigiliae Christianae* 38 (1984) 360–370, pp. 363, 365.

The minority view, which advocated a "realistic" or "economy-of-salvation" interpretation of 2 Cor. 3:6, also continued to exist, of course, throughout the Middle Ages. But its emphasis on literal exegesis, as it came to be associated with the Antiochene school, did little to curve the excesses of the allegorical approach. M.F. Wiles suggests that the reason for its lack of influence was that later generations considered third-century Antioch to be "a training ground for Arians" and the fourth-century Antiochene school 'a nursery for Nestorians."[11] Even John Chrysostom, "the one leading Antiochene scholar of that time to remain free of any suspicion of heretical taint," had little impact on subsequent practice.[12] Smalley attributes this to the fact that his works were not theological treatises, but sermons or exhortations based for the most part on the Pauline epistles. As such they exercised little influence on exegetical practice. For ironically, the very epistles which provided the proof-texts for the legitimacy of the allegorical method were themselves ill-sorted for such a method.[13] Moreover, even those within the "Antiochene School" were concerned with the spiritual character, meaning, and application of the biblical text *(theoria)* in which the prophet expressed *both* a historical *and* future messianic meaning in the one literal sense.[14] Hence, to the proponents of the allegorical method, the position of the Antiochene school seemed quite compatible with that of their own, since an emphasis on the literal sense of Scripture could be accepted as appropriate to those passages not suitable for allegorizing without affecting at all the validity of the allegorical method *per se*. As is often the case, the majority view simply incorporated the minority emphasis as part of its own position, thus essentially nullifying the latter's particular contribution. Consequently,

"Antiochene exegesis as a distinct method had been forgotten by the time it would have been useful, forgotten beyond hope of recovery. It was missing from the vast amount of material to be 'received' in the 12th and 13th centuries from Greek originals."[15]

---

[11] Cf. M.F. Wiles, "Theodore of Mopsuestia as Representative of the Antiochene School," *The Cambridge History of the Bible, Vol. 1, From the Beginning to Jerome*, ed. P.R. Ackroyd and C.F. Evans, 1970, pp. 489–510, pp. 489 f.

[12] Wiles, "Theodore of Mopsuestia," pp. 489 f.

[13] Cf. Smalley, *Bible*, p. 18.

[14] I owe this point to Bradley Nassif's seminar paper, "Spiritual Exegesis in the School of Antioch," "History of Exegesis Section," Society of Biblical Literature Annual Meeting, Nov. 18, 1990. See now his *Mystical "Insight" (theoria) in John Chrysostom's Literal Exegesis of Scripture*, Ph.D. diss., Fordham University, 1991. See too Karlfried Froehlich, *Biblical Interpretation in the Early Church*, 1984, p. 20, who also points out that the contrast between the two approaches to Scripture was never black and white, since even the Antiochene exegetes held to a higher sense of Scripture (i.e., the *theoria),* though their methodological emphasis was certainly different.

[15] Smalley, *Bible*, p. 20. Among the Fathers representing the "realistic" interpretation, Schneider, "Meaning," pp. 164–184, lists Tertullian (d. 215/220), Ephraem (d. 373), Apollinarius of Laodicea (?), Ambrosiaster (?), John Chrysostom (d. 407), Augustine (d. 430),

The history of this unstable merger between the allegorical and literal approaches, with the allegorical method assuming the role of "senior partner," can be traced from Ausgustine[16] to the Reformers.[17] Due to this merger, 2 Cor. 3:6 could be used for over 1200 years to support both a *hermeneutical program* focused on the fourfold sense of Scripture,[18] and a *theological distinction* between two economies of salvation, the Law and the Gospel, the old and the new covenants, or in effect, Judaism and Christianity. In other words, Paul's letter/Spirit antithesis sustained two radically different interpretations and could be used for two very different purposes. It was not until the Reformation that this merger came to an end, and with its dissolution the modern history of the interpretation of the letter/Spirit contrast began.

Severian of Gabala (d. 408), Pelagius (d. after 424), Ps-Jerome (?), Ps-Primasius (?), Theodoret (d. 458), and Gennadius I of Constantinople (d. 471) (dates where available again from the *New Intern. Dict. of the Christian Church*, see above, n. 8). Schneider regards Theodore of Mopsuestia (d. 428) as holding both positions, while Smalley, *Bible*, p. 15 and Wiles, "Theodore of Mopsuestia," pp. 507 f., regard him as a representative solely of the Antiochene school.

[16] Here is not the place to enter into the debate concerning whether Augustine represented the "realistic" view alone, or in fact held to both possibilities. The issue revolves around the relative value of the positions presented in his works *De doctrina Christiana* ("hermeneutical") and *De spiritu et littera* ("realistic"). Ebeling, "Geist," pp. 1292 f., views the latter as the key to Augustine's position, while Smalley, *Bible*, p. 23, and Froehlich, "Biblical Hermeneutics," pp. 23, 31, view the former as Augustine's "hermeneutical handbook" or "philosophy of Bible study" and therefore argue that he represented both positions. But all would agree with Ebeling's conclusion, "Geist," p. 1293, that the "fact that Augustine did not prevent the coexistence of the two interpretations determined the tradition of the Middle Ages."

[17] Cf. K. Froehlich's work, "Biblical Hermeneutics," for an insightful analysis of how this double tradition was questioned and reaffirmed in the 15th cent. Council of Constance (1414–1418). For a helpful survey of the ways in which the two approaches could be combined, especially in the "double literal sense" of Nicholas of Lyra (d. 1349) and Paul of Burgos (d. 1435) and in the identification of the spiritual with the literal or "prophetical literal sense" of Faber in his editions of the Psalms (1509) and commentary on Paul's epistles (1512), see Heiko Oberman, "Biblical Exegesis: The Literal and the Spiritual Sense of Scripture," in his *Forerunners of the Reformation, The Shape of Late Medieval Thought*, 1966, pp. 281–296. As Oberman points out, Faber claimed that the "'precise' or 'historical sense' is the letter which kills the spirit" (p. 287), and that the spiritual sense, which was equated with the literal, is "not available through simple grammatical exegesis" (p. 288). For Faber, this grammatical, objective reading of the OT was to be associated with rabbinic exegesis, with its focus on the "naked letter," the antidote to which was to return to the Scriptures themselves (p. 289). In contrast, Jean Gerson (d. 1429) had, a century earlier, taken this same concern for the true literal sense of Scripture to support a return to the tradition of the Church against the attempts of the Hussites to base their teaching on the Scriptures alone (cf. pp. 289 f.). Oberman thus traces one line of tradition "from Lyra through Burgos, Pérez, Faber, to Luther," in contrast to that which runs from Gerson to the Counter Reformation (p. 291).

[18] I.e. the original literal/spiritual division was expanded by naming three specific modes of the spiritual sense of Scripture: allegory or typology, tropology or morality, and anagogy or eschatology. This expansion first appears in Augustine's contemporary John Cassion's *Conlationes*, XIV.8. Cf. Smalley, *Bible*, pp. 27 f., and Froehlich, "Biblical Hermeneutics," p. 23.

The contribution of the Reformation to the modern understanding of the letter/Spirit contrast was twofold. It was now no longer possible to accept the merger between the allegorical and literal approaches to the Bible which stood at the heart of the interpretive tradition of the Middle Ages. The allegorical method associated with Origen was explicitly rejected (though of course it continued on in practice) in favor of the minority view of the Antiochene school.[19] As a consequence of this reversal, the corresponding and dominant hermeneutical interpretation of 2 Cor. 3:6 was also rejected. Rather than referring to the literal meaning of the Old Testament, γράμμα came to be seen as referring exclusively to the Law, with its ministry of death and condemnation, while πνεῦμα became an equivalent for the Gospel, with its life-producing message of faith.[20] Against the backdrop of the Middle Ages, the unilateral nature of this position stood in bold relief. Both Luther and Calvin take as their starting point an exegetical decision concerning Paul's *one* intention in 2 Cor. 3:6.[21] As a result, the use of 2 Cor. 3:6 to support the classical hermeneutical distinction between the literal and spiritual sense of the Scriptures was now completely replaced by its use as a proof-text for the Reformation contrast between the Law and the Gospel.

Finally, it was the eventual rise of the "historical-critical" method in the modern period, characterized by an insistence on rediscovering an author's one intention,[22] that brought the Reformation impulse concerning 2 Cor. 3:6 to its climax. For when forced to choose, modern scholars almost unanimously decided that Paul's expressed intention in the statement, "the letter kills, but the Spirit makes alive," was to introduce a theological "economy-of-salvation" contrast, *rather than* a contrast which could serve as a basis for a new, distinctively Christian hermeneutic.[23] In this respect, F.W. Farrar anticipated

---

[19] For an example of the explicit rejection of Origen's program, cf. Luther's "Epistel am XII. Sonntag nach Trinitatis" (Sept. 3, 1536) concerning 2 Cor. 3:4–11 in *WA* 22.211–231, esp. 22.219.1, 15–17, 21 f., 28–38; and Calvin's comments to 3:6 (found in T.A. Smail, *The Second Epistle of Paul the Apostle to the Corinthians and the Epistles to Timothy, Titus and Philemon, Calvin's New Testament Commentaries, Vol. 10*, 1964, pp. 41–43).

[20] For examples of Luther's understanding of 2 Cor. 3:6, cf. *WA* 22.219.23–25; 22.219.28–38 and 220.1–14; 22.217.20–37; 22.222.23 ff.; 8.495.15–19; 8.249.3–8; 12.569.18–25; 10 III.207.1–4; 10 III.205 Anm.; 10 III.89.12–15. It is beyond our purposes to investigate the application Luther made of this distinction in his struggle with Rome. For Calvin's view, cf., besides his commentary, *Institutes* II.11.8 and I.9.3.

[21] Cf. Calvin's dismissal of Origen's position with the assertion that "in fact nothing could be further from (Paul's) mind," *Second Epistle*, p. 42.

[22] For just one example of the many modern formulations of this goal, see Norman Perrin, "Eschatology and Hermeneutics: Reflections on Method in the Interpretation of the NT," *JBL* 93 (1974) 3–14, p. 4, who defines the goal of historical criticism to be "the attempt to understand the meaning of a text in its specific and original historical context, the endeavor to recover, so far as is possible, the meaning intended by the author and understood by the first readers or hearers."

[23] But see M. Güdemann, "Spirit and Letter in Judaism and Christianity," *Jewish Quarterly Review* 4 (1892), 345–356, who attempted to argue (unconvincingly) that Paul's con-

our century well when he responded to Origen's use of 2 Cor. 3:6 by concluding that "the foundations of his exegetical system are built upon the sand."[24]
For almost a century later, C.H. Dodd spoke for modern scholarship as a
whole in his judgment that the day Ambrose persuaded Augustine that the let-
ter/Spirit contrast in 3:6 meant that the literal understanding of the OT was
dangerous and the allegorical edifying was "an unlucky day for Christian theology."[25] Until recently, the legacy and dominance of Origen's interpretation
and the allegorical method which it supported had thus been decisively overturned in favor of a "realistic" or theological interpretation of the letter/Spirit
contrast understood almost universally in terms of the Law/Gospel antithesis
inherited from the Reformation. [26] But Dodd's statement appeared in the same
year that E.P. Sanders' programmatic work *Paul and Palestinian Judaism* was
published.[27] And since then, students of Paul have been wondering, in an unprecedented way, if this modern consensus, wedded as it was to the traditional
Reformation Law/Gospel distinction, has not been an equally unfortunate inheritance.

2. The Paradigm Shift in Pauline Studies

For over 400 years, the traditional Reformation understanding of Paul's Law/
Gospel contrast has determined the exegesis of 2 Cor. 3:6. Moreover, due to
its seemingly maxim-like character, its own surrounding context was usually
used merely to support this perspective, which was imported into 2 Cor. 3 on
the basis of Galatians and Romans. Hence, the letter/Spirit contrast has been
repeatedly interpreted as an expression of the Reformation understanding of
Paul's view of the Gospel as the answer to his "quantitative" critique of the

---

trast represented two distinct ways of reading Scripture, the literal (characteristic of
Judaism, from Paul's perspective) and the symbolic or allegorical characteristic of the
Christian approach (cf. pp. 352, 354 f.). To my knowledge, the only scholar in this century
to hold the position that Paul intended both meanings is J. Héring, *The Second Epistle of
Saint Paul to the Corinthians*, 1967 (ET of the French, 1958), p. 23. But he offers no support
for his interpretation.

[24] *History of Interpretation*, 1886, p. 201.

[25] "New Testament Translation Problems II," *The Bible Translator* 28 (1977) 110–112,
p. 110.

[26] For a long list of those scholars who have suggested some sort of "realistic" interpretation of the letter/Spirit contrast up until the early 1950's, cf. Schneider, "Meaning," p. 186,
and his own view on pp. 188–207, esp. pp. 191 f., 196. Nevertheless, as James Barr has
pointed out, modern scholarship's rejection of Origen's allegorical method does not mean
that historical criticism is not characterized by the search for a theological understanding of
the Bible. Rather, it has merely rejected the attempt to interpret texts apart from their contexts or to allegorize texts which are intended to be taken literally in their original context.
See his "The Literal, the Allegorical, and Modern Biblical Scholarship," *JSOT* 44 (1989) 3–
17, esp. pp. 13 f.

[27] Subtitled, *A Comparison of Patterns of Religion*, 1977.

law ('no one can keep the whole law perfectly') and/or its "qualitative" anthropological extension (the law's demands *themselves* lead to sinful boasting and self-righteousness).[28] Viewed from this perspective, the "letter (= Law) kills" because it demands a sinless perfection which cannot be attained and/or because it produces a deluded self-confidence and self-justification in the attempt to do so. In contrast, the "Spirit (=Gospel) makes alive" because it calls for a justification by grace through faith alone, made possible by the cross of Christ.

But as Douglas Moo observed in 1987, "scholarship on Paul and the Law in the last ten years has witnessed a 'paradigm shift.'"[29] All the traditional "assured results" concerning Paul's Law/Gospel contrast are now being so seriously called into question that "the explanation of Paul's understanding of the law is probably the topic about which there is the most debate" among New Testament scholars.[30] The recent destruction of the modern consensus concerning Paul's Law/Gospel contrast merely brings to fruition earlier, but largely unheeded, dissatisfaction in our century with the traditional Reformation understanding of Paul. From Wrede's *Paul* (1908), to Schweitzer's *The Mysticism of Paul the Apostle* (1931), to Stendahl's "The Apostle Paul and the Introspective Conscience of the West" (1963), the modern consensus concerning the central place of justification by faith and the concomitant criticism of the soteriological claims of the Law in Paul's theology had already been increasingly challenged from a number of different fronts and for various historical and exegetical reasons.[31] However, though widely cited for their his-

---

[28] For these helpful descriptive terms, see C.H. Cosgrove, *The Cross and the Spirit, A Study in the Argument and Theology of Galatians*, 1988, p. 10, and Douglas Moo, "Paul and The Law in the Last Ten Years," *SJTh* 40 (1987) 287–307, pp. 297 f., who attributes them to E.P. Sanders. Cosgrove traces both critiques back to Luther himself, though Thomas R. Schreiner, "'Works of Law' in Paul," *NovT* 33 (1991) 217–244, pp. 218 f. n. 6, argues that most likely Luther taught only the quantitative view, i.e. that no one is justified by the Law because all sin and cannot keep the Law perfectly. See Cosgrove, pp. 10 f., for the recent criticism of the "qualitative" interpretation so forcefully presented in this century by Bultmann (see above, n. 4). Representatives of the "qualitative" view are divided and not always clear over whether the Law itself promotes this sinful attitude or whether this extension is a human perversion of the Law's intent. For a more recent and influential presentation of this latter view in regard to Romans, see Hans Hübner, *Das Gesetz bei Paulus, Ein Beitrag zum Werden der paulinischen Theologie, FRLANT 119*, 1980², esp. pp. 76 f., 104, 115 f., 118 ff.

[29] "Paul and The Law," p. 287. Moo is in turn indebted to Robert Jewett for the observation. Moo's article provides a helpful orientation to the blur of recent opinions and literature on Paul.

[30] So Klyne Snodgrass, "Spheres of Influence, A Possible Solution to the Problem of Paul and the Law," *JSNT* 32 (1988) 93–113, p. 93. Snodgrass goes on to detail no less than nine different contemporary views before offering his own!

[31] For an insightful and extended treatment of the debate concerning Paul's view of the Law beginning with Wrede, see Stephen Westerholm, *Israel's Law and the Church's Faith, Paul and His Recent Interpreters*, 1988, pp. 15–101. That this question can now sustain such an extensive review is further evidence of the new, undetermined status of the issue.

torical significance, the works of Wrede and Schweitzer were, until recently, largely overlooked. For its part, Stendahl's work initiated and anticipated in programmatic fashion much of the later criticism of the Reformation approach to Paul, but was itself too brief and undeveloped to turn the tide alone. Moreover, Stendahl's subordination of Paul's Law/Gospel contrast to the relationship between Jews and Gentiles has led to an interpretation of Paul's soteriology as distinct for Jews and Gentiles, a position which seems to compromise many of Stendahl's other insights.[32]

On the other hand, W.D. Davies' *Paul and Rabbinic Judaism* (1948) and H.J. Schoeps' *Paul: The Theology of the Apostle in the Light of Jewish Religious History* (ET, 1961; German, 1959) sought to challenge the traditionally negative view of post-biblical Judaism as legalistic, against which Paul's thought was commonly interpreted. Yet Schoeps did not deny the basic Reformation understanding of the Law in Paul's *own* thinking, but merely sought to show its irrelevance to the Judaism of Paul's Palestinian contemporaries, in contrast to those Hellenistic Jews who, like Paul before his conversion, had perverted the nature and function of the Law into legalism.[33] Such a distinction between Palestinian and Hellenistic Judaism has not held up, however. And Davies, though his work is undoubtedly a landmark in Pauline studies, discounted Paul's critique of the Law too readily as merely polemical, and therefore not essential to Paul's otherwise normal "rabbinic" views. In other words, Schoeps' Paul was not Jewish enough, while Davies' Paul was too Jewish to win the day.

However, within a year of the publication of Stendahl's proleptic study, C.E.B. Cranfield significantly attacked the modern consensus again, this time from within.[34] Cranfield did not deny the centrality of justification by faith for Paul's theology or the Reformation understanding of his opponents as legalists. Rather, he sought to redefine the focus of Paul's criticism of the Law in terms of its *perversion* into legalism by post-biblical Judaism as a whole. This perversion was represented in Paul's thought by the phrase ἔργα νόμου ("works of the law," cf. Rom. 3:20, 28; Gal. 3:2,10, etc.), which Paul coined to signify "legalism," a meaning unique to him.[35] Thus, for Cranfield, when Paul speaks negatively of the "works of the Law," he is not opposing the Law itself,

---

[32] For my own critique of Stendahl's work in regard to this latter issue, see "The Salvation of Israel in Romans 11:25–32. A Response to Krister Stendahl," *Ex Auditu* 4 (1988) 38–58.

[33] Cf. Schoeps, *Paul*, pp. 29, 31 f., 213, 257, 260.

[34] See his "St. Paul and the Law," *SJTh* 17 (1964) 43–68. Cranfield later developed his views in "Some Notes on Romans 9:30–33," in *Jesus and Paulus, FS W.G. Kümmel zum 70. Geburtstag*, ed. E.E. Ellis and E. Grässer, 1975, pp. 35–43, summarized in "Romans 9:30–10:4," *Interpretation* 34 (1980) 70–74. For the development of his view in relationship to Romans as a whole, see *A Critical and Exegetical Commentary on the Epistle to the Romans, ICC, Vol. II*, 1979, esp. the excursus "The OT Law," pp. 845–862.

[35] Cranfield's thesis is based on his premise that Paul had no word in Greek to represent this legalistic perversion and thus coined this phrase since, "in this difficult terrain Paul was to a large extent pioneering," "St. Paul and the Law," p. 157.

but its perversion into legalism. Conversely, Paul's positive statements concerning the Law refer to the Law freed from this legalistic misuse. In arguing this, Cranfield intended to counter the axiom of the modern consensus that, for Paul, Christ had abolished the Law.[36] For while Christ had abolished legalism, he was, for Paul, the "goal" (τέλος) of the Law itself (Rom. 10:4).[37] In 2 Cor. 3:6, it is thus the "legalistic misunderstanding and perversion of the law," not the Law itself, which kills.[38] For Cranfield, the letter/Spirit contrast is consequently

"... a contrast not between the Old Testament law which is written and a spiritual religion which knows no law, but between the legalistic relation of the Jews of Paul's time to God and to His law and the new relation to God and to His law established by the Holy Spirit and resulting from Christ's work."[39]

Cranfield's view has won many followers and has been refined in many directions.[40] But it has also been severely criticized for its reliance on what appears to many to be an artificial linguistic distinction in Paul's writings between the Law and its works (cf. e.g. Gal. 3:10–12, 17–19) and its apparent failure to take into account adequately some of Paul's negative statements concerning the abolition of the Law itself (e.g. Gal. 3:12 par. 4:5; 3:15 ff.; Rom. 6:14; 7:4–6).[41] Moreover, whether correct or not, the advent of Sanders' work has

---

[36] Cf. "St. Paul and the Law," pp. 152–169.

[37] "St. Paul and the Law," p. 152.

[38] "St. Paul and the Law," pp. 155 and 156.

[39] "St. Paul and the Law," p. 159.

[40] Cf. e.g. C.F.D. Moule, "Obligation in the Ethic of Paul," in *Christian History and Interpretation: Studies Presented to John Knox*, ed. W.F. Farmer, C.F.D. Moule and R.R. Niebuhr, 1967, pp. 389–406; Ragnar Bring, "Die Gerechtigkeit Gottes und das Alttestamentliche Gesetz," in his *Christus und das Gesetz*, 1969, pp. 35–72; Bring's *Commentary on Galatians*, 1961, and most importantly, his "Paul and the Old Testament, A Study of the Ideas of Election, Faith and Law in Paul, with Special Reference to Romans 9:30–10:30," (*sic*) *Studia Theologica* 25 (1971) 21–60. The most significant extension of Cranfield's work has been that of D.P. Fuller, "Paul and 'The Works of the Law'," *WJT* 38 (1975) 28–42 and his chapter on "Paul's View of the Law" in his *Gospel and Law: Contrast or Continuum? The Hermeneutics of Dispensationalism and Covenant Theology*, 1980, pp. 65–120.

[41] See most recently Westerholm, *Israel's Law*, p. 110, 121, 127–133, Snodgrass, "Spheres," p. 95, and Thomas R. Schreiner, "The Abolition and Fulfillment of the Law in Paul," *JSNT* 35 (1989) 47–74, pp. 50 f., and now his "'Works of Law' in Paul," *NovT* 33 (1991) 217–244, where he surveys the various basic interpretations of "works of the Law" in Paul, concluding that the traditional Lutheran view is essentially correct, i.e. that Paul was opposing a Judaistic and legalistic works-righteousness as the basis for attaining righteousness because it required perfect obedience to the Law for salvation, which no one can do (p. 241). But contra Bultmann, Schreiner rejects the further extension of this to include the very attempt to obey the law as a means of justification as being sinful (pp. 220, 241, 244). Rather, the problem is simply that no one can keep the Law perfectly, which then leads to the corresponding legalistic "delusion of those who think they can earn merit before God by their obedience to the law, even though they fail to obey it" (p. 244). However, Schreiner does not pose the question of the relationship between "works of the Law" in Paul and the OT Law itself as raised by the work of Cranfield and Fuller.

increasingly caused many scholars to regard the entire historical base for Cranfield's view to be a phantom.

Finally, although from a very different perspective on Paul's theology as a whole, a revitalized interest in Biblical Theology has led Hartmut Gese and Peter Stuhlmacher to reject the traditional Reformation understanding of the Law/Gospel contrast as a theological distinction between two competing ways of salvation. Instead, the Law and the Gospel are seen to represent an eschatological contrast between two periods in God's *Heilsgeschichte*, which may not entail a corresponding distinction between the Mosaic Law and the Gospel as the central characteristics of these two epochs.[42] Though still retaining the Reformation understanding of the centrality of justification by faith in Paul and his corresponding critique of the Law apart from faith, this approach views the Law as a witness to faith before Christ, as well as playing a very positive role within the epoch of the Gospel itself. For example, commenting on Romans 3:27, Stuhlmacher asserts that the boast of the Jew "is not excluded through the Law which demands works (= 'the Law of works')" but "through 'the Law of faith,' i.e. through the Pentateuch, which, for example, testifies through its promises to God's salvific righteousness and his gracious willingness to make atonement (through Christ) (see Ex. 34:6f. [LXX], Lev. 16 and 17:11)."[43] This contrast between the Law, more narrowly conceived, which demands works, and the Law as a whole, which witnesses to faith, is then expressed eschatologically in terms of a distinction between the "Torah of Sinai" and the "Torah of Zion." Through the atonement of Christ and by the power of the Spirit, God redeems not only mankind, but also the Law itself from the power of sin, and thus in the "Zion Torah" gives back to the Law "its original function which it had in paradise."[44] But to date, this approach has not been fully developed, nor has it won widespread support.[45] In addition, since

---

[42] In terms of 2 Cor. 3:6 this view was first suggested by M. Rissi, *Studien zum Zweiten Korintherbrief: Der alte Bund – Der Prediger – Der Tod,* AThANT 56, 1969, esp. pp. 23–25. For variations of this view, though not developed specifically in terms of 2 Cor. 3, cf. Hartmut Gese, "Das Gesetz," in his *Zur biblischen Theologie, Alttestamentliche Vorträge,* BevTh 78, 1977, pp. 55–84, esp. pp. 68–78, 82, who combines this eschatological distinction with a *traditionsgeschichtliche* development of the understanding of the Law itself; and Peter Stuhlmacher, who develops Gese's basic insights in his "Das Gesetz als Thema biblischer Theologie," *ZThK* 75 (1978) 251–280 (now in his *Versöhnung, Gesetz und Gerechtigkeit, Aufsätze zur biblischen Theologie,* 1981, pp. 135–165; ET *Reconciliation, Law and Righteousness, Essays in Biblical Theology,* 1986, pp. 110–133), esp. pp. 270–274, and "Paul's Understanding of the Law in the Letter to the Romans," *Svensk exegetisk årsbok* 50 (1985) 87–104. For the working out of this perspective, see his *Der Brief an die Römer,* NTD Bd. 6, 1989, esp. his excursus "Die paulinische Lehre vom Gesetz," pp. 112–117.

[43] "Paul's Understanding of the Law," p. 97.

[44] "Paul's Understanding of the Law," p. 99. "... in and through Christ, the Law which had become an instrument of sin and death since the fall of Adam, has now become the Law of Christ which protects life" (p. 99).

[45] For the recent critiques of it by Kalusche, Räisänen, and Schreiner, see Schreiner, "Abolition and Fulfilment," pp. 52, 69 nn. 30–31. It must be pointed out against Schreiner's

its criticism of the more traditional view does not strike at its essence, the refinement it offers goes either too far for the traditional view, or not far enough for those seeking to replace the old consensus with a new one.

Thus, though substantial critiques of the prevailing paradigm could certainly be found prior to 1977, they were primarily attacks on the Reformation understanding of *Paul*, and not on its perception of Paul's Jewish or Judaizing opponents. But as long as the traditional view of Paul's opponents remained in place, the attempt to rethink Paul's own view could be dismissed not only as theologically or exegetically unsound, but also as historically misguided. Moo is therefore right in dating the destruction of the modern consensus to the advent of Sanders' contribution to the debate. Sanders' view of Paul is, of course, itself worthy of note and demands a response. But this is not what turned the tide in Pauline studies. Rather, Sanders' work marks a watershed in modern Pauline scholarship due to its comprehensive nature, its intentionally polemical tone and purpose, and its uniform and inclusive presentation of the structure of *both* early Judaism and Paul, the latter viewed not in light of, but over against the former.[46] Specifically, Sanders' presentation of Paul against the backdrop of Palestinian Judaism as a religion of non-legalistic "covenantal nomism" succeeded, where earlier attempts had failed, in forcing scholars to rethink *fundamentally* the nature of the opposition Paul faced in his churches and consequently the character and content of the criticism he raised against it.[47] For according to Sanders, the "covenantal nomism" pervasively found throughout Palestinian Judaism "is the view that one's place in God's plan is established on the basis of the covenant and that the covenant requires as the proper response of man his obedience to its commandments, while providing means of atonement for transgression."[48] Thus, for Palestinian Judaism at the time of Paul, "the intention and effort to be obedient constitute the *con-*

---

understanding of this perspective, that they do not advocate a "new Law" in Christ, but the reestablishment of the Law of God known in the Garden of Eden, within the Pentateuch, and in the future. Nevertheless, this "Law of God" is not identical with the entire Mosaic Law (i.e. the "cultic Torah") but "is the decalogue and the corresponding deeds of love which are based in it;" see Stuhlmacher, "Paul's Understanding of the Law," p. 101. In this regard, Stuhlmacher's view is close to that of Schreiner's own!

[46] At this point the degree to which Sanders is successful in this endeavor is not the issue; the fact that he attempted it and presented a coherent and distinct thesis in this regard over against the traditional view was all that was needed. For a comparison, see Sanders' own evaluation of the relationship between his work and the earlier "motif research" of scholars such as W.D. Davies, Schoeps, Dahl, Scroggs, etc., in *Paul and Palestinian Judaism*, pp. 7–18.

[47] For Sanders' central thesis that an investigation of Palestinian Judaism reveals that it was not a system of legalistic "works-righteousness," see *Paul and Palestinian Judaism*, pp. 59, 100, 180 f., 205, 233 f., 293 and 320 (on Qumran), 383 (on Jubilees), 409 (on the one exception which proves the rule, IV Ezra), 418–427. For his analysis of why the earlier attempts of scholars such as G.F. Moore and C.G. Montefiore and W.D. Davies failed to bring about the same results, cf. pp. xiii, 4 f., 7, 9 f., 34, 47, 54 f., 59.

[48] *Paul and Palestinian Judaism*, p. 75, cf. p. 236.

dition for remaining in the covenant, but they do not *earn* it."[49] With regard to
the dominant "Weberian view" of (rabbinic) Judaism as a religion of legalistic
works-righteousness, Sanders therefore concludes that,

"... the text books and reference works in which that view is found and where it is
presumed to be proved ... are, as far as they deal with Rabbinic religion, completely
untrustworthy. They cannot be corrected by new editions citing different views or by
mitigating some of their harsher and more ill-founded remarks. They proceed from
wrong premises, they misconstrue the material, and they are, like those Jews who cast
off the yoke, beyond redemption." [50]

The comprehensive nature of Sanders' presentation and the forcefulness of
his conclusions concerning Palestinian Judaism, though certainly not without
their critics,[51] could not be ignored. And since completing his original work,
Sanders has solidified his perspective with extensive treatments of the belief
and practice of Judaism in the first century.[52] Despite the serious debate Sanders' work has engendered, for the vast majority of scholars Paul's world had
dramatically changed. Indeed, Sanders' work on Judaism has won such widespread acceptance among NT scholars that just over a decade later C.H.
Cosgrove can affirm *as a matter of course* that "his work serves as an indispensable reminder of at least this much: Torah-obedience was understood in
Palestinian Judaism to be grounded in and enabled by God's grace to no lesser
degree than in early Christianity."[53] But if Sanders and his followers are right
about the nature of Palestinian Judaism in Paul's day, then the traditional Reformation view of "Paul's polemic is left hanging in mid-air, and it is necessary
either to accuse Paul of misunderstanding (or misrepresenting) his opponents,

---

[49] *Paul and Palestinian Judaism,* p. 180 (emphasis his). Sanders' statement in context refers specifically to rabbinic Judaism, but for Sanders the same holds true for the rest of Palestinian Judaism: "... covenantal nomism was *pervasive* in Palestine before 70. It was thus
the basic *type* of religion known by Jesus and presumably by Paul" (p. 426, emphasis his).

[50] *Paul and Palestinian Judaism,* p. 234. Sanders argues the same point for the rest of
Palestinian Judaism as well, cf. pp. 426 f.

[51] Among the many reviews of this initial work, see esp. that of Jacob Neusner, "Comparing Judaisms," *HR* 18 (1978) 177–91, N.A. Dahl and S. Sandmel, "E.P. Sanders, Paul and
Palestinian Judaism: A Comparison of Patterns of Religion," *RelSRev* 4 (1978) 153–160,
and W.D. Davies, "Preface to the Fourth Edition," *Paul and Rabbinic Judaism,* 1980⁴, xxix–
xxxviii.

[52] See now his *Jewish Law from Jesus to the Mishnah, Five Studies,* 1990, and *Judaism,
Practice and Belief 63 BCE – 66 CE,* 1992. For the continuing debate between Sanders and
his most severe critic, see now Jacob Neusner, "Mr. Sanders' Pharisees and Mine," *Bulletin
for Biblical Research* 2 (1992) 143–169, in response primarily to Sanders' evaluation of
Neusner's work in his *Jewish Law,* pp. 309–331. For the fundamental methodological issues
in the current debate, see Jacob Neusner, "The Mishna in Philosophical Context and Out of
Canonical Bounds," *JBL* 112 (1993) 291–304, in response to Craig A. Evans, "Mishna and
Messiah 'In Context': Some Comments on Jacob Neusner's Proposals," pp. 267–289, in the
same volume.

[53] *The Cross and the Spirit,* p. 9.

or to find new opponents for him to be criticizing,"[54] which would entail radically rethinking the nature of Paul's polemic against the "works of the Law" itself. Once accepted, the consequences of the paradigm shift regarding Judaism precipitated by Sanders are thus both far-reaching and decisive for the way in which Paul will be read in the decades ahead.

The investigation of Paul's view of the Law in the last decade has thus been reenergized by a flurry of studies seeking to work out the implications of Sanders' work for "the new perspective on Paul."[55] Often at odds with one another on points of exegesis, these studies are unified by their common conviction concerning the non-legalistic nature of first century Judaism and their corresponding rejection of the traditional Reformation understanding of the Law/Gospel antithesis as the key to both Paul's view of the Law and the nature of his opponents.[56] Thus, though they have mounted a forceful and successful attack on the modern consensus, their own constructive proposals suffer as much from internal dissent as from external critique.[57] And the earlier perspectives represented by scholars such as Cranfield and Stuhlmacher continue to compete for attention, albeit often in modified forms, especially as the eschatological (history-of-salvation) framework of Paul's thinking, rather than his Christology *per se*, receives renewed attention as a key to his thought in general and to his understanding of the Law in particular.[58] Moreover, pro-

---

[54] So Moo, "Paul and The Law," p. 293.

[55] To borrow the title of James D.G. Dunn's article, "The New Perspective on Paul," *BJRL* 65 (1983) 95–122, in which he outlines his own new interpretation of Paul in view of Sanders' work.

[56] In addition to Dunn's 1983 article (n. 55), as representative of this perspective see now his collected essays and responses to critics in his, *Jesus, Paul and the Law, Studies in Mark and Galatians*, 1990 and his two volume commentary on *Romans, WBC Vols. 38A; 38B*, 1988/88; Sanders' own *Paul, the Law, and the Jewish People*, 1983 (an extension and refinement of his earlier work on Paul in *Paul and Palestinian Judaism*, 474–523) and his other articles on Paul listed there; N.T. Wright, "The Paul of History and the Apostle of Faith," *Tyndale Bulletin* 29 (1978) 61–88; Heikki Räisänen, *Paul and the Law*, WUNT 29, 1983 (also published in the US in 1986); his "Galatians 2:16 and Paul's Break with Judaism," *NTS* 31 (1985) 543–553 and "Paul's Conversion and the Development of his View of the Law," *NTS* 33 (1987) 404–419; T. David Gordon, "The Problem at Galatia," *Int* 41 (1987) 32–43; the essays of Lloyd Gaston in his *Paul and the Torah*, 1987; Cosgrove, *The Cross and the Spirit*, 1988, Paula Fredriksen, *From Jesus to Christ, The Origins of the New Testament Images of Jesus*, 1988, pp. 142–176, and Klyne Snodgrass, "Spheres of Influence."

[57] See, e.g. the distinctions between the views of Sanders, Dunn, Wright, and Räisänen on the question of why Paul actually rejected Judaism as outlined by Moo, "Paul and the Law," pp. 293–296, and Westerholm, *Israel's Law*, p. 144.

[58] See now especially the thesis of Frank Thielman, *From Plight to Solution, A Jewish Framework for Understanding Paul's View of the Law in Galatians and Romans*, Suppl. NovT 61, 1989, for such a response to Sanders' central thesis that it was Paul's new found "solution" in Christ which subsequently determined his revisioning of the plight associated with the Law and Judaism, though Thielman too sees no evidence in Paul "that first century Judaism was generally a meritorious religion" (p. 27). See too Thielman's helpful analysis of the course of the debate over Paul and the Law, pp. 1–27. For an application of an escha-

ponents of the more traditional view, now quickly becoming a minority, remain convinced that the "paradigm shift" in Pauline studies has been misguided and that "there is more of Paul in Luther than many twentieth-century scholars are inclined to allow."[59]

The positive result of this great diversity among scholars today is the impetus it gives to return to the text itself with a healthy skepticism concerning *all* paradigms. Nowhere is this more true than in 2 Cor. 3:6 and its surrounding context. In view of the paradigm shift in Pauline studies, to say that a consensus exists among scholars that the letter/Spirit contrast refers to a "realistic" or "economy-of-salvation" distinction between the Law and the Gospel is simply to pose the question of the nature of this distinction itself. And there is certainly no consensus today on how this question should be answered.[60] Indeed, as our brief survey makes clear and as W.D. Davies observed almost a decade ago, the Law/Gospel distinction is "the chief dichotomy which recent scholarship has reopened and even questioned."[61] Yet, despite the many exegetical difficulties presented by 2 Cor. 3:6, certainly the letter/Spirit contrast must provide a key plank in any successful attempt to understand Paul's view of the Law. It comes as no surprise, then, that most recently scholars have begun once again to turn their attention to this strategic text and its elucidation in 3:7–18.[62] For the interpretation and historical background of 2 Cor. 3 will

---

tological framework as the key to understanding Paul's thought as a whole, see now N.T. Wright, *The Climax of the Covenant, Christ and the Law in Pauline Theology*, 1991, and James M. Scott, *Adoption as Sons of God, An Exegetical Investigation into the Background of ΥΙΟΘΕΣΙΑ in the Pauline Corpus*, WUNT 2. Reihe 48, 1992; and in regard to the Law itself, now Scott's "'For as Many as are of Works of the Law are Under a Curse' (Galatians 3:10)," in *Paul and the Scriptures of Israel*, Studies in Scripture in Early Judaism and Christianity 1, ed. Craig A. Evans and James A. Sanders, 1993, pp. 187–221.

[59] Westerholm, *Israel's Law*, p. 173; cf. pp. 109–113, 119 f., 122, 129 f., 146–150, 154, 169, 222. Westerholm, though arguing for the traditional quantitative view of Paul's critique of the Law, nevertheless agrees with the "new perspective" that the Judaism of Paul's day is not to be correspondingly characterized as legalistic or free of grace: "... Paul gave the human dimension of the law (its demand for compliance) an emphasis foreign to Judaism as a whole and to the understanding of his opponents ...," p. 163; cf. pp. 169, 173, 220. For a detailed critique focusing on Sanders' view of Paul's theology, see R.H. Gundry, "Grace, Works, and Staying Saved in Paul," *Biblica* 66 (1985) 1–38; for a criticism of Sander's view of the possibility of keeping the Law, see Thomas R. Schreiner, "Paul and Perfect Obedience to the Law: An Evaluation of the View of E.P. Sanders," *WTJ* (1985) 245–278, and now his "Works of Law."

[60] It is bewildering to realize that in 1977, even before the advent of the work of Sanders, J.A. Sanders could list eight different positions on Paul and the Law then currently being advocated; see his "Torah and Paul," in *God's Christ and His People, FS Nils Alstrup Dahl*, ed. J. Jervell and W.A. Meeks, 1977, pp. 132–140.

[61] "Preface to the Fourth Edition," *Paul and Rabbinic Judaism*, p. xxvii.

[62] For the most thoroughgoing and consistent presentations of the traditional view of 3:6–18, see Otfried Hofius, "Gesetz und Evangelium nach 2. Korinther 3" in his *Paulusstudien*, WUNT 51, 1989, pp. 75–120 (now also found in *"Gesetz" als Thema Biblischer Theologie*, Jahrbuch für Biblische Theologie Bd. 4, 1989, pp. 105–149) and Peter von der Osten-Sacken, "Die Decke des Moses, Zur Exegese und Hermeneutic von Geist und Buchstabe in

have great bearing on how one decides the larger issue of Paul's view of the
Law. In view of the current paradigm shift in Pauline studies, the need for a
detailed reexamination of the letter/Spirit antithesis within its wider context
as a *theological* contrast is therefore manifest.

3. The Letter/Spirit Contrast and the Question of Paul's OT Hermeneutic

To complicate matters further, the last thirty years have also witnessed a renewed attempt to link Paul's contrast between the letter and the Spirit to the
hermeneutical question of how one reads the OT as a Christian, but this time
in a way that avoids the pitfalls of the Origenian approach.[63] Indeed, just one
year after Schneider's study, in which the ascendancy of the "realistic" interpretation was triumphantly proclaimed,"[64] this exclusive approach to the text
was fundamentally called into question in a new way by Ehrhard Kamlah's
brief, but important article, "'Buchstabe und Geist,' Die Bedeutung dieser
Antithese für die alttestamentliche Exegese des Apostels Paulus."[65]

Kamlah accepted the modern repudiation of any attempt to interpret the
meaning of the letter/Spirit contrast hermeneutically as *eis*egesis. In his view
the letter/Spirit contrast was an eschatological contrast between "die Thora
nach ihrer schriftlich-fixierten Gestalt" and the Spirit as the characteristic of
the new covenant (p. 277). But Kamlah rejected modern scholarship's dismissal of any further attempt to find in Paul's letter/Spirit contrast a herme-

---

2 Korinther 3," in his *Die Heiligkeit der Tora, Studien zum Gesetz bei Paulus*, 1989, pp. 87–
115. But unlike Hofius, von der Osten-Sacken argues that we must reject Paul's negative
understanding of the Law as normative for our own understanding of Judaism past and
present, cf. pp. 108–115. For an interpretation of 2 Cor. 3 from within the "new perspective," see now Reinhold Liebers, "2 Kor 3," in his *Das Gesetz als Evangelium,
Untersuchungen zur Gesetzeskritik des Paulus*, AThANT 75, 1989, pp. 96–123; for an interpretation from the perspective of Cranfield, et al., see Thomas E. Provence, "'Who is Sufficient for these Things?' An Exegesis of 2 Corinthians 2:15–3:18," *NovT* 24 (1982) 54–81,
esp. pp. 62–68; and for the attempt to counter the traditional view from the standpoint of
Paul's interpretation of Ex. 34, see now Ekkehard Stegemann, "Der Neue Bund im Alten,
Zum Schriftverständnis des Paulus in II Kor 3," *ThZ* 42 (1986) 97–114.

[63] The last attempts to reject the "realistic" interpretation of 2 Cor. 3:6 by Boaz Cohen,
"Note on Letter and Spirit in the New Testament," *HTR* 47 (1954) 197–203 (in which he
asserted that γράμμα καὶ πνεῦμα were equivalent to the antithesis commonly found in Greek
rhetoric between ῥητὸν καὶ διάνοια) and R.M. Grant, *The Letter and the Spirit*, 1957,
pp. 49–52 (in which he viewed the contrast to be the principle behind Paul's own allegorical
method) were simply too radical to be taken seriously. The theological contrast in the text is
too apparent to be ignored.

[64] See above, n. 26.

[65] Published in *EvTh* 14 (1954) 276–282. Hereafter page references will be given in the
body of the text.

neutical *significance*.[66] In Kamlah's view, Paul *himself* drew from the letter/
Spirit contrast a crucial implication for the development of a Christian hermeneutic. Precisely because of Paul's judgment that the Law is now γράμμα, and
as such done away with in Christ,

"Er will vielmehr gegen das halbe Verstehen das sachgemäße, volle setzen, das allein
vom gekreuzigten Christus auszugehen hat." (p. 281)

This "complete" understanding of the Law, which Kamlah refers to as "die bleibende Bedeutung der Schrift," is thus for Paul no longer the Law viewed as
γράμμα but as γραφή (p. 277). Hence, Paul's *hermeneutical* conclusion, based
upon his *theological* judgment that "the letter kills, but the Spirit makes alive,"
was that the OT, in order to be the abiding expression of the will of God, must
be understood πνευματικῶς (p. 281). As examples of such an understanding
Kamlah pointed to 2 Cor. 3:7 ff. and Rom. 10:4 ff., concluding that

"Das Wort des damit abgetanen γράμμα stellt die Gerechtigkeit auf das Tun des
Menschen. Dem steht die endzeitliche Offenbarung gegenüber, *die Paulus auch im
geistlich Verstandenen Alten Testament findet*, denn in ihm spricht die δικαιοσύνη,
denen Verwandtschaft mit πνεῦμα uns schon 2 Cor. 3:8 f. gezeigt hat. Paulus findet
also das, was er im Kreuz Christi erfahren hat, in den Worten des alten Testaments
wieder, und so kann er es mit ihnen auch entfalten." (p. 281)

Kamlah's conclusion that Paul's γράμμα/πνεῦμα antithesis led him to a new
"spiritual" understanding of the OT (= OT as γραφή) sounded a new note in
the discussion of the letter/Spirit contrast. But perhaps due to its brevity, it had
little impact upon subsequent scholarship.

It was not until 15 years later that Kamlah's challenge to the modern consensus found another, and this time much stronger voice in E. Käsemann's
programmatic essay, "Geist und Buchstabe."[67] Käsemann's goal in writing
was to set forth the "provocative thesis"

"... daß der Apostel nicht nur in seinem ganzen Werk durchaus von einer zentra-
len, sogar lehrhaft formulierbaren Botschaft getragen wird, sondern auch zum ersten
Male in der christlichen Geschichte ansatzweise eine theologische Hermeneutik ent-
wickelte."[68]

---

[66] I am using the terms "meaning" and "significance" in the technical sense established by
E.D. Hirsch, *Validity in Interpretation*, 1967, p. 8: "*Meaning* is that which is represented by
a text; it is what the author meant by his use of a particular sign sequence; it is what the signs
represent. *Significance*, on the other hand, names a relationship between that meaning and a
person, or a conception, or a situation, or indeed anything imaginable."

[67] Published in his *Paulinische Perspektiven*, 1972², pp. 237–285 (ET: "The Spirit and
the Letter," *Perspectives on Paul*, 1971, pp. 138–166).

[68] "Geist," p. 238. Hereafter, pages from this essay will be given in the body of the text.
Although not developed to the degree that it is in Käsemann's work, this same emphasis was
earlier suggested by J. Roloff in his "Der Apostel als bevollmächtigter Ausleger der
Schrift," *Apostolat – Verkündigung – Kirche.Ursprung, Inhalt und Funktion des kirchlichen
Apostelamtes nach Paulus, Lukas und den Pastoralbriefen*, 1965, pp. 98–103. Roloff de-

Moreover, Käsemann contended that both Paul's "central message" and his "theological hermeneutic" come together uniquely in the letter/Spirit contrast found in Rom. 2:27–29, 7:6, and 2 Cor. 3:6. It was in this contrast that Käsemann found the embodiment of the former, as well as the basis for the latter (cf. pp. 244–246, 251–254, 264–267).

Hence, in Käsemann's view, the problem with the modern consensus has not been its understanding of the "meaning" of the letter/Spirit contrast, but its reluctance to develop the interrelationship between this contrast and Paul's OT hermeneutic (p. 240). On the one hand, Käsemann himself reestablished, and even significantly extended, the modern consensus. In his view, the letter/ Spirit antithesis posited a contrast between the will of God embodied in the Mosaic Law itself, now perverted by Jewish tradition into a demand for works (i.e. the Law as "letter"), and the rediscovery in the Gospel of this lost, pre-fall, will of God (p. 252). On the other hand, Käsemann, like Kamlah before him, took the additional step of relating this antithesis to Paul's reading of the OT. 2 Cor. 3:6 therefore also implies a contrast between two "scriptures," the latter not having been written with ink but with the Spirit. As a result, the Spirit takes on the hermeneutical function of assisting one to read the OT "in the light of Christ" in order to rediscover the Scripture's original intention (pp. 265 f.). In Käsemann's words,

"Die Schrift muß von Christus her und auf ihn hin gelesen werden, wobei dann selbst das Gesetz seine ursprüngliche göttliche Intention zurückgewinnt und zur Verheißung des neuen, eschatologischen Gehorsams wird. Der Geist erhält hier eine herme-neutische Funktion." (pp. 266 f.)[69]

But in view of the Law/Gospel contrast itself, Käsemann concluded that read-ing the OT from the perspective of Christ demanded either that the Law as "letter" be transformed into promise, or that a wedge be driven between the two. Paul's new dialectical handling of the OT thus implies a critical interpre-

---

scribes Paul's use of the OT as a "pneumatische Exegese, die Paulus kraft seiner apostolischen Vollmacht vollführt ..." (p. 103).

[69] For a discussion of the dependence upon and relationship between Käsemann's per-spective on the letter and Bultmann's "qualitative" understanding of the Law and σάρξ in Paul, see now Stephen Westerholm, "Letter and Spirit: The Foundation of Pauline *Ethics*," *NTS* 30 (1984) 229–247, esp. pp. 230–232. Westerholm himself rejects a hermeneutical reading of the letter/Spirit contrast, seeing the letter as a direct reference to the Law itself as possessed in written form, "not as perverted by Jewish tradition, but as imposing obligations during one period of salvation-history which for the Christian are no longer binding" (p. 233, cf. p. 234). Westerholm thus agrees in essence with Käsemann's emphasis on the eschatological framework of Paul's thought in 3:6, arguing that Rom. 7:6 and 2 Cor. 3:6 "clearly point to two epochs of salvation-history" (p. 235), but not with the hermeneutical significance which Käsemann draws from this contrast, nor with Käsemann's conclusion that the problem in 2 Cor. 3:6 is not two ways of reading Scripture, a perverted understand-ing of the Law itself, nor the misguided Jewish zeal to keep the Law in order to establish one's own righteousness. Rather, for Westerholm, the letter/Spirit contrast expresses "the essence of service under the two covenants" (p. 240).

tation of Scripture and, for that matter, of all tradition. For to Paul as a Christian, it is now a question of "Scripture against Scripture" or "the Law as promise (which for Käsemann is the Law read in the power of the Spirit) against the Torah as a demand for works" (i.e. the Law perverted into the "letter") (p. 274). In Käsemann's view, therefore, the letter/Spirit contrast is the heart of Paul's message because it summarizes the generative principle of his theology, namely, the Law/Gospel distinction between a demand for works and justification by faith in and because of Christ. For precisely this reason, it also functions as the basis for Paul's OT hermeneutic: "Die durch die Rechtfertigungslehre interpretierte Christologie ist das Kriterium zwischen Geist und Buchstabe, die beide aus der Schrift abgeleitet werden können" (p. 267). But because the doctrine of justification by faith becomes the "hermeneutical key for the Pauline understanding of the OT," Käsemann can conclude that

"Paulus hat keine feste exegetische Methode und kein geschlossenes dogmatisches System entwickelt. Er hat jedoch ein Thema, das seine gesamte Theologie beherrscht, nämlich die Rechtfertigungslehre. Das gab ihm nicht nur einen 'hermeneutischen Ansatz,' sondern bestimmte durchweg seine Auslegung der Schrift, und zwar unter dem Gesichtspunkt der Antithese von Gesetz und Evangelium kritisch." (p. 282)

In other words, Paul's letter/Spirit contrast demands a hermeneutic which "allowed Scripture to be played out against Scripture," and which consequently leads ultimately to the ability to speak both hermeneutically and theologically of "a canon within the canon" (p. 282). For Käsemann, then, the theological *and* hermeneutical significance of the letter/Spirit contrast cannot be overestimated.

More recently, this challenge to the modern consensus has also been taken up by Peter Stuhlmacher in his development of what he calls Paul's "Christological understanding of Scripture."[70] In contrast to the criticism of arbitrariness and artificiality often levied by modern scholars against the OT hermeneutic employed by Paul (and other NT writers),[71] Stuhlmacher argues that it is inappropriate for modern critics to pull rank methodologically over the practices of the first century Christians. Rather, the NT writers, and especially Paul, were only doing what every subsequent Christian generation has done when they interpret the OT in the light of their own Christian experience, namely, use the methodology available to them. What made Paul's exegesis

---

[70] Stuhlmacher's basic position was outlined in his article "Historische Kritik und theologische Schriftauslegung," in his *Schriftauslegung auf dem Wege zur biblischen Theologie,* 1975, pp. 59–127 (ET as *Historical Criticism and Theological Interpretation of Scripture,* 1977), esp. p. 64; and further developed in *Vom Verstehen des Neuen Testaments, Eine Hermeneutik;* Grundrisse zum Neuen Testament, NTD Ergänzungsreihe 6, 1986², pp. 66–74. It should be pointed out, moreover, that Stuhlmacher sees Paul's hermeneutic to be a continuation of Jesus' own interpretation of the Scriptures (cf. *Verstehen,* pp. 64 f.).

[71] This view has been clearly summarized by Morna D. Hooker, "Beyond the Things that are Written? St. Paul's Use of Scripture," *NTS* 27 (1981) 295–309, pp. 296 f.

unique was not a new method (or lack of one!), but the Christian perspective which guided his application of the standard interpretive procedures of his day.[72] For Stuhlmacher, the essence of this perspective, which overwhelmed Paul in his experience on the road to Damascus, was

"die Erkenntnis nämlich, daß auch der angestrengteste Eifer um Verständnis der Tora nicht in die Gemeinschaft mit Gott, der sich in Jesus Christus offenbart, führt, vielmehr eine religiös vertiefte Form von Eigenmächtigkeit und Verschlossenheit gegenüber Gottes Handeln darstellen kann."[73]

Hence, for Stuhlmacher, as for Kamlah and Käsemann before him, the heart of Paul's theology centers in the realization that Christ put an end to the Law (Rom. 10:4).[74] It was in his Damascus Road experience that Paul came to realize that the Law was a deadly trap, i.e. that "the letter kills, but the Spirit makes alive."[75]

From this point it was an easy transition for Paul to move from his new Christian perspective to its implications for reading the OT:

"Der Apostel hat folgerichtig auch hermeneutisch auf den Umstand reflektiert, daß man die hl. *Schrift* mit aller Anstrengung lesen und auslegen kann und dennoch in die Gottesferne gerät (emphasis mine)."[76]

---

[72] *Verstehen*, pp. 67 f. Cf. e.g. too Hooker, "Beyond," pp. 297, 304 f., who also argues that Paul's methods, if not his exegesis, make sense given the contemporary methods of biblical exegesis; and Jost Eckert, "Die geistliche Schriftauslegung des Apostels Paulus nach 2 Kor 3:4–18," in *Dynamik im Wort*, ed. Katholischen Bibelwerk, 1983, pp. 241–256, p. 242, who views Paul's "spiritual interpretation of the Scripture" to be the fact that in 2 Cor. 3, "Paulus betreibt hier in Übereinstimmung mit der biblischen Auslegungsmethode seiner Zeit eine sehr freie, von seinem christlichen Standpunkt beherrschte Exegese der Schrift."

[73] *Verstehen*, p. 68.

[74] For Stuhlmacher's understanding of the implications of Paul's Damascus Road experience for his view of the Law (and consequently for his theology in general) see his essays, "'Das Ende des Gesetzes.' Über Ursprung und Ansatz der paulinischen Theologie," *ZThK* 67 (1970) 14–39; "Achtzehn Thesen zur paulinischen Kreuzes-theologie," *Rechtfertigung, FS E. Käsemann zum 70. Geburtstag*, ed. J. Friedrich, W. Pöhlmann and P. Stuhlmacher, 1976, pp. 509–525 and "Zur paulinischen Christologie," *ZThK* 74 (1977) 449–463 (all of which are now in his *Versöhnung*, pp. 166–191, 192–208, and 209–223 respectively; for the ET, see above, n. 42).

[75] Stuhlmacher himself does not summarize the problem with the Law in terms of 2 Cor. 3:6, but his adaptation of its terminology makes it clear that he would find this contrast a suitable summary of its effects. For as he puts it, *Verstehen*, p. 69, "Seit Paulus und seinen berühmten Ausführungen in 1. Kor 2:6 ff.; 2. Kor 3 und 4:1–6 unterscheiden wir christlich zwischen *gramma* und *graphē*, zwischen tötendem Buchstaben und lebenschaffendem Geist, zwischen den Urkunden des Alten Bundes und der in Christus eröffneten Offenbarung des Neuen Bundes, die zu einem vertieften Verständnis des Alten Testaments führt." For a detailed working out of this basic premise, see Seyoon Kim, *The Origin of Paul's Gospel, WUNT 2. Reihe 4*, 1981, esp. pp. 4, 126–136, 274 f. and 307 f., where he also argues that Paul's experience with the risen Christ led him to the insight that Christ was the end of the Law. Kim's key text for this position is 2 Cor. 3:4–4:6 (cf. pp. 5 ff., 128, and 229 ff.) !

[76] *Verstehen*, p. 68.

Moreover, Stuhlmacher pinpoints the results of Paul's hermeneutical reflection in 2 Cor. 3, especially verse 14. It is in this text that Paul makes explicit the foundation of his hermeneutic. For according to Stuhlmacher, 2 Cor. 3:14 indicates that Paul's experience forced him to conclude that a "veil" lay over the reading and interpreting of the Law which blinded the Jew to its proper meaning and, as a consequence, hindered him from gaining a true understanding of Christ.[77] Conversely, in Christ this veil is removed so that a true understanding of the Law is made possible. It thus follows for Paul

"... daß es seit der Erscheinung Jesu Christi wenigstens zwei Arten von Verständnis der Schrift gibt und damit zugleich zwei Weisen, in denen die Schrift begegnet. Man kann die Schrift lesen als Ansporn und Aufruf zu immer neuer Gesetzesfrömmigkeit. Dann exegesiert und hört man nach Meinung des Apostels mit verbundenen Sinnen, und die Schrift erscheint als ein von Christus wegführender, tötender Buchstabe (... *gramma*). Man kann aber auch aus der Begegnung mit Christus heraus aufbrechen und erkennen, daß alle Verheißungen Gottes in Christus bejaht worden sind (2. Kor 1:19 f.), und findet dann in der Schrift die tröstliche Urkunde der Führungen Gottes. Die so gelesenen Urkunden nennt Paulus immer wieder *graphē*, d.h. 'Schrift.'"[78]

For Stuhlmacher, therefore, like Käsemann before him, the γράμμα/πνεῦμα contrast between the Law of Moses and the Gospel of Christ leads Paul to a γράμμα/γραφή antithesis between the Law read as a death producing demand for works and the Law read in the light of one's encounter with Christ as "die tröstliche Urkunde der Führungen Gottes."[79] But whereas for Käsemann the decisive hermeneutical criterion which emerged from the letter/Spirit contrast was the theological principle of justification by faith, for Stuhlmacher it is Paul's Christological experience which supports both his view of the Law and his OT hermeneutic. It is God's revelation to Paul on the road to Damascus of the new covenant in Christ that not only leads him to an understanding of Christ as the "end of the Law," but also provides him with the key to the "true meaning" of the Law itself.

With the addition of Stuhlmacher's contribution it is now evident that the tendency of past scholars to ignore the wider hermeneutical dimensions of the letter/Spirit contrast has been seriously challenged. This fact has been confirmed by J. Chr. Beker's incorporation of the Kamlah-Käsemann-Stuhl-

---

[77] *Verstehen*, p. 68. Cf. now too his Tübingen colleague Otto Betz, "Der fleischliche Mensch und das geistliche Gesetz, Zum biblischen Hintergrund der paulinischen Gesetzeslehre," in his *Jesus, Der Herr der Kirche, Aufsätze zur biblischen Theologie II*, WUNT 52, 1990, pp. 129–196, p. 181, who argues that one of the two ways in which the Law is established in the new covenant, according to 2 Cor. 3:15 and with an allusion to 3:6, is hermeneutical. In Betz' view, the Spirit removes the veil which lies over the reading of the Law so that the Spirit may open up the prophetic meaning of the Scriptures, which points to Christ and "makes alive."

[78] *Verstehen*, pp. 68 f.

[79] Stuhlmacher's statement from *Verstehen*, p. 69 (n. 75) is also illustrative of this point. Stuhlmacher's contrast between γράμμα/γραφή is thus reminiscent of Kamlah's.

macher perspective into a comprehensive view of Paul's theology in his work, *Paul the Apostle, The Triumph of God in Life and Thought.*[80] Beker too introduces the γράμμα/γραφή antithesis as the heart of Paul's dialectical approach to the Law, which he then combines with Paul's "hermeneutic of 'pneumatic' freedom" based on Christ as its "key."[81] In his words,

"Although the relation of the law to Scripture is complicated in Paul, it demonstrates a new departure for a specifically Christian hermeneutic of Scripture. Despite the fact that Scripture in all its parts is the inspired, authoritative document of God's revelation to Israel, Paul makes its authority subject to Christ as the hermeneutical key to Scripture: (he then quotes 2 Cor. 3:15–17). Christ is the canon within the canon, so that Paul, in certain contexts, makes distinctions within Scripture between the letter and the Spirit (2 Cor. 3:6; Rom. 2:29[?]), between the law and Scripture (Gal. 3:21, 22), and between the promise and the law (Gal. 3:15–21). He can even quote Scripture against Scripture when he contrasts the works of the law to faith-righteousness (Rom. 10:5–9; Gal. 3:11–12)."[82]

As Beker's statements again make clear, at the heart of this new challenge stands the observation that Paul's new perspective "in Christ" forced him to confront not only the *theological* issue of the relationship between the Law and the Gospel (2 Cor. 3:6), but also its *hermeneutical* implications. This observation is buttressed by the context of the letter/Spirit contrast itself, in which the question of the reading of Moses in the light of Christ's coming is said to be directly addressed in 2 Cor. 3:7–18. According to the representatives of this approach, Paul's *own* response to this question was to advocate, both by precept (most explicitly in 2 Cor. 3:6 and 14–17) and by example (i.e. by the way he used the OT in 2 Cor. 3:7 ff. and elsewhere, most notably in Rom. 10:5 ff.), that the new covenant in Christ also implied a corresponding, distinctively Christian hermeneutic. Any reading of 2 Cor. 3 in its context that fails to elucidate these hermeneutical implications thus falls short of rediscovering Paul's *own* intention.

This paradigmatic approach to Paul's use of the Old Testament, in which his interpretation of the Scriptures is seen to be determined by his Christian presuppositions, especially Paul's new view of the Law, rather than by the original intent of the OT Scriptures themselves, has now found support in the massive and detailed 1986 study of Paul's OT hermeneutic by Dietrich-Alex Koch, *Die Schrift als Zeuge des Evangeliums: Untersuchungen zur Verwendung und zum Verständnis der Schrift bei Paulus.*[83] As a result of his insightful

---

[80] 1980, pp. 81 note, 120 f., 251–253, and 344. Although Beker does not refer to either Kamlah or Stuhlmacher, his position is close to that of Käsemann; cf. his reference to Käsemann on p. 252 and cf. Beker, p. 121 with Käsemann, "Geist," p. 282.

[81] Beker, *Paul the Apostle*, p. 120; cf. p. 81 note.

[82] Beker, *Paul the Apostle*, pp. 251 f. In support of this statement Beker refers to Käsemann, "The Spirit and the Letter," p. 166 (p. 390 n. 35).

[83] BHT Bd. 69. Koch's major and important work concludes with the issue of Paul's theological and corresponding hermeneutical convictions (cf. pp. 341–353), though its primary

study of the Pauline corpus, Koch concludes that although Paul shares his basic hermeneutical convictions with both early Christianity and the Judaism of his day, he nevertheless often goes beyond them. This is especially the case when Paul employs the Scriptures in regard to the interrelated themes of the righteousness of God and the Law on the one hand, and the calling of both Jews and Gentiles in relationship to the question of the continuing election of Israel on the other (p. 341). Due to the subject matter itself, it is in regard to these two themes that Paul uses the Scriptures most frequently, and engages his interpretive methods and "kompositorischen Mittel" most intensively (p. 341). For according to Koch, "mit der völligen Umwertung des Gesetzes und der Verkündigung einer neuen eschatologischen Situation, die Juden und Heiden gleichermaßen Zugang zum Heil eröffnet, begibt sich Paulus in einen fundamentalen Gegensatz zur Predigt der Synagoge und ihrer Schriftauslegung" (p. 341). In order to think through this "fundamental antithesis," Paul was forced to posit the question of an appropriate understanding of the Scriptures in order to demonstrate how the Scriptures offer a *present* witness *to* the Gospel as that which now reveals the righteousness of God to all those who believe (Rom. 3:21–22).[84]

But this understanding of the Scriptures as a witness to the Pauline Gospel, understood most clearly within Paul's doctrine of justification, runs counter to the prevailing understanding of the Scriptures. Thus, in Koch's view, Paul's appropriation of the OT as a witness to the Gospel, in view of his distinctively Christian presuppositions, can only succeed

> "a) on the basis of a fundamentally altered context of understanding (i.e. that the Scriptures are now fulfilled in Christ)
> b) through an explicitly selective use of the Scriptures
> c) through, in part, a massive intrusion into the wording of the Scriptural quotation[85]
> d) and through a peculiar 'distance free' use of Scripture to refer to the present, eschatological situation." (pp. 344–347)

---

focus is on the technical ways Paul adopts OT texts and the question of their identification. His detailed study of the various Pauline passages calls for a text by text response. The focus of this work is on one of these passages, 2 Cor. 3:4–18, which Koch himself admits is the pivotal text, since it is the only passage where Paul explicitly addresses the question of his hermeneutic.

[84] *Schrift*, pp. 341–343. Koch substantiates this conclusion by comparing Rom. 3:21 with Rom. 1:2, where the Scriptures are referred to in their prophetic function as "Vorausankündigung auf das εὐαγγέλιον περὶ Ἰησοῦ Χριστοῦ" in accord with pre-Pauline, early Christian, Christological use of the Scriptures, rather than seen as presenting a specifically "soteriological interpretation" of the Gospel, as in Rom. 1:21 (p. 342). As further examples, Koch then points to Rom. 4 and 10:5–8 (pp. 343 f.).

[85] According to Koch, *Schrift*, p. 187, of the 93 texts cited by Paul, 59 are altered in 125 different ways. Of these, the following 11, in addition to 2 Cor. 3:16, contain the most intensive changes (three or more): Rom. 2:24 (Is. 52:5); 3:10–12 (Ps. 13:1–3); 3:15–17 (Is. 59:7,8); 9:17 (Ex. 9:16); 9:25 (Hos. 2:25); 10:6–8 (Deut. 30:12–14); 11:3 (1 Kgs. 19:10); 11:8 (Deut. 29:3); 1 Cor. 14:21 (Is. 28:11 f.); Gal. 3:10 (Deut. 27:26); 3:13 (Deut. 21:23).

Of special significance for this study is the fact that in support of this distinctively Christian hermeneutic, Koch too sees the letter/Spirit contrast in 3:6 as a contrast between the Mosaic Law as a power, which itself judges and brings about death as an instrument of sin, and the Spirit as the transformed "Verstehenshorizont, der der jetzt praktizierten Auslegung und Aneignung der Schrift vorausliegt" (p. 339).[86] For Koch, therefore, the letter/Spirit contrast is not a contrast between the γράμμα and the γραφή, in which the "Scripture" is the inner meaning of the "letter" or in which the letter and the Spirit are two entities within Scripture itself. Rather, "Die Antithese von γράμμα und πνεῦμα markiert somit den fundamentalen Verstehensunterschied, der mit der christlichen Verwendung der Schrift gegeben ist" (pp. 339 f.). In short, the Spirit, which for Paul is interpreted as Christ's salvific work in bringing about freedom from the Law, "opens up the understanding of Scripture" (p. 340). Hence, the letter/Spirit contrast undergirds the fact that for Paul the Gospel concerning Jesus Christ is the "sachgemäße Verstehensvoraussetzung der Schrift" (p. 340).

Koch points to 2 Cor. 3:12–17, which he stresses is not accidentally related to 3:6 f. (!), as a prime example of the conscious application of this fundamental alteration of the "horizon of understanding," based on the presupposition of the Gospel, from which Paul reads the Old Testament (p. 345). This view is supported by Koch's interpretation of 3:14–15 as a reference to the question of the proper interpretation of the Scriptures "in Christ," taking the "reading of Moses" in v. 15 to be equivalent to the "reading of the old covenant" in v. 14 (cf. pp. 334 f.). Moreover, for Koch, the distinctively Christian perspective clearly evident in 2 Cor. 3:12 ff. determines all of Paul's other textual adaptations and selective uses of the Old Testament, even though Paul shares many of the exegetical methods themselves with his contemporaries (cf. pp. 345–350). Koch is careful to make clear, however, that Paul's use of the Old Testament, especially his practice of altering the text itself, is not a sign of an "exegetical freedom" made possible by the Spirit, over against the "tyranny of the words."[87] For as Koch points out, in addition to the fact that the letter/Spirit contrast cannot be read as a contrast between the formal and "real meaning" of the text, for Paul it is precisely the altered quotation *itself* which becomes constitutive for Paul's argument (p. 346). Indeed, in the vast majority of cases the Scriptural quotation is not explained, but itself contains Paul's point and thus functions to establish or further Paul's argument (pp. 346 f.). Rather, what legitimates Paul's ability to adopt the Old Testament in these

---

[86] Koch, *Schrift*, p. 339 nn. 41–43, follows Kamlah and Käsemann in seeing the Law as a power in 3:6, but rejects Käsemann's view that it is the Jewish misinterpretation of the Law, rather than the Law itself, which kills.

[87] *Schrift*, p. 346. Koch is quoting and responding to the position of Grant, *Letter*, p. 51, who concluded in relation to 2 Cor. 3:17 that "this Spirit gives exegetical freedom. He destroys the tyranny of the words. He makes possible a Christian exegesis of the Old Testament, intuitive rather than based on words" (quoted on p. 346 n. 21).

unprecedented ways is his conviction concerning the "consistency *(Selbigkeit)* of God," so that God's present revelation and work in Christ cannot bring him into a self-contradiction (pp. 347 f.). Paul maintains this in spite of the fact that in Christ he comes to the startling conclusion concerning the Scriptures that there is no evidence of a saving and electing work of God between Abraham and the Fathers in the past and the eschatological work of God in the present (p. 348; cf. p. 352). For it is the present work in Christ which is now *definitive* both for Paul's understanding of God and of God's work in the history of Israel as seen in the Scriptures (pp. 349 f.).

In Koch's view, therefore, it is not as if Paul relates the kerygma of God's present work in Christ to the Scriptures as two objective realities to be compared. Instead, the work of God witnessed to in the Scriptures is now related directly to the present work of God in Christ (pp. 349 f.). Instead of a mutual conformity or inner-historical continuum between Scripture on the one hand and the revelation of the righteousness of God and the calling of both Jews and Gentiles in Christ on the other, for Paul it is the latter which defines the former. This distinctively Christian approach to the Scriptures produces the tensions which exist between Paul's interpretation of the OT and its Jewish interpretation, and between Paul's interpretation and alteration of the text for the sake of his new understanding in Christ and the Scripture itself (pp. 350 f.). But inasmuch as the inner consistency of God can be seen in the Christological confession itself and in its explication in Paul's doctrine of justification, there is no need to prove the theological legitimacy of Paul's use of Scripture by questioning whether such discrepancies exist between his use of the OT and the OT itself (since they certainly do). Nor is there any need to establish the legitimacy of Paul's interpretation on the basis of some principle apart from Paul's use of the OT itself (p. 350). For again, 2 Cor. 3:7–18 demonstrates that in Christ the Scripture is no longer the same as it used to be (p. 352). Rather, it has received a "renewed relevance" precisely through this fundamental break between its meaning apart from Christ and its meaning from the perspective of Christ (pp. 352 f.).

Koch's understanding of the various ways in which Paul reinterprets and alters the Old Testament in view of his distinctively Christian hermeneutic, which he marshalls in support of these wide ranging conclusions, can only be responded to on a passage by passage basis. What is significant for this study, however, is his recognition that 2 Cor. 3:6–18 plays a central role in ascertaining the nature of Paul's OT hermeneutic in two ways. First, it provides an extended interpretation of an Old Testament text in which Paul's various methods and perspectives are said to play a decisive role. Second, and even more importantly, Koch rightly points out that 2 Cor. 3 is the only passage where Paul explicitly reflects on the implications of his Christian convictions and presuppositions for the interpretation of the Scriptures. For as Koch emphasizes, early Christianity shared with Judaism the conviction that the Scriptures looked forward to a future salvific event and pointed people to this event

(p. 331). Indeed, prior to Paul the early Church had already concluded that the Scriptures were in fact pointing to the salvation which had taken place in Christ, which in itself introduced a fundamental change in the content of the Old Testament (p. 331). Hence, Paul had inherited the view that the same Scripture could be heard and read from different presuppositions (p. 331). But it is only in 2 Cor. 3:12–17, according to Koch, that Paul himself addresses this problem thematically in his writings (p. 331). 2 Cor. 3:12–18 thus becomes Koch's test case for his conclusion that Paul's Gospel is the explicit presupposition for his distinctly Christian understanding and alteration of the Scriptures (cf. pp. 331–341).

Finally, the recent appearance of Richard Hays' 1989 treatment of Paul's hermeneutic, *Echoes of Scripture in the Letters of Paul*,[88] indicates that this perspective is now firmly entrenched in Pauline scholarship. At the heart of Hays' study lies the conviction that "Israel's Scripture was ... the grand textual matrix within which Paul's thought took shape, the privileged predecessor with which he wrestled ..." (p. 122). It is only "reasonable," therefore, "to ask whether he had a coherent and consciously articulated hermeneutic" (pp. 122 f.). Moreover, although passages like Romans 15:4 and 1 Corinthians 10:11 provide pointers to Paul's hermeneutical practice, "they do not address the theoretical problem of continuity and discontinuity, a problem that Christians later came to know as the problem of the relation between the testaments" (p. 123). Hays recognizes that the answer to this question can only be formulated on the basis of the "one lengthy passage in Paul's surviving correspondence that has traditionally been read as his definitive reflection on this hermeneutical issue: in 2 Cor. 3:1–4:6 Paul contrasts 'the letter' and 'the Spirit' as hallmarks of the distinction between the old covenant and the new" (p. 123). In Hays' words, "Any investigation of intertextuality in Paul's letters must come to grips with the hermeneutical implications of this passage," especially "the heart of the matter" as formulated in the letter/Spirit contrast in 3:6 (p. 123).

As these statements reveal, Hays is also careful to delineate the distinction between the meaning of the contrast in 3:6 itself and its subsequent "implications" for the question of Paul's hermeneutic. In view of 3:6 itself, the key question thus becomes, "... does this new-covenant ministry-competence en-

---

[88] The work of Richard Longenecker, *Biblical Exegesis in the Apostolic Period*, 1975, deals with the entire NT and focuses on the interpretive techniques employed in Jewish literature and their possible parallels among NT authors; for his understanding of Paul's techniques, see pp. 104–132. For a concise survey of the history of research on the use of the OT in the NT, see now E. Earle Ellis, *The Old Testament in Early Christianity, Canon and Interpretation in the Light of Modern Research*, 1992, pp. 53–74. Ellis points out that the two core problems throughout the history of research have been the nature of the textual variations and the theological/hermeneutical interpretations or exegetical explanations of the OT found in the NT (cf. pp. 55, 59, 61, 65, 74). Both of these issues come together explicitly in 2 Cor. 3.

tail a new form of reader-competence ... did Paul find himself given new eyes to read Scripture in a new way?" (p. 123). For Hays, Paul's use of Scripture elsewhere leads one to respond positively to this question. Indeed, 3:12–18 itself "certainly suggests that a new reader-competence is born in the Christian convert" (p. 124).

But again, Hays is careful at this point. He observes that this is the case in spite of the fact that "protest is certainly justified" against the Church's past misuse of the letter/Spirit contrast to support "esoteric allegorical readings," to which must be added the awareness that in 2 Cor. 3:1 ff. "Paul is writing an apologia for his ministry, not an excursus on hermeneutical method" (pp. 124 f.). For Hays, therefore, the issue to be resolved in pursuit of whether or not Paul affirmed such a new, Christian "reader-competence" is the meaning of the letter/Spirit antithesis itself, understood as a realistic contrast, within the context of Paul's larger argument. Such an attempt, however, leads to a subsequent question:

"If Paul is neither a philosophical idealist nor an apologist for the Alexandrian brand of Platonizing allegory, what does he mean by his distinction between *gramma* and *pneuma*, and why does his contrast between the old and new covenants turn into a discussion of minds veiled and unveiled when Scripture is read?" (p. 125)

Like Käsemann, Stuhlmacher, Beker, and Koch, Hays too clearly perceives the contours of the current debate. His insightful analysis also leads to an equally helpful starting point, stressing that "questions such as these are best addressed through a fresh reading of the text" (p. 125). As the interplay between 3:6 and 3:12–18 itself indicates, in this reading "we should pay attention not only to what the text says about the interpretation of Scripture but also to how the text uses Scripture. If the text does offer a hermeneutic, it is reasonable to expect Paul's practice to exemplify – and therefore to illuminate – the theory that he espouses" (p. 125).[89] As a result, Hays' own subsequent analysis of Paul's argument in 2 Cor. 3:1–4:6 becomes the crucial test case for Hays' overall understanding of what he calls Paul's "ecclesiocentric hermeneutic" (cf. pp. 84–87).

---

[89] See now Carol K. Stockhausen, "2 Corinthians 3 and the Principles of Pauline Exegesis," in *Paul and the Scriptures of Israel, Studies in Scripture in Early Judaism and Christianity 1*, JSNT Suppl. Series 83, 1993, pp. 143–164, p. 145, who also argues that Paul does not describe his exegetical process *per se*, but that "we see only its results, as the shape of his arguments express his hermeneutic." In regard to 2 Cor. 3, Stockhausen disagrees with Hays, *Echoes*, pp. 137, 140, 147, that Exod. 34 functioned in Paul's argument only to stimulate Paul's hermeneutical discussion, but played no further role in determining it. In contrast, Stockhausen argues that although Exod. 34 "in itself has nothing to do with the interpretive process ... once chosen by Paul, Exodus 34 did exercise a continuous and dynamic influence on Paul's discussion" (p. 144 n. 4). Yet inasmuch as Exod. 34 itself did not give rise to the theological principles employed by Paul (cf. p. 144), for Stockhausen too Paul's interpretation of the OT in 2 Cor. 3 is guided ultimately by his own presuppositions and hermeneutical principles.

At this point, however, the value of Hays' work resides in the way in which he has joined those already treated in pinpointing the exegetical and theological/hermeneutical questions in 2 Cor. 3:6 ff. and in his recognition of the significance of this text for Paul's hermeneutic in general. Hays is correct that his overall theory concerning the nature of Paul's hermeneutic stands or falls with his interpretation of the letter/Spirit contrast *itself*, read within the context of Paul's *own* subsequent interpretation of the OT in 3:7 ff. For as we have seen, the weight of the emerging historical-critical method crushed the past attempts to justify a hermeneutical interpretation of the letter/Spirit contrast. The new challenge initiated by Kamlah and Käsemann has won the right to a hearing because of its own commitment to take Paul's original intention in 2 Cor. 3:6 seriously. The fundamental thesis of the modern consensus that the attempt to extract a hermeneutical meaning from the letter/Spirit contrast itself is merely a matter of eisegesis is affirmed by Kamlah, Käsemann, Stuhlmacher, Beker, Koch, Hays, and those who follow them. But because they tacitly recognize the important distinction between a text's meaning and its subsequent significance, they are also able to argue that the economy-of-salvation-*heilsgeschichtliche* meaning of the contrast has further implications for the development of a Christian hermeneutic. Moreover, and this is the point that must be emphasized, they assert that the significance of the letter/Spirit contrast for hermeneutics was first recognized and presented by Paul himself! Hence, this new challenge finds its strength in its ability to argue exegetically, and not merely theologically or philosophically,[90] that part of the significance of this contrast, as evidenced by Paul's own writings and the context of 2 Cor. 3:6 itself, was a hermeneutical one. As Käsemann boldly asserts,

"Zum Problem der Auslegung muß ich als Exeget argumentieren, der die erste grundsätzliche hermeneutische Überlegung im Neuen Testament selbst, nämlich die paulinische Unterscheidung von πνεῦμα und γράμμα, ins Auge faßt."[91]

---

[90] In my opinion, therefore, the attempt by Jacob Kremer, "'Denn der Buchstabe Tötet, Der Geist aber macht lebendig,' Methodologische und hermeneutische Erwägungen zu 2 Kor 3:6b," in *Begegnung mit dem Wort, FS Heinrich Zimmermann,* Bonner Biblische Beiträge 53, ed. J. Zmijewski and E. Nellessen, 1980, pp. 219–250, to derive a meaning from 2 Cor. 3:6, interpreted as a gnome, which it does not have in its context is a step backward and must be rejected; see his pp. 219, 231–233, 243–246.

[91] "Zum Gegenwärtigen Streit um die Schriftauslegung," in his *Exegetische Versuche und Besinnungen, Zweiter Band,* 1970³, pp. 268–290, p. 276. Käsemann's impulse was also picked up and developed in terms of the necessary role of the Spirit in interpreting what is "written" (*gramma*) by Peter Richardson, "Spirit and Letter: A Foundation for Hermeneutics," *EvQ* 45 (1973) 208–218. Richardson's thesis is that within the letter/Spirit contrast in 2 Cor. 3 "there is latent the demand for interpretation at the instigation of the Spirit" (p. 209). This Spirit-led interpretation is then evidenced in Paul's own reading of Ex. 34 in 3:7–18 with its emphasis on the Spirit as the interpreter of the old covenant (212 f.) and the unveiler of the true meaning of the ancient writings (214 f.). Paul's purpose in 2 Cor. 3, therefore, is to point to the Spirit as the "foundation for hermeneutics in the life of the Church at Corinth" (215).

Käsemann and those who have followed in his train have thus certainly thrown down the gauntlet in front of the modern consensus concerning the non-hermeneutical interpretation of the letter/Spirit contrast.[92] And not without response.[93] In view of the current proposals in Pauline studies concerning a specifically Pauline hermeneutic anchored in 2 Cor. 3, the need for a detailed reexamination of the letter/Spirit antithesis as implying a *hermeneutical* contrast is therefore also manifest.[94]

4. The Problems Presented by the Letter/Spirit Contrast and Paul's Self-Conception as an Apostle

In once again taking up the letter/Spirit contrast in 2 Cor. 3:6, the interpreter is consequently faced with two interrelated problems. First, the meaning of the contrast itself and its implications for the unresolved debate concerning Paul's view of the Law are open to question in a way unimaginable 25 years ago. In

---

[92] See, especially, the significant work of Samuel Vollenweider, "2 Kor 3: Der transzendente Schein des Gesetzes," in his *Freiheit als neue Schöpfung, Eine Untersuchung zur Eleutheria bei Paulus und in seiner Umwelt*, FRLANT 147, 1989, pp. 247–284. Vollenweider follows the lead of Käsemann and Koch (cf. his pp. 271 n. 377, 272 n. 379, 276 n. 400) in seeing the letter/Spirit contrast as a response to the theological problem of the Law (p. 267) in which the contrast is essentially between two "elementary powers" (p. 271). But it also entails a hermeneutical application in which Paul reads the OT γράμμα as γραφή, i.e. in a distinctively Christian or "spiritual" way that leads to an allegorical and typological rereading of the text (cf. pp. 264 f., 267, 276 f.). Though this aspect of Vollenweider's thesis will be questioned in the work below, many of his exegetical insights and interactions with secondary literature are extremely valuable.

[93] See, e.g., the response of Westerholm, "Letter and Spirit" (cf. above, n. 69) and his conclusion on p. 241, that, against Käsemann, "the letter-spirit antithesis has nothing to do with Pauline hermeneutics. In no case do the terms refer to an inadequate and an adequate way of reading the sacred scriptures, rather they are used of man's obligation to God under the old and new dispensations. The letter-spirit antithesis is thus the key to Pauline ethics, not Pauline hermeneutics." See too now Westerholm, *Israel's Law*, pp. 210–216.

[94] Carol Kern Stockhausen's full length study of this passage, *Moses' Veil and the Glory of the New Covenant, The Exegetical Substructure of II Cor. 3:1–4:6*, AB 116, 1989, p. 8, also suggests that although Origen's view cannot be accepted "without reservation," "it does grasp one of the dimensions of Paul's intention." Stockhausen thus hopes to show that the "two historically adverse positions are not necessarily mutually exclusive alternatives" (p. 9). But for Stockhausen the relationship between the two views is one of degree of appropriateness. Thus, since the letter/Spirit contrast is a contrast between "covenant benefits or characteristics rather than between hermeneutical principles," for Stockhausen the non-hermeneutical view associated with Tertullian, etc. "is *more* correct than the tradition stemming from Origen" (p. 62 n. 57, emphasis mine). The recent work of Linda L. Belleville, *Reflections of Glory, Paul's Polemical Use of the Moses-Doxa Tradition in 2 Corinthians 3.1–18*, JSNT Supplement Series 52, 1991, also raises the hermeneutical issues surrounding Paul's use of the OT, though it does not link these to the letter/Spirit contrast in any substantive way. The focus of the work is rather on 3:12–18 within the overall structure of 2 Cor. 1–7 and against the backdrop of post-biblical Jewish tradition.

view of the panorama of opinions currently being offered in search of a new paradigm, this study seeks to elucidate the meaning of the letter/Spirit contrast within its own context, rather than viewing it merely as a dictum within the larger question of Paul and the Law. Only then can this text offer its distinct contribution to this larger debate. Second, the fundamental challenge posed by the studies of Kamlah, Käsemann, Stuhlmacher, Beker, Koch, and Hays must be taken up and put to the test.[95] But again, it is the context of the letter/Spirit contrast itself that must prove determinative for evaluating this challenge and not some external thesis concerning "Pauline hermeneutics." This is especially apparent in view of the fact that 2 Cor. 3:6 initiates an extended interpretation of a specific OT tradition, within which Paul himself offers explicit statements concerning the reading of the old covenant Scriptures (cf. 3:14–15). Any discussion of Paul's OT hermeneutic, based on the letter/Spirit contrast, must therefore take seriously Paul's own exegetical practice and principles as demonstrated and declared in 3:7–18. These problems and the debate which surrounds them not only provide the rationale for undertaking this study, but also determine its twofold purpose.

In an earlier study I have therefore tried to outline the larger context from which Paul's letter/Spirit contrast takes its bearings and in which it is to be understood.[96] There I argued that by the time of the writing of 2 Cor. 2:14 ff.,

---

[95] See too Peter von der Osten-Sacken, "Die Decke des Mose," pp. 91, 94 f., who points out the need for a monograph to handle the secondary literature on this passage in an attempt to draw out the hermeneutical consequences of one's interpretation of 2 Cor. 3:6 within the context of the chapter.

[96] See my *Suffering and the Spirit*, pp. 1 f., 7 f.; hereafter page references given in the body of the text. Stockhausen's study, *Moses' Veil*, independent of my work, has also presented a strong case for viewing 2 Cor. 3:6 within the context of 3:1–6 (though dated 1989, Stockhausen's work is a publication of her dissertation, which was finished in 1984. She has not incorporated into her book the literature published since that time). She too argues convincingly, on the basis of Ezek. 11 and 36, that at the heart of Paul's argument in 3:3, "the spirit itself in all its manifestations is then the verification of the reality of the new covenant, Paul's recommendation" (p. 76). Her understanding of 3:1–3 varies from mine, however, at significant points. On the one hand, she understands Paul to be arguing in 3:1 ff. not only for the validity of his apostleship, but also for the validity of the Christian standing of the *Corinthians* themselves (p. 38). On the other hand, Stockhausen divorces 3:1 ff. from 2:14–17 (pp. 33–35, cf. esp. p. 35 n. 7). In my view, the status of the Corinthians as genuine Christians was never in question in Corinth (though for some it was for Paul, cf. 2 Cor. 13:5–9) and even becomes the presupposition for Paul's defense in 3:2 f. My study as a whole has tried to demonstrate the extremely close and necessary conceptual links between 2:14–17 and 3:1–3, though I certainly agree that the argument continues in 3:4 ff. But because of Stockhausen's decision to start with 3:1, she does not see the role and question of Paul's suffering in his ongoing apologetic, and therefore can only conclude that in 3:1 ff. "Paul is not being specific enough" and that "He gives very little information about the background events which gave rise to his outright refusal to supply letters of recommendation (3:1) ..." (p. 35). Hence, for Stockhausen, "No previous argument explains Paul's abrupt rejection of such an ordinary means of social legitimation" (p. 36). For an evaluation of her specific views of 3:1–6, see chapter two.

the situation in Corinth had changed. Previously, the appropriateness of Paul's suffering as an apostle was common ground between Paul and the Corinthians (cf. 1 Cor. 4:14–17; 11:1). Now Paul's status as an apostle is itself being challenged and his suffering used as a pivotal argument *against* his apostolic authority (cf. pp. 65–67). The purpose of the catalogs of suffering in 2 Corinthians has therefore also changed. Rather than functioning as a warning to the *Corinthians* (cf. 1 Cor. 4:6 ff.), they now form an essential part of Paul's *self-defense* as an apostle (cf. 2 Cor. 4:7–12; 6:1–10; 11:21–33) (p. 67). Paul's legitimacy as an apostle can no longer be assumed (cf. 1 Cor. 9:1 f.), it must now be defended.

In 2 Cor. 2:14–3:3 Paul thus picks up the διάκονος-terminology and the "theology of glory" motif, most likely introduced into the Corinthian situation by his opponents (cf. 2 Cor. 11:23), in order to use these same categories to demonstrate the genuine nature of his own ministry (pp. 81 f.). Specifically, I have tried to show that, against this attack on his apostolic authority, 2 Cor. 2:14–3:3 is a corresponding compendium of Paul's self-conception as an apostle in which he offers a summary of his twofold apologetic for the legitimacy and validity of his ministry.

On the one hand, I have argued that 2 Cor. 2:14–16a parallels 1 Cor. 4:9 and 2 Cor. 4:11 as a thesis-like declaration of the role of Paul's apostolic "sentence of death" (θριαμβεύειν) in the salvific plan of God (cf. pp. 18–54, 83). But unlike 1 Corinthians, where Paul presented his suffering as the active *corollary* to the *cross* of Christ, in 2 Cor. 2:14–16a Paul portrays himself as a passive *antithesis* to the *glory* of Christ (cf. 2 Cor. 4:4) (pp. 68 f., 81). Rather than calling his apostleship into question, Paul's suffering becomes the necessary platform for the display of God's resurrection power, expressed through God's rescuing and sustaining activity in Paul's life (cf. 2 Cor. 1:3–11; 4:8–12) (p. 82). Interpreted in terms of the death and resurrection-life of Jesus (cf. 2 Cor. 1:9 f.; 4:10–12), Paul's suffering thus affirms the cross and reveals God's resurrection glory in Christ. Moreover, Paul's suffering in Corinth is due, in part, to his own decision to preach the Gospel there free of charge (cf. 1 Cor. 9; 2 Cor. 11:7–15; 12:12–19). As a result, Paul's commitment not to "sell the word of God like a retailer in the market" (καπηλεύοντες τὸν λόγον τοῦ θεοῦ) not only calls his opponents' motives into question, but also establishes the sincerity and divine origin of his own (2:17) (pp. 103–176). For Paul's suffering as a result of his constant anxiety over his church (2 Cor. 2:12 f.; cf. 11:28) and his practice of self-support are evidence of his love for the Corinthians (p. 174).[97] Paul therefore praises God for the very experiences

---

[97] David A. Renwick's subsequent work, *Paul, the Temple, and the Presence of God*, 1991, has added further support to many aspects of my thesis through his study of the structure of Paul's thought in 2:14–3:18 in view of the fact that "the issue of finding God's presence and living within it was a recurrent, and at times, central passion in the broad literary background and experience of faithful Jews in the first century of the common era" (p. 43). See especially his study of the sacrificial and cultic background of ὀσμή and εὐωδία,

of "being led to death" in his suffering that his opponents suggest call his apostleship into question (2:14), because through these experiences he becomes a revelatory agent of the knowledge of God in Christ (2:15–16a).[98]

But Paul's argument for his legitimacy, based on his suffering, is not merely an exercise in "self-commendation" (2 Cor. 3:1). As 3:2 f. make clear, Paul's second evidential argument for the legitimacy of his apostleship is the spiritual existence of the Corinthian Church itself (cf. pp. 177–218). Their own reception of the Spirit through Paul's ministry demonstrates that his suffering is in no way contrary or a hindrance to the full expression of God's power in his ministry (cf. 2 Cor. 3:2 f. with 1 Cor. 2:1–5).[99] The Corinthians cannot deny the

---

κατέναντι θεοῦ, and εἰλικρίνεια in 2:14–16 (pp. 61–94). But Renwick fails to see the evidential nature of Paul's argument in 2:14–17. In his view, 2:14–17 are "assertions without proof," with the necessary "experiential evidence for the validity of his apostleship" first being given in 3:1–3 (p. 50; cf. pp. 94 f., 98). For the import of his thesis that "the theme of God's presence can be understood to function as an interpretive key to Paul's argument not only in II Cor. 2:14–17 ... but also in II Cor. 3:1–18 ..." (p. 76), see the chapters below.

[98] This thesis concerning the relationship between suffering and the Spirit in Paul's thought and experience has now been confirmed by Ulrich Heckel's important study of the relationship between "power" and "weakness" in Paul's life and ministry as portrayed in 2 Cor. 10–13. See his *Kraft in Schwachheit, Untersuchungen zu 2. Kor 10–13*, WUNT 2. Reihe 56, 1993. As Heckel concludes, p. 107, "Wer die äußere Situation der Schwachheit zur Bedingung für das Wirksamwerden der Kraft Christi erklärt, stellt nur den *Ausgangsvorwurf aus 10:7b–10* auf den Kopf und vertauscht die Vorzeichen, aber löst den Widerspruch zwischen Vollmachtsanspruch und schwachem Auftreten nicht auf. Gerade diesen Widerspruch will Paulus aber überwinden und zeigen, daß seine Schwachheit und die Kraft Christi in seiner apostolischen Vollmacht sich nicht verrechnen lassen, weder sich gegenseitig bedingen noch einander ausschließen. Deshalb verkehrt der Apostel, wenn er sich seiner Schwachheiten rühmt, das gegnerische Selbstlob der eigenen Stärken nicht einfach ins Gegenteil. Dem Verlangen nach Kraftbeweisen stellt er nicht einfach seine Schwachheit gegenüber, sondern die Kraft Christi in dieser Schwachheit. Auch für Paulus bildet nicht schon die Schwachheit an und für sich das Gütesiegel seines Apostolats, sondern der Schlüssel zu seinem Amtsverständnis liegt in der Kraft und Vollmacht, die ihm der Herr gegeben hat (10:8; 13:10) und *in* seiner menschlichen Schwachheit zur Entfaltung und Vollendung bringt (12:9a)" (emphasis his).

[99] This fits well with the suggestion of Renwick, *Temple*, p. 51, that, given the cultic context of 2 Cor. 2:14–17, the key question raised against Paul by his opponents was whether Paul's suffering was an indication of God's displeasure with him, which in turn meant his consequent exclusion from God's presence as "blemished" (cf. Lev. 21–22). But Renwick argues that this question was raised not about Paul's apostleship as such, but only about his *continuing* sufficiency, so that the question becomes: "Can Paul, admitting that he was *once* an apostle, yet given the extent of the tribulation that *now* characterizes his life, *still* be conceived as an apostle, one who stands in the presence of God?" (p. 96, emphasis his). But Paul's life as an apostle had always been characterized by suffering (cf. 2 Cor. 11:30–33; Acts 9:23–25). Moreover, if Paul's continuing sufficiency could be separated from his original call and earlier ministry, then Paul's own arguments for his present legitimacy, based on his founding function in regard to the Corinthian church, carry no weight (cf. 1 Cor. 9:1 f.; 2 Cor. 3:1–3; 10:13–18). Renwick himself asserts that "the only real *proof* that Paul provides of his apostleship is that which the Corinthians cannot deny – that it was through Paul's ministry alone [but see above, n. 97] that the Corinthians had found 'life'" (p. 98, emphasis his). For a full discussion of Renwick's thesis, as well as the many other re-

authentic nature of Paul's ministry of the Spirit in the midst of his suffering without denying their own Christian identity and pneumatic experience.[100] Moreover, the Corinthians' own conversion and new life in the Spirit testify to the fact that Paul's ministry represents and *affects* the breaking in of the power of the new age in fulfillment of the eschatological promises of Ezek. 11:19 and 36:26 (cf. Ezek. 37:26 ff.) (pp. 204–208, 215–218). The very existence of the Corinthians as Christians is evidence the new age has dawned and that Paul himself now occupies a crucial role in its establishment as the mediator of the Spirit to the Gentiles (pp. 215 f.).

As the "Spirit-giver" who suffers, Paul thus pictures himself as occupying the intermediary role of a revelatory agent of the glory of God to his people. The essential content of his mediation between God in Christ and the church is the Spirit. The means of his mediation is his suffering. The proof of his mediation is not only his willingness to take on this suffering (2:17), but also the effects of his ministry in the lives of those to whom he is called (2:15–16a; 3:1–3). The result of his mediation is to extend the inbreaking of the new age among the Gentiles. To reject Paul's apostleship, therefore, is to place oneself outside of the work of God in the world (cf. 2 Cor. 13:5, 10) (pp. 220 f.).

This is the context within which the letter/Spirit contrast must be interpreted. For as an introductory thanksgiving, both the tone and the themes of 2:14–4:6 are already clearly outlined in 2:14–16a (pp. 10–12; 87). The tone is apologetic, and the theme is the genuine nature of Paul's role as a mediatory agent between God and his people. Within this context, 2 Cor. 3:6 is not a detached and dogmatic theological maxim to be read first and foremost as part of Paul's larger "view of the Law" (p. 83). Indeed, as the parallel between 2 Cor. 2:17 and 4:1 f. shows, the issue throughout 3:4–18 is still whether or not Paul's ministry of suffering can be integrated with his ministry of the Spirit (pp. 86 f.; 224 f.). The letter/Spirit contrast is therefore an essential aspect of Paul's apologetic for the legitimacy of his apostolic ministry of the Spirit. In the same way, Paul's understanding of the contrast between the letter and the Spirit as outlined in 3:7–18 also first finds its significance as an expression of Paul's self-understanding as an apostle. This is not to deny that the letter/Spirit contrast has significance for understanding Paul's view of the Law. Certainly it does. But its significance is to be derived from its use in the context of 2 Cor. 2:14–4:6, not taken apart from it.

This brings us to the present study. On the basis of these conclusions I went on to posit in my earlier work that Paul implicitly portrayed his apostolic role in 2 Cor. 2:14–3:3 to be the eschatological counterpart to the role of Moses as

---

sponses to my former work, see the forthcoming second, revised edition of my *Suffering and the Spirit*.

[100] Most recently this view has been stressed by Hays, *Echoes*, pp. 127, 138, and becomes the central pillar in his thesis concerning Paul's metaphorical use of Scripture in 2 Cor. 3:7–18 (cf. pp. 149 f.). For my critique of Hays' adaptation of this aspect of Paul's apologetic for interpreting Paul's hermeneutic, see chapter five.

the mediator *par excellence* between YHWH and his people (pp. 216–221). I suggested as a working hypothesis that this is clear both in Paul's conception of his ministry of suffering (2:14–17) and in his conviction that his ministry of the Spirit was a fulfillment of Ezek. 11:19 and 36:26 (3:1–3) (p. 218). For in both cases, Paul's apologetic seems to be explicitly anchored in his *sufficiency* as an apostle (cf. 2:16b: ἱκανός; 3:5: ἱκανοί, ἱκανότης; 3:6: ἱκάνωσεν). And this sufficiency appears to be derived from his call to be an apostle as this is consciously modeled after the sufficiency of Moses in Exodus 4:10 LXX (pp. 98–101; 220 f.). The substantiation of this hypothesis and its implications for understanding 2 Cor. 3:4–6a are the subject of chapters one and two.[101]

But if Paul's authority as an apostle is based in some sense on the *parallel* between his sufficiency and the sufficiency of Moses, it is also equally supported by the *contrast* between his διακονία and the διακονία of Moses (cf. 2 Cor. 3:6–18). Paul is called like Moses to be an intermediary between God and his people, but with a distinctive, and seemingly even contradictory ministry! As an extension of the tension which has long been recognized to exist within Paul's understanding of the contrast between the Law and the Gospel, in which Paul apparently affirms both negative and positive things about the Law, in 2 Cor. 3 Paul is also apparently caught up in an unresolved tension concerning the ministry of Moses in relationship to his own.[102] For as E.P. Sanders has observed, in 2 Cor. 3:7 Paul declares that the Mosaic dispensation of *death*, focused on the letter which kills (3:6), was nevertheless *glorious*, so that Paul "is caught here as elsewhere between two convictions, but here there is no struggle to resolve them; he states them both as facts."[103] The second

---

[101] Confirmation of this thesis is now found in Stockhausen, *Moses' Veil*, pp. 41 f., 83 f., who also argues that Ex. 4:10 (LXX) is the backdrop to 3:5 and to the ἱκανός-terminology as well (now followed by Renwick, *Temple*, pp. 92 f.). Hence, she too sees "the model of Moses" to play a key role not only in 3:7–18, but also in 3:1–6, though with different results in part (see chapter two) and without the explicit tie either to 2:16b or to the prophetic call tradition as outlined below in chapter one. As I am, she too is indebted at this point to the work of Peter Jones, *The Apostle Paul: A Second Moses According to II Corinthians 2:14–4:7*, Ph.D. diss. Princeton Theological Seminary, 1973, and Austin M. Farrer, "The Ministry in the New Testament," in *The Apostolic Ministry, Essays on the History and the Doctrine of Episcopacy*, ed. K.E. Kirk, 1946, pp. 115–182 (cf. Stockhausen, pp. 42 n. 20; 84 n. 84). See now Peter Jones, *La Deuxieme Epitre de Paul aux Corinthiens*, CEB 14, 1992, pp. 56–83.

[102] It is this tension in Paul's thought which has not only led to various interpretations of Paul's view of the Law seen as a conceptual unity (as surveyed above), but also given rise to a developmental understanding of Paul's thought in this regard, as well as to the ideas of those who simply posit that concerning the nature and function of the Law Paul's thought is hopelessly self-contradictory. For a full scale presentation of a developmental view, see Hans Hübner, *Das Gesetz bei Paulus, Ein Beitrag zum Werden der paulinischen Theologie*, FRLANT 119, 1980², and for the view that Paul's thought on the Law is self-contradictory and cannot be reconciled, see now the influential work of Heikki Räisänen, *Paul and the Law*, 1986 (1983).

[103] *Paul, the Law, and the Jewish People*, p. 138. Because he does not take Exod. 32–34 seriously as the generative source of Paul's thinking in 2 Cor. 3, Sanders must therefore also conclude that "Paul does not explain how it is that something which condemns and kills can

major thesis of this work is that the answer to this apparent contradiction is to be found in a renewed investigation of Paul's understanding of Moses' role in the "second giving of the Law" as found in Exodus 32–34 and its relationship to his own call to be a διάκονος καινῆς διαθήκης. An investigation of Paul's interpretation of this OT tradition and its function within his argument are the subject of chapters three through five. Here it will be argued that rather than merely *using* the Scriptural traditions to buttress his own conclusions, which he arrived at independently of the witness of the OT, or *misusing* them under the power of his Christian presuppositions for apologetic reasons, Paul, in fact, *derived* his argument and apology for the nature and legitimacy of his apostolic ministry from the Scriptures themselves.[104]

In the end, then, it is Paul's self-conception and ministry as an apostle, *compared and contrasted to the ministry of Moses,* which becomes the *crux interpretum* for understanding the nature of the letter/Spirit contrast, even as the letter/Spirit contrast becomes essential for understanding Paul's self-conception and ministry as an apostle. But this circularity should not deter us. It is merely evidence that we are at the very center of Paul's thinking. For as Johannes Munck observed over twenty-five years ago,

"We should try to find the key to the life and work of the man whose thought we would investigate. In the case of Paul we would find that he was an apostle."[105]

---

be glorious" (p. 138). Paul does not explain it himself, however, because it is explained in Exod. 32–34, upon which Paul builds his argument.

[104] See too William J. Dumbrell, "Paul's Use of Exodus 34 in 2 Corinthians 3," in *God Who is Rich in Mercy, FS D.B. Knox* , ed. Peter T. O'Brien and David G. Peterson, 1986, pp. 179–194, pp. 185 ff., who clearly sees that Paul is utilizing the OT background of Ex. 32–34 to speak to the meaning of the letter/Spirit contrast in 3:6. This present study was essentially completed before encountering Dumbrell's insightful work, so that the independent overlap in many of our positions has helped confirm the conclusions drawn in this investigation.

[105] "Pauline Research Since Schweitzer," in *The Bible in Modern Scholarship*, ed. J.P. Hyatt, 1965, pp. 166–177, p. 176.

Part One

The Letter/Spirit Contrast within the Context of Paul's Apostolic Calling

Chapter One

The Sufficiency and Call of Moses

In questioning Paul's apostleship, his opponents apparently cast doubt not only on the adequacy of Paul's apostolic ministry, but also on its foundation (cf. 1 Cor. 9:1 f.; 2 Cor. 10:7; 13:6). On what *basis* did Paul have the right to claim equality with the "pillar apostles" from Jerusalem? In 1 Corinthians Paul's prior response to this question functioned not as an apology for his apostolic authority *per se*, but as didactic support for his admonitions to the Corinthians (cf. 1 Cor. 9:1 f.; 15:8 f.).[1] Now, however, in view of the new apologetic situation in which he found himself in Corinth, Paul *himself* raised the question of his sufficiency for the apostolic ministry in 2 Cor. 2:16b in order to affirm his legitimacy. For as I have argued in detail earlier, Paul's answer to the rhetorical question of 2:16b, "and who is sufficient for these things?" (καὶ πρὸς ταῦτα τίς ἱκανός;), though left unexpressed, was equally to the point: he is![2] Moreover, as Austin Farrer observed in 1946, Paul's question and implied affirmation of his sufficiency in 2:16b was framed in terms which alluded to the call of Moses as portrayed in Exodus 4:10 (LXX).[3]

---

[1] This is one of the conclusions of my prior study, *Suffering and the Spirit, An Exegetical Study of II Cor. 2:14–3:3 within the Context of the Corinthian Correspondence*, WUNT 2. Reihe, 1986, pp. 67 ff. Although this is a matter of much dispute, the majority view is that already in 1 Cor. Paul must also defend his legitimacy as an apostle; for this view see now the commentary of Gordon Fee, *The First Epistle to the Corinthians*, NICNT, 1987, to the relevant passages, and pp. 6 f., where he introduces the basic perspective of his commentary, i.e. "that the *historical situation* in Corinth was *one of conflict between the church and its founder*" (p. 6, emphasis his). In contrast, I have argued that at the time of 1 Cor. Paul's legitimacy as an apostle was still in tact among the Corinthians themselves, though there was confusion over the significance of Paul's apostleship and authority for the Corinthians (cf. 1 Cor. 1:12 f.; 4:1, 6, 16–21; 9:1 f., 11:1; 15:11).

[2] Following Windisch, Bultmann, and Lietzmann, etc.; cf. my *Suffering and the Spirit*, pp. 90–98, and the literature cited there. Since then, this understanding of Paul's positive answer to the question of 2:16b has been denied by V.P. Furnish, *II Corinthians*, AB 32A, 1984, pp. 190 f., who, like Georgi, takes it to be a question of resignation like that of Joel 2:11 and concludes that, as such, it cannot be answered either yes or no. But in order to make this reading work, Furnish too must supply the missing thought of an adequacy "in and of oneself," something which Paul does not have in mind in 2:16b (cf. my response to this view, *Suffering*, pp. 94 f.). The view of Georgi, et al. is also adopted by R.P. Martin, *2 Corinthians*, WBC Vol. 40, 1986, p. 49, and F. Lang, *Die Briefe an die Korinther*, NTD Bd. 7, 1986[16], p. 267, but with no additional argumentation.

[3] See his "The Ministry in the New Testament," in *The Apostolic Ministry, Essays on the History and the Doctrine of Episcopacy*, ed. K.E. Kirk, 1946, pp. 115–182, pp. 171, 173. For

Even though Paul's question in 2:16b alludes to the call of Moses, Paul's first defense of his legitimacy in 2 Cor. 2:17 ff. was not to point explicitly to his *own* calling by Christ, as he did, for example, in Gal. 1:11–24, 1 Cor. 9:1, and 1 Cor. 15:8–10. The important question concerning the *basis* of Paul's apostolic ministry is nowhere explicitly addressed in 2:14–3:3, although it is presupposed in the imagery of the "triumphal procession" in 2:14 (as the one led in the procession, Paul had been previously "captured" by Christ) and intimated by the allusion to the call of Moses in 2:16b. Instead, in 2:17 and 3:1–3 respectively Paul first supported his sufficiency as an apostle with evidential arguments based on his suffering and ministry of the Spirit. Rather than reaffirming the basis of his apostleship, which itself could be called into question, Paul first pointed to its *effects* as incontrovertible evidence of his legitimacy. Having offered an evidential argument in 2:17–3:3, in 2 Cor. 3:4–6 Paul can now return explicitly to the theme of his "sufficiency" introduced earlier in 2:16b.

Paul returns in 3:5 f. to the theme of his sufficiency as an apostle in order to complete his defense of the legitimacy of his apostolic ministry by developing further the corollary question of the origin and foundation of his apostleship. As in 2:16b, here too Paul does so by alluding to the call of Moses, now structured in a way that also evokes the subsequent call of the prophets. Since the *effects* of Paul's ministry are genuine, they point to the legitimate nature of his ministry, which, in turn, *is* legitimate precisely because, like Moses and the prophets, his *call* to be an apostle is authentic. Paul thus completes his defense of his apostleship by reminding the Corinthians of his divine calling, a calling portrayed in prophetic terms as an extension of the paradigmatic call of Moses.[4] Hence, as will become clear in chapter two, the allusion to Moses' call in

---

arguments against taking Joel 2:11, the only other possibility, as the relevant backdrop, see my *Suffering and the Spirit*, pp. 96–98.

[4] For confirmation of this fundamental point, see the helpful work of Karl Olav Sandnes, *Paul – One of the Prophets? A Contribution to the Apostle's Self-Understanding*, WUNT 2. Reihe 43, 1991, pp. 7 f., 16 n. 6, 64 f., whose extensive study of the prophetic background to Paul's self-understanding is recognized by him to confirm and support my position in this regard as it was presented in an earlier form in my dissertation. Moreover, Sandnes notes that "it is significant that (Hafemann) establishes this without referring to the 'standard test,' Gal. 1:15–16, for this seems to imply that Gal. 1:15–16 is not an isolated witness in Paul's epistles" (p. 8). For his part, Sandnes investigates the common features associated with the call and ministry of the prophets in both the OT and post-biblical Judaism, as well as the key Pauline text, Gal. 1:15–16a, in order to demonstrate that "the basic structure, call, election, revelation, commission and definition of target group (in Paul's self-understanding as reflected in Gal. 1:15 f.), corresponds to the basic structure of the commission texts of the OT prophets" (p. 4), and that this OT prophetic call-narrative structure was an essential part of Paul's self-understanding as an apostle (cf. pp. 68 f.). Based on this investigation of the essential features associated with the OT prophets, both within the OT and in post-biblical literature, and of Paul's use of them in Gal. 1:15 f., Sandnes goes on to demonstrate that when Paul intentionally presents his self-understanding as an *apostle* to his readers (1 Cor. 2:6–16; 9:15–18; 2 Cor. 4:6; Rom. 1:1–5; 10:14–18; 11:25–36; 1 Thess. 2:3–8; and Eph.

2:16b and the parallels to it in 3:4–6a provide the foundation upon which Paul erects his argument for the legitimacy of his apostolic ministry.[5] But before the force of Paul's argument in 3:4–6a can be appreciated, the canonical tradition of the call of Moses and the prophets must be reviewed. Against this backdrop it will become evident why Paul never portrays his call in terms of the call of Moses *per se*, but always in imitation of the call of the prophets, especially that of Jeremiah.[6] It will also become clear what role Paul's allusion to his call played in his apologetic in view of the social function which call narratives performed in Paul's day as a source of legitimation.[7] It is to the call of Moses and its reception in canonical and post-canonical tradition that we now turn our attention.

2:19–3:7), he consistently does so in terms of common *prophetic* motifs. Although Paul's fundamental category in his self-understanding was that of being an apostle (he never refers to himself as a "prophet"), Paul understood his apostleship and message to be a continuation of the OT prophetic calling and of its prophetically inspired speech, which Paul conducted under the same kind of compulsion as the OT prophets (cf. pp. 2 f., 15, 18, 20, 68 f., 115, 129, 152, etc.).

[5] This corresponds to the basic thesis of Sandnes' work, *Paul*, p. 68, in which he argues that although in Gal. 1:15–16a, "Paul's primary concern in reminding the Galatians of the Damascus revelation was self-defense," this polemical situation does not explain the origin or significance of the prophetic call narrative structure in Paul's self-understanding. Rather, as Sandnes argues, "A situation which demanded Paul's self-defense certainly sharpened and defined his self-concept," but did not create it (p. 69). Instead, Sandnes is correct in maintaining that the prophetic nature of Paul's reference to the Damascus road revelation reflected in Gal. 1:15–16a "refers to Paul's self-concept, and not only to his acquaintance with biblical language; nor is the text totally dependent upon the situation in which Paul found himself," but is to be derived from "important elements in his apostolic commission to preach the gospel in prophetic terms" (p. 69). Sandnes establishes this point by examining other Pauline texts in which Paul "makes a creative use of his call as prophet-like when establishing his apostolic authority vis-à-vis his communities" and/or explaining for various purposes the nature of his "prophet-like apostolic self-understanding" (pp. 70, 241; cf. pp. 18, 77 ff.).

[6] For this point in critique of Peter Jones' attempt, *The Apostle Paul: A Second Moses according to II Corinthians 2:14–4:7*, Ph.D. diss. Princeton Theological Seminary, 1973, to picture Paul as a "second Moses," see my *Suffering and the Spirit*, p. 100; for the view that Paul modelled his understanding of his call on that of the prophets, see pp. 138 f., and the literature cited on p. 138 f. nn. 129–131. This criticism applies to the same attempt of Carol Kern Stockhausen, *Moses' Veil and the Glory of the New Covenant, The Exegetical Substructure of II Cor. 3:1–4:6*, AB 116, 1989, pp. 172, 175, to conclude that Paul is "a second Moses" or "new Moses" within the "Christian covenant" based on the various allusions to Moses not only in 3:6–18, but also in 4:1–6 (though her insights concerning the allusions to Moses in 4:1–6 are especially helpful).

[7] For a study of this point, see the ground breaking work of Burke O. Long, "Prophetic Authority as Social Reality," in *Canon and Authority, Essays in Old Testament Religion and Theology*, ed. George W. Coats and Burke O. Long, 1977, pp. 3–20, and now J. L. Berquist, "Prophetic Legitimation in Jeremiah," *VT* 39 (1989) 129–139.

1. The Septuagint Version of Exodus 4:10

In the biblical account of the call of Moses in Exodus 3–4, Moses's fourth response to YHWH's call is the protest in Exod. 4:10:

"Please, Lord, I have never been a man of words (לֹא אִישׁ דְּבָרִים), neither yesterday nor in time past, nor since Thou hast spoken to Thy Servant (עַבְדֶּךָ); for I am slow (lit. 'heavy,' כְּבַד) of speech and of tongue." (NASB)

As in the first three instances, here too YHWH's response to Moses' objection is to reassure him. The very one who has made mankind's mouth and makes mankind dumb or deaf, seeing or blind (4:11)[8] will be with Moses' mouth and YHWH himself will teach Moses what to say (4:12). It is only when Moses refuses to accept YHWH's assurance concerning his lack of eloquence that the Lord becomes angry and appoints Aaron to speak in his stead (cf. Exod. 4:14–16). Nevertheless, Moses' role as God's spokesman is not eliminated (cf. Exod. 4:30; 7:1 f.). YHWH's promise to teach Moses what to say is now merely extended *through Moses* to Aaron (cf. 4:12 with 4:15). Aaron's relationship of "spokesman" or "prophet" for Moses (Exod. 7:1) thus parallels and defines Moses' relationship to YHWH. Just as Aaron is to be the "mouth" of Moses and Moses is to be his "god," Moses is to be the "mouth" of YHWH (4:16).[9] As a result, although Aaron is the one designated in the narrative to speak directly to the people, it is Moses who becomes known in the OT and post-biblical literature as the first and greatest of the prophets.[10]

The relevance of this fact for Paul's apostolic self-understanding as reflected in 2 Cor. 2:16b and 3:4–6 only becomes apparent, however, in the light of the Septuagint's version of Moses' call. The LXX's rendering of Exod. 3:1–4:17[11] corresponds closely to that of the MT, deviating from it only in matters

---

[8] Even if the attempt of S.T. Lachs, "Exodus 4:11: Evidence for an Emendation," *VT* 26 (1976) 249–250, to emend "seeing" (פִּקֵחַ) to "lame" (פִּסֵחַ) is accepted, the basic sense of the verse remains the same.

[9] This chain-of-command from YHWH to Moses to Aaron is reflected throughout the narrative in the fact that Aaron receives and is installed in his office of priesthood through Moses (see Exod. 28–29; Lev. 6:1; 8; 9:1 f.; 10:12; 16:2; 17:1 f.; 22:1 f.; etc.). Conversely, God is said to speak directly to Aaron only four times: Lev. 10:8; Num. 18:1, 8, 20. Horst Seebass, *Mose und Aaron, Sinai und Gottesberg;* Abhandlung zur evangelischen Theologie Bd. 2, 1962, p. 25, refers to this state of affairs as "die Durchführung der zweiten Bestimmung von 4:16b."

[10] See Exod. 5:22; Num. 12:6–18; Deut. 18:15–18; 33:1; 34:10–12; Hosea 12:13. For surveys of the relevant texts, see Albert Gelin, "Moses im Alten Testament," in *Moses in Schrift and Überlieferung*, 1963, pp. 31–57, esp. pp. 31 f., 46 f.; my "Moses in the Apocrypha and Pseudepigrapha: A Survey," *Journal for the Study of the Pseudepigrapha* 7 (1990) 79–104; and Josef M. Kastner, "Das Mosesbild in der rabbinischen Tradition," in his *Moses im Neuen Testament*, Diss. München, 1967, pp. 74–104, esp. pp. 80–90.

[11] Following the literary analysis of Brevard S. Childs, *Exodus, A Commentary*, OTL, 1974, pp. 51 f., against Noth, et al., who see the larger pericope as extending from 2:11 (or 2:23) through 4:23 (or 4:18, 24; 5:1 and even 6:1).

of detail which do not impact the overall meaning of the narrative.[12] But there is one glaring difference between the two accounts, and it is this difference which provides the clue for understanding the force of Paul's argument. In the MT Moses protests that he is not "a man of words," i.e. eloquent, whereas in the LXX Moses' crucial fourth response is that he is not "sufficient" (ἱκανός). The text reads:

εἶπεν δὲ Μωϋσῆς πρὸς κύριον, Δέομαι, κύριε, *οὐχ ἱκανός εἰμι* πρὸ τῆς ἐχθὲς οὐδὲ πρὸ τῆς τρίτης ἡμέρας οὐδὲ ἀφ' οὗ ἤρξω λαλεῖν τῷ θεράποντί σου· ἰσχνόφωνος καὶ βραδύγλωσσος ἐγώ εἰμι.

The difficulty of relating the LXX version of Exod. 4:10 to the MT was soon felt, as evidenced by the versions of Aquila and Symmachus,[13] and by the textual variant represented in MSS F and M, οὐκ εὔλογος εἰμι,[14] all of which translate the text of Exod. 4:10 in the direction of the MT. But more important is the witness to this tradition preserved in Philo, who refers explicitly to Exod. 4:10 four times, three of which state that Moses was not or refused to be "eloquent" (εὔλογος); cf. *Quod. det.* 38; *De sacr.* 12–13; *De vit. Mos.* I, 83.[15] The fact that Philo was referring to a variant LXX tradition rather than merely giving his own interpretation of the Hebrew is suggested by *Vit. Mos.* I, 83 and *Quis. rer.* 4, where Philo also mentions that Moses was ἰσχνόφωνος and βραδύγλωσσος, direct parallels to the LXX. In addition, *De sacr.* 12 refers to Moses as God's θεράπων, as in the LXX, over against the more literal δοῦλος for עבד as in Aquila, while in *De vit. Mos.* I, 79, Philo follows the LXX against the MT in omitting Moses' leprosy and speaking instead of a mere change in color. Hence, the variant εὔλογος is also well attested as early. Yet the better attested, more difficult, and hence more reliable reading is found in MSS B, S (a), and A. Furthermore, in the light of the otherwise close resemblances between the MT and LXX, K.H. Rengstorf is justified in

---

[12] The LXX omits the description "mountain of God" for Horeb in 3:1; reads τί ἐστιν; for זנה in 3:4; reads γεργεσαίων in 3:8; designates Pharaoh to be βασιλέα Αἰγύπτου in 3:10 f.; explicitly identifies the "king of Egypt" with Pharaoh in 3:18; omits יהוה twice in 3:18; omits the fact that Moses' hand was leprous in 4:6 f., stating rather that his hand merely changed complexion; and adds μου in 4:15.

[13] Aquila reads οὐκ ἀνὴρ ῥημάτων, while Symmachus renders it οὐκ εὔλαλος; cf. F. Field, *Origenis Hexaplorum Quae Supersunt, Vol. I*, 1875, p. 86. On Aquila's and Symmachus' tendency to be more faithful to the Hebrew than the LXX, see H.B. Swete, *An Introduction to the Old Testament in Greek*, rev. ed., 1968 (1914), pp. 33 f., 50 f. As reflected here, Aquila's tendency is to render the Hebrew with wooden literalness, while Symmachus provides a more dynamic equivalent.

[14] I.e. the fifth cent. AD Codex Ambrosianus. This reading is also apparently attested in the fragment of Ezekiel the Tragedian's ἡ Ἐξαγωγή 113 (2nd cent. BC), preserved by Eusebius, *Pr. ev.* 9.29.9 and Clement of Alexandria, *Strom.* V, 14.131.3; see A.-M. Denis, *Fragmenta Pseudepigraphorum Quae Supersunt Graeca*, PVGT Vol. 3, 1970, p. 211 for the text.

[15] Contra Liddell, Scott, and Jones, *A Greek-English Lexicon*, 1958 (1940[9]), p. 721, who suggest that Philo interprets εὔλογος to mean "reasonable" in Exod. 4:10. Such a meaning is common in Philo (cf. *De op. mundi* 27.45; *Leg. all.* III, 161; *De vit. Mos.* I, 174, 196, 244; II, 261), but to my knowledge Philo always uses it to mean "eloquent" when referring to Moses' protest. In fact, Philo's point concerning Moses' lack of eloquence seems to be based on the word play possible between these two meanings of εὔλογος.

his observation that the LXX of Exod. 4:10 seems to be an interpretation rather than a translation of the original.[16] Finally, the similarity between the LXX and the possible play on words preserved in the Targums is striking. Tg. Neofiti, Tg. Onqelos, and Tg. Ps.-Jonathan all render the Hebrew expression לֹא אִישׁ דברים with the phrase גבר לא,[17] which as a substantive means simply "man." But as a verb it means "to be strong," or "uppermost."[18] This same word play is possible in Hebrew between גֶּבֶר ("man") and גָּבַר ("to be strong, mighty").[19] Thus, גבר in the verbal sense could be seen as a parallel to ἱκανός, but the late date of the targums in relationship to the LXX forbids positing a dependence, nor does the parallel solve all of the problems. For example, even in the targumic tradition the original sense of the Hebrew is maintained, so that the impulse of the LXX to drop the notion of Moses' lack of eloquence remains unexplained.[20] Moreover, although the semantic field encompassed by ἱκανός could very well include the idea of "strong enough," the link between ἱκανός and גבר is not direct, though ὁ ἱκανός can be used for שַׁדַּי ("the mighty one"/"sufficient one") in Ruth 1:20 f.; Job 21:15; 31:2; 39:32; Ezek. 1:24; and in Aquila to Gen. 17:1 and Exod. 6:3. The question of the relationship between the MT, LXX, and the targums must therefore be left open.

The first observation to be made concerning the LXX of Exod. 4:10 is that in comparison to the MT the protest itself has been broadened out and left indefinite, although the reason for Moses' response remains the same as in the MT.[21] For whereas in the MT Moses objects to his calling because he is "not a

---

[16] Art. ἱκανός κτλ., *TDNT* 3 (1965), p. 294 n. 6.

[17] Cf. Alejandro Diez Macho, *Neophyti I, Vol. II,* 1970, p. 21; A. Sperber, *The Bible in Aramaic, Vol. I,* 1959, p. 94; and M. Ginsburger, *Pseudo-Jonathan,* 1903, p. 103.

[18] Cf. M. Jastrow, *A Dictionary of the Targumim …, Vol. I,* 1903, pp. 208 f.

[19] Cf. Jastrow, *Dictionary of the Targumim,* p. 208 and Brown, Driver, and Briggs, *A Hebrew and English Lexicon of the Old Testament,* 1976, pp. 149 f.

[20] For example, J. Levy, *Chaldäisches Wörterbuch über die Targumim, Bd. I,* 1881³, p. 161 to דברן, translates Ps. Jon. to Exod. 4:10 to be "ich bin nicht ein Redner."

[21] Cf. ἰσχνόφωνος καὶ βραδύγλωσσος ἐγώ εἰμι with כי כבד פה וכבד לשון אנכי and the article of Jeffrey H. Tigay, "Moses' Speech Difficulty," *Annual of Jewish Studies* 3 (1974) 29–42, who demonstrates that the adjective "heavy" (כבד), when applied to bodily organs, means in the first instance a medical-physical disorder or malfunction. When applied to the mouth and tongue it could mean a speech defect such as stammering or stuttering (cf. pp. 31 f. and Ezek. 3:5 f.). It is this meaning which is reflected in the LXX, as well as the haggadic tradition that Moses had a speech impediment as a result of burning his tongue on a hot coal in his infancy (cf. Deut. Rab. I, 7 and Philo, *Quis rer.* 3 f.; see Tigay, pp. 29 nn. 1,3,4, for additional primary and secondary literature). There is, however, a problem in understanding the MT itself. For as Tigay has pointed out, the concrete medical diagnosis of a "heavy tongue" has also been extended to refer metaphorically to speech which is unintelligible because of its foreignness (cf. Tigay, p. 32, and Is. 28:11; 33:19; Ezek. 3:5 f.; and his examples from Greek, Sanskrit, Arabic, Sumerian, and Akkadian on pp. 32 f.). Hence, the tradition preserved in Philo, *De vit. Mos.* I. 83; *Quod. det.* 11.38; Tanhuma Deut. § 1, Exod. Rab. 4:10; etc., which understands Exod. 4:10 to mean that Moses was unskilled in public speaking or had forgotten his Egyptian in the 60 years he had been away from Egypt (cf. Exod. 2:11 f.; 7:7; and Tigay, pp. 29, 38 f.) also has a point of departure in the text. For although the LXX prefers the former, the Hebrew could mean either that Moses suffered from a speech impediment (so the Old Latin, Vulgate, Tg. Onq.; Tg. Neof.; and Tg. Ps.-J.), or that he lacked eloquence because he was the "speaker of a foreign tongue" (Rashbam). For an-

man of words," in the LXX Moses simply states that he is not "adequate" or "sufficient." As a result, the structure of the passage has been altered as well. In the LXX we are left uninformed concerning the nature of Moses' inadequacy until the following assertion that he has a "speech impediment" (ἰσχνόφωνος) and is thus "slow of tongue" (βραδύγλωσσος).[22] This may also explain why the logical conjunction ־כ found in the MT (... כבד כי) is missing in the LXX. For in the LXX the statement concerning Moses' speech impediment provides the specific interpretation of his inadequacy and in so doing provides the reason for his insufficiency, while in the MT this statement functions to support directly Moses' prior statement that he was not "eloquent."[23] In contrast to the MT, the LXX makes it possible to regard Moses' fourth response to his "apostolic" calling[24] to be a general statement (οὐκ ἱκανός εἰμι) whose exact nature and reason must be filled in with the specific circumstances involved.

Second, in the LXX Moses' "insufficiency," like his protest found in the MT, is *overcome* by God's twofold provision: YHWH himself not only will instruct Moses in what he is to say,[25] but also provide Aaron to communicate to the people what Moses has received from the Lord (Exod. 4:15 f.). As in the first three instances (cf. Exod. 3:11, 13; 4:1), here too YHWH provides for the insufficiency of Moses' call, but now, in addition, God compensates for the insufficiency of Moses *himself*. For Moses' first response in Exod. 3:11

---

other version of this same article, but with an extensive bibliography, cf. Tigay's "'Heavy of Mouth' and 'Heavy of Tongue,' On Moses' Speech Difficulty," *BASOR* 231 (1978) 57–67.

[22] Following Liddell and Scott, *A Greek-English Lexicon*, pp. 327 and 843, with reference to Exod. 4:10.

[23] This is assuming that the MT also speaks of a speech impediment in Exod. 4:10b. Tigay, "Moses'," p. 30, points out that Moses did claim to be ineloquent. "The question is whether 'heavy of mouth and tongue' and 'uncircumcised of lips' (i.e. from Exod. 6) repeat the idea or express something new, a reason for the ineloquence (as Jer. 1:6b, 'for I am a youth' adds a reason) ..." That this is the original intention of the text seems to be indicated by the use of ־כ itself (cf. pp. 39–41 for Tigay's other arguments in favor of this reading).

[24] Note that שלח, whose technical nature is well known, is rendered by ἀποστέλλω in Exod. 3:10, 12 and 4:13, 28 to describe Moses' being sent by God. This suggests a broader meaning for שליח than the often too narrowly conceived notion of a "representative" who may only pass on the verbal message entrusted to him. If Moses is an example of such a representative, then the meaning ought to be enlarged to include the broader prophetic concept of one who speaks for God, but who also occupies an office of his own, with a sometimes independent function of mediating between God and his people. For a development of this dual function in post-biblical literature, cf. Jan-A. Bühner, *Der Gesandte und sein Weg im 4. Evangelium*, WUNT 2. Reihe Bd. 2, 1977, pp. 285–314.

[25] Cf. LXX of Exod. 4:12b: καὶ ἐγὼ ἀνοίξω τὸ στόμα σου καὶ συμβιβάσω σε ὃ μέλλεις λαλῆσαι. Here too the LXX seems to go beyond the MT tradition, which simply states that YHWH will "be with Moses' mouth." For as Tigay, "Moses'," pp. 40 f. points out, according to the MT Moses is not cured by God, so that the force of Exod. 4:11 is: "'If your speech is defective, it is because I made you that way.'" But the LXX need not be understood to imply that Moses is cured, but merely that God will give Moses the words to speak, i.e. "open his mouth."

("Who am I, that I should go to Pharaoh [LXX adds 'the king of Egypt'] and that I should bring the sons of Israel out of Egypt?") does not focus on a deficiency in Moses himself, but on his authority to act in the prescribed manner. This is indicated by God's answer in 3:12, "I will be with you," which provides Moses with his authority for acting, rather than affecting Moses' personal ability in some way.[26] The narrative as it now stands reaches its highpoint when the focus of attention switches from the sufficiency of God's revelation to the sufficiency of his messenger.

It is not concluding too much, therefore, to posit that Moses' call demonstrates the *sufficiency* of Moses to be God's appointed prophet, despite his *own insufficiency* (οὐκ ἱκανός εἰμι), in order that the role of Moses, like that of the hardening of Pharaoh's heart, the plagues, the Passover, and the Exodus itself, might demonstrate that the election and power, and therefore the glory, i.e. *the sufficiency*, is God's alone.[27] For there is no indication that after God's gracious compensation Moses remains in a position of insufficiency, despite his speech defect. In fact, his attempt to claim this very thing only causes God to become angry (cf. Exod. 4:13 f.)! Instead, from the call of Moses on, the consistent emphasis is on Moses' effective and assumed role as the servant of YHWH.[28] Hence, when Moses once again brings up the fact that he is unskilled in speech in Exod. 6:12 and 30, the narrative passes over his complaint, pausing only to remind Moses of God's mandate (6:13) and his promise to use Aaron as Moses' prophet (7:1 f.). In other words, from the standpoint of the narrative, the issue of Moses' sufficiency to be God's prophet is settled in 4:10–16.[29]

---

[26] So U. Cassuto, *A Commentary on the Book of Exodus*, 1967, p. 36, on Exod. 3:11: "This is not, as most commentators explain, a refusal to accept the mission or an expression of doubt as to his ability to implement it. The doubts will be mentioned in chapter IV ... At this stage, when Moses is confronted with the plan as a whole ... his initial response is to voice his sense of humility and to stress his unworthiness relative to the magnitude of the enterprise. That is the meaning of such phrases as 'Who am I?' or 'Who is your servant?' and the like, whether they occur in the Bible, in the Lachish letters, or generally in the idiom of the ancient East." See also his comments on Exod. 4:1a on pp. 45 ff., and Martin Noth, *Das zweite Buch Mose, Exodus*, ATD Bd. 5, 1959, pp. 28 f., 32, who also makes a distinction between 3:11 and 4:10: 3:11 refers to "wie er denn das große Werk vollbringen solle," while 4:10 is "die Weigerung dessen, der beauftragt und beglaubigt worden ist, und zwar mit einem Vorwand (V.10) ..."

[27] See esp. the purpose clauses in Exod. 6:7; 7:5; 9:14–16; 10:1 f.; 14:4, 17 f.; the significance of the Passover in 12:26 f.; 13:3,8; the conclusion to the Exodus narrative itself in 14:31, and to the entire Pentateuch in Deut. 3:10–12.

[28] Again Cassuto, *Exodus*, p. 51, who in noticing that the command to Moses to "go and do so-and-so" is not repeated again after 4:10 remarks, "This silence creates a deeper impression than any confirmatory injunction: there is no need to say that you are duty bound to go, and that you will go and carry out your commission. Moses is only told how, and by what means, he should execute his task."

[29] This doublet is usually attributed to the fact that Exod. 6:2–7:13 is "P" material in contrast to the "JE" sources behind Exod. 3–4. See e.g. G. Fohrer, *Überlieferung und Geschichte des Exodus, Eine Analyse von Ex 1–15*, BZAW 91, 1964, pp. 24 ff., and H. Seebass, *Mose und Aaron*, pp. 5–13. But my goal here and below is not to ascertain the his-

This is not to suggest that Moses' role is to be limited to that of a prophet, but to recognize that Moses' call in Exod. 3:1–4:17 is given in terms of his most immediate and predominant task, that of speaking for God to Israel and Pharaoh (cf. 3:10, 13, 15 f.). As the narrative continues, Moses' prophetic function becomes one of his many roles, which also include that of leader, miracle-worker, priest, and law-giver, among others. For this reason, when faced with the almost impossible task of classifying Moses' role in the Pentateuch, scholars have most often chosen the more comprehensive designation *mediator*.[30] The nature and significance of Paul's own dependence in 2 Cor. 2:16b and 3:4–6 on the LXX version of the call of Moses and his ensuing role as the prophetic mediator between YHWH and his people will become evident, however, only after the various ways in which the biblical tradition of the call of Moses was taken up, interpreted, and adapted in biblical and post-biblical literature have been examined. For by Paul's day the call and figure of Moses had taken on a theological and apologetic significance which not only explains Paul's allusion to Moses in 2 Cor. 2:16b and the structure of the argument in 3:4–6, but also provides an important clue for understanding Paul's ongoing defense of his apostolic ministry in 3:7–18 and 4:1–6. The first stage in this development is the *structural parallels* established within the Old Testament between the call of Moses and the various prophetic call narratives.

2. The "Mosaic Pattern" in the "Sufficiency" of the Old Testament Prophets

Ever since Walther Zimmerli sketched the form-critical relationships which exist between the various "calls" of the prophets, including those of Moses, Gideon, and Saul,[31] it has become customary to speak of the general form or *Gattung* of the *"Berufungsbericht"* as underlying and unifying the various prophetic calls preserved in the Old Testament.[32] Yet scholars have by no

---

tory of the text, but to read the narrative in the way in which it was read in Paul's day, i.e. as the unified work of Moses. Source criticism has therefore been intentionally put aside.

[30] Cf. e.g. G. von Rad, *Old Testament Theology, Vol. 1*, 1962, pp. 289–296; C. Westermann, *Theologie des Alten Testaments in Grundzügen*, ATD Ergänzungsreihe, Bd. 6, 1978, pp. 39 f., 42 f., 62–71; H. Seebass, *Mose und Aaron*, pp. 27–31, 129 f., 150 f., and Lothar Perlitt, "Mose als Prophet," *EvTh* 31 (1971) 588–608, who sees "Prophet" and "Fürbitter" to be the two central understandings of Moses developed in the later tradition and then brought together via "Analogieschlüsse und Kombinationen" based on Moses as mediator (cf. pp. 599 f., 606).

[31] Originally published in the first section of his commentary on Ezekiel in 1955, but now to be found in his completed work, *Ezechiel, 1.Teilband*, BKAT Bd. 13/1, 1979², pp. 16–21.

[32] In fact, the form "Prophetic Call Narrative" has been further refined to the point that scholars now distinguish between it and an "act of commissioning" on the one hand, and an "installation" form on the other; cf. Kenneth W. Schmidt, "Prophetic Delegation: A Form-Critical Inquiry," *Biblica* 63 (1982) 206–218, pp. 206 nn. 2–3, 207 n. 6. More recently, Die-

means reached a consensus concerning the nature or contours of the form itself. The basic point of contention is whether or not Zimmerli is right in maintaining that there are two different types of prophetic calls, i.e. one in which the *word* of YHWH dominates and the prophet responds to his call with an objection, as in the call of Jeremiah, and one in which the *vision* of YHWH dominates and the prophet offers no objection, as in the call of Isaiah. Those who oppose this distinction argue that both expressions can be understood as the outworking of one basic generative structure.[33]

But regardless of whether one aspect of the prophetic call dominates over another in any particular call narrative, it is evident that the various calls, as they now stand, all exhibit a similar pattern or "schema."[34] For as Zimmerli, Reventlow, Habel, Kilian, Long, and Vieweger have all observed, both a theophany and a reception of the prophetic word occur in all the accounts regardless of whether they may have had separate literary histories and/or distinct emphases.[35] Past scholarship has also demonstrated that the calls of Gideon, Jeremiah, Isaiah, and Ezekiel all follow the same basic structure found in the call of Moses read as a unified whole. Indeed, Long has pointed out that the account of Moses' call in Exodus 3–4 demonstrates that "it is not at all clear that we have to do with two types of call report (Zimmerli), but rather with essentially one type, whose roots go deeply into ancient Near Eastern culture

---

ter Vieweger, *Die Spezifik der Berufungsberichte Jeremias und Ezechiels im Umfeld ähnlicher Einheiten des Alten Testaments*, Beiträge zur Erforschung des Alten Testaments und des Antiken Judentums, Bd. 6, 1986, pp. 95–105, 131–135, has argued that the "Beauftragungsberichte" of Ezekiel and Jeremiah, with their emphasis on a call to an indefinite, lifelong office as prophet, ought to be distinguished from the "Berufungsberichte" of Moses, Gideon, and Saul, which are time-limited and focused on a specific task. For Vieweger, the calls of Ezekiel and Jeremiah are thus independent, though literarily derived "sub-genres" ("Untergattungen") of the form found in the calls of Moses, Gideon, and Saul, both of which belong to the "Obergattung" of the divine sending-narrative. In contrast, he follows Jenni, Steck, and Koch in separating out the narratives of Is. 6 and 1 Kgs. 22:19–22 as a separate trajectory of tradition and genre because they present the "bestowal of an extraordinary mandate in the assembly of the heavenly throne room," which serves to legitimate a concrete sending within the prophetic sphere and is not an initial call to the prophetic office as such (p. 134; cf. pp. 20–24).

[33] For a concise summary of the main lines of research, see Rudolf Kilian, "Die Prophetischen Berufungsberichte," in *Theologie im Wandel*, Tübinger Theologische Reihe, Bd. I, 1967, pp. 356–376, pp. 356–358, and for the debate since then see Vieweger, *Spezifik*, pp. 11–24. This aspect of the debate need not detain us.

[34] See Burke O. Long, "Prophetic Call Traditions and Reports of Visions," *ZAW* 84 (1972) 494–500, who follows Richter in arguing that a schema of elements shaped the various accounts by being "taken up in varied circumstances and brought into texts belonging to other genres," rather than defining them in the tight sense of a literary form (p. 495). Long's point is that the element of the epiphany, as well as the call itself, was vital in shaping the various accounts since both were used as "legitimating devices" in ancient literature (p. 500).

[35] Cf. Zimmerli, *Ezechiel*, pp. 35 f., 75 f.; Henning Graf Reventlow, *Liturgie und prophetisches Ich bei Jeremia*, 1963, pp. 52, 63 f.; N. Habel, "The Form and Significance of the Call Narratives," *ZAW* 77 (1965) 297–323, pp. 307, 309–11; R. Kilian, "Berufungsberichte," pp. 358 ff.; Long, "Prophetic Call Traditions," pp. 495 ff. and Vieweger (see n. 32).

and literature."[36] The point is not to propose a direct literary dependence among the various accounts, but simply to recognize that the call of the prophet in Israel's tradition followed a definite and recurring structure which contained several essential elements. This is now generally accepted in contemporary scholarship.[37] Moreover, the priority of Moses as the one like whom God would raise up subsequent prophets for Israel (Deut. 18:18) justifies the designation of this recurring pattern from the perspective of the canon and history of Israel as "Mosaic." Wolfgang Richter and N. Habel have thus listed five and six elements of the pattern respectively.

W. Richter lists 1) die Andeutung der Not;[38] 2) der Auftrag; 3) der Einwand; 4) die Zusicherung des Beistandes; and 5) das Zeichen.[39] N. Habel identifies the following six elements, together with the various examples: 1) Divine confrontation (Jud. 6:11b–12a; Exod. 3:1–3, 4a; Jer. 1:4; Is. 6:1–2; Ezek. 1:1–28); 2) Introductory Word (Jud. 6:12b–13; Exod. 3:4b–9; Jer. 1:5a; Is. 6:3–7; Ezek. 1:28–2:2); 3) Commission (Jud. 6:14; Exod. 3:10; Jer. 1:5b; Is. 6:8–10; Ezek. 2:3–5); 4) Objection (Jud. 6:15; Exod. 3:11; Jer. 1:6; Is. 6:11a; Ezek. 2:6,8); 5) Reassurance (Jud. 6:16; Exod. 3:12a; Jer. 1:7–8; Is. 6:11b–13; Ezek. 2:6–7); 6) Sign (Jud. 6:17; Exod. 3:12b; Jer. 1:9–10; none in Is. 6, though possibly in Is. 7; Ezek. 2:8–3:11).[40]

For the purposes of this study the form can be simplified into these four fundamental aspects:

(1) the theophany/divine encounter
(2) the word of YHWH/commission
(3) the obstacle to be overcome in the prophet's situation
(4) the act of God's grace and/or promise of his presence (sometimes with a sign to overcome the obstacle)

In this way, both the unity and diversity of the various calls may be accounted for in a scheme which avoids the artificial necessity of deciding whether or not Isaiah's response in 6:5 that he is a man "of unclean lips," or Ezekiel's fear

---

[36] "Prophetic Call Traditions," p. 500. This fact is true whether or not one joins Long in accepting the traditional source analysis of these accounts.

[37] See again Long, "Prophetic Call Traditions," p. 494: "There is general agreement regarding the correspondence in both form and content between the call reports of classical prophets (Jeremiah, Ezekiel, Isaiah), and the materials about figures who antedate them (Moses, Gideon, Saul)."

[38] Vieweger, *Spezifik*, pp. 36–44, accepts the same basic five-fold structure, but understands the first element in the calls of Jeremiah and Ezekiel to be biographical introductions rather than indications of the need as in the calls of Moses, Gideon, and Saul (cf. pp. 38, 91). For helpful charts of the parallels between the fivefold scheme in the various calls, see his pp. 139–141.

[39] *Die sogenannten vorprophetischen Berufungsberichte, Eine literaturwissenschaftliche Studie zu 1 Sam 9:1–10, 16; Ex 3f. und Ri 6:11b–17*, FRLANT Bd. 101, 1970, p. 139. See too p. 138, for his table of the parallels between the calls and pp. 182 f., for his synopsis of the two "Faden," i.e. J and E, in the call of Moses.

[40] "Form and Significance," pp. 309 ff.

in 2:6, 8, is an objection in the same sense as Moses' response in Exod. 3:11 or 4:10, Gideon's in Jud. 6:15, or Jeremiah's in 1:6.[41] Such a question is important for understanding the call and message of each prophet. But when it comes to the broader question of form, it is clear that in each prophetic call narrative there is an obstacle to be overcome before God's word can be delivered, which is then removed by an act of God's grace or promise of his presence. It is this pattern of a *"sufficiency in spite of insufficiency,"* so clearly presented in the call of Moses, which is of primary interest for our study and to which we now turn our attention.

a) The Call of Moses

The structure of the prophetic call narrative is clearly found in the call of Moses in Exod. 3:1–4:17. In fact, the narrative actually repeats the basic pattern found in all prophetic calls four times! The initial call in Exod. 3:1–12 already contains, in and of itself, the basic elements of the prophetic call: 1) the theophany in 3:1–9; 2) the word of YHWH in 3:10; 3) the obstacle in 3:11; and 4) the promise of God's presence, confirmed with a sign, in 3:12. This pattern is then reduplicated in 3:13–22, 4:1–9, and 4:10–12, based on the three further objections in 3:13, 4:1, and 4:10. That the entire narrative in 3:1–4:17 is nevertheless intended to be read as the report of Moses' *single* call is evident in that the three repetitions of the call-structure all presuppose the initial theophany in Exod. 3:1–9. Moreover, the use of the objection-obstacle motif to introduce the other three patterns indicates that the emphasis of the narrative is on the *overcoming* of Moses' protests through God's gracious provision. Hence, according to the LXX, the point of Moses' call is that, although Moses is not ἱκανός to be God's apostle (cf. Exod. 4:10, 12 and 4:13, 28 LXX), God himself has made him sufficient by the promise of his presence (3:12a, 4:12), the giving of a sign (3:12b), and the provision of the miracle-working rod (4:2–9). Even Moses' outright refusal to go in Exod. 4:13 is met with God's provision of Aaron to be his spokesman (4:14 ff.). The structure of Moses' call, culminating in the conquest of Moses' insufficiency in 4:10 ff., may thus be summarized as follows:

(1) the theophany (3:1–9)
(2) the mandate to Moses (3:10, 12, 15–18)
(3) the objections (3:11, 13; 4:1, 10)
(4) the promise of God's presence and acts of grace to overcome the obstacles, which lead to a renewed mandate (3:12, 14; 4:2–9, 11–12, 14–16).[42]

---

[41] It is striking that like Habel, even Zimmerli sees Ezek. 2:8 as implying a sort of objection on Ezekiel's part, cf. *Ezechiel*, p. 76. For a recent representative of those who argue that there is no objection in Isaiah's call, see now Vieweger, *Spezifik*, pp. 39–42. But as the analysis below will show, such a position remains unconvincing.

[42] This analysis is based on the assumption that Moses' response in Exod. 4:13 is not part of the obstacle motif, as indicated by God's reaction of anger rather than provision in 4:14.

b) The Call of Gideon

This same fourfold structure, with its emphasis on the prophetic "sufficiency-in-spite-of-insufficiency-as-a-result-of-the-grace-of-God" is also apparent in the call of Gideon in Judges 6:11–24.[43] This is more than just coincidence. For although a general pattern for the call of leaders may have existed as a social form in the ancient near east, within the canonical context the parallels between the call of Moses and that of Gideon take on a legitimating function in which the historical sequence from Moses to Gideon points to a *paradigmatic role* for the call of Moses. Gideon's call thus establishes him as a Moses-like authority among the people. For as W. Beyerlin has pointed out,

"Wird hier die Überwindung der Midianitergefahr analog der Herausführung aus Ägypten verstanden, so kann es nicht wundernehmen, daß entsprechend auch Gideon selbst von der Tradition *dem* zur Seite gestellt wird, der Jahwes Volk aus Ägypten geführt hatte: *Mose* nämlich. Der Überlieferung in Ri 6:11b–17 steht es ganz offensichtlich fest, daß Gideons Berufung in genau derselben Weise verlaufen sein muß wie die des Mose."[44]

Here too Gideon's call is initiated by a theophany (6:11 ff.), which immediately leads to the word of YHWH as his mandate (6:14). Like Moses, Gideon responds with an objection (6:15), which is then overcome by YHWH's promise to be with him and an accompanying sign to testify that Gideon has found favor in God's sight (6:17–21). In the same way, YHWH's promise to be with Moses after Israel's sin with the golden calf was also based on the fact that Moses had found favor in God's sight (cf. Exod. 33:12–17).

What is most significant for our study, however, is that the structure of the narrative again makes it clear that the stark contrast between Gideon's God-given sufficiency and his own insufficiency lies at the heart of his call. In God's eyes Gideon is a "a mighty man of strength" (6:12) who will "defeat Midian as one man" (6:16), even though his "family" (אֶלֶף) is the "weakest" (דַּל, LXX ταπεινοτέρα) in Manasseh and he is the "youngest" in his father's house (6:15). And unlike the simple pattern found in the call of Moses, Gideon's call is both introduced and concluded with a pronouncement of his

---

Nowhere else within the calls of the prophets do we encounter such a response on YHWH's part to the obstacles raised. Exodus 4:13 is therefore to be understood as an outright refusal of the call rather than as an expression of insufficiency. Since this refusal calls into question God's ability to overcome the obstacles, God's response is now anger; but anger followed by grace!

[43] The basic form-critical work on this text has been done by E. Kutsch, "Gideon's Berufung und Altarbau, Jdc 6:11–24," *ThLZ* 81 (1956) 75–84. He identified four basic elements in the call of Gideon (as well as that of Moses, Jeremiah, Saul and John the Baptist!): "1) Auftrag; 2) Einwand des Berufenen; 3) Abweisung des Einwandes; 4) Zeichen als Bestätigung;" see p. 79. I would combine numbers 3 and 4 and include the additional category of the initiatory theophany (cf. Jud. 6:11–14).

[44] "Geschichte und heilsgeschichtliche Traditionsbildung im Alten Testament, Ein Beitrag zur traditionsgeschichte von Richter VI–VIII," *VT* 13 (1963) 1–25, p. 9.

"strength" due to God's promise to be "with him" in his "weakness" (cf. the
parallels between 6:12 and 16).[45] Gideon's objection that he is the "weakest of
the weak" (i.e. the youngest son of the weakest tribe) is framed between its
two adversative disclaimers, so that the emphasis falls on Gideon's strength
due to God's provision. As N. Habel has summarized it, the point of Gideon's
call is that

"... the total insufficiency of the chosen individual seen from a human perspective
stands in direct contrast to the character of the same individual from *God's vantage
point* ... In this portrait the theme of YHWH's elective grace becomes prominent."[46]

c) The Call of Isaiah

It is precisely this theme of God's "elective grace" which characterizes the
call of Isaiah in Is. 6:1–3.[47] Whether one interprets Isaiah's cry in 6:5 to be an
objection to his call,[48] or merely Isaiah's natural response to being confronted

---

[45] The close connection between 6:12, 15, 16 becomes even more evident when we realize that דל in 6:15 can mean "weak" in a military sense. Cf. 2 Sam. 3:1, where דל is used in
this sense in reference to the family of Saul, in contrast to the increasing "strength" (חזק) of
David's family. See Brown, Driver, and Briggs, *Hebrew-English Lexicon*, p. 195.

[46] "Form and Significance," p. 300. He also points to 1 Sam. 9:21 as evidence of this same
pattern. For a detailed comparison of the calls of Moses, Gideon, and Saul, see W. Richter's
work, *Berufungsberichte*. Richter concludes concerning the element of the objection in these
reports: "In diesem Glied kann keine feste Wendung erkannt werden, vielmehr weichen die
Formulierungen überall voneinander ab. Um so mehr fällt auf, daß dennoch wiederholt ein
Einwand bei Berufungen steht" (p. 145).

[47] I am following the vast majority of scholars who see Is. 6 to be the account of Isaiah's
call. For the opposing view, see the paradigmatic work of Mordecai M. Kaplan, "Isaiah 6:1–
11," *JBL* 45 (1926) 251–259, who argues that this text "merely pictures the sense of despair
which came over Isaiah in the course of his career" (p. 251). Kaplan's main objection that
the call to harden the people in Is. 6, devoid of the message of repentance, "could not have
constituted the burden of an inaugural message" (p. 253), has been answered by Ivan
Egnell, *The Call of Isaiah, An Exegetical and Comparative Study*, Uppsala Universitets
Arsskrift, Bd. 4, 1949, pp. 25 f., and more recently Joseph Jensen, "Weal and Woe in Isaiah:
Consistency and Continuity," *CBQ* 43 (1981) 167–187, who both argue that Isaiah's message included, from the beginning, both judgment and repentance. See too Wolfgang
Metzger, "Der Horizont der Gnade in der Berufungsvision Jesajas, Kritische Bedenken zum
masoretischen Text von Jesaja 6:13," *ZAW* 93 (1981) 281–284, who argues for the original
nature of 6:13bβ, against those who try to excise this positive reference as the gloss of a later
disciple.

[48] So Reventlow, *Liturgie und prophetisches Ich bei Jeremia*, p. 52. Habel's attempt,
"Form and Significance," pp. 310–312, to see Is. 6:11a as the objection fails on two counts.
First, Isaiah's reaction in v. 5 is not simply one of terror, as Moses' in Exod. 3:6, but one of
sinfulness. Moses' removal of his shoes cannot, therefore, be equated with the cleansing of
Isaiah's lips, as Habel proposes. Hence, Is. 6:3–7 should not be considered as part of the
"introductory word." Second, if Is. 6:11a were to be construed as an objection to the call, it
would lack the necessary divine compensation. Is. 6:11bf. is a response to Isaiah's question,
not an overcoming of an obstacle. Thus, Is. 6:11ff. is best construed as part of the mandate
which YHWH gives to Isaiah. For an insightful response to Habel's attempt to see v. 11 as
the prophet's objection, based on an analysis of the mixed genre of Is. 6, see N.L.A. Tidwell,

with the glory of God,[49] it is evident that Isaiah's participation in the sinfulness of his people is the obstacle needed to be overcome (cf. Is. 6:6f.). It is only *after* his forgiveness-purification that Isaiah hears the word of God, so that, as V. Herntrich has emphasized, "Er ist neugeschaffen zu einem bestimmten Dienst."[50] It is this objection concerning the prophet's lack of suitability and the divine compensation which follows that makes Isaiah 6 distinctive in comparison to the other biblical accounts of the heavenly council.[51] Thus, Tidwell is right in emphasizing that Is. 6 represents a mixed genre in which the "council-*Gattung*," i.e. "a narrative of events in the heavenly council when it is assembled to make some fateful decision concerning the affairs of men,"[52] has been modified by a prophetic call-narrative.[53] For nowhere else in these scenes does a prophet (or the spirit in 1 Kgs. 22:19–21) offer an objection to his call, nor is the one sent out from the council subsequently made sufficient by God for the task. Isaiah's objection and God's response in Is. 6:5–7 thus render this narrative a prophetic call, rather than merely a commissioning for a particular task, despite its unique setting within the heavenly council.[54] In Tidwell's words, Is. 6 is "a council-scene into which, at a suitable point, the objection element of the call-*Gattung* has been introduced, i.e. at v. 5."[55] Indeed, that the council-*Gattung* has been modified by the objection motif from the call narrative, and not vice versa,[56] makes it all the more apparent that the emphasis of the narrative falls on Isaiah's objection and the divine response, as well as on the message itself.

"WA OMAR (Zech 3:5) and the Genre of Zechariah's Fourth Vision," *JBL* 94 (1975) 343–355, pp. 351 f., who shows that v. 11 parallels not the objection of the prophets, but the responses of those who hear God's deliberations and plans in the divine council (cf. Zech. 1:12; 3:5; Is. 6:8; 40:6; 1 Kgs. 22:21; Job 1:9; 2:5).

[49] So Richter, *Berufungsberichte*, p. 146; Zimmerli, *Ezechiel*, p. 20; Hans Wildberger, *Jesaja, 1. Teilband*, BKAT Bd. X/1, 1972, p. 251.

[50] *Der Prophet Jesaja, Kapitel 1–12*, ATD Bd. 17, 1957³, p. 105.

[51] Cf. e.g. Zech. 1:7–21; 3:1–10; Is. 40:1–8 and esp. 1 Kgs. 22:19–21.

[52] "Genre," p. 350.

[53] "Genre," p. 354.

[54] Contra e.g. Vieweger, *Spezifik*, pp. 14, 20, 24, 134, who, because of its specificity and setting, attributes Is. 6 to an entirely different genre than the prophetic calls of Moses, etc. on the one hand, and Ezekiel and Jeremiah on the other; and John D.W. Watts, *Isaiah 1–33*, WBC 24, 1985, pp. 70 f., who rejects Is. 6 as a call narrative due to its emphasis on the sending (שלח) of the prophet, which is never mentioned elsewhere in reference to a call, "but always of a particular task and message" (p. 70). But the mixed nature of the genre answers this objection, especially when one recognizes that this particular message of Israel's judgment becomes the distinctive task of Isaiah. Hence, even Watts refers to Is. 6 as an "authenticating vision" (p. 71), though he leaves open the question of the identity of the speaker in Is. 6 (cf. pp. 71, 73 f.).

[55] "Genre," p. 354.

[56] Contra Habel, "Form and Significance," p. 310, who sees the call-narrative being modified by its distinct setting rather than the setting being modified by the introduction of the call motifs; for this latter view, see Tidwell, "Genre," pp. 349 f., 354.

Moreover, the clear cultic backdrop to Isaiah's confession of "uncleanness" and his corresponding purification in 6:6 f.[57] emphasize that Isaiah's call is based on an act of God's grace, since it is parallel to the acts of atonement carried out regularly in the temple.[58] Against this backdrop, Isaiah's famous response הנני שלחני in 6:8 is to be read as the *recognition* that he is the one who has been *chosen* and *prepared* for the task by the theophany and act of grace in 6:1–7, rather than as the spontaneous response of one who is volunteering for service. Thus, the dichotomy often drawn between the calls of Moses and Jeremiah, in which the prophet is elected by God, and that of Isaiah, in which the prophet supposedly volunteers as an act of "perfectly free choice,"[59] is a false one. As Ivan Egnell stressed over forty years ago,

"This is ... a modernistic over-interpretation strengthened by a failing understanding of the literary form. The voluntariness should by no means be emphasized that much. For, as held forth already by Duhm and Mowinckel, Yahweh's question is rhetorical, actually implying the vocation." [60]

Viewed in this light, Isaiah's vision embodies the pattern we first saw in the call of Moses, where the prophet's obstacle is overcome by God's grace in order that he might be made sufficient to be God's messenger in spite of his own insufficiency. The very fact that Isaiah himself responds to God's query in 6:8, after first being able to react only with fear (cf. 6:5), makes this emphasis especially clear. Like Jeremiah and Ezekiel, as we will see below, Isaiah's objection is his own person. God's touching Isaiah's mouth in 6:7 and Jeremiah's in Jer. 1:9 are not only parallel linguistically, but functionally.[61] Further-

---

[57] On the cultic backdrop to Is. 6, cf. Egnell, *The Call of Isaiah*, pp. 35–39; Rolf Knierim, "The Vocation of Isaiah," *VT* 18 (1968) 47–68, p. 56; C. Westermann, *Theologie*, p. 108 and O. Eissfeldt, *Introduction*, pp. 74, 119.

[58] Cf. H. Gese, "Die Sühne," in *Zur biblischen Theologie, Alttestamentliche Vorträge*, BevTh Bd. 78, 1977, pp. 85–106, pp. 88 f.: "Der Sühnevorgang wird als reinigende Verbrennung mit dem kultischen Feuer abgebildet," and Otto Kaiser, *Das Buch des Propheten Jesaja, Kapitel 1–12*, ATD Bd. 17, 1981⁵, p. 131, on Is. 6:6 f.: "Sprache und Vorstellungswelt sind kultisch: Was der Priester bei jedem Sündopfer und der Hohepriester am großen Versöhnungstag für sich, sein Haus und Israel bewirkt, vgl. 3. Mose 4:26, 35 und 3. Mose 16:17, vollbringt der Himmlische mit seiner außergewöhnlichen Sühnehandlung." Kaiser, pp. 124 f., also argues against those who, like Kaplan, attempt to deny that Is. 6 is an initiatory call on the basis of the parallels between 1 Kgs. 22:19 ff. and Is. 6.

[59] So G.B. Gray, *A Critical and Exegetical Commentary on the Book of Isaiah I–XXXIX, Vol. I*, ICC, 1912, p. 109. For the continuation of this view, see Kaiser, *Jesaja*, pp. 123 f., and now Watts, *Isaiah 1–33*, p. 75, who refers to the prophet here as "the volunteer."

[60] *The Call of Isaiah*, p. 42, pointing to the Akkadian parallel as evidence that "these words are also bound by tradition, having the character of a formula" (cf. p. 42 nn. 2–5 for the relevant literature).

[61] Contra Vieweger, *Spezifik*, p. 42, who sees Jer. 1:9 f. to be a sign overcoming Jeremiah's objection, but not Isaiah's experience, though he too acknowledges the linguistic parallel between the two and observes that the objections in the call narratives all have to do with one's own person. The lack of explicit reference to cultic purity in Jer. 1 does not overcome this similarity in function.

more, the fact that the obstacle to be overcome in this instance is Isaiah's sinfulness highlights the gracious nature of God's call in a way we have not seen before. At the center of Isaiah's call is the recognition that the prophet is *made* sufficient by the *grace* of God.[62] "Der schuldige Prophet hat von seiner Seite nichts beizutragen."[63] Here too, then, we see the same four elements illustrated in the call of Moses: 1) the theophany in Is. 6:1–4; 2) the word of YHWH, here transposed to the end, in 6:8–13; 3) the obstacle to be overcome in 6:5; and 4) the act of God's grace in 6:6–7.

d) The Call of Jeremiah

Against the background investigated thus far, it should not be surprising that the same pattern of elective grace (i.e. "sufficiency in spite of insufficiency because of God's election and merciful provision") found in the calls of Moses, Gideon, and Isaiah also occurs in the call of Jeremiah in Jer. 1:4–10. What is surprising, however, is the way in which the call of Jeremiah so closely resembles that of Moses, not only in form, but also in content. Now both the content of the obstacle to be overcome in Jer. 1:6, as well as God's gracious provision for it in vv. 7–9, parallel what we found in Exod. 4:10 ff. Moreover, the very formulation of the various elements of Jeremiah's call is also found in the classic passage concerning the coming of a "prophet like Moses" in Deuteronomy 18:18:

Moses	*Jeremiah*	*Prophet like Moses*
1. אתה תדבר את כל אשר אצוך (Exod. 7:2a; cf. 4:12a)	1. ואת כל אשר אצוך תדבר (Jer. 1:7)	1. ודבר אליהם את כל אשר אצונו (Deut. 18:18c)
2. בי אדני לא איש דברים (Exod. 4:10a)	2. אהה אדני יהוה הנה לא ידעתי דבר (Jer. 1:6)	2. –
3. אהיה עמך (Exod. 3:12a)	3. אתך אני להצלך (Jer. 1:8)	3. ונתתי דברי בפיו (Deut. 18:18b)
ואנכי אהיה עם פיך והוריתיך (Exod. 4:12)	... ויגע על פי הנה נתתי דברי בפיך (Jer. 1:9)	–

(1 = Mandate; 2 = Objection; 3 = Promise)

---

[62] So too G. von Rad, *Theology, Vol. 1*, p. 271 n. 195, who comments concerning Is. 6:8 f.: "What takes place in Is. 6:8 f. is also to be understood as an expiatory cleansing of an object, the lips, which were as a result made capable of sufficing for a function that God laid upon them."

[63] Wildberger, *Jesaja*, p. 252 on Is. 6:6.

This twofold relationship between the call of Jeremiah and the Mosaic tradition, confirmed by the direct parallel between Jeremiah and Moses in Jer. 15:1, demonstrates that "Jeremiah claims to stand in the prophetic succession of Moses."[64] For our purposes it is not important whether this dependence is historical and literary, as William L. Holladay has repeatedly argued, so that the book of Jeremiah reflects the historical reality "that it was in the light of the figure of Moses that Jeremiah lived out his own ministry,"[65] whether these parallels are simply the result of a common call tradition, or, as Christopher R. Seitz has recently maintained, that later editors depicted Jeremiah in view of the originally unrelated conceptions of Deuteronomy.[66] Even if the latter is true, Moses' historical and theological precedence clearly provides the force of the comparison, and to Paul the formulation of Jeremiah's call would certainly be seen as subsequent to both Exodus 4 and Deuteronomy 18. In either case, Jeremiah's call and role as a prophet testifies clearly to the fact that, as Seitz has again pointed out, "Moses is the first prophet, the type against which others are measured."[67]

Hence, as a "prophet like Moses," Jeremiah's call can only be the result of God's election, as Deut. 18:18 makes clear: *YHWH* is the one who raises up the prophet, puts his words in the prophet's mouth (cf. Jer. 1:9), and commands him to speak (cf. Jer. 1:7). As a result, when the true prophet speaks, he speaks in *YHWH's* name (cf. Deut. 18:19).[68] God's sovereign election is thus an essential aspect of the self-consciousness of the prophet. This is reflected

---

[64] Habel, "Form and Significance," p. 306; cf. too Vieweger, *Spezifik*, pp. 28–31, who argues against the view that Jer. 1:7–9 are later Deuteronomistic redaction. Rather, the backdrop of Deut. 18:15–22 shows that Jer. 1:2, 4–10 are consciously built on the "Mosebild" from Deuteronomy (p. 31).

[65] "The Background of Jeremiah's Self-Understanding, Moses, Samuel, and Psalm 22," *JBL* 83 (1964) 153–164, p. 153, cf. 156 f. Holladay argues not only from Jeremiah's call and the parallels between Moses and Jeremiah concerning their call and intercessory roles, but also from the confessions in Jer. 15:1–4 and 20:17–18, the dating of Jeremiah's birth, not his call, to 626 BC, so that Jeremiah could have known Deut. 18:18 after its discovery and thus be influenced by it in the verbalization of his call, and from the parallels between the covenant/new covenant as associated with Moses and Jeremiah respectively. Holladay strengthened his argument in his subsequent study "Jeremiah and Moses: Further Observations," *JBL* 85 (1966) 17–27, by pointing to the parallels between Deut. 32 and various passages throughout Jeremiah and to the meaning of Jer. 15:16. For the continuation of this view that "Jrm evidently understood his vocation to be the prophet like Moses set forth in Deut. 18:18," see now his *Jeremiah 2, A Commentary on the Book of the Prophet Jeremiah*, Hermeneia, 1989, pp. 38 f., 54–56, 60, 78 f., 197–201.

[66] "The Prophet Moses and the Canonical Shape of Jeremiah," *ZAW* 101 (1989) 3–27. Of these three options, Holladay's position is to be preferred.

[67] "Prophet Moses," p. 5.

[68] Cf. Holladay, *Jeremiah 2*, p. 38, where he points to the parallels between Exod. 5:23, Deut. 18:19–22, and Jer. 20:9 on speaking in YHWH's name; and to his "Jeremiah's Self-Understanding," p. 155, where he points out that only in Jer. 1:7, Exod. 7:2 (addressed to Moses), and Deut. 18:18 do we find the pairing of the concepts of "commanding" and "speaking."

in the call of the prophets not only by the abrupt coming of the vision and the word of YHWH from "outside," as in the case of Isaiah, but also by the emphasis on the prophet's being "known" and "consecrated" by YHWH before his birth, as in Jer. 1:5.[69] As von Rad summarized it,

"Being a prophet is never represented as a tremendous intensification or transcendence of all previous religious experience. Neither previous faith nor any other personal endowment had the slightest part to play in preparing a man who was called to stand before Jahweh for his vocation." [70]

As a paradigmatic illustration of von Rad's point, Jeremiah's election before his birth, together with God's gracious promise in response to his objection, simply confirms the Mosaic pattern that *the sufficiency of the prophet* is, in reality, the sufficiency of the one who has not only elected him, but also enabled him to fulfil his task, i.e. *the sufficiency of God himself.*[71] Moreover, Vieweger has called attention to the striking fact that the objections in the call narratives all relate either to bodily inabilities or the inferiority of one's person or status, and not merely to an expression of humility before God.[72]

e) The Call of Ezekiel

Finally, the call of Ezekiel brings the development of this motif to its climax by extending the two central elements of the call narrative, i.e. the theophany (cf. Ezek. 1:1–28) and the word of YHWH (cf. Ezek. 2:1–3:11), to their outermost limits.[73] The significance of W. Zimmerli's extensive work on Ezekiel for our study is thus twofold. First, Zimmerli has insisted on the unity of Ezek. 1:1–3:11 in the light of the *Traditionsgeschichte* of the prophetic call itself. As these narratives demonstrate, the throne scene of chapter one need not necessarily be separated from the word of YHWH in chapters two and three. Second, Zimmerli has worked out the parallels between Ezek. 1 and Is. 6 on the one

---

[69] Cf. the close parallels to the "servant" in Is. 44:2; 49:1, 5, 6. Since there is no explicit call narrative among the Isaianic Servant texts (note the absence of the objection-motif!), I have not included this tradition in my survey. For a development of the Isaianic Servant of YHWH as a "prophet like Moses" or "second Moses" see Jones, *Second Moses*, pp. 118–137.

[70] *Theology*, Vol. 2, p. 57.

[71] This link between Moses and Jeremiah may also be reflected in the LXX version of Jer. 1:6 itself in which אֲהָהּ is translated by ὁ ὤν, apparently reflecting the same designation for God in Exod. 3:14. Holladay, "Jeremiah's Self-Understanding," p. 154 n. 3, thus comments concerning Jer. 1:6 LXX that "this rendering immediately suggests the reading אֶהְיֶה, the self-designation of God to Moses in Exod. 3:14. Is the Alexandrian exegetical tradition associating Jeremiah's call here with the 'I am' revelation to Moses?"

[72] *Spezifik*, p. 39. Contra Vieweger, p. 40, this same thing is true of the call of Isaiah.

[73] Vieweger, *Spezifik*, pp. 50, 59, 83, who argues in addition that the units are 1:4–28a and 2:3–11, with 3:12–15 closely related to the former in providing a vision framework for the unit and 1:28b–2:2 being transitional.

hand, and Ezek. 2–3 and Jeremiah on the other.[74] Against this background, it is significant for our study that the contrast between Ezekiel's falling on his face before the vision of God's glory in 1:28 and his being summoned to stand up in order to receive YHWH's word in 2:1 are directly juxtaposed in the narrative. Vieweger has pointed out that this transitional scene highlights the "smallness of the prophet" over against "the greatness, the power, and the distance of Jahweh" as the natural outcome of the vision in chapter one, now portrayed in a concrete event.[75] But even more significant in view of Paul's use of Ezek. 36:26 f. in 2 Cor. 3:3 (see chapter two), is that the summons to Ezekiel to stand is accompanied in Ezek. 2:2 by the coming of a "revitalizing and energizing spirit."[76] The text does not explicitly identify whether or not this spirit is the Spirit of YHWH. But as Block argues, "the fact that the raising of the prophet occurs concurrently with the sound of the voice suggests a dynamic and enabling power in that voice. We should probably associate the *rwh* ["spirit"] that vitalizes the wheels [in Ezek. 1:12, 20] with the *rwh* ["spirit"] that energizes the prophet."[77] Block portrays the scene in the following way:

"Ezekiel's experience is described in royal court language. Having been ushered into the presence of a monarch, a person would signify his subjection with the act of prostration. Only when the king had authorized one to arise would one dare to do so. Ezekiel realized that he had been ushered into the court of the divine king and that Yahweh was seeking an audience with him. But only the divine spirit could give him the authority or the energy to stand erect before God. To fall before a god is appropriate, but to remain on one's face once he has indicated a desire to speak is insulting to the deity. Ezekiel may have been a … 'mere mortal,' but infused with the *rwh* he may – yea, he must – stand in God's presence."[78]

The fact that Ezekiel is unable to stand up on his own, but must be set on his feet *by the Spirit* (cf. Ezek. 2:2 and 3:23 f.) graphically illustrates that, like Moses and the other prophets, Ezekiel is also *made sufficient* for his call by God himself, *in spite of his insufficiency*.[79]

---

[74] See esp. *Ezechiel*, pp. 21, 35, 36, 70, 71, 75 f. Similarly, though with more caution, Vieweger, *Spezifik*, pp. 59, 61, 68–70. In contrast to Zimmerli, see Bernhard Lang, "Die erste und die letzte Vision des Propheten, Eine Überlegung zu Ezechiel 1–3," *Biblica* 64 (1983) 225–230, who argues that the call narrative and the vision narrative are two separate events which have been brought together by a later redactor (p. 229). Nevertheless, Lang's analysis stresses that as the text now stands the two accounts are interwoven into a unity, so that Lang, like most modern critics, agrees that the vision of Ezek. 1–3 is essentially one literary unit; cf. Robert R. Wilson, "Prophecy in Crisis: The Call of Ezekiel," in *Interpreting the Prophets*, ed. James Luther Mays and Paul J. Achtemeier, 1987, pp. 157–169, p. 160.

[75] *Spezifik*, p. 59.

[76] So Daniel I. Block, "The Prophet of the Spirit: The Use of *RWH* in the Book of Ezekiel," *JETS* 32 (1989) 27–49, p. 37.

[77] "Prophet of the Spirit," p. 37.

[78] "Prophet of the Spirit," p. 37.

[79] A connection between Moses and Ezekiel might also be seen in Num. 16:22 and 20:6, where Moses and Aaron are reported to have fallen on their faces before YHWH as an act of

Lastly, here too God acts in Ezek. 2:6 and 8 to overcome the implied obstacles of the prophet's fear before a hardened people by placing his words in the mouth of the prophet with his outstretched hand (cf. Ezek. 2:8–3:3 and 3:27).[80] The divine act vividly recalls God's similar acts of grace in Is. 6:6 and Jer. 1:9, as well as God's promise to Moses in Exod. 4:12 and 15 and the corresponding prophecy of Deut. 18:18.[81] Indeed, as in the call of Moses, Ezekiel's call also repeats the motif of the obstacle and its resolution more than once. In Ezek. 3:7–10 God restates his warning that Israel will not be willing to listen, since the nation is stubborn and obstinate (cf. 3:7 with 2:4 f.). But then God reassures Ezekiel that he has provided him with what is necessary to withstand Israel's rebelliousness (cf. 3:8 f.). Once again, Ezekiel's obstacle, i.e. his fear in the face of Israel's "hard" rebelliousness, is overcome by God's gracious provision: Ezekiel is made just as "hard" as the people to whom he must go *by YHWH himself*.[82] Hence, although embellished, the pattern detected in the call of Moses is also evident in the call of Ezekiel:

(1) The Theophany: 1:1–28
(2) The Word of YHWH: 2:1–5, 7 and 3:4–7, 10–11
(3) The Obstacle to be Overcome: 2:6, 8a; 3:9b
(4) The Act of God's Grace: 2:8b–3:3; 3:8–9a.

f) Conclusion

It is now possible to draw some general observations about the call narratives as found in the call of Moses and the prophets. The first thing to note is the central role which the objection/obstacle motif plays both structurally and theologically.[83] In each case it is the response of the prophet which provides the structural rationale for God's further action within the call itself. But the obstacle to be overcome also determines the *nature* of this action. It is only

---

worship; cf. also Exod. 34:8, where Moses "bows low towards the earth" when the Lord passes before him. See Zimmerli, *Ezechiel*, p. 36, for these parallels and others.

[80] Zimmerli, *Ezechiel*, p. 70, calls 2:8–3:3 the "Hauptakzent" of Ezekiel's call, i.e. the "ordinationsartigen Handeln Jahwes am Propheten." Vieweger, *Spezifik*, p. 73, refers to the "theme of the objection" which can be seen in the contextual flow of the narrative in 2:3–3:3.

[81] On the parallels between Jer. 1:9; Is. 6:6 and Ezek. 2:9–3:3, see H.G. Reventlow, *Liturgie und prophetisches Ich bei Jeremia*, 1963, pp. 63–65. For other examples of God stretching forth his hand, he points to Num. 22:38; 23:5, 12; Deut. 18:18; Is. 51:16; 59:21 (p. 64).

[82] Contra those who, like Tidwell, "Genre," p. 351 n. 44, suggest that Ezekiel's resistance to his call "has nothing to do with his own insufficiency."

[83] This constitutive nature of the obstacle motif has also been underscored positively by its existence in similar call-structures outside of the OT and Ancient Near East, and negatively by its absence in the closely related "messenger formulas" (e.g. Exod. 4:16; 7:1; 16:9; 1 Kgs. 14:1–18; 2 Kgs. 9:1–10; 22:15–20; Jer. 21:1–4; 27:1–11; 36:1–8) and "symbolic act accounts" (e.g. Jer. 51:59–64a; Hos. 3:1–5) within the OT. For the former, see Martin J. Buss, "An Anthropological Perspective upon Prophetic Call Narratives," *Semeia* 21 (1982) 9–30, pp. 13 f., and for the latter, Kenneth W. Schmidt, "Prophetic Delegation," pp. 206 f.

because Moses questions and finally objects to God's call that he learns God's name, is given the miracle-working rod and signs, and receives Aaron as his mouthpiece! The same can be said about Isaiah's purification/forgiveness, the promise to Gideon and Jeremiah, and Ezekiel's "hard forehead." The prophetic response to God's call becomes the structural axis upon which the narrative turns.

Moreover, the objection/obstacle motif, with its resolution in the additional activity of YHWH beyond the theophany, also provides the platform from which the central theological assertion of the call narrative is displayed. It is this motif which demonstrates that the call of the prophet is a result of God's elective grace alone, since in each case the response of the prophet makes it clear that he would be insufficient for the task in and of himself. The prophet's obstacle demonstrates that it is only because *YHWH* has overcome his particular inadequacy that the prophet is able to speak on YHWH's behalf. It is therefore important to recognize that as a result of the prophet's call the obstacle has been overcome, but not removed! Moses' speech impediment is not cured, Gideon's family status cannot be altered, Jeremiah is still young, and the people to whom Ezekiel must go will continue to be hard-hearted.[84] In this way the objection/obstacle motif demonstrates that the prophet owes "his" sufficiency to the grace of God.[85]

Second, the conclusion of this study that the center of gravity in the prophetic call narratives is the objection/obstacle motif supports the current consensus of scholars that the *purpose* of the prophetic call in its canonical form is not primarily autobiographical, but apologetic.[86] The *negative* emphasis in the obstacle motif on the *insufficiency* of the prophet implies and underscores a *positive* emphasis on the *sufficiency* of the prophet as a result of God's grace. As Berquist has emphasized in relation to the call of Jeremiah, it does so by pointing to God as the one who is responsible for the prophet's message, while at the same time stressing that the prophet has no personal benefit to be gained from his message. The prophet's only motive is service to YHWH.[87] The prophet's call aims to *legitimate* the claim of the prophet and the authority of his oracles in spite of his obvious insufficiency. Recent studies have emphasized that this legitimation depended historically upon the community's acceptance of the prophet as won by the prophet's own actions, while the literary tradition functioned in a subsequent situation to establish the prophet's au-

---

[84] The only exception to this pattern seems to be that Isaiah's impurity is cleansed once and for all.

[85] This point has been well put by Zimmerli, *Ezechiel*, p. 71.

[86] See already Klaus Baltzer, "Considerations Regarding the Office and Calling of the Prophet," *HTR* 61 (1968) 567–581, p. 568: "Formerly, the aspect of personal experience often was emphasized in these stories. But today we can see more clearly that their real point is the vindication and legitimation of the prophet in his office." For this point see too Berquist, "Prophetic Legitimation," p. 131.

[87] "Prophetic Legitimation," p. 131.

thority as he now "lives" in the tradition. [88] It is precisely this latter function beyond the prophet's own situation which is of significance for our study, since it is the literary form and function of the prophetic call narrative which provide the ongoing basis of authority within the tradition. Scholars have therefore pointed out that the very existence of the prophetic call narratives is an indication of their apologetic purpose and function in the tradition. The subsequent inscripturation of the prophet's experience indicates that he (or his school) must now legitimize his prophetic claim before those who reject his authority or calling. In von Rad's words,

"This makes clear that the writing down of a call was something secondary to the call itself, and that it served a different end than did the latter. The call commissioned the prophet: the act of writing down an account of it was aimed at those sections of the public in whose eyes he had to justify himself." [89]

The fact that the prophetic call is expressed in terms of a stylized *Gattung*, which itself contributes to the purpose of the report, is further evidence of the apologetic nature of the prophetic call narrative or schema. Function is always related to and reflected by form. Thus, as N. Habel has put it,

"By employing this form the prophets *publicly* identify themselves as God's ambassadors. The call narratives, therefore, are not primarily pieces of autobiographical information but *open proclamation* of the prophet's claim to be Yahweh's agent at work in Israel ... The employment of the literary form in no way negates the reality of the call encounter itself, but underscores the relevance of this form for the *public affirmation* of the claims which the prophet is making as Yahweh's spokesman." [90]

As a result, when it became necessary to make the prophet's private experience public, a form was already available to do so, and one which carried with it an implied claim to authority which was presumably recognizable to its hearers. The established purpose of the call schema itself was "to announce publicly that Yahweh commissioned the prophet in question as His representative."[91]

This brings us to our third and, for this study, most significant point. As we have seen, both the structure and theological meaning of the prophetic call narratives are also found in the call of Moses. From the standpoint of the history and canon of Israel, no one in the first century A.D. would question the historical priority of the Mosaic accounts, even if today many would question the historical dependence of the prophetic call narratives on the call of Moses.[92]

---

[88] For this point see esp. the paradigmatic work of Long, "Prophetic Authority," pp. 4, 7, 13, and now J.L. Berquist, "Prophetic Legitimation in Jeremiah," pp. 130 f.

[89] *Theology*, Vol. 2, p. 55. See his pp. 50–69 for what is still one of the best introductions to the subject of the prophet's call, and p. 54 n. 9 for important literature.

[90] "Form and Significance," p. 317, emphasis mine.

[91] Habel, "Form and Significance," p. 323. For this same point see Kilian, "Berufungsberichte," p. 375, and R. Knierim, "The Vocation of Isaiah," p. 62.

[92] See e.g. B. Childs, *Commentary on Exodus*, pp. 55 f, who argues that "the evidence points ... toward seeing the setting of Exod. 3 in the prophetic office. This is not to suggest

Looking back from this first-century perspective, it becomes evident that the prophetic call schema carries its implicit apologetic force in part because it is patterned after the call of *the* prophet Moses. Inasmuch as the "prophet like Moses" is also *called* "like Moses," he can claim the same "sufficiency in spite of one's own insufficiency because of the grace of God" that Moses had. In other words, the call of Moses provides not only the prototype for the later prophetic call narratives, but also the precedent for their claim to authority in spite of the circumstances which might call that very authority into question. If YHWH used Moses in spite of his speech defect, then the insignificance of Gideon, the sin of Isaiah, the youth of Jeremiah, or the timidity of Ezekiel cannot be adduced as reasons to doubt the validity of their respective calls. In fact, far from disqualifying the prophet, these very obstacles are an essential part of the call itself, demonstrating that God, not the prophet himself, is the source of the prophet's message and sufficiency. As a result, as Kilian has summarized it,

"Wer sich später als Berufener Gehör und Autorität verschaffen wollte, tat deshalb gut daran, sein eigenes Berufungserlebnis *in die Formen der Mosesberufung zu kleiden ...* so aber konnten die durch die Übertragung auf Moses vollends sanktionierten Berufungsschemata geradezu *Legitimationscharakter* erhalten. Wer nach der Weisen des *Moses* berufen war, der konnte Anspruch darauf erheben, gehört zu werden, weil er von Gott gesandt war. Damit wiederum erlangte der so gestaltete Berufungsbericht die Bedeutung einer *Legitimationsurkunde.*"[93]

The existence of this "Mosaic pattern" of "sufficiency in spite of one's own insufficiency because of the grace of God" in the call of the prophets thus becomes an integral part of the prophetic claim to authority. From a canonical standpoint, however, it also witnesses to the accepted authority of Moses himself as God's first and foremost prophet-mediator. As such, this call schema not only provides a paradigm for later expressions of God's call in the life of his servants, but also points forward to the central, authoritative place which Moses comes to occupy in non-canonical, Jewish literature.

---

that the form of prophetism which developed in the monarchial period was simply read back into the Mosaic period. Rather, the reverse movement seems closer to the truth. The tradition linked Moses' call as Yahweh's messenger with the later phenomena of classic prophetism ... However, it is also clear that the later prophetic office influenced the tradition of Moses' call." Cf. Kilian, "Berufungsberichte," p. 374, who speaks of the "exemplarische Bedeutung" and "normative Auswirkungen" which the call of Moses possessed. The question of the degree and direction of influence need not detain us, given the obvious canonical relationship.

[93] "Berufungsberichte," pp. 374 f., emphasis mine.

3. The Authority of Moses as a Legitimizing Presupposition in the Apocrypha, Pseudepigrapha, and the Literature from Qumran

The first thing that strikes one in turning to the literature outside the Hebrew bible is that the use of Moses to legitimize one's own authority, which was only evident *implicitly* in the Old Testament, now becomes *explicit* in a variety of ways throughout this literature. In post-biblical literature the figure of Moses takes on significance as a source of authority and basis of legitimacy to a degree not found in the biblical tradition. Indeed, outside of 1 Esdras, whenever Moses is mentioned in this literature, his authority is first assumed and then used to legitimize either a particular theological point (e.g. in Sirach, the Letter of Aristeas, The Martyrdom of Isaiah, 2 Baruch), or the work of the author as a whole (e.g. in 2 Maccabees, Jubilees, 4 Ezra, and the Testament of Moses). The sufficiency of one's theology, one's leaders, or one's own ministry can all be tied in the Hasmonean and Herodian periods to the undisputed authority and reverence for the person of Moses.[94] In *The Testament of Moses* (TM) this reverence reaches its climax when Moses is appropriated to be "the pre-eminent spokesman of God's plans for world history."[95] The portrait of Moses in TM is thus a classic proof text for J. Jeremias' observation that in post-biblical Judaism, "as distinct from the basic OT approach to Moses ... his person is now panegyrically magnified ...."[96] This is so much the case that G. Vermes even suggests that in TM Moses takes the place of the Messiah.[97] Hence, by the end of the Herodian period (4 B.C.–A.D. 34) Moses can be referred to not only as "the mediator of (God's) covenant" (TM 1:14), but also as "the divine prophet for the whole earth, the perfect teacher in the world" (TM 11:16), or as we read in the late first century work, *The Biblical Antiquities of Philo* (LAB), "the first of all the prophets" *(primus omnium prophetarum*; LAB 35:6).[98]

---

[94] For the support and development of these points see my "Moses in the Apocrypha and Pseudepigrapha." The references to Moses in 1 Esdras 1:6, 5:48, and 9:39 highlight Moses' authority to a degree not found in the MT, but lack an explicit legitimizing function.

[95] David L. Tiede, "The Figure of Moses in the Testament of Moses," in *Studies on the Testament of Moses,* SBL Septuagint and Cognate Studies, Nr. 4, 1973, pp. 86–92, p. 86.

[96] Art. Μωϋσῆς, *TDNT* 4 (1967) 848–873, p. 849.

[97] "Die Gestalt des Moses an der Wende der beiden Testamente," in *Moses in Schrift und Überlieferung,* 1963, pp. 61–93, p. 78.

[98] Translation of TM by J. Priest, "Testament of Moses," in *OTP, 1,* ed. J.H. Charlesworth, 1983, pp. 927 ff. R.H. Charles, "The Assumption of Moses," *Apocrypha, Vol. II,* 1913, p. 424, renders this verse: "God's chief prophet throughout the earth, the most perfect teacher in the world." The Latin reads, *divinum ... profetem* (Charles, p. 424 n. 16). Translation of LAB by D.J. Harrington, "Pseudo-Philo," *OTP, 2,* pp. 304 ff. The Latin text is from D.J. Harrington, J. Cazeaux, C. Perrot and P.M. Bogaert, *Pseudo-Philo, Les Antiquites Bibliques, Tome 1,* SC Nr. 229, 1976. Although this cannot be developed here, the actual focus on Moses as the supreme prophet in the TM and LAB is on his function as intercessor; see my "Moses in the Apocrypha." For Moses as prophet, see too Martyrdom of Isaiah 3:7–

But of even greater significance for our study of Paul's self-defense in 2 Cor. 3:4 ff. is the contemporary use of Moses as the source of legitimation for the authority and call of Israel's subsequent leaders. This is true whether it be Joshua, Kenaz, Gideon, or Samuel in *The Biblical Antiquities of Philo*, the apocalyptic seer Ezra himself in *4 Ezra*, or the Teacher of Righteousness in the Qumran community. Of this literature, LAB provides the most extensive look at how the biblical traditions concerning Moses were being viewed and used in Paul's day.

The narrative recounting the life of Moses in LAB encompasses 11 chapters of the 65 chapter work, occupying more space within the author's account of Genesis through 2 Samuel than that of any other figure or event.[99] It is significant, therefore, that in LAB Israel's other most important leaders are also explicitly linked to the call and authority of Moses.[100] Hence, as in the biblical tradition, Moses is not only presented in his own right, but also becomes the basis for legitimizing Israel's future leaders. For to those who look to Moses as their mediator and intercessor par excellence, the natural next step is to look to their subsequent leaders as the embodiment of this Mosaic ideal.

Thus Joshua is commanded to take the "garments of (Moses') wisdom and clothe yourself, and with his belt of knowledge gird your loins, and you will be changed and become another man," just as God had previously promised Moses concerning Joshua (LAB 20:2). As a result, Joshua, like Moses, also comes to be called "a servant of the Lord" as Moses' successor (LAB 30:1; 20:5; 24:6). In a similar way, Kenaz, the second most prominent figure in LAB and one that is uniquely developed in this work,[101] begins his own tenure as Israel's judge by twice referring to the prior words of Moses, "the friend of the Lord," as the reason and legitimation for his initial actions (LAB 25:3,5). Conversely, when Gideon resists his call to deliver Israel out of the hand of the Midianites (cf. LAB 34:4–5; Jud. 6:15) and God reassures him of his presence (35:5), Gideon's immediate response is to ask God for a sign, using Moses as his precedent for doing so (35:6). The connection between the call of Gideon and Moses which is established formally in the biblical account (see above) is now made explicit in LAB. Finally, Samuel's call is also introduced with a reference to God's prior election of Moses (LAB 53:8). Moreover, since Samuel is "like (God's) servant Moses," God's decision to approach Samuel with the voice of a man is compared by God to his prior encounter with Moses. Despite their likeness, God decides not to reveal himself directly to Samuel for fear of overwhelming him, since Moses was 80 when he saw the burning bush, but Samuel is now only eight (53:2; cf. 1 Sam. 3:4 ff.)! In addition, in LAB 57:2 Samuel himself draws a comparison between his ministry and that of Moses in order to assert his innocence in the light of Israel's desire to have a king. And even

---

10; TM 3:11–13; LAB 53:8; 56:1; 57:2; 1 Esdras 8:84; Sir. 46:1; 2 Bar. 59:2–12; Philo, *Quaes.Gen.* I, 86; *Quaes.Gen.* IV, 8; and Vermes, "Gestalt," pp. 62, 64 f., 81–84.

[99] Pointed out by M.R. James, *The Biblical Antiquities of Philo*, 1917, p. 146.

[100] For the following survey, see too my "Moses in the Apocrypha."

[101] For the name Kenaz in the bible, cf. Num. 32:12; Josh. 15:17; Jud. 1:13; for a survey of the Kenaz-tradition in LAB and its relationship to the biblical narrative and other non-biblical traditions, see James, *Antiquities*, p. 146.

though Saul's appointment is seen to be a transgression, Saul's first recorded act as king is commanded by Saul as a fulfillment of the words which Moses has spoken (LAB 58:1; cf. Exod. 17:14). In fact, even the appointment of the king itself, though not approved, is nevertheless said to be a fulfillment of a prior prophecy of Moses (see LAB 56:1 and Deut. 17:15).

Just as in the parallel between the call of Moses and the biblical tradition of the call of the prophets, here too Moses' authority as Israel's law-giver and first prophet can be seen to undergird the authority of Israel's subsequent servants and prophets.[102] In LAB, God's accreditation of those whom he has chosen is displayed in the establishment of a direct link between the one who is called and the call and life of Moses. Moses is not only a paradigm for how Israel's leaders should act toward God; Moses' experience is a model of how God acts toward Israel's leaders. Moreover, in the call of Gideon in LAB 35, we encounter a motif similar to that of the prophetic "insufficient-but-sufficient-by-the-grace-of-God" motif which we have seen in the OT – but this time *directly* and *explicitly* linked to the call of Moses (cf. LAB 35:6). On the one hand Gideon is said to have the "inner" qualities which make him suitable for God's call (LAB 35:5). But on the other hand, his own desire for a sign reflects the same tension between sufficiency in and of oneself and the call of God which is evidenced in the OT in the calls of Moses, Gideon, and the prophets. As Gideon himself puts it in LAB 35:6, "But who am I, unless perhaps the Lord has chosen me? May he give me a sign so that I may know that I am being guided."

In the same way, in 4 Ezra 14 Ezra's commission to remember and record all that he has seen and heard in the seventh vision is explicitly modelled after the theophany to Moses in the burning bush and God's later revelation to him on Mt. Sinai in Exod. 3:8 and 34:28 respectively. The purpose in doing so is not only to lend credence to the constitution of the biblical writings associated with the work of Ezra (i.e. if Moses wrote the law, Ezra, as his successor, "re-wrote" it), but also to accredit the apocalyptic visions of the author, and the apocalyptic tradition in general (i.e. the 70 secret books which can only be delivered to the "wise among the people," cf. 4 Ezra 14:38–48), by presenting Ezra as a "second Moses."[103] Moreover, Michael P. Knowles has recently demonstrated on the basis of the two periods of 40 days which provide the framework for the visions recorded throughout 4 Ezra that, as a "second Moses," Ezra is commissioned to restore to Israel the Law/wisdom which has been destroyed with the destruction of Jerusalem (14:23–36).[104] For as

---

[102] Joshua is called a servant in LAB 30:1; Samuel is a prophet (LAB 56:4; 57:4); Kenaz is called "the ruler" in LAB 28:3, though he too prophesies (see 28:6–9); and Gideon, though never referred to in the narrative by a specific title, is one of the judges.

[103] So Charles, *Apocrypha*, Vol. II, note to ch.14, p. 620, and G.W.E. Nickelsburg, *Jewish Literature Between the Bible and the Mishnah, A Historical and Literary Introduction*, 1981, p. 292.

[104] "Moses, the Law, and the Unity of 4 Ezra," *NovT* 31 (1989) 257–274, pp. 269–271, 273. For the significance of this in relation to Israel's hard-heartedness and their sin with the

Knowles has observed, the 40 days that Ezra spends in God's presence rewriting the Law and the secret books in 14:38–48 correspond to the prior 40 days of revelation during which Ezra received his prior visions in 3:1–14:37.[105] Chapter 14 thus becomes the key to the entire book both structurally and theologically by making explicit Ezra's authority and role as the prophet like Moses. As this chapter makes clear, through these two periods of 40 days Ezra's role parallels that of Moses in his 40 days of fasting and interceding for Israel after their sin with the golden calf and his subsequent 40 days on Mt. Sinai to receive the Law for the second time (cf. Exod. 34:28; Deut. 9:25; 10:1–11).[106]

Finally, whether or not one agrees with N. Wieder's equation of the "interpreter of the law" in CD 7:18–21 with the Greek god Hermes , thus creating a parallel between the leader of the Qumran community and Moses (who was also referred to as Hermes in the fragment attributed to Artapanus),[107] his overall thesis that the דורש התורה in Qumran was portrayed in the image of Moses is surely correct. Wieder's insistence that "it is not a mere accident that the sectarian leader is described in terms applied to Moses," since "this is related to the eschatological role of the 'Interpreter of the Law': He was regarded as the Second Moses,"[108] is supported by his observation that the attributes of "interpreter of the law" (דורש התורה), "stave" (מחוקק), and "vessel" or "tool" (כלי), which are applied to the community's leader in CD 6:7–8, are all attributes applied to Moses in Jewish and Samaritan tradition.[109]

In addition, the structure of the wider context of CD 5:11–6:14 also leads to this conclusion.[110] The enemies of the community described in CD 5:11–15a as those who "defile their holy spirit and open their mouth with a blaspheming tongue against the laws of the Covenant of God saying, 'they are not sure,'" etc.[111] are likened in CD 5:17f. to "Jannes and his brother" who rose up against Moses and Aaron in "ancient times." This parallel allows the author to

---

golden calf, Ezra's own role, and the nature of the Law itself in 4 Ezra, see below, chapter six.

[105] Cf. "Unity of 4 Ezra," pp. 261–264, for a discussion of the time references throughout 4 Ezra.

[106] "Unity of 4 Ezra," p. 265.

[107] I.e. based on the Greek equivalent of הכוכב, ἀστήρ, taken to mean the planet mercury/ Hermes, rather than its more general meaning "star," cf. N. Wieder, "The 'Law-interpreter' of the Sect of the Dead Sea Scrolls: the Second Moses," *JJS* 4 (1953) 158–175, pp. 165–167, for his view of CD 7:18. For a criticism of this one aspect of Wieder's thesis, but a general assent to the thesis as a whole, see D.L. Tiede, *The Charismatic Figure as Miracle Worker*, SBL Dissertation Series 1, 1972, pp. 185 f., 192–194.

[108] Wieder, "Second Moses," pp. 167 f.

[109] See Wieder, "Second Moses," pp. 161–165, for the relevant parallels.

[110] It is surprising that Wieder does not call attention to the structural argument, which so closely supports his position, even though he emphasizes that Num. 21:18 is used in CD 6:4f. as a prediction of the sect's existence and investigates the equation of the "well" with the "law" in depth; cf. "Second Moses," pp. 159–161.

[111] English translations of the Qumran texts are taken from G. Vermes, *The Dead Sea Scrolls in English*, and the Hebrew from E. Lohse, *Die Texte aus Qumran*, 1971.

construct a typical pesher interpretation in which those who "preached rebellion against the commandments of God given by the hand of Moses and of His holy annointed ones" in CD 5:21–6:1 are equated with the present enemies of the community, while those who remained faithful and "dug the well" (Cf. Num. 21:18) become "the converts of Israel who went out of the land of Judah to sojourn in the land of Damascus" (6:5). Since for the author of the Damascus Document the "well" of Num. 21:18 is the Law, the "staves" used to dig it are now provided by the community's own "Interpreter of the Law." The "staves" thus become that correct interpretation of the law of Moses now possessed by the community, given by the hand of their teacher, in which "they should walk in all the age of wickedness ..." (6:7–10, 14).

The task of the "Interpreter of the Law" (דורש התורה) was to provide the faithful community with the "exact interpretation of the law" (CD 6:14) by which one was to live in the last days of wickedness before the dawn of the messianic age.[112] In this role he occupied the same position in relationship to the faithful of Qumran as Moses did to those who were faithful in the wilderness. Such a parallel is part of the well-known typological correspondence developed by the Qumran community in which the present eschatological experience of the community is interpreted in view of Israel's experience in the wilderness.[113] Wieder is right, therefore, in asserting that this typological correspondence "demands categorically the presence of a second Moses, as the representative of the principle figure who held the very centre in the drama of the exodus and the life in the desert."[114] The study of the Torah in Qumran had a messianic significance (cf. 1QS 8:12–16), since the "Interpreter of the Law," i.e. the Teacher of Righteousness (CD 1:10f. and 6:11), was preparing the way into the messianic era, just as Moses had prepared the way into the promised land (1QS 9:17–21).[115] Hence, to join the Qumran community meant "to

---

[112] See CD 1:12–13; 4:2–4; 20:15; 1QpHab 2:8–10; 7:1–5; 1QM 1–2; 4Qp Ps 37 2:5–7.

[113] See 1QM 3:12–4:11; 7:3–7; 11:8; CD 20:26; 1QS 6:2; 8:12–14; 1QM 1:3 and F.M. Cross, *The Ancient Library of Qumran and Modern Biblical Studies*, rev. ed., 1961, p. 78, who in referring to these texts concludes, "... the Essenes prove to be an apocalyptic community, a *Heilsgemeinschaft*, imitating the ancient desert sojourn of Mosaic times in anticipation of the dawning kingdom of God." On the parallel between the ordering of the camp in Qumran and the ordering of the wilderness generation, cf. Deut. 1:15 with 1QS 1:14–15; 1QM 4:1–4; CD 13:1–2; and Tiede, *Charismatic Figure*, pp. 185f.

[114] Wieder, "Second Moses," p. 172. See too P.R. Jones' extensive treatment of the Teacher of Righteousness as a second Moses in his *Second Moses*, pp. 187–202 and "Apostolic Authority," pp. 230–233, and his development in *Second Moses*, pp. 232–236, of the point that the wilderness typology in the Qumran writings necessitates the presence of a second Moses figure. For a list of 21 scholars holding the position that the Teacher was viewed as a second Moses, see his *Second Moses*, p. 186 n. 1. However, against Wieder's attempt to attach a special salvific-eschatological significance to the Teacher of Righteousness himself and this "second Moses" typology, see the definitive study of the Teacher of Righteousness by Gert Jeremias, *Der Lehrer der Gerechtigkeit*, SUNT 2, 1963, esp. pp. 273–275.

[115] G. Vermes, "Gestalt," pp. 81–84, suggests in line with this that the Interpreter of the Law in Qumran could also possibly be described as a "new Moses."

return to the law of Moses with a whole heart and soul" (CD 15:7, 12; cf. 16:1–5) *as it was being interpreted in the Qumran community* (cf. 1QS 5:7–9). As a result, what is taught in the Manual of Discipline can be identified with what God commanded "by the hand of Moses" and perceived as the means by which the latter is fulfilled (cf. 1QS 1:1–3).[116]

Unlike 4 Ezra 14:1–8, therefore, the Teacher of Righteousness does not receive an entirely new revelation, but merely the inspired and infallible interpretation of what Moses and the prophets have already revealed (see 1QpHab 7:4–5; CD 6:14). This is true even in the *Temple Scroll*, where Moses' authority is still foundational, even though the work contains an extensive rewriting of large portions of the Pentateuch itself. This can be seen in the fact that the scroll as a whole is written in the first person, with God himself as the speaker who apparently addresses Moses (cf. 11QT 44:5: 'the Sons of Aaron your brother[s]'[117]). The scroll is thus conceived as a Torah given to Moses by God. In pointing to these facts, Dimant concludes that "...the author was undoubtedly convinced that he was writing the truly divine Torah as revealed to him through tradition and divine inspiration."[118] But he does so by taking on the role of Moses! For this reason, it seems more appropriate in view of his non-messianic character to view him as the "prophet like Moses" sent to reveal the true meaning of the Law (and perhaps therefore to be identified as the unexpressed subject of Deut. 18:18 f. in 4Q175 5–8). Nevertheless, it remains clear that the portrayal of the Interpreter of the Law/Teacher of Righteousness in Qumran as a Mosaic figure implied a claim to authority which, because of its obvious nature, need not be explicitly expressed. Nowhere is the *legitimizing* function of Moses more evident, therefore, than in the writings of the Qumran community as the deposit of those who went into the wilderness to study the law of Moses (1QS 8:15), equipped with its correct interpretation by the Mosaic Teacher of Righteousness (CD 1:10f.; 6:4–11).

Having come this far, we are, in effect, back where we began with our examination of the relationship between the call of Moses and that of the prophets in the Old Testament. An investigation of the Apocrypha, Pseudepigrapha, and Qumran literature reveals that Moses continues to be associated principally with the Law, and, indeed, even derives his authority from having been chosen to receive it.[119] Nevertheless, the figure of Moses now takes on a

---

[116] So too A.R.C. Leaney, *The Rule of Qumran and Its Meaning; Introduction, Translation and Commentary*, 1966, p. 171 to 1QS 5:7. See the parallels he lists.

[117] Because of the ambiguity of אחיכה it is not clear whether the singular or plural is to be preferred; for the singular cf. Yigal Yadin, *The Temple Scroll*, Vol. 2, 1983, p. 186; for the plural, see Johann Maier, *Die Tempelrolle vom Toten Meer*, 1978, p. 47. Even if taken as a plural, the reference may still be, by extension, to "Moses."

[118] Devorah Dimant, "Qumran Sectarian Literature," *Jewish Writings of the Second Temple Period*, CRINT Section 2, Vol, 2, ed. Michael E. Stone, 1984, pp. 483–550, pp. 527 f.

[119] For Moses as the recipient of the laws or as the law-giver in the Apocrypha and Pseudepigrapha, cf. e.g. 1 Esdras 1:6 in contrast to 2 Chron. 35:6; 1 Esdras 1:12; 5:48; 7:6, 9; 9:39 in contrast to Neh. 8:1; Tobit 1:8; 6:13; 7:11, 13; Test.Zeb. 3:4; 2 Macc. 6:23; 7:30;

significance not explicit in the biblical tradition. In these writings Moses' authority as Israel's law-giver and first (and most authoritative, cf. Martyrdom of Isaiah 3:7–10) prophet becomes a canon and legitimizing presupposition for those who wish to speak authoritatively to the people of God. As a result, Moses himself is rarely discussed in this literature.[120] Instead, when referred to, his authority and status in Israel's history are *assumed* and then used to *legitimate* the author's own standing and/or purpose.

4. Moses in the Literature of the Jewish Apologists

The distinctive approach to Moses in the Apocrypha, Pseudepigrapha, and the Dead Sea Scrolls becomes clear when we compare it to the view of Moses found in the writings of those Jewish authors of the same period whose aim was to present an apology for Judaism and its traditions. For as I have pointed out elsewhere,[121] in the literature of the Jewish apologists (i.e. Eupolemus, Philo, Josephus, Ezekiel the Tragedian, Artapanus, and Aristobulus)[122] the very authority and respect which could otherwise be *assumed* for Moses, and then used as a legitimizing presupposition, now becomes the burden and subject matter of the various portrayals found throughout this literature. What is common ground in the Apocrypha, Pseudepigrapha, and Qumran writings, now becomes the battle ground for the apologists. This is reflected in that in the apologetic literature Moses is no longer presented in categories supplied primarily by the biblical tradition, but, instead, by the Hellenistic world which it is trying to persuade, whether that world be Jewish or Gentile, Egyptian or Greek.[123] Fortunately, the basic, though diverse, contours of the Moses-tradition in this literature have already been thoroughly examined.

Sir. 24:23; 45:5; Letter of Arist. 139, 144; Jub. 1:4; 2:1; 30:9–12; 33:10–13; 33:18; TM 1:5, 14, 16; 3:11–13; 10:11; 11:1; LAB 9:7 f.; 11:2; 9:7 f. (Hebrew fragments); 19:1 f.; 53:8, etc. and my survey, "Moses."

[120] The exception is LAB, whose intent was to focus on Israel's history. But in the three works which depend directly on Moses' authority, i.e. Jubilees, TM, and the Temple Scroll, the life and authority of Moses himself receives surprisingly little attention.

[121] For this following summary, see my "Moses," though the actual listing of the views of Moses presented here were not included at that time.

[122] I have excluded the Letter of Aristeas due to its dual nature. Though its purpose is also apologetic, Moses' authority and wisdom continue to be assumed throughout the letter as the legitimizing presupposition used to support the validity of the Law; cf. Letter of Arist. 139, 144, 147–153, 161, 168, 240, 313, etc.

[123] This basic distinction is an extension of the contrast Tiede, "Figure of Moses," p. 86, observed between the view of Moses in the TM and that found in Artapanus, Philo, and Josephus. See too John J. Collins, *Between Athens and Jerusalem, Jewish Identity in the Hellenistic Diaspora*, 1983, esp. pp. 33, 40 f., 175 f., 207 f. As Collins rightly stresses, the distinction between apologetic/non-apologetic is not an absolute one, since the apologetic literature also aims to persuade and encourage Jews as well as non-Jews. The distinction

See, for example, 1) the view of Moses in the Hellenistic tragedy entitled the *Exagoge*[124] as the divinely appointed king and prophet with a royal upbringing, 2) Moses as the "first wise man" (πρῶτος σοφός) responsible for giving the knowledge of the alphabet (γράμματα) to the Jews (who then passed it on to the Greeks by way of the Phoenicians) as found in the fragment from the Greek-educated Palestinian Jew Eupolemus;[125] 3) the description of Moses by Aristobulus, the "first Jewish 'philosopher' in Alexandria,"[126] who called Moses an inspired prophet because of his endowment with "wisdom" and a "divine spirit" (Eusebius, *P.E.* 8.10) and asserted that his teaching in the law was followed by the Greek poets and philosophers, including Plato, Socrates, Orpheus, and Pythagoras (cf. Eusebius, *P.E.* 13.12); 4) Artapanus' presentation[127] of Moses as the great inventor (e.g. of ships, weapons, devices for drawing water, philosophy, etc.) and miracle worker who, as the "master of Egyptian culture," was "worthy of being honored like a god" and "was called Hermes because of his interpretation of the sacred letters" (τῶν ἱερῶν γραμμάτων);[128] 5) the more comprehensive Philonic interpretation of Moses as a man of divine stature who not only is prophet, priest, legislator, and interpreter, but also the divine and "most excellent king" and "perfect ruler" *(Vit.Mos.* I, 155–158; 334; II, 1–7), hierophant and mystagogue *(Mig.* 14; *Leg.all.* III, 151, 173; *Post.* 164; *Conf.* 95–97);[129] and finally, 6) Josephus' view of Moses as Israel's commander (στρατηγός, *Ant.* II, 268; IV, 165, 329) and legislator (νομοθέτης, *Ant.* I, 18, 24; II, 6, 18, 20, 23, 24; III, 180; IV, 13, 150, 156; *C.Ap.* II, 75, 145, 154, etc.), based on the model of an ideal founder of a Greek πόλις, whose laws form the πολιτεία of the state (cf. *Ant.* I, 6; III, 322; *C.Ap.* II, 185), and as the θεῖος ἀνήρ, who is both prophet *(Ant.* IV, 165, 329; *C.Ap.* I, 40, etc.) and intercessor *(Ant.* III,

developed here focuses on the distinctive mode of argumentation found in these two basic types of literature.

[124] Written in Alexandria by the virtually unknown poet Ezekiel sometime in the second century B.C. and preserved in Clement of Alexandria, Eusebius, and Epiphanius. For the texts see A.-M. Denis, *Fragmenta*, pp. 207–216; Howard Jacobson, *The Exagoge of Ezekiel*, 1983, as well as his introduction; and C.R. Holladay, "The Portrait of Moses in Ezekiel the Tragedian," in *SBL 1976 Seminar Papers*, SBL Seminar Papers Series 10, 1976, pp. 447–452.

[125] Preserved in Eusebius, *P.E.* 9.26 and Clement of Alexandria, *Strom.* 1.23; see Denis, *Fragmenta*, pp. 179 f. For a discussion, cf. M. Hengel, "The Jewish historian Eupolemus," in his *Judaism and Hellenism, Vol. 1*, 1974, pp. 92–95; Tiede, *Charismatic Figure*, pp. 138–140; and the extensive treatment by Ben Zion Wacholder, *Eupolemus, A Study of Judaeo-Greek Literature*, 1974, esp. pp. 71–96 on Moses.

[126] The description is dated 175–170 B.C. and preserved in Clement of Alexandria and Eusebius. See again Denis, *Fragmenta*, pp. 217–226; Hengel, *Judaism and Hellenism, Vol. 1*, pp. 163–169, and Tiede, *Charismatic Figure*, pp. 140–146.

[127] Preserved in Eusebius, P.E. 9.27, and also originating in Egypt in the second century B.C. See Tiede's extensive study of Artapanus' view of Moses in his *Charismatic Figure*, pp. 146–177, and his convenient compilation of the text, with English translation, on pp. 317–324.

[128] Text and translation from Tiede's *Charismatic Figure*, p. 318.

[129] On Moses' divine status in Philo, see *Q.E.* II, 54; *Vit.Mos.* I, 27; *Sac.* 9; *Post.* 28; *Gig.* 47 ff.; *Quod deus* 23; *Conf.* 30 f. For Moses' various roles see the entire treatise *Vita Mosis* and the now standard treatments of Philo's view of Moses by W. Meeks, *The Prophet-King, Moses Traditions and the Johannine Christology*, SuppNovT 14, 1967, 100–131, and his "Moses as God and King," in *Religion in Antiquity, FS E.R. Goodenough*, ed. J. Neusner, 1968, 354–371; and Tiede, *Charismatic Figure*, pp. 101–137.

6–7, 22–26; IV, 194, etc.), though, in contrast to Philo, is never called a king or priest (cf. Ant. IV, 223; III, 188–192).[130]

As this brief overview illustrates, Moses is portrayed in the apologetic literature in ways one could hardly have expected on the basis of the biblical tradition alone. The identity and ministry of Moses now come to occupy a position of importance in the apologetic literature which has no parallel in the non-apologetic literature. For as David Tiede has observed, "The figure of Moses was one of the most important propaganda instruments that Jews of the Hellenistic period appropriated for their competition with non-Jewish schools and cults, as well as inter-Jewish sectarian disputes."[131] Hence, in turning to the Jewish apologetic literature from the Apocrypha, Pseudepigrapha and the writings from Qumran, we take a step into a new conceptual world. With this basic contrast in mind, we can now turn our attention to the specific motif of the call of Moses as it is found in non-canonical Jewish literature.

5. The Call of Moses in the Apocrypha and Pseudepigrapha

There are five references to Moses' call found within the extant corpus of the Apocrypha and Pseudepigrapha,[132] a surprising number when one considers how infrequently Moses' life as such is treated in this literature. Like the Old Testament tradition, here too Moses' call-election by God to be the recipient of the Law and his resulting authority to be God's prophet-mediator are the presuppositions upon which the portraits of Moses in these works rest. This becomes especially clear in the two more extended treatments of Moses' election in the *Testament of Moses* (TM) and the *Biblical Antiquities* of Pseudo-Philo (LAB).

In TM 1:14 Moses declares to Joshua that to accomplish God's sovereign plan for history, which entails blinding the Gentiles to God's divine purposes in order to convict them (see 1:13 and the introductory conjunction *itaque* // καί in 1:14a),[133] God

---

[130] Again taken from Meeks, *Prophet-King*, pp. 131–146, where he investigates Josephus' view of Moses. For the specific theme of Moses as prophet in Philo and Josephus, see Howard M. Teeple, *The Mosaic Eschatological Prophet*, JBL Monograph Series 10, 1957, pp. 34–39; Meeks, *Prophet-King*, pp. 112 f., 137 f., 162–164, 176–200, and Tiede's chapter, "Images of Moses in Hellenistic Judaism," *Charismatic Figure*, pp. 109–137 and 207–240, esp. pp. 112–120, 127–129, 207, 230, 234.

[131] *Charismatic Figure*, p. 101.

[132] I.e. Sirach 45:2; 1 En. 89:17 f.; 4 Ezra 14:3 f.; Jub. 48:1; and Exagoge 113–115. For the idea of Moses' election by God, see Lives of the Prophets, Jer. 8; Sir. 45:4; and perhaps an implication of Moses' election in his title "man of God" in 1 Esd. 5:48, while this is certainly the case in the "servant" title in LAB (see above).

[133] See Charles, *Apocrypha*, Vol. II, p. 415 n. 13, 14. See TM 1:17; 12:4 for the other references to God's control of the world's events from the beginning of creation; and 3:11–13, where Moses' prophecies and suffering also function to underscore the author's emphasis

"... did design and devise me, who (was) prepared from the beginning of the world, to be the mediator of his covenant." [134]

Thus, the first thing we learn about Moses in TM is that he owes his office as the prophetic mediator of the covenant to God's having chosen him "from the beginning of the world." Just as Jeremiah's call is cast in Mosaic terms in the biblical canon, now Moses' call is cast in terms of Jeremiah 1:5 in TM, which is also the case in LAB 9:7 f. (see below). In line with this emphasis on God's election, the last thing Moses tells us in TM is that he also owes his other and most important role as prophetic intercessor to God's sovereign grace:

"(God has) established me for them (i.e. Israel) and for their sins (•••) and (•••) on their behalf. Yet (this is) not on account of either my strength or weakness, (it is) simply that his mercies and long-suffering have lighted on me." (12:6–7)[135]

This emphasis is especially significant as the basis for the crescendo of accolades heaped upon Moses in TM 11:16, where Moses is described as

"... that sacred spirit, worthy of the Lord, manifold and incomprehensible, master of leaders,[136] faithful in all things, the divine prophet for the whole earth, the perfect teacher in the world ..."

For as Tiede has pointed out, the emphasis on God's call and election in TM make it clear that

"... even the hyperbole which is used to describe Moses' pre-eminent role in God's plan ... is not allowed to develop into a full-blown doctrine of the person of Moses. In spite of Moses' lofty calling as God's chief prophet, it is God's nature as architect and ruler of world history that is fundamental." [137]

In the Testament of Moses, Moses' authority does not derive from his own qualifications, but from the fact that he has been called by God according to "his mercies and long-suffering." At the same time, it is striking that the weakness of Moses, which is so important in the biblical account, is now simply left ambiguous and in this way played down. Nevertheless, although the contrast in the biblical tradition between the prophet's insufficiency and his sufficiency by the grace of God is not made explicit in TM, we still encounter

---

on God's sovereign control – this time to stress that even the exile was part of God's plan. For both the Latin and Greek texts, see Denis, *Fragmenta*, p. 63.

[134] Translation of TM by J. Priest, "Testament of Moses," *OTP, Vol. 1*, pp. 927 ff.

[135] TM 12:7 is difficult to render; cf. Charles, *Apocrypha, Vol. 2*, p. 424, and Egon Brandenburger, "Himmelfahrt Moses," in *Jüdische Schriften aus hellenistisch-römisches Zeit, Bd. V/5, Apokalypsen*, 1976, pp. 57–84, p. 80, who translates it: "Denn nicht auf Grund meiner Tüchtigkeit oder (Fertigkeit), sondern (durch die Milde) seiner Barmherzigkeit und durch seine Langmut ist mir das zugefallen."

[136] Literally, "master of the word," see J. Priest, *OTP, Vol. 1*, p. 934, and Charles, *Apocrypha, Vol. 2*, pp. 423 ff.

[137] "Figure of Moses," pp. 90 f.

the emphasis on divine election and grace as the source and basis for the authority of God's prophetic mediator and intercessor.

In LAB, like TM, the double tradition of Moses as the spokesman for God and intercessor for the people, because of his election to receive God's law, is once again made the focal point of the biblical tradition inherited by the author (cf. LAB 10:4f.; 11:2, 14; 12:8–10; 19:3, 6, 8f., 11, etc.). Here too Moses' call is determined before his birth. But now what is merely asserted in TM 1:14 is fleshed out in an extended speech by God himself in response to Amram's refusal to join the others in not fathering children because of his hope in God's commitment to the covenant (see LAB 9:1–7). God thus decrees before Moses' birth:

"Because Amram's plan is pleasing to me, and he has not put aside the covenant established between me and his fathers, so behold now he who will be born from him will serve me forever, and I will do marvelous things in the house of Jacob through him and I will work through him signs and wonders for my people that I have not done for anyone else; and I will act gloriously among them and proclaim to them my ways. And I, God, will kindle for him my lamp that will abide in him, and I will show him my covenant that no one has seen. And I will reveal to him my Law and statutes and judgments, and I will burn an eternal light for him, because I thought of him in the days of old, saying, 'My spirit will not be a mediator among these men forever, because they are flesh and their days will be 120 years'." (9:7–8)[138]

The exercise of divine providence in Moses' election and the corresponding greatness of Moses are then further highlighted by the fact that his birth is revealed to Amram's daughter in a dream by "the spirit of God" (LAB 9:10) and is said to take place "in the covenant of God and the covenant of the flesh" (9:13). Similarly, the daughter of Pharaoh goes down to bathe in the river "as she had seen in dreams" (9:15). His being raised by Pharaoh's daughter then leads to the pronouncement that

"... the child was nursed and became glorious above all other men, and through him God freed the sons of Israel as he had said (9:16)."

In LAB, Moses' authority and role as law-giver, miracle worker, and intercessor is thus also solely dependent upon his election by God. Even though Moses can be described as "glorious above all other men" and certainly occupies a unique status before God, here too Moses is never directly deified, but remains the one whom God foreordained and chose to be his servant and prophet (see LAB 53:8).

---

[138] Translation from D.J. Harrington, "Pseudo-Philo," *OTP*, Vol. 2, pp. 304 ff. M.R. James, *Antiquities*, p. 102 n. 8, points out that the quotation from Gen. 6:3 harks back to LAB 3:2 and refers to the fact that Moses was 120 years old when he died; cf. too LAB 19:8.

6. The ἱκανός-motif in Philo and Josephus

The distinctive nature of this emphasis in LAB and TM becomes evident, however, only when we compare it to those writings such as the *Letter of Aristeas* and Eupolemus, in which Moses' authority resides in his own wisdom; Artapanus, in which the greatness of Moses results from his military and civil accomplishments; or Philo's development of the call of Moses and the ἱκανός-motif within his allegory of the life of Moses as a whole.[139]

In stark contrast to the more literal account of Moses' call in *De Vita Mosis* I, 83–84, in *De Fuga et Inventione* 163–165, Philo understands the call of Moses through the burning bush to be an allegorical illustration of the truth that "no human being is capable (ἱκανὸν εἶναι) of dealing with the study of causation."[140] Philo supports this by interpreting Moses' inquiry in Exodus 3:2 f. concerning the burning bush (i.e. "Why is it that the bush is burning and not being consumed?" *De fuga* 161) to be an inquiry into "the causes by which the most essential occurrences in the universe are brought about" *(De fuga* 161). Conversely, in the same passage God's response in Exod. 3:5 that Moses not draw near to the bush is taken to be a prohibition against taking up such an inquiry, since it is "too great for human ability." The place upon which Moses stands becomes the topic of causation, a subject reserved for God alone, i.e. it is "holy ground" (cf. *De fuga* 163).[141] This is buttressed by the fact that Moses is told in Exod. 33:23 that he will only be allowed to see God's back, which for Philo means that

"... it amply suffices the wise man to come to a knowledge of all that follows on after God and in His wake (i.e. what is created), but the man that wishes to set his gaze upon

---

[139] The text and translations for Philo's works are taken from F.H. Colson and G.H. Whitaker, *Philo*, LCL, Vols. 1–10, 1958–1962. On the phrase ἱκανὸν εἶναι meaning "to be capable/sufficient" in Philo, see *Leg.all.* I, 10; III, 171; *Quis rer.* 39; *De conf.* 17; *Quod deus* 157; *De post.* 21; *De fuga* 40, 202; *De mut.* 46. For an interpretation of Philo's allegorization of Moses' life, see Erwin R. Goodenough's "The Mystic Moses," in his *By Light, Light. The Mystic Gospel of Hellenistic Judaism*, 1935, pp. 199–234, esp. pp. 202–204, on Philo's view of the call of Moses. In Goodenough's words, for Philo "Moses' life is throughout the life of the perfect man turned to war against the forces of evil in the world" (p. 203).

[140] This same contrast between Philo's treatment of Moses in his *Vita Mosis* and elsewhere in his writings is reflected in the nature of Moses' identity itself. In the *Vita*, Moses is primarily the Hellenistic king, while in his allegory Moses becomes the hierophant or mystagogue (cf. *Post.* 16, 173; *Spec. leg.* I, 41, etc). The reason for this contrast lies in Philo's two *different* purposes. In the *Vita*, Philo intends to present an "introduction to Judaism for the Gentile inquirer," while elsewhere, "Moses' essential importance for Philo is as the prototypical mystic and the guide for those of his 'disciples' who, like Philo himself, long to participate in the true 'Exodus,' an escape from the 'Egypt' of the senses and passions," cf. Meeks, *Prophet-King*, pp. 117, 121; and for the quotes, pp. 129 and 130 respectively.

[141] For the similar theme of humanity's not being capable (ἱκανός) of enjoying divinity or wisdom completely, cf. *De fuga* 202, 213; *De mut.* 15.

the supreme Essence, before he sees Him will be blinded by the rays that beam forth all around Him." *(De fuga* 165)[142]

This same theme of Moses' noble search for that which no human being is capable of knowing, i.e. the essence of God himself, is also picked up in *De Posteritate Caini* 13–16. Here Philo once again emphasizes the unceasing and intense nature of Moses' desire to "see God" (Exod. 33:13), only to point out the futility of such a desire. For according to Philo, Moses' request in Exod. 33:13 (i.e. "manifest yourself to me") reveals not only "his earnest endeavour," but also that "the holy Guide" (ὁ ἱεροφάντης),[143] i.e. Moses, "seems ... even before he began this search to have discerned its futility." Furthermore, Moses' request that God reveal himself demonstrates

"... quite clearly ... that there is not a single created being capable of attaining *by his own efforts* the knowledge of the God who verily exists (... ἱκανὸς οὐδὲ εἷς ἐξ ἑαυτοῦ ...)." *(De Post.* 16, emphasis mine)[144]

Therefore, even Moses, although he is the "perfect man" *(De sac.* 10) and "wise man" *par excellence (De sac.* 9), was not able (ἱκανός) to understand causation, which is the nature and essence of God himself.[145]

Yet the fact that Moses shares the insufficiency of all humanity when it comes to understanding the nature of God ought not to blind us to the fact that, for Philo, Moses is also the *only one* who *is* sufficient to receive what God has revealed about himself.[146] In an extended discussion in *Legum Allegoria* III, 125–135, based on an allegory of Moses' offering of the breast of the ram in Leviticus 8:29 (in which the "breast of the ram" is the "passion of anger," *Leg. all.* III, 131), Philo argues that only Moses could bear the word of reason revealed by God, since, in contrast to Aaron, Moses was willing to cut out his heart of passion completely rather than try to cure it or live with it in a state of

---

[142] For a helpful discussion of this text and its relationship to *De mut.* 7–10, where Moses is said to have penetrated into "the invisible and immaterial substance," cf. Goodenough, *Light,* p. 213. Cf. *De fuga* 141; *De mut.* 134; *Vita Mos.* I, 66, where we learn that, in reality, Moses did not see God, but an angel.

[143] Cf. *De cher.* 49, where Jeremiah is also referred to as a ἱεροφάντης ἱκανός ("worthy minister") of the holy secrets.

[144] See too *De Som.* II, 25, where Moses' statement in Deut. 1:17 ("judgment belongs to God only") is said to teach that we ought never "entertain thought that we ourselves are sufficient (ἱκανοὺς εἶναι ἑαυτούς) apart from the divine overseeing guidance to cleanse our life ..."

[145] See *Leg. all.* III, 205, where Philo states that no one but God himself is able to bear witness to God, "for who else would be capable (ἱκανός) of bearing witness to Him?" In the context this refers to the legal act of verifying God's oaths, but it is grounded in the fact that God has shown his nature "to no one" (cf. *Leg. all.* III, 206).

[146] The corollary is that the true Jews are those who are capable of understanding the symbolic meaning of the Torah and, as a result, become ʋιe true disciples of Moses; cf. *Spec. leg.* I, 59, 319 ff., 345; *Det.* 86; *De Post.* 12; *Conf.* 39; etc. and Meeks, *Prophet-King,* pp. 101 ff.

moderation *(Leg. all.* III, 128 f.).[147] So, when the issue becomes who is "suffi-cient (ἱκανός) to bear the word (of reason) upon his breast with the virtues that belong to it" *(Leg. all.* III, 126), the answer can only be the one who, like Moses, "goes in in the sight of the Lord, that is he who does all things for God's sake ..." *(Leg. all.* III, 126). But Moses' sufficiency is not due to God's sovereign call *per se*, but to his own excellence, virtue, and perfection, illus-trated by his willingness to "cut out his heart of passion" *(Leg. all.* III, 128 f.).[148] Moses is sufficient to bear the word *by nature*, having been "sent" on loan by God into the earthly spheres and "gifted" with the excellency of being "god" over his passions *(De sac.* 9). For Philo, Moses is not called to bear God's word in spite of his insufficiency, but because of his excellency and perfection – though even Moses is insufficient when it comes to seeing God.

Against this backdrop it is not surprising that Philo's two interpretations of Moses' objection to God's call in Exodus 4:10 also serve to highlight Moses' moral superiority. In *De Vita Mosis* I, 83–84 Moses is said to object to his call, in spite of the fact that he believes the signs which God has demonstrated, because he considered human eloquence to be "dumbness" (ἀφωνίαν εἶναι) when compared with the speech of God. Moses' objection that "he was not eloquent, but feeble of voice and slow of tongue" (ἰσχνόφωνον καὶ βραδύγλωσσον οὐκ εὔλογον) becomes, for Philo, an expression of Moses' modesty! Conversely, rather than reacting with anger, as in the biblical ac-count, God now approves of Moses' response and simply reassures him that he will enable Moses to be as articulate as the stream which flows from an "undefiled fountain."

A similar point is also made in *Quis Rerum Divinarum Heres* 4, where Moses is given as an example of one who, like Abraham, is struck dumb when confronted with the majesty and greatness of God. Philo derives this point by emphasizing the second aspect of Exod. 4:10, namely, that Moses became

---

[147] Cf. *De sac.* 10, where this same point is made based on Exod. 7:1; i.e. Moses becomes "god" over the passions, in contrast to the kings who merely "hold sway and sovereignty" over them.

[148] H.A. Wolfson's standard treatment, *Philo, Vol. 1*, 1948², pp. 47 f., is consequently mis-leading when it includes Moses with Isaac and Jacob as those from whom God took away their passions as an act of "special grace," based on *De Cher.* 50 and *Leg. all.* III, 219. In the context of the former Philo is not discussing Moses at all, but rather God's way of acting with the soul in general, using Sarah as the example; while in the latter, although the exam-ple is Isaac, the principle quoted by Wolfson from this passage, i.e. that God himself begets happiness in people's souls, is again related as a general principle to the one initiated. Rather, as Goodenough, *Light*, pp. 198 f., points out, for Philo Moses is to be distinguished from Jacob on the one hand, and from humanity in general on the other hand. Like Isaac, he is a "special incarnation" (cf. *Sac.* 9), though there is no mention of Moses being miracu-lously conceived as Isaac was (cf. *Som.* 173). However, Moses excels Abraham, Isaac, and Jacob as the one called to stand beside God himself (cf. *Conf.* 192 and the "Index to Names," *Philo, LCL Vol. 10*, pp. 385–389, for the uniqueness of Moses).

"feeble of voice and slow of tongue (ἰσχνόφωνος ὁμολογεῖ καὶ βραδύγλωσσος γενέσθαι), *ever since* God began to hold converse with him (ἀφ᾽ οὗ ἤρξατο ὁ θεὸς αὐτῷ διαλέγεσθαι)." But again, Moses' objection is an expression of his *virtue*, even if, for Philo, being rendered speechless before God's majesty is not the ultimate expression of a slave's duty and loyalty to his master (cf. *Quis rer.* 5–9). For as Philo goes on to emphasize,

"... courage and well-timed frankness (παρρησία) before our superiors are admirable virtues also ..." *(Quis rer.* 5)[149]

The question consequently becomes *when* one ought to speak frankly or with boldness to his/her master (πότε οὖν ἄγει παρρησίαν οἰκέτης πρὸς δεσπότην; *Quis rer.* 6). And Philo's answer is clear:

"Surely it is when his heart tells him that he has not wronged his owner, but that his words and deeds are all for that owner's benefit. And so when else should the slave of God open his mouth freely to Him who is the ruler and master both of himself and of the All, save when he is pure from sin and the judgments of his conscience are loyal to his master, when he feels more joy at being the servant of God than if he had been king of all the human race ...?" *(Quis rer.* 6–7)

In *Quis rer.* 19–25 Moses becomes, for Philo, a model of the wise "man of worth" who has the "courage of speech" (χρῆται παρρησίᾳ) that comes from being a friend of God (pointing to Exod. 33:11),[150] as testified to by Moses' willingness to cry out on Israel's behalf in Exod. 5: 22f., 32:32 and Num. 11:12, 13, 22 *(Quis rer.* 19–21). But at the same time, such mortal confidence must be seasoned with caution, since God is the "master" (δεσπότης) who inspires fear and terror *(Quis rer.* 22–23). This recognition of one's proper place before the sovereign cause of all things is then illustrated by Philo *not* by pointing to Moses, but to Abraham, even to the point of using God's promise in Exod. 4:12 to overcome Moses' inability to speak as a description of *Abraham's* experience *(Quis. rer.* 25)! It is thus Abraham, not Moses, who is given as the model of the kind of humility and nothingness before God that creates speech before God that is "neither bold without caution, nor cautious without boldness" *(Quis rer.* 29), thus preserving Philo's emphasis on Moses' superior moral character and wisdom.

This is confirmed by Philo's other interpretation of Moses's objection, based on the play on words made possible by the double meaning of εὔλογος, the Greek equivalent of דברים אִישׁ אֹל found in the LXX version of Exod. 4:10 and also represented in Philo and in the *Exagoge* 113–115.[151] On the one hand,

---

[149] Note Paul's use of this same motif of "boldness" (παρρησία) in his comparison to Moses in 2 Cor. 3:12 and see below, chapter five, for a development of this theme.

[150] Cf. Philo's maxim in *Quis rer.* 21 that "Frankness of speech (παρρησία) is akin to friendship."

[151] In Ezekiel the Tragedian 113–115, Moses responds to his call with the protest, "I am not by nature eloquent (οὐκ εὔλογος πέφυκα); my tongue with difficulty speaks, I stammer

εὔλογος can mean simply "eloquent," while on the other hand it can denote that which is "probable" or "reasonable" in contrast to that which is certain. [152] The semantic link between the two meanings seems to be the recognition that the use of sophisticated rhetorical devices becomes known in the ancient world as a substitute for certainty. Consequently, Colson and Whitaker choose to translate εὔλογος in this second sense as "the conjectural and insecure myth-making of eloquence (or 'the eloquent')." [153] In *Quod Deterius Potiori insidiari solet* 38, Philo can therefore interpret Moses' flight from "Egypt" to be a flight from the "tricks and deceptions of sophistry" (σοφισμάτων) precisely because Moses asserts that he is not "eloquent," i.e. εὔλογος. Philo then emphatically states that Moses is not merely not eloquent, but absolutely "speechless" (ἄλογος, referring to Exodus 6:12). [154] For according to *De Sacrificiis Abelis et Caini* 12,

"Moses sets no value on probabilities and plausibilities, but follows after truth in its purity (since) ... when he comes alone to God apart from all, he frankly says (μετὰ παρρησίας φησί) that he has no gift of speech (μὴ εἶναι εὔλογος) (by which he means that he has no desire for eloquence or persuasiveness (ἴσον τῷ μὴ τῶν εὐλόγων καὶ πιθανῶν ἐφίεσθαι) ..." (Exod. 4:10)

Conversely, Israel's problem in the wilderness was that she was prone to believe that which was merely plausible (τοῖς εὐλόγοις) or probable *(Vit. Mos.* I, 174), rather than that which was clearly proved, i.e. God's "unfailing truthfulness" *(Vit. Mos.* I, 196; cf. II, 261). Hence, as Goodenough put it, Moses ob-

---

(γλῶσσα δ' ἐστί μοι δύσφραστος, ἰσχνόφωνος), so that I cannot speak before the king;" cf. R.G. Robertson, "Ezekiel the Tragedian," *OTP*, Vol. 2, p. 813, for the translation, and Eusebius, *P.E.* 9.29.9, for the text, as provided in C.R. Holladay, *Fragments from Hellenistic Jewish Authors, Vol. II, Poets*, Texts and Translations 30, Pseudepigrapha Series 12, 1989, p. 372. Holladay renders the text a bit more freely, "I am not a convincing speaker; in fact my speech is too coarse, even halting, for any words of mine to come before a king" (p. 373) and points to the poet's "tendency to deemphasize the extent of Moses' resistance" in his handling of the biblical tradition, in which he omits Exod. 3:11 and 3:13–4:1; 4:11, 13 f. (p. 461). For the question of the possible relationship between the *Exagoge* and Philo, together with the relevant literature, cf. Holladay, pp. 461 f. However, the reference to Moses' objection itself in the *Exagoge* does not receive further elaboration. But see H. Jacobson, *Exagoge*, p. 107, who discusses the significance of the fact that the order of the events in the call are now reversed, i.e. the signs follow Moses' objection rather than precede it as in the biblical account.

[152] See Liddell-Scott, *A Greek-English Lexicon*, p. 721.

[153] *Philo, LCL,* Vol. 2, 1958, p. 489, commenting on *De Sac* 13. But εὔλογος can also mean that which is "reasonable" or "probable" apart from any reference to the eloquence of one's speech; cf. *De opif.* 27, 45, 72; *Leg. all.* III, 161; *Quod deus* 127; *De agr.* 156; *De plant.* 54, 176 f.; *Vit.Mos.* I, 244.

[154] Cf. the parallel text in *De migr. Ab.* 76, where Moses "excuses himself from investigating well-worded and specious arguments" which are characteristic of the "sophists in Egypt, from whom specious sounding fables are of more value than the clear evidence of realities." For the origin of the sophists who dwell in Egypt, cf. *De som.* I, 220, where we are told that they arose from "many large portions of false, probable, plausible, conjectural matter."

jects that he cannot speak well when called by God because "sophistic rhetoric ... vanishes from one who has had a vision of the truth."[155]

From Philo's perspective, Moses' objection is thus no longer an expression of his inadequacy *per se*, but rather an acknowledgement of the supremacy of the truth of God which he is called to convey. On the one hand, this truth renders one mute, and on the other hand, it cannot be contained in the physical instrument of speech, since speech, being a physical act, is linked with the passions of the body (cf. *Quod det.* 38; *De migr. Ab.* 76). In either case, the biblical motif of the inspired spokesman's "sufficiency-in-spite-of-one's-insufficiency-because-of-the-sovereign-call-of-God" is now transformed by Philo into an apologetic for the character of Moses himself. In Philo's view, Moses' objection that he was not "eloquent" is not an objection at all, but rather a badge of honor as an expression of his superiority over all those who are still tied to the material world of the body and passion. Moses' complete denial of passion has freed him from the need to resort to the physical instrument of speech to express his understanding of God to those still enslaved to the physical world (cf. *De sac.* 12; *De migr. Ab.* 77). As such, Moses' "objection" becomes another example, among many, of why he is the only one who is sufficient (ἱκανός) to receive God's word.

In contrast to Philo's detailed development of the ἱκανός-motif, Josephus nowhere uses this terminology in direct reference to Moses or to his call. Although the phrase εἶναι ἱκανός, meaning "to be capable, strong, proficient," etc. is well attested in Josephus,[156] it is only used three times to describe a capability in speech, once in reference to Joshua *(Ant.* III, 49), once in reference to the two "eloquent speakers" sent by the Zealots to the Idumaens *(Bell.* IV, 230), and once to describe Korah in his attempt to lead the people in rebellion against Moses *(Ant.* IV, 14). Nevertheless, in this last context the idea of Moses' sufficiency as a speaker is implied in the comparison Josephus develops between Korah and Moses. Just as Korah is said to be "a capable speaker" (ἱκανὸς δ' εἰπεῖν), Moses too is described as one who "with all his other talents, was so gifted in moving a crowd" *(Ant.* IV, 25). It is because Moses can speak so well that he is able to avert the impending rebellion, as illustrated in his extensive speech recorded in *Ant.* IV, 25–34.[157]

In keeping with this emphasis on Moses' ability to move a crowd with his oratory, Josephus' account of Moses' call in *Ant.* II, 264–276 nowhere explic-

---

[155] *Light*, p. 204. Cf. *Quod det.* 39 and *De migr. Ab.* 76, however, where we are told that Moses goes on to learn rhetorical skills before he returns to Egypt in order to deal with the sophists!

[156] Cf. e.g. *Bell.Jud.* III, 352; IV, 638; *Ant.* I, 29, 227; IV, 3; V, 178; X, 187; XVI, 298; etc. The texts and translations are taken from H.St.J. Thackeray, *Josephus, LCL,Vols. I–IX*, 1961–1965.

[157] So too Josef M. Kastner, *Moses im Neuen Testament*, p. 54: "Der 'Gesetzgeber' und 'Prophet' besitzt in hohem Maße die Rednergabe (IV.25); wenn er redete, konnte man glauben, Gott selbst sprechen zu hören (IV.329) ..."

itly refers to Moses' objection in Exodus 4:10, nor does it mention the con-comitant provision of Aaron to be Moses' spokesman. Instead, Josephus fo-cuses his attention on the objection from Exodus 3:11 and God's act of re-assurance in providing the miracles of the rod, the hand, and the water (see Exod. 4:1–9 and *Ant.* II, 271–274). Although Josephus alludes to Exodus 4:10 in his formulation of Moses' objection,[158] the motif is dismissed in passing (cf. *Ant.* II, 272) in order to recount in detail the three miracles and their sig-nificance (cf. *Ant.* II, 272–275). The biblical narrative of Moses' call is then abruptly broken off after the exhibition of the signs, with the revelation of God's name now usurping the place originally occupied by Moses' final ob-jection in Exod. 4:10–16. As a result, the emphasis in Josephus' account does not fall on the call of Moses in spite of his insufficiency, but rather on his en-dowment with the power of God "to use miracles to convince all men ..." *(Ant.* II, 274). For Josephus, the call of Moses thus lays the foundation for his life's work as the "commander and leader of the Hebrew hosts," who "found those miracles at his service ... at all times whensoever there was need of them" *(Ant.* II, 268, 276).[159] The main point of the call of Moses for Josephus, therefore, is his endowment with the power to work the miracles that will verify him as God's spokesman (i.e. to provide him with the necessary σημεῖα).

Within this context it is not surprising that in Josephus' portrayal the voice of God from the burning bush does more than call Moses and provide him with his mandate. In direct opposition to the biblical account, it also commends Moses for his courage in approaching the place of divine presence (!), and predicts "the glory and honour that he would win from men," albeit "under God's auspices" *(Ant.* II, 268–269).[160] For this reason, according to Josephus, Korah's later criticism of Moses was that he was "hunting round to

---

[158] I.e. in *Ant.* II, 271 Moses responds to God's call with the words, "... I am at a loss to know how I, a mere commoner, blest with no strength (μηδεμιᾶς ἰσχύος εὐπορῶν), could either find words to persuade my people to quit that land that they now inhabit and follow me ... or ... how I should constrain Pharaothes to permit the exodus ...." Sandnes, *Paul*, p. 8, disagrees and suggests that this text is a direct and explicit reference to Exod. 4:10. But even if it is more than an allusion, it is still not the focus of Josephus' attention.

[159] For the meaning of "signs" (σημεῖα) in Josephus as that which legitimizes the messen-ger of God, in distinction to the "miracle," cf. Otto Betz, "Das Problem des Wunders bei Flavius Josephus im Vergleich zum Wunderproblem bei den Rabbinen und im Johannes-evangelium," in *Josephus-Studien, FS Otto Michel*, ed. O. Betz, K. Haacker, and M. Hengel, 1974, pp. 23–44, pp. 27–30. Betz concludes that "Die Berufung und das erste Auftreten des Mose zeigen am besten, was Josephus unter einem Semeion versteht" (p. 28). Betz empha-sizes that, in contrast to the miracle, a sign must still be believed in order to perform its function; cf. *Ant.* II, 280, 284–287, and Betz, pp. 28 f.

[160] Klaus Haacker, "Nachbiblische Traditionen vom Tod des Mose," in *Josephus-Studien, FS Otto Michel*, 1974, pp. 147–174, p. 147, points to this text as a key example of Josephus' "grundsätzlichen Tendenz, die Größe des Gesetzgebers herauszustreichen." As Haacker puts it, "Josephus geht sogar so weit, die δόξα καὶ τιμή, die Mose bei den Menschen erlangen soll, im Rahmen der Berufung am Dornbusch von Gott weissagen zu lassen *(Ant.* 2,268)."

create glory for himself" in the "pretended name of God" *(Ant.* IV, 15).[161] Hence, without developing the ἱκανός-motif itself, Josephus, like Philo, uses the call of Moses to focus his reader's attention on the person, work, and authority of Moses himself. But unlike Philo, Josephus traces the source of Moses' authority to his possession of the miracle-working power of God, rather than to his innate and superior moral nature. Yet for Josephus, as for Philo, the biblical emphasis in the LXX on Moses' sufficiency in spite of his insufficiency no longer stands at the heart of the narrative. With this in view, it will be helpful to survey the call of Moses in rabbinic literature before turning our attention to Paul.

7. The Call of Moses in Rabbinic Literature

In spite of the serious methodological problems concerning the use of rabbinic literature in investigating the New Testament,[162] it will nevertheless be helpful to see some of the ways in which the tradition of the call of Moses was taken up by the rabbis and preserved in the post-Pauline period.[163] The first thing to note in this respect is that two of the central emphases in regard to Moses himself, which are often kept separate in earlier works, are now brought together in the Palestinian targumic tradition. On the one hand, in contrast to the tendency evident in Philo, there is no attempt in either *Tgs. Pseudo-Jonathan* or *Neofiti* to mitigate the force of Moses' objection in Exod. 3:11, 4:1, and especially 4:10. Nor is God's anger with Moses because of his objections played down in

---

[161] A similar reproach is also attested in the rabbinic tradition as preserved in Tanhuma B, Book 4, p. 86 (ed. Buber, 1885) and Exod. Rab. 18.4, etc., in which Moses and Aaron are accused by Korah of lifting themselves up "above the congregation;" cf. L. Ginzberg, *The Legends of the Jews, Vol. III,* 1954[4], pp. 291–292, and *Vol. VI,* p. 101.

[162] See e.g. Geza Vermes, "Jewish Literature and New Testament Exegesis: Reflections on Methodology," *JJS* 33 (1982) 361–376, who argues correctly that we must see the NT "as part of a larger environment of Jewish religious and cultural history," so that "the stages of religious thought preceding it and following it are not merely relevant but essential to an historical understanding and evaluation of its message ..." (p. 375). Rabbinic literature thus provides part of the necessary "broader canvas" against which the peculiarities of the NT become evident (and vice versa!) (cf. p. 375). This does not mean, however, that rabbinic literature becomes the "key" to Paul's thinking. See my conclusion below and the discussion of methodology in Jacob Neusner's "Die Verwendung des späteren rabbinischen Materials für die Erforschung des Pharisäismus im 1. Jahrhundert n. Chr." *ZThK* 76 (1979) 292–309.

[163] For an overview of how Moses is understood in rabbinic literature, see R. Bloch, "Die Gestalt des Moses in der rabbinischen Tradition," in *Moses in Schrift und Überlieferung,* 1963, pp. 95–171; and for a compilation of the various traditions, although joined together without any historical differentiation, see Aaron Rosmarin, *Moses im Lichte der Agada,* 1932, and in English, L. Ginzberg, *Legends, Vol. II,* pp. 258–375 and *Vol. III,* with the corresponding notes in volume five. For a concise summary of the material, but with few references to the original sources, cf. Josef M. Kastner, *Moses im Neuen Testament,* pp. 74–107. Finally, see J. Jeremias, art. Μωυσῆς, *TDNT* 4 (1967) 848–873, esp. for his extensive compilation of secondary literature.

these accounts.[164] On the other hand, Tg. Ps.-J. also preserves the tendency among the Jewish apologists as a whole, and especially evident in Josephus, of emphasizing Moses' role as a miracle worker. Thus, Tg. Ps.-J. preserves a tradition, now inserted into the biblical account between Exodus 2:20 and 2:21 (Exod. 2:21–22 in the targum), which functions to explain the origin of the rod which Moses later uses to work his miracles during the exodus event proper. According to Tg. Ps.-J., upon his arrival in Midian, Moses was first thrown into a pit for 10 years by Reuel, the priest of Midian, before he is accepted into the family and given Zipporah, the one who has secretly sustained Moses during his confinement. Upon his release, Moses is said to have entered into Reuel's bed chamber and, after praying to the Lord, ("who by him would work miracles and mighty acts," דעבד עמיה ניסין וגבורן),[165] the rod miraculously appears in the bed chamber. The rod is then described as an equally supernatural creation by God, upon which "the great and glorious name" (שמא רבא ויקירא) is engraved (cf. Tg. Ps.-J. Exod. 4:20 f.).[166] Hence, even before his call, Moses is identified in Tg. Pseudo-Jonathan as the one elected by God to work miracles and endowed with divine power as manifested in his possession of the wonder-working rod. Furthermore, the inextricable association of Moses with the Law, which also characterizes the view of Moses in the Apocrypha, Pseudepigrapha, Qumran literature, Philo, and Josephus,[167] now comes to occupy center stage within the call of Moses itself in Tg. Ps.-J. Exod. 3:5. The "holy place" upon which Moses stands when confronted with the theophany of the burning bush is now explicitly identified as the place upon which Moses is "to receive the law (אורייתא) to teach it to the sons of Israel."

---

[164] These biblical passages are not extant in either the *Fragmentary Targum* or the targumic traditions discovered in the Cairo Geniza and Qumran.

[165] English translation of Tg. Ps.-J. taken from J.W. Etheridge, *The Targums of Onkelos and Jonathan Ben Uzziel on the Pentateuch with the Fragments of the Jerusalem Targum*, 1968 (reprint). The text is from M. Ginsburger, *Pseudo-Jonathan*, 1903.

[166] See Pirqe R. El. 40 for another version of the miraculous origin of Moses' rod as created by God and given to Adam, who passes it on to Enoch, and then by means of Noah, Shem, Abraham, Isaac, Jacob, and Joseph it arrives in Pharaoh's court, where Jethro steals it. Moses then finds the rod planted in Jethro's garden and is the only one able to draw it out of the ground as the sign that he will redeem Israel; cf. Gerald Friedlander, *Pirke de Rabbi Eliezar*, 1916, pp. 312–313. The motif of the miraculous creation of the rod and its reception by Moses was widespread throughout rabbinic literature; cf. e.g. Exod. Rab. 8.3 and the many traditions listed by Rosmarin, *Moses*, pp. 75–77 nn. 266–274.

[167] This seems self-evident until one realizes, as J.J. Collins has pointed out, that among the Jewish apologists Artapanus, Eupolemus, and Ezekiel the Tragedian, Moses, as well as the identity of Judaism as such, is no longer exclusively tied to the Law! See his *Between Athens and Jerusalem*, pp. 36, 42, and 210 f. So too Ben Zion Wacholder, *Eupolemus*, 1974, p. 71, who comments concerning the view of Eupolemus that "Moses was important not, as in the Scripture tradition, as the transmitter of God's law to his chosen people Israel, but in his role as the father of Oriental and Greek civilizations." Therefore, G. Vermes' conclusion, "Gestalt," p. 62, that "die Ereignisse des Exodus, die Gestalt des Moses und der Empfang der Thora für das gesamte nach-exilische Judentum den Mittelpunkt bildeten" must be qualified, at least in terms of the subject of some apologetic literature.

In this tradition Moses is commanded to bring Israel to Mt. Horeb to worship not because it is the place of the theophany *per se*, but specifically "because ye shall have received the law upon this mountain" (Tg. Ps.-J. Exod. 3:12).[168]

In keeping with this emphasis, Moses is pictured throughout the Palestinian targumic tradition as a rabbinic master committed to investigating and teaching the Law. In the context of Moses' call this is seen in the fact that Aaron's role in Exod. 4:16 is no longer that of a prophet to his god, as in the biblical tradition, but is now interpreted in *Tgs. Neofiti*, Ps.-J., and the *Fragment Targum* (Vatican MS Ebr. 440) as that of an "interpreter" or "dragoman" (תורגמן) to his "master."[169] As K.G. Kuhn points out in his note to Sifre Numeri § 140 to Num. 27:18, the תורגמן was the interpreter or assistant assigned to the rabbinic master, whose task it was to communicate the rabbi's rulings to the people.[170] Thus, in *Tg. Neofiti* and the *Fragment Targum* Moses is no longer described as Aaron's "god," but as "his source" (lit. his "seeker") of instruction from before the Lord" (לתבע אולפן מן קדם ייי).[171] In turn, in Tg. Ps.-J. Moses is Aaron's רב. Even in the later redaction of Onqelos,[172] which no longer preserves either the legend of the rod or the emphasis on the Law in Exod. 3:5 and 12 found in Tg. Ps.-J., Aaron is still portrayed as Moses' "interpreter" (מתורגמן), while Moses is again his "rab" (רב).[173]

The targumic presentations of the call of Moses thus offer a picture of Moses as the one who, as in the biblical tradition, objects to God's call because of his lack of eloquence, but who, at the same time, is the miracle worker who receives not only the divine rod, but also God's name *in order that* he might then receive God's law and teach it to Israel. In fact, the reception of the Law now becomes the main point of the Exodus itself (contrast Exod. 2:24; 3:12; 6:2-7,

---

[168] Cf. Exod. Rab. 3.4, where Israel is delivered from Israel "for the sake of the Torah which they will receive on this mountain from thy hands ..." (trans. S.M. Lehrman, *Exodus, Midrash Rabbah, Vol. 3*, 1951, p. 63.

[169] For the Frg. Tg., both text and translation, see Michael L. Klein, *The Fragment-Targums of the Pentateuch According to their Extant Sources, Vols. I and II*, AB 76, 1980. For the text and translation of Tg. Neofiti, cf. Alejandro Diez Macho, *Neophyti 1, Tomo II, Exodo*, 1970. In contrast, both MSS of the Samaritan Targum follow the Hebrew closely at this point; cf. Abraham Tal, *The Samaritan Targum of the Pentateuch, A Critical Edition, Part I, Texts and Studies in the Hebrew Language and Related Subjects, Vol. 4*, 1980, pp. 232–233.

[170] *Der tannaitische Midrasch Sifre zu Numeri, übersetzt und erklärt*, 1959, p. 574 n. 9.

[171] The translation is that of Klein to the Frg. Tg. Cf. the translation given by Diez Macho, *Neophyti 1*, p. 415: "you shall be for him as one seeking instruction from before the Lord."

[172] Following Gerard J. Kuiper, *The Pseudo-Jonathan Targum and its Relationship to Targum Onkelos*, Studia Ephemeridas 'Augustinianum,' Nr. 9, 1972, who, on the basis of the agreements between Ps.-J. and the Pal. Tg. (i.e. Cairo Geniza and Neofiti) and their differences to Onqelos (he examines Gen. 4:7-10, 16; Exod. 20:1-18, 25-26; Lev. 22:27; 23:29, 32), argues that Tg. Ps.-J. is one strand of the Palestinian Tg. tradition and that Onqelos is a later, authoritative redaction of it, rather than a late compilation of Onqelos and the Pal. Tg. as has often been assumed (cf. his summaries on pp. 99–107).

[173] Tg. Onq. Exod. 4:16. Translation from Etheridge; for the text, see Alexander Sperber, *The Bible in Aramaic, Vol. I, The Pentateuch according to Targum Onkelos*, 1959.

etc.). Hence, although Moses' objection is maintained in the tradition, the point of the narrative now highlighted in regard to Moses is his greatness as Israel's first rabbinic "master." The distinctiveness of this view again becomes evident when we realize that for Josephus and Philo Moses is the lawgiver or legislator, while for the rabbinic literature surveyed here Moses is the one who teaches the Law, since only God can be said to have given the Torah. Thus, in Abot R. Nat., rec. A, 1 the Law comes merely "by the hand of Moses," so that the typical title for Moses becomes "Moses our master" (משה רבינו).[174]

Against this backdrop it is surprising that in the later midrashic compilations we encounter the same attempt to explain Moses' objection or hesitancy to take up his mandate in Exodus 4:10 in the *positive* manner that we found in Philo.[175] A classic example of this recasting of the biblical tradition can be seen in *Exodus Rabbah* 3.14–17. In Exod. Rab. 3.14 to Exod. 4:10 Moses' objection is no longer interpreted to be a comment on Moses' own inability, but is taken to be the proper scriptural response to the fact that Pharaoh has a hard heart. Since Pharaoh is a "slave" who "will not accept reproof" (cf. Prov. 39:19), Moses responds to his call by declaring that words will be useless in persuading him. As Moses puts it in Exod. Rab. 3.14, "I see no place for words here," or put positively, "I will only go if I can chastise him with suffering."[176] In this same passage, this positive reevaluation is also evidenced in the fact that Moses' response in Exod. 4:10 is said to indicate that God was forced to plead with Moses for seven days to take up his mission before he accepted it. This was not, however, because Moses refused God's call as such, but rather because Moses was too humble to believe that he could be God's messenger (שליח).

It is significant, moreover, that Moses' objection itself is now portrayed in Exod. Rab. 3.15 as an integral part of God's predetermined plan to "create" Moses "anew." Exodus 4:11 is thus interpreted to mean that God had purposely created Moses not to be a "man of words" (איש דברים) in order that he might "perform a miracle" with him.[177] This is supported by the fact that a

---

[174] Cf. Josephus, *Ant.* I, 18, 20, 23; II, 180; IV, 13, 150, 156; *C.Ap.* II, 75, 145, etc.; Philo, *Leg.all.* II, 14; III, 145; *Cher.* 40, 53; *De sac.* 16, 72; *Det.* 62, 105, etc.; though see *Vit.Mos.* II, 48, where God is the true lawgiver; for the rabbinic perspective, cf. *b.*Ber. 33b, 34a; *b.*'Erubin 18b, 54b, 63a; Abot R. Nat.a 23, 27, etc. I owe this basic insight to W. Meeks, *Prophet-King*, p. 132, who points this out to highlight the distinctiveness of Josephus' view. As he puts it, "To call Moses νομοθέτης, then, is already to adapt for Gentile understanding his primary role in Jewish sacred history."

[175] To my knowledge there is no extant tannaitic tradition concerning the call and/or objection of Moses in Exod. 3 and 4.

[176] English translations for Exod. Rab. are taken from S.M. Lehrman, *Exodus, Midrash Rabbah, Vol. 3*, 1951. For the Hebrew text, see A.A. Halevi, *Midrash Rabba, Bd. 3, Shemot Rabba, Part I*, 1959.

[177] Cf. J. Tigay, "Moses' Speech Difficulty," *AJS* 3 (1974) 29–42, p. 41, who argues that "the most natural reading of v. 11" is "'If your speech is defective, it is because I made you that way.'"

play on the word הוריתיך ("I will teach you") enables Exod. 4:12 to be interpreted to mean that God now promises to create Moses "into a new being" (cf.
ותהר from Exod. 2:2: הרה = "to conceive").[178] As the midrash continues, the
emphasis on Moses' objection as a positive expression of his humility is
picked up once again when his plea that God send someone else in Exod. 4:13
is taken to be a reference to Moses' unworthiness and deference, first in comparison to the angels whom God has used in the past to deliver Lot and Hagar,
and then in reference to Aaron, his older brother (cf. Exod. Rab. 3.15).[179] It is
thus somewhat unexpected that, as in the biblical account, here too God responds with anger to Moses' request, and that Moses is then punished for his
hesitancy. In Exod. Rab. 3.17 the high priesthood is taken away from Moses
and given to Aaron, while God declares that Moses will not be allowed to
speak to the people as he would have been able to do otherwise, since he has
been "created anew."

But of even more significance for our study is the midrashic tradition concerning Exod. 4:10 preserved in *Pirke de Rabbi Eliezer* 40:

"The Holy One, blessed be He, said to him: 'Come and I will send thee (אשלחך) unto
Pharaoh' (Exod. 4:10). He answered before Him: Sovereign of all worlds! Have I not
spoken thus to thee three or four times, *that I have no power* (אין בי כה) for I have a
defective tongue (שאני נפלם בלשוני) as it is said, 'And Moses said unto the Lord, O
Lord, I am not eloquent' (לא איש דברים אנכי, Exod. 4:10). Not only this, but moreover thou doest send me (משלחני) into the power of my enemy who seeks my hurt. For
this reason I fled from him, as it is said, 'But Moses fled from the face of Pharaoh'
(Exod. 2:15). He answered him: Do not fear him, for all the men who sought thy life
are already dead."[180]

Moses' statement in the biblical tradition that he is "not a man of words"
(לא איש דברים) is here interpreted to mean that Moses has no "power" (כה)
because of his "defective tongue." As in the LXX version of Exodus 4:10, the
repetition of the motif of Moses' lack of eloquence is now also replaced by a
more general statement, which is then grounded by the fact that Moses cannot

---

[178] See too Tanhuma B, Exodus I, § 18, where Moses' call is referred to as a "new creation." For in commenting on Exod. 4:12 we read, "R. Jehuda b. Simon sagte: Der Heilige,
g.s.er! sprach zu Mose: Ich mache dich zu einem neuen Geschöpf, wie eine Frau, die
schwanger ist und gebiert, wie es heißt: 'und dich lehren, was du sagen sollst' (ebda.)."
Trans. Han Bietenhard, *Midrasch Tanhuma B, Bd. 1*, Judaica et Christiana Bd. 5, 1980,
p. 304. This same idea of Moses' being created anew, as evidenced by his being given the
ability to speak, is also reflected in the midrasch Tanhuma B, Deut. Ia, § 1, where Deut. 1:1
("the words which Moses spoke") is taken in conjunction with Exod. 4:10 as evidence that
God gave Moses the ability to speak the 70 languages of the world, just as he created Adam
with the ability to name the animals, cf. H. Bietenhard, *Midrasch Tanhuma B, Bd. 2*, Judaica
et Christiana Bd. 6, 1982, pp. 440–441.

[179] For this same motif, see Tanhuma B, Exod. I, § 18 and Lev. I, § 5; cf. Bietenhard,
Midrasch Tanhuma B, Bd. I, p. 304 and *Bd. II*, pp. 11 f.

[180] English trans. taken from G. Friedlander, *Pirke*, pp. 314–315. The Hebrew text is from
Pirque R. Eliezer, Warsaw ed., 1946, p. 846.

speak well. The parallel between the *structure* of the argument in the LXX version of Exod. 4:10 and the midrashic exegesis in Pirqe R. El. 40 is thus striking:

	LXX to Exod. 4:10	*Pirqe R. El. 40 on Exod. 4:10*
Principle:	οὐχ ἱκανός εἰμι	אין בי כח
Reason:	ἰσχνόφωνος καὶ βραδύγλωσσος ἐγώ εἰμι	שאני נפלם בלשוני

At the same time, the *content* of Moses' objection, as understood in Pirqe R. El. 40, is strikingly similar to that found in the LXX. The fact that Moses objects that he has no "power" or "strength" (כח)[181] is close, though of course not identical, to the semantic field encompassed by the ἱκανός-motif. The context of Pirqe R. El. 40 demonstrates that the "power" being spoken of is not that of the special authorization given to one sent by God, which is usually expressed with רשות/רשותא,[182] but rather "power" in the sense of physical strength or ability: Moses is afraid because God is sending him "into the hand",[183] i.e. the power of Pharaoh, who will certainly harm him if he has the chance.[184] Thus, far from being mitigated or justified in some way as in Exod. Rab. 3.14–17, Moses' objection in Exod. 4:10 is here interpreted to be a confession of his weakness or powerlessness. Moreover, as in the LXX, here too Moses is sent (שלח) by God in spite of his weakness.

This brings us to the common and related motif in rabbinic literature of Moses as the one called by God to be his "sent one" (שליח, cf. Exod. Rab. 3.14) and "prophet."[185] This identification is so well established that in Lev. Rab. 1.1 Moses' role as the messenger sent by God (לישלח מלאך) to deliver Israel from Egypt in Numbers 20:16 can be used to support the fact that the prophets are also called "messengers" (מלאכים), on the basis of the unexpressed premise that Moses was God's prophet.[186] It is of interest for our study, therefore, that in Exod. Rab. 4.3 to Exod. 4:18 Moses' call to be God's "prophet" is given as one of the classic examples, together with Balaam,

---

[181] Cf. M. Jastrow, *A Dictionary of the Targumim ... and the Midrashic Literature*, p. 628.

[182] I owe the suggestion of this contrast to a discussion with Prof. Dr. Otto Betz. For רשות as "authorization," cf. Jastrow, p. 1499.

[183] For the figurative use of יד meaning "power" or "authority" in rabbinic literature, cf. Jastrow, *Dictionary*, p. 563.

[184] So too A. Rosmarin, *Moses*, p. 82 n. 290, who lists parallels to this motif from throughout the literature.

[185] This motif has been investigated in depth in both rabbinic and extra-rabbinic literature by Jan-A. Bühner, *Der Gesandte und sein Weg im 4. Evangelium*, 2. Reihe, Bd. 2, 1977, pp. 285–314, so that it will suffice to highlight those emphases in the tradition which relate to our own study. For Moses as שליח cf. Mek. 3.5; Exod. Rab. 3.9 to 3:14; 4.1 to 4:18; 4.4 to 4:18; 12.1 to 9:3; 42.1 to 32:7; and Abot R. Nat.b 25.

[186] For this same tradition, cf. Tanhuma B, Lev. I, § 1. For the Hebrew, see M. Margulies, *Midrash Wayyikra Rabbah, Part One*, 1953, pp. 1 f.; and for the translation, J. Israelstam and J.J. Slotki, *Leviticus, Midrash Rabbah, Vol. IV*, 1951, p. 1.

Jonah, and Jeremiah, that those so called by the decree of God cannot revoke God's word once he has pronounced it. In spite of the fact that Moses is reluctant to take up his "mission" or "sending" (בשליחותו), like Jeremiah, he too is compelled to fulfill the task assigned to him by God.[187]

In this context it is also important to note that in Exod. Rab. 3.4 to Exod. 3:12 the biblical tradition אהיה עמך ("I will be with you") is now combined with the "Rechtsformel"[188] אנכי שלחתיך ("I have sent you") in such a way that the sign that Moses has been sent by God now becomes not only God's presence, but also his promise to "do all (Moses') wishes," which in the context means performing the miracles necessary to accomplish his mission. Bühner is therefore right in emphasizing that here "... Mose ist in ein Vertrauensverhältnis zu Gott gestellt, das ihn als charismatischen Wundertäter erscheinen läßt," so that "das Motiv des Botenschutzes, also die Erweisung der Sendung und Autorisierung durch Gott, in einer charismatischen Vollmacht ausgedrückt (ist)."[189] As in the targumic literature, here too Moses' call to be God's "sent one" means that he owes his very call itself to the irresistible decree of God (i.e. Moses is forced to go against his will!), and that this decree or mandate is attested and verified by Moses' ability to perform the necessary signs and wonders.

Finally, Moses' identity as the prophet and שליח of God is also the presupposition behind the tannaitic midrash *Sipre to Deuteronomy*, § 5 to Deut. 1:6a, where Moses says, "the Lord our God said to us in Horeb." The midrash takes this statement to mean that Moses' ability to speak for YHWH is evidence that Moses does not speak "from himself," but "from the mouth of the Holy One."[190] Conversely, and even more significant, this same principle ("I [Moses] said to you") can be adduced in Sipre Deut. § 9 and 19 (to Deut. 1:9 and 1:20 f. respectively) to designate Moses' speech as equally divine in origin and authority. The assumption seems to be that if Moses can pronounce the word of YHWH in Deut. 1:6a, then it must be true that when Moses himself speaks in Deut. 1:9, 20 f. he is speaking "from the mouth of the Holy One." As the one entrusted with the oracles of God, Moses takes on an authority which allows him to speak in his own right with divine sanction.

This same point seems to be implied in the tradition preserved in Exod. R. 19.3 to Exod. 12:43 and b. Shab. 87a, where we learn that Moses did three things on the basis of his own initiative which were nevertheless approved of by God.[191] For as Bühner points out,

---

[187] See too Tanhuma B, Lev. I, § 4, where Moses is again used as an example of this same motif, under the principle that no one can flee from the sovereignty of God; i.e. "Jeder, der vor der Herrschaft flieht, dem läuft die Herrschaft nach" (Bietenhard, *Midrasch, Bd. II*, pp. 11 f.).

[188] So Bühner, *Gesandte*, p. 290.

[189] *Gesandte*, p. 290.

[190] Cf. L. Finkelstein, *Siphre ad Deuteronomium*, 1939, p. 13; cf. also pp. 16, 31.

[191] I.e. according to Exod. Rab. 19.3 he decided not to engage in conjugal relations since he was the one appointed to receive God's word; he broke the tablets of the Law after Israel sinned in making the golden calf; and he refused to enter the Tent of Meeting without God's

"... gilt grundsätzlich, daß jedes Handeln מדעתו (i.e. from one's own initiative or understanding) die Auflösung des Auftragsverhältnisses zur Folge hat, so besteht desungeachtet daneben die Möglichkeit, daß der משלח einzelne Handlungen im Rahmen einer sonst gültigen שליחות für die speziell vom Auftrag her keine Deckung besteht, nachträglich als in seinem Sinne geschehen anerkannt und sie damit für sich rechtsverbindlich macht." [192]

Moses' call to be God's שליח or prophet is thus not merely a call to perform a predetermined set of commands or tasks, but rather the call to occupy a specific *office*, which is characterized by a "Wort-dienst" that carries the authority of God himself.

The significance of this last point for the rabbis cannot be overemphasized, since the authority of Moses becomes the legitimizing presupposition for the specific rabbinic claim that the oral law, and hence the entire rabbinic program as such, carries the same divine sanction as the written law. As is well known, according to rabbinic tradition the oral law was also delivered by God to Moses on Mount Sinai and has been faithfully handed down through the generations. Hence, it too is as binding as the written law, since, like the Torah, it also originates in Moses' Sinai experience.[193] For inasmuch as Moses is God's chosen spokesman, all his words are reliable and authoritative. We thus read in Pirqe R. El. 41:

"The rest of the commandments He (God) spake through the mouth of Moses, and concerning him the text says, 'As the cold of snow in the time of harvest, so is a faithful messenger to them that send him'." (Prov. 25:13)[194]

As Bühner has pointed out concerning this text, "Dem Midrasch kommt es auf den Gedanken des Botengehorsams und der Zuverlässigkeit des Gottesboten Mose an. Die Existenz Israels beruht auf der Zuverlässigkeit seiner Tradition und hängt daran, daß Mose das Gotteswort unverfälscht Israel übergeben hat."[195] It is no coincidence, therefore, that for the rabbis Moses is a rabbi – not because they intend to recreate Moses in their image, but because they wish to portray themselves in his. In rabbinic tradition Moses does not exist as a rabbi because rabbis exist, but the rabbi exists because Moses was a rabbi. Moses himself is the legitimizing presupposition for their rabbinic identity and authority as teachers of the Law.[196]

---

permission. According to *b*. Shab. 87a the third action was Moses' decision to add a third day to the command by God that he "sanctify them today and tomorrow."

[192] *Gesandte*, p. 299.

[193] This tradition is widespread; cf. e.g. Pirqe Aboth I.1–12; Abot R. Nat. a+b 1; *p*. Sanh. 10:1; Eccl. Rab. 12.11; 3 Enoch 48 (D).3–4; and Hekhalot Rabbati 68b (cf. H. Odeberg, *3 Enoch*, 1928, p. 178 n. 7).

[194] Trans. G. Friedlander, *Pirke*, pp. 325–326.

[195] *Gesandte*, p. 297.

[196] Cf. *b*. Shab. 30a; 92a; etc. for the title "Moses our Teacher," and *b*. 'Erubin 54b, where the rabbinic method of teaching is derived from the way in which Moses taught Aaron, his sons, the elders, and the people.

In completing our survey we find ourselves back where we began. The one motif which can be found throughout the literature we have examined, with the exception of the apologists,[197] is the concept of Moses as an authoritative presupposition, which can then be used to support one's own theological program and/or authority in a variety of ways. In the literature of this period, from the Apocrypha and Pseudepigrapha to the rabbinic traditions, to be like Moses, or to speak in the name of Moses, is to claim to speak authoritatively to the people of God, while at the same time implicitly supporting this claim. And in the case of the OT prophets, this link between their ministries and that of Moses is seen most directly in the structural similarities between their respective calls to be God's spokesmen.

8. A Concluding Note on Methodology

Having come this far, we are once again confronted with the suggestion that Paul's understanding of his own sufficiency as an apostle in 2 Cor. 2:16b and 3:4 f. is modelled after and built upon the call and sufficiency of Moses, the one sent (שׁלח, ἀποστέλλω) by God to be a minister of the Sinai covenant.[198] But before we turn our attention to Paul's argument in 2 Corinthians, a word needs to be said concerning the purpose of this survey in order to avoid any possible misunderstanding of its value. In coming to the conclusion concerning the ways in which the call of Moses and the motifs of his sufficiency and authority were understood in the biblical and non-canonical literature, the reader may be disappointed to realize that the temptation to compose a synthetic picture of "the call of Moses in Jewish literature," although a strong one, has been resisted. Instead, this study has been limited merely to offering a few general comparisons and contrasts between the various traditions. The reason for this restraint is that the purpose of such a survey is not to construct a composite picture of the call and sufficiency of Moses as it was understood in "Judaism" by somehow combining the various traditions into one gigantic mural, which in turn then becomes the key to unlocking Paul's thinking in 2 Cor. 2:16 ff. and elsewhere. Even if this were possible, not only would it force the

---

[197] But cf. Josephus, *Ant.* XVIII, 85–87; XX, 97–98; and *Bell.* II, 258–263, etc., where the false prophets support their claims by recourse to Sinai motifs and often with parallels to Moses and the theme of the Exodus! As Tiede, *Charismatic Figure*, p. 205, points out, although a definite link with the Deuteronomic prophecy of the coming of a prophet like Moses cannot be established, it is nevertheless clear that "these figures wanted to be regarded as the true successors of Moses," so that Joshua becomes their primary model. See his helpful discussion of the false prophet texts in Josephus on pp. 197–206.

[198] See Sandnes, *Paul*, pp. 17–19, for support of the fact that the common distinction usually drawn between "prophet" and the rabbinical institution of the שׁליח, based on the work of Rengstorf, is no longer tenable, since the latter designation was also used of prophets in post-biblical Judaism.

diversity of the literature and points of view of the period into an artificial unity,[199] but it would also be useless historically. Such a *"Gesamtbild"* would be based on the unexpressed presupposition that Jews in the first century in general, and Paul in particular, actually carried such a composite picture in their minds, something for which we have no literary evidence whatsoever.

Rather, the purpose of this survey is to outline the various ways in which the call of Moses and the motif of his sufficiency were understood in different literary contexts and periods of history in order to provide an indication of the ways in which the biblical account in Exodus 3–4 *could*, and in fact, in certain cases, *was* being understood in the milieu in which Paul lived. But such a survey can only indicate the interpretive possibilities that existed in Paul's day (and later). It can never provide, in and of itself, the exegetical key to Paul's own thinking. What Paul himself did with the biblical tradition can only be determined on the basis of an exegesis of Paul's own writings understood synchronically.[200] Moreover, we must carry out this exegesis with the possibility in mind that Paul does something novel with the tradition he inherited.

With this caution in view, the value of this survey is not that it provides *the* background to Paul's thought, but rather the backdrop, or in Vermes' words, the "broader canvas" against which Paul's own thinking becomes more distinct.[201] The purpose of our survey of the interpretation of the biblical account of Moses' call in Jewish literature from the bible to the rabbis is to highlight the distinctiveness and/or continuity of Paul's thought in the light of the heritage to which he belonged, and in so doing, to provide clues to Paul's own adaptation of the tradition. In turning to Paul we do not come with a pocket full of "parallels" with which we can develop a theory of Paul's literary antecedents, but with an awareness of the tendencies and exegetical "moves" which were possible and current in Paul's day (and later) as an aid to observing Paul's own "exegesis" of the tradition. Moreover, in using rabbinic traditions we must be especially careful to avoid confusing a parallel with literary dependency. For regardless of the widely accepted view that the targumic and midrashic literature are compilations of already long-standing traditions, the

---

[199] For a concise survey of this diversity and its implications for the study of early Christianity's "Jewish heritage," see Robert A. Kraft, "The Multiform Jewish Heritage of Early Christianity," in *Christianity, Judaism and Other Greco-Roman Cults, FS Morton Smith, Part Three: Judaism Before 70*, ed. J. Neusner, 1975, pp. 174–199.

[200] This same point has been well made by Vern S. Poythress, "Analysing a Biblical Text: Some Important Linguistic Distinctions," *SJTh* 32 (1979) 113–137, p. 115, with his emphasis on the distinction between "diachronic" and "synchronic" analysis of a text, i.e. between an analysis which compares languages and meanings at two different temporal stages (diachronic) and that which takes a cross section of languages, meanings, people, and cultures at a given point in time (synchronic). As Poythress emphasizes, "the meaning of a discourse for St. Paul or for his hearers can depend *only* on what Paul and his hearers know and remember about their language and culture" (p. 115). The synchronic analysis is thus the definitive one for understanding Paul (cf. p. 116).

[201] See above, n. 160.

problem still remains that there is no methodological certainty concerning the date and provenance of any individual tradition within that corpus of literature.[202] What holds true as a generalization cannot be asserted, with methodological surety, in respect to any single example. To assert that rabbinic literature preserves older tradition is to make a statement about its nature, not a historical judgment about the antiquity of any one particular tradition or saying within that literature. With this reminder in view, we can now turn out attention to Paul's argument in 2 Cor. 3:4–6.

---

[202] For an excellent discussion of the indiscriminate way in which scholars continue to use rabbinic literature, and a constructive appraisal of the way it ought to be carried out, see J. Neusner, "Anthropology and the Study of Talmudic Literature," in *Method and Meaning in Ancient Judaism*, Brown Judaic Studies 10, 1979, pp. 21–40, esp. pp. 25–29 and his "Method and Substance in the History of Judaic Ideas: An Exercise," in *Jews, Greeks and Christians, Religious Cultures in Late Antiquity, FS W.D. Davies*, ed. R. Hamilton-Kelly and R. Scroggs, 1976, pp. 89–111, esp. pp. 91–95. For a full length treatment of this problem, see now his forthcoming *What We Cannot Show, We Do Not Know: Rabbinic Literature and the New Testament*, 1993.

Chapter Two

The Sufficiency and Call of Paul
(2 Cor. 3:4–6)

As noted above, Paul's argument in support of his apostolic authority began in 2:14–16a and 3:1–3 with an emphasis on the present and ongoing *evidence* of his legitimacy as an apostle. The evidence Paul adduced was his ministry of the Spirit mediated through his experiences of suffering as an apostle (3:3). Paul's apostolic life of faith in the midst of adversity thus mediated the same glory and power of God revealed in the death and resurrection of Christ both to those who were being saved and to those who were perishing (2:14–16a; cf. 2 Cor. 1:8–11; 4:7–12). Rather than calling his apostolic ministry into question, Paul's suffering was therefore the very vehicle by which the power and authority of the Gospel were being revealed through the pouring out of God's Spirit to redeem, deliver, and sustain his people as the inaugural work of the promised new age.[1]

In 2:16b Paul grounded the legitimacy of his ministry in his *calling* to be an apostle by picturing his "sufficiency" (ἱκανός) in terms of the call of Moses, and then, in 2:17, by pointing to the consequences of his calling "from God" (ἐκ θεοῦ) for the way in which he conducted his ministry "before God" (κατέναντι θεοῦ), that is, in the very presence of God[2] as judge. Paul's ministry as an apostle was not an exercise in self-recommendation or self-delusion (3:1), nor was it an elaborate attempt to swindle his churches (2:17 and 3:2), because it was accredited by the work of the Spirit through Paul on the one hand (3:1–3a), and by his own suffering for the sake of the Corinthians on the other (2:14–16a; 2:17). The Spirit, in making alive those who accepted Paul's Gospel, testified to the genuine nature of Paul's apostolic ministry, as well as to its claim that the eschatological new age of the Spirit pictured in Ezekiel

---

[1] See my *Suffering and the Spirit, An Exegetical Study of II Cor. 2:14–3:3 within the Context of the Corinthian Correspondence*, WUNT 2. Reihe 19, 1986, pp. 219–221, for a summary of the main points of this previous study.

[2] Following David A. Renwick, *Paul, the Temple, and the Presence of God*, 1991, pp. 44, 50, 61–74, who argues that κατέναντι θεοῦ refers to being in the very presence of God in a literal sense. This provides the basis for my emphasis that Paul is mediating to others what he himself experiences as the very heart of the gospel, namely, the promise and experience of God's presence as manifest in his Spirit. This also supports my earlier argument that to be "before God" is to stand before God's judgment, since to be in God's presence is at the same time to be (have been) judged by him; see below, n. 17.

11:19 and 36:26 had now arrived among God's people through Paul's role as its intermediary agent (3:3b).[3]

Having offered this evidential argument for his sufficiency as an apostle in 2:17–3:3, in 2 Cor. 3:4–6 Paul now returns explicitly to the theme of his calling introduced earlier in 2:16b–17. It will become clear below that Paul's purpose in doing so is to complete his defense of the legitimacy of his apostolic ministry by developing further the corollary question of the origin, foundation, and purpose of his apostleship. Paul completes his self-defense by reminding the Corinthians that the results of his ministry are genuine, and therefore point to the "sufficiency" (ἱκανότης) of his ministry (3:5), because his prior call to be an apostle has "made him sufficient" (ἱκάνωσεν) for his new covenant ministry of life and death (2:15–16; 3:6a).[4]

1. The Confidence of Paul in 2 Cor. 3:4

This understanding of the underlying basis of Paul's argument in 2 Cor. 2:16–3:3 is confirmed by the fact that Paul's immediate response to his prior assertions in 2:14–3:3 is to summarize this self-understanding as the "confidence" (πεποίθησις) he has διὰ τοῦ Χριστοῦ πρὸς τὸν θεόν (3:4).[5] Paul is confident

---

[3] For confirmation of my earlier thesis that the Corinthians' experience of the pouring out of the Spirit through Paul's ministry in fulfillment of Ezek. 11:19; 36:26 and Jer. 31:31 ff. becomes "the focal point in Paul's authorization that he is the Spirit-giver to the Corinthians, the one through whom God's revelation is brought," see now Karl Olav Sandnes, *Paul – One of the Prophets? A Contribution to the Apostle's Self-Understanding*, WUNT 2. Reihe 43, 1991, p. 135, quoting his summary of my thesis. Sandnes, p. 135, rightly sees this to be the point of 3:18 (see my own corresponding view of 3:18 in chapter five below). For the contrary view, see now Peter Jones, *La Deuxieme Epitre de Paul aux Corinthiens*, CEB, 1992, pp. 67–68, who, following Baird and the earlier work of his own dissertation, *The Apostle Paul: A Second Moses according to 2 Corinthians 2:14–4:7*, Diss. Princeton Theological Seminary, 1973, pp. 28–34, argues that the "tablets of fleshly hearts" in 3:3 is a reference to Paul's own heart in parallel to 3:2. Thus, though Jones clearly sees the evidential nature of Paul's apologetic in 3:1–3, he denies the allusions to Ezek. 11:19 and 36:26 in 3:3. But such an interpretation has difficulty in explaining the transition from 3:3a to 3:3b.

[4] This point has been well put by Erich Gräßer, *Der Alte Bund im Neuen, Exegetische Studien zur Israelfrage im Neuen Testament*, WUNT 35, 1985, p. 80, who sees Paul's answer to why he has the right to claim what he does in 2:16 as twofold: "1. das Recht gibt ihm das geleistete Werk (d.h. Gottes Handeln durch ihn), 3:1–3; 2. das Recht gibt ihm sein Amt (d.h. Gottes Handeln an ihm), 3:4–6." Cf. too p. 82, where Gräßer sees Paul's reference in 3:4 f. to be to his call as an apostle.

[5] For the view that the demonstrative pronoun τοιαύτην in 3:4, and thus 3:4–6 as a whole, refers back to Paul's entire argument in 2:14–3:3, see e.g. G. Barth, "Die Eignung des Verkündigers in 2 Kor. 2:14–3:6," in *Kirche, FS G. Bornkamm zum 75. Geburtstag*, ed. D. Lührmann and G. Strecker, 1980, pp. 257–280, pp. 266, 269 n. 39; Michael Theobald, *Die überströmende Gnade, Studien zu einem paulinischen Motivfeld*, 1982, p. 170, who rightly argues that 3:4 functions like a joint or pivot ("Gelenk") in the argument, summing up the preceding material and leading by way of conclusion to the following; J. Lambrecht,

that his suffering is the vehicle through which the Spirit is being poured out in his ministry. This has been substantiated by Stanley Olson's study, in which he shows that the focus of Paul's expressions of confidence in 2 Cor. 1–7 is not on Paul's *feeling* of confidence, but on the *content* of that confidence.[6] Rather than being merely incidental reports of Paul's state of mind, such expressions are fixed forms used persuasively to further Paul's goals in writing.[7] Moreover, Paul's use of this confidence expression in 2 Cor. 3:4 indicates the continuing polemical context of his writing. Hence, in 3:4 Paul's purpose is to state the "goal" of his apologetic by emphasizing his claim to be "God's messenger to the Corinthians."[8] As Olson observes on the basis of a survey of related literature, "such expressions are most frequently found in sections of apologetic or self-commendation" and "the confidence expression usually states the view of the writer's character which he hopes his readers (hearers) will have and for which he *argues* if there is an extended section of apologetic or self-commendation."[9] This has been confirmed more recently by Linda Belleville's argument that the structure of 2 Cor. 1–7 and the repetition of the commendation theme indicate that the genre of 2 Cor. 1:8–7:16, as the body of the letter, is best understood to be that of an apologetic letter of self-commendation (cf. the introduction of the theme in 1:12 and the related themes of "confidence" and "boldness," throughout 2 Cor. 1–7).[10] Moreover, I have ar-

---

"Structure and Line of Thought in 2 Cor. 2:14–4:6," *Biblica* 64 (1983) 344–380, pp. 352 f.; and C.K. Barrett, *A Commentary on the Second Epistle to the Corinthians*, HNTC, 1973, p. 110. For the opposing view that 3:4–6 jumps over 3:1–3 to 2:16b–17, see Hans Windisch, *Der zweite Korintherbrief*, KEK Bd. 6, 1970[9], p. 107, who is led to this view because he sees a contradiction between 3:1 and 3:4–6 in that the latter gives a kind of self-recommendation. For the rebuttal of this view, see below.

[6] *Confidence Expressions in Paul: Epistolary Conventions and the Purpose of 2 Corinthians*, Ph.D. Diss., Yale University, 1976, p. 162. For the other expressions in 2 Cor. 1–7 of Paul's confidence in his ministry or character (in contrast to his expressions of confidence in his addressees), which are not limited to a specific set of terminology, see e.g. 1:7, 12, 13–14, 15; 2:3, 14; 3:12; 4:1, 7, 13, 16; 5:6–9, 11; 6:1; 7:1, 4, 16. Cf. his pp. 37–39 and 99–101 for a list of Paul's expressions of confidence in 2 Cor. and their parallels elsewhere in the NT and in Greek literature of the period. For a brief overview of Paul's uses and parallels in contemporary literature, see his "Epistolary Uses of Expressions of Self-Confidence," *JBL* 103 (1984) 585–597.

[7] Olson, *Confidence*, p. 5.

[8] Olson, *Confidence*, p. 162. In his summary article, "Epistolary Uses," p. 587, Olson points out that "in other Hellenistic letters and speeches, expressions of self-confidence are found almost exclusively in the immediate context of apologetic or self-commendation."

[9] "Epistolary Uses," pp. 596, 587, emphasis mine. Olson is also correct in stressing that the commendation in 3:1–3 which provides the basis for Paul's confidence, "is the evidence of the Spirit's working in the Corinthians themselves," *Confidence*, p. 147. For his exegesis of 3:1–3, which despite our basic agreement differs at several points from my own, cf. his pp. 145–148.

[10] See her "A Letter of Apologetic Self-Commendation: 2 Cor. 1:8–7:16," *NovT* 31 (1989) 142–163, esp. pp. 153–156 and p. 149, for the analysis of 1:12 as the theme of the following chapters as introduced at the beginning of the letter's "body middle" (1:12–7:2). In support of this evaluation, Belleville points to the related themes of καύχησις, καυχάομαι

gued earlier not only that the theme of "self-commendation" is the key to the development of Paul's argument in 2 Corinthians, but also that Paul responds to the charge that his authority is based merely on his own "self-commendation" by pointing to the objective evidence in his ministry which testifies that God is the one who commends him as an apostle (cf. 2 Cor. 10:18).[11] Hence, given their literary and apologetic role as Paul's answer to the accusation of "self-commendation," to quote Olson yet again, "the expressions [of confidence in one's own character] frequently function as thematic statements for their context and may ... help one to discern the point of an argument."[12]

This is certainly the case in 2 Cor. 3:4–6. Paul's apologetic purpose is to offer further support for the fact that in commending himself to the Corinthians he has not engaged in an unattested self-commendation (3:1 f). Rather than commending *himself*, Paul's confidence is that the Spirit, as *God's* commendation (cf. 2 Cor. 10:18), is at work in his ministry to transform the hearts of those to whom he proclaims the cross of Christ (3:3–4).[13] This confidence testifies that he has been made sufficient to be a "minister"[14] of the new covenant (3:5–6a). Paul's proof for this confidence is once again the work of the Spirit in his ministry, which, due to its objective nature as seen in the lives of the Corinthians themselves, provides a commendation for Paul that cannot be

---

(1:12, 14; 5:12; 7:4, 14), πεποίθησις, πέποιθα (1:9, 15; 3:4), παρρησία (3:12; 7:4), θαρρέω (5:6, 8; 7:16), and συνίστημι (3:1; 4:2; 5:12; 6:4), with συνιστάνειν ἑαυτούς (3:1; 4:2; 5:12; 6:4) being "the phrase that is characteristic of the dialogue at this stage in Paul's relationship with Corinth" (p. 152).

[11] See my "'Self-Commendation' and Apostolic Legitimacy in 2 Corinthians: A Pauline Dialectic?" *NTS* 36 (1990) 66–88. For confirmation of this point and its place within Paul's argument in 2 Cor. 10–12, see now Ulrich Heckel, *Kraft in Schwachheit, Untersuchungen zu 2. Kor 10–13*, WUNT 2. Reihe 56, 1993, pp. 191–214. Heckel demonstrates the decisive influence of Jer. 9:22 f. on Paul's thought in this regard, concluding, in comparison to 1 Cor. 1:31, "daß Paulus die Unterschiede zwischen den Aposteln nicht durch den Hinweis auf das Heil in Christus relativiert, sondern im Gegenteil großen Wert auf seine Erfolge legt, diese jedoch nicht als eigenes Werk ausgibt, sondern auf den Herrn zurückführt und dadurch den Affront gegen Gott vermeidet" (p. 192).

[12] "Epistolary Uses," p. 596. See too Jones, *Second Moses*, p. 143, who observed that the confidence language introduced at 3:4, 12; 4:1 forms a consistent pattern in which it both looks backward to the previous argument and leads into the subsequent assertions so that they "seem therefore to be the point of each section."

[13] Cf. already K. Stalder, *Das Werk des Geistes in der Heiligung bei Paulus*, 1962, pp. 52 f., and before him R. Birch Hoyle, *The Holy Spirit in St. Paul*, 1927, p. 97, who pointed out that although Paul alludes to signs and miracles in his ministry, "the evidence he delighted to dwell upon was that given in the changed ethical lives of his converts ..." In support of this conclusion he points to 2 Cor. 3:3 f. and Gal. 3:2–5. Commenting on 2 Cor. 12:18, Hoyle, p. 106, thus observes that "the Spirit, known and possessed by all believers, was the standard to which the apostle appealed in the last resort in justification of his action and conduct ..."

[14] Though technically better translated as "servant" (see below), for the sake of preserving the word play between the various διακον-stems, διάκονος will at times also be rendered "minister."

equated with a subjective "self-commendation" (3:1, 4, 6b).[15] Paul's confidence comes διὰ τοῦ Χριστοῦ πρὸς τὸν θεόν, which, as the chiastic formulation κατέναντι θεοῦ ἐν Χριστῷ in 2:17 indicates,[16] certifies that Paul's confidence was given by means of Christ's work within him and in the knowledge that he stands approved before the judgment of God (cf. the further parallels in 2 Cor. 12:19; 4:2; 5:9–11; 7:9–12; 8:16–21; 10:7 and the important parallel in Rom. 15:15–19). God, not the Corinthians, is the one who judges Paul and before whose presence his defense stands or falls.[17]

Paul's argument in 2:14–3:4 thus exhibits the same structure as his prior thesis-like summary in 2 Cor. 1:21 f., which serves to introduce the theme of 2 Cor. 1–7 as a whole.[18] In both cases Paul moves from an emphasis on the Spirit as the corroboratory evidence for the validity of his ministry to a statement of assurance that his authority as an apostle is based on God's own authority as attested by the outpouring of the Spirit. The logical link between 3:3 and 3:4, indicated grammatically only by the ambiguous connective δέ, is thus best understood as an *inference* based on Paul's prior assertion of the Spirit's work in his ministry. Olson's conclusion concerning 2 Cor. 1:21 f. can therefore by applied equally well to our present text:

---

[15] For this distinction between an unattested "self-commendation" (ἑαυτοὺς συνιστάνειν) in the negative sense (cf. 2 Cor. 3:1; 5:12; 10:12, 18) and the kind of appropriately supported "commendation of oneself" (συνιστάνειν ἑαυτούς) that Paul offers (cf. 2 Cor. 4:2; 6:4; 12:11), see my "Self-Commendation," pp. 74 ff., and Carol Kern Stockhausen's *Moses' Veil and the Glory of the New Covenant, The Exegetical Substructure of II Cor. 3:1–4:6*, AB 116, 1989, p. 76: "The Spirit itself in all its manifestations is then the verification of the reality of the new covenant, Paul's recommendation." Stockhausen, however, fails to connect this with Paul's suffering since she divides 3:1–4:6 from 2:14–17 and 4:7 ff.

[16] For the meaning of this phrase as a reference to Paul's standing before the judgment of God, see my *Suffering and the Spirit*, pp. 170–172. See too Gräßer, *Der Alte Bund*, p. 79: "Κατέναντι θεοῦ meint immer das eschatologische Stehen vor Gott im Gericht (vgl. 12:19)." For the use of διά in the sense of "the causal usage in relation to persons," so that in 3:4 "the whole Christ is the Author of apostolic authority" (cf. Rom. 1:5; Gal. 1:1; 1 Thess. 4:2), see A. Oepke, art. διά, *TDNT* 2 (1964) pp. 65–70, p. 68.

[17] Following Renwick's emphasis on the literal nature of the presence of God in 2:17; cf. *Temple*, pp. 61–74. But Renwick, *Temple*, pp. 51 f., though correctly emphasizing that Paul's confidence is related to the fact that he had access to God's presence, has reversed the order of Paul's argumentation. In Renwick's view, the imparting of the Spirit "gave him the confidence which he needed to claim that he had access to God (and thus, *implicitly*, to claim that his apostolic status was valid)" (emphasis mine). But Paul's explicit argument does not concern access to God's presence, but the validity of his apostleship, which implicitly means that he has access to God! Renwick's desire to see the theme of God's presence as the key to Paul's thought throughout 2:14–3:18 leads him to read this motif into texts where it is only implicit. Hence, in speaking of the point of 3:5–6, Renwick states, "... *the access to God* which he enjoyed had not been granted to him because of any worthiness within his life ..." (p. 52, emphasis mine), when Paul is explicitly speaking of his confidence and sufficiency as an apostle (see below). This same concern leads him to play down the motif of the judgment of God referred to in 2:17. But what takes place in God's presence fundamentally is the judgment and/or vindication of God's creation.

[18] So Belleville, "Apologetic Self-Commendation," p. 149.

"The Spirit is the present guarantee of Paul's trustworthiness, the guarantee that he is established and certified by God, or perhaps, the proof that he is 'sealed' and 'anointed' and therefore that his confident assertions about himself are justified." [19]

But as the parallel between διὰ τοῦ Χριστοῦ πρὸς τὸν θεόν in 3:4 and κατέναντι θεοῦ ἐν Χριστῷ in 2:17 indicates, the confidence Paul has in his ministry also picks up the theme of 2:17, and thus of 2:14–17 as well.[20] This is also seen in the resumption of the ἱκανός-motif in 3:5 f. In referring back to 2:16b, therefore, the "sufficiency" motif in 3:4 must incorporate Paul's apostolic ministry of suffering in 2:14–16a, since it is this ministry which provides the referent for the ταῦτα of 2:16b. Paul's statement of confidence in 3:4 refers not only to his ministry of the Spirit, but also to his ministry of suffering as an equally significant argument that his apostleship has been ordained by God himself.[21] Moreover, the fact that Paul once again introduces the theme of his confidence at precisely this point highlights the apologetic nature of Paul's argument in 2:14–16a, as well as its more obvious presence in 2:17–3:6.

2. The Sufficiency of Paul in 2 Cor. 3:5 f.

Of even more importance for this study is the reintroduction of the sufficiency motif from 2:16 in 3:5 f. (cf. ἱκανός/ἱκανότης/ἱκανόω). As the extension of his affirmation in 3:4, it is this motif which ties Paul's present declaration of confidence to his prior assertion of sufficiency in 2:16b., since Paul's confidence in 3:4 is now explicitly identified with his sufficiency in 3:5 f. The work of the Spirit to transform hearts in fulfillment of Ezekiel 11:19 and 36:26 (3:3–4) *is* the basis of his "sufficiency" and "confidence" as a minister of the new covenant (2:16b; 3:6a). Paul's authority is built on his self-understanding

---

[19] *Confidence*, p. 136. Olson refers to Paul's argument in 1:21 f. as the "certification (cf. βεβαιόω) of the Spirit" (p. 130). Cf. pp. 131–137 for his exegesis of this passage.

[20] So too R.P. Martin, *2 Corinthians*, WBC 40, 1986, p. 52 (following Strachen, Godet, Windisch, and Provence) and Olson, *Confidence*, p. 145 n. 2. But because they do not see 2:17 as a reference to a specific aspect of Paul's suffering, i.e. that suffering incurred as a result of his practice of self-support (cf. 1 Cor. 4:11 f.), which continues the theme of suffering from 2:14–16a, they fail to include 2:14–16 as part of Paul's referent in 3:4.

[21] See now Renwick, *Temple*, p. 52 n. 9, who takes τοιαύτην in 3:4 to point to the new covenant "referred to implicitly by reference to the spirit in 3:3, and explicitly in 3:6." Contra those who, like Bultmann, *Zweiter Korintherbrief*, p. 78, insightfully show that Paul's sufficiency in 3:4 f. is based upon the character of the new covenant as that which gives life (p. 78), but then relate the confidence theme to what follows, which then allows them to deny any visible evidence for Paul's confidence. On the other hand, in his art. πείθω κτλ., *TDNT* 6 (1968) 1–11, p. 8, Bultmann correctly stresses that the reference of Paul's confidence in 3:4 is to the "specific self-awareness of the apostle" in parallel to the παρρησία of 3:12 and in view of the fact that τοιαύτην refers back to 3:1–3, though this too offers for him no evidence for Paul's assertions. For a response to this attempt to rob Paul's argument in 2 Cor. of its evidential force, see now my "Self-Commendation."

as the mediatory agent of the Spirit, through which the eschatological promises of Ezekiel are being fulfilled in the preaching of the cross and its embodiment in his life of suffering (cf. 2:14–16a).

But Paul's assertion that he is "sufficient" for the life and death ministry of
the gospel in 2:16b and his "confidence" that the Spirit is at work through his
suffering in 3:4 are both significantly qualified in 3:5 f. Just as Paul was careful in 2:17 to emphasize that his sufficiency to preach the word of God came
about as a result of the work of God's grace in his life (ἀλλ' ὡς ἐξ εἰλικρινείας),
i.e. as a result of his call and gifting from God (ἀλλ' ὡς ἐκ θεοῦ),[22] now too
Paul immediately stresses in 3:5 that he is not "sufficient" (ἱκανοί) to consider
this aspect of his ministry or anything else as originating *from himself* (ἀφ'
ἑαυτῶν, ἐξ ἑαυτῶν).

This qualification takes on added significance against the backdrop of
1 Cor. 15:9, where Paul told the Corinthians that he is the "least of the apostles" and that he is not "sufficient" (ἱκανός) to be called an apostle because he
persecuted the church "*of God*, thus standing over against God himself and
God's work in the world through Christ."[23] As in 2 Cor. 2:16 f. and 3:4 f., here
too Paul points to the specific manifestation of the grace of God in his call
as that which overcame his own past insufficiency (1 Cor. 15:8; cf. Gal. 1:15;
1 Tim. 1:12–16) and now enables him in spite of it to occupy the apostolic role
of preaching the gospel (cf. 1 Cor. 15:11): "But by the grace (χάριτι) of God
I am what I am, and his grace (χάρις) toward me was not in vain. Rather I
worked harder than all of them, though not I, but the grace (χάρις) of God with
me" (1 Cor. 15:10).[24] Against this backdrop, Paul's reference to his lack of

---

[22] For a demonstration that 2:17 refers to the divine sincerity given to Paul by God's grace
(cf. 2 Cor. 1:12; 1 Cor. 5:8) and to his call "from God" (cf. 1 Cor. 1:30; 2:12; 7:7; 8:6; 11:12;
12:4–6; 2 Cor. 5:18), see my *Suffering and the Spirit*, pp. 164–168. For the thesis that 2:17
actually functions as the key to 2:14–4:15 by introducing the three subjects of 3:4–18
("from God"), 4:1–6 ("before God"), and 4:7–15 ("in Christ"), see now Theobald, *Gnade*,
pp. 172–177. Though in a general sense this may be true, the first relationship is built upon
Theobald's conviction that a contrast between human and divine qualifications for one's
ministry is determinative for the contrast between the Mosaic and apostolic ministry in 3:7–
18 (cf. p. 172), contra the view argued in this study.

[23] Gordon D. Fee, *The First Epistle to the Corinthians*, NICNT, 1987, p. 734. Fee rightly
points out that "out of this encounter comes the basis of (Paul's) theology of grace. Since
God was gracious to him, God's enemy, in this way, (Paul) came eventually to realize that
this is the way God is toward all, Jew and Gentile alike, making no distinctions" (pp. 734 f.).
For the point being made here, see now Sandnes, *Paul*, p. 8 n. 19, who qualifies my earlier
stress on Paul's personal weakness and unimpressive speech as that which calls Paul's sufficiency into question by pointing out that Paul's previous persecution of the Church is the
obstacle to his sufficiency in 1 Cor. 15:9 and Acts 22:17–21. But it is not an either/or situation. Paul's persecution of the Church called into question his commission to be an apostle
at the level of his conversion-call, just as his suffering and lack of impressive speech called
into question his ministry at the level of his performance.

[24] Again, cf. Fee, *First Corinthians*, p. 735: "Thus, 'grace' in this sentence does not so
much refer to God's gracious favor on behalf of sinners, although that is not very far behind,
but in a way similar to (1 Cor.) 1:4 to the concrete expression of that grace in his apostleship.

self-sufficiency and the source of his sufficiency in God in 3:4 f. clearly picks up and draws out the logical conclusion implied in the prior discussion of his apostolic status in 1 Cor. 15:9–11. In himself, Paul is not "sufficient" (ἱκανός) to be an apostle because of his past (1 Cor. 15:9). Nevertheless, Paul *is* sufficient to be an apostle (2:16), but his "sufficiency" (ἱκανότης) is "from God" (ἐκ τοῦ θεοῦ) (3:4 f.).

In the same way, in Col. 1:12, Paul encourages the church to give thanks to God because he has *made them* (or "us," depending on the variant chosen) *sufficient* (ἱκανώσαντι) to share in his inheritance. Both in terms of Paul's own life as an apostle (2 Cor. 3:4 f.), as well as for the life of believers in general (Col. 1:12 f.), one's sufficiency comes from the grace of God manifested in the redemption of Christ. Paul's sufficiency from God to be an apostle in 2 Cor. 3:5 f. is merely his own particular experience of the sufficiency given by God which is needed to inherit the kingdom of God's Son, as expressed in Colossians 1:12–14. God is the one who has made all believers sufficient (ἱκανώσαντι, Col. 1:12) by delivering them from the "authority of darkness" and transferring them into the kingdom of Christ (Col. 1:13), in which they experience the redemption of the forgiveness of sins (Col. 1:14). As a result, the believer's sufficiency is grounds for praising and thanking *God* (Col. 1:3, 12). Hence, in Col. 1:12–14 the allusion to Paul's call carried by the sufficiency terminology in 2 Cor. 3:5 f. is extended to the call of all believers (cf. Col. 1:4–6). Moreover, in Col. 1:8, as in 2 Cor. 3:4–6, the evidence of the genuine nature of their calling is also their manifestation of the Spirit. Read in this way, the all-important qualification of Paul's sufficiency in 3:4 f. establishes an exact parallel between the content and structure of Paul's argument in 2:16b–17 and 3:4–5, with the latter extending the thought of the former:[25]

Paul's Sufficiency (2:16b)	Paul's Confidence/Sufficiency (3:4)
before God	before God
(κατέναντι θεοῦ)	(πρὸς τὸν θεόν)
based on	*based on*
The Call of God (2:17)	The Call of God (3:5)
(ἐξ εἰλικρινείας, ἐκ θεοῦ)	(ἐκ τοῦ θεοῦ)

The structure of Paul's argument also demonstrates that the hinge between the two texts is the work of the Spirit through Paul's apostolic life of suffering as the evidence of God's call. 2 Cor. 2:16b–3:6 thus exhibits an ABC–ABC pattern of argumentation which highlights the three essential aspects of Paul's apologetic, with the following implicit logical connections between them:

Thus he speaks in the succeeding clauses of God's 'grace *to* me,' and finally of 'the grace of God that was *with* me.'"

[25] So too Windisch, *Korintherbrief*, p. 108, who sees 3:5 f. to specify the origin and contents of the confidence spoken of in 3:2 f. and previously in 2:14–16a. As Windisch thus points out, Paul's self-evaluation in 3:5 flows normally out of 2:17 as the "prophet-apostle" who speaks from/before God (p. 108).

(A) Paul's Sufficiency (2:16b)
    based on
       (B) The Call of God (2:17)
         as evidenced by
           (C) The Work of the Spirit (3:2–3)
            therefore
(A) Paul's Confidence concerning his Sufficiency (3:4–5)
    based on
       (B) The Call of God (3:5–6a)
         as evidenced by
           (C) The Work of the Spirit (3:6b)

In each case, Paul asserts his sufficiency in spite of the suffering which seems to call his legitimacy into question (cf. 2:14, 17a; 3:4). And in each case Paul's affirmation of his sufficiency is based upon the call of God in his life, the evidence for which is the subsequent work of the Spirit in his ministry. Paul's "sufficiency" is not "from himself." Hence, as Furnish has emphasized, Paul's assertion of his sufficiency and its qualification in 3:4 f. are not "an expression of religious humility but ... an expression of his *confidence before God ... through Christ* that his apostolic service is fit and proper ... This dialectic of inadequacy/adequacy or unworthiness/worthiness is present whenever, as here, Paul considers his call to apostleship ...."[26] But whereas in 1 Cor. 15:10 Paul refers to the dialectic involved in his call by theological terms under the rubric of God's grace (see above), in 2 Cor. 2:16 f. and 3:4 f. he does so by alluding to the call of Moses.

3. The Call of Paul in 2 Cor. 3:5–6a and the Call of Moses

Against the backdrop of the LXX version of Exodus 3 and 4, especially 4:10 (see chapter one), the rhetorical question in 2:16b and its ἱκανός-terminology recollect the call of Moses.[27] In addition, the survey in chapter one makes it

---

[26] Victor P. Furnish, *II Corinthians*, AB Vol. 32A, 1984, p. 197, pointing to the work of Georgi and the parallel in 1 Cor. 15:9–10.

[27] So too Jones, *Second Moses*, pp. 37–41, and now his *La Deuxieme Epitre*, pp. 71 f., who notes both the allusion to the call of Moses and that the "sufficiency" terminology in 2:16b and 3:5 f. refers to Paul's call on the road to Damascus (see esp. *La Deuxieme Epitre*, pp. 71 f., where he points to the parallels in 1 Thess. 2:4; Eph. 3:8; 2 Cor. 5:18 f.; Gal. 1:15; 1 Cor. 15:8), though Jones then develops this parallel in terms of the second Moses expectation from Deut. 18:18 rather than in terms of the call of Moses and the prophets *per se* (see below). For the common and contrary attempt to read 2:16b as a cry of resignation in face of the magnitude of the apostolic ministry, parallel to that of Joel 2:11, see Windisch, *Korintherbrief*, p. 100, and Dieter Georgi, *Die Gegner des Paulus im 2. Korintherbrief. Studien zur Religiösen Propaganda in der Spätantike*, WMANT 11, 1964, p. 223 f. For a detailed response to the arguments of Windisch and Georgi, see my *Suffering and the Spirit*, pp. 96–98. Georgi is right, however, that the context of Paul's assertion of his confidence is not primarily the opinion of the Corinthians, but the judgment of God. See too now R.P. Martin,

clear that the structure of 3:5 recalls its parallels throughout the OT tradition concerning the call of the prophets.[28] Hence, even if the reference to the call of Moses in 2:16b appears "only as ... reflected through the later prophetic experience," as Brevard Childs has maintained for Paul in general,[29] the terminology in 2 Cor. 2:16b and its development in 3:4 f., together with the contrast between the ministries of Moses and Paul as the driving force of the argument in 3:7–18, demonstrate that in this context the underlying Mosaic prototype for Paul's assertion of sufficiency cannot be denied. Indeed, unlike the references in Gal. 1:15 f., 1 Cor. 9:16, and 1 Thess. 4:15, where the prophetic motifs certainly dominate, in 2 Cor. 2:16b and 3:5 the call of Moses even stands in the foreground.[30] Moreover, as we have seen in chapter one, within the ca-

---

2 Corinthians, p. 53, who posits the possibility of an allusion to Joel 2:11, but leaves the question open apparently due to his misreading of Georgi as being unconvinced of the allusion, and Lloyd Gaston, "Paul and the Torah in 2 Corinthians 3," in his *Paul and the Torah*, 1987, pp. 151–168, pp. 154, 156, who follows Georgi and thus misreads the central issue of 2 Cor. 2:14 ff. to be a contrast between "two competing concepts of ministry, one which claims competency and one which claims sincerity, claiming to be from God," which in view of 3:4 f. Gaston then interprets as "one which claims self-competence and one whose competency comes from God." But it is hard to imagine how Paul's opponents, if they did base their ministry on supernatural experiences which they had had, as Gaston supposes, would then claim that this was a "self-competency."

[28] See now Theobald, *Gnade*, p. 171 n. 15, who follows Vos in the latter's observation that "Die Frage nach der menschlichen Fähigkeit zum göttlichen Dienst ist eine stereotype Frage aus den prophetischen Berufungsgeschichten," pointing to Ex. 3:11; 4:10 (LXX); Jes. 6:5; 40:6 f.; Jer. 1:6; and Mark 1:7 in explicit rejection of Georgi's thesis that the background is the question of resignation from Joel 2:11. Theobald, however, contra the position argued in *Suffering and the Spirit*, pp. 90 ff., takes the implied answer of 2:16b to be "no one."

[29] *Exodus, A Commentary*, OTL, 1974, p. 83. Childs offers the following reasons for the lack of reference to Moses in the call of Paul: 1) Moses' initial response of resistance "did not find a ready place in the New Testament's understanding of apostleship;" 2) Moses' call to deliver from physical slavery is replaced with spiritual deliverance; and most importantly, 3) the dominant motif of suffering in the prophets made this form more suitable for NT appropriation (pp. 83 f.). But the recognition of the context of Paul's suffering in 2 Cor. 2:14 ff., Paul's emphasis on the parallel between the ministries of the old and new covenants and the development of the sufficiency in spite of insufficiency motif overcome these objections.

[30] This point has been confirmed and supported by Sandnes' very helpful and detailed study of the prophetic motifs in Paul's self-understanding (cf. his study, *Paul – One of the Prophets?*). Sandnes is correct in concluding that 2 Cor. 3:4–18 is the only place in Paul's writings where "an analogy to Moses is found with reasonable explicitness" and that "the reference to Moses' call appears as reflected through a broader framework of prophetic experience and self-concept" (p. 16 n. 6, in reference to my earlier dissertation). Sandnes investigates 1 Cor. 2:6–16; 2 Cor. 4:6; Rom. 1:1–5; 10:14–18; 11:25–36; 1 Thess. 2:3–8; and Eph. 2:19–3:7 as the other key passages which, when taken together with Gal. 1:15 f., establish Paul's view of himself as a latter day, eschatological prophet (cf. his conclusions on pp. 240–242). Cf. too Paul Demann, "Moses und das Gesetz bei Paulus," in *Moses in Schrift und Überlieferung*, 1963, pp. 205–264, p. 207 n. 4, who not only sees the theme of the "prophet like Moses" related to Jesus in Acts 3:22; 7:37, but also sees allusions to Ex. 3:1–5 in the three accounts of the call of Paul, and points out that the texts concerning the servant from Is. 49:6 and Is. 42:7, which are applied to Paul in Acts 13:47 and 26:17 f. respectively, are also often applied to Moses in Jewish tradition.

nonical perspective from which Paul undoubtedly read the call of Moses and the prophets, the OT prophetic call narratives merely extend and stand in continuity with the call of Moses. It has even been suggested by Stockhausen that the καί of 3:6a, since it has no explicit antecedent within the context, refers to Moses' being made competent in Exod. 4 to be a minister of the old covenant.[31] If this is so, then 3:6a itself indicates that Paul's implied point is that, like Moses, God has *also* made him sufficient to be a minister. In any case, the introduction of the sufficiency theme in 2:16b and the contrast between the ministries of the Spirit and the Law in 3:3b make it clear that in introducing the theme of his "sufficiency" in 3:4–6 Paul had such a comparison in view. Paul's call is elsewhere no doubt modeled after the call of the prophets, but 2 Cor. 2:16b and 3:5 demonstrate that Paul can also maintain that within the biblical tradition, the call of the prophets, like that of his own, follows the pattern of the call of Moses.

In picking up this tradition, however, Paul is not attempting to picture himself as the fulfillment of the Jewish expectation for a "second Moses" based on Deut. 18:18.[32] There is no allusion, verbal or conceptual, to this expecta-

---

[31] *Moses' Veil*, p. 84. In her words, "Without this reference to a previous making-competent by God, the καί of II Cor. 3:6a is superfluous" (p. 84). Renwick, *Temple*, p. 93, agrees. Though certainly possible, it could also simply be taken to refer to an additional action beyond what is stated in 3:5. In any case, Stockhausen, *Moses' Veil*, pp. 84, rightly sees the backdrop of 3:5 to be Exod. 4:10 and points to the prior work of Jones and Farrer (p. 84 n. 84), concluding that "... the situations reported in the two texts are so similar that a relationship must be assumed" (p. 84).

[32] Contra the main point of Peter R. Jones' very thorough and insightful work, *Second Moses,* and his "The Apostle Paul: Second Moses to the New Covenant Community, A Study in Pauline Apostolic Authority," in *God's Inerrant Word: An International Symposium on the Trustworthiness of Scripture,* ed. J.W. Montgomery, 1974, pp. 219–241, applied now in his *La Deuxieme Epitre,* pp. 25–28, 75 f. Concerning this point, J. Munck, *Paul and the Salvation of Mankind,* 1959, p. 57, was right in observing that, "If we think of Paul's relation to the figures of Old Testament redemptive history, there are no grounds for giving him any pre-eminent connection with any one of them." Jones may be right, therefore, to emphasize an understanding of Christ as a "second Moses" figure (albeit, without the function of giving a new law!), but he wrongly jumps categories from the Mosaic-call tradition to that of the "second Moses" expectation in the case of Paul. Paul can view his call as like that of Moses without viewing himself as a "second Moses" (as demonstrated in the call of the prophets other than Jeremiah), since to do so could imply either a confusion with the work of Christ, or a misunderstanding of his role. Technically speaking, Paul is not called to establish or mediate another covenant (Christ does that), nor does he mediate a new law (there is no new law in the new covenant, see below). Hence, if there were a clear "Second Moses" expectation in the first century (see next note), these material differences keep Paul from broadening out his argument from the call of Moses to an explicit self-understanding as a "second Moses." This and the absence of any allusion to Deut. 18:18 in the Pauline corpus cause me to "stop short of using the term 'Second Moses' in relation to Paul," quoting Jones' critique of my position in his review of my prior work, *EvQ* 4 (1987) 370–374, p. 373. In this case, what is in a name is quite significant, and it is not correct that I say "virtually everything about the Second Moses except the name" (p. 373). That Paul mediates the Spirit and not the law *per se* is a crucial distinction. For this same reason, however, Jones' critique, p. 374, of my use of the phrase "the Spirit-giver" for Paul is well taken and needs to be

tion in 2 Cor. 3 or elsewhere in the Pauline corpus. Nor does Paul use any fulfillment language in developing parallels between his ministry and the ministry of Moses. Indeed, although it is beyond the scope of this work to settle this issue, Robert Banks has argued that there is no evidence for a pre-Christian speculation concerning the return of Moses or a figure fashioned in Moses' likeness and given his particular functions. Rather, "where the expectation of a 'prophet like Moses' does occur the emphasis is laid more on God's action in raising up a prophetic spokesman than on any specific similarity to the ministry of Moses himself."[33] This is confirmed by Paul's argument in 2 Cor. 2:16–3:6. As his adaptation of the *structure* of Moses' call indicates, Paul is a fulfillment of this expectation only to the degree that *all* the legitimate prophets were understood to be prophets "like Moses" (Deut. 18:18). On the other hand, the expectation for a single, messianic "second Moses," if it did exist as a crystalized belief, is focused in the New Testament on Jesus alone. Rather, as Sandnes has now argued in detail, Paul conceived "of his apostolate and his commission to preach the gospel to the Gentiles in prophetic terms," while an investigation of the current post-biblical traditions concerning the OT prophets demonstrates that Paul's audience would also recognize "that Paul was presenting himself in a manner reminiscent of the ancient prophets."[34] In

---

nuanced, since it is Christ, not Paul, who grants the Spirit (cf. 1 Cor. 15:45). But despite our differences on the existence of an explicit second Moses conception in Paul's thinking, the conclusions Jones reached concerning the *function* of the comparison between Paul and Moses in 2 Cor. 3 are fundamentally the same, thus confirming much of the present study. Jones' final suggestion that, in order to bring the insights of our two studies together, we thus speak of a "*deutero*-mosaic prophecy of the *New* Covenant for the *eschatological* people of God" (p. 374) is therefore much more satisfying.

[33] R. Banks, "The Eschatological Role of Law in Pre- and Post-Christian Jewish Thought," in *Reconciliation and Hope, New Testament Essays on Atonement and Eschatology presented to L.L. Morris on his 60th Birthday*, ed. R. Banks, 1974, pp. 173–185, pp. 182 f. According to Banks, the earliest evidence for a return of Moses himself or a figure like him in his function as law-giver is Sifre Deut. 33:21 (attributed to R. Ishmael, 120–140 AD, though Sifre Deut. itself is at least 7th cent.). Cf. the expectation of "a (faithful) prophet" in 1 Macc. 4:46; 14:41. Banks sees only three references to a "prophet like Moses" in rabb. literature, each of which relates the figure to a past prophet (Pesik. 112a; Sifre Deut. 18:15, 16), rejecting the Deut. 18:15–18 background for Test. Levi 8:14 and viewing Test. Benj. 9:2 as a Christian interpolation. And rather than being a "second Moses" figure as often argued, Banks sees the Teacher of Righteousness in Qumran as a "law-interpreter" whose instructions are valid only to the dawn of the Messianic era (p. 180).

[34] This is the conclusion of his study, *Paul*, p. 240. See now Alan F. Segal, *Paul the Convert, The Apostolate and Apostasy of Saul the Pharisee*, 1990, pp. 8–11, who suggests that "Luke equally intended Paul's conversion to be understood as a prophetic call," so that the contrast often drawn by scholars between Paul's description of himself as "commissioned prophetically" and the Lukan portrayal of Paul as a convert is overdrawn. Yet Segal himself concludes that even though "Paul may cast his mission to the gentiles in terms of a prophetic commission ... Paul's great change of direction is better understood as a conversion" (i.e. from one Jewish sect to another, cf. p. 33), since his use of prophetic forms of speech is "restricted" and his Hellenistic cultural context was one in which conversion, rather than merely a prophetic calling to a vocation, was possible in a way not found in "traditional

short, "the apostle Paul is, then, as a preacher of the gospel of God's Son a latter day prophet,"[35] or as Peter Jones has now suggested, "Paul is conscious of participating, with Jesus and the other apostles, in the establishment of the *deutero*-mosaic prophecy of the *New* Covenant for the *eschatological* people of God."[36]

For Paul the parallel between his call and the call of Moses serves another function. As we saw in chapter one, the one motif associated with Moses which can be found throughout the literature we have examined, with the exception of the apologists,[37] is the concept of Moses as an authoritative presupposition for one's own ministry. We have also seen that when parallels were established between a later figure and the call or personage of Moses in the literature of Paul's tradition, these structural parallels were intended to support the latter's own theological program and/or authority. Hence, for Paul, as for the prophets and leaders of Israel before him,[38] the parallels to Moses in 2 Cor. 2:16 and 3:4 f. carry an *implicit* claim to speak with divinely sanctioned authority to the people of God. And like the OT prophets before him, this link between the ministry of Paul and that of Moses in 2 Cor. 2:16; 3:4 f. is seen most directly in the structural similarities between their respective calls to be God's spokesmen.

In a move that is thus well-prepared for in the prophetic writings and by the Moses-tradition in post-biblical Judaism, Paul's own use of this tradition serves a distinctly apologetic role in support of his authority and legitimacy as an apostle. By alluding to the call of Moses and its development in the call of the prophets, Paul associates his own argument for his "sufficiency" with the

---

first-temple Israelite society" (pp. 9, 14, 30). Nevertheless, Segal's point in comparing Luke and Paul is to show that prophetic commissioning and conversion were analogous in first century Jewish experience (cf. pp. 19–20), so that one cannot rule out the other. Moreover, in line with the argument of this present work, Segal argues that Luke's portrayal "draws on the Hebrew Bible for themes of prophetic calling," as found in the commissioning of Jeremiah, Isaiah, and Ezekiel, and that "these themes include an encounter with God, a divine commissioning, demur and resistance by the prophet, divine assurance, and preparation for the task by signs and wonders" (p. 9). It is questionable, however, whether Luke ever viewed Paul's experience of prophetic conversion as "the model experience for other believers" (p. 11) or as "the model for gentile conversion" (p. 35; cf. p. 14), as Segal maintains. The larger question raised by Segal's study, i.e. the relationship between Paul's conversion-call and Jewish mysticism and apocalypticism, except where it touches on the interpretation of 3:18 (see chapter five) is beyond the scope of this study.

[35] Sandnes, *Paul*, p. 65. An evaluation of the distinction which Sandnes then draws between Paul's "prophet-like apostolic self-understanding" and the identity of non-apostolic early Christian prophets, so that there are, in effect, two kinds of prophets in the early Church, is beyond the scope of this study (cf pp. 14 f. and his summary on pp. 244–246).

[36] "Review," p. 374.

[37] But cf. chapter one, n. 197.

[38] Sandnes, *Paul*, p. 65, is correct in arguing "that Paul did not understand his commission in terms of any particular prophet. He describes his call (in Gal. 1:15 f.) in terms and motifs that are analogous to the call of Isaiah, Jeremiah and the Servant of the Lord," pointing to Is. 49:1–6; Jer. 1:5–6; and Is. 50:4 (p. 63).

argument implicit in Moses' call and later developed throughout the OT prophetic call narratives (see chapter one).[39] Specifically, in alluding to the call of Moses and the prophets, Paul could effectively silence the criticism of his opponents that his prior persecution of the Church and present ongoing weakness rendered him insufficient for the apostolic ministry. By picturing his own call in terms of the call of Moses in 2:16b and 3:5, Paul is tacitly claiming that, like Moses, God's prophets have always been called by YHWH in spite of their own personal insufficiency in order to underscore the sufficiency of the God who called them (cf. 1 Cor. 15:9 f.; 2 Cor. 4:6 ff.; 12:7–9). As in this biblical tradition, in 2 Cor. 2:16b Paul asserts his sufficiency both *in spite of* his suffering and, as 2:17 makes clear, *because* of his suffering. That which apparently renders Paul unfit to be an apostle is the very thing which God uses as the revelatory vehicle and legitimating foundation of his ministry (cf. 2 Cor. 12:9 f.).

Paul's summary in 3:4–6 confirms this understanding. The Mosaic/prophetic pattern of "sufficiency-in-spite-of-insufficiency-by-the-grace-of-God," which was evident in the biblical call narratives and is implicit in Paul's argument in 2:14–17,[40] is now made explicit when the ἱκανός-theme is resumed and summarized in 3:5 f.[41] In 2 Cor. 3:5 Paul is simply drawing out the theological implication inherent in the structure of the OT call narratives themselves, while in 3:6a he alludes directly to his own call to be an apostle when he states that God[42] was the one who also ἱκάνωσεν ἡμᾶς διακόνους καινῆς διαθήκης.[43]

---

[39] For the apologetic role of the prophet's commission in the OT and in Paul's corresponding self-understanding as a prophet-like apostle, see Sandnes, *Paul*, pp. 67 f., 126–128, and his conclusion on p. 242. In his words, "Paul utilizes his call apologetically, that is to legitimize his claim to be an apostle. This has an interesting correspondence to how call-narratives function in OT" (p. 67). Hence, elsewhere "it is by recalling the tradition of the biblical prophets that Paul is able to lay a legitimate foundation for his apostolate" (p. 242), whereas in 2 Cor. 2:16 and 3:5 f. Paul alludes specifically to the paradigmatic call of Moses. For his support of my conclusions concerning the call-narrative pattern of God's overcoming the insufficiency of the one called as an act of divine grace and its function in Paul's self-understanding, see his pp. 64 f.

[40] For the basis of Paul's sufficiency in the call of God as referred to in 2:17, see my *Suffering and the Spirit*, pp. 163–174.

[41] See too Stockhausen, *Moses' Veil*, pp. 84, who also sees the parallel structure between the call of Moses and that of Paul. In her words, "II Corinthians 3:5–6 mimics Moses' attitude in this scene from Exodus perfectly. Exodus 4:10–12 is appropriated in the Pauline version: 'Not that we are competent in ourselves so as to reckon anything as coming from ourselves' – like Moses in Exod. 4:10; 'rather our competence is from God' – like Moses in Exod. 4:11–12" (p. 84).

[42] Plummer, *Second Corinthians*, p. 85, even suggests that the connection between ἱκανότης and θεοῦ in 3:5 f. might be an allusion to the divine name ἱκανός found in the LXX of Ruth 1:20 f.; Job 21:15; 31:2; 39:32: "It is just possible that St. Paul had this in his mind here; 'Our sufficiency comes from the Sufficient One.'"

[43] Jones has argued convincingly that 3:5 f. refer to Paul's call; see his *Second Moses*, pp. 36–39, and "Apostolic Authority," pp. 225 f., and the literature he cites. Furnish, *II*

With this resumption and resolution of the sufficiency motif in 3:5–6a Paul has come full circle in his argument. In 3:4–6 Paul moves from focusing on the evidence of the Spirit (cf. 2:14–3:3), in which he simply alluded to his call in 2:16b and 17b, to focusing on the nature of his call *itself*, in which he now simply recalls the work of the Spirit in 3:6b. In 2 Cor. 3:4–6, the focus of Paul's attention now falls on his sufficiency from God as one who was called like Moses. The sufficiency which Paul asserted to be his in 2:16f., and then supported with evidence from his ministry of suffering and the Spirit in 2:14–3:3, is now appropriately anchored in the source of both his call and his resulting ministry, God himself (cf. ἡ ἱκανότης ἡμῶν ἐκ τοῦ θεοῦ ὅς καὶ ἱκάνωσεν ... in 3:5f. and 1 Cor. 15:9f.). Paul's statement in 3:5f. thus also recapitulates Paul's starting point in 2:14, i.e. that God is the one who has triumphed over Paul and now leads him to death as his conquered slave (θριαμβεύειν). Paul's imagery in 2:14 presupposes what is now made explicit in 3:5f.: Paul owes his ministry to the conversion-call of God which rendered him the slave of Christ. It is not going too far, therefore, to suggest that the motif of praise which introduces Paul's argument in 2:14 (τῷ δὲ θεῷ χάρις) is also present in Paul's conclusion in 3:5–6a. For as Helmuth Kittel observed over 50 years ago concerning 3:4–6, inasmuch as Paul received his call and power from God, the praise of his work is, at the same time, praise to God.[44]

This doxological *inclusio* ought not blind us, however, to the apologetic point of Paul's *theo*logically based argument in 2:14–3:3. Paul's theology was forged in battle. Viewed in this light, the implication of Paul's argument of praise in 2:14–3:6a becomes clear. As we concluded in our earlier study,

"... if Paul's suffering and his ministry of the Spirit are, in fact, convincing evidence for the validity of his apostolic authority and ministry, a ministry which he attributes directly to God (cf. 2:14; 2:17b; 3:5f.), then the Corinthians' decision to reject that ministry becomes, from Paul's perspective, a rejection of God as well. It is for this reason that Paul ends his second canonical letter to the Corinthians, of which 2:14–3:6 is the 'theological heart,' with the severe warning to the Corinthians to test themselves in order to make sure that they are still 'in the faith.' For upon his arrival, Paul will be forced to use his power, revealed in his weakness, to tear down all those who have failed this test by rejecting his apostleship (cf. 13:5, 10)."[45]

Corinthians, p. 184, also suggests that the aorist ἱκάνωσεν ("he made sufficient") "would seem to look back to a specific call and commissioning to apostolic service (Gal. 1:15–16; cf. 1 Cor. 15:8)," but he does not point out the parallels to the call of Moses.

[44] *Die Herrlichkeit Gottes: Studien zu Geschichte und Wesen eines neutestamentlichen Begriffs*, BZNW 16, 1934, p. 203.

[45] *Suffering and the Spirit*, p. 221.

4. The Significance of Paul's Allusion to Moses
in 2 Cor. 2:16b and 3:4–5

As argued in my previous study, Paul's apologetic for the validity of his apostolic ministry was occasioned by the apparent contradiction between the profound life- and death-producing effects of the apostolic ministry on the one hand, and Paul's apparent insufficiency for this task because of his weakness and suffering on the other hand. This tension is both reflected and resolved within 2 Cor. 2:12–15 through Paul's assertion that his suffering itself, patiently endured in the power of the Spirit, served as the vehicle for the revelation of the cross of Christ and glory of God.[46]

In view of the investigation of the tradition of the "sufficiency" of Moses and its development presented in chapter one, the ἱκανός-motif in 2 Cor. 2:16b and 3:4 f. takes on an added significance beyond its explicit meaning of asserting Paul's own sufficiency for the apostolic ministry. In alluding to the call of Moses in 2:16b and 3:4 f., Paul once again responds to this same critique by implicitly emphasizing that his own weakness, i.e. his "insufficiency," like that of the insufficiency of Moses, cannot be regarded as that which disqualifies him for the apostolic ministry. Rather, as in the call of Moses, Paul's insufficiency provides the counterpart to God's elective grace. Moses was chosen and made sufficient for his ministry in spite of his "insufficiency," which in the biblical account is linked to his *speech defect* (see above, pp. 44 f.). In the same way, Paul can assert his sufficiency in spite of his own suffering and personal weaknesses, the latter of which, according to 2 Cor. 10:10 and 11:6, consist in part in his *unimpressive speech*, as well as his prior persecution of the church as stated in 1 Cor. 15:9 and Gal. 1:13. Paul's allusion to the call of Moses in 2 Cor. 2:16b and 3:4 f., like the similar allusions in the OT prophetic call narratives and in the non-canonical literature examined in chapter one, thus establishes a parallel between Paul and Moses which supports Paul's own claim to authority and "sufficiency" in spite of those aspects of his life which would seem to call such sufficiency into question.[47]

---

[46] For the development of these themes, see my *Suffering and the Spirit*, pp. 7–87. Heckel, *Kraft in Schwachheit*, has now made this same point on the basis of 2 Cor. 10:10 and 12:9, from which he concludes, pp. 119 f., that although both Paul and his opponents derived their authority from the power of Christ, "Der Unterschied entsteht jedoch dadurch, daß die Gegner von einer Analogie zwischen der Vollmacht eines Apostels und seinem kraftvollen Auftreten ausgehen ... während Paulus die Schwachheit gerade als Wirkungsfeld göttlicher Kraft erkannt hat (12:9a). Der *Gegensatz von Kraft und Schwachheit* ist *für die Gegner ein kontradiktorischer, für Paulus ein polarer*. Syntaktisch läßt sich dieser Unterschied daran ablesen, daß der Ausgangsvorwurf in 10:10 als Antithese formuliert ist (μὲν ... δέ), während Paulus sein Schlußresümee in 12:10b in einem Iterativ zusammenfaßt (ὅταν ... τότε)" (emphasis his; cf. his summary on pp. 323–325).

[47] See now Stockhausen, *Moses' Veil*, p. 42, who also sees that the force of Paul's argument is that, "like ... Moses, Paul's competence stems directly from God. Therefore, letters of recommendation are superfluous for him. Only his actions can prove whether or not he

Moreover, if the link made in later rabbinic literature between the overcoming of Moses' speech defect in Exod. 4:10 f. and the new creation was current in the tradition of Paul's day,[48] the allusion to the call of Moses in 3:4 f. might well prefigure Paul's explicit statement about the new creation in 2 Cor. 5:17–21. If so, it too forms part of that larger new creation motif which recent scholarship has recognized to be an integral part of the basic structure of Paul's thought in 2 Cor. 2:14–7:1.[49] There Paul's call to the ministry of reconciliation is an example of this divine act of new creation in Christ which comes "from God" (ἐκ τοῦ θεοῦ, 5:18), a close parallel to Paul's statement of the divine origin of his sufficiency as an *apostle* "from God" (ἐκ τοῦ θεοῦ) in 3:5. Hence, as Sandnes has now demonstrated, the very fact that Paul understands himself to be a prophet-like *apostle* of Jesus Christ, rather than a prophet *per se*, is itself an indication of Paul's eschatological perspective.[50] For as Sandnes has shown, Paul is declaring that his gospel and ministry are a fulfillment of the promises of the OT prophets and thus transcends the OT office of prophet in two ways: in the Christological foundation of his ministry and in his correspondingly different role within the history of redemption.[51] *Phenomenologically*, Paul's ministry can be seen as that of a "prophet," while *theologically* and *eschatologically* he is an apostle.[52] As Sandnes summarizes it,

"... Paul placed the prophets and himself in different positions vis-à-vis the gospel: the prophets as predicting it, he himself as proclaiming it ... This means that Paul's identification of the time in which he was acting separated him from the prophets and put

---

comes from God." But she does not trace this to the explicit allusions to the call of Moses in the text, but to the criticism of Paul's opponents which brought about the comparisons between "Paul's covenant and the covenant of Moses," as "the fulcrum of his argument and the basis of the reproaches of his opponents." The theme of the call of Moses, though recognized by Stockhausen (see above, n. 31), thus remains relatively undeveloped in her work (cf. e.g., p. 85).

[48] For the development of the new creation motif in 2 Cor. 5:17, see P. Stuhlmacher, "Erwägungen zum ontologischen Charakter der καινὴ κτίσις bei Paulus," *EvTh* 27 (1967) 1–35. See esp. pp. 27–29, in which Stuhlmacher demonstrates that for Paul partaking in the new creation meant being put into the realm of and experiencing the reality of the Spirit through one's calling and baptism as a proleptic realization of the future new creation (cf. Rom. 6:3; 1 Cor. 12:13; Rom. 8:10 f.). The reality and power of the new creation is that of the Spirit in his work of making the word of God effective (cf. pp. 27, 35). For the sources in which the link between the call of Moses and the new creation is made, see p. 27 n. 99.

[49] It is beyond the scope of this present work to develop this crucial insight in detail. But see now the important works of G.K. Beale, "The Old Testament Background of Reconciliation in 2 Corinthians 5–7 and its Bearing on the Literary Problem of 2 Corinthians 6.14–7.1," *NTS* 35 (1989) 550–581), C. Marvin Pate, *Adam Christology as the Exegetical & Theological Substructure of 2 Corinthians 4:7–5:21*, 1991, and now William J. Webb, *Returning Home, New Covenant and Second Exodus as the Context for 2 Corinthians 6.14–7.1*, JSNT Suppl. 85, 1993, who surveys the new covenant and second Exodus traditions throughout 2:14–7:4.

[50] See his *Paul*, pp. 18, 243 f.

[51] Cf. Sandnes, *Paul*, p. 18.

[52] Sandnes, *Paul*, p. 18.

them into different epochs of God's plan of salvation ... We think Paul would have put it this way: The eschatological prophets proclaiming the final comfort in the Last Days are the apostles of Jesus Christ proclaiming the gospel."[53]

Due to the well established Mosaic/prophetic call tradition inherited by the early church, Paul's allusion to the call of Moses in 2:16 and 3:4 f. was already enough to support Paul's claim to apostolic legitimacy in view of the evidential arguments already presented in 2 Cor. 2:14–3:3.[54] In the non-canonical tradition of the call and sufficiency of Moses, however, the glory and sufficiency of Moses become increasingly exaggerated, while his weakness, if not completely neglected, at least receives little notice. In stark contrast to this, we find no hint of such a development in the Pauline corpus. In this respect Paul returns to the biblical account rather than picking up the themes that are present, for example, in the Testament of Moses and the Biblical Antiquities of Pseudo-Philo, and which find their extreme representation in the apologetic literature in one direction, and in the rabbinic materials in the other (see chapter one).

Finally, the allusion to the figure of Moses in 2 Cor. 2:16 corresponds to the fact that Moses' preeminent authority stands without question and could thus be used freely as an authoritative presupposition for Paul's own ministry. In this regard Paul's reference to the call of Moses in 2:16 and its further development in 3:4 f. stand in a long line of tradition, both within and outside of the canon. In addition, Paul's allusion to Moses is motivated by his conception of the parallels in function between his own ministry and the ministry of Moses. Of all the OT figures, only Moses embodies the functions of mediator,[55] prophet,[56] and priest,[57] all of which are vital aspects of Paul's self-conception.

---

[53] Sandnes, *Paul*, pp. 243 f.

[54] The allusion to Moses' call found in 2 Cor. 2:16b and 3:4 f. may also be present in the call of Paul as reported in Acts 9, 22, and 26, though the allusions are general enough to be regarded merely as typical of theophanies, rather than explicitly referring to the call of Moses. For the point that Moses is explicitly in view in Acts, see Paul Demann, "Mose und das Gesetz bei Paulus," pp. 205–264, p. 207 n. 4, and Jones, *Second Moses*, pp. 72 ff. But Jones' corresponding attempt to link 2 Cor. 4:5–7 to these accounts from Acts in order to argue that 2 Cor. 4:5–7 also refers to the call of Moses remains unconvincing to me.

[55] For Paul as mediator, see my previous study, *Suffering and the Spirit*, pp. 51 f., 54, 63 f., 67–69, 71 f., 76 f., 83–89, 220; and below, chapter three.

[56] Besides the well-known use of prophetic call motifs in Paul's descriptions of his own call (cf. the programmatic article of Traugott Holtz, "Zum Selbstverständnis des Apostels Paulus," *ThLZ* 91 (1966) 322–330 and the discussion of J. Chr. Beker, *Paul*, pp. 10, 115–118), see now O. Hofius, "Unbekannte Jesusworte," in *Das Evangelium und die Evangelien*, WUNT 28, ed. P. Stuhlmacher, 1983, pp. 355–382, pp. 357–359, who argues convincingly that 1 Thess. 4:15–17 represents an example of Paul's ability to speak as an authoritative prophet, and the insightful work of Karl Olav Sandnes, *Paul – One of the Prophets?* WUNT 2. Reihe, 43, 1991.

[57] See e.g. Rom. 15:16, 19 and D.W.B. Robinson, "The Priesthood of Paul in the Gospel of Hope," in *Reconciliation and Hope, FS L.L. Morris on his 60th Birthday*, ed. R. Banks, 1974, pp. 231–245, and the helpful summary by Konrad Weiß, "Paulus – Priester der Christlichen Kultgemeinde," *ThLZ* 79 (1954) 355–364.

Moreover, like Moses,[58] Paul too was called to suffer for his people, an aspect of Paul's ministry which we argued previously to be of central importance in 2 Corinthians as a whole.[59] Thus, we ought not to be surprised that Paul turns to Moses in order to provide support for his own sufficiency in 2 Cor. 2:16b and 3:4 f., just as he can picture his own willingness to suffer on behalf of Israel in Mosaic terms in Romans 9:3.[60] In doing so, Paul joins a long standing tradition, though his own sober use of it distances him from certain developments within it. And naturally, if Paul's opponents in Corinth were themselves referring to Moses in some way to support their own ministry,[61] and/or criticizing Paul's attitude toward the Law as the ministry of Moses, then the introduction of this theme in 2:16b becomes all the more understandable.[62] But whatever the case, against the background we have outlined in chapter one, Paul's question in 2:16b and its development in 3:4 f. not only explicitly assert his sufficiency, but also *implicitly* support this assertion by casting Paul's call in the mold of the call of Moses.

5. Paul, the "Servant" (διάκονος) of the New Covenant (2 Cor. 3:6a)

The specific confidence that Paul has, then, as a result of his call like that of the call of Moses, is that God has made him sufficient in spite of his own personal insufficiency (ἱκάνωσεν ἡμᾶς) to be a "servant" (διάκονος) of the new covenant. A survey of Pauline usage makes clear that unlike his common and favorite self-designation of "apostle" (ἀπόστολος),[63] which points directly to the divinely granted authority and office of Paul's ministry, the designation "servant" (διάκονος) refers to his own particular *activity* of service which he

---

[58] On Moses' willingness to suffer for his people, see chapter three, and Albert Gelin, "Moses im Alten Testament," in *Moses in Schrift*, pp. 49 f., who makes this point in reference to Num. 11:12 and Exod. 32:31 f.; the parallels between the Isaianic Servant of YHWH and Moses developed by Jones, *Second Moses*, pp. 118–137; G. Vermes, "Gestalt," p. 80; and R. Bloch, "Gestalt," pp. 130–140.

[59] See my *Suffering and the Spirit*, pp. 41–87.

[60] On Romans 9:3 as an allusion to Exod. 32:31 f., see G.P. Wiles, *Paul's Intercessory Prayers*, SNTSMS 24, 1974, p. 256 (who points to J. Munck, *Christus und Israel*, 1956, pp. 27 f.); Otto Betz, "Die heilsgeschichtliche Rolle Israels bei Paulus," *ThB* 9 (1978) 1–21, p. 17; and now P. Stuhlmacher, *Der Brief an die Römer*, NTD 6, 1989, p. 132, who also points to the parallel between Rom. 9:3 and 2 Cor. 3:4 ff., albeit without reference to the call of Moses in the latter passage.

[61] So e.g. D. Georgi, *Gegner*, pp. 258–282, and Jones, *Second Moses*, pp. 41–59, 79.

[62] As Jones, *Second Moses*, p. 33, suggests, "the cruciality and appropriateness of demonstrating the legitimacy of his apostolate may well have enabled Paul to compare the experience of his call and the exercise of his ministry with the call and ministry of Moses in the Old Covenant."

[63] Cf. Rom. 1:1; 11:13; 1 Cor. 1:1; 9:1 f.; 2 Cor. 1:1; Gal. 1:1; Eph. 1:1; Col. 1:1; 1 Tim. 1:1; 2:7; 2 Tim. 1:1, 11; Titus 1:1.

exercises as an apostle, i.e. the proclamation of the gospel as the revelation of God and the mediation of God's Spirit.[64] Moreover, Paul can share this title with those who are also engaged in the proclamation of the gospel or function as authoritative delegates on behalf of a church.[65] Indeed, even Satan has his "servants" (διάκονοι) in 2 Cor. 11:15 and a pagan ruler used by God to accomplish his purposes can be called a "servant" (διάκονος) of God (Rom. 13:4), while Christ himself is described in the function of his earthly ministry as a διάκονος to the circumcised in Rom. 15:8 and Moses' ministry of the Law is called a διακονία in 2 Cor. 3:7,9.

In this regard Paul's use of "servant" (διάκονος) parallels his use of the title "slave [of Christ Jesus]" (δοῦλος [Χριστοῦ Ἰησοῦ]), which can refer to Paul's own identity and function in ministry, as well as to that of others.[66] In Col. 1:7 and 4:7, Paul can even use "fellow slave" (σύνδουλος) and "servant (διάκονος) of Christ" as tandem, overlapping descriptions of Epaphras and Tychicus. Moreover, Paul's role as a "servant" and "slave" is tied closely to the corresponding "service" or life of enslavement to others or to God which characterizes those who are "servants" or "slaves of Christ."[67] And as with διάκονος, in Phil. 2:7 Christ can also be referred to as a δοῦλος in regard to his

---

[64] For Paul's use of διακον-terminology to describe his apostolic ministry in service to the Gospel, cf. Rom. 11:13; 2 Cor. 3:3, 6, 8 f.; 4:1; 5:18; 6:3 f.; 11:8; Eph. 3:7; Col. 1:23, 25; 1 Tim. 1:12. For a full-length treatment of the meaning of the διακον-terminology in the NT within its historical and linguistic environment, see now John N. Collins, DIAKONIA, Reinterpreting the Ancient Sources, 1990, esp. pp. 195–215 on Pauline usage. Collins' central thesis that for Paul the terminology refers to the function of proclaiming the Gospel ("spokesman") and, specifically in 2 Cor. 2:14–6:13, to Paul's role as a "medium" of God's revelation and glory, rather than to a general Christian service by the church as a whole or to the work of "deacons," supports the view and interpretation being argued here (cf. pp. 197 f., 203–205). In addition, as 1 Cor. 16:15–18 indicates, εἰς διακονίαν can also refer to a Gospel-centered mission or delegation which focuses on representing a church in an authoritative manner (cf. p. 224 and 1 Tim. 1:12; 2 Tim. 4:11; Acts 11:29). To take up the details of Collins' work is beyond the scope of this study.

[65] Cf. 1 Cor. 3:5 (with Apollos); 16:1 (with Phoebe); 1 Cor. 16:15 (with the household of Stephanas); 2 Cor. 11:23 (ironically with his opponents!); Eph. 6:21; Col. 4:7 (with Tychicus); Col. 1:7 (with Epaphras); 4:17 (with Archippus); 1 Tim. 4:6 (with Timothy).

[66] For δοῦλος in reference to Paul as an apostle, cf. Rom. 1:1; Gal. 1:10; Phil. 1:1; Titus 1:1; for its use in reference to others, cf. Phil. 1:1; Eph. 6:6; Col. 4:12; 2 Tim. 2:24.

[67] For the Spirit-endowed ministries of "service" (διακονία) exercised by those set aside by the church to preach and represent it, see Rom. 12:7; 1 Cor. 12:5; 16:15; Eph. 4:12; 2 Tim. 4:11; Phm 13; Phil. 1:1; 2 Tim. 1:18; and 1 Tim. 3:8, 10, 12 f.; for the use of διακονία/ διακονέω to refer to the collection for Jerusalem as an expression of the grace of God and ministry of the saints to one another, in which Paul participates as a servant, cf. Rom. 15:25, 31; 2 Cor. 8:4, 19, 20; 9:1, 12 f.; for the ministry of an evangelist, cf. 2 Tim. 4:5. For the use of δοῦλος/δουλεία/δουλεύω/δουλόω terminology to express one's relationship of service or "enslavement" to God/righteousness (or sin), cf. Rom. 6:6, 16 f., 18–20, 22; 7:6, 25; 8:15, 21; 12:11; 14:18; 16:18; 1 Cor. 7:22; Gal. 4:3, 8 f.; 5:1; Eph. 6:7; Col. 3:24; 4:1; 1 Thess. 1:9; Titus 2:3; 3:3; for its use to describe the believers' service to one another, cf. 1 Cor. 9:19 (though free, Paul makes himself a slave to all); 2 Cor. 4:5 (Paul preaches himself as a slave of the Corinthians on account of Christ); Gal. 5:13; Phil. 2:22; 1 Tim. 6:2.

earthly life of humble obedience in taking on the likeness of humanity and taking up the cross.

In view of this widespread overlap in usage and application, even to Christ, it is saying too much to argue that the διάκονοι were a special *class* of co-workers who were engaged especially in preaching or teaching,[68] or to suggest that its special connotation was one of lowliness or humility, anymore than that of δοῦλος, or even ἀπόστολος, especially since all three speak of one's subordinate allegiance to God or Christ against the backdrop of their use in profane literature and in Judaism.[69] Rather, the stress of the term διάκονος is on one's *function* or *act* of mediation and representation, or in Collins' words, "messengers on assignment from God or Christ."[70] Moreover, unlike Paul's use of the description δοῦλος, διάκονος is never used by Paul as a title of authority or introduction, most likely because the former is that "predicate of honor" which in the OT "was a title of honor to refer to those chosen by God and predestined for his service"[71] and thus retains in Paul's use a titular connotation not found in διάκονος. The designation "servant" is therefore a more general term which can be used to describe those engaged in a particular work of service (διακονία).

In the context of 2 Cor. 3, therefore, Paul's use of διάκονος to describe himself points to his *role* or *function* as an apostle,[72] rather than to his authority as

---

[68] Contra E.E. Ellis, "Paul and His Co-Workers," *NTS* 17 (1970–71), pp. 437–452, though J.D.G. Dunn, *Jesus and the Spirit*, 1975, p. 288, goes too far in arguing against Ellis that, in accordance with the more common view, διάκονος "makes better sense as a general description of anyone whose activity served Christ, the gospel, or one of his churches."

[69] Sverre Aalen, "Versuch einer Analyse des Diakonia-Begriffes im Neuen Testament," *The New Testament Age, Essays in Honor of Bo Reicke, Vol. 1*, ed. W.C. Weinrich, 1984, 1–13, p. 8, points to the similarity between διάκονος, δοῦλος in Mtt. 20:26 f.par. and Col. 4:7 and to the fact that in Jewish literature עֶבֶד can stand for both, and encompass the שַׁמָּשׁ in the synagogue. Hence, a "servant" is one upon whom responsibilities are laid (p. 9). Aalen points out that διάκονος is one of the few theological concepts in the NT which is developed independent of the OT in that it occurs only a few times in the LXX to mean "Dienerschaft," while διακονέω does not occur at all (p. 9). Its Aramaic equivalent שַׁמַּשׁ/שְׁמַשׁ (cf. Dan. 7:10) comes to refer to serving at meal times and is equated with עֲבַד in *Tg. Onq.* Gen. 18:8 (p. 106), whereas profane Greek also used διακονία to mean a "business," or "occupation" (p. 11).

[70] *DIAKONIA*, p. 195, with reference to 1 Cor. 3:5; 2 Cor. 3:6; 6:4; 11:23.

[71] Peter T. O'Brien, *Colossians, Philemon*, WBC Vol. 44, 1982, p. 15. O'Brien points to Abraham (Ps. 105:42), Moses (Ps. 105:26; 2 Kgs. 18:12), David (2 Sam. 7:5; Ps. 89:4, 21), and the prophets (Amos 3:7) as examples of God's slaves in the OT. In Paul, cf. Rom. 1:1; Phil. 1:1; Gal. 1:10. In addition, see cf. Bar. 2:28; Wis. 10:16 for the continuation of Moses as the servant of God *par excellence*.

[72] Cf. J. Roloff, *Apostolat – Verkündigung – Kirche. Ursprung, Inhalt und Funktion des kirchlichen Apostelamtes nach Paulus, Lukas und den Pastoralbriefen*, 1965, pp. 121–123, who argues for the close relationship in Paul's usage between δοῦλος and διάκονος, with the latter carrying the nuance of Paul's call, while the former refers to the christological components of Paul's apostleship, and in particular his suffering (p. 122). But this study has shown that the latter can be used in the context of Paul's calling, especially if necessitated by the presence of Paul's opponents (see Conclusion). Roloff's point is well taken, however, that

an apostle *per se.*[73] In using this designation, Paul is calling attention to the way in which his ministry actually works, i.e. his activity as an apostle as a result of God's calling.[74] As the parallel to 2 Cor. 3:3 and 6a in 1 Cor. 3:5–7 makes clear, for Paul to call himself a "servant" is to recognize that his particular act of service is directly under the sovereignty of God and that the effectiveness of his ministry is utterly dependent upon God as the one who both gives the opportunity for faith and causes the subsequent growth. Hence, as Kleinknecht has pointed out, "Der Skopus all dieser Aussagen ist: sie sind nichts aus sich selbst, nicht ihrer kann man sich rühmen."[75] In 1 Cor. 3 and 4, this service is Paul's stewardship of the "mysteries of God" which bring about faith (1 Cor. 3:5; 4:1). Moreover, as Käsemann has rightly emphasized, the διαχονία ("ministry") of Paul "receives as its content, namely, suffering as the actual form of appearance ("Erscheinungsform") of the apostolic service of Christ."[76] As we have seen above, the activity primarily in view in the context of 2 Cor. 3 is Paul's corresponding role as a mediator of the *Spirit* (cf. 3:3), which is now further defined in terms of Paul's having been called and made sufficient to be in service *of the new covenant.* Paul's role as a mediator of the Spirit through his suffering is thus first and foremost to bring about faith and spiritual growth in Christ (cf. 1 Cor. 3:1–3), which comes about as a result of being "the temple of God" in that "the Spirit of God dwells in you" (1 Cor. 3:1; 16).

---

the use of the terminology of "servant" by Paul recalls its use in Mk. 10:45 and Lk. 22:27, so that in 2 Cor. 3 it points in particular to Paul's suffering in light of the suffering of Christ and at the same time calls into question the legitimacy of Paul's opponents.

[73] Contra the emphasis of Collins, *DIAKONIA*, pp. 197 ff., that the term itself refers to a "specific entitlement" (p. 197) and is a "technical expression" of Paul's claim to authority (p. 198, with reference to 2 Cor. 6:4) which conveys the "precise connotations of a person entrusted with God's full message, charged with the duty to deliver it, and endowed with the right to be heard and believed" (p. 197). Collins concludes concerning Paul's apology in 2 Cor. 3:4–4:6 that Paul's claim to legitimacy is "explicit in the phrase 'having this ministry (διαχονίαν)'" in 4:1, even though Collins himself recognizes, as will be argued below, that "if (Paul) can convince the Corinthians that by virtue of his preaching the glory (of God which he mediates) has reached them unimpeded and resides in them unimpaired, his status as God's authorized preacher is established" (p. 204). Thus it seems more accurate to argue that Paul's assertion of authority in 3:4 ff. is not carried by the διαχον-terminology, but by his evidential arguments, which may explain why he avoids using the terminology of apostle in favor of the functional designation "servant."

[74] This corresponds to Sverre Aalen's thesis, "Analyse des Diakonia-Begriffes," pp. 2, 4, 6, that in the NT in general, διαχονία, διαχονέω, διάχονος should not be taken in a general sense as synonyms for love of neighbor or as a general ethical principle, but in the limited sense to refer to activities in the church as a sign of the fellowship of faith. As its application to the collection in Rom. 15:25 f. and 2 Cor. 8:4; 9:13 demonstrates, this means that "service" and "fellowship" are not a subjective feeling, but an activity whose basis is in the confession of the Gospel (p. 7).

[75] K. Kleinknecht, *Der leidende Gerechtfertigte*, WUNT 2. Reihe 13, 1984, p. 188.

[76] "Die Legitimität des Apostels. Eine Untersuchung zu II Korinther 10–13," *ZNW* 41 (1942) 33–71, p. 53.

That the focus of Paul's being a "servant" (διάκονος) in 3:6a is on his role as a mediatory agent of the Spirit is confirmed first by the fact that Paul's statement in 3:6a picks up his prior use of the related verb form διακονηθεῖσα [ὑφ' ἡμῶν] ("being ministered [by us]") from 3:3, where it is explicitly tied to his apostolic role of mediating the "Spirit of the living God."[77] In using the διακον-terminology in 3:3 in reference to the Corinthians as a "letter of Christ," Paul's point is to "extend the preceding metaphor of the Corinthians as Paul's 'letter of recommendation' by stressing that the Corinthians owe their existence as Christians to Christ as he was made known to them by the Spirit in the gospel ministry of Paul (cf. 1 Cor. 2:1–16; 4:15; 2 Cor. 10:13 f.)."[78] Second, it is supported by the development of Paul's "ministry of the Spirit" (ἡ διακονία τοῦ πνεύματος, 3:8) under the rubric of the letter/Spirit contrast in 3:6b–18. In referring to himself as a "servant of the new covenant," Paul emphasizes that he has been called to perform those activities that are in accord with the new covenant ministry of the Spirit as already experienced by the Corinthians as a result of Paul's apostolic ministry of suffering and proclamation of the gospel. This is confirmed by Paul's reference to himself as a "servant" (διάκονος) of the gospel in Colossians 1:23 and Ephesians 3:6 f. Why Paul is called to this particular activity of the Spirit, and the exact nature of this apostolic ministry of the new covenant in relationship to that of the ministry of Moses under the old covenant, are then made clear in 3:6b–18.

---

[77] Contra E. Stegemann, "Der Neue Bund im Alten, Zum Schriftverständnis des Paulus in II Kor 3," *ThZ* 42 (1986) 97–114, p. 107, who suggests that the plural in 3:6 refers to Paul, together with his addressees. For the arguments against those who, like W. Baird, "Letters of Recommendation. A Study of II Cor. 3:1–3," *JBL* 80 (1961) 166–172, pp. 168–171, and J.D.G. Dunn, argue that rather than being a reference to Paul's apostolic ministry of the gospel, διακονηθεῖσα in 2 Cor. 3:3 ought to be translated "deliver" or "carry" in reference to the fact that Paul delivers this "letter" as "Christ's postman," *(Baptism in the Holy Spirit, A Re-Examination of the New Testament Teaching on the Gift of the Holy Spirit in Relation to Pentecostalism Today,* 1970, p. 137), so that Paul is merely the courier (Baird, p. 169) of a "Himmelsbrief" (so Windisch, Lietzmann. Wendland, Georgi, etc.), see my *Suffering and the Spirit,* pp. 195–203. In construing the meaning of διακονέω in 2 Cor. 3:3 and in reference to the collection in Rom. 15:25; 2 Cor. 8:19–20, one ought not to draw a hard distinction between Paul's "ministry (διακονία) of the Gospel to the Gentiles" (Rom. 11:13; 2 Cor. 5:18; 6:3; 11:8) and his role in delivering the collection, which is also called a διακονία (see n. 67 above). In both cases the work is done to the glory of God (cf. 2 Cor. 8:19; 9:12 f.) and derives from the grace of God (cf. 2 Cor. 4:15; 8:1, 6 f., 19; 9:12 f.). Moreover, Gal. 2:7, 9 makes it clear that Paul's mandate to remember the poor is an integral part of his larger gospel ministry (p. 197). Hence, "the collection is designated a διακονία and is said to be 'ministered' (διακονέω) by Paul and his co-workers precisely because it is part of Paul's larger διακονία of the gospel" (pp. 197 f.).

[78] *Suffering and the Spirit,* p. 199.

Excursus: Διάκονος in the LXX, Pseudepigrapha, Josephus and Philo and Its Connotation in Paul

It is well-known that διάκονος occurs infrequently in the Septuagint, as does διακονία,[79] while διακονέω does not occur at all. In Esther 1:10; 2:2; 6:3, 5 διάκονος refers to various servants of the king, and in the first passage one group of these servants is also defined as the εὐνοῦχοι ("eunuchs") who governed the king's harem (cf. Esth. 2:14). In Proverbs 10:4 and 4 Macc. 9:17 it refers to a servant in general, with the connotation of the servant's low status.[80] A direct line of influence from the LXX to the New Testament, and to Paul in particular, is thus not supported by this meager backdrop. Nor is there any evidence of the development of a special Christian use of the terminology. Rather, as the extensive work of Collins has now demonstrated, its use in Paul reflects its common parlance in the culture and literature of the day, from which it has also infiltrated Hellenistic Jewish conceptions.[81] It is this latter context, especially as developed in Josephus and Philo, that sheds special light on Paul's usage.

Among the pseudepigraphical writings preserved in Greek, the noun διάκονος occurs only in the T. Judah 14:2, where wine is called the "servant (διάκονον) of the spirit of promiscuity."[82] The verb διακονέω is found eight times, while the corresponding noun διακονία occurs in T. Job 11:1-3 and 15:1.[83] In the T. Abraham 9:3, Abraham refers to himself as "a sinner" and the "completely worthless servant" (ἀνάξιον

---

[79] Cf. Esth. 6:3, 5, where οἱ ἐκ τῆς διακονίας is used in Alexandrinus for οἱ διάκονοι and 1 Macc. 11:58, where it refers to the table service.

[80] In Esth. 1:10; 2:2; 6:3 it translates שׁרת ("to minister, serve" in Piel, usually of higher domestic or royal service, Brown, Driver, Briggs, *A Hebrew and English Lexicon*, 1976, p. 1058), and in Esth. 2:2; 6:3, 5 it represents נער ("servant" in the sense of a "personal attendant," or "household servant," *Hebrew Lexicon*, p. 655).

[81] See his *DIAKONIA*, pp. 73-194. It will be helpful to quote part of his conclusion at length: "Thus, the words show no signs of having developed in meaning over the course of changing literary eras, the sense of 'to serve at table' cannot be called 'the basic meaning' – in fact that sense has to be perceived as a particular application of a word capable of signifying doing messages and being another person's agent – and the more comprehensive idea of 'serving' is vague and inadequate. If the words denote actions or positions of 'inferior value,' there is at the same time often the connotation of something special, even dignified, about the circumstance, and though they may truly be said to be unbiblical, they have wide religious connotations ... the idea expressed by the words is that of the go-between ... the words ... speak ... of an action done in the name of another. This, which applies also to actions done in the service of God, means that the words do not speak directly of 'attitude' like 'lowliness' but express concepts about undertakings for another, be that God or man, master or friend. In accepting such undertakings or in having them imposed on him, the agent has a mandate as well as a personal obligation ..." (p. 194, quoting the common view of the meaning of the word as expressed by Eduard Schweizer, *Church Order in the New Testament*, ET, 1961, pp. 173-178).

[82] Text from M. De Jonge, *The Testaments of the Twelve Patriarchs, A Critical Edition of the Greek Text*, PVTG 1,2 1978, p. 67; trans. from H.C. Kee, "Testaments of the Twelve Patriarchs," *OTP, Vol. 1*, p. 799.

[83] According to the *Concordance Grecque des Pseudepigraphes D'Ancien Testament*, ed. A.M. Denis, 1987, p. 258.

δοῦλον) of Michael the "commander-in-chief"[84] when he beseeches him to take yet another message back to the Lord, asking Michael "to serve" (διακονῆσαι) him by doing so. In a text also related to Michael, a fragment of the *Ass. Mos.* refers to the fact that Michael served (δεδιηκονηκέναι) at the tomb of Moses.[85] In Joseph and Aseneth 2:11 the verb is used to describe the action of the seven virgins who wait on Aseneth as her servants. In Joseph and Aseneth 13:12, it is then used to describe her prayer that she be given to Joseph as his "maidservant" (παιδίσκην), ἵνα ἐγώ ... διακονήσω αὐτῷ καὶ δουλεύσω αὐτῷ forever. The parallel use of διακονέω and δουλεύσω in this passage highlights the connotation of slave status that sometimes accompanies the use of this terminology.[86] Playing on this connotation of the slave status of the one who serves, "repentance" is personified or even allegorized in Joseph and Aseneth 15:7, where we read that although she is in the heavens and is exceedingly beautiful and good as the daughter of the most high, nevertheless repentance herself will "serve" (διακονήσει) forever those who repent by being a go-between between them and God.[87] With this same connotation of slave status, διακονία is used in T. Job 11:1–3 for the "service" of feeding the poor (at tables?) which Job and others, with Job's help, engage in.[88] In the T. Job 12:2 διακονῆσαι is then used for the one who is not rich enough to give to the poor himself, but who nevertheless humbles himself instead by serving the poor at Job's table. In T. Job 15:1 διακονία is used to refer to the "ministry of the service" (τὴν ὑπηρεσίαν τῆς διακονίας) of Job's practice of feeding the widows and afterwards leading them in worshipping God with hymns and psalms (cf. 14:1–5), while in 15:4,8 διακονοῦσιν and διακονοῦμεν refer to the serving at table done by slaves and by Job's children respectively, concerning whom Job is worried that they might complain, "We are sons of this rich man, and these goods are ours. Why then do we also serve?" (15:8).[89] The point is that both Job and his children (who may complain about it) are models of righteousness in that they exercise their piety by joining the servants in providing for the poor and widows like those of a slave-status.

Josephus too employs διάκονος for the servant or attendant who serves as a helper or middleman for others. But what is striking is the way Josephus employs this designation in religious contexts in which the διάκονος speaks and/or acts on behalf of God.[90] In *Bell.* III.354 Josephus portrays his surrender to the Romans not as the act of a traitor, but as the act of God's servant (διάκονος).[91] Josephus' subsequent prediction of Vespasian's rise to power in *Bell.* IV.626 is described in terms of his being a "servant

---

[84] Greek (Recension A): ἀρχιστράτηγος; text from Michael E. Stone, *The Testament of Abraham, The Greek Recensions,* Texts and Translations 2, Pseudepigrapha Series 2, 1972, p. 20; Trans. from E.P. Sanders, "Testament of Abraham," *OTP, Vol. 1,* p. 886.

[85] As quoted in Oecumenius, *Comm. in N.T., II,* in *Jud. Apost. cath. epist., I* (to Jude 9); text from A.M. Denis, *Fragmenta pseudepigraphorum quae supersunt graeca,* PVTG 3, 1970, p. 67. A variant on this tradition reads διηκόνησε (cf. n.k, p. 67).

[86] Text from Marc Philonenko, *Joseph et Aseneth, Introduction, Texte Critique, Traduction et Notes,* Studia Post-Biblica 13, 1968, pp. 134, 176.

[87] As argued by Collins, *DIAKONIA,* p. 123.

[88] Greek text from Robert A. Kraft, et al., *The Testament of Job according to the SV Text,* Texts and Translations 5, Pseudepigrapha Series 4, 1974, pp. 32 ff.

[89] Trans. from R.P. Spittler, "Testament of Job," *OTP, Vol. 1,* p. 845.

[90] For a detailed study of Josephus' many references, see Collins.

[91] Trans. and text of Josephus are taken from H. St. J. Thackeray, Ralph Marcus, Allen Wikgren, and Louis H. Feldman, *Josephus, Vol. I–IX,* LCL, 1966–1969.

of the voice of God" (διάκονον τῆς τοῦ θεοῦ φωνῆς). In a related way, the Zealots of the revolt are described in *Bell.* IV.388 as servants of the prophet's pronouncements, i.e. the instruments through which they come to pass. And in *Ant.* VIII.354 Elisha is called the "servant and disciple" (μαθητὴς καὶ διάκονος) of Elijah.

In the same way, a διακονία can be the service rendered by the servant class *(Bell.* III.70), a cup-bearer *(Ant.* II.65; XI.163), or even that of Balaam's ass *(Ant.* IV. 65). But it can also refer to the "service of God" (διακονία τοῦ Θεοῦ) rendered by Samuel as a prophet *(Ant.* V.344, 349), or the "service" of the sacrifices to God in the temple *(Ant.* VIII.101; X.57). Josephus also employs the related verb διακονέω to express the action of the ministry of the priest *(Ant.* III.155; VII.365; X.72) or Jeremiah's service as a prophet to those who asked him to entreat God on their behalf *(Ant.* X.177).[92] In non-religious contexts it can correspondingly refer to being sent with a message *(Bell.* IV. 252) or on a mission *(Bell.* VI. 298), and in *Ant.* XVIII. 261–262, 265, 269, 277 it is used for the rendering of service by an envoy or ambassador (πρεσβευτής), who, like Paul in 1 Cor. 9:16, is under constraint (ἀνάγκη) as a steward-slave (cf. οἰκονομίαν in 1 Cor. 9:17 and 1 Cor. 4:1) to perform his duty or be punished, and in 2 Cor. 5:20 is compelled (συνέχει) by the love of God to speak the message of reconciliation on Christ's behalf as his ambassador (πρεσβεύομεν).[93] This corresponds to the emphasis

---

[92] Cf. too William L. Lane, "Covenant: The Key to Paul's Conflict with Corinth," *TynB* 33 (1982) 3–29, p. 17, who points to Epictetus, Diss. 3.22, 26, 28, 69; 4.7, 20, 24, 65 for the use of διάκονος to refer to the wise man as God's servant in his function as an instrument and witness of God.

[93] Though in this case Petronius finally rejects his orders to set up the statue of Gaius in the temple and pledges himself instead to serve on behalf of the Jews in attempting to avoid this sacrilege (cf. *Ant.* XVIII.283, 304). For the common use of πρεσβευτής ("envoy," "legate") in Josephus, see *Bell.* I.541; II.207, 420; VII.163; *Ant.* V.104, 166; VII. 120 (where it refers to envoys sent by David, cf. 2 Sam. 10:5; 1 Chron. 19:5), etc. For πρεσβεύω (intransitive: "to be an envoy, be sent as an envoy"), cf. *Bell.* I.255, 384; II.111, 429; IV. 414; *Ant.* IV. 103; X.2, and often. And for πρέσβεις ("envoys"), cf. *Ant.* IV.76, Moses sends envoys (πρέσβεις) to the king of the Idumaeans; *Bell.* I.245, 371, 378, 661; IV.105 (ambassadors from Balak to Balaam), 256. For the development of the ambassador-terminology and institution in the Greco-Roman world and the relevant secondary literature, see now Cilliers Breytenbach, *Versöhnung, Eine Studie zur paulinischen Soteriologie*, WMANT 60, 1989, pp. 65 f. Though the political and military use of this terminology is clear, Breytenbach's central thesis that this backdrop also determines the reconciliation motif in 2 Cor. 5:18 ff. and related texts is not persuasive. Cf. his central thesis on pp. 80, 135, 137 and his application of it from the "ambassador" motif in 5:20 on p. 67: "Es ist bemerkenswert, daß Paulus in Röm. 5,1–11 durch die Verwendung von εἰρήνη, ἐχθροί und in 2 Kor 5,18–21 durch die Verwendung von πρεσβεύειν aufzeigt, daß ihm der profane Gebrauch unserer Wortgruppen (i.e. καταλλάττειν κτλ. and διαλλάττειν κτλ.), die auf die Aufhebung eines Kriegszustands referieren, geläufig war." In using the ambassador language, Paul is simply choosing a metaphor in 2 Cor. 5:18 ff. which will communicate his relationship to what God has accomplished in Christ, the latter of which is still best understood against the backdrop of the OT and post-biblical Judaism's understanding of atonement, both here and in Rom. 5:1–11, as the references to Christ's death in both contexts, his being "made sin" in 2 Cor. 5:21, and the justification and transgression language make clear. For the development of this more appropriate backdrop to the reconciliation concept in Paul, see still P. Stuhlmacher, "Das Evangelium von der Versöhunung in Christus," in P. Stuhlmacher and H. Claß, *Das Evangelium von der Versöhnung in Christus*, 1979, pp. 13–54, and his "Sühne oder Versöhnung? Randbemerkungen zu Gerhard Friedrichs Studie: 'Die Verkündigung des

in the targumic and rabbinic literature, where we have seen in chapter one that Moses' call to be God's "sent one" means that he owes his very call itself to the irresistible decree of God (i.e. Moses is forced to go against his will!).

This instrumentality and typical bonded or even slave status of the διάκονος are both expressed in Philo's writings.[94] On the one hand, in *De Post.* 165, the ears can be said to act as "servants" or "ministers" of those foolish ones who spread myths about the reality of idols, while in *Vit.Mos.* II.199 they are the servants of cursing. On the other hand, Philo makes a point of stressing in *De Vit. Cont.* 75 that the "servants" (διάκονοι) at the Jewish Pentecost banquet were not slaves as one would expect. In this regard, the verb διακονέω is used of the serving of slaves in *De Vit. Cont.* 70, while the noun "service" (διακονία) is used of the duties of slaves (δοῦλοι) in *De Spec. Leg.* II. 90–91 and *De Virt.* 122. In *De Io.* 167 and *In Flac.* 113, the "service" is simply that of one who has been sent with a task, with the latter again referring to a household servant.

But Philo too can use this terminology in religious contexts. In *De Gig.* 12, those divine souls which do not inhabit bodies, but are devoted to the service of God, are called "servants" (διάκονοι), while Joseph can say to his brothers in *De Io.* 241 that God willed to use him as his "servant" (διάκονος), which is coupled with his description as God's ὑπηρέτης ("servant to a master").

Against this background, Paul uses διάκονος in 2 Cor. 3:6a as an integral part of his larger self-conception as an obedient slave of Christ, whose duty is to serve him in the proclamation of the gospel of reconciliation as a "steward of the mysteries of God" (1 Cor. 4:1) and an "ambassador" on Christ's behalf (2 Cor. 5:20). Moreover, the "servant" was very often a slave. In calling himself a "servant" (διάκονος), Paul is pointing to, by way of connotation, the constraint he has in his ministry, since he has been called by the grace and will of God to this life of apostolic service. This lack of freedom functions as a testimony to the trustworthy nature of his message – he has no choice but to deliver the message of the one who sent him and has entrusted him with it (cf. 1 Cor. 9:16; 2 Cor. 5:14). Finally, the use of "servant" language in Josephus, Philo, and the Pseudepigrapha illustrates how this terminology, though profane in origin, could be used of God's servants, including the prophets, inasmuch as they, like Paul, could be viewed as in a position of submission to God as their master and called to serve him and others as a result.

But here too, as in the parallel passage of 2:14–17, Paul's "confidence" in 3:4 and his assertion in 3:5–6a that he has been made sufficient to be a "servant of the new covenant" could be interpreted as unsubstantiated expressions of

---

Todes im Neuen Testament,'" in *Die Mitte Des Neuen Testaments, FS E. Schweizer*, 1983, pp. 291–316; and Otfried Hofius, "Erwägungen zur Gestalt und Herkunft des paulinischen Versöhnungsgedankens," *ZThK* 77 (1980) 186–199; "Gott hat unter uns aufgerichtet das Wort von der Versöhnung (2Kor 5:19)," *ZNW* 71 (1980) 3–20; and his "Sühne und Versöhnung. Zum paulinischen Verständnis des Kreuzestodes Jesu," in *Versuche, das Leiden und Sterben Jesu zu verstehen*, 1983, pp. 25–46. For the OT backdrop, see Bernd Janowski, *Sühne als Heilsgeschehen*, WMANT 55, 1982. For Stuhlmacher's explicit response to Breytenbach's thesis, see now his "Cilliers Breytenbachs Sicht von Sühne und Versöhnung," *JBTh* 6 (1991) 339–354.

[94] Trans. and texts from F. H. Colson and G.H. Whitaker, *Philo, Vols. VI, VII*, LCL, 1950 and F.H. Colson and G.H. Whitaker, *Philo, Vol. V*, LCL, 1949.

"self-commendation" (cf. 3:1). Hence, in 3:6bc Paul must once again point to evidential support for his legitimacy as the foundation for the assertions of 3:4–6a.[95] It is Paul's portrayal of his own call in terms of the call of Moses which occasions the subsequent argument from the "letter" and the "Spirit" in 3:6bc, just as his allusion to the call of Moses in 2:16b occasioned his argument from the Spirit in 3:1–3. It is to this evidence that we now turn our attention.

6. The "New Covenant" in 2 Cor. 3:6bc:
Its Function and Meaning in Paul's Argument
against the Backdrop of Jeremiah 31:31–34

a) The Covenant Context of 1 and 2 Corinthians

The object of Paul's ministry and service as an apostle and "servant" is said in 3:6a to be the "new covenant" (καινὴ διαθήκη). The only other explicit use of this terminology in the Pauline corpus also occurs in the Corinthian correspondence, 1 Cor. 11:25, where it is part of the Lord's Supper tradition which Paul "received from the Lord" (1 Cor. 11:23). According to Paul's own testimony, then, the immediate source of the "new covenant" terminology is its use by Jesus to explain the significance of his death, a tradition in the early Church which Paul faithfully handed down (παρέδωκα ὑμῖν, 1 Cor. 11:23) as an essential part of the rationale behind the celebration of the "Lord's Supper" (cf. 1 Cor. 11:20, 23).[96] The point of the tradition is clear. Through the shedding of Christ's blood on the cross, God has eradicated the believer's sin and

---

[95] Contra the many who, like Jost Eckert, "Die geistliche Schriftauslegung des Apostels Paulus nach 2 Kor 3:4–18," in *Dynamik im Wort*, ed. Katholischen Bibelwerk, 1983, pp. 241–256, p. 247, posit that "the life giving power of the Spirit is of course only able to be perceived in faith in Jesus and cannot be simply demonstrated." This view derives from Eckert's conviction that there is a spiritual interpretation of Scripture which opens one's eyes to see the salvific meaning in relationship to Christ (p. 247; cf. p. 242).

[96] Cf. e.g. M. Hengel, "Leiden in der Nachfolge Jesus," in *Der leidende Mensch, Beiträge zum unbewältigten Thema*, ed. H. Schulze, 1974, pp. 85–94, p. 87, and his important work, *The Atonement, The Origins of the Doctrine in the New Testament*, 1981, pp. 34 ff.; P. Stuhlmacher, "Das Evangelium von der Versöhnung in Christus," in P. Stuhlmacher and Helmut Claß, *Das Evangelium von der Versöhnung in Christus*, 1979, pp. 13–54, p. 23 and his important, "Existenzstellvertretung für die Vielen: Mk 10:45 (Mt 20:28)," now in his *Versöhnung, Gesetz und Gerechtigkeit*, 1981, pp. 27–42; and F. Lang, "Gesetz und Bund bei Paulus," in *Rechtfertigung, FS E. Käsemann zum 70. Geburtstag*, ed. J. Friedrich et al., 1976, pp. 305–320, pp. 306 f., who also argues that the use of the new covenant tradition to explain the death of Christ had to go back to a pre-Pauline stage in the tradition since Paul nowhere explicitly quotes Jer. 31:31 ff. in contrast to Heb. 8:8 ff. and 10:16 f. "Ginge die Interpretation des Kelchworts mit Jer 31 auf Paulus selbst zurück, dann wäre bei der Art, wie der Apostel seine theologischen Thesen mit at. Schriftzitaten zu begründen pflegt, zu erwarten, daß er auch diese Stelle irgendwo in seinen Briefen direkt zitiert" (p. 307).

established a new relationship between God and the believer so that the substitutionary atonement of Christ brings about the eschatological new covenant as God's great act of redemption for both Jews and Gentiles.[97] This corresponds to the point made in Jer. 31:31–34, in which the basis of the promised knowledge of God is the anticipated forgiveness of sins.[98] Moreover, Paul's introduction of the "new covenant" in 2 Cor. 3:6 without explanation presupposes that through their own celebrations of the Lord's Supper and catechesis the Corinthians were well aware of the significance of the "new covenant"[99] as that which Jesus' death had brought about (cf. 1 Cor. 1:17 f., 23 f.; 2:2), and of their own identity as members of it (cf. 1 Cor. 1:2; 1:26–31; 3:16; 6:19; 7:23; 12:13, 27; 2 Cor. 6:14–7:1; etc).[100] Indeed, in 1 Cor. 11:17–34 Paul makes it clear to the Corinthians that because they are part of the cov-

---

[97] Cf. again F. Lang, "Gesetz und Bund," pp. 307 f., for this point. He points to Is. 25:6–8; 42:6; 49:8; 53:11; and Ps. 22:28 as examples of the expectation that Gentiles would be included in the eschatological salvation.

[98] See Christian Wolff, *Jeremia im Frühjudentum und Urchristentum*, Texte und Untersuchungen zur Geschichte der altchristlichen Literatur 118, 1976, p. 117. Wolff, however, argues that Jer. 31 is not in view either in the Lord's Supper traditions in Paul and Luke, or in 2 Cor. 3. For the former he sees Exod. 24 as decisive in the Markan/Matthean tradition, which implied a new covenant based on the fact that the Mosaic covenant was no longer valid. The Pauline/Lukan tradition simply made this implication explicit without reference to Jer. 31 (see pp. 131–133). In 2 Cor. 3:6 he sees Paul following this Exodus-based tradition, rather than looking to Jer. 31, since Jer. does not refer either to the Spirit or to its life-giving work (pp. 135–137). More recently, Dietrich-Alex Koch, *Die Schrift als Zeuge des Evangeliums: Untersuchungen zur Verwendung und zum Verständnis der Schrift bei Paulus*, BHT Bd. 69, 1986, pp. 45 f., has also argued that Jer. 31:31 is not behind 2 Cor. 3:6, since the reference to the "new covenant" alone is not enough to establish this connection. Rather, Paul merely took this concept over from the Lord's Supper tradition. But contra Wolff and Koch, it must be emphasized that 3:6 combines Ezek. 36 with Jer. 31 and that the reference to the Law as γράμμα is explicable only on the grounds of Jer. 31, and not Ezek. 36, since only Jer. 31:31 ff. offers the reason for the need of the new covenant summarized in Paul's use of the "letter" motif (see below). Moreover, the striking terminology of the "new covenant," unique to Jeremiah, and the central role that Jer. 31 played theologically in the Scriptural tradition, would have made the association of Exod. 24 with Jer. 31 both natural and immediate. Indeed, the explicit quotations of Jer. 31 in Heb. 8:8–12 demonstrate that Jer. 31 was an important part of early Christian thinking and catechesis. There is thus no compelling reason to deny the influence of Jer. 31 either on the Pauline Lord's Supper tradition, or on 2 Cor. 3:6. Nor is there any evidence that Paul has taken up the terminology in an unreflected manner. The argument of the immediate context leads one to the exact opposite conclusion. It is beyond the scope of this work to evaluate further the contentions of Wolff and Koch that Jeremiah also played no role in any other Pauline text (cf. Wolff, pp. 137–142; cf. p. 146 for his conclusion that Jeremiah's prophecy played no role in early Judaism and is found only in Hebrews within the NT; and Koch, pp. 45 f., that there are no citations from Jeremiah, Ezekiel, or Daniel in the Pauline corpus).

[99] Following A. Schlatter, *Paulus, Der Bote Jesu. Eine Deutung seiner Briefe an die Korinther*, 1969⁴, p. 504.

[100] This extends back to 3:6ab what Samuel Vollenweider, "2 Kor 3: Der transzendente Schein des Gesetzes," *Freiheit als neue Schöpfung*, FRLANT 147, 1989, 247–284, pp. 247 f., maintains for 3:6c, i.e. that Paul's letter/Spirit contrast "bringt anscheinend nur in prägnante Form, was er bei seinen Lesern weitgehend voraussetzen darf."

enant community established by the death of Christ, a divine discipline is now being meted out against their unworthy participation in the church's fellowship and worship (11:32; cf. 1 Cor. 5:2–5), centered around their mockery of the common bread and cup of the "Lord's Supper," which is identified as the covenant meal of this "new covenant."

The link between the "new covenant" and the death of Christ in 1 Cor. 11:25 thus made it evident to the Corinthians that the "new covenant," like its counterpart in the history of Israel, inaugurates a relationship between God and his people that is wholly initiated by God's act of redemption (now having culminated in the cross of Christ) and the consequent divine promises of protection and provision. Conversely, the pronouncement of God's judgment on the community in 1 Cor. 11:30, as well as the warning in 1 Cor. 11:27 that such judgment will continue if their behavior does not change, makes it equally clear that the "new covenant" also entails a corresponding responsibility of God's people to depend upon the God of the covenant and to be faithful to his will. If they are not faithful, God's discipline will be poured out on them, with a corresponding threat of an ultimate divine judgment for those who, together with the rest of the unrighteous, continue to dishonor God by failing to trust his promises and, as a result, are unable to obey his commandments (besides 1 Cor. 11:32, cf.1 Cor. 4:19–21; 5:9–13; 6:9–11; 15:1 f.; 16:22; 2 Cor. 5:10 f.; 6:1–3; 12:19–21;13:2–10).[101]

---

[101] Although it is beyond the scope of this present work to develop this in any detail, Paul's understanding of the new covenant is itself therefore also a "covenantal nomism" *like* that found within the Old Testament and Judaism of Paul's day, contra the central thesis of E.P. Sanders that, in contrast to such a covenantal nomism, Paul's "pattern" of religion is best understood as a "participationist eschatology" which represents an entirely different religious perspective and scheme and leads within Paul's thinking to "a more general theological conception than is generally realized: Christianity versus Judaism;" cf. his *Paul and Palestinian Judaism, A Comparison of Patterns of Religion*, 1977, pp. 491, 549; cf. pp. 422 f. for the definition of "covenantal nomism," 496 f., 552, and esp. p. 514, where he rejects the idea that Paul's thought can be construed in covenantal terms as a "new covenantal nomism" primarily because "that term does not take account of his participationist transfer terms, what are the most significant terms for understanding his soteriology." Sanders recognizes that Paul uses the term "new covenant" in 1 Cor. 11:25 and 2 Cor. 3:6 to describe the community which Christ has established by his death, but he does not take its content seriously, relegating Paul's references to "traditional Christian terminology" that can be reinterpreted and subsumed under the "new creation" motif (p. 514). But this is to prejudice the text in favor of one's theory and to drive a wedge between covenant and eschatology in Paul's thought where none exists, since as Paul's admonitions within 1 Cor. 11 itself reflect, his "participationist eschatology" is expressed within a covenant framework. The view presented here is also contra those who, like Jack T. Sanders, *Ethics in the New Testament, Change and Development*, 1975, pp. 48 f., follow Käsemann in arguing that the threat of eschatological judgment as found in the so-called "sentences of holy law" (i.e. 1 Cor. 3:17; 5:3–5; 14:38; 16:22; Gal. 1:9) represents only the exception to Paul's usual grounding of ethical admonitions on the indicative of justification. Rather, the ethical admonitions are grounded both in the past indicatives of justification and in the future indicative reality of eschatological judgment, which flow from one another instead of being in conflict. Nor do

Hence, Lane is correct when he concludes that "Paul's pastoral response to the disruptive situation at Corinth" entailed "an appeal to the New Covenant and the administration of its provisions."[102] Like the Old Testament prophet who was called to be a "messenger of the covenant lawsuit of God," Paul was called to express the "divine complaint against the rebellious Corinthians and to call them back to the stipulations of the covenant."[103] As Lane points out, this is confirmed by the fact that in 2 Corinthians Paul portrays his ministry in terms of the covenantal tasks of "building up" and "tearing down" derived from Jeremiah 1:10 (see 2 Cor. 10:8; 13:10; cf. Gal. 2:18). It is this covenant lawsuit against the Corinthians which provides a necessary key for understanding the character, content, and unity of 2 Corinthians,[104] especially in view of the link between the new covenant and second Exodus motifs in 2 Cor. 2:14–7:1 now established by Beale and Webb.[105] This is also confirmed by the fact that these covenantal tasks which Paul understands himself to be fulfilling toward the Corinthians "recur in the preamble to the promise to establish the New Covenant" in Jeremiah 31:28.[106]

"The explicit allusion to Jeremiah 31:28 indicates that Paul understood his task as the eschatological ministry of establishing the New Covenant, an act of God prophesied through Jeremiah and achieved through Paul as the servant of the covenant."[107]

---

we need to make a distinction between the ethics of Jesus, with their thoroughgoing eschatological orientation, and those of Paul, as Sanders maintains, even though for Sanders Paul's ethics are also based completely in Paul's "already but not yet" eschatology so that all of the indicatives in Paul are implied imperatives (cf. pp. 14, 23, 26, 29, 50, 53–56). Nevertheless, for Sanders, because the imperatives are implied in the indicative, inheriting the kingdom for Paul cannot be dependent upon one's fulfilling the ethical commands (p. 56). Yet this is precisely what Paul affirms, due to his understanding of the *necessary* link between obedience and faith within the covenant framework.

[102] Lane, "Covenant," p. 6. Thus, Paul's "pastoral ministry is an expression of covenant administration" (p. 8).

[103] Lane, "Covenant," p. 10. Lane admits, however, that there is no explicit covenant lawsuit pattern in the structure of 2 Cor. (pp. 15 f.).

[104] Lane, "Covenant," p. 10; cf. p. 13. In developing his thesis, however, Lane does not take adequate account of the fact that throughout 2 Corinthians Paul is also defending himself. Lane thus neglects the significance of the arrival of Paul's opponents or the direct attack on Paul's apostolic authority in his reconstruction of the historical situation (cf. pp. 10–15). In 2 Cor. 3 the reference to the new covenant is not given directly to support a covenantal lawsuit against the Corinthians in order to bring them back to its stipulations, but in order to support Paul's legitimacy as an apostle. Lane's conclusion, p. 16, that the point of 2 Cor. 3:1–7:1 is "to call the Corinthians to renew their commitment to the Lord and to complete the obedience they have already begun to manifest in response to his 'letter of tears'" is the ultimate purpose of the section, but not its immediate one. Contra Lane, p. 18, the focus of attention in 3:6 is not the disobedient Corinthians, but Paul, though Lane, p. 19, recognizes that "reconciliation to God demanded reconciliation to his messenger" as made clear by the citation of Is. 49:8a in 2 Cor. 6:2 (cf. his insightful analysis of 6:2 on p. 20).

[105] See above, n. 49.

[106] Lane, "Covenant," p. 9. Lane points to the development of these themes in Jer. 12:14–17; 18:7–11; 24:6 f.; 31:27–28; 42:10; 45:4.

[107] Lane, "Covenant," pp. 9 f.

Thus, the Corinthian correspondence makes it clear that even Paul's warnings of judgment are part of God's gracious "new covenant" provision (cf. e.g. 1 Cor. 10:6–23), since at the center of this "new covenant" is the death and resurrection of Christ, to whom the Spirit of God brings one for the forgiveness of sins and for new life (or "new creation," cf. 2 Cor. 5:17) "in Christ" and under his Lordship, to whom one can swear allegiance and remain faithful only by the power of this same Spirit (cf. 1 Cor. 2:9–13; 6:11; 12:3, 13; 2 Cor. 3:3, 17 f.; 4:13 f.). The church in Corinth was thus well aware that the inextricable link in Paul's thinking between the redemptive work of Christ on the cross and the corresponding ethical admonitions of the Gospel is based on the conviction that those who do possess the Spirit of God as their "seal" and "guarantee" of salvation (2 Cor. 1:22; 5:5; cf. Rom. 8:23) will grow in faith from being "babes in Christ" to "spiritual men" (πνευματικοί, 1 Cor. 3:1; cf. 1 Cor. 6:20; 9:24; 10:7–10, 14; 15:58; 16:13 f.; 2 Cor. 7:1; 8:7 f.; 9:13; etc.) by responding to the call to repent when they are caught in sinful disobedience (1 Cor. 5:5; 2 Cor. 1:23–2:11; 7:2–16). Continuing perseverance in the obedience which is brought about by faith, marked by repentance from sin and dependence upon God for forgiveness and the power of a new life in Christ, is therefore the mark of genuine Christian experience produced by the Spirit[108] in response to the redemption and provision of the new covenant made possible by Christ.

By the use of the word "covenant" to translate διαθήκη in 1 Cor. 11:25 and 2 Cor. 3:6, therefore, there is *no* intention to imply any "agreement" or "treaty" or "Bund" that is *mutually* initiated, arranged, disposed, or carried

---

[108] For a working out of this Pauline perspective on perseverance and the tension in Paul's thought between the assurance of God's saving work and the reality of the ethical admonitions and warnings of judgment aimed at believers, see now the helpful study of Judith M. Gundry Volf, *Paul and Perseverance, Staying in and Falling Away*, WUNT 2. Reihe 37, 1990, esp. pp. 21 ff. 83 ff., 217 ff., 277 ff., 283–287. While in agreement with Volf's central thesis concerning the certainty of salvation for those who are indeed Christians, based on the faithfulness of God, and the continual "fruit of victory over the obstacles which stand in its way" (p. 284), I question her conclusion that when Paul argues "vehemently against various forms of misconduct which have arisen he does not threaten Christians with the possibility of losing salvation" (p. 285). It appears as if in face of the persistent rejection of his authority and the Gospel by his opposition in Corinth that Paul finally does precisely that in 2 Cor. 12:19–13:10 (as he does in the polemical context of Gal. 5:16–26), in the conviction that this threat of losing one's salvation will be the very means used by God to keep one persevering. Is it true, as Volf maintains, that Paul's point in such contexts is to make it clear that those who think themselves to be Christians have not yet "made the initial step of repentance and conversion (2 Cor. 12:20, 21; 1 Cor. 5:1–13; 10:1–12), that is, that they are not even saved yet" (p. 285), or is is that for Paul a continual willingness to repent is evidence that one has been and is being saved? My understanding is that Paul is confident that those who are *genuinely* Christian will not lose their salvation, but he threatens all those who *consider* themselves Christian but refuse to repent of their disobedience with the final judgment of God, and holds out this prospect for the consideration of all believers (cf. 1 Cor. 10:1 ff.; 15:1 f.). For my reading of this strategy in 2 Corinthians, see *Suffering and the Spirit*, index to 2 Cor. 13:1–10.

out.[109] Paul's emphasis throughout the Corinthian correspondence on the centrality of the cross in salvation and on the work of the Spirit in sanctification makes it evident that the initiative, inauguration, and sustenance of the new covenant, like God's covenant with Israel at Sinai, is solely the gracious work of God on behalf of his people (cf. again 1 Cor. 1:17–31; 2:1–5; 15:3 f.; 2 Cor. 1:19 f., etc.). Moreover, as Hofius has pointed out, the parallels between 2 Cor. 2:14–17 (cf. v. 17) and 3:5 f. on the one hand, and 3:5 f. and 4:1–3 on the other, demonstrate that the content of the new covenant is to be paralleled with the "word of God" (ὁ λόγος τοῦ θεοῦ) in 2:17 and 4: 2, which is the "Gospel" (τὸ εὐαγγέλιον) in 4:3 f.[110] In the light of 2 Cor. 5:18 f., this new covenant is

---

[109] See the helpful observations of James Barr, "Some Semantic Notes on the Covenant," *Beiträge zur Alttestamentlichen Theologie, FS für Walther Zimmerli zum 70. Geburtstag,* ed. H. Donner, R. Hanhart, and R. Smend, 1977, pp. 23–38. Barr points out that the various etymological attempts to explain the meaning of בְּרִית in the OT are of no real help in determining its OT usage (p. 26), and that there are, in fact, no real synonyms to it in the OT (pp. 31 f.). In addition, the use of different prepositions with the noun does not distinguish different kinds of covenants, but that the phrase "to cut a covenant" can be used to refer to a promise placing an obligation on oneself, on another, or to a reciprocal obligation (p. 33). Finally, our use here follows Barr's conclusion that the English translation "covenant" is in fact suitable when used to refer not to an alliance or agreement, but to a unilateral undertaking, as is the case here (cf. pp. 36 f.). Moreover, Barr's caution that Kutsch's "insistence that *bᵉrit* consists always and only in obligation and that it does not include the establishment of a relationship seems to be strange; and the whole discussion seems dominated by a strong sense of the opposition between grace and law, which makes the reader uncomfortable" is to be accepted (see below). In support of the view taken here, see the survey in Gräßer, *Alte Bund,* pp. 2–16, and his observation concerning the meaning of διαθήκη in Greek literature outside the NT as a legal technical term: "Die einseitige Rechtssetzung des Testators und die Rechtsverbindlichkeit seines Testaments, das von niemandem ungültig gemacht order verändert werden darf, stehen dabei ganz deutlich im Vordergrund" (p. 3), and now O. Hofius, "Gesetz und Evangelium nach 2. Korinther 3," *Paulusstudien,* WUNT 51, 1989, pp. 75–120, p. 75, for the rejection of the translation "Bund" for "Setzung Gottes" for this reason. See J. Behm, "The Greek Term διαθήκη," *TDNT* 2 (1964) 124–131, for a helpful discussion in which he suggests the translation *dispositio* or that of a one-sided "disposition" of the divine will (pp. 125–127). The point to be emphasized is the "exclusively determinative will of the divine author" of this declaration or disposition (p. 127). This is confirmed by the LXX's choice of διαθήκη rather than συνθήκη to translate בְּרִית in 260 of its 287 occurrences, cf. Lang, "Gesetz und Bund," p. 310, and Gräßer, *Alte Bund,* p. 4. Here too Gräßer emphasizes that even when διαθήκη "an einigen Stellen an einen Bund oder Rechtsvertrag denkt (z.B. Gen. 21:27, 32), so ist doch ganz eindeutig nicht der Vertragsabschluß zwischen zwei Partnern der Leitgedanke, sondern die Idee der einseitigen Verfügung oder autoritativen, eine Ordnung setzenden Anordnung" (p. 4, pointing to Num. 25:21 f. as an example). He thus concludes that when it is used, above all, to refer to "die göttliche Willenskundgebung am Sinai" (Exod. 31:18; 34:27; Deut. 4:13; 9:9 ff., etc.), "Der Gedanke der Verfügung Gottes ist der beherrschende ... (and that the dominant meaning in the Greek environment of early Christianity is): Gott als absoluter Souverän verfügt seinen Willen. Διαθήκη muß deshalb klar unterschieden werden von συνθήκη = 'Übereinkunft,' 'Verabredung,' 'Vertrag,' dem die Vorstellung gemeinsamen Handelns mit wechselseitiger Verpflichtung zweier Partner zugrunde liegt ... Das NT hat den Begriff gar nicht" (pp. 4 f.).

[110] Hofius, "Gesetz und Evangelium," p. 78. Contra Hofius, however, these terms are not to be "equated" *per se,* as he maintains, since "covenant" refers to a larger semantic domain

also to be equated with the "word of reconciliation" (ὁ λόγος τῆς καταλλαγῆς) that forms the heart of Paul's "ministry of reconciliation" (ἡ διακονία τῆς καταλλαγῆς). These parallels underscore that the new covenant is identified with and based upon God's divine act of redemption in the cross of Christ,[111] just as its further identification with the Spirit points to its promise and/or consequence in the lives of the believer.

Nevertheless, in *response* to God's initiative and gracious act of redemption, both parties are obligated within the new covenant to remain faithful to their covenant partner.[112] The one-sided initiative and sustenance of the divinely established covenant does not preclude that God's people would incur covenant stipulations in the Law which must be kept for the covenant to be maintained by God.[113] For Paul, as for the Sinai covenant before him, obedi-

---

which includes the "word of God" and the "gospel," but is not, strictly speaking, synonymous with them (cf. pp. 77 f.).

[111] But this does not mean that in 3:6 Paul is contrasting directly "zwei klar zu bestimmende Größen ... das *Gesetz* vom Sinai und das *Evangelium* Jesu Christi," as Hofius, "Gesetz und Evangelium," p. 78, concludes (see below). Paul does not use "law" and "gospel" in this passage, but rather the "letter" and the "Spirit" to develop his contrast in order to point to the two operating functions of the old and new covenants respectively.

[112] So too Prümm, *Diakonia Bd II/Teil 1*, pp. 195–198, in which he rightly concludes that "Ungleichheit der Beteiligten zieht nicht jeweils sofort auch Einseitigkeit des Vertrags nach sich" (p. 197). But unfortunately, Prümm still maintains the traditional Law/Gospel distinction and simply tries bringing the two together, rather than seeing that the covenant structure is completely one of faith based on grace, but that faith inextricably produces obedience as part of its very nature (i.e. the "obedience that comes from faith," Rom. 1:5; 15:26).

[113] See E. Kutsch, "Von der Aktualität alttestamentlicher Aussagen für das Verständnis des Neuen Testaments," *ZThK* 74 (1977) 273–290, who rightly argues that there is no evidence in the Old Testament for God and mankind entering together as bilateral partners into a mutual agreement, as is possible on the human level (p. 280), whereas on the human level ברית can refer to the imposing of an obligation on another (Ezek. 17:13–14), to an obligation imposed by a third party (Hos. 2:18; 2 Kgs. 11), or to the bilateral acceptance of mutual obligations (1 Kgs. 5:12) (cf. pp. 276–280). He then argues that the one-sided action taken by YHWH in establishing the covenant with Abraham means that there is no obligation laid upon Abraham for the continuing of the covenant, but only a "Selbstverpflichtung" on God's part, but that in Ex. 24:8 we see that God has imposed a "Verpflichtung" on Israel in the "blood of the covenant," which must be kept (pp. 280 f.). Though this cannot be argued here, in my view such a distinction between the Abrahamic and Sinai covenants remains unconvincing. But Kutsch goes on (rightly) to contrast the covenant at Sinai, with its imposed "Verpflichtung" ("obligation") and possibility of being broken, with the new covenant in Jer. 31, which, though it contains God's law and hence a "Verpflichtung" of its own, will not be broken. But again, his conclusion concerning the early Christian understanding of Jer. 31 as containing the promise of forgiveness instead of the Law is to be rejected, once one sees that the act of redemption in Christ inaugurates the new covenant, as did the early act of redemption at the Exodus, but in both cases these covenants included imposed stipulations that must be kept as evidence of genuine faith. For the development of his position, see now E. Kutsch, *Neues Testament – Neuer Bund?, Eine Fehlübersetzung wird korrigiert*, 1978 and "Bund," *Realenzyklopädie*, Vol. 8, 1980, pp. 397–410. For a concise presentation of the idea that the OT divine covenants included both a one-sided pledge and "mutual commitments," in response to Kutsch, see M. Weinfeld, "Bᵉrit-Covenant vs. Obligation" (review of E. Kutsch, *Verheissung und Gesetz*, 1973), *Biblica* 56 (1975) 120–128, pp. 124 f., 128,

ence to the Law is the inextricable result of trusting in God's promises.[114] As for his part, God will remain faithful to his people, fully committed to ruling over them in justice and love and meeting their needs according to his wisdom so that his people might be able to endure in the midst of adversity and persevere in faith (1 Cor. 1:8 f.; 10:13; 2 Cor. 1:7; cf. 1 Thess. 5:9; Phil. 1:6). There is therefore no excuse for a continuing, habitual disobedience and rebellion that results from failing to trust God's gracious provisions and promises in Christ (cf. 2 Cor. 1:20), given God's work in the lives of his people to forgive them and the power of his Spirit to sanctify them (cf. 1 Cor. 5:7; 6:19 f.; 10:13; 13 [love as the work of the Spirit]).

---

though Weinfeld too draws some distinction between the covenant with the Patriarchs and that at Sinai, even though both contain mutual commitments, and Gräßer, *Alte Bund*, p. 7. For a helpful history of the debate concerning the background, origin, antiquity, and history of the covenant in the OT since Wellhausen (1878), see now Ernest W. Nicholson, *God and His People, Covenant and Theology in the Old Testament*, 1986, pp. 3–117.

[114] Cf. H. Gese, "Der Dekalog als Ganzheit betrachtet," in his *Vom Sinai zum Zion*, pp. 63–80, p. 66, who stresses that "Der Dekalog formuliert nicht ein Israel wesensmäßig fremdes Gesetz, das zu halten Voraussetzung für eine gnädige Zuwendung Gottes ist, sondern der Dekalog konstituiert jenen salom-Zustand, in dem sich Israel als Empfänger der Offenbarung befindet. Das Gesetz ist nicht die Bedingung des Bundes, sondern sein heilvoller Inhalt." See too Peter von der Osten-Sacken, "Befreiung durch das Gesetz," in his *Evangelium und Tora, Aufsätze zu Paulus*, 1987, pp. 197–209, p. 199, who argues that it is essential for Paul's understanding of the word of God that the divine promise precedes the demand of God and that the Gospel itself is the dynamic unity of promise and Law which serves to save mankind. The Law is only opposed to grace when it is separated from it and used to relate to God based on one's own actions and strength (p. 201). Rather, one is to expect and depend upon the gift of the Spirit as the power of God as that which enables one to fulfill the Law (pp. 201, 204). But von der Osten-Sacken also thus separates the Law and Gospel as representing two distinct responses, doing and receiving (cf. p. 201), instead of seeing the Law itself calling for mankind to receive God's sanctifying work just as much as the Gospel demands that one act in dependence and obedience to God, while both are acts of God's grace. Nevertheless, he is right in emphasizing that for Paul there is no doubt that the Law is to be fulfilled, and that only under this presupposition can Paul speak of the righteousness of God, which is conformity to the will of God (p. 203). Thus, both pre- and post-conversion one's relationship to God is explained in terms of the Law (cf. Rom. 8:2 f.), so that "Das Verhältnis des Menschen zum Gesetz ist konstitutives Merkmal des paulinischen Menschenbildes" (p. 203). For the crucial theological and anthropological link between faith, hope, and obedience, see D. P. Fuller, *Gospel and Law: Contrast or Continuum*, 1980, pp. 105–117. As Fuller insightfully argues, though obedience is absolutely essential as the result of faith, for Paul "sanctification, like justification, is by faith alone," since "according to Paul, a faith which banks its hope on the promises of God can never by devoid of the works of love, and therefore faith is all that is needed for carrying on the Christian life" (cf. Gal. 5:6) (p. 115). Conversely, "any teaching that implies that good works are done alongside of and coordinately with faith, instead of as the result of faith, is Galatianism" (p. 115). Hence, Prümm's answer to the unity of faith and obedience, as it is for all those who follow E.P. Sanders in making the distinction between "getting in and staying in," is ultimately that of the Galatian heresy itself, in which obedience or works are added to faith as a distinct and separated act needed in order to maintain a covenant relationship (cf. n. 91 above, and Prümm, *Diakonia Bd II/Teil 1*, p. 200).

Hence, although the immediate source for the "new covenant" terminology in 1 Cor. 11:25 is in all probability the "Lord's Supper" tradition,[115] Paul's own development of the implications of the cross, resurrection, and Spirit in the Corinthian correspondence speaks against the supposition that Paul's return to this language in 2 Cor. 3:6 was either unreflective, or simply a "catchword" reference to its OT backdrop. In the first view, Paul's reference to the "new covenant" in 3:6 is merely due to its place in the important Jesus-tradition cited in 1 Cor. 11:25. In the second, it is another instance in which Paul reinterprets the OT in view of his new Christian presuppositions, robbing the OT of its terminology, but omitting its substance. In both cases, although Paul may be alluding to the OT, the force and content of his thought come from outside the OT, and even go against it, since as a result of his own experience "in Christ" Paul fills the notion of the "new covenant" with a distinctly new content. Rather than simply adopting either of these basic approaches to understanding 3:6, the covenantal structure of Paul's thinking in general, and his dual emphasis within the Corinthian correspondence itself on the redemptive act of Christ, and on the ethical demands for obedience, point *materially*, as well as verbally, to the "new covenant" tradition in Jeremiah 31:31–34 as the background to Paul's argument.[116] This should not be surprising in that, as Erich Gräßer has pointed out, 31 of the 33 uses of διαθήκη in the NT "in der *theologischen* Tradition des atl. Zentralbegriffes בְּרִית steht, den die LXX-Übersetzer regelmäßig mit διαθήκη wiedergeben. [117]

---

[115] So too E. Gräßer, *Alte Bund*, p. 16. But Gräßer, pp. 81 f., is wrong to follow those who cast doubt on the influence of Jer. 31 on 3:6 (though the view that Jer. 31 influenced 3:3 is to be rejected); see next note. Because Gräßer does not take Jer. 31 seriously as the backdrop to 3:6, he is able to maintain the radical Bultmannian view that in 3:6 ff. Paul maintains a strict Law/Gospel antithesis and discontinuity between the content and nature of the old and new covenants, with the "letter" referring, "nicht grundsätzlich, sondern *faktisch*," to the Law itself over against the Spirit as representing two powers, the Law being that power which confronts one as a demand and thus forces one back "in die Leistung aus eigner Kraft" (p. 83, quoting Bultmann). Moreover, because he identifies the letter of 3:6 with the Law and the Law with Moses, while he takes 2 Cor. 3:17 to mean that Christ is identified with the Spirit, Gräßer, p. 82, can also see in 3:6 a mutually exclusive contrast between Moses and Christ parallel to that between Adam and Christ in Rom. 5:12 ff. where no such contrast exists (see below).

[116] Contra those who, like Heikki Räisänen, *Paul and the Law*, 1986 (1983), pp. 240–245, reject the influence of Jer. 31 on 3:6, concluding that "Paul did *not* derive his theology of the law from the promise of the new covenant in Jer. 31" (p. 245). Though Räisänen is correct in rejecting Jer. 31 as decisive for Paul's point in 3:3, he is wrong to extend this to 3:6 as well. He does so, however, because of his *prior* conviction that in 2 Cor. 3 Paul is rejecting the Law itself (see below, nn. 161, 192, 203), and thus, for Räisänen, Paul's understanding cannot be squared with that of Jer. 31, since he rightly observes that Jer. 31 does not predict either the abrogation of the Sinai law or the establishment of a new law as part of the new covenant (cf. pp. 241 f. and my own discussion below). But once 2 Cor. 3:6 ff. is also seen not to be teaching such a view, Jer. 31 and 2 Cor. 3 coalesce. As the terminology of the "new covenant" itself indicates, Paul *is* building his understanding of the Law on Jer. 31.

[117] *Alte Bund*, p. 9. As the exceptions, he points to Gal. 3:15 and Heb. 9:16 f., which use it in accordance with the secular Greek forensic meaning of a last will or testament. Gräßer, in

The suggestion that in 2 Cor. 3:6 Paul is alluding to Jeremiah 31:31 (LXX = 38:31),[118] the only explicit reference to the terminology "new covenant" (ברית חדשה, διαθήκη καινή) in the OT, is of course certainly not new.[119] But few interpreters of Paul have attempted to take this background, in its original context, seriously as the key to understanding the force of Paul's assertions in this passage.[120] When one does, however, the meaning and significance of Paul's self-designation as a "servant of the new covenant" not only correspond to the structure of his argumentation in general, but also make eminent sense within 2 Cor. 3:1–18.

---

contrast to the position taken here, does not see the covenant structure as constitutive for the NT writings, largely because of the relative infrequency of its occurrence and his conviction that the Christological and eschatological focus of the NT renders the OT covenant structure inadequate as a paradigm, cf. pp. 11–16. But this assumes a radical discontinuity between Israel and the Church in which the Christology and the eschatological perspective of the NT writings, and for Gräßer even their *theology* proper (following Barth) (!), are indeed no longer concerned with the history of Israel or the fulfillment of the OT covenant (cf. esp. p. 15). Thus, those passages such as 2 Cor. 3:6, in which Jer. 31:31 ff. is in view, as well as those such as Rom. 9:4 and Eph. 2:2, in which God's covenants of promise in a more general sense are in view, have in common the fact that they do not speak of a renewal of the OT covenant, but "von deren eschatologischer Vollendung *und insofern von ihrer Auf-Hebung* (im *dialektischen* Wortsinn) durch das Christusereignis" (p. 15, emphasis mine; cf. pp. 77–95, where he applies this perspective to 2 Cor. 3). In his view, 3:6 and 14 present a "schroffe *Antithetik* von Mosediatheke und Christusdiatheke" (p. 78). This present work is a response to such a perspective.

[118] For the sake of clarity, the numbering of the MT will be followed in referring to all passages from Jeremiah, unless specifically noted. In the case of Jer. 31:31–34, this will be always be the case since in the LXX the versification is the same, while only the chapter number, 38, is different.

[119] Besides the multitude of commentators who have maintained this view, cf. W. C. van Unnik, "'Η καινή διαθήκη – A Problem in the Early History of the Canon," in *Studia Patristica Vol. IV/Part II*, ed. F.L. Cross, TU Bd 79, 1961, pp. 212–227, who argues that the new covenant concept is "completely unintelligible without the OT" (p. 216) and that the first unequivocal connection between the terminology of the "new covenant" and Christian *literature* is found in a refutation of Montanism by an anonymous author in 192/193 A.D. (cf. Eusebius, *Historia Ecclesiastica* V, 16, 3) (p. 216). Van Unnik argues that Paul's distinction between the old and new covenants "was not the incentive to the distribution of the two names to two parts of one Bible," since Paul's point had no influence on the church Fathers in this respect (p. 220). Moreover, ever since the studies of J. Behm, *Der Begriff Διαθήκη im Neuen Testament*, 1912, and E. Lohmeyer, *Diatheke*, 1913, it has been clear that, apart from Gal 3:15 and Heb. 9:16 f., the term is not used in the NT to refer to the usual Greek sense of a "will" or "testament," but is derived from the LXX translation of ברית. See van Unnik, p. 221, who makes this same point.

[120] For a very insightful exception to this rule, see the programmatic work of William J. Dumbrell, *The End of the Beginning, Revelation 21–22 and the Old Testament*, 1985, pp. 79–96, on the meaning of the new covenant in Jer. 31:31 ff. (including its relationship to Ezek. 36:25 f.), and its application to 2 Cor. 3 on pp. 107–112. Although worked out independently of Dumbrell, many of the following conclusions concerning Jer. 31:31–34 are collaborated by his work.

Excursus: The Meaning of the "New Covenant" in Jeremiah 31:31–34[121]

The first thing to note concerning the "new covenant" in Jer. 31:31–34 is that it is the divinely promised answer to the perennial problem of Israel's hard-hearted rebellion against YHWH, which according to Jeremiah has always characterized the people. Hence, God declares that in the *present* not even the intercession of a Moses, not to mention Jeremiah himself, can now avert God's coming wrath and the judgment of the exile (Jer. 15:1; cf. 9:12–16; 11:14; 14:11). For as Jeremiah declares,

> "... since the day that your fathers came out of the land of Egypt until this day, I have sent you all my servants the prophets, daily rising early and sending them. Yet they did not listen to me or incline their ear, but stiffened their neck; they did evil more than their fathers." (Jer. 7:25 f.)[122]

Despite the chance to repent offered to the nation (cf. e.g. Jer. 26:1–3; 36:1–3, 7, etc.), there is no longer any hope left for the people in their present condition. As their responses and the responses of their leaders in 26:8–11 and 36:23–25 demonstrate, they will not, indeed in view of their hardened condition cannot, repent so that God might forgive them (cf. 36:31).[123] What is needed, therefore, is nothing less than a new begin-

---

[121] For a detailed study of the promise of the new covenant from Jer. 31:31 ff. within its canonical context (and its relationship to Ezek. 11 and 36), in which this promise occupies the very center of the OT canon, representing as it does the "perspektivische Fluchtpunkt" of the OT (a point of departure which lies in the future!), see now Christoph Levin, *Die Verheißung des neuen Bundes in ihrem theologiegeschichtlichen Zusammenhang ausgelegt*, FRLANT 137, 1985. Unfortunately, this work cannot be given here the careful treatment that it deserves. Suffice it to point out Levin's central thesis that the promise of the new covenant combines with the fundamental promise to Israel that, "I am the Lord, your God," as that which encompasses and expounds all of the promises of the OT (p. 12). Furthermore, Levin's central point concerning the role of the Law in Jer. 31 is that it functions as the concretizing of the covenant theology and is applied to Israel's history in the light of the breaking of that covenant (cf. p. 132). Hence, the promise of Jer. 31:31 ff. is to bring the Law back to its original purpose, namely, to renew the relationship of Israel and Judah to YHWH, which has been destroyed (p. 132). Finally, Levin stresses the promise of forgiveness within Jer. 31:31–34 as that which makes the new covenant presence of God and relationship with his people possible. Indeed, as Levin points out, it is hardly possible anymore for the reader of the Bible who stands within the NT tradition to recognize to what degree the message of forgiveness was heard at that time as a new and liberating gospel (pp. 134, 138). Nevertheless, Levin concludes that it is impossible to read the promise of the new covenant in Jer. 31 as something qualitatively new and in contrast to the past, but as a renewal of what God had already promised and revealed concerning himself and his intended relationship with Israel, but which has been lost due to Israel's history of unfaithfulness (cf. pp. 138–141 for his word study of חדשה and conclusions in this regard). The covenant promised in Jer. 31 is thus "new" in the sense that it is a radical break with the past, but it is not new in its structure, content, or purpose. In this latter case it is a "renewal" (cf. pp. 140 f.). These central points of Levin's work all undergird the position argued here.

[122] For this same motif of the "stubbornness" (שררות) of Israel's evil heart in relationship to the perpetual disobedience of the people, see Jer. 3:17; 7:24; 9:13; 13:10; 16:12; 17:23; 18:12; 19:15; 23:17. For the implications of this theme in relationship to Ex. 32–34 and the ministry of Moses, see below, ch. 3.

[123] Contra Aurelius, p. 123, who argues that since Jer. 31:31–34 stands between Jer. 26:1–3 and 36:1–3 it is the promise of the new covenant that makes this offer of repentance pos-

ning, a "new covenant," in which Israel will be decisively changed in her relationship to God. Jer. 31:31–34 thus looks to a *future* in which Israel's present state of rebellion and "stubbornness" will no longer determine her covenantal relationship. As the wider context confirms, the adjective "new" in Jer. 31:31 points to an eschatological reality yet to be fulfilled, which Jeremiah holds forth as Israel's only hope after the destruction of the exile (cf. 31:1–30, 35–40).[124] Jeremiah's twofold call in 1:10 to break down and destroy as well as to plant and build up is consequently fulfilled in his preaching of destruction in the present and its eventual reality on the one hand, and in his promise of God's restoration in the future, a restoration that centers on the establishment of a "new covenant" between God and his people (cf. Jer. 1:10 with its promised fulfillment in Jer. 31:28) on the other.

Second, the nature of this "new covenant," though future, is described in Jer. 31:32–33 by *contrasting* it to the Mosaic/Sinai covenant made with the fathers at the Exodus.[125] This covenant is rehearsed in Jer. 11:3–5, followed by the grim news that both the fathers "in the day that I brought them up from the land of Egypt" (11:7) and the Israel and Judah of Jeremiah's own day (11:9 f.; cf. 22:9 f.)[126] have broken this covenant "in the stubbornness of their evil heart" (11:8) and stand under the wrath and judgment of God (11:11). Hence, according to v. 32, the essential difference between this new covenant and the Sinai covenant is not that a new *type* of covenant or a new *content* within the covenant will be established, but that the new covenant will not be broken like the previous one, in spite of the fact that under the Sinai covenant God was faithful to his covenant commitments; i.e. although he was a "husband" to them. The new covenant is thus an "everlasting covenant that will not be forgotten" (Jer. 50:5).[127]

The reason for this confidence concerning the new covenant is given in verse 33 (note the כִּי in v. 33a; ὅτι in LXX 38:33a). Unlike the Sinai covenant, the new covenant

---

sible, i.e. that the move from the reference in 26:3 to God's repentance of the judgment planned to the offer of forgiveness in 36:3 is not self-evident, "aber als eine Nachwirkung der Verheißung Jer 31:34 erklärlich ist" (p. 123), and that "Hinter Moses Fürbitte Ex 34:9 steht mittelbar die Verheißung des neuen Bundes Jer 31:31–34" as well (p. 123). But the people's obvious rejection of repentance in both texts in Jeremiah, as well as the declaration concerning their hardened state in Ex. 33:3,5 and 34:9, makes this view impossible to hold. The point is that in their current condition the people cannot repent, while the promise of the new covenant assures a change in the people themselves.

[124] Cf. Rudolf Schrieber, *Der Neue Bund im Spätjudentum und Urchristentum, Diss. Tübingen*, 1954, pp. 8 f., who also points out that "new" in this context is eschatological, as the word "behold" (הִנֵּה) in v. 31 indicates, which is used to introduce warnings or promises for the future.

[125] Though it has been argued that the covenant from the past in view in Jer. 31:32 f. is some pre-exodus covenant (so, e.g. S. Herrmann and L. Perlitt), the reference to the Exodus seems decisive for seeing it as the Sinai covenant, especially in view of the parallel passage in 11:1–6 in which the "fathers" are specifically identified as those of the exodus generation; cf. the helpful article by Helga Weippert, "Das Wort vom Neuen Bund in Jeremia xxxi 31–34," *VT* 29 (1979), 336–351, pp. 336 f. for this latter position.

[126] For the point that the covenant people and their leaders have continued to break the covenant, see Jer. 2:8; 5:31; 6:13, 17; 10:21; 14:18; 23:13 f.; 27:16; 28:2; etc.

[127] As Dumbrell observes, *End of the Beginning*, p. 90, "What is 'new' is the avoidance of the fallibility of the old covenant ... Yahweh had maintained his fidelity to that earlier commitment in spite of Israel's unceasing provocations. In the new arrangement *both* parties would be loyal."

will not be broken because God declares that in this new covenant he will place his law (the preferred LXX MS tradition reads plural "laws," νόμους) "within them" (בקרבם) or "in their mind" (εἰς τὴν διάνοιαν[128]) and "write it on their heart" (על לבם אכתבנה, ἐπὶ καρδίας αὐτῶν γράψω αὐτούς). A writing of the Law on their hearts, as the will of God, is the counterpart and reversal of the present situation in which the *sin* of Judah is "written down with an iron stylus; with a diamond point it is engraved upon the tablet of their heart" (Jer. 17:1). In the context of the problem of Israel's stubborn rebellion from the Exodus onward, repeated throughout Jeremiah, this can only mean that in the new covenant Israel's rebellious nature will be fundamentally *transformed* so that her hardened disobedience is replaced with an open obedience to God's covenant stipulations in his Law.

In contrast to the conflict which now exists between God's commandments and the desires of one's heart (cf. e.g. Num. 15:39), under the new covenant there will be a harmony between God's law and the inward desires, as well as the decisions, of his people, i.e. their "heart."[129] This then is the point of God's declaration in v. 33 that he will "put (his) law within them" and its synonymous expression in v. 33 that he will "write it on their heart" when read against the backdrop of Jeremiah as a whole.[130] As such, the promise of the new covenant in Jer. 31:31–34 is the divine response to Israel's inability and failure to heed the call that they "circumcise (themselves) to the Lord and remove the foreskins of (their) heart" (Jer. 4:4). Apart from this divine work, Israel will suffer God's punishment against "all those who are circumcised and yet uncircumcised," since "all the house of Israel are uncircumcised of heart" (Jer. 9:25 f.; cf. 4:4b and Deut. 10:16). Indeed, Weippert argues that in the context of Israel's hardness as portrayed throughout Jeremiah, the promise of the new covenant that God will write his Law in their hearts indicates such a "thoroughgoing change of the person, that one may speak of a new creation."[131]

The Law "within" and "written on the heart" are thus images for a people who accept God's Law as their own and obey it willingly, rather than repulse it as foreign to

---

[128] This translation corresponds to the OT use of the "heart" as representing one's intellectual and rational functions; cf. Hans Walter Wolff, *Anthropology of the Old Testament*, 1974, pp. 46, 51.

[129] See again Wolff, *Anthropology* , pp. 43–46, 51–54, where he outlines the use of the "heart" as the inward place where one's vital decisions of the will are made and as that which represents one's driving desires and longings.

[130] For the development of this theme, see Weippert, "Wort vom Neuen Bund," pp. 339–346, where she develops the theme of Israel's hardened condition and lack of knowledge throughout Jeremiah (cf. e.g. Jer. 2:21 f.; 5:20–25; 8:7; 13:23; 14:22; 17:1; 18:13–15a; etc.) to demonstrate that the new covenant promise is the answer to this need for a change in Israel's condition. She concludes that "das ins Herz geschriebene Gesetz bedeutet eine grundlegende Veränderung des Menschen" (p. 339).

[131] "Wort vom Neuen Bund," p. 347. Dumbrell, *End of the Beginning*, pp. 94 f., points out, however, that the reference in Jer. 31:34 to God's "not remembering" their sin any longer also points beyond the NT age into the final new creation in which sin will be "foreign to all human experience," since forgiveness is already offered freely in both testaments. I would argue that for Paul this final consummation is understood to be the extension of the present experience of the OT remnant and new covenant people of God in which forgiveness for Israel's disobedience and the Gentiles' rejection of God is now being extended anew under the impetus of the cross and the new epoch of salvation history (cf. 1 Cor. 15:42–57; Rom. 11:25–36).

them and obey it either grudgingly or not at all.[132] In the "new covenant," unlike the Sinai covenant, the Law will not be rejected by Israel, but kept, since it will no longer encounter a stubborn "evil heart," but be inculcated by God within the heart of the people. As a result of this acceptance of God's Law, i.e. his covenant stipulations, the covenant will be kept by the people and their relationship of faithfulness to YHWH will be maintained, rather than continually broken. The consequence of the "new covenant," unlike that of Sinai, will be the realization of the covenantal relationship between God and his people in which God declares, in typical covenant formulary, that "I will be their God, and they will be my people" (31:33c).

Third, the movement of thought from Jer. 31:32 to 33 makes clear that essential to the new covenant, as in the Sinai covenant before it,[133] is keeping the Law in *response* to God's prior act of redemption (cf. Jer. 31:1 ff.), which maintains the covenantal relationship between God and his people. Rather than suggesting that the Law is somehow negated or done away with in the new covenant, Jeremiah 31:31–33 emphasizes just the opposite. According to Jer. 31:31–33 it is rather the ability to *keep* the Law, as a result of having a transformed nature, and thus to keep rather than perpetually break the covenant between God and his people, that distinguishes the new covenant from the covenant at Sinai. There is no indication in this text, or in Jeremiah as a whole, that the future eschatological restoration will entail the giving of a new Law or that the Law is now being thought about only in the abstract sense as a revelation of the general will of God.[134] The Law written on the heart is the Sinai Law itself as the embodiment of

---

[132] So too Holladay, *Jeremiah 2, A Commentary on the Book of the Prophet Jeremiah*, Hermeneia, 1989, p. 198, who points out that the Law in the heart "is commonly understood as Yahweh's move to plant his law within the interior intentionality of the people, so that obedience becomes natural." On the theme of the Law written on the heart Dumbrell, *End of the Beginning*, pp. 91 f., rightly points to Deut. 6:4–5; 10:16; 11:18 to show that the Law was always intended to be in the heart, and to Ps. 40:8; Is. 51:7 to show that doing the will of God depends on the placing of the Law in the heart. Hence, "Jer. 31:33 may plausibly be viewed as simply saying Yahweh is returning to the idealism of the Sinai period in the New Covenant relationship" (p. 92).

[133] Cf. Georg Braulik, "Gesetz als Evangelium. Rechtfertigung und Begnadigung nach der deuteronomischen Tora," *ZThK* 79 (1982) 127–160, pp. 135–138, who points to Deut. 6:20–25, esp. v. 25, as a classic example of the context of God's prior deliverance from Egypt out of slavery as a "Rechtsakt" which then leads to the Law (p. 135). As a result, the commands are given and the keeping of them is thus salvation and life (v. 24) and righteousness (v. 25). "Was diese beiden Termini (i.e. salvation and life from v. 24) anthropologisch umschreiben, interpretiert *sedaqa* juristisch-theologisch als die 'Gerechtigkeit' des schon Gerechtfertigten vor Gott" (p. 140). But Israel will only remain in this "Heils (zu) stand" if she keeps the law, "d.h. wenn seine Recht'*fertigung durch Gott* auch ihren Ausdruck findet im Halten des ganzen Gebotes, nämlich des Deuteronomium ... Von anderer Seite her formuliert: Daß Israel gerecht (fertigt) ist, wird dann offenkundig, wenn es das Gesetz hält. Aufgrund dieses Verhaltens also kann Israels Gerecht (fertigt) sein festgestellt, kann ihm *durch Menschen* 'Gerechtigkeit *zugesprochen* werden'." (p. 140, emphasis his).

[134] The LXX MS tradition which reads the plural νόμους for the singular תורתי in Jer. 38:33 (MT 31:33) underscores this point. Cf. too Richard B Hays, *Echoes of Scripture in the Letters of Paul*, 1989, p. 217 n. 22, who follows the work of H.W. Wolff and R.P. Carroll in pointing out that "In Jeremiah's prophecy, the problem with the old covenant lies in the disobedience of the people, not in some inherent deficiency of the Mosaic Law." Hays observes that in Jer. 31 even the terminology of "new covenant" indicates "a positive correlation between the Mosaic covenant and the new covenant, although, in contrast to the posi-

the will of God.[135] The contrast between the new and Sinai covenants is not a contrast between a covenant with and without an external Law; nor is it a contrast between two different kinds of Law.[136] Rather, the contrast between the two covenants is a contrast between the two different *conditions of the people* who are brought into these covenants and their correspondingly different responses to the *same Law*.[137]

Finally, verse 34 indicates both the result of this new covenant transformation of God's people and its ultimate ground. As a result of having God's law written on their

---

tion argued here, he sees this expectation of continuity in Jeremiah as "immediately disturbed" by Paul in 3:3b, since there is "an implicit dissonance" in 2 Cor. 3:1–3 between the Mosaic and new covenants (pp. 128 f.). Hays' view is based on the common attempt to see Paul "imputing negative connotations to the stone tablets on which God once wrote at Sinai" (p. 129). For a refutation of this view, see my *Suffering and the Spirit*, pp. 204–218, and its summary below. Positively, see now Otto Betz, "Der fleischliche Mensch und das geistliche Gesetz, Zum biblischen Hintergrund der paulinischen Gesetzeslehre," in his *Jesus, Der Herr der Kirche, Aufsätze zur biblischen Theologie II*, WUNT 52, 1990, pp. 129–196, pp. 174 f., who argues that already in Jeremiah the Law is spiritual since it comes from God who is Spirit (Jer. 31:3) and thus already possesses the nature of the end times and hence is complete and eternal (cf. 1 Cor. 15:45).

[135] This point is strengthened historically if Holladay's reconstruction, *Jeremiah 2*, pp. 60, 197, is correct that the parallels between Jer. 31:31–34 and Deut. 4:45–5:33; 6:6–9; 11:18–21 point to a setting for Jer. 31 in which the Deuteronomic Law was recited during the feast of booths in the autumn of 587 after the destruction of Jerusalem.

[136] Contra the main thesis of Rudolf Schrieber, *Der Neue Bund im Spätjudentum und Urchristentum*, who represents the classic Lutheran position. Although "Berith und Gesetz in einem unlöslichen Zusammenhang stehen" (p. 11), he nevertheless sees Jer. 31:33 as the opposite of Deut. 30:11–14, since in Jer. 31 there are no imperatives or conditions, only the Law as "Gabe" (p. 14). In his words, "Im ersteren Falle ist das Gesetz eine Gabe, die zur Forderung wird, und im letzteren Falle eine Forderung, deren Erfüllung zur Gabe wird" (p. 14). Schrieber must then conclude that Jer. 11:1–14 is also in contrast to Jer. 31 (p. 15)! Moreover, for Schrieber, in the old covenant the way of life and death are both open possibilities, while in the new covenant only the positive way of life is possible and determinative (p. 18). For him, therefore, the fulfillment of the Law is no longer the condition for the promise of salvation in the new covenant so that the possibility of disobedience and condemnation is gone (p. 20). The new covenant contains "ausschliesslich eine Heilsweissagung" because God himself effects the fulfillment (p. 20). The old covenant is not forgotten, however, but becomes a basis for accusing the people (p. 23). The old covenant has the character of demand, while the new that of promise (p. 26). This view fails to find support not only in Jer. 31:31–34, but also in the covenant structure of Paul's thought, as well as in the understanding of the new covenant in the book of Hebrews (cf. Heb. 8:8–12, where the central point concerning the new covenant from Jer. 31:31–34 is that it is built upon "better promises" (8:6) in that it provides access to God through the sacrifice of Christ as our high priest (8:1 f.; 9:11–13, 15; 12:18–24; cf. 4:14–16). The consequence of Christ's work, however, is not only access to the presence of God and the corresponding "promised eternal inheritance" (9:15), but also the imperatival obligations and implications concerning the judgment of God that stem from the fact that Christ's work purifies one's conscience "from dead works to serve the living God" (Heb. 9:14; cf. 3:12–4:13; 6:1–8; 10:19–31; 12:25–29).

[137] Contra Holladay, *Jeremiah 2*, p. 197, who maintains that the new covenant implies that YHWH "had learned something from the failure of the old covenant," referring to Jer. 2:5, since the new covenant does not have "the defects of the old one" and YHWH "could improve on the old one." But Jer. 2:5–8, like Jer. 31:32, points to the faithfulness and faultlessness of YHWH, so that the covenant relationship and stipulations were both maintained by YHWH, thus showing the problem to lie clearly with the people.

hearts, the people of the new covenant will not need to be taught to "know" the Lord, since they will all know him directly. The new heart which is promised as essential to the new covenant thus provides the conceptual transition from v. 33 to v. 34 in that in OT anthropology the "heart" (לב) is not only the seat of volition and desire, but also the organ most often associated with the function of understanding and intellectual knowledge. In Wolff's words,

> "… there is an easy transition in the use of the word from the functions of the understanding to the activity of the will. The Israelite finds it difficult to distinguish linguistically between 'perceiving' and 'choosing,' between 'hearing' and 'obeying' … Thus the heart is at once the organ of understanding and of will."[138]

The consequence of having their hearts transformed so that they desire and are able to keep God's Law and thus maintain their covenant relationship with YHWH is that there will no longer be any need for a mediator to stand between God and his people. In the context of the Sinai covenant, which as we have seen forms the point of comparison, verse 34 points to a time when the role of Moses as the mediator of the will, knowledge, and presence of God is no longer necessary. The need for the continual teaching spoken of in Deut. 6:6–9 and 11:18–21, so that the Law might be on one's heart, will be fulfilled. In turn, this new covenant transformation will mean the overturning of the lack of trust that now characterizes relationships between brothers and neighbors in which they do not teach the truth but speak lies to one another, and through their deceit "refuse to know" the Lord (Jer. 9:4–6). Hence, it is not as if the knowledge of God has been in some way altered or intensified or made more real or easier to comprehend. Instead, in the new covenant God will renew the people's ability to know God directly,[139] whereas under the Sinai covenant, beginning with the sin of the golden calf, the glory and presence of God had to be kept veiled and separated from the people in order to protect them from destruction due to their sinful, "stiff-necked" state (cf. Jer. 7:26; 19:15 with Exod. 32–34, esp. 33:3, 5 and Deut. 9:6, 13 one the one hand, and the many parallels between Deut. 32 and Jeremiah on the other).[140] Holladay even sug-

---

[138] Wolff, *Anthropology*, p. 51. Cf. his pp. 46 f., where he points to passages like Deut. 29:3 to illustrate that the heart is "destined for understanding" and Prov. 15:14 and Ps. 90:12 to show that the "essential business" of the heart is to seek knowledge and wisdom. It is significant that the use of the "heart" occurs most often in the Wisdom literature (99 times in Proverbs; 42 times in Ecclesiastes), and second in the "ṣtrongly didactic Deuteronomy" (51 times) (p. 47). As that which describes "the seat and function of reason," the heart "includes everything that we ascribe to the head and the brain – power of perception, reason, understanding, insight, consciousness, memory, knowledge, reflection, judgment, sense of direction, discernment. These things circumscribe the real core of meaning of the word לב" (p. 51).

[139] For this point, see again Weippert, "Wort vom Neuen Bund," p. 339, who argues against those who, like J. Swetnam, maintain that a new kind or degree of knowledge was to be revealed. For the position taken here that the placing of the Law within the heart implies the direct knowledge of God, see H. Gese, "Das Gesetz," *Zur biblischen Theologie, Alttestamentliche Vorträge*, BevTh 78, 1977, pp. 55–84, p. 74.

[140] See ch. 3 below and Holladay, *Jeremiah 2*, p. 39, who argues that the phrase "stiffen the neck" in Jer. 7:26; 19:15 is an adaptation of the description of Moses' generation from Exod. 32–34 and Deut. 9:6, 13, and on pp. 54–56 lists the 9 persuasive and 8 suggestive parallels to Deut. 32 from throughout Jer. to support his conclusion that this special terminology of Israel's rejection of YHWH derives from these prior biblical traditions (p. 55).

gests that the emphasis on the Law being placed "within (קֶרֶב) them" recalls the emphasis on Jerusalem within the land in Jer. 6:1 and the temple within the city in Jer. 6:6, so that against the backdrop of the Lord's being within the temple of the holy city (cf. e.g. Ps. 46:5–6; 55:11 f.) this new covenant promise also suggests a renewed worship of the Lord in the temple.[141] If so, then our emphasis on the direct knowledge of God would take on the connotation of approaching his presence in worship without fear.

This is why the foundation of the new covenant (cf. the כִּי in v. 34b)[142] is the fact that, despite the past sin of Israel, a new possibility for forgiveness will be opened up in the new covenant (v. 34). Both the changed condition of God's people and their resultant obedience to the covenant, together with their renewed access to the knowledge of God, are based upon this divine forgiveness that makes the new covenant possible. The argument of Jer. 31:31–34, separated into its constituent propositions, runs as follows:

v. 31: "Behold, the days are coming," declares the Lord, "when I will make a new covenant with the house of Israel and with the house of Judah.

v. 32a: *Specifically,* I will not make it like the covenant which I made with their fathers …

v. 32b: *since* they broke this covenant of mine

v. 32c: *even though* I was a husband to them," declares the Lord.

v. 33a: *"The reason the new covenant will be different in this regard (כִּי) is that* this is the covenant which I will make with the house of Israel after those days," declares the Lord, "I will put my Law within them, and I will write it on their heart.

v. 33b: *The result of this new covenant will be that* I will be their God, and they shall be my people.

v. 34a: *The ultimate consequence of this new covenant relationship in which I am their God and they are my people is that* they shall not teach again each man his neighbor and each man his brother saying, 'Know the Lord,'

v. 34b: *because (כִּי)* they shall all know me, from the least of them to the greatest of them," declares the Lord.

v. 34c: *"The basis for all of this (כִּי) is that* I will forgive their iniquity, and I will remember their sin no more."

b) The Significance of 2 Cor. 3:6 in View of Jer. 31:31–34

Against the backdrop of Jeremiah 31:31–34, Paul's assertion in 2 Cor. 3:6 that he is a servant of the "new covenant" both confirms and summarizes the structure of his thought and thrust of his ministry as reflected in the Corinthian correspondence as a whole. From Paul's perspective that which was promised

---

[141] *Jeremiah 2*, p. 198.
[142] Weippert, "Wort vom Neuen Bund," p. 338, emphasizes that this כִּי is not accidental, but is the supposition upon which everything rests.

in Jeremiah 31:31–34 is now being fulfilled through his own ministry.[143] Specifically, Paul sees himself as a servant (= "mediator of the message," see above) of the eschatological reality of the new covenant, since fundamental to Paul's self-understanding is his conviction that he is participating with those "upon whom the end of the ages has come" (1 Cor. 10:11). As the context of 1 Cor. 10 demonstrates, this conviction determines his understanding of the applicability of the Scriptures to the church, as well as his ethical expectations for the people of God who now find their identity in Christ, since as believers they are the eschatological ἐκκλησία τοῦ θεοῦ which is being gathered from among both Israel and the Gentiles (1 Cor. 10:32; cf. Gal. 6:15 f.). Paul is convinced that those who have been justified and set apart in the name of Christ and are living in the Spirit are *now already* participating in the present reality of the kingdom of God, while the unrighteous will not inherit the kingdom of God when it comes in its fullness (1 Cor. 6:7–11; cf. Gal. 1:4 with Gal. 5:21).

Second, and as a direct implication of this first Pauline perspective, in view of Jer. 31:31 ff. Paul's operating assumption is that those who are in the church have had their "hearts" transformed by the work of God so that their response to his will as revealed in the Mosaic law ought to be one of compliant obedience to the Sinai law *itself*.[144] Though this assumption may certainly have to

---

[143] Cf. R.P. Martin, *2 Corinthians*, p. 46, who sees 3:1–6 to be a positive statement of what Paul's ministry has accomplished in that the Holy Spirit has changed lives through his ministry. But contra the view taken here, Martin sees this new covenant reality to be "in some tension with Moses' law" (p. 54).

[144] The view argued here is distinct therefore from that of W.D. Davies, "Paul and the People of Israel," *NTS* 24 (1978) 4–39, p. 11, who concludes that "just as the new covenant conceived by Jeremiah, Jubilees and the sectarians at Qumran did not unambiguously envisage a radical break with the Sinaitic covenant but a *reinterpretation*, so Paul's new covenant. Thus Jer. 31:33 does not look forward to a new law but to 'my law,' God's sure law, *being given and comprèhended in a new way* ... [T]he new covenant of Paul, as of Jeremiah, finally offers *reinterpretation of the old*" (emphasis mine). For Davies, the new covenant in Christ does not abolish the Law, but reinterprets and reestablishes it in a *new* form. This is in line with his earlier work, *Torah in the Messianic Age and/or the Age to Come*, JBL Monograph Series 7, 1952, in which he traced the expectation within Jewish tradition of a new, messianic Torah in the age to come (equal in some ways to the Torah from Sinai, but "new in some sense," p. 28), since there is no clear indication that either Jer. 31:31 ff. or Ezek. 36:27 f. envisioned doing away with a written Law (cf. pp. 11, 13, 20–23, 42 f.). Yet, according to Davies, it is not clear in Jer. 31 whether the new covenant implies a new Torah or better obedience to the old Torah (p. 48). As time went on, tradition, esp. rabbinic tradition, took it to refer to the latter, but with modifications (pp. 48, 66, 70, 72). Hence, in his earlier work he follows Moore in concluding that in the OT and Jewish tradition "it is natural that the law should not only be in force in the Messianic Age, but should be better studied and better observed than ever before; and this was indubitably the common belief" (p. 48). Indeed, the doctrine of the "immutability of the Torah ... almost dominated Judaism" (p. 78; cf. 51 f.). With the possible exception of Jer. 31, which, according to Davies, was ambiguous concerning whether obedience would be directed to the written Torah, the "profound conclusion" of the OT and post-biblical literature, including rabbinic literature, was "that obedience to the Torah (generally conceived as the Torah in its *existing* form) would be a dominating mark of the Messianic age ..." (p. 84, emphasis mine). Nevertheless, according to

be qualified in the light of the significance of Christ's death, the dawning of the new creation, and the fact that Christ's reign on earth has not yet been consummated,[145] Paul nevertheless uses as his starting point the fact that under

---

Davies, the *minority* view persisted (as represented only by a relatively few and late rabbinic traditions!) that there would be a "new messianic Torah" which would replace the Sinai Law, evidenced by the early Christians who held to such a view (pp. 85, 90)! Paul saw this expectation for the new Law in the messianic age fulfilled in the "personification of Torah in Christ" (p. 93). Thus, for Davies, Christianity is "a movement which not only denies the old Torah on one level, and affirms and fulfills it on another, but also introduces a New Torah" (p. 91). But there is no evidence in Jer. 31:31–34 that the Law was being reinterpreted (the reference to "my law" in 31:33 is certainly to be equated with the Law of Sinai), nor in Paul, though certain aspects of it were for Paul no longer applicable or binding (e.g. circumcision, ritual purity laws, etc.) in view of the work of Christ and dawning of the new covenant. Therefore, if one rejects Davies' view of the early Christian understanding of the existence of a new Torah, then there remains no compelling evidence for the existence of this minority view in either Jewish or in the earliest Christian tradition. For another critique of Davies' view, see Paul Demann, "Moses und das Gesetz bei Paulus," pp. 230 f., who argues that there is no evidence of a tradition at the time of Paul in which a new, messianic Torah would replace the Sinai Torah. He maintains that even those texts from later rabbinic literature which speak of a "new Torah" can simply be taken to mean that there will be a new understanding and observance of the eternally valid Law. For this view, see also F. Lang, "Gesetz und Bund," p. 311 (following P. Schäfer), who therefore must conclude that the Pauline antithesis between the Law and the New Covenant has no parallel in Judaism, including Qumran, since for Paul the Sinai covenant and new covenant stand over against one another in "the contradictory opposition of the righteousness of the Law and the righteousness of faith" (pp. 312, 313). As for the meaning of γράμμα, he follows those who see it as the perversion of the Law of Moses into a works-righteousness and boasting, though other places he sees the contrast to be with the Law itself (pp. 316, 318 f.). See too e.g. Morna D. Hooker, "Beyond the Things that are Written? St. Paul's Use of Scripture," *NTS* 27 (1981) 295–309, p. 303: "Attempts have been made to find in rabbinic writings indications of an expectation that the Law would be abolished by the Messiah, or replaced by a new Law; but the whole idea runs counter to Jewish belief in the Torah as the revelation of God ... Paul himself, asked if he is abrogating the Law, replies with a characteristic μὴ γένοιτο! (Rom. 3:31). Closer to Paul's attitude is the idea that the age of the Law will be succeeded by the age of the Messiah, an idea which suggests fulfillment rather than cancellation." But Hooker, pp. 303–304, sees the "age of the Law" as entailing a relationship with God on the basis of "works of the Law" and "on obedience to letter of that Law," taken to be legalism, an understanding of obedience to the Law that has now of course been seriously challenged by the "new perspective" and which 2 Cor. 3, read against the backdrop of Jer. 31 and Ezek. 36, also calls into question. Finally, cf. R. Banks, "The Eschatological Role of Law," p. 179, who after surveying all of the literature usually adduced to support the views of Davies, Teeple, Longenecker, Schoeps, etc., concludes that "the view that within the framework of a doctrine of the immutability of Torah expectations of its partial modification or abrogation are occasionally to be found, exceeds the evidence adduced in its support." Rather, "such alterations as were to take place only enhanced its authority and indicated that in the future it would be understood more accurately and observed more closely. It would be unwarranted to infer from the presence of an untypical opinion to the contrary (viz. Midr. Tehillim on Ps. 146:7) or from the occasional anti-Christian polemical utterance on the subject (e.g. Dt. R. 8:6) that there was a more widely-held minority belief in the coming of a new Torah within pre-Jamnian Judaism." (p. 184).

[145] Cf. e.g. the fact that the ritual purity laws surrounding the sacrificial system are no longer needed, that all things are now "clean" in the new covenant/creation [cf. Mark 7:19

the new (renewed) covenant the Sinai law is to be obeyed. It is this eschatological assumption and expectation that fuel his indignation concerning the
Corinthians' continuing lack of spiritual growth and flagrant, habitual disobedience on the one hand (cf. e.g. 1 Cor. 3:1–4, 16 f.; 5:1–13; 6:1–8, 15–20;
10:14–22; 11:17–22; 2 Cor. 2:4; 6:14–7:1; 12:19–13:10), and his insistence
that those who refuse to repent be cast out from the people of God on the other
(1 Cor. 5:2, 9–13; 2 Cor. 12:21; 13:2, 10). For even if the "law of Christ"
(1 Cor. 9:21) is only partially identical with the Sinai law, or even if it is merely to be identified with the commandment to love one another, it is nevethe-
less significant that elsewhere Paul derives the command to love from the
Law itself (Lev. 19:18) and views it to be the fulfillment of the entire Law (cf.
Gal. 5:14; Rom. 13:8 f.). Indeed, it is striking that even in the context of the
predominantly Gentile community in Corinth, Paul argues from the Law for
specific ethical injunctions (cf. 1 Cor. 9:8–11), for general moral principles (1
Cor. 10:6–10), and for the pattern of Christian worship (1 Cor. 14:34), in each
case being convinced, as recent scholarship has convincingly emphasized,

---

and Paul's application of this point to the Law in Rom. 14:1–15:13] and that even physical
circumcision is no longer the sign of the covenant! It is beyond the scope of this work to
develop this further, though what can be demonstrated, once the eschatological framework
of Paul's thought is taken seriously, is that Paul does have a coherent theoretical viewpoint
from which he evaluates the applicability of the Law within the new covenant (see below).
This is contra the thesis of E.P. Sanders, *Paul, the Law*, p. 103, that "Paul himself offered no
theoretical basis for the de facto reduction of the law." Moreover, like Westerholm, Sanders
too sees the ultimate basis of Pauline ethics to be the Spirit and love of neighbor rather than
the Law itself (cf. pp. 103 f., 107). Finally, Sanders' failure to take the OT promises from
Jer. 31 and Ezek 36 seriously as the backdrop to Paul's thinking leads him to conclude that
"the flesh/Spirit distinction does not explain Paul's de facto changes in the content of the
law ... If the basic thing 'wrong' with the law is that humans are unable to fulfill it, there is
no reason to have those in the Spirit, who have been given the ability, fulfill only part of it.
In the Spirit one should certainly be able to obey the laws governing circumcision, food, and
days" (p. 147). For Sanders what is "basically wrong with the law is that it does not provide
entry to the people of God for Gentile as well as Jew ...," which explains why Paul elimi-
nates these aspects of it (p. 147). Sanders is correct in insisting that those who argue as I do
must "consider concrete cases" in order to demonstrate their thesis (p. 147). As the work of
Instone Brewer, Theilman, and Tomson now demonstrates (see next note), such a perspective can be brought to bear on even the most difficult texts. Rather than simply regarding
passages such as 1 Cor. 7:19 to be "amazing" and offered by Paul "without explanation,"
and concluding that Rom. 2 must be a "self-contradiction," as Sanders does (pp. 102 f.,
147), such concrete cases must be reexamined in view of Paul's explicit statements of principle about the Law and its function within the new covenant. To make one of these statements clear, i.e. 2 Cor. 3:6–18, is the purpose of this work. For an application of the same
fundamental perspective pursued here to Paul's view of the Law in Gal. 2–3, in which the
eschatological framework of restoration/second Exodus, etc. is seen to be the key to Paul's
thinking, see now the important work of James M. Scott, "'For as Many as are of Works of
the Law are under a Curse,' (Gal. 3.10)," in *Paul and the Scriptures of Israel*, ed. Craig A.
Evans and James A. Sanders, JSNT Suppl. 83, 1993, pp. 187–221, and his development of
this framework for Galatians as a whole in his *Adoption as Sons of God, An Exegetical Investigation into the Background of* ΥΙΟΘΕΣΙΑ *in the Pauline Corpus*, WUNT 2. Reihe 48,
1992, pp. 121–186.

that the Law was written ultimately for the church and is to be obeyed (cf. 1 Cor. 9:10; 10:6, 11; 14:33b, 36).[146]

This basic conviction concerning the new covenant work of writing the Law on the heart is further confirmed by the transition in Paul's thought from 2 Cor. 3:3b to 3:6. Here he brings together by way of allusion the conceptually related passages from Ezekiel and Jeremiah concerning the future restoration of Israel, having introduced them sequentially in order to emphasize different aspects of his ministry.[147] In 3:3b Paul began by picturing his ministry as the fulfillment of the eschatological new age of the Spirit pictured in Ezekiel 11:19[148] and 36:26 f., which has now arrived among God's people through Paul's own role as its intermediary agent. At that point the contrast was between God's work in the past, in which he engraved on the stone tablets of the Law,[149] and his

---

[146] For the development of this perspective in regard to the Corinthians, see now the important work of Peter J. Tomson, *Paul and the Jewish Law, Halakha in the Letters of the Apostle to the Gentiles*, CRINT III/1, 1990, Frank Thielman, "The Coherence of Paul's View of the Law: The Evidence of First Corinthians," *NTS* 38 (1992) 235–253, and D. Instone Brewer, "1 Corinthians 9.9–11: A Literal Interpretation of 'Do Not Muzzle the Ox,'" *NTS* 38 (1992) 554–565. Contra those who, like E.P. Sanders, *Paul, the Law, and the Jewish People*, 1983, pp. 145–148, conclude that Paul's view and use of the Law are unsystematic in character and not ultimately determinative for his *Christian* ethics, and those who, like F. Hahn, "Die alttestamentlichen Motive in der urchristlichen Abendmahlsüberlieferung," *EvTh* 27 (1967) 337–374, p. 370 n. 127, argue that the typology of correspondence and renewal in 1 Cor. 10 does not apply to the Law of Sinai, since in regard to the Law only an antithetical typology exists.

[147] For the conceptual relationship between Ezek. 36:27–28 and Jer. 31:33 see now Daniel I. Block's very helpful survey, "The Prophet of the Spirit: The Use of *RWH* in the Book of Ezekiel," *JETS* 32 (1989) 27–49, pp. 38 f. and below. Block argues convincingly for taking the reference to the "spirit" in 36:26 f. in both cases to be the divine Spirit. For the arguments in favor of seeing in 2 Cor. 3:3 an allusion only to Ezek. 11:19 and 36:26 f. (so too e.g. A. Schlatter, H. Räisänen), rather than to a broader and less descript collage of these texts from Ezek. together with Jer. 31 (LXX 38):31 ff., and perhaps including Jer. 17:1; Prov. 3:3; 7:3, or even as an allusion to the texts from Proverbs alone with no allusion to either Ezek. or Jer. (so Christian Wolff and now too A.T. Hanson, *Studies*, pp. 171 f.), see *Suffering and the Spirit*, pp. 204–207. There it is argued that one ought not to collapse 3:3 and 3:6 together, interpreting one in view of the other. In particular, one ought not to read 3:3 from the perspective of 3:6 (contra e.g. Bultmann), nor vice versa (contra Hickling and Hughes), cf. p. 206. For the opposite view, see now Stockhausen, *Moses' Veil*, pp. 42, 63, 75 f., 76 n. 72, who views 3:3 as requiring both Jer. 31 and Ezek. 11/26 as background, together with Exod. 34:1, 4.

[148] There is some question whether the reference to the "spirit" in Ezek. 11:19 refers to the human seat of mental activity, or to the divine Spirit; cf. Block, "Prophet of the Spirit," p. 45. Block argues that the reference "appears to be intentionally ambiguous," though he contends that the former dominates (p. 41). But in any case, as Block observes, "when the contends theme resurfaces in Ezek. 36:26–27 the nuance of seat of intellect and will recedes … and gives way to Yahweh's own spirit, which will be infused into the nation" (p. 41). But inasmuch as Paul has Ezek. 36 primarily, if not exclusively, in view, the exact referent in 11:19 need not concern us here.

[149] Cf. the LXX of Ex. 24:12; 31:18; 32:15; 34:1 and Deut. 9:10 as the backdrop to the "tablets of stone" imagery in 3:3b (cf. ἐν πλαξὶν λιθίναις), rather than as an allusion to Jer. 38:33 (LXX); cf. *Suffering and the Spirit*, p. 205.

present work, in which he "engraves" on "tablets of human hearts" by means of the Spirit which is being poured out through Paul's ministry. The motif of the new "fleshly heart" and the explicit reference to the Spirit, which are so central to Paul's thought in 3:3, both derive from Ezekiel 11:19 and 36:26 f.[150] Viewed against this background, Paul's concern in 3:3 was not with the relationship between the new covenant and the Law, as in 3:6, but with "the two 'materials' of God's activity as 'writer'."[151]

Thus, the significance of the contrast in 3:3b between ink and the Spirit, and then between the tablets of stone and of fleshly hearts, is twofold.[152] First, read as a fulfillment of the promises from Ezekiel concerning the future restoration of God's people, the contrast between the stone tablets of the Law and the heart of flesh is not a contrast between the nature of the Law and the heart.[153] Nor is it a contrast between the Law and the Spirit, which in turn would create a contrast between two conflicting qualities or ways of salvation. Rather, 2 Cor. 3:3b establishes a

"... contrast between the two spheres of God's revelatory-salvific activity, i.e. the 'law' and the 'heart' ... as a contrast between the two basic ages in the history of salvation ... represented by these two fundamental rubrics. For while in the 'old age' the locus of God's activity and revelation was the law, in the 'new age,' according to Ezekiel, God will be at work in the heart." [154]

In view of the history of Israel's hardened rebellion against God (see below, ch. 3), Paul's allusion to the promise from Ezekiel in 3:3b picks up the common theme in post-biblical Jewish literature of "the nation's 'hard heart,'" while at the same time expressing hope in God's corresponding eschatological promise to replace the 'heart of stone' with a *new* heart of flesh and a new spirit/Holy Spirit so that his people might keep the law and thus remain faithful to the covenant."[155] This becomes especially apparent in those passages where the motifs of the heart and/or Spirit and faithfulness to the Law come together.

---

[150] The view of Koch, *Schrift*, p. 45, that the language of καρδίαι σαρκίναι in 3:3 is indeed biblical terminology which goes back to Ezek. 11:19; 36:26, but that an allusion to these passages is not in view, remains unconvincing. The language is specific enough that it is hard to imagine that Paul would use it here without intending a reference to the passages from which it comes.

[151] *Suffering and the Spirit*, p. 206.

[152] For these points and their support, as well as a critique of opposing positions, see *Suffering and the Spirit*, pp. 207–218.

[153] Failure to take this into account has led G. Theißen, "Die Hülle des Mose und die unbewußten Aspekte des Gesetzes," in his *Psychologische Aspekte paulinischer Theologie*, 1983, pp. 121–161. pp. 146 f., 152–154, to read Paul's reference to the "heart" in 3:2, 3, 15, and 4:6 to be a reference to mankind's inner reality, which must come to grips with the law as internalized "aggressive norms." This leads to a psychological reading of the "letter" in Freudian terms which cannot be sustained by the text (cf. pp. 147, 152, and see below).

[154] *Suffering and the Spirit*, p. 214.

[155] *Suffering and the Spirit*, p. 213; cf. p. 213 n. 150 for a listing of various traditions which reflect this perspective, from 4 Ezra 3:19–21, 36; 7:23 f., 45–49, 72; to Jub. 1:7, 10,

Excursus: The Heart, Spirit, and the Law in the Apocrypha and Pseudepigrapha

The relationship between the heart, the Spirit, and the Law which provides the framework of Paul's thought in 2 Cor. 3:3–6 corresponds to the way in which these motifs are interrelated in post-biblical literature in the few instances where they come to expression. [156] In particular, the heart is consistently viewed as the locus of true obedience, and when the Spirit is mentioned in connection with the Law and the heart it is portrayed as the agent of empowerment which makes obedience to the Law from the heart possible. A simple cataloging of the various assertions which surround these themes will demonstrate these points. [157]

In 1 Esdras 1:18 f., 22, the passover of Josias is described as better than those of all the previous kings, since the people were wicked "and the words of the Lord were established against Israel."[158] The reason given in v. 21 for Josias' exemplary actions is that, unlike the parallel in 2 Chron. 35:19 f. where such a reference is omitted, Josias' "works before his Lord" (τὰ ἔργα Ιωσιου ἐνώπιον τοῦ κυρίου αὐτοῦ) are done "in a heart full of godliness" (ἐν καρδίᾳ πλήρει εὐσεβείας). 2 Macc. 1:3 f. reflects this same view of the heart in relationship to obedience and the law when it prays, "may he give you all a heart to worship him and do his pleasure ... may he give you an open heart for his Law and for his statutes." Similarly, in 2 Macc. 2:2 f. Jeremiah sends the people into exile with the charge that "the Law should not depart from their heart," which in the context parallels "neither be led astray in their minds." In Tobit 4:19, at the end of his instructions, Tobit says to his son, "remember these commandments, and let them not be blotted out of thy heart," though the commandments in view here are not those of the law, but those given by Tobit. In the same way, in Sirach 2:16 f. we read that "they that love Him will be filled with (his) Law," which is linked to the affirmation that "they make ready their hearts." Conversely, in Sirach 1:26–30, it is "in the midst of the synagogue" (ἐν μέσῳ συναγωγῆς) that disobedience to the "fear of the Lord" as expressed in the commandments is revealed by the Lord and judged, a statement which may be related to Paul's point in 2 Cor. 3:14 f. (see ch. five below). This disobedience

---

21–23; Apoc.Mos. 13:3–5; T. Levi 18:10–11; Odes of Sol. 4:3; to Ps.-Philo, LAB 30:6 and Bar. 1:17–21, etc. See now Hofius, "Gesetz und Evangelium," p. 81, who also emphasizes that this new heart is the gift of the new διαθήκη (Jer. 31:33; 32:39 f.) based on forgiveness, which he rightly calls "das zum Gehorsam befreite Herz." But Hofius stops short of speaking of the Law itself as written on the heart in Jer. 31 and speaks rather of a general and abstract "Willensforderung" or "will of God," or "life of obedience" (pp. 81, 83), since he sees no room for the Sinai Law in the new covenant in Paul's thought.

[156] A treatment of these themes in the Qumran literature will appear in a forthcoming work on the new covenant in the Qumran writings.

[157] Besides those texts mentioned below, see 2 Macc. 1:3 f.; 2:2 f.; Tobit 4:19; Sir. 2:16 f.; Adam and Eve 29:8 f.; Apoc. Mos. 13:3–5; 1 Enoch 5:4; 14:3; 16:3; 94:5; 98:11; 99:2, 8; 100:8; T. Reub. 3:8 f.; T. Sim. 2:7 f.; 5:2; 6:2 (cf. the use of the motif of "stiff-neckedness" here); Test. Jud. 18:3; 20:3–5; Test. Naph. 2:8; 3:1; and 2 Bar. 15:5. For this theme viewed from the standpoint of "reason" as that which controls the passions, so that the Law can be obeyed and said to have been given "to the mind," see 4 Macc. 1:17, 34 f.; 2:1–14, 23; 5:16, 23; 16:1–5; 18:1–4.

[158] Translations for this text and all the other apocryphal writings, unless otherwise noted, are my own, while the text and versification follows that of A. Ralph, Septuaginta, 2 Vols, 1935.

finds its root in approaching the fear of the Lord "in a double heart" (ἐν καρδίᾳ δισσῇ, 1:28), i.e. with "your heart full of deceit" (ἡ καρδία σου πλήρης δόλου, 1:30). By implication, obedience to the Law comes about as a result of being able to approach the "fear of the Lord" with a clean heart intent on keeping its commandments as the expression of the wisdom of God (cf. Sir. 1:10, 11–21, 26 f.; 2:15 f.; 9:15 f.; 17:11; 21:11; 24; 38:34; 39:1, etc.).[159]

In Baruch 2:30–33, a passage with special affinities to Paul's argument in 2 Cor. 3:3–6 due to its allusions to Jeremiah 31:31–34; 32:38–41 and Ezekiel 36:24–28, as well as to 2 Cor. 3:12–18 (see below, ch. five), God promises to overcome the fact that Israel is "stiff-necked," which caused them to be judged and led into exile. For

"... in the land of their captivity ... I will give them a heart, and ears to hear: and they shall praise me in the land of their captivity, and think upon my name, and shall return from their stiff neck (ἀπὸ τοῦ νώτου αὐτῶν τοῦ σκληροῦ), and from their wicked deeds: for they shall remember the way of their fathers, which sinned before the Lord. And I will bring them again into the land which I swore unto their fathers, to Abraham, to Isaac, and to Jacob, and they shall be lords of it: and I will increase them, and they shall not be diminished. And I will make an everlasting covenant with them to be their God, and they shall be my people: and I will no more remove my people of Israel out of the land that I have given them."

Baruch here applies the promises from Jeremiah and Ezekiel, linking them explicitly to the motif of Israel's "stiff-neck" and the sinful ways of the fathers, which recalls the history of Israel's rebellion beginning with the golden calf (see below, ch. three). The future redemption of God's people is thus pictured in terms of a reversal of the hardened condition first displayed in Israel's sin with the golden calf (cf. Ex. 32:9; 33:3, 5; 34:9). But unlike Paul, according to Bar. 2:30 this return to the Lord as a result of having received a new heart was to have taken place already in the "land of Israel's captivity," at which time God would bring them back into the promised land and make an "everlasting covenant" with them (Bar. 2:35). For Paul, however, although the "new covenant" has indeed been inaugurated in Christ, Israel's rejection of the messiah demonstrates that such a redemption and restoration of the nation has not yet occurred. They remain hardened "until this very day" (2 Cor. 3:14 f.).

Finally, in a related restoration text, Jubilees 1:23 f. declares that in the future God "shall cut off the foreskin of their heart and the foreskin of the heart of their descendants. And I shall create for them a holy spirit, and I shall purify them so that they will

---

[159] For a very helpful and detailed study of the interrelationship between the wisdom of God, the Law, and the fear of God, see Eckhard J. Schnabel, *Law and Wisdom from Ben Sira to Paul, A Tradition Historical Enquiry into the Relation of Law, Wisdom, and Ethics*, WUNT 2. Reihe 16, 1985, esp. his comprehensive survey of terminology and uses of these concepts on pp. 16–60. As Schnabel also points out, for Sirach the fear of the Lord is considered to be the basis for obedience to the Law (p. 45), while "the fact that Ben Sira often includes references to the law in passages which contain traditional wisdom material (cf. 1:5, 26; 19:17, 20, 24; 24:23; 32:14–18, 22–23) seems to indicate that the great didactic pericopes on wisdom, on the fear of the Lord, on the destiny of man, on creation, and on the wise man all aim at establishing the Torah as the 'vanishing point' of the activity of the sage. For Ben Sira, a priest and scribe, the law and the commandments formed the very basis of his life and thought" (p. 30). Hence, wisdom does not replace the Law in Sirach, but functions to establish it.

not turn away from following me from that day and forever. And their souls will cleave to me and to all my commandments. And they will do my commandments." As the covenant formula in 1:25 then indicates, this new "circumcised heart" and the obedience by the power of the Spirit which characterizes it form the essential content of this renewed, and certainly in the sense of Jer. 31, "new" covenantal relationship. [160] For as we read in Jub. 23:26, the eschatological restoration begins in the midst of God's judgment of the people for their disobedience, when "in those days, children will begin to search the law, and to search the commandments and to return to the way of righteousness."

Second, rather than being a negative assessment of the nature of the Law itself, or functioning to introduce a negative nuance concerning the Law,[161] the reference to the Law under the rubric of the "tablets of stone" in 3:3 is part of a long tradition in which this designation is at least a normal, neutral way of referring to the Law, and more probably is a way to emphasize its divine authority, honor, and glory (cf. 3:7, 9, 11).[162] Once read against the backdrop of Ezekiel and the new covenant from Jeremiah 31, there is no indication in the context that Paul is intending to qualify this common ground assumption negatively.[163] Instead, "if anything is to be assumed as implicit in

---

[160] Jub. 1:16–25 (cf. Jer. 4:3 f.; Deut. 6:5, 10; 8:11; 28:13, 44) refers to the old covenant, but not explicitly to the new one.

[161] For just one example of this common view, see Räisänen, *Paul and the Law*, p. 45 (cf. p. 83), who sees Paul to be making "a deprecatory reference to the *tablets of stone* – the very core of God's law in as original a form as possible. *Here* is the killing letter to be found!" (emphasis his).

[162] Cf. now Reinhold Liebers, "Paulinische Rezeption und Kritik des frühjüdischen Gesetzesverständnisses, 2 Kor 3" in his *Das Gesetz als Evangelium, Untersuchungen zur Gesetzeskritik des Paulus,* AThANT 75, 1989, pp. 96–123, p. 101, who argues based on the parallel between the stone tables and the covenant in Deut. 9:9,11 that the stone material does not devalue the Law, but the Law retains its value and validity through its origin in YHWH. Liebers supposes, therefore, that there is some tension between the divine origin of the Law and its form as written on stone. But besides the references from the OT which support the point argued here (cf. Ex. 24:12 with 31:18 and the reference to the tablets as the "work of God" in Ex. 32:16 [LXX] and as written with the finger of God (Ex. 31:18; Deut. 9:10), cf. the development of the stone tablet motif in Jub. 1:1; 1:26 f.; 2:1; 3:10, 31; 6:22; 16:30; 32:10 f.; etc.; 1 En. 81:1 f.; 103:2–4; T. Levi 5:4; 7:5; 2 Apoc. Bar. 6:7–9; Lives of the Prophets, Jer. 14; Tg. Ps.-J. Ex. 31:18; Exod. Rab. 41.6; 46.2; Lev. Rab. 32.2; 35.5; Num. Rab. 9.48; b.Ned. 38a; Pirqe R. El. 45, and the other texts from post-biblical Judaism surveyed in *Suffering and the Spirit*, pp. 208–212, after which it is concluded that "there is, to my knowledge, no indication at any period in Jewish-tradition that the stone-nature of the tablets of the law ever carried a negative connotation similar to the heart of stone imagery used in Ezekiel 11:19 and 36:26" (p. 212). In addition to these traditions listed in my earlier work, see Eupolemus, Frag. 4 (Eusebius, *Praeparatio Evangelica* 9.39.5) and 2 Macc. 2:1–10 for the tradition of Jeremiah's preserving the tablets after the destruction of Jerusalem, which in view of Paul's reference to Jer. 31 may be of special significance as underscoring the abiding validity of the Law in the new covenant; and for the tablet motif in general. Also of interest in view of the development of the new covenant motif in Qumran is the fragment entitled "The Ages of the Creation" (4Q180), where it is said that the events of every age were "engraved on [heavenly] tablets ... the ages of their domination." Finally, see Philo, *Quaes. Exod.* II, 41, where he gives his answer to why the commandments were written on tablets of stone, i.e. to signify their permanence by providing a material that would make it possible for them to be spread abroad without corruption.

[163] Contra now Vollenweider, "2 Kor 3," pp. 262, 267, who concedes that the tablets were viewed positively within Judaism, but rejects my view of 3:3 and 3:6, taking Paul's refer-

Paul's contrast in regard to the law, it is that the law is now being kept by those who have received the Spirit, as Ezekiel prophesied!"[164] The implication of the contrast in 3:3, based on the allusions to Ezekiel, is that

---

ence to stone tablets as a negative qualification of the tradition because of 3:6, which, together with 3:3 and the contrasts in 3:7–11, he takes as a negative statement about the Law itself, since the entire passage is a working out of the letter/Spirit contrast (cf. p. 265). In his view, the Law written on stone tablets "wird negativ qualifiziert; mit Christus ist es abgetan und nunmehr symbolisch, typologisch und allegorisch zu deuten" (p. 267, emphasis removed). In contrast to the view of 3:6 argued here, Vollenweider supports his view by rejecting the fact that in pointing to Jer. 31 Paul is referring to the Law itself, though he supports the view that Jer. 31 is in view (cf. p. 269 n. 366), and by pointing to the Greek antithesis between the written and divine law in addition to Jer. 31 and Ezek. 11:19 and 36:26 as the essential background to Paul's thought in 3:6 (and in Rom. 2:14 f., 26 f.), since Vollenweider recognizes that in the OT prophets it is the heart and not the Law which is changed (cf. pp. 265 ff.) ! Hence, his understanding of Paul's view of the Law (in which this prophetic view of the Law cannot be maintained!) brings him to look outside the OT for a possible conceptual background (p. 266). But once his understanding of Paul's purportedly negative view of the Law is not brought to 2 Cor. 3:6, in which the "letter" refers to the written Sinai Law characteristic of Judaism over against the unwritten ethical law that is binding on Jews and Gentiles (p. 267), such a decision is not necessary. For my corresponding view of 3:7–11, see chapter four.

[164] *Suffering and the Spirit*, p. 214. This conclusion is directly opposite to that drawn by Schoeps, *Paul, The Theology of the Apostle in the Light of Jewish Religious History*, 1961, whose central point is that, as a Diaspora Jew influenced by Hellenistic Judaism, Paul misunderstood the role of the Law as separated from the covenant and thus, alienated from the faith of his fathers, reduced it to a mere ethical principle of self-justification and ritual performance, which after his conversion he came to see had failed and been dissolved or subsumed in the new age (cf. pp. 200, 213 f., 259–262). Schoeps is right that "Paul's consistently eschatological mode of thought" is the key to Paul's thinking concerning the Law (p. 170), but wrong in the conclusions he draws from it concerning the establishment of a new law in Christ and the abrogation of the Sinai law (cf. pp. 29, 171; for a critique of the idea that in the messianic age God will give a new law through the Messiah, see above, n. 144). Moreover, for Schoeps, the origin of Paul's original misunderstanding is the LXX itself and Hellenistic Judaism, whose interpretation of תורה ("Torah") with νόμος ("Law") was "a shift of emphasis towards legalism" (p. 29; cf. p. 32), and in whose translation of ברית ("covenant") with διαθήκη ("testament") "the idea of reciprocity has ceased to exist" (p. 217), two distinctions now widely and correctly rejected. Schoeps thus concludes that "the Pauline theology of law and justification begins with the fateful misunderstanding in consequence of which he tears asunder covenant and law, and then represents Christ as the end of the law" (p. 218; cf. pp. 168 f., 171–174). For Schoeps, as for those who follow in his train on this point (e.g. E.P. Sanders), "The abolition of the law is a Messianological doctrine in Pauline theology" (p. 171). Of significance for this study is the fact that once Jer. and Ezek. are taken seriously as the backdrop for 2 Cor. 3, rather than it's being true that Paul "had ceased to understand the totality and continuity of the Berith-Torah" (p. 198), Paul's point becomes the continuity and fulfillment of this unity in the new covenant! The integral unity of faith and obedience which Schoeps rightly emphasizes for the Sinai covenant, but sees torn apart in Paul, is actually reaffirmed and established by Paul (cf. pp. 200–202), though it must be emphasized that for both the Law and for Paul, the imperative covenant stipulations always follow and are based upon the indicatives of God's divine redemptive acts upon which the covenant is based. Hence, Schoeps is able to establish his view only because he is convinced that for Paul, "not the meaning of scripture, but Christ is the *a priori* for his judgment of the law" (p. 175).

"Paul affirms that the age characterized by the law as the locus of God's revelatory activity is over. In contrast, the Corinthians owe their relationship to Christ not to the revelation of God in the law, but to God's work in changing their hearts through his Spirit. As such, the conversion and new life of the Corinthians are evidence that the new age has arrived, i.e. the age of the 'fleshly heart' prophesied by Ezekiel."[165]

c) The New Covenant and the Spirit

Having made this point in 3:3b, Paul now makes it explicit in 3:6a that he sees his *apostolic ministry of the Spirit* in fulfillment of Ezek. 11:19 and 36:26 f., with its focus on the work of the Spirit on the renewed heart, to be conceptually at one with his role as a *servant of the new covenant* in fulfillment of Jer. 31:31–34. Paul "serves" or "delivers" (διακονηθεῖσα) the "letter of Christ" (= the conversion of the Corinthians) by means of the Spirit (3:3b) as a "servant" (διάκονος) of the new covenant. And as Jer. 31:31–34 and Paul's own preservation of the Lord's Supper tradition in 1 Cor. 11:25 make clear, the new covenant which Paul ministers is built squarely on the atoning death of Christ which has made possible the forgiveness of sins and reception of the Spirit with a renewed heart.[166] Hence, his being a servant (= minister) of the new covenant based on the cross of Christ means that his ministry will be a ministry of the Spirit as the manifestation of the presence of God.[167] As a result, since Paul's "confidence" and "sufficiency" are based upon this work of the Spirit in and through his ministry (3:4–5; see above), Paul supports the fact that his sufficiency is from God by pointing to the existence of the Corinthians themselves as "demonstrable proof of the gospel of the new covenant."[168] Paul's new covenant ministry (3:6 based upon Jer. 31:31–34) is a ministry of the Spirit (3:3b based upon Ezek. 36:26 f.) and vice versa. In typical Pauline style, the relative pronoun clause which begins 3:6 (ὃς καὶ ἱκάνωσεν ἡμᾶς διακόνους καινῆς διαθήκης) thus functions to *ground* Paul's prior assertion in 3:5b that his sufficiency is from God. It does so by pointing to the reality of

---

[165] *Suffering and the Spirit*, p. 215.

[166] For this point, see Stegemann, "Neue Bund," p. 109. He rightly observes that "Das Element also, das bei Jeremia den Gegensatz bildet, ist dasselbe wie bei Paulus, nämlich die Sünde" (p. 109). Jeremiah promises the eschatological "overcoming of sin," and Paul sees it established in Christ among the Gentiles (p. 109). Finally, Stegemann, p. 109, rightly emphasizes that the other point connected with the Law written on the heart in Jeremiah is the promise of the immediacy of God to his people, which finds its corollary in Paul's thought as well.

[167] I owe the emphasis on the Spirit as the manifestation of the presence of God in this passage to Renwick, *Temple*, p. 52, who suggests that, already at this point in Paul's argument, it is crucial that in the new covenant access to God's presence has been opened up to all Christians. But Renwick goes on to link this with the problem of Paul's suffering, which does not seem to be in view. It was precisely the suffering righteous who anticipated one day being in God's presence. The issue, rather, in view of Jer. 31 and Ezek. 11 and 36 is the condition of one's heart.

[168] Jones, *Second Moses*, p. 33 n. 2.

what is being fulfilled through his apostleship and its consequences in the lives of the Corinthians.[169] Paul's support for his "confidence" and "sufficiency" as an apostle is therefore implicit already in his choice of the designation "new covenant" to depict that which he serves. At the same time, Paul's reference to the new covenant supports his prior point that he does not consider any aspect of his sufficiency to derive from his own human ingenuity or distinctives, but from God, precisely *because* God made him sufficient as a servant of the new covenant, a covenant which revolves around the work of the Spirit in the hearts of God's people. It is *God's* work of pouring out his Spirit that is the basis of Paul's sufficiency as an apostle.

In addition, inasmuch as Ezek. 11:19; 36:26 f. and Jer. 31:31–34 are related conceptually, but not in their essential terminology, the fact that Paul brings these two passages together in 2 Cor. 3:3 and 6 alerts the reader that Paul's references to these texts function as more than just OT proof texts from which he borrows helpful terminology. In moving from one passage to another, Paul is following their train of thought, rather than merely establishing a slim linguistic link or "catch-word" connection as is common in Jewish literature.[170] Indeed, the only common element between them is the reference to the "heart," and even here Ezekiel significantly modifies this term in ways not

---

[169] For uses of ὅς to introduce a relative pronoun clause functioning as a ground or support in the argument, see Rom. 2:6; 4:16, 18; 8:32; 1 Cor. 1:8; 1:30; 4:5, 17; 10:13; 1 Cor. 15:9; 2 Cor. 1:10; 13:3; Phil. 2:6; 3:21; Col. 1:7, 13, 15 (?), 18; 2:10; 1 Tim. 2:4; 4:10; Titus 2:14.

[170] See e.g. Stockhausen, *Moses' Veil*, p. 26, who helpfully defines the Jewish practice of *gezera shawa* as building analogies between texts based on similar verbal expressions which are then used to interpret one another based on this "linking through hook words." For Stockhausen, it is this "hook-word association of Scriptural texts around a central theme" (p. 54) which explains the combination of Jer. 31 and Ezek. 36 in this passage. Moreover, her central thesis is that the exegetical background behind 3:1–18 was not ad hoc, but reflected part of a *pre-Pauline* Christian exegesis based on an independent existence of this cluster of texts, which Paul tapped into based on the "hook word" γράφω (p. 23; see next note). In her view, "The structure of Paul's own text [i.e. 3:1–18] hangs on a single link with the text-group discovered, γράφω, and consists of an argument which relies heavily on ideas drawn from the group" (pp. 58 f.). The key word γράφω is thus "the thread on which Paul's argument from scripture is strung" (p. 71; cf. pp. 72 f.). She sees this pre-Pauline cluster of texts to have been built on the catch words καρδία (Jer. 38:31 ff. and 39:39 with Ezek. 11:16 ff. and 36:26 LXX), διαθήκη (Jer. 38 with Jer. 39), and πνεῦμα (Ezek. 11 with Ezek. 36), and the covenant formula in Jer. 38:33; 39:38 (LXX) and Ezek. 11:20; 36:28 (pp. 56 f.; 60 f.). Hofius, "Gesetz und Evangelium," p. 79, who also sees the connection to be made on the basis of the Jewish practice of analogy *(gezera shawa)*, but instead of hook words points to the four themes they have in common: 1) the promise of a new/everlasting covenant (Jer. 31:31; 32:40; Ezek. 37:26); 2) the promise of forgiveness and cleansing (Jer. 31:34; Ezek. 36:25, 29); 3) total renewal of the human heart (Jer. 31:33; 32:39 f.; Ezek. 36:26); and 4) the covenant formula (Jer. 31:33; 32:38; Ezek. 36:28; 37:27). But notice how Hofius overlooks their common understanding of the Law in the new covenant (Jer. 31:33; Ezek. 36:27), which needs to be added as a fifth correspondence. Hofius does this because he sees only a negative function for the Law in the new covenant, while the old covenant which is brought to an end is a "Gesetz-διαθήκη" to be equated with the Torah from Sinai (p. 80).

found in Jeremiah. Nor does Ezekiel have any reference to the Law being written on it, speaking rather of the work of the Spirit, while he nowhere uses the terminology of the new covenant to refer to the eschatological reality of a Spirit-enabled obedience to the Law. On the other hand, Jeremiah lacks any reference to the Spirit, which is the main focus of the texts from Ezekiel.[171]

Nevertheless, the two texts *are* clearly related conceptually. The "Law written on the heart" from Jer. 31:33 is clearly equivalent to the new obedience to God's statutes, which Ezekiel explicitly says will be the brought about by the Spirit *as its purpose* in the future restoration (cf. Ezek. 36:27).[172] Paul's allusion to the passages from Ezekiel in 3:3b calls one's attention to the corresponding point of the new covenant from Jer. 31:31–34 in 2 Cor. 3:6a, with its clear emphasis that in this covenant God will write his Law on their hearts, i.e. transform them so that they accept his Law and respond with obedience.[173]

As was true for Jeremiah (see above), for Ezekiel too this eschatological promise of a new heart and a Spirit-caused obedience to the Law of God is a reversal of the hard-heartedness that has characterized Israel since the Exodus (cf. the "stone heart" imagery in Ezek. 11:19b; 36:26b with Ezek. 2:1–8; 20:1–31; and see chapter three below). Ezekiel also parallels Jeremiah in emphasizing that this new heart and relationship to God's Law will be made possible only by a divine act of redemption and forgiveness, which for Ezekiel is pictured in the priestly terms of God's cleansing the people from their uncleanness and idolatry (Ezek. 36:25, 29). In bringing these two texts together,

---

[171] Stockhausen's catch-word connections are thus misleading in that her references to the Spirit and covenant serve only to link Jeremiah with Jeremiah and Ezekiel with Ezekiel, which surely would have been done naturally. She admits that Jeremiah has no reference to the Spirit, while Ezekiel 11 and 36 do (p. 62), but argues that the other association between the texts makes the connection between the two texts legitimate (pp. 62, 67). In reality, however, the only other connections remaining, besides the common use of heart, are conceptual, exegetical connections, which speak against an exclusive reliance on the "hook word" theory.

[172] See now Block, "Prophet of the Spirit," p. 39, who concludes that Ezekiel's reference that God will cause Israel to walk in his statutes parallels Jeremiah's reference to the law written in the heart, both of which signify keeping the "covenant standards." In his words, "What Jeremiah attributes to the infusion of the divine Torah, Ezekiel ascribes to the infusion of the *rwh*. In both the result is the renewal of the covenant relationship." There is no reason to mitigate this equivalency by making a distinction between Ezekiel's antithesis as "moral" and Jeremiah's as "heilsgeschichtlich," as Hickling, "Sequence," p. 389, suggests, since in both passages the context is the eschatological restoration of Israel after the exile (cf. Ezek. 11:13–18; 36:19–25; cf. 37:15–23; and Jer. 31:23–28, 38–40). On the other hand, both prophets refer to the eschatological keeping of the Law. Hence, in both cases the hope is moral and "heilsgeschichtlich." See Werner E. Lemke, "Jeremiah 31:31–34," *Int* 37 (1983) 183–187, p. 186: "both Jer and Ezek envisaged a similar restoration and internalization of the relationship between Yahweh and his people ..."

[173] See too F. Lang, "Gesetz und Bund," p. 308, who makes this same point concerning Jer. 31 and Ezek. 36, but then sees Paul going against this view in his own theology (based on the widespread view of Schoeps' distinction between the Jewish Christian and Hellenistic-Jewish Christian attitudes toward the Law, with Paul inheriting the latter, cf. pp. 308 f.).

Paul emphasizes that being a servant of the new covenant essentially involves mediating the work of the Spirit, which in turn brings about the transformation of the heart, making obedience to the Law possible. The passages from Ezekiel supply Paul's references to the work of the Spirit in 3:3b, while Jer. 31:31–34 provide the focus on the new obedience to the Law found in 3:6, as the subsequent letter/Spirit contrast confirms (see below).

d) The New Covenant and the Presence of God

This brings us to the promise of the new covenant itself from Jer. 31, which again finds its parallel and confirmation in Paul's prior allusion to the passages from Ezekiel. In both passages the result of the Law being written on the heart by God (Jer.), or of its being kept because of the work of the Spirit in one's heart (Ezek.), is that God will be known directly by his people, since they have been forgiven and now have both the desire and ability to keep his covenant. The "new covenant" of Jer. 31:31–34, which is described as the "everlasting covenant" (ברית עולם) in Jer. 32:40 in which God gives them "one heart and one way, that they may fear (him) always, for their own good, and for the good of their children after them" (32:39) and in which God "will put the fear of (him) in their hearts so that they will not turn away from (him)" (32:40), is thus of a piece with the statement concerning the "everlasting covenant" (ברית עולם) in Ezek. 37:24b–28, which functions as a summary of the significance of the prior passage of restoration in 36:25 f.:

> "... and they will walk in my ordinances, and keep my statutes, and observe them ... And I will make a covenant of peace with them; it will be an everlasting covenant with them. And I will place them and multiply them, and will set my sanctuary in their midst forever. My dwelling place also will be with them; and I will be their God, and they shall be my people. And the nations will know that I am the LORD who sanctifies Israel, when my sanctuary is in their midst forever." (Ezek. 37:24b–28, NASB)[174]

Hence, both Jeremiah and Ezekiel have at the center of their expectations concerning the future "everlasting covenant" the relationship between God and his people which is expressed in the typical formula, "I will be their God and they shall be my people" (Jer. 31:33; cf. 31:1; 32:38; Ezek. 37:27). In both prophets this entails God's dwelling in the midst of his people (Jer. 31:34; Ezek. 37:26 f.). As the combination of Ezekiel 36:25 f. and Jer. 31:31–34 in 2 Cor. 3:3 and 6 makes clear, for Paul this is already taking place through God's

---

[174] Cf. Moshe Greenberg, "The Design and Themes of Ezekiel's Program of Restoration," *Int* 38 (1984) 181–208, p. 182 on 37:24b–28 as a summary of chs. 34–37: "The hearts of the people will be bent to observe God's laws; as a result they will possess their patrimony forever under God's pious chief. The five-fold repetition of 'forever' stresses the irreversibility of the new dispensation. Unlike God's past experiment with Israel, the future restoration will have a guarantee of success; its capstone will be God's sanctifying presence dwelling forever in his sanctuary amidst his people. The vision of the restored Temple (and God's return to it) in chapters 40–48 follows as a proleptic corroboration of these promises."

Spirit, which dwells within and in the midst of the new covenant people who now make up God's eschatological "temple" of the Spirit (1 Cor. 3:16; 6:19).[175] The lives of the Corinthians as believers, as well as Paul's apostolic preaching and way of life, are consequently continually attributed to and defined by their origin and participation in the Spirit.[176] Moreover, as Block has emphasized, Ezek. 39:29 makes it clear that the promise of the Spirit in Ezek. 36, "poured out upon his people, served as the permanent witness and seal of the *bryt slwm* ["covenant of peace"] and the *bryt 'wlm* ["eternal covenant"] ... When we think in terms of the OT understanding of the *rwh* of Yahweh, of which *to pneuma to hagion* is the counterpart, we should think first and foremost of the divine presence on earth."[177] It is this participation in the Spirit which is the focal point of the promised new covenant reality, which for Paul is already being realized among those who are now in Christ. In 2 Cor. 1:22, Paul's reference to the Corinthians' being sealed in the Holy Spirit can thus be seen to be a reference to the divine confirmation of the covenant relationship in which they now stand.[178] It is this eschatological perspective, in which the proleptic fulfillment of the new age restoration is understood as taking place in the present experience of the Spirit, that provides the presupposition for the structure of Paul's thought.[179]

---

[175] Again, for the development of this theme in 2 Cor. against its OT and Jewish backdrop, see now Renwick, *Paul, the Temple, and the Presence of God*.

[176] For the Spirit as that which defines the Corinthians (and all believers), see 1 Cor. 2:10–14; 3:16; 6:11; 12:3 (it is the Spirit which brings one to confess Jesus as Lord!); 12:7–13; 2 Cor. 3:18; for the Spirit as the origin and force at work in Paul's ministry, see 1 Cor. 2:4; 7:40; 2 Cor. 4:13. Of course, examples could be multiplied from the other Pauline epistles. In this sense W. Klaiber, *Rechtfertigung und Gemeinde. Eine Untersuchung zum paulinischen Kirchenverständnis*, FRLANT 127, 1982, p. 159, is correct that the congregation is the "Urkunde des neuen Bundes," though he follows Käsemann in seeing the letter/Spirit contrast to be a Law/Gospel contrast pertaining to the doctrine of justification (p. 162, cf. pp. 166 f.).

[177] "Prophet of the Spirit," p. 48. Block, p. 47, refers to Joel 3:1; Zech. 12:10; Is. 32:15; 44:1–4 in addition to Ezek. 39:29 as texts pointing to the pouring out of the Spirit as that which "signified the ratification and sealing of the covenant relationship." Block notes too the implications of this for Acts 2 and the subsequent pouring out of the Spirit in Acts 8:14–17; 10:44–48; 19:6 (pp. 47 f.).

[178] Following Block, "Prophet of the Spirit," p. 48, who also points to Eph. 1:13; 4:30 for this same concept.

[179] See P.W. Meyer, "The Holy Spirit in the Pauline Letters: A Contextual Explanation," *Int* 33 (1979) 3–18, pp. 12–14, who argues against "the long-established and conventional dictum that for Paul the Christian has been transported into 'the age to come'" (p. 14 n. 13), since the Spirit is not "a partial resurrection ... It does not heal a 'defect' in man's nature ..." (p. 13). Meyer is certainly right that in 1 Cor. 15, Rom. 8, and 1 Cor. 6 Paul "reserves the transformation of human existence by God's life-giving Spirit to the future resurrection" (p. 16). The point, however, is not that Christians have been transported into the age to come, but that the age to come has invaded *this* age. For the classic presentation of this latter thesis, see Oscar Cullmann, *Christ and Time, The Primitive Conception of Time and History*, rev. ed., 1964, and its extension by George Eldon Ladd, *The Presence of the Future, The Eschatology of Biblical Realism*, 1974.

This becomes even more apparent when Paul's thought in 2 Cor. 3:6 is compared to the extensive development of the "new covenant" motif and its implications in the writings associated with Qumran. It is well known that apart from Jeremiah 31:31–34, the only explicit reference to the "new covenant" in pre-rabbinic Jewish literature outside of the New Testament is found in these documents.[180] Moreover, in the Qumran writings it is widely recognized that the new covenant conception is derived from Jeremiah 31.[181] As such, the new covenant theme in the Qumran writings provides an important contemporaneous tradition with which Paul's thought concerning the new covenant might

---

[180] For the related rabbinic texts, see below, n. 199. According to Schreiber, *Bund*, p. 29, 4 Ezra 6:26 ("and the heart of the earth's inhabitants shall be changed and converted to a different spirit" in reference to the future restoration) is reminiscent of Jer. 31:31–34, which he characteristically, but in my view wrongly, distinguishes from Paul's use since in 4 Ezra Schreiber sees no tension between the old and new covenants (p. 32). For another possible allusion, cf. 4 Ezra 9:31. There we read that at Sinai God declares, "I sow my Law in you, and you shall be glorified through it forever," although Israel's disobedience overturned this hope, so that the "sowing" in view here does not refer to the transformed heart (see below). Baruch 2:35 most probably refers to the covenant formula and the "everlasting covenant" in allusion to Jer. 31:31–34 and 32:40, though Wolff, *Jeremia*, pp. 117–119, 122, disputes this. In the later rabbinic literature, Jer. 31:31–34 is not cited in either the Babylonian or Jerusalem Talmud, with the only verbatim reference to the new covenant found in *Sifra* Lev. 26:9.

[181] Contra Wolff, *Jeremia*, pp. 124–130, who argues that in spite of the parallel terminology, the decisive characteristics of Jer. 31 are not found in the Qumran texts and that the detailed instructions concerning the Law in Qumran speak against Jer. 31, in which the Law is superfluous. But this is a misreading of Jer. 31 itself. Moreover, the point of this section is to show that the other key characteristics are also in view. In the Qumran texts, the full designation "new covenant" is found in CD 6:19; 8:21; 19:33–34; 20:12; 1QpHab 2:3, always with the designation "in the Land of Damascus," which may refer either to an actual place in which the community existed for a time (i.e. Babylon; cf. the use of Damascus for Babylon in Amos 5:26 f. and Acts 7:43, or to the area of Damascus itself), or to the community as a symbolic name reflecting their self-understanding as the continuation and fulfillment of the remnant within the nation which had been preserved through the Babylonian exile. The latter view is that of the majority; for the former, see Jerome Murphy-O'Connor, "The Essenes and Their History," *RevB* 81 (1974) 215–244, pp. 221 f., who argues that the sect originated in Babylon; and Devorah Dimant, "Qumran Sectarian Literature," *Jewish Writings of the Second Temple Period,* CRINT Section 2, Vol, 2, ed. Michael E. Stone, 1984, pp. 483–550, p. 494, who suggests that the sect migrated to "the land of Damascus" at some early point in their history during the lifetime of the Teacher of Righteousness, but before the major periods of occupation at Qumran. In either case, contra, U. Luz, "Der alte und der neue Bund bei Paulus und im Hebräerbrief," *EvTh* 27 (1967) 318–336, p. 318 n. 3, this reference to Damascus provides no compelling reason to conclude that Jer. 31:31–34 is not in view, since in both readings the community sees itself as the beginning fulfillment of the promise of restoration from Jer. 31. Luz' position also derives from his conviction that because the new covenant in Qumran is not opposed to the old, but is viewed as its reestablishment, it cannot be based on Jer. 31:31 ff. (cf. p. 318 n. 3). But this too is based on a radical antithesis between the old and new covenants in Jer. (and Paul!) that need not be maintained. The concept of the "covenant" itself is, of course, one of the major themes in the Qumran documents, occurring among the major writings 36 times in CD, 38 times in 1QS; 13 times in 1QM; 23 times in 1QH; and 3 times in 1QpHab; cf. A.M. Haberman, *Megilloth Midbar Yehuda, The Scrolls from the Judean Desert,* 1959, pp. 28 f.

be compared.[182] What is striking, therefore, is that the Qumran community also viewed itself as the people of this new covenant.[183] This becomes immediately evident in the introduction to the Damascus Rule, where the Qumran community is portrayed as the continuation and final fulfillment of the righteous remnant of Israel which, in accordance with his covenant with the Fathers, God had earlier preserved in the midst of Israel's rebellion and kept from the destruction of the Exile (CD 1:4–5; cf. CD 3:13–14).[184] As a

---

[182] A detailed investigation of the new covenant motif in the Qumran writings is beyond the scope of this present work. For our purposes it is not necessary to enter the current debate concerning the identity of the Qumran community itself, nor the thorny question of the relationship between the Qumran community and the documents found in their vicinity. The basic point to be made is that the Qumran community (whether to be strictly identified with the Essenes or not) can no longer be simply understood as an isolated, monastic community on the shores of the Dead Sea, but is seen to encompass a much broader constituency, which included city dwellers. This new perspective means their views were more pervasive and influential than previously thought, thus making these parallels even more significant.

[183] See the work on Qumran of E.P. Sanders, *Paul and Palestinian Judaism*, pp. 239–328, p. 240, in which he points out that there are two ways of formulating God's covenant with the Essenes, both of which "appear to amount to the same thing": God had made a new covenant with the community (CD 6.19; 8.21; 20:12; 1QpHab 2.3 f.), and the more frequent one that "God made a covenant with Moses (or the patriarchs) but that it contained hidden things understood only in the community, so that the community comprises the only adherents to God's covenant with Israel." (p. 240). As Sanders observes, in CD 15:5–11 "it is clear ... that 'returning to the Law of Moses' is in fact equivalent to joining the 'new covenant', for we learn that a man may not learn the individual laws (*mishpatim*) of the covenant until he is proved to be acceptable" (p. 241). This same equation is seen in 1QS 5.8 f., where "returning to the Law of Moses" means obeying the Law as revealed to the sons of Zakok. "Their covenant" in this context refers to the covenant of the priestly founders of the community; their covenant = God's covenant in 1QS 1.2 f. (p. 241). The "covenant of the community" (1QS 8.16 f.) or the "covenant of the everlasting community" (3.11 f.) is more regularly called "God's (Thy; His) covenant" (cf. 1QS 5.7 f.; CD 7.5; 20.17; 14.2) (p. 242). Sanders is also correct in emphasizing that in Qumran the establishment of the "new" covenant does not mean God has denied or replaced the Mosaic covenant. "New" means that the Mosaic covenant (i.e. the law and prophets) "contained secrets which have been only recently revealed" (p. 241). Thus, according to CD 3.10–14, the new covenant was established by God revealing the "hidden things concerning which all Israel had gone astray" to and through the Teacher of Righteousness, to whom was given the meaning of the mysteries of the prophets; cf. 1QS 5.11 f.; 1QpHab. 7:4 f. (p. 241).

[184] With John J. Collins, *The Apocalyptic Imagination, An Introduction to the Jewish Matrix of Christianity*, 1989 (1984), p. 119, the traditional view is here assumed that there is an essential (if not complete) unity of theological conception throughout the scrolls, evidenced by the fact that "the major documents of the sect were composed early on and continued to circulate throughout the history of Qumran." In making this statement, Collins points to 1QS, CD, segments from and perhaps the framework of 1QM, and the Thanksgiving Hymns in the assumption that, to a large degree, they reflect the thought of the Teacher of Righteousness (p. 119). Moreover, although the actual copies of the pesharim belong to the later history of the sect, Dimant, "Sectarian Literature," p. 489, is most likely correct in emphasizing that "the material they expound may go back to the beginnings of the sect." Finally, our survey confirms Collins' conclusion that evolutionary theories based on the use of source criticism in the scrolls should be approached "with caution," since although there was no doubt "a process of development, at least in the formative period of the sect," yet "there is little doubt

fulfillment of the prophetic hope for restoration, the Qumran community was raised up by God "390" years after the Exile in order to inherit the promises of the land and abundance given to Abraham, Isaac, and Jacob (CD 1:5–6; 3:13; cf. Ezek. 4:5). The need for this divine act is traced to Israel's past sin and history of rebellion in which the "eternal covenant" made with the fathers (cf. CD 1:4; 6:2; 8:18; 19:31) was broken by the nation as a whole and hence now becomes applicable only to the Qumran community as the beginning of the faithful remnant from within the people (cf. 1QH 6.7 f; 1QM 13.8; 14.8 f.; CD 3:5, 12–13; 8:17–18).[185] God therefore established a "new covenant" with the Qumran community as a renewal and fulfillment of his past covenant with the Patriarchs (cf. CD 2:2; 4:9–10; 6:2; 1QS 1:1–2:12). In doing so he "raised for them a Teacher of Righteousness to guide them in the way of His heart" so that they might remain faithful to the Law in contrast to the rebellion of the nation and in response to the new revelations and instruction being granted them concerning the coming eschaton (CD 1:12–13; cf. 1QpHab 2:8–10; 7:3–4;

... that such documents as 1QS and CD continued to function as authoritative documents after they reached their present form, and indeed were in their present form for most of the history of the Qumran settlement" (pp. 119 f.). Hence, Collins is correct in emphasizing that "we must ... respect the coherence of the way in which their various components have been put together" (p. 120). Dimant, p. 497, also following this approach, warns that "the exaggerated search for distinct literary sources and corresponding historical situations may often distort the original intentions of the work and obscure more fundamental historical considerations." She too concludes that the "sect's literary corpus attests to an overall unity of thought, terminology and style," despite its diversity in manner of expression, literary forms, purposes, and nuances in detail (p. 532). Hence, "even if divergencies exist, they should be seen as various components of basically one system which originated in a relatively short span of time" (p. 532).

[185] For this point see now Michael O. Wise, "The Covenant of Temple Scroll 29:3–10," *RevQ* 53 (1989) 49–60, p. 58. But see E.P. Sanders, *Paul and Palestinian Judaism*, pp. 250 f., who argues that the use of "remnant" refers to the eschatological existence of the saved, when the others have been destroyed (1QM 13.8; 14.8 f.), so that the sect did not entitle itself 'remnant' during its historical existence. According to Sanders, "the term is used in the biblical sense of those who survive the judgment (thus 'survivors' is parallel to 'remnant' in 1QH 6.8 and 1QM 13.8)" (pp. 250 f.), though Sanders too recognizes that CD 1.4 uses remnant to refer to those saved from destruction in the past, while 1QH 6.8; 1QM 13.8; 14.8 f. uses it to refer to the eschatological people of God (p. 250 n. 35). The remnant is therefore wider than the sect, since the sect will form the core of a larger community to be gathered around it (similarly Jaubert), p. 251. As Sanders points out, "The 'Qumranizing' in 1QM here (i.e. in 1QM 14.8 f. over against the parallel text in 4QMa) consists of specifying God's people as the adherents to the sect, who will be the only Israelites available for the final war against the Gentiles" (p. 252). The sect and "Israel" thus become identical at the time of the eschaton (so too 1QSa 1.20 f.) in contrast to the Gentiles and wicked among Israel who will be judged and destroyed during the eschatological war (cf. 1QpHab 5:3–6; 4QpPs37 2.19; 4.10) (p. 254). But the hesitancy of the Qumran community to call themselves Israel and the remnant may be explained by the fact that they viewed themselves as part of the *preparation* for the coming eschatological deliverance, in contrast to the church, which saw itself as already in it!

4Q171 3:15).[186] In 1QM 14:8–10, the remnant at the end of the age is thus composed of those who have remained faithful to the "covenant with our fathers" in the midst of the "dominion of Satan." As a result, their self-understanding as the people of the eschatological reality promised by Jeremiah becomes pivotal to their understanding of the way in which their lives of faithfulness to God relate both to the history of Israel on the one hand, and to the previous Sinai covenant on the other. Once 2 Cor. 3:6a is interpreted in the way suggested above, Paul's understanding of what it means to be living in the new age of the new covenant provides a striking parallel to the central themes associated with the new covenant in the Qumran writings, i.e. that of obedience to the Law from the heart, the role of the Spirit, and the identity of the community with the remnant of the Old Testament.[187] The essential dis-

---

[186] See again the helpful insights of Sanders, *Paul and Palestinian Judaism*, who concludes that "It would thus appear to be inaccurate to hold that the only reason for the establishment of a new covenant was that 'the old one had been disregarded by the majority of people', for the sectarian covenant contains new revelations" (p. 242). Sanders concludes that the new covenant is more than a renewal of the old, contra Thyen, though it is true that they did not view the new covenant as modifying the Mosaic covenant, since the new revelations were secret things hidden in the Bible itself (p. 242 and 242 n. 9; 250 n. 35). Therefore Sanders calls it "the full and true covenant" (p. 242). In his words, "… it is a prime sectarian tenet that the sectarian covenant is the only true covenant and that all who do not seek to know and accept the 'hidden things' are outside the covenant (and consequently beyond God's saving mercy)" (p. 242). Those outside the covenant are Gentiles, non-Essene Jews and apostate Essenes (p. 243). Yet the community did not simply appropriate the title "Israel" for itself, even though they viewed themselves as the elect people of the true covenant (p. 245; contra e.g. those like Vermes, Ringgren, Cross, Leaney, Jaubert, etc. who argue that the community saw themselves as the "true Israel"). Instead, they saw themselves as being "chosen from out of Israel, and as being a *forerunner of the true Israel*, which God would establish to fight the decisive war" (p. 245, emphasis his). Cf. 4QpPs37 3.1 on the designation "those who turn (from sin) in the desert" as the designation of those who have repented and joined the covenant, not as all Israel (cf. CD 4.2; 6.4 f.; 8.16; 20.17. 1QH 14.24; 2.9; 1QS 10.20, p. 245). "In short, in spite of confident scholarly assertions that the sectarians considered themselves to be the only true Israelites, and in spite of the substantial truth in that statement – the sectarians did consider that only they knew the entirety of the covenant and that those outside their covenant were 'wicked' – they generally refrained from simply calling themselves 'Israel' …." Instead they viewed themselves as being "a specially chosen part of Israel" (p. 247; so too Klinzing). The point to be made in the context of the present study is that this too distinguishes the "eschatology" of the Qumran community from that of the church, which *did* see itself as the inauguration of eschatological Israel *per se*, since the eschaton had now dawned in Christ.

[187] The purpose of The Community Rule (1QS) is to enable the people of the new "Covenant of Grace" to "seek God with a whole heart and soul, and do what is good and right before Him as He commanded by the hand of Moses and all His servants the Prophets; that they may love all that He has chosen and hate all that he has rejected; that they may abstain from all evil and hold fast to all good; that they may practice truth, righteousness, and justice upon (the) earth and no longer stubbornly follow a sinful heart and lustful eyes committing all manner of evil" (1QS 1:2–7). Conversely, "all those who embrace the Community Rule shall enter into the Covenant before God to obey all His commandments so that they may not abandon Him during the dominion of Satan because of fear or terror or affliction" (1 QS

tinction between Paul and Qumran thus becomes the person and work of Christ as that which, for Paul, inaugurates the new covenant reality. This ultimately becomes the question of whether Jesus is accepted as the messianic Son of David and Son of God in spite of, and ultimately because of, the cross, once it is understood in the light of his resurrection (cf. 1 Cor. 1:18–24; 15:1–5; Rom. 1:2–4). Although both the Qumran community and the early Christians were convinced that Israel as a nation could no longer be identified as the people of God due to their continual rebellion against the covenant, the question becomes *which* "new covenant" community is, in reality, the continuation of the faithful remnant from Israel's past.

In view of the prophetic promise of the New (Everlasting) Covenant that the Spirit will write the Law within the heart, and in the light of the significant conceptual parallels between the structure of Paul's thought and that found in the Qumran writings, Paul's reference to the spiritual gift of knowledge, with which all the Corinthians have been enriched by God (cf. 1 Cor. 1:4–7), and his corresponding emphasis on the Spirit who reveals to believers the things and thoughts of God (1 Cor. 2:9–11), take on particular significance as

---

1:16–18). To enter into the "covenant" can thus be paralleled with keeping the Law in 1QS 5:7–11 and 6:13–15, while the community itself can be described as the "community of truth," so that entering the new covenant is equated with returning to the truth of God measured by the commandments of the Law as now interpreted and obeyed within the community (cf. 1QS 1:11 f.; 2:24; 6:15). I owe this point to Gnilka, *Die Verstockung Israels*, pp. 155–185, esp. p. 157. For the corollary and foundation of this point, see too e.g. 1QH 4:7–12, one of the Psalms of the community which is often attributed to the Teacher of Righteousness himself. For the interpretation of the everlasting new covenant from Jer. 31:31–34 in terms of the promise of a new heart from Ezek. 36:26 brought about by the work of the Holy Spirit, see too Herbert Braun, *Qumran und das Neue Testament, Band II*, 1966, pp. 175 f. Braun rightly stresses that for the Qumran community their experience of the Spirit was viewed as a new beginning in Israel's history as part of the eschatological fulfillment, and that it had an important dynamic quality as well in that it was through the Spirit that one's predestination to life came into effect (he points to 1QH 4:31; 7:6; 9:32; 1QS 4:6–8). But Braun agrees with Davies that in Qumran the Spirit is not linked to the coming of the messiah in the way that it is in Paul and in this sense is not "eschatologisch bestimmt" (p. 177). Such a distinction is based, however, on the view that the coming of the Spirit for Paul was something completely new. And even if Qumran did see itself more in continuity with the experience of the remnant in the OT than Paul (which is open to question), this does not diminish the eschatological role that the Spirit does play in Qumran as the community of the end-times. As Braun himself points out, what is new in the Qumran doctrine of the Spirit in contrast to contemporary Judaism is the "volle Gegenwart des Geistes," so that it was the possession of the Spirit which showed Qumran to be the "Endzeitgemeinde" (p. 252). Hence, like Paul, "auch die Qumrangemeinde versteht sich als eschatologischen Neuansatz, und die Kraftwirkung des Geistes fehlt in Qumran mehr der Vokabel als der Sache nach" (p. 259). The issue is rather whether the coming of the Spirit as the sign of the eschaton had preceded that of the coming of the messiah as in the Qumran conception, or whether it is the result of the coming of the messiah as in early Christianity. Moreover, Braun also agrees with Davies' emphasis that in Qumran the Law and the Spirit are brought together, whereas in Paul they are separated (cf. pp. 176 f. and below). At this point I would differ with both Braun and Davies.

fulfillments of this new covenant promise.[188] Once again the point needs to be emphasized that the Spirit, now being revealed and poured out through Paul's ministry and at work in and among the Corinthians, becomes concrete evidence of their legitimacy, both for Paul as God's apostle, and for the Corinthians as God's people.[189] Paul's reference to himself as a servant of the new covenant in 3:6a is a reminder that his ministry is to bring about new life in the Spirit, a life which derives its identity from the fact that those in Christ experience the presence of God himself in a way that sanctifies (cf. 1 Cor. 1:2) rather than condemns. Indeed, it will become evident in 2 Cor. 3:7–18 that, in contrast to Israel's experience in the wilderness and beyond, encountering the glory of God in Christ by the power of the Spirit now becomes the very focus of what it means to be the people of the new covenant which "remains" (2 Cor. 3:11).[190] Hence, Paul's allusion to Jer. 31:31 ff. and Ezek. 36:25 f. in 3:3–6 points to the prophetic promise of the Spirit's work in the future, which in Jeremiah and Ezekiel is linked explicitly to Israel's past failure in keeping the covenant. It is therefore striking in view of Paul's thought in 2 Cor. 3 that in Is. 63 this failure is tied to their grieving the *Holy Spirit* as that which guided and saved them (cf. Neh. 9:20), so that in the future the Spirit is again promised to Israel.[191] This positive promise of the Spirit is in view in 3:4–6, while the

---

[188] Contra e.g. those like F. Lang, "Gesetz und Bund," pp. 312–319, Stockhausen, *Moses' Veil*, p. 44, Furnish, *II Corinthians*, p. 199, and already George Johnston, "'Spirit' and 'Holy Spirit' in the Qumran Literature," in *New Testament Sidelights, FS Alexander Converse Purdy*, 1960, pp. 27–42, p. 41, who agree with H. Braun in seeing a stark contrast between Qumran and Paul concerning the relationship between the new covenant and the Law. For Furnish, the two are "fundamentally different" in that "the Qumran sectarians regarded themselves as constituting a 'household of the Spirit' devoted entirely to obeying the law; they seem to have had no sense whatever of any incompatibility between 'life in the Spirit' and 'life under the law.' For Paul, on the other hand, these stand over against one another as two radically different and mutually exclusive modes of existence."

[189] For the Spirit and its gifts as evidence of God's grace at work in the Corinthians, see 1 Cor. 1:4–9; 2 Cor. 1:22; 2:2–3; 5:5; for the Spirit as the evidence of Paul's apostolic standing, see 2 Cor. 3:3; 6:6; 11:4; *Suffering and the Spirit*, pp. 183–218; and the discussion of 3:7–18 below. Again, examples could be multiplied from the other Pauline epistles. The only discussion to my knowledge which takes as a starting point Paul's experiences of the Spirit in relationship to his writings is still Hoyle's *The Holy Spirit in St. Paul*, cf. esp. his chapter "The Spirit in the Life of Apostleship," pp. 91–112, in which he distinguishes between Paul's experiences of the Spirit in his personal ethical and religious life, which Paul regarded as typical of Christians, and his experiences of the Spirit in his ministry as an apostle.

[190] See now Renwick, *Temple*, p. 97, who rightly concludes that Paul's specific concern in 2 Cor. 3 is "to demonstrate that through Christ access to God's presence, the location of every true apostle, has now been granted to *all* Christians, who, without fear of death, are free to gaze upon and to be transformed by the revelation of God's presence."

[191] Cf. Is. 63:10–14, where the "presence" of God from 63:9, which saved Israel in the wilderness, is interpreted in terms of the "holy spirit" (63:10, 11) and the "spirit of YHWH" (63:14), as pointed out by John Wright, "Spirit and Wilderness: The Interplay of Two Motifs within the Hebrew Bible as a Background to Mark 1:2–13," in *Perspectives on Language and Text, FS Francis I. Andersen*, ed. Edgar W. Conrad and Edward G. Newing, 1987, pp. 269–298, pp. 287 f. Wright goes on to emphasize that "The spirit in this chapter is not the spirit of

negative point concerning Israel's past "grieving the Spirit" is the central subject of 3:7 ff.; together they form the foundation for the meaning and legitimacy of Paul's ministry of the "new covenant." But at this point, Paul's immediate concern in referring to the new covenant is the relationship between the Spirit and the Law, prepared for by the reference to the stone tablets in 3:3 and confirmed by the continuation of Paul's argument with the letter/Spirit contrast in 3:6bc.

7. The Letter/Spirit Contrast Against the Backdrop of Jeremiah 31:31–34 and Ezekiel 36:25 f.

As our introduction to the exegetical problems surrounding the letter/Spirit contrast in 3:6bc made clear, the current disparity concerning its significance is a result of the corresponding consensus concerning its fundamental meaning. The majority of students of Paul are now convinced that the contrast is a "realistic" or "economy of salvation" distinction between the Law and the Gospel, rather than a hermeneutical contrast between two ways of reading the Scriptures (though it may have hermeneutical significance). Yet once the letter/Spirit contrast is placed within the larger question of Paul's view of the Law, the present lack of consensus surrounding the Pauline Law/Gospel contrast itself means that opinions concerning the precise meaning of the letter/Spirit contrast again diverge drastically according to the larger paradigm which the interpreter brings to the text.

In view of this very lack of consensus, it is crucial that we temporally suspend judgment on the whole of Paul's thought in order to examine this specific part on its own terms. In doing so, one must entertain anew the possibility that the arguments from Scripture in 2 Cor. 3:3b and 3:6a may provide the backdrop for understanding the meaning of the letter/Spirit contrast in this context, rather than prejudice the exegesis of this passage by deciding in advance that Paul could not have derived his thinking from the OT passages to which he explicitly alludes.[192] Indeed, if Ezekiel 36:25 f. and, especially, Jeremiah 31:31–34 are taken as the initial keys to Paul's thinking in 3:6bc, then

---

the special endowment as of the leaders of old, but is the very presence of God himself manifested in power and in operation, yet there is a degree of personification here as well (note the use of the verb 'to grieve'), which is developed further in the New Testament."

[192] See as one paradigmatic example Räisänen, *Paul and the Law*, pp. 241 f., 244 f., who concludes that since "there is no basis for a theology of an abrogation of the law in Jer. 31 or the related texts (he points to Ezek. 11:20; 36:27; cf. p. 242 n. 71)," "Paul could not seize on Jer. 31 if he understood the passage in its original meaning or in consonance with contemporary Jewish understanding" (p. 242); see too *Suffering and the Spirit*, pp. 212 f., where Räisänen's view is critiqued in relationship to 3:3, which he reads in light of 3:6 understood to speak of the abrogation of the Law. For similar positions, see too Hays and Vollenweider (cf. above, nn. 134 and 163).

the meaning of the letter/Spirit contrast, despite the volumes of ink which have been spilled over it, becomes readily apparent.[193] At this point, then, we will proceed by interpreting the letter/Spirit contrast against this prophetic backdrop.[194] This is done in the awareness that the so-called "negative" view of the Law in Paul's thinking, which is usually buttressed in this context from the continuation of Paul's argument in 3:7–18, is assumed by most commentators to make such a reading impossible. The substantiation of this thesis remains to be seen in the interpretation of 3:7–18 against its OT backdrop given in Part Two of this study. For now, however, it is important to make clear what Paul is saying if the letter/Spirit contrast is read against the OT backdrop from Ezekiel and Jeremiah alluded to in 2 Cor. 3:3 and 6.

The first observation in this regard is that the contrasting genitive clauses of 6b, οὐ γράμματος ἀλλὰ πνεύματος ("not of the letter but of the Spirit"), most naturally pick up the verbal assertion of 6a, ἱκάνωσεν ἡμᾶς διακόνους ("he made us sufficient to be servants"), which has been elided in 6b. This structure parallels Paul's similar use of the contrasting prepositional phrases in 3:3b, οὐκ ἐν πλαξὶν λιθίναις ἀλλ' ἐν πλαξὶν καρδίαις σαρκίναις ("not in stone tablets but in tablets of fleshly hearts"), to define further the verbal assertion ἐγγεγραμμένη ("having been engraved"), rather than to relate directly to the immediately previous reference to ink and Spirit.[195] Syntactically, 6b is a subsequent assertion concerning Paul's ministry, rather than an epexegetical interpretation of the "new covenant." The letter/Spirit contrast therefore functions to define further ἱκάνωσεν ἡμᾶς διακόνους ("he made us sufficient to be servants") by *replacing* the previous genitive "of the new covenant."[196] As

---

[193] See now Stockhausen, *Moses' Veil*, p. 54, "There is no line of argument without the full force of this scriptural background, as the scholarly confusion over Paul's meaning amply attests." Her thesis is correct that Jer. 38 (LXX) and Ezek. 11 and 36 have influenced not only Paul's vocabulary, but also the structure and content of his argument (p. 54), though she too ends up disregarding the original argument of Jer. and Ezek. themselves as materially significant for Paul's own position by ignoring completely the theme of the Law in both of the prophetic texts (cf. p. 63)!

[194] Contra now Liebers, *Das Gesetz als Evangelium*, pp. 101–104, 115, who sees the key to Paul's argument not to be a reconstructed pre-Pauline text taken over from his opponents (à la Georgi), but an equally hypothetical composite "Jewish" view of the Law which he draws based upon diverse traditions and which itself fails to take into consideration the most relevant streams of tradition for Paul's argument in 2 Cor. 3, i.e. those built upon Exod. 32–34 itself (cf. his summary on p. 115). In a similar way, Vollenweider, "2 Kor 3," pp. 248 n. 241, 265, 267, suggests that the letter/Spirit contrast (in his view as a critique of Judaism!) was already existent among the pre-Pauline, Hellenistic, Jewish Christian churches and tradition. Such a supposition, however, must remain a matter of speculation. And even if true, the relevant point is that Paul has applied this viewpoint within his own argument in 2 Cor. 3, which is the only context we have that is capable of rendering his statements intelligible.

[195] For this reading of 3:3b, cf. my *Suffering and the Spirit*, pp. 200–202.

[196] Contra those who, like Furnish, *II Corinthians*, p. 199, and Stockhausen, *Moses' Veil*, pp. 34, 62, take it to be a qualitative genitive referring to the nature of the new covenant. See too now Hofius, "Gesetz und Evangelium," p. 82 n. 45, who points out that though both views are possible grammatically, the *content* of the contrast makes it necessary to relate

such, the letter/Spirit contrast does not further elucidate the nature of the new covenant *per se* (although by implication it certainly does this[197]), but rather makes explicit what Paul sees as the important *consequence* of having been made a servant of the new covenant. This is confirmed by Paul's statement in 2:15–16a, in which Paul's *ministry* itself brings about the consequences of life and death, and 3:3, where Paul describes his *ministry* in terms of mediating the Spirit. Having referred to himself as a servant of the "new covenant" from Jeremiah 31:31–34 in 6a, Paul then goes on to assert that *as a result* of being identified with this covenant, he has not been made sufficient to be a servant of "the letter, but of the Spirit." The letter/Spirit contrast in 3:6b thus brings together the concerns from both Ezek. 36:25 f. and Jer. 31:31–34 as expressed in 3:3b and 3:6b respectively. Inasmuch as Paul is a servant of the new covenant, he has been made sufficient to be a revelatory agent of the Spirit, since the new covenant ministry is essentially one in which the Spirit of God is now being poured out upon all the people of God in order that they might be brought into the new covenant and that they might keep it faithfully.

Second, we have seen that the very purpose for the pouring out of the Spirit in Ezekiel in conjunction with the promise of the new covenant from Jer. 31 is that God's people might now keep the Law with transformed hearts. The development of the new covenant theme in the Qumran writings confirms this, as does the common conception in post-biblical Judaism and rabbinic literature that the Law will not be abolished, reinterpreted, or altered in some way in the age to come, but reestablished, fulfilled, and kept.[198] Of special interest are those later rabbinic traditions which take God's writing of the Law on the heart in Jeremiah 31:33 to mean that in the age to come the Law will not be forgotten, which in some traditions is attributed to the fact that God himself

---

them to the new covenant. Here too we see that one's view of the role of the Law in general can prove determinative. But in context the contrast is not between two covenant natures, but two ministries (cf. 3:3, 7, 8, 9, 13; 4:1). For the view taken here, see H.A.W. Meyer, *Critical and Exegetical Handbook to the Epistles to the Corinthians*, 1979 (1883), p. 465, who also argues that the phrase is dependent upon διαχόνους "as an appositional more precise definition" to the new covenant, translating it, "to be ministers not of letter ... but of Spirit."

[197] The difference becomes one of emphasis. Cf. H. Lietzmann, *An die Korinther I–II*, HzNT Bd. 9, 1969⁵, p. 111: "Ob γράμματος und πνεύματος von διαχόνους oder διαθήκης abhängig ist, läßt sich auch durch v. 7 διαχονία τοῦ θανάτου nicht sicher entscheiden, ist auch inhaltlich gleich."

[198] For examples of this widespread tradition in post-biblical literature, see Wis. 18:4; Bar. 4:1; 4 Ezra 6:28; 9:36–37; Ps. Sol. 17:37; Test. Levi 18:2–9; Jub. 3:31; 6:17; 15:26 f.; 23:26; 32:10; 33:10–13; 49:8; 50:13 33:17; 1 En. 99:2, 14; 2 Apoc. Bar. 59:2; 77:15; Ps-Philo, LAB 11:2, 5; 32:7; Philo, *Vit. Mos.* II, 14; Josephus, *C. Ap.* II, 277 (cf. too Hofius, "Gesetz und Evangelium," p. 82 n. 44 and H. M. Teeple, *The Mosaic Eschatological Prophet*, JBL Monograph Series 10, 1957, p. 16, from which several of these texts were taken, though Teeple sees those passages which speak of new knowledge as implying a new law). For a response to the thesis of W.D. Davies in this regard, see above, n. 144.

will then teach his people.[199] Moreover, in Song of Songs Rab. 1,2, § 4, we read that when Israel heard the divine voice directly in Exodus 20:2, the Torah was at that time fixed in their hearts, only to be forgotten when they demanded that Moses become their mediator, since he himself is also mortal and transient. Yet when they cry out to Moses for a second chance to hear a direct word from God in order "that He would fix the knowledge of the Torah in our hearts as it was!", Moses refuses. His reason is that "'This cannot be now, but it will be in the days to come,' as it says, 'I will put My law in their inward parts and in their heart will I write it'" (Jer. 31:33).[200] The midrash continues by paralleling this to the tradition in which the evil inclination itself was removed from Israel's heart in Exod. 20:2, but then returns to Israel when they asked for Moses to be an intermediary between them and God. But this time when asked for a second chance, Moses again responds negatively, but now quotes Ezekiel 36:26 to support his assertion that they must wait for the days to come for the removal of their evil heart. That the link in these traditions between Moses' role as mediator and Israel's lack of the Law or possession of an evil heart is consonant with the original meaning of the Exodus 20–34 narrative will become clear in chapter three. Important here is the way in which the future remembrance of the Law and its validity is tied to Jer. 31:33 on the one hand, and the way in which Jer. 31 and Ezek. 36 are seen as conceptually related on the other hand, so that the remembering of the Law in the age to come corresponds to the future removal of the evil inclination that characterized Israel ever since she turned to Moses as mediator under the Sinai covenant.

Hence, as the argument in 3:7–18 will substantiate (see below, chapters five and six), Paul is already cognizant of this same implication. Paul is therefore careful in 3:6 *not* to establish a contrast between the Law itself and the Spirit. This is reflected in the fact that Paul does not refer to the Law (ὁ νόμος) *as such* in introducing this contrast, a fact which must be taken seriously. In accord with both Ezek. 36:25 f. and Jer. 31:31–34, the letter/Spirit contrast in 3:6b is not simply between the Law in its written form, with its command-

---

[199] Cf. Eccl. Rab. II, 1, where Jer. 31:33 is taken to support the idea that the Torah learned in this world (i.e. the "pleasure" of Eccl. 2:1!) is "vanity" in comparison with the Torah learned in the world to come because then it will not be forgotten. There is also an undeveloped reference to Jer. 31:33 in Pesiq. Rab. Kah. 10.6. But in Pesiq. Rab. Kah. 12.21, Jer. 31:33 is explicitly related to Is. 54:13 to make the same point as in Eccl. Rab. II, 1 that in the world to come God himself will teach the people so that they will not forget. Similarly, in Gen. Rab. 95.3 God declares to Abraham that whereas Abraham has taught his sons the Torah in this world, in the future world God himself will teach them the Torah, quoting Is. 54:13. In addition, see Strack-Billerbeck, *Kommentar, Bd. 3*, 1926, p. 704 for later traditions making the same point, also in association with Is. 54:13. Cf. Midr. Ps. 21.1, where God himself, in contrast to the Messiah, is the one who teaches Torah in the age to come, since the Messiah is sought, but does not teach.

[200] Trans. M. Simon, *Song of Songs, Midrash Rabbah, Vol. 9*, 1939, p. 26.

ments, and the Spirit, with the latter rendering the former invalid.[201] Indeed, Paul's reliance on Ezekiel 36, Jeremiah 31, and Exodus 34 in 2 Cor. 3 confirms that in viewing the Sinai covenant his predominant use elsewhere throughout his epistles of νόμος ("Law") for the Hebrew תורה, in reliance on the Septuagint, is meant to refer to the Torah as a whole, and not some subset of it in terms of its legal requirements. And there is no reason to suspect that Paul's reliance on the Septuagint has led him away from the original meaning of "Torah" as the covenant history, promise, and stipulations found in the books of Moses, or, indeed, in the Scriptures as a whole.[202] Instead, Paul's use of γράμμα reflects his conviction that the work of the Spirit in the new covenant is a fulfillment of the promises of Ezekiel 36:25 f. and Jer. 31:31–34 concerning the Law as a constitutive part of the Sinai covenant, rather than a break with it in view of a supposed Christian reworking of the OT expectation based on the traditional Law/Gospel distinction,[203] or on the Law/Gospel dis-

---

[201] Contra the thesis of Vollenweider, "2 Kor 3," pp. 267–270, 272, and Stephen Westerholm, "Letter and Spirit: The Foundation of Pauline *Ethics*," *NTS* 30 (1984) 229–248, esp. pp. 238, 241, 244, and his *Israel's Law and the Church's Faith*, 1988, pp. 209–216, as well as those who, like Stockhausen, *Moses' Veil*, p. 105, argue that both Jeremiah and Paul recognized that failing to remain in the covenant was due to a failure of the people, but that both nevertheless have the "similar focus on the extrinsic legal expression of the covenant itself as the ultimate source of and solution to the problem," so that the covenant itself must be improved (p. 105, 105 n. 39). The problem with the old covenant, as symbolized by the stone tablets, is again, as is typical in this traditional view, "exteriority" as such (p. 105). Hence, though Stockhausen recognizes that the Law is promulgated in the new covenant of Jer. 31, she too does not extend this to 2 Cor. 3.

[202] The supposed negative consequences of the LXX translation of the Hebrew תורה with νόμος ("Law") for understanding the Torah have often been pointed out; cf. S. Talmon, "Torah as a Concept and Vital Principle in the Hebrew Bible," *GOTR* 24 (1979) 271–289, pp. 279 f., who points to the "momentous consequences" of reducing Torah as "instruction" to "law"; and esp. H.J. Schoeps, *Paul*, pp. 29, 32, 35, 260, who saw Paul's supposedly negative view of the Law to be derived from his postulated reliance on the LXX translation and what it represented in Hellenistic Judaism rather than on the Hebrew traditions (see above, n. 164). I see no evidence for this distinction either in the LXX or in the Judaism of Paul's day, nor is there any indication in Paul that he drew a distinction between תורה and νόμος, but rather saw the latter as a translation equivalent of the former. For the view taken here, see too e.g. W. Zimmerli, *The Law and Prophets, A Study of the Meaning of the Old Testament*, 1965, pp. 11 f.; who also emphasizes, p. 14, that in the NT there is no tension between the Law and the Prophets, with the former sometimes being used for the latter (cf. Mtt. 5:17 f.; Rom. 3:19; 1 Cor. 14:21).

[203] So too Lloyd Gaston, "Paul and the Torah in 2 Corinthians 3," p. 156, who also stresses that γράμμα is not to be equated with the Law (pointing to Rom. 2:27, 29 and 7:12, 14 as evidence). Gaston too sees that the subject in view is two contrasting ministries, though, contra the view taken here, Gaston understands this contrast to be between the ministries of Paul and his opponents (who are using Moses as their model), rather than between Paul and Moses *per se*. For Gaston, the "letter" refers "neither to the Law nor to Scripture but specifically here to the ministry of the rival missionaries" and represents a "certain type of ministry" which, like sin and the flesh, can be seen as "a power that kills" (p. 157). But this interpretation fails to take seriously the OT backdrop to Paul's argument, as well as the obvious connection between the letter and the Law. Without such a backdrop, Gaston must recon-

tinction taken to represent two powers now at work in the world.[204] Again, the problem is not with the Law itself, but with the people whose hearts have remained hardened under the Sinai covenant.[205] Paul's choice of the "letter" to

---

struct his own, thus positing that Paul's opponents came to Corinth either with "heavenly texts" or the Hebrew Scriptures, both of which the Corinthians could not read. Against this hypothetical backdrop, Gaston proposes that the letter/Spirit distinction, based on the use of written texts to enhance the glory of the divine man in Hellenistic Judaism (as argued by Georgi), "may well (have) its origin in Paul's very practical suggestion to the Corinthians that they need not be intimidated by Hebrew characters, for the Septuagint read in the Spirit was perfectly adequate for them" (p. 158). There is, however, no textual evidence to support such a fanciful thesis. The view being argued here is also in stark contrast to that of those like H. Räisänen, *Paul and the Law*, pp. 25, 45 f., who sees 3:6, which is then reinforced by v. 7, to be one of "Paul's sharpest negative comments about the law" (p. 25), since for him the so-called moral law itself is in view. Räisänen thus takes the letter as a direct deprecatory reference to the Decalogue itself, so that he must conclude [*unnecessarily*] that there is a tension between 2 Cor. 3:6 and Rom. 13:9 on the one hand, and "an irreconcilable contradiction to Rom. 7:14" on the other (cf. pp. 25, 45). Hence, in Räisänen's view, "Both in Gal. 3 and in 2 Cor. 3 Paul speaks quite clearly of the inferior, transient, and temporary character of the law given at Sinai" (pp. 45 f.). Most recently, see now Stockhausen, *Moses' Veil*, p. 77 n. 75, who assumes that what is "exceptional" about Paul is "the negativity" that comes to be attached to the Sinai covenant represented by the "letter" (= "what is written," pp. 34, 78), given that, as she rightfully emphasizes, "Nothing in the preceding verses has prepared for this radically negative assessment of the 'written thing' with which Paul is now concerned, the Sinai covenant mediated by Moses" (p. 78). In her view, the whole covenant narrative from Exodus is "radically excluded" from Paul's understanding of the covenant concepts derived from the prophets so that "nothing which is proper to the new covenant may be present in the old covenant" (p. 79). For Stockhausen, p. 76 n. 73, "what Paul is saying *theologically* has been clear since Tertullian ..." But this surprise "negativity" in Paul's theological evaluation of the Sinai covenant, so out of place in the context, ought to raise serious questions about its propriety in the text at all. See too the earlier substantial work of Seyoon Kim, *The Origin of Paul's Gospel*, WUNT 2. Reihe 4, 1981, pp. 4, 126–136, 273–275, 307 f., who, in support of his very traditional law/Gospel contrasts (cf. e.g. his discussion of the "law-free Gospel" on pp. 131–133, 269–311), sees 2 Cor. 3:4–4:6 as the key text for his argument "that at the Damascus revelation Paul realized that Christ had superseded the Torah and is therefore the true Wisdom ...," since it is this text which brings together Paul's call and his view of the Law (p. 128; cf. pp. 5 ff., 229 ff.). He thus sees in 2 Cor. 3 a clear Torah/gospel contrast in which Christ is the end of the old covenant, equated with the Law (p. 128), since at the Damascus road, as confirmed by 2 Cor. 3:4–4:6, Paul knew "that Christ had brought the Torah to an end as the embodiment of the divine will and as the means of salvation, that Christ himself superseded it ..." (p. 127). For Kim, similar to Davies, Christ replaces the Law as the "embodiment of divine wisdom" (Sir. 24:23; Bar. 3:37 f.; 4 Macc. 1:17; 7:21; 23; 8:7), though he stops short of following Davies in calling Christ a "New Torah" (p. 127, 127 n. 3). The point of this study, however, is that the Law is not brought to an end as "the embodiment of the divine will," nor was it ever conceived of as "the means of salvation"!

[204] Contra Käsemann's view (cf. Introduction), now taken up by Vollenweider, "2 Kor 3," pp. 271 f. Both Käsemann and Vollenweider wed this view to the idea that the "letter" also refers to a misunderstanding or misuse of the Law, but see this misuse to be itself the instrument and power of death and condemnation. It is argued here, however, that γράμμα also does not refer to a misunderstanding of the Law *per se*, though the Law encountered without the Spirit may certainly produce such misuses (see below).

[205] Cf. now Reinhold Liebers, *Das Gesetz als Evangelium,* p. 94, who concludes that for Paul there is no polemic against "Verdienstdenken," "Selbstruhm," or human striving after

designate the Law in 3:6 is therefore best explained by the prophetic expectation for a time in which the Law would not remain merely the rejected expression of the will of God by a rebellious people.[206] Here again, Paul's thought parallels closely the development of the new covenant motif in the Qumran documents, rather than contradicting them as Herbert Braun has argued and as those who support the traditional view of the Law/Gospel contrast accept.[207]

"Leistung" *per se*, at least not in the center of Paul's thinking; nor is there any rejection of works of the Law as such. Rather, Paul's critique of the Law centers on "die Relation von Tora und Täter" as "das eigentliche Problem." The issue for Paul thus becomes the Law as "Heilsmittler" over against "derjenige Heilsweg Gottes, der nach Paulus allein in der Person Christi seinen Ausgangspunkt hat" (p. 93). But contra the position argued here, for Liebers 2 Cor. 3 becomes a key text (together with Gal. 3:15–22; Rom. 2:17–20; 9:31; 10:6–8; 11:33–36) for seeing how Paul evaluates the Jewish view of the Law by *altering* the Jewish understanding of it, since Paul denies what the Jews assert, i.e. that the ministry of Moses leads to life (pp. 95, 116).

[206] Cf R. Banks, "The Eschatological Role of Law," who argues that in the prophets the Law refers to much more than just the specific Sinai Law, but includes the basic ethical principles equated with the "word of the Lord" (cf. Is. 2:3) but with the prophetic message itself (cf. Is. 1:10; 8:16, 20; 30:9; 42:1 f.; 51:4 f.; Jer. 2:8; 6:19; 9:12–13; 16:10–12; 26:4 f.; 44:18) (pp. 174 f.). Thus, the knowledge of the Lord in Jer. 31:31–34 is "much more" than obedience to the Law (cf. Jer. 2:8; 3:15; 5:1–4; 8:7; 11:18; 24:7; 32:8; 44:29) (pp. 174 f.); and because Ezek. 40–48 "contains items which have no parallel in the Mosaic Law" the reference to the "statutes" in Ezek. 36:27 must be broadened beyond the Law (p. 175; cf. Ezek. 43:11–12; 44:5). This may certainly be true, and hence my use of the broad category of the "will of God as embodied in the Law" in this section. But this does not mean that the "law" in Jer. 31:31–34 and Ezek. 36:26 f. is something *less* in emphasis than the Law, so that Banks can conclude that Torah in Jer. "refers primarily to the survival of Yahweh's prophetic instructions beyond the disintegration of the present covenantal framework" and not to the Law *per se*, though the prophetic instruction includes the traditional Law as secondarily in view (pp. 174 f., 184 f.).

[207] In comparing Paul and Qumran, Braun, *Qumran und das Neue Testament, Band II*, 1966, p. 167, supports the traditional view, based on his work on Rom. 7: "Paulus hat als Christ entdeckt und spricht es in Römer 7 aus, daß nicht nur die Toraübertretung, sondern die Torabejahung in Sünde und Gespaltenheit und Tod führt. Diese Einsicht liegt in Qumran nicht vor; dort gilt der Toragehorsam unbedenklich als ein Weg, auf den die Gnade führt." For him faith in Christ for justification presupposes a "Gegensatz" to the Law as a way of salvation (p. 167). Braun thus follows Daníelou in concluding that "Qumran nehme den Glauben mit der Tora zusammen, Paulus setze beides gegeneinander" or with Burrows that "Qumran kombiniere Glaube und Werke, Paulus behandle sie antithetisch" (p. 170). The essential difference is "daß Glaube und Toraweg in Qumran zusammengehören, bei Paulus aber sich ausschließen" (p. 172). According to Braun, therefore, "Der neue Bund von II Kor. 3 würde auch die Essener als Leute mit einer Hülle auf ihrem Angesicht bezeichnen müssen" (p. 170). Yet Braun himself points out that both Paul and the Qumran texts agree concerning justification that 1) God alone gives righteousness; 2) it is a justification of sinners and not a result of good works; 3) it is an act of divine grace; 4) the superiority of mankind is attributed to the act of justification; 5) only God can be trusted to justify; 6) good works are ascribed only to God's work in his people; and 7) mankind is totally dependent upon God (pp. 167 f.). Moreover, though their respective terminology is not at all places the same (cf. Rom. 5:11; 8:4; 2 Cor. 5:18 f.), in 2 Cor. 3:7–9 Paul uses the same terminology as that found in Qumran (p. 168). The difference, of course, is the "christologische Verklammerung" of the Pauline doctrine of justification (p. 168). Contra Braun, the point is not that the Law leads to legal-

Viewed from this perspective, the letter/Spirit contrast is not between the Law and the Gospel as two distinct ways of relating to God. Nor is it between two distinct ways of God's relating to us (i.e. an externally written one in the Law/old covenant and an internally written one by the Spirit/new covenant), since what distinguishes the ministry of the new covenant in Jer. 31:31–34 is that the Law itself is now kept as a result of a transformed heart. Rather, the contrast inherent between the letter and the Spirit is the eschatological contrast which stands at the center of the Scriptural understanding of the history of redemption and the corresponding two-age conception within which it unfolds.[208] But unlike the eschatology of the Qumran documents, for which the

ism, but that for Paul Christ had come as the Messiah. The difference between Paul and Qumran is essentially an eschatological and Christological one, not a theological one in regard to the role of the Law in the new covenant. In Qumran, as in Paul, the problem is the lack of the Spirit in the old covenant, i.e. the Spirit was not at work among those outside of the remnant and hence they did not and could not keep the covenant. In contrast to Qumran, Braun argues that Paul places the Spirit and the Law against one another (p. 173), but in reality both see the Spirit at work in relationship to the Law in fulfillment of Jer. 31:31–34 and Ezek. 36:26 f. For Braun, "Das Wirken des Geistes führt in Qumran zur Tora und ist mit ihr eng verbunden; bei Paulus stellen Geist und Christus den Heilsweg dar, welcher dem der Tora strikt zuwiderläuft, wie W.D. Davies zutreffend unterstreicht ... der neue Bekehrungswandel schließt in Qumran den Heilsweg der Tora ein, bei Paulus aus" (p. 260). For Braun, therefore, the essential difference between Qumran and Paul centers on their different understanding of the relationship between the messiah and the Spirit (here he is right) and the different view of the relationship between the Spirit and the Law (pp. 260 f.) On the latter point, he is right for Qumran, but wrong for Paul.

[208] As stated earlier in *Suffering and the Spirit*, p. 215 n. 156, apart from the implications he draws from this concerning the nature of the law and the old covenant, Ridderbos, *Paul*, p. 215, is (thus) right in emphasizing that the letter/Spirit contrast in 3:6 is a "redemptive-historical contrast, namely, as the two dominating principles of the two aeons marked off by the appearance of Christ;" or as he puts it on p. 216, "two regimes" (cf. pp. 221–223). For the development of the Spirit/flesh, old/new covenant, and letter/Spirit contrasts in Paul as "redemptive-historical" contrasts (i.e. "as the two dominating principles of the two aeons marked off by the appearance of Christ"), and not primarily as metaphysical or anthropological contrasts, see H. Ridderbos, *Paul, An Outline of His Theology*, 1975, pp. 215–219, and for the significance of the Spirit as the eschatological gift of God which was not a "theological theory" but an "empirical experience, which one sought to explain," see L. Goppelt, *Theologie des Neuen Testaments, Bd. 2*, UTB 850, 1978³, pp. 447–453, quotes from p. 449. For this same point in post-biblical Judaism, see W.D. Davies, *Paul and Rabbinic Judaism, Some Rabbinic Elements in Pauline Theology*, 1980⁴, pp. 208–216, who argues that in early rabbinic Judaism the messianic age was regarded as the "era of the Spirit" (p. 216), so that for Paul, "what lent reality to the Messianic claims of Jesus was the presence of the Spirit, the advent of the power of the Age to Come ..." (p. 217); and W. Foerster, "Der Heilige Geist im Spätjudentum," *NTS* 8 (1961–62) 117–134, pp. 117–122, esp. his point that "Das Pendant zu dem Gefühl, daß Gottes Heiliger Geist seit dem Exil nicht mehr in bevollmächtigten Propheten dem Volk gegeben war, ist die Erwartung, daß er in der Endzeit ihm wieder verliehen würde" (p. 119). He points out that Ezek. 36:26 f. and Joel 3:1 f. were key texts in this expectation. Foerster observes as well that the Spirit was also seen to be at work in the present in anticipation of the messianic era, e.g. esp. in the Qumran community, where it was related to the unveiling of the previously hidden understanding (pp. 120, 122). For a helpful discussion of the tension in rabbinic literature between the tradition which saw

creation of the new covenant community takes place *prior* to the coming of
the messianic deliverance, so that their messiahs work through the faithful
community already established by the Spirit as part of the final deliverance,
for Paul the coming of the messiah *precedes* the pouring out of the Spirit and
establishment of the new covenant community. For Paul, as for the New Testament as a whole, the new covenant community is created by the messiah
himself in the midst of this evil world and in anticipation of its final redemption as part of its distinctive eschatology, i.e. the "overlapping of the ages."
Unlike Paul, therefore, the Qumran community did not view the new age as
already having dawned. Instead, as Dimant has put it, the knowledge that the
Teacher of Righteousness "imparted to the sect unveiled to its members the
fact that they are living in the final generation, on the threshold of the
Eschatological Era."[209] Rather than participating in the end, for Qumran their
experience of the Spirit and faithfulness to the Law were an expression of the
fact that they stood on the "threshold of the eschaton" in which "the sect announces the approaching End, and initiates the beginning of the eschatological process."[210] In stark contrast, the present experience of the Spirit for
Paul is a proleptic participation in the age to come which has *already* been
inaugurated in Christ. Because the new age of the new covenant has dawned
in Christ, Paul has not been made a minister of the letter, but of the Spirit,
since, in accordance with Ezekiel and Jeremiah, the Spirit is the central mark
of the new age of God's rule by which the people of God no longer break the
covenant, but keep its Law. In this regard Paul's thought remains closer to the
original intention of Ezekiel and Jeremiah than that found in the Qumran writings.

---

the activity of the Holy Spirit cease with the end of the prophetic period or steadily decline
afterward (cf. e.g. 1 Macc. 9:27; b.Yoma 9b; b.Sota 48b; b.San. 11a; Tos.Sotah 13.2; Sifre
Deut. 173) and that minority tradition which saw the Spirit continuing among the rabbis as
the continued presence of prophecy (cf. e.g. Lev. R. 6.1; 15.2; 35.6; Cant. R. 1.8; Mekh.
33b; 65b; Sifre Deut. 352; Exod. R. 5.23), see A. Marmorstein, "The Holy Spirit in Rabbinic
Legend," in *Studies in Jewish Theology, The Arthur Marmorstein Memorial Volume*, ed. J.
Rabbinowitz and M.S. Lew, 1950, pp. 122–144. For the centrality of eschatology in Paul's
thought, see too U. Luz, *Das Geschichtsverständnis des Apostels Paulus, BEvTh 49*, 1968,
pp. 127, 130. The view argued above is contra that of Vollenweider, "2 Kor 3, " p. 272, who
rejects the heilsgeschichtlich perspective being argued here and in my prior work (cf. p. 272
n. 379), though he too sees that the letter/Spirit contrast divides "die Zeiten." But for
Vollenweider, the "times" in view are the unalterable structures of the past over against the
"eschatological dynamic" of a present which is open to the future. In his words, therefore,
"Gramma ist in sich verschlossene Vergangenheit, Pneuma eschatologische Präsenz des
Künftigen" (p. 272). For Paul, however, the eschatological present cannot be understood
apart from the history of Israel and the history of the eschatological people of God in Christ
and their interrelationship as expressed in their respective covenants. Though I am not in
agreement with his paradigm at every point, this fundamental perspective has now been well
argued by N.T. Wright, *The Climax of the Covenant*, 1991.

[209] "Qumran," p. 536.
[210] Again quoting Dimant, "Qumran," pp. 538 f.

Finally, Paul's choice of the "letter" (γράμμα) terminology as that which characterizes the previous covenant and age is his novel[211] attempt to encapsulate the distinction between the role of the Law within the Sinai covenant and its new role within the "new covenant" in Christ.[212] At the center of this choice is again the Spirit as the mark of the new covenant reality, since, as Cosgrove has rightfully called to our attention, "Primitive Christianity understood itself as a people upon whom God had poured out the Spirit of the last days. The manifest presence of the Spirit among them, perhaps more than anything else, gave the church as a whole its sense of distinct 'eschatological identity' over against the synagogue and the world at large."[213] Viewed from this perspective, and buttressed by the point of Ezekiel and Jeremiah, Paul naturally rivets his attention in 3:6b on the fact that in the Sinai covenant the Law was given to Israel without the Spirit, with the result that it remained "outside their hearts" (cf. Jer. 31:33).

But as Ezekiel and Jeremiah also make clear, the problem with the Law was not the Law itself, which remains for Paul, as it did for the Jewish traditions of his day, the holy, just, and good expression of God's covenantal will (Rom. 7:12). The Law is thus characterized as "spiritual" (πνευματικός, Rom. 7:14), and when kept from the heart by the mercy of God becomes the pathway to life before God (Ps. 119:2, 11, 17, 32, 34, 77, 105, 112, 116).[214] Rather, against the backdrop of Ezekiel and Jeremiah, the problem was the people themselves, whose hearts, ever since the time of the fathers in the wilderness, had not been transformed by the power of the Spirit so that they might remain faithful to the covenant.[215] This corresponds to the common Jewish tradition

---

[211] A proximity search of the *Thesaurus Linguae Graecae* data base for the combination γράμμα/πνεῦμα turned up no significant parallels in pre-Pauline literature. Following Furnish and Käsemann, the use of the singular "letter" here to refer to the Law is therefore best attributed to Paul himself; cf. Furnish, *II Corinthians*, p. 185, contra those who, like Liebers and Vollenweider, attribute it to a pre-Pauline Jewish or Jewish-Christian tradition (see above, n. 194).

[212] This is confirmed by F. Hahn's study of the Lord's Supper traditions, "Die alttestamentlichen Motive," in which he demonstrates that when OT texts are taken up in the NT a single motif is not used in isolation, but represents, designates, and picks "an entire complex of tradition" from that passage. Conversely, this is true within the New Testament itself, which follows the same pattern (p. 373). This, of course, was the programmatic thesis of C.H. Dodd, *According to the Scriptures, The Sub-Structure of New Testament Theology*, 1952, cf. esp. pp. 57, 72, 126 f.

[213] *The Cross and the Spirit, A Study in the Argument and Theology of Galatians*, 1988, pp. 43 f.

[214] Cf. the saying attributed to Hillel in Aboth II, § 8, "more Torah, more life," since "He who has acquired words of Torah has acquired for himself the life of the world to come" (trans. R. Travers Herford, *Pirke Aboth*, 1962, p. 48). Thus, the Law is identified with eschatological life itself! For just one example of this theme from later rabbinic tradition, see Song of Songs Rab. I.2, § 3, where we read that "Torah is a source of life for the world" in reference to Prov. 4:22 (trans. M. Simon, *Song of Songs, Midrash Rabbah*, Vol. 9, 1939, p. 33).

[215] In this regard my conclusion is in fundamental agreement with the important work of Frank Thielman, who, against the thesis of E.P. Sanders, argues that for Paul, as for the

which emphasizes that obedience and disobedience to the Law are a matter of the disposition of the heart.[216] Moreover, as the introduction to the fourth vision in 4 Ezra 9:28–37 makes clear, this perspective concerning the abiding validity of the Law on the one hand, and the corresponding problem of Israel's "heart" on the other, continued to live on through Paul's day:

"And my mouth was opened, and I began to speak before the Most High, and said, 'O Lord, you showed yourself among us, to our fathers in the wilderness when they came out from Egypt and when they came into the untrodden and unfruitful wilderness; and you said, 'Hear me, O Israel, and give heed to my words, O descendants of Jacob, For behold, I sow my Law in you, and you shall be glorified through it forever.' *But though our fathers received the Law, they did not keep it, and did not observe the statutes; yet the fruit of the Law did not perish – for it could not, because it was yours. Yet those who received it perished, because they did not keep what had been sown in them.* And behold, it is the rule that, when the ground has received seed, or the sea a ship, or any dish

---

Judaism around him, there was indeed a "plight" which was widely recognized in the tradition and manifest in Israel's history and the history of the world and which, therefore, for Paul preceded the "solution" brought about by Christ. See his "From Plight to Solution in Ancient Judaism," in his *From Plight to Solution, A Jewish Framework for Understanding Paul's View of the Law in Galatians and Romans*, Suppl. NovT 61, 1989, pp. 28–45. Without separating the Law from the covenant, Thielman argues from the biblical and post-biblical traditions concerning humanity's inclination toward sin and Israel's own history of disobedience that "authors sometimes spoke of Israel's failing in terms of disobedience to the law and of Israel's redemption in terms of God's intervention on her behalf to enable her to keep the law. Israel, these writers frequently said, had become entangled in a web of sin from which only God could extract her, and God would rescue her at some future time" (p. 28). It is this plight and the expectation of an eschatological solution that Thielman argues is the pattern of thinking which "lies behind much of what Paul says about the law and its place both in the human plight and in eschatological redemption" (p. 28). In developing this theme he naturally points to Ezek. 20 and 36:26 f. and Jer. 31:31–34, among other key biblical and post biblical texts (cf. pp. 35 f.). For this same approach, see now the significant work of James Scott, "Works of the Law," (cf. above, n. 145), who builds his interpretation of Gal. 3:10 on the biblical and post-biblical understanding of Israel's history in terms of a "sin-exile-restoration" pattern in which Israel's "curse" and "exile" due to her sinful state extends beyond the end of the sixth century B.C., as does her need for a final redemption and restoration (cf. Deut. 27–32; Ezra 9:6–15; Neh. 9:5–37; Ezek. 4:4–8; Dan. 9:4–19; and the recapitulation of these biblical texts and pattern in Bar. 1:15–3:8; 4:21–5:9; Dan. 3:26–45 LXX; Tobit 13:5–18; 14:4–7; Sir. 36:1–17; 2 Macc. 7; 1 En. 85–90; T. Levi 14–18; T. Judah 24:1–3; Jub. 1:24; CD 1:3–11a, cf. his pp. 194–213). As Scott rightly points out, "It is unfortunate that Sanders' notion of covenantal nomism has so stressed continuity in the covenantal relationship between God and his people, and readily available atonement for sin by means of repentance, that texts on the exile which, like Daniel 9, emphasize prolonged discontinuity as punishment for sin, have gone practically unnoticed or have been labelled aberrant" (pp. 201 f., pointing esp. to Sanders' view of 4 Ezra as an idiosyncratic example of "'legalistic perfectionism,'" p. 202 n. 47). In the context of this study, Scott's earlier work on 2 Sam. 7:14 as the basis of the expectation in T. Judah 24:1–3 and Jub. 1:24 that after this period of protracted exile Israel will be adopted as God's son and endowed with the Spirit as an essential element of their messianic restoration is also of particular importance as collaboration of the thesis being argued here; cf. his *Adoption as Sons*, pp. 96–105, 107–117.

[216] See above, n. 157.

food or drink, and when it happens that what was sown or what was launched or what was put in is destroyed, they are destroyed, but the things that held them remain; yet with us it has not been so. *For we who received the Law and sinned will perish, as well as our heart which received it; the Law, however, does not perish but remains in its glory"* (emphasis mine).[217]

In accordance with this prophetic perspective on the Law and its later development in post-biblical Judaism as seen in this passage from 4 Ezra and the Qumran documents (see above and chapter three), Paul's particular choice of terminology in 3:6 takes on a heightened significance. It must be emphasized once again that Paul did *not* use his most common term νόμος, which does not call attention to the nature of the Law as an external, written document or declaration, but is used by Paul to refer to the Torah and its content as part of the Scriptures, or even to the Scriptures as a whole. Nor did he choose the designation γραφή ("Scripture"), which carries the nuance of authority, but is not specific either in regard to the section or content of Scripture in view or in regard to the nature of Scripture as written and external. Instead, Paul's decision to characterize the Law apart from the Spirit in 3:6 as the "letter" (γράμμα) follows conventional usage in calling attention to the *nature* of the Law as the *written* expression of God's will.[218] This is brought out further by

---

[217] Trans. B.M. Metzger, "The Fourth Book of Ezra," *OTP, Vol. 1*, 1983, p. 545. I am in agreement with Scott (see above, n. 215) that 4 Ezra is not an aberration within post-biblical Judaism (contra Sanders), but representative.

[218] See G. Schrenk, γράφω κτλ., *TDNT* 1 (1964) 742–773, p. 761, who concludes that "γράμμα is properly what is 'inscribed' or 'engraven' and then what is 'written' in the widest sense," while "γράμματα can also be 'symbols' or 'letters' without the idea of engraving." Hence, "it will be seen that γράμμα always connotes 'what is written'" and "γράμμα, γράμματα are most commonly used for various kinds of 'written pieces'" (p. 762; cf. his documentation on pp. 761–763). In much of the discussion that follows, we will focus on Schrenk's work since it is so representative as well as influential due to its widespread use as part of *TDNT*. The range of meaning pointed to by Schrenk is reflected in the NT itself, with its use in Gal. 6:11 to refer to actual handwritten characters; in Lk. 16:6 f. in the plural to refer to a written bill; in John 5:47 in the plural to refer to the writings of Moses; in John 7:15 and Acts 26:24 in the plural representing literature (esp. the Law) and thus the educational reading it represents; and in Acts 28:21 in the plural to refer to written epistles. See e.g. the 171 uses of γράμμα in Josephus, in which it refers to various kinds of writings and is used to refer to the actual alphabet or characters of various languages in *Bell.* 5, 194; 6,125; *Ant.* 12, 15; 14, 197; 14, 319; *C. Ap.* 1, 10–11; 1, 22; and most often in the plural to refer to actual epistles sent from one party to another (approximately 102 times!), often synonymous with ἐπιστολή; see K.H. Rengstorf, *A Complete Concordance to Flavius Josephus, Vol. 1*, 1973, pp. 391–393. Of significance for Paul's use is that it can also be used in the plural in *Bell.* 5, 235 and *Ant.* 3, 178 (cf. Philo's *De Vit. Mos.* II, 114, for this same use and see below) to refer to the "sacred letters" (τὰ ἱερὰ γράμματα) representing God's name on the high priest's head-dress and to refer to the (holy) Scriptures or Writings in *Bell.* 6, 312; *Ant.* 5, 61; 10, 210; 13, 167; 20, 264; *C. Ap.* 1, 42, 54, 127, 128, 160, 218. In *Ant.* 1, 5 they are called the "Hebrew records" or "writings" (...Ἑβραϊκῶν ... γραμμάτων), which are then equated with the sacred writings (τὰ ἱερὰ γράμματα) in *Ant.* 1, 13. In *Ant.* 3, 322 the Law is referred to as the "writings left by Moses" (τὰ καταλειφθέντα ὑπὸ Μωϋσέος), which "have such authority (ἰσχύν) that even our enemies admit that our constitution was established by God himself through the agency of

his unusual use of the singular form γράμμα ("letter"), rather than the typical plural form γράμματα ("writings"/"Scriptures"), which is more idiomatic in reference to the Law as that which is written.[219] Moreover, when Paul's choice of γράμμα is read against the prophetic background behind 2 Cor. 3:3, 6 it carries the nuance of the Law as being *merely* expressed in writing rather than being incorporated into one's heart by the Spirit.[220] The new covenant becomes the reversal of this state of affairs. The letter/Spirit contrast thus in no way points to the termination or devaluation of the Law due to its material content.[221] Nor does it present a contrast between two natures of revelation or

---

Moses and of his merits," while in *Ant.* 10, 79 Lamentations is designated as the writings (γράμμασι) left behind by the prophet. Finally, the positive nature of the "writing" or "letters" of the Law is seen in *Ant.* 12, 89, where the LXX version of the Law is said to be written on leather skins "in letters of gold" (χρυσοῖς γράμμασιν), while in *C. Ap.* 1, 42 the γράμματα of the Scriptures is said to be the δόγματα θεοῦ ("decrees of God"), which no one ventures to remove or even alter a syllable and for which one is willing to die. Texts are from H. St. J. Thackeray and R. Marcus, *Josephus, Vols. III, IV, VI, VII*, and *The Life, Against Apion Vol. I*, LCL, 1979 (1928) –1987 (1937) and 1976 (1926).

[219] Cf. the plural use in the immediately following passage, 2 Cor. 3:7, and the full use of ἱερὰ γράμματα to refer to the Scriptures in 2 Tim. 3:15 as that which continues to have value for salvation! This speaks against the attempt of many who, like Schrenk, γράφω, p. 768, argue that "γράμμα is not used when (Paul) speaks of the positive and lasting significance of Scripture," but "the positive task is always stated in terms of γραφή." See too the position of Stuhlmacher (cf. above, Introduction). On the other hand, Paul certainly does prefer both νόμος and γραφή to γράμμα/γράμματα to refer to the Law and the Scriptures, since in most cases he does not have its nature as external and written in view, but its authority. This follows the LXX, where γράμμα is never used in either the singular or the plural to refer to the Law or to the Scriptures in general (it is doubtful, contra Schrenk, γράφω, p. 763, that Esther 6:1 refers to canonical Chronicles). It is used in Ex. 36:39LXX to refer to the letters engraved on the priest's golden plate (cf. Sir. 38:27, where it may also be found in reference to engraved letters), as also found in both Josephus and Philo (see above and below). In Lev. 19:28 it refers to letters or marks tattooed on one's skin. In Dan. 1:4, Esther 4:3; 6:1, 2; 8:5, 10, 13; 9:1, 1 Macc. 5:10, and 1 Esdras 3:9, 13, 15 it is used in the more common meaning of written epistles, records, and statements.

[220] Cf. Peter von der Osten-Sacken, "Die Decke des Mose, Zur Exegese und Hermeneutik von Geist und Buchstabe in 2 Korinther 3," in his *Die Heiligkeit der Tora*, 1989, pp. 87–115, pp. 100, 100 f. n. 64, who sees γράμμα as referring to the "geschriebene Forderung" in general, as well as indicating a certain way of interacting with the Law as in Rom. 7:6 ff. This more general interpretation is based on his view that the letter/Spirit contrast refers to the written versus the oral form of Paul's ministry, the latter accompanied by the power of God (p. 100). But such a view looses sight of the OT background to both terms as well as the clear connection between 3:6 and 3:7 ff.

[221] So too now Betz, "Der fleischliche Mensch," pp. 183 f., who points out that since the Law remains in the new covenant (cf. Rom. 3:31), this demands that the person be changed by the Spirit, since only then can one fulfill the Law. Hence, "Was durch Christus wesenhaft geändert wird, ist nicht etwa das Gesetz, sondern der Mensch unter dem Gesetz; er wird durch den ihm geschenkten Geist dem geistlichen Gesetz nahegebracht" (p. 186). See too Schlatter, *Bote*, p. 506: "Das γράμμα macht Gottes Willen offenbar, seine διαθήκη, sein Recht, das mit absoluter Geltung den Anteil des Menschen an Gott bestimmt." For Schlatter, however, the coming of the new covenant means that the γράμμα as equivalent to the Law is done away with, since there is no longer any "holy letters" in Paul's message (pp. 506, 509),

authority, an external, written one, versus an internal spiritual one, so that Paul ends up "contending against a religion of the book."[222] It s not an expression of the fact that "moral demands (in a general sense) can be experienced as anxiety-producing signals in an archaic level of the human psyche" and experienced as "threatening," as Gerd Theißen has maintained.[223] It is also not a

---

though he does not set up any antithesis between God's word and the "letter" (pp. 507, 509). Contra too the traditional view represented by Furnish, *II Corinthians*, p. 185, who understands it to be used "as the destructive power of *what* is *written* is specifically accented ..." (first emphasis mine); and Hofius, "Gesetz und Evangelium," p. 84, who sees the Law to refer to the "Wesen, Auftrag und Funktion der Sinai-Tora." Hence, for Furnish, et al., the Spirit must free one *from* the Law in order to make one alive or provide a new way of understanding it, seeing the problem with the Law to be material rather than functional (cf. Furnish, pp. 189, 197 f.). See Hofius, p. 84, who argues that this is so since the Law can do nothing but kill, being given by God for no other purpose. He thus sees *only* a negative function for the Law in 2 Cor. 3, though the will of God expressed in the Law is of course not abolished by the Gospel (pp. 84 n. 64; 120). Yet Furnish also sees a positive function for the Law that Hofius does not and argues that the description of the new covenant reflects Paul's "eschatological perspective on God's redemptive work in history," which is effected through Christ and not the Law (p. 200). Hence, for Furnish, the Law is not rejected as such, since the "letter" is not "fully synonymous" with the Law (p. 200). Nevertheless, when describing the problem with the Law, Furnish follows Käsemann and returns to a material distinction: what Paul rejects is "that way of using the law which presumes that its 'letter' provides a sure way to righteousness and life," yet "what is written kills because it enslaves one to the presumption that righteousness inheres in one's doing of the law, when it is actually the case that true righteousness comes only as a gift from God" (pp. 200 f.). Hence, Furnish translates the letter/Spirit contrast to mean, "not written but spiritual" (p. 199).

[222] Schrenk, γράφω, p. 768, and Windisch, *Korintherbrief*, p. 111. Contra also those who do not go as far as Schrenk and Windisch, but still draw a similar conclusion by joining Schrenk in contrasting the written Law and the Spirit, often in contrast to Paul's use of γραφή. As Schrenk puts it: "γράμμα represents the legal authority which has been superseded, while γραφή is linked with the new *form* of authority determined by the fulfillment in Christ and by his Spirit, the determinative *character* of the new no longer being what is written and prescribed. The word which is near (R. 10:8) is not the γράμμα but Scripture, which is self-attesting through the Spirit of Christ" (p. 768, emphasis mine). See most recently, Hays, *Echoes*, p. 130, who moves from rightly seeing that γράμμα as a verbal noun refers to "'that which is inscribed,'" to interpreting it to refer to "script" in contrast to the non-inscribed form of the writing of the Spirit on the heart from 3:3. Hays then concludes that Paul's ministry is not of the "script," but of the Spirit, which he takes to mean that Paul's ministry centers not on "texts," but on the "Spirit-empowered transformation of human community." This subtle (and in Paul unsupported) shift from the character of the Law as written to written scripts enables Hays to contrast γράμμα with Scripture, the latter of which is a living presence. For in Hays' view, "the problem with the old covenant lies precisely in its character as a written thing" (p. 131). But since Scripture is also a "written thing," the distinction Hays makes between γράμμα and Scripture has no real referent for the latter; nor is the problem in 3:6 with the nature of the Law, but with the nature of the human heart. Yet Hays is correct and helpful when he goes on to observe that "The problem with this old covenant is precisely that it is (only) written, lacking the power to effect the obedience that it demands. Since it has no power to transform the readers, it can only stand as a witness to their condemnation" (p. 131).

[223] "Die Hülle des Mose," p. 152 (translation mine). Though he makes insightful exegetical observations on individual aspects of 3:1–4:6 (see below, chapters 4 and 5), Theißen can only maintain his central thesis because of his reconstructions of Paul's experience behind

designation of a particular use or misuse, interpretation, or subset of the Law, whether that be a divine intention in the Law to kill, a Jewish or "Hellenistic-Jewish" perversion of the Law into legalism or works-righteousness, or merely those ceremonial aspects of the Law which created distinctions between Jew and Gentile in contrast to the abiding moral law.[224] Although such

---

the text, his assumption that they are typical of all human experience (read from a Freudian *and* Jungian perspective (!), cf. p. 147), and his psychological reinterpretations of Paul's explicit statements (cf. e.g., pp. 148 f., 154–156, 160). As such, his reading of Paul, though in my view completely unconvincing, is, strictly speaking, impossible to refute.

[224] So too E.P. Sanders, *Paul, the Law, and the Jewish People*, pp. 82–86, in regard to Paul's statements that Christians die to the Law or are freed from it (cf. e.g., in his view, Rom. 6:14 f.; 7:4,6; 10:4) and the Law's ability to condemn and kill (2 Cor. 3:6), who acknowledges his debt to Räisänen at this point. But in sharp contrast to the position argued here, for Sanders "the virtual equation of the law with sin and the flesh in some passages (e.g. Rom. 6:14; 7:4–6; Gal. 5:16–18) is not part of a harmonious view of the law which held in balance its destructive and its productive power, depending upon human response" (p. 84). Sanders does not take the OT Scriptural backdrop to Paul's various positive and negative statements concerning the Law seriously enough, but rather sees them within his overall paradigm for understanding Paul's thought in which the solutions now found "in Christ," as advocated by Paul, are understood to precede and determine Paul's subsequent delineation of the "problems" which they are seen to solve (cf. his *Paul and Palestinian Judaism*, pp. 442 f., 499–501, 509–511, for succinct statements of his view). Such an approach allows Sanders to evaluate Paul's apparently positive and negative statements concerning the law and/or its function as distinct answers to different questions, without having to integrate them (cf. *Paul, the Law*, pp. 144–147). This can be seen in his treatment of 2 Cor. 3 (cf. his *Paul, the Law*, pp. 138–140). Hence, for Sanders, the negative statements concerning the law, of which 2 Cor. 3:6 is a central example (cf. p. 83), and the related "virtual equation of the law with sin and the flesh" arise "most immediately from Paul's assigning the law a negative role in God's plan of salvation, an assignment which itself arose from his view that righteousness is only by faith in Christ and that God must have given the law with *that* righteousness ... ultimately in view" (p. 84). Moreover, this negative evaluation of the Law and the "black and white contrast" between the Law and the Spirit in 3:6, which is then picked up in 3:7,9, is not integrated with Paul's subsequent statement in 3:9 that the Mosaic ministry of death was *glorious* (cf. p. 138). For inasmuch as Sanders equates the letter with the Law itself, and because he ignores the OT background to Paul's argument in 2 Cor. 3:6–18, all Sanders can conclude concerning 3:6 ff. is that "Paul does not explain how it is that something which condemns and kills can be glorious. He is caught here as elsewhere between two convictions, but here there is no struggle to resolve them; he states them both as facts" (p. 138). But as we will see in chapter four, Paul is neither "caught" nor without explanation in establishing this equation. Cf. Räisänen, *Paul and the Law*, p. 45, who thinks the attempt to see 3:6 as referring to some particular aspect or function of the law is "impossible" in view of Paul's reference to the activity of Moses in v. 7, rather than Pharisaic teachers, as the ministry of death. As he rightly observes, "The association of this reference to the Decalogue with the talk of the 'letter' in the previous verse is unmistakable. There is no allusion at all to a later misinterpretation or misuse of the stone tablets" (p. 45). Though correct in what he denies, Räisänen's own view of 3:6 ff., is also to be rejected (see above on 3:6 and chapter four on 3:7 ff.). For given his view of the identity of the letter and the Law, if there is a legalism it is an "*original* legalism inherent in the law" as that which "would merely denote slavery to precepts and ordinances (cf. Gal. 4:25) without taking into account the attitude of the man under law" (p. 46). The view that the letter represents a perversion of the law into some sort of legalism has been championed most widely by C.E.B. Cranfield

perversions and misuses of the Law may *result* from encountering the Law as "letter," and although there does exist an implied distinction in Paul's thinking between what has traditionally been called the ritual purity and ceremonial laws on the one hand and the moral law on the other,[225] neither is the referent of "letter" in 3:6.[226] Rather, the letter/Spirit contrast is between *the Law itself without the Spirit*, as it was (and is! cf. 3:14 f.) experienced by the majority of Israelites under the Sinai covenant, and *the Law with the Spirit*, as it is now being experienced by those who are under the new covenant in Christ.[227] As Thomas E. Provence concluded over a decade ago,

---

from one perspective, and E. Käsemann from another; for the former, see Cranfield's paradigmatic article, "St. Paul and the Law," *SJTh* 17 (1964) 43–68, developed further by T. Provence, "'Who is Sufficient for These Things?' An Exegesis of 2 Corinthians 2:15–3:18," *NovT* 24 (1982) 54–81, and for the other, see the Introduction above. In the commentary literature, see now R.P. Martin, *2 Corinthians*, p. 55, who considers Cranfield's view the most satisfactory of the various interpretations which have been given (pointing to T. Provence, esp. his pp. 62–68 for a helpful summary of the various views). Martin himself, however, intimates a degree of uncertainty concerning this view since, in his words, "a more severe attitude to Moses will occupy Paul as he moves into ... 3:7–18." But that such a severe attitude toward Moses or the Law exists in 2 Cor. 3 is called into question by this present study. For the application of Käsemann's view, see now F. Lang, *Die Briefe an die Korinther*, NTD 7, 1986[16], pp. 270 f., for a succinct presentation of the view that the eschatological character of 3:6 means that the new covenant is determined by the Spirit rather than the letter of the Law, since the contrast in 3:6 is between "Gesetzesgerechtigkeit und Glaubensgerechtigkeit," in which the "letter" refers to the holy Law as it is misused as a basis for self-justification (p. 270). Lang asserts that the problem with the Law is not only that one does not have the power to keep it perfectly, but also that "die Zweckentfremdung des Gesetzes zur Selbstbehauptung des Menschen Gott die Ehre raubt ..." (p. 271).

[225] For a defense of this distinction, see Thomas R. Schreiner, "The Abolition and Fulfillment of the Law in Paul," *JSNT* 35 (1989) 47–74, esp. pp. 59–65, although not all aspects of his paradigm are convincing to me, e.g., his view that "Paul departs from Judaism in his insistence that the law must be obeyed perfectly by non-believers in order to merit salvation," and that "Paul views such perfect obedience as impossible, and thus he claims that one can only be saved by believing in Christ" (p. 65). In my view, the distinction between the ritual purity laws and the moral laws derives from the eschatological work of Christ (see above, n. 145). For this same view, argued on the basis of the relationship between Rom. 12:1 f. and 14:1–15:13, see A.J.M. Wedderburn, *The Reasons for Romans*, 1988, pp. 77 f.

[226] Contra now, e.g., Segal, *Paul the Convert*, pp. 151 f., who argues that the letter/Spirit contrast "means that the ceremonial laws of Judaism, understood strictly rather than allegorically, cannot bring one to transformation, as does the Holy Spirit" (p. 152). Segal is correct, however, in stressing that the issue at stake in the contrast is the actual transformation of the believer's life and that, as we shall see in chapters four and five, this transformation comes about as a result of encountering the presence/glory of God as Moses did (cf. p. 152). But see already K. Prümm, *Diakonia Pneumatos, Bd. II/Teil 1*, 1960, p. 209, who emphasized that there is no evidence at all for a distinction between the moral and ceremonial laws in this context: "Die Stellungnahme Pauli in der Gesetzesfrage ist durchaus Einheitlich" (p. 210). Prümm, however, takes this to mean that Paul is teaching the abrogation of the Law in order to assert the primacy of the promise, which was itself also taught in the Law, but ignored and thus perverted by the Pharisees into a legalistic nomism (pp. 210 f., 213).

[227] This is close to the position taken by Stegemann, "Neue Bund," p. 108, who argues that the letter/Spirit contrast is not a contrast of Scripture vs. the Spirit, but Scripture under the

"... the contrast between the Old and New Covenants cannot consist in the distinction between the law and the Spirit since the law is good (Rom. 7) and is placed within the heart in the new covenant (Jer. 31). The law is common to both covenants ... The Old Covenant was the ministry of the law without the empowering work of the Spirit; the new covenant is the ministry of the law along with the Spirit's empowerment to accomplish the law's demands (cf. Ezek. 36:26 ...).".[228]

Hence, the letter/Spirit contrast in 3:6 is not primarily between two ontological realities, but is a *functional* contrast between the two ways in which God's will encounters those under the Sinai and new covenants respectively, either as an external letter which is unable to be accepted, or as the transformation brought about by the Spirit.[229] The letter/Spirit contrast is therefore not a con-

---

two aspects of the letter and the Spirit, each with distinct functions. But for Stegemann, pp. 108 f., the letter is the perversion of the Scriptures into that which condemns (on the basis of his reading of Rom. 7), rather than the Law itself as that which condemns when it encounters the hard hearted. On the other hand, this conclusion runs counter to the thesis of Liebers, *Das Gesetz als Evangelium*, p. 241, which concludes that Paul critiques the promise of Jer. 31:33 and Ezek. 11:19; 36:26 f. that the Law or the wisdom it generates can transform the heart of the person if one turns to it. But as this study has argued, the promise of Jer. and Ezek. is not that the Law can transform, but that the agent of transformation is the Spirit.

[228] "Sufficient," p. 77. But there is no need to posit that the "letter" therefore refers directly to a legalistic perversion of the Law as Provence (following Cranfield, et al.) argues (see n. 224). Provence points to Hughes, *Second Corinthians*, p. 94, in support of this point. Cf. too Hughes' perception of the implications of these points on p. 90: "To overlook these considerations leads to the postulation of an erroneous and unscriptural antithesis between law and Gospel, which by its equation of divine love with divine 'injustice,' or disregard of law, undermines the whole structure of the Christian redemption." As the corollary to this, Hughes rightly points out that "there were, of course, lovers of the law in the Old Testament period, but as such they did not differ radically from believers of the New Testament era: their love of the law was by means of divine grace granted to them, not by reason of any self-adequacy ..." (p. 94).

[229] Contra Liebers, *Das Gesetz als Evangelium*, pp. 96 f., who sees γράμμα in 3:6 as referring primarily to the Law itself rather than to the Law's function, though he admits that the meaning of γράμμα as "letter" is "nahe" and that 3:7 refers to the form of the Law as written on stone tablets (p. 98). Liebers rightly sees that one cannot equate the Law with the γράμμα, since it is always contrasted with something positive and therefore expresses a "negative function" (p. 98). But because of his failure to take the OT backdrop seriously as the key to Paul's thinking (cf. p. 102), Liebers fails to see Paul's point concerning the negative function of the Law when it encounters the hard heart, concluding instead that γράμμα refers to the Law "under a particular aspect, in which it exclusively picks up the negative side of the Law" in terms of its "character as a power" which kills (p. 98, following Kamlah and Luz). Moreover, Liebers fails to see the role of the Spirit in Ezekiel as the promised power of the new covenant. Nor does he see the significance of Jer. 31 for Paul's argument. He consequently attributes to the "Jewish view of the Law" behind 2 Cor. 3, which Paul opposes, the idea that under the Sinai covenant the Law already naturally belongs together with the Spirit and that this life of Spirit-empowered obedience to the Law was already a reality for Israel, since only when the Law comes together with the Spirit can they bring about proper conduct, (pp. 102, 104). Liebers thus concludes, pp. 116 f., that in 3:6 Paul is denying the "Jewish view" of the unity of the Law and the Spirit, the very unity which this study argues Paul affirms as the promise of the new covenant! In addition, Liebers' view is based on the standard interpretation of καταργέω and the veil in 3:7 ff. (cf. p. 117 and see

trast between two kinds of covenants, but between two distinct *ministries*, a contrast that will become explicit in 3:7–18.[230] Paul's assertion in 3:6b that God has made him sufficient to be a servant of the Spirit, in contrast to serving the "letter," thus points to Paul's underlying assumption that, unlike Moses, who was called to mediate the Law under the Sinai covenant, he has been called to mediate the new life of the new covenant in which the Law now functions under the power of the Spirit (cf. 3:3b). Moses was called to mediate the Law to a stiff-necked people under the Law who could not obey it. Paul is called to mediate the Spirit now being poured out as a result of the cross of Christ to a people whose hearts are being transformed to obey the covenant stipulations of the Law.[231]

a) The letter/Spirit Contrast in Aristobulus

This functional understanding of the letter/Spirit contrast finds a striking parallel in the one passage from Jewish literature in which the written nature of the Law given by Moses is contrasted to the power of the Spirit, Aristobulus, Frag. 2, found in Eusebius, *Praeparatio Evangelica* 8.10.4–5. There we read concerning Moses that "... those who are able to think well marvel at his wisdom and at the *divine spirit* (τὸ θεῖον πνεῦμα) in accordance with which he has

---

below chs. 4 and 5). In Lieber's view, the Law cannot be equated in Paul's thought with the true way and judgments of the Lord or with the wisdom of God (cf. his conclusion on pp. 241 f.). And this remains true even in the new covenant. In his words, "Für Paulus erweist sich die Verheißung der Tora im Herzen des Menschen, die sein Denken und Handeln bestimmt und 'erneuert,' als nicht erfüllt" (p. 243). Liebers is careful, however, to reject the view that "letter" refers to the Law perverted into a works righteousness or into a principle of human endeavor (p. 98 n. 8).

[230] This is the main emphasis of W.D. Davies, "Paul and the People of Israel," who states the point well that "It is important to recognize that in II Cor. 3 Paul is concerned essentially with the contrast between two ministries, not with that between two covenants on which two distinct religions were founded" (p. 11). U. Luz, *Gesichts*, p. 123, thus rightly warns that 3:7 makes it clear that the letter/Spirit contrast must be understood from the standpoint of these two ministries. He argues that γράμμα cannot be equated directly with the Law, nor with the Scriptures, for which Paul uses γραφή (p. 124). As for the meaning of γράμμα itself, Luz takes as his key its parallel to Spirit (p. 125). He concludes that γράμμα is the Law of God when it is *misunderstood* as human and therefore able to be fulfilled "nach Menschenweise" without being confronted by its radical requirement (pp. 125 f.). He goes on to associate γράμμα exclusively with the old age as a human, enslaving "Machtprinzip" and the Spirit with the new as a divine, liberating "Machtprinzip," the former being determined by mankind's misuse of the Law and the latter by God's work of the Spirit (pp. 126 f., 130 f., 146).

[231] Cf. Betz, "Der fleischliche Mensch," p. 181, who concludes that the second way in which the Law is established in the new covenant is that it can now be obeyed by the "spiritual person". Betz asserts that this takes place in that the Law is summarized and fulfilled in the command to love one's neighbor (Rom. 13:8–10). Betz thus draws a parallel between the "spiritual person" (ἄνθρωπος πνευματικός) and the "spiritual law" (νόμος πνευματικός) on the one hand, and the "fleshly person" (ἄνθρωπος σάρκινος or ψυχικός) and the "other Law in one's members" (ἕτερος νόμος ἐν τοῖς μέλεσιν, Rom. 7:23) on the other (p. 181).

been proclaimed as a prophet also" (emphasis mine).[232] In recognition of Moses' wisdom and prophetic endowment with the Spirit, philosophers and poets are then said to have taken "significant material from him and are admired accordingly" (8.10.4).[233] Of significance for our interpretation of the letter/ Spirit contrast in 2 Cor. 3:6 is that these statements about Moses are made in the context of anthropomorphisms in the Law to describe God (cf. 8.10.1), concerning which it is said that "... to those who have no share of *power and understanding* (δυνάμεως καὶ συνέσεως), but who are devoted to the *letter alone* (τῷ γραπτῷ[234] μόνον), he does not seem to explain anything elevated" *(Praeparatio Evangelica* 8.10.5, emphasis mine). In the context, this "power" must be the same "divine spirit" which Moses had when he wrote the Law, which gives one understanding into the meaning of the "letter," especially because in 8.10.1, 8 the references to God's hands, arms, feet, etc. are explicitly seen to be references to the "divine power" (ἐπὶ τῆς θείας δυνάμεως ἐπὶ δυνάμεως εἶναι θεοῦ). Strikingly, those things which are offered as the "elevated" understanding of the anthropomorphisms in the Law concerning God are based on common ground understandings of the meaning of "metaphors" such as "hands" (8.10.9), and not on an interpretation derived from esoteric revelation (cf. 8.10.6–12). The work of the Spirit appears to be to enable one to accept these explanations as valid. Aristobulus therefore prefaces his explanations with the disclaimer that "if I miss the point or fail to be persuasive, attribute the lack of reason not to the lawgiver but to my inability to interpret his thoughts" (8.10.6), something which would not be said if the elevated understandings came about as a result of a special divine revelation! Indeed, the onus lies on Aristobulus himself to provide an accurate and persuasive interpretation of the Law already given by Moses under the power of the Spirit. As for Paul, here too reading the Mosaic Law as a mere "letter" is to read it without the Spirit so that it fails to be persuasive, thus remaining unaccepted (and disobeyed).

b) The "letter" in Philo

In contrast, Ronald Williamson has pointed out that for Philo it is the terminology of "speaking or being spoken in a riddle or darkly," i.e. in Williamson's words, being "under a figure" (αἰνίττεται), which is "the technical term used for the language of Scripture which has a meaning below the surface level hidden, until it is appropriately decoded, by the figures which make up the literal

---

[232] Trans. A. Yarbro Collins, "Aristobulus," *OTP Vol. 2,* 1985, p. 838. Greek text from Karl Mras, *Eusebius Werke, Bd. 8, Die Praeparatio Evangelica,* GCS 8/1, 1982², p. 452.

[233] Cf. Frag. 3, Eusebius, *Prae. Evan.* 13.12.1 for this same point applied explicitly to Plato and Pythagoras, Frag. 4, Eusebius 13.13.4, 6 to Socrates, Orpheus, and Aratus, and Frag. 5, Eusebius 13.12.13, 16 to Homer, Hesiod, and Linus.

[234] Cf. γραπτός, ή, όν meaning "written"; Liddell and Scott, *Greek-English Lexicon,* 1968, p. 359.

meaning."[235] On the other hand, γράμμα ("letter") refers to the letters of the alphabet,[236] or in a more extended fashion to something in particular which has been written or engraved.[237] In *De migratione Abrahami* 195 and *De somniis* I, 57 it refers to the specific phrase of a poet, which in both cases is then quoted. Indeed, of the 49 uses of *gramma* (γράμμα) in Philo's writings,[238] it is most often used either with reference to the Law or to specific statements or commandments in the Law which are then quoted by Philo, or as a positive description of the Scriptures as the "holy writings" (τὰ ἱερὰ γράμματα).[239] For example, in *De migratione Abrahami* 139, Numbers 31:28 ff. is first called τὸ ἱερώτατον γράμμα ("the all-holy writ"), and is then designated as a specific "law" (νόμος). In *Quod deus immutabilis sit* 6 it is used to refer to the writing of Moses in Numbers 28:2 as "the most sacred letter of Moses" (τὸ ἱερώτατον Μωυσέως γράμμα). In *De confusione linguarum* 50 κατὰ τὸ Μωυσέως γράμμα ("according to the letter of Moses") is used to introduce Numbers 16:15. And in *De specialibus legibus* III, 8 γράμμα is used to refer to the specific commandment, "Thou shalt not commit adultery," from Exodus 20:14.

This is even more significant given Philo's view of the superiority of that which can be known from nature and directly within one's soul over that which is set down in the writings (γράμματα) of the wise men.[240] In *De*

---

[235] *Jews in the Hellenistic World: Philo*, Cambridge Commentaries on Writings of the Jewish and Christian World 200 BC to AD 200, Vol. 1/2, 1989, p. 189. For an example of this use of αἰνίττεται, see *De Vit. Mos.* II, 131.

[236] Cf. *De mut. nom.* 64; *De vit. Mos.* I, 23; *De vit. Mos.* II, 132, where it refers to the four letters representing the name of God on the priest's golden plate; *De spec. leg.* I, 336 and II, 230, where it refers to "letters" over against numbers, music and arithmetic, or geometry, music, and philosophy respectively. The texts and translations are taken from F.H. Colson and G.H. Whitaker, *Philo*, LCL, Vols. 2–10, 1979 (1927) –1984 (1934), except where noted with the brackets [].

[237] Cf. *De plant.* 131, 173; *De spec. leg.* I, 58; *Quod omnis prob.* 104, 158; *In Flaccum* 108, 131; *Leg. ad Gaium* 231, 253, 260; and esp. *Quis rerum* 176, where θεῖα γράμματα ("divine graving" [letters]) refers to the names of the 12 patriarchs engraved on the two emeralds of the priestly robe; *De Ios.* 168, where it refers to a written summons; *De Vit. Mos.* I, 23, where it refers to the "holy inscriptions [letters]" (ἱεροῖς γράμμασιν) of the Egyptians; *Leg. ad Gaium* 69, where it refers to the "Delphic motto" (τὸ Δελφικὸν γράμμα); *De dec.* 140, where it is used as the counterpart to λόγος as that which is "written" rather than "verbal"; *Quod omnis prob.* 95, where it refers to written words as more durable than spoken words; *De spec. leg.* IV, 30, where it refers to written documents and IV, 162, where it refers to that which is written down.

[238] According to Günter Mayer, *Index Philoneus*, 1974, p. 66, who lists 50 occurrences, though no use of γράμμα could be found in *In Flaccum* 57 as listed.

[239] Cf. *Quis rerum* 258, where γράμμα ῥητόν ("word written") refers to something written in the "holy Scriptures [books]" (ἱεραῖς βίβλοις); and *De vit. Mos.* II, 290, 292; *De spec. leg.* II, 159; II, 238; *De vita cont.* 28, 75; *Leg. ad Gaium* 195, where it is used to refer to the "Holy Scriptures [Writings];" *De spec. leg.* IV, 142, where it refers to the Laws written on the door posts of houses and IV, 161, where it refers to the written law; and *De praem. et poen.* 79, where it refers to the Holy Writings, specifically the Law and its commandments.

[240] Cf. Windisch, *Zweite Korintherbrief*, p. 111, who traces this idea back to Plato, who thought that writing was an inferior means of preservation of spiritual products in compari-

sacrificiis Abelis et Caini 79 these writings are to be sought, yet considered inferior to the "self-inspired [taught] wisdom" (αὐτοδίδακτος σοφίας) that God causes to spring up in one's soul, which abolishes the things gained from such teaching (τὰ ἐκ διδασκαλίας). In *De Abrahamo* 60 γράμμα refers to those divine commands made clear through writing over against those manifested through speech (διὰ φωνῆς) and through nature (διὰ τῆς φύσεως), with the last being the most superior. In *De Abrahamo* 275 Abraham is thus said to have obeyed the divine law (Gen. 26:5) not taught "by written words" (οὐ γράμμασιν ἀναδιδαχθείς) but by "unwritten nature" (ἀγράφῳ τῇ φύσει). And in *De mutatione nominum* 63 the γράμματα ("letters") are themselves not the "gifts of God's grace," but merely the disposal of human wisdom, as seen in mankind's naming of the animals. Thus names are a sign (χαρακτήρ) of hidden values or realities (cf. *De mut. nom* 67).

Although to speak of the Law in its written form points for Philo to its need to be understood and correctly taught by the use of allegory, and even though it may be merely an expression of that which can be learned and obeyed more directly from nature or God, it is nevertheless not a criticism of the Law itself nor of the nature of the Sinai covenant to recognize that it was written on tablets. In *De migratione Abrahami* 85, Philo can even use γράμμα to refer to Exodus 8:19 as a specific point from the tablets (τὰς πλάκας) upon which "the holy word" (ὁ ἱερὸς λόγος) was written "by the finger of God" (referring to Exodus 32:16).[241] And in *De somniis* I, 202 Philo can point to the fact that the Law is "engraved with inscriptions [letters]" (γράμμασιν ἐγκεκολαμμένα) as a positive demonstration of that which is "speckled" (ποικιλία) in diversity and yet works together to produce a harmony (reading Gen. 31:10 together with Exod. 36:15 and 39:8). Indeed, in *De specialibus legibus* I, 31 Philo uses γράμμα to refer to writing recorded on the tablets of nature, which endures with nature "to all eternity."

In the same way, Paul can move from referring to the Law in terms of "the tablets of stone" in 2 Cor. 3:3 to describing the Law in its written form as a "letter" in 3:6, without in either case intending a negative evaluation of the nature of the Law itself. And even if 2 Tim. 3:15 is deutero-Pauline, it still reflects the fact that Paul (or a Paulinist) viewed the Scriptures in their form as "holy writings" (ἱερὰ γράμματα) to be inspired (3:16) and able to lead one to salvation "through faith in Jesus Christ." At the same time, his choice of the singular form γράμμα ("letter," "that which is written") to refer to the Law calls attention to the same basic reality highlighted by Philo's insistence on the need for allegory, i.e. that the Law by itself as a written expression of

---

son to their being impressed in the soul (cf. the various references given by Windisch). Contra the view argued here, Windisch sees Paul influenced by this antithesis between written and unwritten law, whereas Philo is the one who weakens it!

[241] Cf. too *De congr. quae.* 58, where γράμμα is used to refer to Deut. 32:8, which is then described as "graven as on a stone" or "recorded."

God's will is not efficacious to bring about its acceptance and obedience.[242] But unlike Philo, Paul's solution is not an allegorical reading of the text, but, like 4 Ezra (!) and the prophetic tradition, the power of the Spirit.

c) *The letter/Spirit Contrast in Romans 2:27–29 and 7:6*

More importantly, this interpretation is supported by the two other contexts where Paul discusses the Law as γράμμα ("letter") in direct contrast to the Spirit, Romans 2:27–29 and 7:6.[243] In both texts the point is that possession of the written prescription of the Law is of no value for salvation if not accompanied by obedience to what the Law teaches (cf. Rom. 2:25 f.; 7:6; cf. 8:3 f.):[244]

---

[242] Cf. *De vita cont.* 78, where the exposition (αἱ ἐξηγήσεις) of the Holy Writings (τῶν ἱερῶν γραμμάτων), specifically the Law, is said to treat its inner meaning by means of allegory (δι' ὑπονοιῶν ἐν ἀλληγορίαις).

[243] It is beyond the scope of this work to treat these difficult texts in detail, and methodologically the common attempt to read 2 Cor. 3:6 in view of a perspective on the Law gained from Rom. 2:27–29 and 7:1–6 is to be rejected. For this reason the immense exegetical tradition on these passages is consciously avoided here, although for orientation to the issues and the basic perspective which I believe is to be followed, see Klyne R. Snodgrass, "Justification by Grace – to the Doers: An Analysis of the Place of Romans 2 in the Theology of Paul," *NTS* 32 (1986) 72–93. Nor can we deal with the function of the analogy from marriage and divorce in Rom. 7:1–3 within Paul's argument, though it is my opinion that the "husband" in view in this analogy does not represent the Law, but the flesh, which then renders the analogy consistent both internally and in relationship to Rom. 7:4 ff., contra e.g. Joyce A. Little, "Paul's Use of Analogy: A Structural Analysis of Romans 7:1–6," *CBQ* 46 (1984) 82–90, p. 87, who, because she equates the husband with the Law, concludes that "Viewed as analogy or allegory, this section, if not a failure, certainly limps very badly."

[244] See too Schrenk, γραφή, p. 765, "Without this doing of the Law, however, the two gifts of the older phase of revelation confer no advantage as compared with the ἔθνη." Though of course it must be noted that Israel has been given the great advantage of prior and first access to the "oracles of God" (Rom. 3:2) and the list of blessings in Rom. 9:4 f. Moreover, Schrenk, p. 765, overstates the contrast when he asserts that "the fashioning of the καρδία afresh to obedience is the antithesis not merely to a false use of the Law but to *every* pre-Christian use" (emphasis mine). On the one hand, one of the *legitimate* functions of the Law in both the old and new covenants, as well as the Gospel, is to bring about judgment on those who reject it, so that the function of the Law as γράμμα is not in itself a "false" use of the Law, though it may not have been its intended (Rom. 7:10) or ultimate use (Rom. 9:22 f.). On the other hand, though they were certainly a minority, according to Paul there was always a "remnant" of the faithful in Israel, the "children of the promise" (Rom. 9:8) who, like Moses, were known for their transformed hearts and possession of the Spirit, with its resultant obedience to the Law/Gospel as the expression of the will of God (cf. Is. 63:10–14; Rom. 11:4 f.; see below). Westerholm, "Letter and Spirit," pp. 236–240, is right to counter Bultmann and Käsemann in showing that the problem in Rom. 7:6 ff. is not a misguided zeal of the legalist to keep the Law in order to establish one's own righteousness, but failing to keep the Law itself! But he is wrong to substitute the Spirit for the Law as the key to Paul's argument so that the "letter" and the "Spirit" refer to different ways of rendering service to God in the old and new epochs of salvation history respectively; in the age of the Spirit (the "sphere of Christ") one is now freed from the law's demands and sanctions since "'Spirit' refers to the spirit of God whose determining of the Christian's conduct from within has replaced obligation to the laws of Torah ..." (cf. pp. 236, 238, 239, quote from p. 239). For

In Rom. 2:27 mere possession of the Law apart from obedience (διὰ γράμματος) leads to or is the instrument[245] by which transgression of the Law results in judgment.[246] In Rom. 7:5, when the Law encounters one who is still in the "flesh," it stirs up the sinful passions "to bear fruit (fit) for death."

On the other hand, in Rom. 2:28–29 obedience to the Law (i.e. the circumcision of value) is associated with the "circumcised" heart of Jeremiah 4:4. But because "all the house of Israel is uncircumcised in heart" (Jer. 9:26), this new heart cannot be brought about simply by the Law itself, since the Law is merely the *written* expression of God's will. Instead, it must be accomplished by the transforming work of the new covenant (Jer. 31:31–34; Ezek. 36:26 f.; cf. Deut. 30:6), which, as we have seen for Paul, is explicitly the work of the Spirit. The motifs of the new, circumcised, obedient "heart" from Jeremiah and the emphasis on the Spirit from Ezekiel thus both come together again in Paul's words in Rom. 2:29, where he declares that "circumcision is of the heart by means of the Spirit, not by means of the letter" (περιτομὴ καρδίας ἐν πνεύματι οὐ γράμματι[247]). Similarly, in Rom. 7:6, the new life of obedience is brought about in that the believer "serves in the newness of the Spirit and not in the oldness of the letter" (δουλεύειν ἡμᾶς ἐν καινότητι πνεύματος καὶ οὐ παλαιότητι γράμματος). This parallels Paul's earlier assertion in 6:17 that although they were "slaves of sin," they have now become obedient "from the heart" (ἐκ καρδίας). The recurrence of the slavery terminology from Rom. 6:14–22 in Rom. 7:6 (cf. δουλεύειν) makes it clear that the "service" in 7:6 is the new life of concrete obedience to God in Christ. Freed from the dominance of sin (6:18a, 22a), the believers now live as "those enslaved to righteousness"

---

this same understanding of Rom. 7:1 ff., see now Volf, *Paul and Perseverance*, pp. 210 f., who concludes that "Romans 7:2,6 pictures the reverse of Gal. 5:4: the complete end of the law for Christians and their total incorporation into the rule of Christ," which she then associates with the leading of the Spirit.

[245] Taking διά plus the genitive to be instrumental rather than adversative, see again Schrenk, γράφω, p. 765.

[246] For this same point, see Westerholm, "Letter and Spirit," pp. 234 f., who argues that in Rom. 2:27 those who are transgressing the Law are not those who misunderstand it, but those who fail to keep it. Hence, circumcision in Spirit and in letter "mark the distinction between a true observance of the commandments of God and physical circumcision which … as the sign of the covenant, carries with it the requirement that its commands be fulfilled, but which hardly guarantees that they will be" (p. 235). Westerholm therefore insightfully sees that in Paul's view the "letter" is not a liability, since the fault of the Jew "lies not in what he lacks, but in what he possesses" (p. 235). Hence, the "letter" and circumcision are not negative entities, but "real benefits," yet benefits "which entail the obligation to fulfil the commands of the law; would that obligation not be met, the benefits are of no value" (p. 236). In substantiating this, Westerholm rightly points to the motif of the "circumcised heart" from Deut. 10:16; 30:6; Jer. 4:4; cf. Lev. 26:41; Jer. 9:2, 26; Ezek. 44:7,9; and 1QpHab. 11:13; Jub. 1:23; and Philo, *Spec. leg.* I.304 f. (p. 235). But as we have seen, Westerholm takes these insights in the wrong direction (see n. 245).

[247] Again, as Schrenk, γράφω, p. 765, points out, "in both cases the ἐν is to be taken strictly instrumentally."

or "to God" (6:18b: ἐδουλώθητε τῇ δικαιοσύνῃ; 22b: δουλωθέντες τῷ θεῷ), the "fruit" of which is "*sanctification*" (τὸν καρπὸν ὑμῶν εἰς ἁγιασμόν).[248]

According to Rom. 7:4, this new life of obedience from the heart by the Spirit is brought about because the believer has "died to the Law." But in view of Paul's emphasis on obedience in Rom. 6, and in the light of Rom. 8:1–3 and the fact that the locus of sin is explicitly identified as life "in the flesh" with its sinful passions in 7:5 and 11 (cf. the parallel thought in Gal. 5:18, 23 f.),[249] this is best interpreted to mean "having been freed from the Law's condemnation and curse of death over sin," rather than from its commands as the expression of the character and will of God (cf. Rom. 3:31; 7:12;13:9 f.). For the one who is in Christ "has died" with Christ and is now "freed from sin" (Rom. 6:7), and hence from the Law's condemnation of it. The Law as "letter," the fixed declaration of God's will, when it encounters the life in the flesh of those who are apart from Christ, condemns and kills as God's declared punishment for sin (Rom. 6:23). In contrast, the "free gift of God is eternal life in Christ Jesus our Lord," a gift brought about by the work of the Spirit in producing a new life of obedient service (δουλεύειν) to God (Rom. 6:23; 7:6). In this sense the believer is no longer "under Law, but under grace," since sin no longer "rules over" (κυριεύσει) him or her (Rom. 6:14). In both Rom. 2:27–29 and 7:4–6 it thus

---

[248] This interpretation is confirmed by the close conceptual parallel found in Jub. 1:22–24 (see above), and the relationship between the Law, the heart, sin, and the flesh as expressed in passages such as 4 Ezra 3:19–20; 9:32–33, 36–37; Odes Sol. 6:7–14; Ps-Philo, LAB 33:1–4; 1QS 4:20–21; 4 Macc. 7:18–20. Besides Jub. 1:23, Liebers, *Das Gesetz als Evangelium*, p. 114 n. 84, points to Odes Sol. 11:1 f. as a further example of the link between the circumcision of the heart and the Holy Spirit. Cf. now also Liebers, p. 96, who argues that in Rom. 2:25–27 and 7:6 the issue is fulfillment of the Law, though he does not see γράμμα itself to indicate the function of the Law as written. He does, however, see that Rom. 2:27 makes a simple equation of the letter with the Law impossible (p. 98). For Liebers, however, the "Jewish view" of the Law and old covenant behind 2 Cor. 3 and Rom. 2 and 7 is that the Sinai covenant gave to all Israel both the Law and the Spirit (p. 115), something about which, as we have seen, the tradition itself is by no means unified, nor does that view appear to be dominant.

[249] See now Betz, "Der fleischliche Mensch," p. 135, who argues that the "Fehlleistung" of the Law (cf. Rom. 7:7, 12) has to do with the fleshly nature of mankind, in contrast to the holy and spiritual nature of the Law itself (cf. Rom. 7:14). Betz points to Jer. 31:3 as biblical support, and especially to Gen. 2:16 f.; 3:1–6 as the key background to Rom. 7:7–14, with Gen. 2:7, 19, 23; 4:7; 6:3–13 as the backdrop for the idea of the rule of sin over the fleshly man in Rom. 6:12 ff.; 7:23 (cf. too p. 180). For the concept of the "Law of the Spirit of life" and the "Law of sin and death" in Rom. 8:2; 7:23 (cf. Rom. 3:27), he points to Gen. 6:3–17 (cf. pp. 167 f.). But Betz's view, p. 177, that the import of this background is that the Spirit was taken away from mankind in Gen. 6:3 and given again to Christ in his baptism is questionable. More important for this study is the fact that Betz traces the contrast between the unholy person and the holy Law in Rom. 7:12–14 to Exod. 19 f. and 32 (pp. 165–167). Betz, p. 169, argues that those who are in Christ and have received the gift of the Spirit "possess the power to obey the law, to fulfill its just demands (Rom. 8:4), to satisfy it through the keeping of the love command (Rom. 13:8–10)." But again, one may question Betz' conclusion that the Law of Moses retained in the new covenant has been "reduced" to the love command as the "Law of Christ" (p. 178; cf. pp. 183 f.).

becomes clear that the "letter" and the "Spirit" are instruments by which their corresponding consequences of death and life are accomplished, thereby undergirding the functional interpretation of the letter/Spirit contrast in 2 Cor. 3:6.[250]

d) "The letter kills, but the Spirit makes alive" (2 Cor. 3:6c)

The essential confirmation of this interpretation of the meaning of γράμμα ("letter") in 3:6b is found in 3:6c itself, where Paul offers the explicit grounds (γάρ) for why it is that God has made him sufficient to be a minister of the Spirit under the new covenant, rather than merely to serve the Law devoid of God's transforming power.[251] Against the backdrop of Ezekiel and Jeremiah the reason is clear. Apart from the transforming work of the Spirit, the letter "kills." In other words, the Law pronounces both the covenant stipulations and their blessings, as well as the consequence for disobeying them, which under the Sinai covenant (as well as under the new covenant, cf. 2:15–16a; 1 Cor. 6:9 f.; Gal. 5:21!) is death.[252] This consequence of disobedience to God's commands is not only proclaimed in the Law from Genesis 2:17 to Deuter-

---

[250] Schrenk, γράφω, pp. 766, 768 f. is thus right to emphasize that the letter/Spirit antithesis "is absolute in so far as the γράμμα can never accomplish what is done by the πνεῦμα," and that for Paul the Spirit is "giving power to fulfil the innermost intentions of what is written" as a "miraculous power," though this ought not be taken to mean that the Spirit works independent of or as a replacement for the Law itself, as Schrenk's following discussion implies. Schrenk simply equates the γράμμα with the Law, without distinction, because he sees the problem to be in the Law itself, since "in virtue of its character as ἐντολή the νόμος brings sin and death to fruition ... The killing is a consequence of the fact that this Law is only what is written or prescribed (= ἐντολή). Neither here (i.e. 2 Cor. 3:6) nor in R. 7 can this killing be attributed only to a false use of the Bible or the Law" (pp. 766–767). But Paul's point is that this same Law, when encountered by the changed heart in the Spirit, brings righteousness to fruition! The issue is not the nature of the Law as written or as command *per se*, but whether it is the Law alone which one encounters, devoid of the Spirit. The "killing" is not a consequence of the Law *per se*, but of the hardened heart which it encounters.

[251] Cf. J. Kremer, "'Denn der Buchstabe tötet, der Geist aber macht lebendig'. Methodologische und hermeneutische Erwägungen zu 2 Kor 3:6," in *Begegnung mit dem Wort. FS Heinrich Zimmermann*, ed. J. Zmijewski and E. Nellessen, BBB Bd. 53, 1980, pp. 219–250, p. 223, who argues that the γάρ of 3:6b is explanatory, but then goes on to include a grounding function as well since it serves to show the superiority and necessity of the new covenant and the special status of Paul as its servant. Cf. too his discussion of the text-critical issue in v. 6 between ἀποκτέννει/κτένει, p. 220, in which he supports NA 26, but recognizes that there is no essential semantic difference between the two readings.

[252] Cf. now Betz, "Der fleischliche Mensch," p. 182, who stresses that as a spiritual entity, the Law belongs to God, so that those who transgress it injure God's glory. Hence, prior to the new covenant, its function is to judge, since the Law demands obedience to God's righteousness but is not able to give the power of the Spirit necessary for it (cf. Gal. 3:21). But Betz goes on to conclude from this, pp. 184 f., that the Law was meant to lead to life only indirectly by pointing to the powerlessness and need of mankind in preparation for the cross, since the Law's demand for perfection cannot be met in order to demonstrate the "Unerfüllbarkeit" of its demands (cf. Gal. 3:10; 5:3). This conclusion, however, does not necessarily follow from Paul's assertions concerning the Law's death-bringing function, especially if the Law's demands themselves are not the problem.

onomy 32:19–27, but also demonstrated in the history of Israel from the wilderness to the Exile (see below, chapter three). And in 1 Cor. 10:1–13 Paul has already made it clear to the Corinthians that they are to learn this lesson from Israel's history in the wilderness. Apart from the Spirit which "makes alive" (ζῳοποιεῖ), those encountered by the Law cannot obey it due to their hardened hearts (cf. e.g. Exod. 32:9; Deut. 29:4, 19 and chapter three).[253] The Law declares God's will but is powerless to enable people to keep it. Paul's assertion in 3:6c that the "letter kills" therefore summarizes the function of the Law when it confronts those whose hearts are hardened against God. In contrast, Paul's affirmation that the Spirit makes alive is his summary of the central promise of the new, everlasting covenant as outlined in Ezekiel and Jeremiah, against the backdrop of the well-known OT concept of the (divine) "spirit" (רוח) or "breath" (נשמה) which gives life to creatures.[254] In our context this

---

[253] Cf. the role of the "spirit (of wisdom)" on Joshua (Num. 27:18–23; Deut. 34:9) and Caleb (Num. 14:24) as the successors of Moses, and on the elders who help Moses in his ministry (Num. 11:17, 24–30), as well as the reference in Is. 63:10–14 to the fact that although Israel had grieved his Holy Spirit, God had placed his Holy Spirit in the midst of Israel by granting it to Moses as the shepherd of the flock, and that it was the Spirit which had delivered and led Israel. As an example of the extension of this emphasis on the Spirit (here esp. in regard to prophecy) as that which marks out God's people, see *Tg. Ps.-J.* Exod. 33:16, where we read that what distinguishes Israel from the nations is not only "the converse of Thy Shekinah with us," but also that "distinguishing signs may be wrought for us, in the withholdment of the Spirit of prophecy from the nations, and by Thy speaking by the Holy Spirit to me and to Thy people ..." Translation according to J.W. Etheridge, *The Targums of Onkelos and Jonathan ben Uzziel on the Pentateuch*, 1968, p. 556. W.D. Davies, "Reflections on Tradition: The Aboth Revisited," now in his *Jewish and Pauline Studies*, 1984, pp. 27–48, p. 31, sees in Num. 11:16–17 the point that Moses as mediator of the Torah was also a "man of the Spirit," so that "so far from there being any opposition between law and Spirit the opposite seems to have been the case ...."

[254] Cf. now Block, "Prophet of the Spirit," pp. 34 f., who points to the biblical phrase "breath of life" and its Akkadian counterpart on the one hand, and to the close semantic relationship between רוח and נשמה on the other hand (see e.g. Gen. 7:22; 2 Sam. 22:16; Ps. 18:16; Is. 42:5; 57:16; Job 27:3; etc.). For one example of this theme in the OT, see רוח as the Spirit of God which accomplishes God's work in creation in Gen. 1:2 and נשמה as the "life-giving breath" given to man in Gen. 2:7, so that lack of רוח and נשמה means death (Job 34:14–15; Ps. 104:29–30), since the divine Spirit is the creative and judging power of God (Exod. 15:8; Job 4:9; 33:4; Is. 30:21–22, 33). In contrast, idols lack רוח (Hab. 2:19), while to have this Spirit taken away is to experience death (cf. Job. 34:14–15; Ps. 104:29–30). For these examples (apart from Gen. 1:2) and a discussion of their relevance, see besides Block, Wright, "Spirit and Wilderness," pp. 282 f. Wright then points out, p. 283, that "This divine 'breath,' life-giving force, is often translated by 'spirit,' and especially so when there occurs the special invasive power which is interpreted as coming from God and is manifested in several ways, such as in prophetic-group ecstasy (1 Sam. 10:5–6) and those who come in contact with them (1 Sam 10:6, 10); which endowed prophets (1 Kgs 18:12; Mic 3:8), cultic craftsmen (Exod. 31:3; 35:31), leaders and 'judges' (Num. 11:17, 25; Jud. 3:10), wise men (Gen. 41:38; Dan. 4:5, 6, 15), the 'Messiah' (Isa. 11:2; 32:15; 61:1), the 'Servant' (Isa. 42:1), the contemporary Israel (Isa. 59:21; Hag. 2:5), and the new Israel (Isa. 44:3; Ezek. 36:27; 37:14; 39:29)." For Gen. 1:2 as a reference to the Spirit of God, rather than merely to a "mighty wind," taking v. 2 with the following verse as the beginning of

takes on special significance given the fact that, "judging by frequency, for Ezekiel the employment of *rwh* to denote the animating, vitalizing force was more important than any other."[255] As we have seen, it is the future bestowal of this life-giving (divine) Spirit which forms the core of the prophetic expectation for restoration.[256] Stockhausen is thus correct that the concept of the Spirit making alive in 3:6c is traceable to the restoration vision of new life for the dead bones in Ezekiel 37:6, 10, and 14, which is the conclusion to be drawn from the context of Ezekiel 36:24–32 and the realization of the promise of Ezekiel 36:26–27.[257] And as Block has observed, "No text in the entire OT portrays the vivifying power of the divine spirit as dramatically as 37:1–14."[258] In his words, the point of Ezek. 37:1–10 is that "the *rwh* that will revitalize Israel is not the ordinary, natural life-breath common to all living things; it is the spirit of God himself. Only he is able to restore to life a nation that has been destroyed and whose remnant now languishes hopelessly in exile."[259] *The startling implication of 2 Cor. 3:6 is that this promised restoration from the exile, never fully experienced by Israel at her "return," is now said to be taking place in and through Paul's new covenant ministry.*[260] Since the work

---

God's work in creation, see now J.H. Sailhamer, "Genesis," *The Expositor's Bible Commentary*, Vol. 2, 1990, pp. 3–284, p. 25. Besides the use of the verb "hovering" in v. 2, Sailhamer also points to the parallel in Deut. 32:11 and the parallels between the creation account and the construction of the tabernacle in Exodus in support of this reading. As he points out, "in both accounts the work of God (... Gen. 2:2; Exod. 31:5) is to be accomplished by the 'Spirit of God' ... As God did his 'work' ... of creation by means of the 'Spirit of God' ..., so Israel was to do their 'work' by means of the 'Spirit of God.'" (p. 25).

[255] Block, "Prophet of the Spirit," p. 34. Block points out that of the 52 uses of רוח in Ezekiel, 17 refer to the Spirit as the agency of animation (cf. pp. 28, 31).

[256] As Wright, "Spirit and Wilderness," has again summarized it, p. 284: After the people have been punished and purged and brought through the wilderness again in a "new Exodus," "they will be given new life, new breath, new power, transformation, a new *ruah*. This is seen in Ezek. 11:19; 18:36; 36:26 (cf. 36:27; 37:14), and the whole parable of the Valley of Bones in Ezek. 37 symbolizes this. On all Israel 'I will pour out my *ruah*' (Ezek 39:29; Isa. 32:15, 44:3). A *ruah* of grace and supplication will be poured on the people of Jerusalem (Zech. 12:10), and the *ruah* will be poured on 'all flesh' (Joel 3:1, 2). The *ruah* will be given to the restored community (Ezek. 36:27; 37:14)."

[257] *Moses' Veil*, pp. 68–70, following too Chevallier, Cohen, Schoeps, Richard, etc. (p. 70 n. 64). As she argues, "Paul's verbal link with Ezekiel 36:26, 27, the verbal links between Ezekiel 36:26, 27 and Ezekiel 37:1–14, and the similarity of expression between Paul's τὸ δὲ πνεῦμα ζῳοποιεῖ and Ezekiel's δώσω πνεῦμά μου εἰς ὑμᾶς καὶ ζήσεσθε all indicate clearly that Paul has based his statements directly on Ezekiel 37" (p. 70). The Corinthian Christians are therefore equated with the new, recreated Israel (p. 70). For the link between Ezek. 36 and 37, see now Block, "Prophet of the Spirit," p. 39, who sees the announcement of the infusion of God's Spirit in 37:14 as the fulfillment of 36:26 f., "suggesting that the entire unit (37:1–14) is an exposition of the notion introduced in 36:26–27."

[258] "Prophet of the Spirit," p. 37. Block points to the tenfold use of "Spirit" (רוח) in this passage and its clustering in vv. 8b–10 as confirmation that the giving of the Spirit of life so that reconstituted bodies might live (cf. v. 8) is the main point of the passage (cf. pp. 37 f.).

[259] "Prophet of the Spirit," p. 38.

[260] For the OT and post-biblical Jewish backdrop for this implication, see the work of James Scott (see above, nn. 145, 214). For the recognition of this same basic plot and the

of the Spirit thus distinguishes the Sinai covenant from the new covenant, it is the Spirit's work on the "tablets of the human hearts" (3:3b) of "making alive" (3:6bc) which provides the ground for why Paul's ministry does not focus directly on mediating the Law, but on the Spirit; it is the Spirit which makes obedience to God possible as the sign of the beginning of the eschatological restoration.

On the other hand, in the light of the *resurrection* of Christ as a "life-giving Spirit" (1 Cor. 15:45), Peter von der Osten-Sacken is right in drawing out the parallels between Christology and Ecclesiology in Paul's thinking as the context for the work of the Spirit as the presence of God and Christ in and among his people.[261] The resurrection of Christ by the power of the Spirit (Rom. 1:4) parallels the baptism-conversion of believers in/by the Spirit into the body of Christ (1 Cor. 12:12 f.; Rom. 8:11; cf. Jesus as the "first fruits" of the resurrection in 1 Cor.15:20, 23 with believers who possess the Spirit as the "first fruit" of the future restoration in Rom. 8:23). The resurrected work of Christ in establishing his reign as the Son of God (1 Cor. 15:25) parallels the life in the Spirit of believers as sons of God as they wage war against the flesh (Rom. 8:14 in the context of 8:9–16; cf. Gal. 5:17). And the return of Christ parallels the resurrection of the faithful (1 Cor. 15:23).[262] Furthermore, all of this takes place within the context of the suffering of God's people who live in the power of the Spirit while they await the future consummation, thus being "saved in hope" (Rom. 8:17–25). Read in this way, Paul's argument in 2 Cor. 3:4–6 is derived directly from the prophetic hopes expressed in Ezekiel 11, 36 and Jeremiah 31[263] as fulfilled by, in, and through Christ in the lives of his new covenant people. Paul's argument can thus be presented as follows:

---

early Christian conviction that "the crisis out of which the Christian movement arose is regarded as the realization of the prophetic vision of judgment and redemption" as the keys to the use of the OT scriptures in the NT, see already C.H. Dodd, *According to the Scriptures*, pp. 72 f., 88 (quote from p. 72). As Dodd concludes, the consistent testimony of the NT use of the OT is that "the 'hardening' of Israel, the 'stone of stumbling,' and in general the judgment of God upon His disloyal people, are conceived as already within the experience of those who witnessed the events of the life and death of Jesus; and equally the calling of the 'remnant,' the inauguration of the New Covenant, the designation of 'Lo-ammi' as 'Ammi' and the abiding presence of 'God with us' (Immanuel) are conceived as realized in the emergence of the Church, which thus figures as the new (and true) Israel of God, revealed through a process of πτῶσις καὶ ἀνάστασις (Lk. 2:34)" (p. 88). It is well-known, however, that Dodd took this realization too far in down playing the significance of the promises and events of salvation history still to be fulfilled. Hence, I have intentionally used the terminology of "inauguration" to describe what Paul sees taking place in and through his ministry.

[261] P. von der Osten-Sacken, "Die paulinische theologia crucis als Form apokalyptischer Theologie, *EvTh* 39 (1979) 477–496, pp. 481–482.

[262] These parallels are based on the insightful points made by P. von der Osten-Sacken, "theologia crucis," pp. 481–483. For the expectation of the coming of the Spirit on the elect in the end times, he points to Jub. 1:23; 4 Ezra 6:26; Test. Jud. 24:3; Test. Levi 18:11.

[263] The interpretation offered here thus falls prey to what Stockhausen, *Moses' Veil*, p. 58, considers one of the "common mistakes" in interpreting 3:1–6, i.e. "the attempt to view Paul's own text as a direct exegesis of, or a hook-word association of, this group of Old

4a: *Therefore (δέ) we have this confidence through Christ to God (since it is through Christ that the Spirit is poured out in my ministry).*

5a: *It is therefore also clear that I am not (οὐχ) saying that (ὅτι) we are sufficient from ourselves to reckon anything as from ourselves.*

5b: *But instead (ἀλλ')* our sufficiency is from God

6a: *because he is the one who (ὅς) also made us sufficient to be servants of the new covenant.*

6b: *For God has not (οὐ) made us sufficient to be servants* of the letter,

6c: *but (ἀλλά) God has made us sufficient to be servants* of the Spirit.

6d: *The reason (γάρ) this is the focus of the New Covenant ministry is that* the letter kills,

6e: *but on the other hand (δέ)* the Spirit makes alive.

8. Conclusion: The Letter/Spirit Contrast and the Necessity of 3:7–18

As we have seen, the Scriptural background adduced in 3:2–6 allows Paul to affirm *that* the "letter kills, but the Spirit makes alive" as a description of the essential difference in *function* between the old and the new covenants because of the nature of the respective covenant people. But it does not explain *how* it is that the Spirit actually does so. Nor is Paul's statement in 3:6c that the "letter kills," picked up in his subsequent description of Moses' ministry as a "ministry of death" in 3:7, without ambiguity, leading naturally to the assertion that the ministry of the Law still participated, without a doubt, ἐν δόξῃ ("in glory")! Indeed, as the diatribal "false conclusion" in the parallel passage Romans 7:7 illustrates, the "natural" (but false!) implication of Paul's assertion of the letter/Spirit contrast (cf. Rom. 7:6) seems to be that, far from being glorious, the Law is sin![264] Moreover, Romans 7:7, written from Corinth (!),

---

Testament texts. Paul does indeed reflect such a hook-word association of the texts assembled ... but the exegetical process itself cannot be traced in II Corinthians 3:1–6." For in her view, the links between Jer. and Ezek. have all been made prior to Paul as part of the "background" of his text (p. 58). Unfortunately, there is no textual evidence of any such preformed package of texts based on a *gezera shawa* series of analogies like she constructs on pp. 60 f., while the conceptual links between the prophetic texts themselves provide strong support for their connection, especially in view of their linkage in the Qumran tradition and the Apocrypha and Pseudepigrapha (see above).

[264] The foolishness of this conclusion seems self-evident until one realizes, as J.J. Collins has pointed out, that among the Jewish apologists Artapanus, Eupolemus, and Ezekiel the Tragedian, the authority of Moses, as well as the identity of Judaism as such, is no longer exclusively tied to the Law at all! See his *Between Athens and Jerusalem*, pp. 36, 42, and 210 f. So too Ben Zion Wacholder, *Eupolemus*, 1974, p. 71, who comments concerning the

indicates that Paul had already suffered the barb of this blasphemous accusation, just as the subsequent history of the Church from Marcion to Harnack evidences that he would be read that way again. Thus, Windisch declares that, taken by itself, the letter/Spirit contrast in 3:6 is "a genuinely 'marcionite' antithesis."[265] That this is *not* the case must be demonstrated.[266] Paul's assertion in 3:6bc therefore leads directly and, given the apologetic context of 2 Corinthians, *necessarily* to the discussion of the glory of Paul's ministry and the veil of Moses in 3:7–18.

Seen in this light, Paul's assertion of the *similarity* between his call and the call of Moses in 2:16b and 3:4 f. demands that he explain their *differences*, as he does in terms of the thesis-like declaration of the letter/Spirit contrast in 3:6.[267] But having done so, Paul must now substantiate and clarify the letter/ Spirit contrast itself in order to keep it from being either rejected out of hand or misunderstood. For as W.D. Davies pointed out over 40 years ago, the key question within the Old Testament and post-biblical traditions concerning the role of the Law in the messianic age of the new covenant revolves around "the marked significance of the Exodus and of Moses not only in Israel's history but also in its Messianic expectation."[268] The same is true for Paul, as the transition from 3:6 to 3:7–18 demonstrates. As will become clear in chapters four and five, the connection between 3:4–6 and 3:7–18 is closely and consciously integrated in the actual flow of Paul's argument, rather than being connected by a series of loosely related themes or catch-words in accordance with the

---

view of Eupolemus that "Moses was important not, as in the Scripture tradition, as the transmitter of God's law to his chosen people Israel, but in his role as the father of Oriental and Greek civilizations." Therefore, G. Vermes' conclusion, "Gestalt," p. 62, that "die Ereignisse des Exodus, die Gestalt des Moses und der Empfang der Thora für das gesamte nach-exilische Judentum den Mittelpunkt bildeten" must be qualified at least in terms of some apologetic literature.

[265] *Zweite Korintherbrief*, p. 110.

[266] Contra e.g. the extensive work of K. Prümm, *Diakonia Pneumatos, Bd. I*, pp. 118, 122, who fails to see this connection between 3:4–6 and 3:7–18 and must import Rom. 7:7–25 to explain how the law kills and the Spirit makes alive, which he then argues is the presupposition of 3:7–18: "Im Abschnitt 2 Kor 3:7–11 setzt Paulus das volle Einverständnis der Leser mit ihm über die Gewißheit beider Teile des Satzes von 3:6 einfach als gegeben voraus. Statt Beweise zu bringen, beleuchtet er nur den Inhalt" (p. 118). Prümm forgets the apologetic context in which Paul is writing, in which no such assumptions could be made, especially if, as Prümm himself argues, Paul's opponents have accused Paul of the "Verkleinerung (oder Mißachtung) der Doxa des AT und seines Mittlers Mosas (Gal. 3:19)" (p. 123).

[267] See too Jones, *Second Moses*, who insightfully structures his dissertation around this fundamental point, i.e. that in 2:14–3:6 Paul describes himself as *like* Moses (cf. pp. 14–78), over against 3:7–18 in which Paul brings out the *dissimilarity* between his ministry and the ministry of Moses (cf. pp. 79–109). Cf. esp. pp. 58 f., 79, in which Jones then relates this to the accusation of Paul's opponents, who charge that he does not act like a glorified Moses though he claims that his call and ministry are like that of Moses (accepting Georgi's reconstruction of Paul's opponents' view of Moses as a θεῖος ἀνήρ, cf. pp. 54–56). For my own understanding of the function of 3:7 ff. in Paul's apologetic, see below.

[268] *Torah in the Messianic Age*, p. 7.

practice of later rabbinic proof-texting.[269] It will also become clear that 3:7–18 is not an attempt on Paul's part to correct 3:4–6 as an overstatement of his position concerning the old covenant.[270] The first argument against this view has already been given above in maintaining that in 3:4–6 the problem was not with the content of the old covenant itself, but with the hardness of Israel's hearts. But the thesis-like nature of the letter/Spirit contrast in 3:6 and the continuation of these themes in 3:7 ff. point to the conclusion that the meaning and function of the letter/Spirit contrast are to be confirmed in large measure from the following argument in 3:7–18 and not the other way around. Our interpretation of 3:6c will therefore only be as good as our exegesis of 3:7–18, *understood on its own terms*, is persuasive.

It could certainly be objected at this point that to speak of 3:7–18 as further *support* and *clarification* of the letter/Spirit contrast in 3:4–6 is to prejudice the issue from the beginning. For the overwhelming consensus is that 2 Cor. 3:7–18, like 3:4–6 before it, offers no real, common ground support for Paul's legitimacy. Rather, Paul's argument in 3:7–18 is seen to be based on his own proof-texting of the Scriptures in line with his particular Christian presuppositions. Paul's "support" for his thesis statement of 3:6 in 3:7–18 is merely an additional expression of Paul's Christian presuppositions in which he simply undergirds one "in-house" assertion with another. The question of the relationship between 2 Cor. 3:4–6 and 7–18 thus poses the more fundamental question of his Old Testament hermeneutic.[271] This question will continue to occupy us in part two of our study.

---

[269] Contra again most recently Stockhausen, *Moses' Veil* (see above, nn. 170, 171, 193, 263), who leaves the logical connection between the various themes which the two passages have in common largely undeveloped, except to read the references to the Law in view of a common interpretation gained from outside of 2 Cor. 3. See too Fitzmyer, "Glory," pp. 634–637, who also views Paul's mode of argumentation in 2 Cor. 3:7 ff. to be closest to that kind of "rabbinic logic" based on an "inference by analogy" *(gezerah shawa)* (pp. 634 f.), and thus understands the connection to be based on a series of six sets of "free association of ideas that runs through the entire passage" (p. 634). While these "associations" serve to strengthen the connection between 3:4–6 and 7–18, they do not explain why or how the two texts relate.

[270] Contra Richard, "Polemic," p. 353, who sees the purpose of 3:7–11 to be to "serve as a corrective to 3:6b ..." since Paul "wishes to correct what might be taken as a totally negative evaluation of the old covenant ..." since in vv. 4–6 Paul was led "in contrasting the old covenant with the new ... to overstate his case" (p. 362). "Therefore, in vv. 7–11, drawing upon Ex. 34, he compares more equitably the ministries of the two covenants ..." (pp. 362 f.).

[271] The question has been well formulated by P. Stuhlmacher, "'Das Ende des Gesetzes,' Über Ursprung und Ansatz der paulinischen Theologie," p. 23 n. 20, who in response to his observation, "Daß Paulus das Alte Testament nicht nur faktisch herangezogen, sondern theologisch bewußt festgehalten hat," asked, "was bedeutet unter diesem Vorzeichen hermeneutisch der offenbar reflektierte Anschluß des Paulus an alttestamentlich-jüdische Sprach- und Denktradition, gerade wenn es um die Verkündigung des Christusevangeliums geht?"

Part Two

The Letter/Spirit Contrast within the Context of the Second Giving of the Law

Chapter Three

The Ministry of Moses: Exodus 32–34 in Canonical Tradition

In 1924 Hans Windisch argued that 2 Corinthians 3:7–18 was a Christian "midrash" on Exodus 34:29–35 in which Paul refashioned the text and its meaning according to his own Christian presuppositions in order to serve his own apologetic purposes.[1] Since then, almost all interpreters have assented to this view, though the appropriateness of the designation "midrash" itself is sometimes questioned. The seemingly self-evident nature of this observation today is merely a reflection of how pervasive this perspective has become.[2]

But if Paul is offering his own reinterpretation of Exodus 34 in 2 Cor. 3:7 ff., it seems only natural that the first and most basic matter to be settled in order to discern Paul's adaptation of this tradition should be the original meaning of the OT text which Paul interprets. It is surprising, however, how quickly NT exegetes presume to understand precisely how Paul used and misused (!) his OT source without first examining the source itself carefully. The conventional wisdom that Paul read Exod. 34:29 ff. atomistically has apparently led his interpreters to do so as well. Yet only against the background of the OT narrative is it possible to probe the supposedly "midrashic" nature of Paul's exegesis.[3] It is also evident that the Old Testament background provides the foundation for

---

[1] Windisch's work appeared in 1924 as the 9th edition of *Der Zweite Korintherbrief,* MeyerK, 6. Abteilung. It was reissued in 1970, edited by G. Strecker. Surprisingly, Windisch argued that Paul had drastically reinterpreted Exod. 34 only in regard to the meaning and purpose of the veil – i.e. as hiding the fact that the glory was fading – in order to bring to expression as blatantly as possible the inferiority of the Mosaic revelation (cf. pp. 119–120). But as the study of Exod. 32–34 offered here will demonstrate, such a position is difficult to sustain.

[2] For just two examples of the widespread acceptance of Windisch's basic perspective, from differing traditions, cf. Richard Longenecker, *Biblical Exegesis in the Apostolic Period* , 1975, pp. 104 f., 206 f., and James L. Kugel and Rowan A. Greer, *Early Biblical Interpretation,* 1986, pp. 128–136.

[3] This was called for programmatically by William J. Dumbrell, "Paul's Use of Exodus 34 in 2 Corinthians 3," in *God Who is Rich in Mercy, FS D.B. Knox,* ed. Peter T. O'Brien and David G. Peterson, 1986, pp. 179–194, p. 180, who argued that in approaching Paul's use of the OT in 2 Cor. 3, Exod. 34:29–35 "needs to be looked at again closely both in terms of its content and its function within the thematic covenant unit, Exod. 19–34. The significance of 34:29–35 in our judgment has been generally undervalued." Dumbrell's study led him to the same basic conclusion reached here, i.e. that "once the setting of Exod. 34:29–35 is correctly understood, then its use and application by St. Paul in 2 Corinthians 3 is not only apparent but also self-consistent" (p. 190).

addressing the larger question of the hermeneutical significance of the letter/ Spirit contrast.[4] Part two of our study therefore begins with a reading of Exod. 34:29–35 within its canonical context as the essential background for approaching Paul's interpretation of this text in 2 Cor. 3:7–18.

But before turning our attention to Paul's interpretation of the biblical tradition, it will be necessary to survey briefly the ways in which the themes of Exod. 34:29 ff. were understood and reinterpreted in the canonical[5] and post-biblical tradition.[6] Such a survey will provide a basis for comparing Paul's understanding and application of Scripture to the canonical and post-biblical trajectory within which he offered his interpretation. An essential, if not *the* essential part of this history is the Hebrew tradition as understood in its Septuagintal adaptation and its impact on establishing some crucial links between the various canonical traditions. The Septuagint provides a particularly

---

[4] So too now Carol K. Stockhausen, "2 Corinthians 3 and the Principles of Pauline Exegesis," in *Paul and the Scriptures of Israel*, ed. Craig A. Evans and James A. Sanders, JSNT Suppl. 83, 1993, pp. 143–164, who argues against R. Hay's view that Exod. 34 simply stimulated Paul's hermeneutical discussion, but had no further role in determining it (Stockhausen refers to Richard B. Hays' *Echoes of Scripture in the Letters of Paul*, 1989, pp. 137, 140, 147). Stockhausen suggests that Paul's exegetical principles did not derive directly from the literary or theological features "intrinsic to Exodus 34," but that "once chosen by Paul, Exodus 34 did exercise a continuous and dynamic influence on Paul's discussion" (p. 144, 144 n. 4). Stockhausen thus rightly advises that since Paul does not describe his exegetical process *per se*, "we see only its results, as the shape of his arguments express his hermeneutic," so that "Paul's interpretations of Scripture are often only to be recovered from behind or beneath his text as it stands" (p. 145). But this requires that we know Paul's Scripture well, especially in view of the fact that, as Stockhausen also emphasizes, Paul shows a "consistent attention to the context of cited passages" as "an extension of his narrative interest" (p. 145).

[5] As in our study of Exod. 32–34, in this overview the canonical form and interrelationship of the various writings has been assumed. For the historical and source-critical questions, see the commentaries; for a traditional source-critical treatment of the texts concerning Israel's disobedience in the wilderness, see George W. Coats, *Rebellion in the Wilderness, The Murmuring Motif in the Wilderness Traditions of the Old Testament*, 1968; and for the role of Moses in Exodus, Numbers and Deuteronomy, see Erik Aurelius, *Der Fürbitter Israels, Eine Studie zum Mosebild im Alten Testament*, CB Old Testament Series 27, 1988.

[6] The relevant material from post-biblical Judaism is best incorporated directly into our treatment of 2 Cor. 3:7–18 in chapter six in order to provide an immediate basis for comparison. The rationale for such a study has been clearly stated by Peter Stuhlmacher, "Theologische Probleme der Römerbriefpräskripts," *EvTh* 27 (1967) 374–389, pp. 379 f.: "Jener paulinische Rückverweis auf den nach dem Zeugnis des Alten Testaments seit Urzeit gnädig erwählenden Gott läßt sich heute nur dann bewältigen, wenn wir uns aufschwingen können nicht nur zu einem geschichtlich reflektierten Urteil über das Alte Testament, sondern auch über die jüdische Überlieferungsgeschichte, in welche hinein das Alte Testament in neutestamentlicher Zeit mündet. Erst aus der jüdischen Überlieferung heraus haben sich ja für die Autoren des Neuen Testaments und den Apostel die maßgeblichen Verständnis-Kategorien für die Erfassung der alttestmentlichen Tradition ergeben!" It is also true, of course, that Paul can go against his tradition and/or build his argument directly on the basis of the OT text itself!

important window into Paul's understanding of Exod. 34 within its context, not only because of Paul's well-known familiarity with the Greek version of the Old Testament,[7] but also because of its thoroughgoing verse-by-verse "commentary" on the original text. As such, it supplies clues into how the communities in which Paul found his identity understood the tradition. For as Moshe Greenberg has observed concerning the use of versions in general for detecting interpretive problems in the text, "Here the versions offer a powerful stimulus: a substitution, a small omission or addition may point up a carrier of meaning that would otherwise go unobserved."[8] The value of the LXX is seen most clearly, therefore, in *comparison* to the Hebrew tradition as its *Vorlage*.

1. Reading Exodus 34 as a Narrative

In turning to Exodus 34, a few comments on the method to be used in interpreting this passage are in order. Exodus 34 is part of the *narrative* of a great human tragedy and an even greater divine mercy as found in Exodus 32–34. But as such, ever since the second half of the 18th century, it can be read in one of two very distinct ways. On the one hand, the exegete can seek to penetrate *behind* the text as it now stands in search of the narrative's tradition-historical prehistory, its literary sources, the stages in its redaction, or its historicity. Once dismembered in this way, the narrative itself is largely ignored or devalued as simply the ultimate deposit of these prior, and implicitly more important, oral, written, and historical sources.[9] For the historian, the real subject matter of the text is no longer the text's story, but rather the story *of* the text; or for those with religious interests, some referent (historical or religious) behind, within, or beyond the text.

---

[7] For the consensus view that Paul's "citations characteristically follow the Septuagint (LXX)," with the relatively few cases where Paul agrees with the MT seen to be examples of variant LXX text forms "that have been subjected to 'hebraizing revisions,'" see most recently Hays, *Echoes of Scripture*, p.xi. This perspective has been supported by Dietrich-Alex Koch's detailed study, *Die Schrift als Zeuge des Evangeliums, Untersuchungen zur Verwendung und zum Verständnis der Schrift bei Paulus*, Beiträge zur Historischen Theologie 69, 1986.

[8] "The Use of the Ancient Versions for Interpreting the Hebrew Text: A Sampling from Ezekiel 2:1–3:11," *Supplements to Vetus Testamentum*, Vol. 29, *Congress Volume 1977*, 1978, pp. 131–148, pp. 147 f.

[9] Cf. Hans Frei, *The Eclipse of Biblical Narrative, A Study in Eighteenth and Nineteenth Century Hermeneutics*, 1974, esp. pp. 1–50, who has shown so clearly that since the middle of the 18th century, this "critical" reading of the text presupposes that the history-like narratives as received in the biblical account and the reality which they seek to relate must be divorced and investigated separately, so that the "literal explicative sense" and the "actual historical reference" can no longer be identified. The result is what Frei called an "eclipse of biblical narrative" in favor of some source, tradition, religious, or historical interpretation of the text, quite apart from what the narrative itself purports to relate.

No doubt it has been this predominant approach to OT texts that has influenced the NT exegete away from a serious study of Exod. 34 within its own context as the backdrop to 2 Cor. 3:7–18. It has apparently been assumed that Paul read Exod. 34 in the same disconnected way that most modern scholars have approached the passage. One cannot help wondering, therefore, if Paul's approach to the text appears atomistic because the OT is usually read atomistically by modern exegetes. What *is* clear, however, is that students of Paul have been content to look merely at the one verse that Paul quotes from Exodus 34:29–35 (cf. Exod. 34:34 in 2 Cor. 3:16) or to the allusions to Exodus 34:30, 33, 35 in 2 Cor. 3:7, 13, rather than to take Exod. 34 seriously as part of the larger biblical narrative in which it is anchored.[10] The implications of a critical reading of biblical narratives have thus inadvertently carried over into the interpretation of Paul's own reading of the biblical tradition.

On the other hand, one can read Exod. 34 "pre-critically" in the way in which Paul himself would have read the text. In such a reading of the text it is assumed that there is no distinction between the literal meaning of Exod. 34 and its historical referent. The question of pre-literary and literary sources is not raised. Moses is the author of Exod. 34 and this is his account of what happened at the foot of Mt. Sinai. Moreover, Exod. 34 is part of a larger narrative, i.e. that of the Golden Calf and Moses' intercessions in Exod. 32–33, which itself is part of the larger narrative of the Exodus and the "first giving of the Law" in Exodus 1–31. Therefore, to understand Paul, the quotes and allusions to Exod. 34 in 2 Cor. 3 demand that we approach Exod. 34 as a unity in its final form and interpret it within its larger narrative context. For as Frei has pointed out, a "figural" or typological reading of a biblical narrative, which we certainly have in part in 2 Cor. 3 (cf. 3:14), depends for its very existence and credibility upon a prior literal reading of the story.[11]

---

[10] For this same critique of past scholarship and a similar call to reinvestigate the content and function of Exod. 34:29–35 within the "thematic covenant unit, Exod 19–34," as the backdrop to 2 Cor. 3:7 ff. see Dumbrell, "Paul's Use of Exodus 34," p. 180 (see above, n. 3). For the similarities and differences in our respective positions concerning Exod. 34 itself, see chapters four and five. Recently, Carol Kern Stockhausen, *Moses' Veil and the Glory of the New Covenant, The Exegetical Substructure of II Cor. 3:1–4:6,* AB 116, 1989, p. 96, has also emphasized the importance of remembering that Exod. 34:29–35 is a narrative so that Paul's "verbal echoes call to mind the whole *story* and not just isolated snatches of it" (emphasis hers, cf. p. 101 n. 30 for the same point and her work cited above, n. 4). It is surprising, then, that she limits her reading to Exod. 34:29 ff., which has serious implications for her understanding of 2 Cor. 3:7 ff. (see below, chapters four and five).

[11] In Frei's words, *Eclipse*, p. 28 (see too pp. 34, 37), "In a precritical era, in which literal explicative sense was identical with actual historical reference, literal and figurative reading, far from contradicting each other, belonged together by family resemblance and by need for mutual supplementation." For further contextual evidence of the fact that Paul did in fact read Exod. 34:29–35 within the context of Exod. 32–34 as a whole, and thus presumably within the larger narrative as well, see chapters four and five.

The problem is that such an approach to the text is as unnatural to most modern scholars as it was natural to Paul. Fortunately, we are helped by the recent resurgence of a literary and canonical approach to OT narratives which once again focuses its attention on the final form of the biblical narratives.[12] Indeed, as Bernhard Anderson has pointed out, the traditional approach of attempting to discover a *Sitz im Leben* for the various levels of the text's prehistory is now increasingly being supplemented, and for some even replaced, by an attempt to discover a passage's *Sitz im Text*.[13] No longer "pre-critical" historically, contemporary literary criticism nonetheless attempts to look at the biblical narrative not merely as having literary *features*, but as being a work of literature *itself*. The aspects of plot, theme, character, narrator, structure, literary patterns, and contextual setting are taken seriously as the essential ingredients of the intended meaning of the text.[14] Following the lead of this literary approach, this study attempts to read Exod. 34 within its narrative context, first that of Exod. 32–34 and then, to a lesser degree for our purposes, Exod. 1–18, 19–24, and 25–31.[15] The methodological corollary to this point, and the basis for un-

---

[12] For a very helpful introduction to and display of the bewildering array of current literary approaches to the OT, see now Paul R. House, ed., *Beyond Form Criticism, Essays in Old Testament Literary Criticism*, Sources for Biblical and Theological Study, Vol. 2, 1992, esp. House's own essay, "The Rise and Current Status of Literary Criticism of the Old Testament," pp. 3–22.

[13] B. Anderson, "The New Frontier of Rhetorical Criticism: A Tribute to James Muilenburg," in *Rhetorical Criticism, Essays in Honor of James Muilenburg,* ed. Jared J. Jackson and Martin Kessler, 1974, pp. ix–xvii, pp. xiv–xv.

[14] The extension of a literary approach to the text into a reader-response criticism and all that follows from this is therefore not in view here; nor in my opinion should it be in approaching biblical texts. In many ways the pioneering work in this area is that of Robert Alter, *The Art of Biblical Narrative,* 1981. But cf. already in regard to the Pentateuch as a whole, M.H. Segal, *The Pentateuch, Its Composition and Its Authorship, and Other Biblical Studies,* 1967, p. 22. For the distinction between literary features and literature and an extensive working out of its exegetical implications for reading biblical texts, see now Meir Sternberg, *The Poetics of Biblical Narrative, Ideological Literature and the Drama of Reading,* 1987, and Richard L. Pratt, Jr., *He Gave us Stories, The Bible Student's Guide to Interpreting Old Testament Narratives,* 1990. For a more general introduction to reading narratives in general, see now Michael J. Toolan, *Narrative, A Critical Linguistic Introduction,* 1988.

[15] R.W.L. Moberly's literary-exegetical study of Exod. 32–34, *At the Mountain of God, Story and Theology in Exodus 32–34, JSOT Supplement Series 22,* 1983, provides a model of the kind of "straightforward reading of the text" which undergirds this study (quote from p. 35). As Moberly has pointed out, p. 24, such a literary analysis of the text looks for unity and pattern in the narrative in search for the text's present coherence, in contrast to the traditional search of historical-criticism for the tensions and apparent dislocations which are assumed to indicate prior sources and redaction. For his description of his approach within a discussion of the broader methodological considerations of a literary approach to the text and its relationship to the more historical-critical methods, see his pp. 15–43. For an attempt to argue for the unified composition of Exod. 32–34 from a single hand on the basis of its literary and theological structure, see Dale Ralph Davis, "Rebellion, Presence, and Covenant: A Study in Exodus 32–34," *WTJ* 44 (1982) 71–87, though the question of whether the unity of the text derives from a single, original hand or from the work of a final redactor is not important for this study. And for a study of Exod. 32–34 as "a carefully crafted narrative

derstanding Paul's use of the biblical tradition from Exod. 32–34, is the assumption that in reading a narrative, "the important thing is to grasp what is being said."[16]

Finally, it must be recognized that for Paul Exod. 32–34 is not simply a story, but a *biblical* narrative. This means, above all, that the interpreter must be alert to the theological intention and significance of the story. For as Hartmut Gese has observed, "Das Alte Testament als literarisches Werk entwickelt sich aus kerygmatische Intentionen."[17] One of the contributions of literary approaches to biblical texts has been to show that this is nowhere more true than of the final form of the text. In our case, Moberly has argued this point for Exod. 32–34 based on the inclusion of the laws in 34:11–16 and the formation of the role of YHWH in 33:18–34:9.[18] Indeed, once we join Paul in positing the Mosaic authorship, historical accuracy, and above all, divine authority of Exod. 32–34, we must seek to read the text as a narrative with *direct* theological import and relevance for his world-view.

Such a synchronic reading of Exod. 32–34, with a focus on its final narrative form and explicit theological themes, is the necessary first step in approaching Paul's reception of this text in 2 Cor. 3.[19] Certainly studies concerned with the more traditional historical-critical questions will not be ignored. But their results will be gleaned for those insights which highlight the narrative and theological meaning of the text as it now stands.[20] Questions

---

in the service of a single theme" by a single author who "made use of an episodic narrative technique to weave a tapestry-like presentation of a theological principle," see Herbert Chanan Brichto, "The Worship of the Golden Calf: A Literary Analysis of a Fable on Idolatry," *HUCA* 54 (1983) 1–44, quote from p. 4. Brichto, p. 4, goes so far as to assert that such an approach to the text will uncover "a deployment of sophisticated literary devices which will seem to have resurfaced in modern literary art after floating, barely submerged and unrecognized, for some two millennia and a half." For a contrary evaluation, see now Pier Cesare Bori, *The Golden Calf and the Origins of the anti-Jewish Controversy*, 1990, p. 85, who views Exod. 32–34 as "full of dark corners, contradictions and problems" with a "confused order of the narrated events in chapters 33 and 34" (p. 90). But apart from a brief survey of the various scholarly approaches to this text (pp. 86–88) and a short reconstruction of the text (pp. 89–90), it is beyond the scope of Bori's work to substantiate this common view further.

[16] Moberly, *Mountain of God*, p. 35.

[17] "Erwägungen zur Einheit der biblischen Theologie," *ZThK* 67 (1970) 417–436, p. 424. Note B. Anderson's observation, "Tradition and Scripture in the Community of Faith," *JBL* 100 (1981) 1–21, p. 10, that the recognition of the theological content of biblical texts is the "Achilles' Heal" of traditio-historical investigations since "our only access to this prehistory is through the final scriptural formulations, and therefore we are led into a realm of uncertainty and hypothetical reconstruction. Can biblical theology, if it intends to be historical in nature, flourish in this shadowy realm?"

[18] *Mountain of God*, p. 38.

[19] For a good discussion of the difference between synchronic and diachronic analyses and its exegetical implications, see Vern S. Poythress, "Analysing a Biblical Text: Some Important Linguistic Distinctions," *SJTh* 32 (1979) 113–137, esp. pp. 115 f.

[20] Though often forgotten by those who followed him, this was the goal of Martin Noth himself in his investigation of literary traditions; cf. his *A History of Pentateuchal Tradi-*

concerning the oral and literary sources of the passage, the original identity of the deity of the Golden Calf and the method of its construction and destruction, the nature of this text as a cult legend or a misplaced polemic against the North (cf. 1 Kings 12:26–33), the history of its redaction, and the historicity of the various aspects of the narrative, therefore all play a minor role in the following discussion. Rather, to follow Paul, we must return to Exodus 32–34 as a theological narrative, before it was eclipsed by critical study.[21]

2. The Golden Calf[22] (Exodus 32:1–29)

As is well-known, Paul's citation and allusions to Moses in 2 Cor. 3 come from the point in the narrative when Moses has received the tablets of the Law the second time and has once again entered the camp with these signs and testimonies of the covenant. It will become clear that Moses' final descent from the mountain in Exod. 34:29 ff. is intended to be read as the climax of the narrative concerning YHWH's self-revelation at Sinai which actually begins at Exod. 19:3, when Moses "went up" (עלה) to the Lord for the first time.[23] As such, the second giving of the Law in Exod. 34 is the narrative counterpart to its first reception in 19:1–20:20. His descent in chapter 34 cannot, therefore, be understood apart from this larger context. But within its immediate context Moses' final descent, originally not foreseen in the narrative (cf. 24:18 and 31:18), is now made necessary by the events recorded in chapter 32 (cf. 32:15–19). For this reason the significance of Exod. 34:29 ff. only becomes clear when anchored within the immediate context of Israel's sin with the golden calf and its implications on the one hand (Exod. 32:1–34:28), and when compared to the first giving of the Law on the other (Exod. 19:1 ff.).

---

tions, 1972 (ET of 1948 German ed.), p. 248: "all literary-critical and traditions-historical investigation must be regarded only as a means for the fulfillment of this task."

[21] The following analysis is not intended to be exhaustive; instead I have tried to focus on those aspects of the narrative which are of importance for this study, while at the same time not doing damage to the flow of the argument as a whole. For a more detailed treatment, see especially the commentaries of U. Cassuto and B. Childs, the article by H.C. Brichto, and above all the monograph of R.W.L. Moberly, all of which have contributed significantly to my understanding of this passage.

[22] Though the best translation of the figure made in Exod. 32 is not a "calf," but a "young bull" (עגל), the traditional translation has been retained because of its familiarity; for this point and a detailed survey of the translation problems and the history of scholarship on this passage since 1550, including references to the early Jewish and Christian interpretations of the text through the middle ages, see Joachim Hahn, *Das "Goldene Kalb" Die Jahwe-Verehrung bei Stierbildern in der Geschichte Israels*, Europäische Hochschulschriften Reihe 23, Theologie, Bd. 154, 1981, pp. 13–217.

[23] Cf. Moses' other ascents in Exod. 19:8, 20; 20:21; 24:9; 24:13, 15, 18 and then in 34:4.

a) Exodus 32:1–6: The Breaking of the Covenant

The fact that the immediate context of Exod. 34:29 ff. begins in Exod. 32:1 is clear from 31:18, where the conclusion of the revelation to Moses concerning the tabernacle and the cult brings Moses' long period on Mt. Sinai to an end (cf. 24:18). Moreover, it is precisely this extended period of time that provides the impetus for the events to follow. Hence, in 32:1a the scene suddenly shifts from the top of the mountain, where God is instructing Moses, to the people of Israel waiting at the bottom. This time, however, the shift in focus is not brought about by Moses' *presence* to deliver the covenant stipulations,[24] but by his very *absence*. The people act in response to Moses' delay in coming down from the mountain (32:1). This in itself signals the distinct and ominous nature of what is about to happen as Israel acts independently of Moses' leadership.

This ominous tone is then heightened by the use of the idiom "to gather to" (קָהֵל עַל) to describe the people's assembling around Aaron, which in view of Num. 16:3 and 20:2 carries "threatening implications."[25] The people demand that Aaron make a "god" (אֱלֹהִים) to lead them in Moses' absence. The striking thing about this request is not the use of the plural form for the deity, since אֱלֹהִים can be used with singular or plural forms of the verb to refer to YHWH.[26] What *is* surprising is the assumed role of Moses as the mediator of God's guidance at this point in the narrative. As 32:1b states explicitly, the problem for the people is not the absence of God, but the unknown whereabouts of Moses. According to the flow of the narrative at this juncture, the theophanic cloud into which Moses disappeared in 24:15–18, and hence the glory of God itself, was still apparently visible on the mountain (cf. 31:18). Thus, YHWH's own presence is certainly not absent from view while the calf is being made! The people's demand for a "god" to lead them should not be understood as a desire for an idol to take the place of YHWH himself as Israel's God, but for an image representing YHWH to replace Moses as "a rival means of mediating Yahweh's presence to the people" (32:1b)![27] The point is

---

[24] Cf. Moses' other descents in Exod. 19:7; 14, 25; 24:3; and then in 32:15, each of which functions to bring about the shift in scene.

[25] Moberly, *Mountain of God*, p. 46, and earlier, U. Cassuto, *A Commentary on the Book of Exodus*, 1967 (ET of Hebrew original, 1951), p. 411. As Edward Keazirian, *Old Testament Parallels in Romans 1:23*, unpubl. Th.M. thesis, Gordon-Conwell Theological Seminary, 1993, pp. 21 f., has observed, the link between Exod. 34 and Num. 16 and 20 is further substantiated by the fact that both of these latter passages are then cited in Ps. 106 (105 LXX) in conjunction with Israel's sin with the golden calf.

[26] Cf. e.g. Gen. 1:1 f.; 2:2, 21 f.; 8:1; 9:1; 17:3, 7; Exod. 2:23 f.; 3:1; 3:14 (!); 4:5; 20:1–3 (!); 32:16, 11; Deut. 4:7; 2 Sam. 7:23; Neh. 9:18, etc. See Moberly, *Mountain of God*, p. 48, for this point and some of the examples.

[27] So Moberly, *Mountain of God*, p. 46. That the calf was intended to replace Moses has also been argued by, e.g., U. Cassuto, *Exodus*, p. 411, and George W. Coats, "The King's Loyal Opposition: Obedience and Authority in Exodus 32–34," in *Canon and Authority, Essays in Old Testament Religion and Theology*, ed. G.W. Coats and Burke O. Long, 1977,

not that YHWH can or should be replaced as Israel's God, but that due to his prolonged absence on the mountain, *Moses* must be replaced as the one to represent YHWH to the people. This is confirmed by the parallel between the people's interpretation of the golden calf as the *god* "who brought you up from the land of Egypt" in verse 4 as a clear echo of Exod. 20:2, and their prior declaration in verse 1 that Moses was the *man* who delivered them (cf. 32:23).[28] The interplay between YHWH and Moses as the deliverers of Israel indicates that the golden calf is now to take the place of Moses as a similar concrete and "real embodiment"[29] of YHWH's presence around which the people can be gathered (cf. חג ליהוה, v. 5).

Brevard Childs has suggested, however, that 32:5 reveals an ambiguity in the text in which Aaron is portrayed as having a different intention for the calf than that of the people. According to Childs, Aaron (as in 1 Kings 12, which he considers to represent the original form of the tradition) intended for the calf to be incorporated into the feast as a syncretistic representation of YHWH, while the people saw it as an idol to replace YHWH himself.[30] But this seems unlikely in that after the golden calf is fashioned, Aaron's priestly decision to consecrate a feast is given in direct response to the people's interpretation without correction (32:4 f.). Moreover, if Childs is correct, Brichto poses the question of the narrative's credibility in asking the reader "to believe that mature adults would hail as their liberator from Egypt a man-made image which had not come into existence until that very moment."[31] It thus seems difficult to consider the calf to be a rival god. And even if Aaron is trying to mitigate the people's request in some way, the move is certainly subtle and Aaron is still held accountable for this sin (cf. 32:21). Whether interpreted as a replacement for YHWH or as his representation, the construction and use of the golden calf in worship are a grave breech of the primary covenant stipu-

---

pp. 91–109, p. 95, and now his *Moses. Heroic Man, Man of God*, JSOT Supplement Series 57, 1988, p. 190, and J. Hahn, *Goldene Kalb*, p. 23. This interpretation corresponds to the understanding of the function of cult statues in Mesopotamian religions as often "a promise, a potential, and an incentive to a theophany, to a divine presence, no more"; see Thorkild Jacobsen, "The Graven Image," in *Ancient Israelite Religion, FS Frank Moore Cross*, ed. P. Miller, et al., 1987, pp. 15–32, p. 29. For this same point and its support in the work on Mari and Ugaritic iconography by Eissfeldt and C.F.A. Schaeffer, see Thomas W. Mann, *Divine Presence and Guidance in Israelite Traditions: The Typology of Exaltation*, The Johns Hopkins Near Eastern Studies, 1977, pp. 155, 265–268.

[28] Cf. this with the same alteration between the function of the theophany to cause the people to believe in Moses "forever" in Exod. 19:9 and its function to keep them from sinning against YHWH in 20:20. See too Jack M. Sasson, "Bovine Symbolism in the Exodus Narrative," *VT* 18 (1968) 380–387, p. 384, who due to this equation calls the calf a "substitute for Moses."

[29] So Moberly, *Mountain of God*, p. 47. Cf. M. Noth, *Das Zweite Buch Mose, Exodus, ATD Bd. 5*, 1968[4], pp. 203 f., for a development of this same point.

[30] Brevard S. Childs, *The Book of Exodus, A Critical, Theological Commentary*, 1974, pp. 565 f.

[31] "Golden Calf," p. 6.

lations which they had accepted (cf. Exod. 19:8; 24:3). Its golden material, tooled manner of construction as "fashioned with a stylus" (ויצר אתו בחרט, 32:4; cf. Is. 8:1),[32] and function as an altar or throne (not to mention as a god itself!) in a cultic practice[33] are all expressly forbidden (cf. Exod. 20:3 f., 23–26 with 32:2–6). In Moses' absence, the people have made a substitute for the mediation of God's presence in direct disobedience to the Law of God and as an affront to the very nature of YHWH himself (cf. Exod. 20:19 f.). The people's idolatry, portrayed in a crisp and decisive manner, implicitly annuls their position as God's "own possession among all the peoples" (Exod. 19:5).

b) Exodus 32:7–10: The Divine Response

YHWH's reaction is equally decisive. He orders Moses to return to the people in their sinful act and declares that he will destroy them for it (32:7–10). God's intense anger is underscored in verse 8 by his own recounting of Israel's sin as

---

[32] On this traditional meaning of חרט in Exod. 32:4 and Is. 8:1, cf. Brichto, "Golden Calf," pp. 5 f.n. 2, and Childs, *Exodus* , pp. 555 f. The question of the difficulty of engraving (יצר) with a writing instrument need not detain us; the important point in view of Exod. 20:25 is that the calf was tooled. For a survey of the problems and the counter suggestion that חרט should be rendered "bag" (repointed *harit*) rather than "stylus" (cf. 2 Kings 5:23; Is. 3:22), so that 32:4 refers to Aaron gathering (ויצר) the gold in a bag or cloak, cf. S.E. Loewenstamm, "The Making and Destruction of the Golden Calf," *Biblica* 48 (1967) 481–490, pp. 481, 487. This position has been challenged by Leo G. Perdue, "The Making and Destruction of the Golden Calf – A Reply," *Biblica* 54 (1973) 237–246, pp. 244 f. Cf. Loewenstamm's reply in "Making and Destruction of the Golden Calf: A Rejoinder," *Biblica* 56 (1975) 330–343, p. 336 f. Most recently, Loewenstamm's position has been defended by S. Gevirtz, "חרט in the Manufacture of the Golden Calf," *Biblica* 65 (1984) 377–381. The debate goes back to M. Noth's support of this reconstructed pointing in his "Zur Anfertigung des 'Goldenen Kalbes,'" *VT* 9 (1959) 419–422. This textual problem is a difficult judgment call which has long been recognized (J.J. Petuchowski, "Nochmals 'zur Anfertigung des Goldenen Kalbes,'" *VT* 10 (1960) 74, traces the attempt to repoint the text back to Rashi); but on the principle of *lectio difficilior* it seems best to retain the reading found in the MT (cf. the LXX rendering of 32:4: καὶ ἔπλασεν αὐτὰ ἐν τῇ γραφίδι). For a defense of the traditional reading, see now Bori, *Golden Calf*, p. 89, who points to the fact that *Tg. Onqelos* also follows the pointing of the MT and the LXX. For a survey of the various possibilities, see esp. Hahn, *Goldene Kalb*, pp. 144–170.

[33] The exact determination of the actual cutic function of the golden calf has been much debated. For the predominant interpretation of the calf as a throne for YHWH, see, among others, U. Cassuto, *Exodus*, p. 407, who points out that this use nonetheless still constituted breaking the prohibition against graven images. For unlike the cherubim, who were to be used for the same purpose (!), the calf was an earthly creature. For the alternative position that the calf was a representation of a false god, perhaps of the moon god Sin, see L.R. Bailey, "The Golden Calf," *HUCA* 42 (1971) 97–115, esp. pp. 98–101, 112. If Bailey is correct, then the move to replace Moses eventuated in an even more heinous form of idolatry. For the mediating position, based primarily on the parallels in Ps. 106:19–20 and 32:31, that the calf was a symbol of YHWH himself, see now M. Haran, *Temples and Temple-Service in Ancient Israel, An Inquiry into the Character of Cult Phenomena and the Historical Setting of the Priestly School*, 1978, p. 29.

evidence of how "quickly" they have turned away from his commandments, by his distancing himself from Israel as *Moses'* people (cf. 32:7 with Exod. 19:5 f.) whom *Moses* has brought up from Egypt (cf. 32:7 with Exod. 20:2), and by his pronouncement in verse 9 of their hardened "stiff-necked" condition. The people have forgotten that God's "way" with his people includes both blessing and curse, a fact which stands at the heart of the covenant as expressed in Exod. 20:5 f. Hence, they now stand under God's wrath as those who, by their idolatry, have shown that they "hate" YHWH (cf. 20:5).[34] Apparently, God's only choice is to annihilate them in order to start over by building a nation around the faithful one Moses (32:10).

c) Exodus 32:11–14: Moses' First Intercession

At this point in the narrative an unexpected twist in the plot occurs which propels the story to its equally unexpected climax in 34:25 ff. This turn of events takes place in regard to both of the main characters, YHWH and Moses, though Moses is now clearly the focal point of attention. For in response to God's command to leave him alone so that he might destroy Israel in order to start over, Moses refuses both this command and God's suggestion that Moses become the nucleus of a new people.[35] Instead, Moses approaches God with a counter argument which at first glance seems to border on disrespect. Yet, as Brichto as pointed out, it is YHWH's command *itself* which invites Moses to respond. As is common in prophetic discourse, "God tells His servant what it is that his people deserves, so that His servant may fulfill his role as intercessor."[36]

On close inspection, the point of Moses' intercession is clearly not an accusation against God, but a response of "loyal opposition" which springs from trust in his word.[37] Moses accepts YHWH's analysis of the people's sin, his declaration of their sinful state, and the justified nature of his anger. So Moses

---

[34] I am indebted to Robert A. Hammer, "New Covenant of Moses," *Judaism* 27 (1978) 345–350, p. 348, for calling my attention to the parallel between 32:8 and Exod. 20:5 f., though I disagree with his view that the basis of Moses' subsequent intercession in 32:11–13 is based on a distinction between the nature of the Abrahamic and Mosaic covenants (cf. p. 346).

[35] For the word play between God's command to be left alone in v. 10 (הניחה) and Moses' refusal to do so by beseeching him to change his mind in v. 12 (הנחם), see Cassuto, *Exodus*, p. 416.

[36] Brichto, "Golden Calf," p. 9. This understanding is confirmed by *Tgs. Neof.*, *Ps.-Jon.*, and *Onq.* to 32:10 and *b. Ber.* 32a, in which the MT tradition "let me alone" is interpreted in terms of Moses' intercession on the behalf of the people.

[37] To borrow both the phrase and central thesis of Coats, "Loyal Opposition," p. 92, though I disagree with his analysis of the underlying premise of Moses' argument in 32:12 f. in which Coats makes a (in my opinion, false) distinction between God acting to maintain his reputation and God violating a previous promise, arguing that Moses appeals to the latter but not the former (cf. pp. 97 f.).

renders no excuse for the people's idolatry. He offers no plea for mercy based on their character or situation. He expresses no direct concern for their welfare. Rather, Moses boldly points out the eventual consequence of YHWH's anger for maintaining the glory of his own character! From Moses' perspective, it is not primarily Israel's future which is now at stake, but the future of God's purpose to reveal his glory to Egypt and the nations through the Exodus in fulfillment of his own covenant promises. The reference to the Egyptians in 32:12 harkens back to God's prior declarations in Exod. 9:16; 14:4, 17, 18 and their beginning fulfillment in 14:25; 15:1, 6, 11, 21 and 16:6 f., 10. In the same way, the seemingly abrupt transition in 32:13, in which Moses adjures YHWH to remember his oath to Abraham, Isaac, and Israel, recalls that the entire Exodus account takes place in fulfillment of his covenant promises to the Patriarchs (cf. Exod. 2:24). As a result of his own gracious initiative, YHWH's character is now inextricably intertwined with Israel's destiny.

Moses' intercession finds its force, therefore, in the implied biblical premise that "the most fundamental characteristic of God's righteousness is his allegiance to his own name, that is, to his honor and glory."[38] It is not just that God's reputation will be ruined if he does not keep his promise, but that it would be *evil* for God not to keep his promise precisely because it would call his own trustworthiness and honor into question. Knowing this, Moses reminds YHWH that these people are *his* people, whom *he* (not Moses; cf. 32:7!) delivered from the land of Egypt (32:11 f.), and that God's original commitment to this people was motivated only by his *own* sovereign will (32:13). Nothing outside of YHWH's own character and gracious desire compelled him to call Abraham and deliver Israel.[39] But now that God *has* made this promise and identified himself with this people, the glory of his own "name" (cf. Exod. 3:13–15!) is at stake. YHWH ought to turn from his anger not because the people deserved to be spared or because his covenant with the Patriarchs is of a different nature than that with Moses,[40] but because to de-

---

[38] John Piper, *The Justification of God: An Exegetical Study of Romans 9:1–23*, 1983, p. 90. For a development of this point in relation to Exod. 33:19 and on the basis of passages such as Pss. 23:3; 31:1–3; 79:9; 143:1–2, 11; Dan. 9:7, 13–19; Isa. 43:6–7, 21, 25; 44:23; 46:13; Jer. 13:11; 14:7, 9, 20–21; Ezek. 16:59–63; 20:9, 14, 22, 44; etc., see his discussion on pp. 55–101.

[39] Contra Brichto, "Golden Calf," p. 9 (cf. pp. 19, 21, 30), who suggests that the point of 32:13 is to remind YHWH of the merit of the Patriarchs, which is then invoked on behalf of the present generation. The explicit reference to the origin of YHWH's action within himself speaks against such an interpretation.

[40] Contra, e.g. Hammer's central thesis in "New Covenant," pp. 346, 348 f., following Weinfeld, that unlike the Sinai covenant, the Abrahamic covenant was a "grant" which carried "absolutely no conditions with it" and as such is "binding upon the ruler." This position finds many adherents both at the exegetical and theological levels. The questions of the genre of the OT covenant and the relationship between the Abrahamic and Sinaitic covenants raise complex issues that cannot be resolved here. Suffice it to say that Weinfeld himself has pointed out that even "grants" are reciprocal (cf. M. Weinfeld, "Bᵉrit-Covenant vs. Obligation," *Biblica* 56 (1975) 120–128), and that even Hammer, p. 346, must admit that the

stroy them now would defame his own glory, something which God cannot do.[41]

Based on this premise, Moses' intercession is effective. God grants Moses' request not to destroy the people. Indeed, the narrator intimates in verse 14 that YHWH once again even regards them as "his people," in spite of their having broken the covenant. But the same righteous commitment to his own glory that motivates God not to destroy Israel also demands that he judge the nation for her sin. Israel has broken the covenant and God's own covenant commitments necessitate that he punish her for it. It is to this judgment that the narrative now turns.

d) Exodus 32:15–29: The Judgment of the Law

Moses' descent from the mountaintop with the tablets of the Law in 32:15 signals not only the switch in scene, but also an omen of what is to come. For the repetition at this point in the narrative of the divine origin of the tablets as God's work and writing (cf. 32:15 with 31:18) is the most elaborate description of them anywhere in the OT. As such, it serves not only to emphasize that Moses is now returning with the witness and seal of the very covenant which the people have just broken, but also to raise the question of what will happen when God's covenant Law, with its divine nature and sanction, encounters those who have rebelled against it. Moses is bringing the divine testimony of the covenant to those who have already rejected it! Moreover, this ironical juxtaposition underscores that Moses is once again the mediator of the covenant. Just as Moses previously functioned to mediate God's commandments and guidance in blessing, the narrative now implicitly poses the question of how Moses will mediate the Law given the reality of Israel's rebellion.[42]

The answer is clear. Just as YHWH desired to "burn with anger" (וַיִּחַר־אַפִּי) on top of the mountain in view of Israel's sin (32:10), Moses himself "burned

---

Abrahamic covenant demanded circumcision as "a kind of condition of it" and that "God fully expected the descendents to be worthy of the grant, following the ways of Abraham and ready to 'keep the way of the Lord by doing what is just and right' (Gen. 18:19) ..." One can even ask what would have happened in Gen. 12 had Abraham not left for the promised land. But my point here is that Moses does not play one covenant off against another, but appeals directly to God's concern for his own glory. It was God's own honor and not some external agreement that bound him to respond to Moses' request.

[41] For another clear example of this same argument from God's glory as the basis for his actions toward sinful Israel, cf. Ezekiel 36:16–38, esp.vv. 20–23, 32; 39:21–29. On this point, Yehezkel Kaufmann, *The Religion of Israel, From Its Beginnings to the Babylonian Exile*, 1960, p. 333, points to Num. 14:13 f.; Deut. 9:28 f.; Pss. 44:16 f.; 74:10, 18, 22 f.; 79:10 ff.; and 115:1 ff. as additional examples of arguments based on God's honor in order to conclude that "Israel's fate and the fate of YHWH's name in the world are inseparable."

[42] The many interior exegetical questions inherent in this passage concerning the nature of the cultic ceremony, the destruction of the calf, the purpose of the ordeal in v. 20, the exact role of Aaron, and the role of the sons of Levi need not concern us, since the main lines of the narrative are clear.

with anger" (וַיִּחַר־אַף מֹשֶׁה) when confronted with Israel's idolatrous feast (32:19). And even though YHWH's intention to destroy Israel for her sin had been adverted by Moses' first intercession, Moses' act of breaking the tablets signifies that the covenant between YHWH and Israel is now broken and nullified. This point is supported in the narrative literarily by the use of the same verb to describe Moses' action in throwing down the tablets which is used in Aaron's description of throwing the gold into the fire to make the calf (cf. שׁלך in 32:19, 24).[43] Hence, though they may not be destroyed physically, Israel's status as God's people is obviously now in jeopardy. Against the backdrop of the clue in verse 14 that Israel is still considered in some sense "YHWH's people," the drama of the narrative raises the question of how, in fact, YHWH will continue to be Israel's God. But before this question can be answered, YHWH's punishment falls.

In his anger Moses now occupies the same role in relation to Israel that YHWH formerly held on top of Mt. Sinai. Conversely, Aaron takes Moses' place as intercessor on behalf of the people. Just as earlier exhibited in relationship to Pharaoh, Moses is now to Aaron as YHWH is to Moses (32:22; cf. Exod. 7:1). But unlike their counterparts, Moses acts to punish rather than destroy, while Aaron must plead for himself as well as for the people. The result is mercy toward Aaron, once again in full view of the people's hardened sinful condition (cf. 32:21 f.), and in the midst of the judgment of death on those who had been involved in the idolatry (32:27–28).[44] Moreover, the sons of Levi, who testify to their loyalty to YHWH by slaying the guilty, receive God's approval and his commitment to favor and protect them (32:29).[45]

As the narrative unfolds, two corresponding realities concerning Israel are yet to be reconciled with the fact that God's commitment to be Israel's God, i.e. her deliverer, defender, provider, and guide (Exod. 6:7–8; cf. Lev. 26:1–13),[46] has not yet been restored. On the one hand, the text has emphasized that the people are "stiff-necked" (32:9) and exist "in evil" (32:22). God's anger against them is thus justified, while Moses' anger with Aaron ought to be tempered by this same fact. Moses should not be surprised that they demanded the calf; what else can be expected from such a people? On the other hand, the direct implication of this reality is that the people deserve only the judgment

---

[43] I owe this observation to Brichto, "Golden Calf," p. 13, though he does not draw out the theological implication of this verbal repetition.

[44] For an analysis of the parallels between Exod. 32:1–14 and 15–29, see Dale Ralph Davis, "Rebellion, Presence and Covenant: A Study in Exodus 32–34," *WTJ* 44 (1982) 71–87, pp. 73–75.

[45] So Brichto, "Golden Calf," p. 17. It is not clear whether the Levites slay only others from within the priestly family, presumably those priests who led in the worship with the golden calf, or whether they also killed the guilty throughout the camp. The point is not decisive for our purposes.

[46] For the recurring theme and implications of YHWH as Israel's God and Israel as YHWH's people in Exodus, cf. 3:7, 10; 5:1; 7:4, 16; 8:1, 8, 20 f., 22 f.; 9:1, 13, 17; 10:3 f.; 15:26; 16:12; 20:2, 5; 23:25; 34:24.

of God. There may be a faithful remnant within the people,[47] represented by the sons of Levi, but as a whole the only possible verdict of the Law upon Israel as a people is death. For as Dumbrell has pointed out, "what Exod. 32 has ... done is to throw into prominence the essential character of national Israel."[48]

At this point in the narrative the tension between these realities and the overarching problem of the future of sinful Israel as God's people is palpable. No solution to the dilemma is in view; the two opposing characters, Israel and YHWH, appear to be at a stalemate. The only one who initiates any action at this point is Moses. He is the one who brings about both the judgment upon the people and the blessing upon the Levites. This in itself is striking since, as M. Walzer has pointed out, Exod. 32 is the only place within the wilderness narratives where YHWH does not directly punish the rebellion of Israel himself through fire, plague, serpents, etc., but does so through Moses (cf. Num. 11:1 ff.; 16:41–49; 21:5 f.).[49] In fact, YHWH gives no direct command concerning Israel's punishment, whereas the *Lord's* command in 32:27 is interpreted as the word of *Moses* in 32:28. This is consistent, however, with the fact that at this point in the narrative God has only consented not to destroy the people. His distance from them and inactivity, in contrast to Moses' activity, further illustrates that the covenant between YHWH and Israel remains broken.

It is precisely at this point that a ray of hope shines through the narrative which provides the bridge to the next stage in the relationship between God and his people. For despite her sin, Moses is *still* active as mediator between YHWH and Israel.[50] In addition, it is significant that the judgment of God and the demonstration of one's loyalty to YHWH both come about in obedience to Moses and his commands. Thus, Exod. 32:7–29 demonstrate that "refusing belief in Moses is tantamount to refusing belief in Yahweh."[51] Of equal significance is the fact that Moses' execution of judgment upon Israel has shown that there *does* exist a remnant within the people who have remained loyal to the covenant and are promised God's blessing (v. 29b).[52] It may be posited,

---

[47] I owe this point to Moberly, *Mountain of God*, p. 55, who sees in this account an implicit contrast between "the faithful few (remnant?) and the disobedient many."

[48] "Paul's use of Exodus 34," p. 184.

[49] "Exodus 32 and the Theory of Holy War: The History of a Citation," *HTR* 61 (1968) 1–14, pp. 2 f.

[50] See too Dumbrell, "Paul's use of Exodus 34," p. 184, who points to Moses' mediatorial role from Exod. 33 onward as reflecting the fact that although the covenant would not be abrogated, in spite of the fact that Israel broke it, "yet the character of that breach had been such as to remove any confidence that from this point onwards her 'national' nature within the OT would change."

[51] Coats, "Loyal Opposition," p. 95.

[52] If, as many commentators argue, the ordeal in v. 20 was intended to determine who was guilty among the Israelites (cf. Num. 5:27), this could be the backdrop for the selection of the remnant in v. 27. But cf. R. Grodwohl, "Die Verbrennung des Jungtiers, Exod. 32:20," *ThZ* 19 (1963) 50–53, who argues on the basis of the lack of mention of any results of the

therefore, that it is on this basis that Moses feels justified in returning to YHWH as mediator, this time not to receive further revelation from YHWH, but to present his second petition. Though it is God's own glory which ultimately motivates him, a faithful remnant among his people must be present for God's righteousness not to be mocked by his grace.[53] Thus, in the midst of a seemingly hopeless situation, Moses again becomes Israel's hope. With his new petition, a possibility for a relationship between Israel and YHWH begins to open up as the problem of the presence of God in the midst of a sinful people is addressed directly.

3. The Problem of the Presence of God (Exodus 32:30–33:11)

The next episode in the narrative begins with Moses' determination to return to YHWH in the attempt to "bear the offense" for Israel's sin (אולי אכפרה בעד חטאתכם, 32:30). Following Brichto, this translation of 32:30 indicates that Moses is not asking YHWH "to wipe the slate clean," but "to withhold punishment, to carry the debit on the books, to refrain from foreclosing."[54] As this statement of purpose itself makes clear, YHWH's prior decision not to destroy the people has not entailed a renewal of their covenant relationship, nor has it "covered" Israel's sin in YHWH's eyes. The judgment against the 3,000 has not served to satisfy completely God's wrath. As a result, Moses is not yet satisfied with Israel's precarious position, in which she exists before God as his *unforgiven* people. For as such, Israel continues to exist, but to exist without God's covenant promise to be her "God" in protection and provision. Without this promise, her future can only eventuate in judgment. It is this covenant promise, therefore, that Moses now attempts to secure in his second intercession.

---

ordeal, the text's earlier declaration of the people's guilt, and the reference to the stream in Deut. 9:21 that this ordeal functioned not to determine guilt but simply to signify the total destruction and falsity of the cult object. For this same conclusion and a complete skepticism about our ability to understand its precise function in its present context, see O. Hvidberg-Hansen, "Die Vernichtung des Goldenen Kalbes und der Ugaritische Ernteritus. Der rituelle Hintergrund für Exod. 32:20 und andere alttestamentliche Berichte über die Vernichtung von Götterbildern," *Acta Orientalia* 33 (1971) 5–46, esp. pp. 10, 32. Cf. now too Hyatt, *Exodus*, NCB, 1971, p. 308, who rejects the view of v. 20 as an ordeal and interprets it to be part of the punishment for Israel's sin. Regardless of how one decides this issue, the point remains that in spite of the seeming general declaration of guilt in 32:7 f., 11, 14, 21, verses 26–29 make clear that not all of the people were in fact guilty of this idolatry. For my own view of the relationship between 32:20–26 and 35, see below.

[53] For this point, see Gerhard F. Hasel's extensive treatment of the concept and function of the remnant in his, *The Remnant. The History and Theology of the Remnant. Idea from Genesis to Isaiah*, 1972, esp. pp. 389, 391. For an attempt to show how this same concept of the preserving function of the remnant is also used by Paul in Romans 9–11, see my "The Salvation of Israel in Romans 11:25–32," *Ex Auditu* 4 (1988) 38–58, pp. 48–52.

[54] Brichto, "Golden Calf," p. 18.

a) Exodus 32:30–33:6: Moses' Second Intercession

As before, Moses' intercession begins with a confession of the people's sin. As in his first intercession, here too Moses' plea is not based on the people's action or character. When Israel's sin as described in 32:31 is read against the backdrop of Exod. 20:23, the people are clearly without excuse. But the precise nature of Moses' prayer in 32:32 is unclear, due to the anacoluthic structure of his request in which Moses' request is broken off by his sudden declaration that he too is willing to be punished with the people's curse if they are not forgiven.[55] Read in this way, the basis of Moses' plea in v. 32 parallels his appeal to God's glory in 32:12 f. Earlier Moses appealed directly to God's own gracious initiative and sovereign promise as that which obligated him to act on behalf of Israel. But now, after the judgment against those most directly involved has been executed, Moses can appeal to the faithful "remnant," as embodied in himself, as the basis for God's subsequent mercy. The reference to the number of those slain in 32:28, the role of the Levites in selecting those to be killed, and the principle of divine judgment in 32:33 all support the supposition that the judgment already meted out has been against those who were somehow more culpably involved in the idolatry.[56] Those directly responsible for Israel's sin have been representatively judged. Though not without guilt, and certainly still "stiff necked" (32:9) and "evil" (32:22), the people now remaining can be considered to be under the umbrella of those who, like Moses, remained faithful.

Moses now stands before YHWH, therefore, as the faithful among the unfaithful. His own eventual punishment is offered as the basis for his request that YHWH forgive his people. For in his righteousness, God cannot "blot out from his book" those who trust in him. Hence, if God were not to forestall judgment against those among whom the faithful now find their place, his glory would be equally tarnished. Hence, Moses' second intercession is based not only on his identification with the people as their intercessor, as often pointed out,[57] but also upon God's same righteous concern for maintaining his own glory that undergirded Moses' first request.

Again the intercession is effective. YHWH implicitly grants Moses' request to spare his people by referring to his principle of judgment in verse 33, a principle which demands that Moses' prayer be answered, since he has certainly

---

[55] As Cassuto, *Exodus*, p. 423, and Moberly, *Mountain of God*, p. 199 n. 57, have pointed out, Moses' statement is not an offer of vicarious atonement.

[56] Cf. Cassuto's view, *Exodus*, pp. 422 f., that 32:30–35 deals with those who did not oppose the sin, but also did not actively participate in it; hence they are still guilty, but not punishable by death. For this same interpretation in terms of a distinction between those who were guilty of a sin of "commission" versus one of "omission," see Brichto, "Golden Calf," p. 18.

[57] For a clear presentation of this point, see Moberly, *Mountain of God*, pp. 57 f.

not sinned.[58] God will not utterly destroy his people for the sake of the "remnant," but bear with them. The reality of this answer can be seen in v. 34a; Moses can now resume leading them out from Sinai.

YHWH's patience at this point, however, does not mean that the covenant has been restored in all its fulness. The narrative intimates that all is not yet well. For YHWH himself will no longer lead the people in the pillar of cloud and fire, since an angel will now take his place as the one who directly guides and protects Israel (32:34a). Moreover, the dialogue between YHWH and Moses ends in verses 34b–35 with a word of warning and judgment. YHWH threatens that when he does once again visit Israel with his presence, it will not be to deliver, but to punish the nation for her sin (34b). This warning anticipates the explanation in 33:3,5 why YHWH himself can no longer guide Israel on their way. In the word of judgment, the narrative sums up the incident with the golden calf by reminding the reader that God has not been and will not be mocked by Israel's sin. To quote Brichto again, "a reprieve has been asked and granted, but not absolution."[59] As a concluding statement, verse 35 indicates that YHWH's past judgment against the 3,000, his withdrawal of his presence from Israel, and his future visitation to judge the nation clearly demonstrate that the "Lord smote the people, because of what they did with the calf which Aaron had made" (32:35).[60] The people may now continue on toward Canaan, but the terrible implications of their sin remain.

The next section of the narrative, 33:1–6, maps out these implications. In so doing, it provides the key transition in the development of the plot, both theologically and in terms of its story-line. In regard to the former, the statement from 32:34 is expanded in 33:1 as Moses is again directly commanded to depart from Sinai. This time, however, the place to which Moses has been told to lead the people (32:34) is defined in terms of the *promised* land (33:1b). In this way the departure from Sinai is explicitly linked with Moses' earlier recourse in 32:13 to this same divine promise given to the Patriarchs. God has not reneged on his prior promise. Nevertheless, the fulfillment of this promise will no longer be executed as the direct result of YHWH's own saving presence. The account in Exod. 23:20–23 and 27–30 of the way in which YHWH himself will drive out the inhabitants of the land with his own "terror," i.e. through the angel who bears YHWH's "name" and by the hornets who do his

---

[58] For this view and the other alternative, i.e. that v. 33 is a general statement of God's righteousness which leaves "little room for mercy to the guilty," a problem that must then be dealt with later in the narrative (33:19; 34:6 f.), see Moberly, *Mountain of God* , pp. 57 f. Moberly opts for the latter interpretation, though the close connection between vv. 32 and 33 and the resumption of God's commitment to Israel in v. 34 lead me to favor the former.

[59] "Golden Calf," pp. 18 f.

[60] For the view of v. 35 as a summary statement, see too Hvidberg-Hanson, "Vernichtung," p. 32. For the view that vv. 20, 25–29, and 34 represent three unrelated punishments, see M. North, *Zweite Buch*, pp. 201 f. The attempt of Brichto, "Golden Calf," p. 19, to read 32:35 as a future tense goes beyond the explicit statement of the text.

bidding, is now picked up by the assertion that the angel will still go before Israel to drive out the peoples (cf. 33:3,5). In view of the explicit statement in 33:3a that YHWH will not "go up in Israel's midst," together with Moses' later request in 33:12 (see below), the angel is not, as often interpreted, a representation of God's presence with his people.[61] The angel's role is not to accompany Moses in leading Israel on her way. Rather, the angel is to go "before" the people as a vanguard for her entrance into the land. Thus, as the first person identification of YHWH with the action of the angel in 33:2 demonstrates, YHWH will keep his promise to drive out the peoples in preparation for Israel's conquest. But Moses, not God, is to lead the people (32:34a). There is consequently no mention here of the pillar of cloud and fire, the visible manifestation of God's own presence with his people.[62] The promise to the Patriarchs of the land is restored, but the promise of the sustaining presence of God in the very midst of his people is no longer in force (cf. Exod. 13:21 f.; 14:19 f., 24; 16:10; 25:8; 29:46).[63] YHWH's mercy and judgment are therefore both clearly visible. God will ensure that the people are brought into the promised land through the work of his angel (mercy), but not through his own intimate presence (judgment).

The reason for this tragic turn of events is clear. The incident with the golden calf has illustrated that Israel is hardened against her Lord (33:3,5; cf. 32:9, 22). As a result, and as the text emphasizes through its repetition, were YHWH to continue in their midst "for one moment" (!) Israel would be destroyed (33:3,5). Due to Israel's sin with the golden calf, the earlier promise of God's presence to guide Israel on her way, once the very expression of his blessing, has now become the instrument of his judgment. But that God would

---

[61] Contra, e.g. Moberly, *Mountain of God*, p. 60, who views the angel as a modified form of YHWH's presence with his people. For Moberly, God's presence is still with his people, but it has been "severely qualified by the absence of some particularly intimate role of Yahweh's presence 'in their midst' that otherwise might be expected." But the text indicates that the situation is even more dire. For the view that 32:1–6 refers to a movement toward the land without God's presence, see Coats, "Loyal Opposition," p. 100; for the distinction between YHWH and the angel, see too George A.F. Knight, *Theology as Narration. A Commentary on the Book of Exodus*, 1976, pp. 192 f.

[62] For the theme of the cloud as an expression of God's presence, cf. Gen. 9:13; Exod. 19:9, 16; 24:15 f.; 40:34 f.; Num. 11:25; 12:5; 16:42; Deut. 5:22 and 31:15. For the theme of YHWH's later guidance of Israel in the pillar of cloud and fire after the events of Exod. 32–34, cf. Exod. 40:36–38; Lev. 16:2, 13; Num. 9:15–22; 10:11 f., 34., and the summary statements in Deut. 1:33 and Num. 14:14. For the various views concerning the origin and significance of this imagery for the presence of God, see Thomas W. Mann, "The Pillar of Cloud in the Reed Sea Narrative," *JBL* 90 (1971) 15–30. Mann's own view, cf. pp. 23 ff., is that this imagery parallels its use with Baal as the Storm God and refers to YHWH's presence as a divine military escort which functions, like the ark, to guide and accompany the people in battle (cf. Exod. 13:21 with Num. 10:33; Josh. 3:4 and Exod. 14:24 with Josh. 3–4; Num. 14:44 f.; 1 Sam. 4). The other most viable possibility is that the cloud and fire represent a cultic protection of YHWH's glory, as in Lev. 16:2 (so, e.g. Beyerlin).

[63] So too Coats, "Loyal Opposition," p. 96, and Cassuto, *Exodus*, p. 426.

consent to withdraw his presence is also an ironic expression of his long-suffering grace. Given the "stiff-necked" nature of the nation, God's withdrawal of his presence from Israel's midst is not only part of his judgment upon the people for their sin (32:34), but also a necessary act of divine *mercy which makes it possible for Israel to continue on as a people.*

This two sided nature of YHWH's removal of his presence from their midst is then illustrated in the people's sad reaction on the one hand, and in the institution of the tent of meeting on the other. In the first instance, the people receive the word of YHWH's judgment with remorse, illustrated by their mourning and the stripping of their ornaments (33:4, 6). Conversely, YHWH commands the people to remove their ornaments. Israel is now spoiled for her rebellion by YHWH just as Egypt was previously spoiled by Israel (cf. Exod. 3:22; 12:36).[64] The long-term implications of her idolatry have become apparent to the people. Israel will leave Mt. Sinai stripped of her former glory, both the glory of YHWH's presence and the glories of her previous triumph over the Egyptians as God's people.[65] Those who arrived at the mountain in victory now leave in defeat and under the judgment of God.

But again the narrative hints that this divine word of judgment is not YHWH's last word to his wayward people. The initial hint, as we have already seen, was implied in YHWH's willingness to lead the people by means of an angel and thus continue to preserve them despite their hardened condition. The second and more direct hint is given in verse 5 when YHWH "leaves the door open" for further deliberations concerning Israel's fate. Like the previous statement in 32:10, here too YHWH invites Moses to approach him with an intercession on behalf of the people. But before that takes place, the divine provision for Moses' contact with YHWH once they leave Mt. Sinai is described in 33:7–11.

---

[64] I owe this parallel to Moberly, *Mountain of God*, p. 61. On the use of a "synoptic-resumptive narrative technique" in 33:4, 6, see Brichto, "Golden Calf," p. 22.

[65] For this same point concerning the implications of Israel's sin with the golden calf, see Ps. 106:20, in which Israel's glory is equated with YHWH, a glory which the people "exchanged" for that which had no glory when they insisted on worshipping the form of a bull rather than God's presence which has no "form" (cf. Deut. 4:15 f.). Israel thus lost her glory. As the close verbal ties indicate, this interpretation of the golden calf in Ps. 106:20 (LXX 105) as an exchange of God's glory for that of an idol is the background alluded to by Paul in Romans 1:23! I am indebted to Keazirian, *Old Testament Parallels*, pp. 85 f., for calling my attention to this. For this same recognition that Rom. 1:23 is an allusion to Ps. 106:20, which in turn is an allusion to Israel's worship of the golden calf, see Terrance Callan, "Paul and the Golden Calf," *Proceedings* 10 (1990) 1–17, p. 5. As Callan observes, "This suggests that Paul may consider Israel's idolatry, and particular its worship of the golden calf, something which puts Israel and the Gentiles on the same footing with regard to idolatry" (p. 5). More precisely, Keazirian, p. 86, has argued that Paul's use of Israel's idolatry with the golden calf to describe the sin of all people illustrates that just as the Gentiles have committed the same kind of idolatry as Israel, Israel too has followed in the footsteps of all humanity, and therefore both are equally guilty before God. In his words, in terms of the ancient morality play, "Israel is Everyman."

b) *Exodus 33:7–11: The Tent of Meeting*

As the divine counterpart to Israel's judgment in 33:4–6, the tent of meeting represents God's further mercy towards his people. With the creation of this alternative to YHWH's direct presence in the midst of his people, Israel is assured of God's continuing guidance and given access to his revelation through their mediator Moses. The narrative is consistent in its emphasis, however, that in view of Israel's hard-heartedness the tent had to be erected "outside the camp, a good distance from the camp" (33:7). Hence, in seeking the Lord, Moses and the people had to "go out" from the midst of the people (33:7 f.).[66] Moreover, it is emphasized that YHWH's glory does not continuously dwell in this tent in a cultic sense, but merely comes periodically as a theophany (33:9).[67] And when the theophany does take place, only Moses experiences it directly (33:9), while the rest of the people must remain in the camp and worship from afar (33:10). Finally, during Moses' absence from the tent, Joshua stands guard outside it.

The tent of meeting thus illustrates the same dual nature of God's mercy and judgment that is portrayed in 32:30–33:6, but now with an emphasis on YHWH's mercy rather than his judgment. Israel is still separated from God's presence, but need not suffer total separation from his will and guidance. Reflecting on the function of the angel, tent of meeting, and motif of God's "face" (פָּנִים) within the flow of the narrative, von Rad therefore summarizes the theological point of the text well when he writes that,

"On the one side therefore, these institutions are a sign of the wrath of Jahweh, since his holiness might destroy Israel. But on the other hand, they are a proof of his will to save. Jahweh himself protects his people from this annihilating encounter, and takes precautions in order that his design to 'give Israel rest' (Exod. 33:14) may achieve its end. *In* actual fact, from now on Israel's relationship to *Jahweh is to some extent a mediated one.*"[68]

The second point that becomes clear is that Moses is now the only link between Israel and her God. On the one hand, "in the case of Moses ... when he

---

[66] On the sphere "outside the camp" as the place of separation from the people, cf. Lev. 4:12, 21; 13:46.

[67] On the tent of meeting as a place of oracles where YHWH declares his will, rather than a place of permanent dwelling, see esp. Rainer Schmitt, *Zelt und Lade als Thema alttestamentlicher Wissenschaft*, 1972, pp. 185 f., 209 f., 274, who, in support of this distinction, draws attention to the absence of cultic activities, objects, and priests in 33:7–11 on the one hand, and to the role of Moses as mediator on the other. See now too M. Haran, *Temples and Temple Service*, pp. 263–269. The later identification of the tent with the tabernacle (cf. Exod. 38:21; 39:32, 40; 40:2, 6, 29; Num. 1:50, 53; 9:15; 10:11; 17:23; 18:2; 1 Chron. 6:17 and the connection of priestly matters with the tent of meeting in Lev. 1–9) need not concern us here.

[68] Gerhard von Rad, *Old Testament Theology, Vol. 1,* 1962, p. 288 (emphasis mine). For my own interpretation of 33:14 as referring only to Moses, see below. But von Rad's basic point still stands.

came to the tent he did so as the representative of all Israel – as indicated by the formal stance of attention and homage which is assumed by the individual Israelites at their own tent-entrances."[69] On the other hand, the divine voice which earlier thundered from the cloud for all to hear is now replaced by an intimate experience in which YHWH carries on his conversations with Moses "face to face, just as a man speaks to his friend" (33:11). Hence, despite Israel's hardened condition, Moses *continues* to meet with God, and it is his intimacy that opens up the possibility for a third and decisive intercession on behalf of the people. As Brevard Childs has pointed out, "There is a clear line connecting ch. 33 with ch. 32 in the speech of judgment in 32:34. An angel – not Jahweh – will accompany Israel. In the same way a line connects ch. 33 with what follows in ch. 34, both in terms of the theophany (34:6 ff.) and the promise of accompaniment (v. 9)."[70]

Exodus 32:30–33:6 therefore functions as the key transition within the narrative in two ways. First, it provides the transition from the sin with the golden calf to YHWH's final response to his people's "stiff necks" by indicating how and why Moses feels free to approach YHWH on Israel's behalf yet again. The tent of meeting is the medium through which Moses can meet with God on the way to the promised land, so that continual access to God is now assured, while the intimate nature of Moses' contact with YHWH is the basis upon which Moses' final intercession can be made. Second, this section provides the pivotal transition within the narrative *theologically* by indicating that the ground for YHWH's distance from his people is not the single incident with the calf, but the underlying problem of their hardened condition. It is not merely what they have done; it is who they *are* that causes YHWH to institute a substitute for his direct presence and to limit the experience of his glory to Moses alone. With the covenant broken, God's continuing mercy towards Israel can only take place within the context of his continuing judgment on the people. The tent of meeting itself, though certainly an expression of divine mercy, must consequently be interpreted as the lesser counterpoint to the motif of God's judgment which runs throughout this section (cf. 32:35 with the role of Joshua in 33:11b). Although Moses speaks with God "face to face" within the tent, this remains a penultimate solution to the problem of the absence of God's presence from his people. As Moberly has pointed out, "... when Moses calls this tent 'the tent of meeting' (... twice in v. 7), it is natural to see it as a substitute for the proper tent in the middle of the camp, pending the restoration of Yahweh's favour and the renewal of the covenant."[71] What

---

[69] Brichto, "Golden Calf," p. 23.

[70] *Exodus*, pp. 585 f.

[71] *Mountain of God*, p. 64, in reference to Exod. 27:21; 28:43; 29:4, 10, 11, 30, 32, 42; 30:16, 18, 20, 36; 31:7. See too Hammer, "New Covenant," p. 348, and Knight, *Theology as Narration*, p. 194, who concludes from the function of the tent of meeting that "the whole apparatus of reconciliation described in chaps. 25–31 is now null and void."

remains to be seen, therefore, is how the covenant with Israel can be renewed in such a way that the problem of God's presence among his people can be solved in spite of their rebellious state. This, then, becomes the subject of Moses' final intercession.

4. Moses, the Mediator of God's Glory (Exodus 33:12–34:35)

In a crescendo-like effect, the flow of the narrative has been moved along at every point by the prayers of Moses on Israel's behalf, with each intercession providing the basis for the next one. Moreover, in each case the basis for Moses' request is his concern for the glory of God as it manifests itself through his relationship with his people. In the first intercession Moses wins back the life of the people because of God's prior intentions and promises to the Patriarchs (32:14). In the second he receives back the promise of the land and the corresponding pledge that God will drive out its inhabitants (33:1–3). God also commits himself to continue to reveal his presence to the people, but now only through Moses as his mediator (33:7–11). Moses, not God, must therefore now lead the people (32:34). Here too the basis of Moses' prayer is the reflection of the glory of God among his people. But, as the distance which exists between YHWH and his people testifies, the Sinai covenant still remains broken and the hearts of the majority of the people are still hardened. Now, in his final request, Moses seeks to secure the reestablishment of the Sinai covenant itself, with its granting of the direct presence of God in the midst of his "possession" (cf. Exod. 19:5 f., 9).[72] It is no surprise that the final resolution to the tension between Israel's idolatry as a result of her "stiff-necked" condition, the broken covenant, and the continuing presence of God among his sinful people will come about as a result of Moses' third intercession. Nor will it be surprising that the basis of Moses' appeal is once again YHWH's concern for his own glory. What is completely unexpected, however, is *how* this tension and the problem of God's presence in the midst of his people will be resolved.

---

[72] See R.E. Clements, *God and Temple. The Idea of the Divine Presence in Ancient Israel*, 1965, p. 112, who points out that the presence of God with his people in the Sinai covenant is to be seen as the fulfillment of the Abrahamic promise (cf. Gen. 17:4, 7 f.; Exod. 6:7 f.). Dumbrell, "Paul's Use of Exodus 34," pp. 182 f., notes the distinction between Moses and the people which is already introduced in Exod. 20:19–21, but also emphasizes that the focus of the prior narrative is on the fact that the commandments in 20:1–17 have been given without an intermediary and that the 70 elders in Exod. 24:1–11, who go up with Moses to "see" God, represent all Israel. Dumbrell thus rightly concludes that prior to Exod. 32–34, "in terms of any mediatorial role, when Moses goes up to Sinai at the end of chapter 24 to receive the commandments reduced to writing, there has only been the vestigial exercise of such a role" (p. 183).

a) Exodus 33:12–23: Moses' Final Intercession

Moses' final request, like his previous ones, is also based on YHWH's prior commitment to his own name and glory. But this time the strength of Moses' prayer is not found in YHWH's identification with Israel, but in Moses himself. Three times Moses grounds his petition in the fact that he has "found favor in YHWH's sight" (33:12 f.,16). In accord with the common use of this idiom, such "favor" refers to one's special regard in the opinion ("eyes") of another, which is then often used as the basis for a further request, even toward YHWH.[73] Conversely, YHWH's blessings are seen as evidence that someone has been given this position of acceptance or approval.[74] Against the backdrop of Moses' call in Exod. 3:10–17, YHWH's "favor" toward Moses has already been evidenced in the experience and promise of God's presence, both in a theophany (Exod. 3:2–6, 12) and in a knowledge of his character or "name" (Exod. 3:13 f.). Moses' intimacy with YHWH within the tent of meeting further validates his claim to be known by name by YHWH and to have found "favor" (חֵן) in his sight (33:12b). Moses is confident, therefore, that he has God's approval. It is this confidence that becomes the basis for his entreaty for a further expression of this divine regard. In other words, as the explicit logical relationships within 33:13 make clear, Moses argues *from* his favor in YHWH's eyes *for* further favor in his sight (cf. אִם־נָא ... נָא ... לְמַעַן). It is not Moses' merit or character that should motivate YHWH to act in the future, but the evidence of God's own bestowal of his "favor/grace" on Moses in the past.[75] As in Moses' prior requests, the power of Moses' petition rests in God's commitment to maintain his own glory, which would be compromised if he refused to act on behalf of some (faithful) one to whom he has already so obviously granted his blessing.

Moses' initial prayer is twofold. YHWH has commanded Moses to lead the people to the promised land (33:1), but he has not yet shown Moses who will lead him on the way (33:12). So Moses' first request is that YHWH would "make known his ways in order that he might know him in order that he might find favor in his sight" (הוֹדִעֵנִי נָא אֶת־דְּרָכֶךָ וְאֵדָעֲךָ לְמַעַן אֶמְצָא־חֵן בְּעֵינֶיךָ),

---

[73] For this use of חֵן cf. Gen. 6:8; 19:19; 30:27; 32:6; 33:8, 10, 15; 34:11; 39:4, 21; 47:25, 29; 50:4; Exod. 3:21; 11:3; 12:36; Num. 32:5; Deut. 24:1; 1 Sam. 1:18; 16:22; 20:3; 2 Sam. 14:22; 16:4; Prov. 3:4; Ruth 2:2, 10, 13; Esth. 2:15, 17; 5:2, 8:5 etc.; for חֵן as a basis for a petition to YHWH, cf. Gen. 18:3; Judg. 6:17; Ps. 119:58; and for the prayer for God's favor or grace, see especially the Psalms, e.g. 4:2; 6:3; 25:16; 26:11; 27:7; 30:11; 31:10; 51:3; 56:2; 119:132; etc.

[74] Thus, when things again go badly in Num. 11:1 ff., Moses questions why he has not found such favor in the eyes of YHWH, and if he has, he requests to be killed rather than continue to be treated this way (cf. Num. 11:11, 15) ! Cf. e.g. 2 Sam. 15:25 f.; Ps. 41:10 f.

[75] This is confirmed by the fact that, as Walter Brueggemann, "The Crisis and Promise of Presence in Israel," *Horizons in Biblical Theology* 1 (1979) 47–86, pp. 51, 75 n. 15, has pointed out, the use of the idiom "find favor in eyes" characteristically occurs in contexts of abasement before kings or others who hold power and authority over one, so that the phrase itself implies "postures of superiority and subordination."

33:13). A possible double entendre, Moses' prayer is to know YHWH's character, i.e. his "ways," so that this more intimate knowledge of God himself would provide the needed direction concerning the "way" to the promised land.[76] In short, Moses first requests that YHWH himself would again be the one who accompanies him on the way to the promised land. Moses' second petition is that YHWH consider that the people are indeed his people (cf. the imperative form ראה in 33:13).

But before the implications of this second request can be drawn out, YHWH answers. His "presence (lit. "face") will go" and he will give *Moses* "rest," i.e. protection from annihilation[77] (33:14). The translation "presence" for פנים in 33:14 f. reflects the common use of this idiom as a periphrasis for the personal pronoun and its use, as in verse 11, for the "enjoyment of personal contact with someone else (especially one's superior) ..."[78] YHWH is promising that he himself will accompany Moses. But the promise is directed to Moses *alone.*[79] Moberly has shown, moreover, that there is a "deliberate vagueness" about YHWH's declaration "in that no preposition is used after 'will go' to indicate the nature of Yahweh's going, whether with the people in their midst, or not."[80] As the continuation of Moses' speech in 33:15–16 indicates, Moses is not yet satisfied with the selectivity and ambiguity of this answer. He will not desist until YHWH promises to be with Moses *and* the people. Moreover, Moses insists that there is an inextricable relationship between his second request and the first, so that he links his "favor" before YHWH with the divine "favor" already bestowed on the people and ties his own desire for God's presence directly to the significance of God's presence among Israel. The promise of protection is not enough. Both Moses and the people, even with the prom-

---

[76] On the meaning of דרכך as a reference to a person's character and the play on its literal meaning as the "route for a journey," see Moberly, *Mountain of God*, p. 73. YHWH's response to Moses in 33:19; 34:6 f. alludes to Exod. 20:5 f. as the prior description of YHWH's character probably in view. See too Hammer, "New Covenant," p. 348.

[77] On the significance of "giving rest" (נוח) as protection from annihilation, see J. Muilenburg, "The Intercession of the Covenant Mediator (Exod. 33:1a, 12–17)," in *Words and Meanings, FS David Winton Thomas*, ed. Peter R. Ackroyd and Barnabas Lindars, 1968, pp. 159–181, p. 172 n. 4 (following von Rad).

[78] For its use as a pronoun, cf. Gen. 31:21; 1 Kgs 2:15; Jer. 42:15; Ezek. 6:2; and of God in Lev. 17:10; Num. 6:26; Deut. 31:17 f.; Judg. 18:23; 1 Kgs. 8:14; Job 13:24; Is. 54:8; 64:6; Jer. 2:27; 21:10; 32:33; Ezek. 39:23 f.; Ps. 13:2; 34:17; 51:11; etc.; and for the latter sense, cf. Gen. 32:21; 43:3,5; Exod. 10:28 f.; 23:15; 2 Sam. 3:13; 14:24; 2 Kgs. 25:19; Job 33:26; Ps. 17:13,15; 24:6; 27:8; 89:15; 95:2; 105:4; etc. For this quote and the relevant passages, see A.R. Johnson, "Aspects of the use of the term *panim* in the Old Testament," *Festschrift Otto Eissfeldt zum 60. Geburtstag*, ed. J. Fück, 1947, pp. 155–160, p. 158. He prefers to translate its use in 33:14 f. as "I myself" and "You yourself" respectively. Von Rad's view, *Theology, Vol. 1*, p. 285, that its use here takes on an "almost hypostatising independence" which is unique in the OT need not be posited, once it is seen that the promise of YHWH's presence is not given to Israel at this point, but only to Moses. The "face" of YHWH does not represent him as a mediator, but is his very own presence.

[79] This is also emphasized by Coats, "Loyal Opposition," p. 102.

[80] *Mountain of God*, p. 74.

ised land securely ahead of them, are nothing without the presence of God in their midst. It is not the land, but YHWH which marks out the people of God as different from all other peoples on the earth (33:16). Moses pleads, therefore, that God's "face" go "with us" (עִמָּנוּ), thus demonstrating that they are indeed YHWH's "own possession among all the peoples" (Exod. 19:5). In other words, Moses is now asking for nothing less than the renewal of the Sinai covenant.[81]

Again YHWH answers. But this time he unambiguously grants Moses' specific request precisely because Moses has indeed found favor in his sight (33:17). The covenantal promise of God's presence, the "thing of which Moses had spoken" (33:17a), will be given. The covenant will be reestablished.[82] It appears that with this answer the narrative has reached its climax. But the question of the *means* of this restoration must still be addressed. How will God be able to place his presence in the midst of his people when nothing has changed concerning her rebellious nature? The motif of Israel's "stiff-neck" and "evil" nature, so central in the development of the narrative to this point (cf. 32:9, 22; 33:3, 5), cannot be ignored.[83] That the narrative is not oblivious to this question is intimated by the basis given for YHWH's answer in 33:17. Although Moses presented his request on the basis of the favor which *both* he and the people had found before YHWH, YHWH's response is based on Mo-

---

[81] See F. M. Cross, *Canaanite Myth and Hebrew Epic, Essays in the History of the Religion of Israel*, 1973, p. 299: "The prime benefit of the Sinaitic covenant in the view of the Priestly tradent was the 'tabernacling' presence of Yahweh in Israel's midst." Cf. pp. 306 f.

[82] Contra Brueggemann, "Crisis and Promise," p. 50, who argues that in 33:12–17 nothing is granted to Moses. But in addition to the explicit statement of v. 17 itself, the structure of Moses' intercessions shows that each new petition is based on the granting of the previous one; Moses' request in 33:18 presupposes that v. 17 is a positive answer. In support of my view, cf. Moberly, *Mountain of God*, pp. 67 f. Both Brueggemann, pp. 48, 51–55, 60, and Moberly, pp. 68, 74 f., see the request for YHWH's "face" to be with Israel as a request for a cultic embodiment. But if 33:17 is taken positively, then Brueggemann's central thesis that YHWH denies Moses' request for a "static" presence in favor of a historically "dynamic" one remains unsubstantiated. Brueggemann's thesis depends on his conviction that 33:12–17 and 18–23 were originally in conflict with one another, something which their present unity may call into question. Moreover, as the narrative progresses, the cultic manifestation of God's presence is in fact restored, without a pejorative evaluation; cf. Exod. 40:34 f. Finally, it may be asked whether such a distinction between "historical trust" (p. 53) and "static presence" can be maintained since Israel's trust in YHWH's covenantal promises led to the establishment of his cultic presence (Exod. 25 ff.), while the renewal of the covenant in Exod. 34:10 ff. stresses just this cultic aspect of YHWH's presence. As a result, Israel is called to trust in YHWH precisely in response to his cultic presence in her midst (cf. Exod. 40:36 f.). Brueggemann's distinction between cultic presence and trust in the historical acts of YHWH, so that the theological point of Exod. 33 becomes a polemic against "religious certitude" (p. 56), thus seems overplayed.

[83] Contra, e.g. Muilenburg, "Intercession," pp. 173 f., and Ronald Clements, *Exodus, The Cambridge Bible Commentary*, 1972, p. 210, who posit that the issue at stake is one of geographical distance from Mt. Sinai. For a good critique of this view based on the function of the tent of meeting itself in 33:7–11, see Mann, *Divine Presence*, pp. 156 f., who argues that the problem is "more theological than spatial."

ses' favor *alone*. Moreover, that the resolution of the theological problem of the text does not take place at 33:17 is made explicit by the fact that Moses takes YHWH's answer as the basis for a final petition that aims at solving this fundamental problem. It is the third petition of Moses' third intercession which consequently brings the tension of the narrative to its dramatic resolution.

The shock that hits the reader at this point is completely unexpected, though within the narrative as a whole certainly not without warrant. Moses accepts the hardened condition of Israel. YHWH cannot place his presence in the midst of his people without destroying them. The answer to the problem of YHWH's presence is therefore not a petition on behalf of Israel, or the hope that God will again dwell in her midst, but a request that Moses himself now experience the solution to the problem![84] As a consistent development of the central role of Moses as the mediator of the covenant, Moses sees the answer to be a *private* theophany of the glory of God (33:18). Moses alone will experience the glory of God and then bring it back with him into the midst of his people, since in their hardened state they can no longer encounter it themselves.

In one of the most profound passages in Scripture, YHWH again agrees to meet Moses' plea (cf. 33:19–23). It is beyond our present purposes to discuss the exact nature and meaning of this important text. Suffice it to say that YHWH declares that his glory will pass before Moses more immediately than has ever been experienced by a person before or after. As a result, YHWH will make known his character ("name") as revealed in his sovereign freedom to bestow grace and compassion (33:19). The magnitude of this revelation is reflected in God's own protection of Moses, who in his mortality cannot directly perceive God's "face" and live (33:20–22).[85] In experiencing God's presence in this way, Moses will become the means through which God will renew his covenant with Israel (cf. 34:29 ff., see below). For as the wilderness narrative makes abundantly clear,[86] the condition of the people's hearts remains rebel-

---

[84] Contra Hammer, "New Covenant," p. 347, who interprets 33:14,19 to be requests for God's presence itself to accompany Israel.

[85] Contra Brueggemann, "Crisis and Promise," pp. 58, 80 n. 1, who suggests that in its present context YHWH covers Moses and shows him only his "back" in order to protect his own sovereignty and to keep Moses from gaining "full assurance." Again, Brueggemann's own understanding of the non-verifiable nature of genuine faith (i.e. faith is based on "the promise unencumbered by visible assurances," p. 52; cf. p. 55) seems to determine his interpretation. In support of the unity between theophanic revelation/faith and cultic presence in the OT, see Menahem Haran, "The Divine Presence in the Israelite Cult and the Cultic Institutions," *Biblica* 50 (1969) 251–267, p. 257, and R. Clements, *God and Temple*, p. 37, and the literature cited there; for this same unity between history and faith in the NT, esp. in Paul's thought, see my "'Self-Commendation' and Apostolic Legitimacy in 2 Corinthians: A Pauline Dialectic?" *NTS* 36 (1990) 66–88.

[86] Cf. Exod. 15:24; 16:2–12, 28; 17:2 f.; Num. 16:1–35, 41; 25:1–15; and esp. Num. 11:1 ff.; 12:1 ff.; 14:10 ff; 32:10 ff.

lious. Nevertheless, Moses' intercessions have been successful so that, as Walter Brueggemann has said, chapter 33 functions as the "bridge over the abyss between the forfeiture of 32 and the 'second coming' of Yahweh in 34, characterized by law, theophany and covenant, grounds for a continued history."[87]

b) Exodus 34:1–9: Moses' Private Theophany

For our purposes two aspects of the theophany in 34:1–9 are striking, both of which stand out against the backdrop of the prior theophany and giving of the Law in Exod. 19:9–20:26. In contrast to the first giving of the Law, where it is repeatedly emphasized that the coming of the Law is preceded by and incorporated within a theophany that is experienced by the entire people (cf. 19:9, 11, 17, 18, 20, 22), now Moses alone will experience the glory of God and receive the Law (34:1–3, 6).[88] This is consonant with the reality of Israel's hardened nature, a theme which is repeated once again in the midst of the theophany itself (cf. 34:9). Furthermore, it underscores Moses' central role as mediator within the restoration of Israel's covenant relationship with YHWH. Only Moses can endure the glory of God. The fact that Moses, not YHWH (cf. Exod. 24:12; 31:18), is entrusted with the task of cutting the stone tablets upon which the Law will be written also seems to underscore the crucial role Moses has played in the reestablishment of the covenant.[89]

The second striking aspect is that its purpose is the same as the earlier one in 19:9 ff, namely, to accredit and establish the Law of the covenant. The theophany promised to Moses in 33:18 is now explicitly presented as the context within which the tablets of the Law will be reinstated. Against the backdrop of the breaking of the tablets in 32:15 f. this can only mean that the covenant is now being restored. This is confirmed by Moses' prayer in 34:9, in which he asks for YHWH's presence in the midst of the people and that Israel once again become his "possession," which clearly echo the earlier covenant promises (cf. Exod. 19:5 f.). What makes this aspect so striking, however, is that, unlike the theme of the private theophany, the reestablishment of the covenant is not consonant with the reality of Israel's "stiff-neck." This is indicated by the adversative relationship which exists between the granting of the

---

[87] "Crisis and Promise," p. 48. See Davis, "Rebellion," p. 79, who suggests therefore that the theme of Moses' intercession forms a central unifying thread within Exod. 32–34. See too now Bori, *Golden Calf*, p. 90, who observes that the "essence of the history" is "the overturning of the catastrophe with the renewal of the covenant and the return of Moses to his glorious role," although as we have seen, Moses' role is now actually substantially altered over against his original function!

[88] So too, among many, Childs, *Exodus*, p. 597, and Moberly, *Mountain of God*, p. 84.

[89] I owe this insight to Brichto, "Golden Calf," p. 30. For the significance of the theme of the tablets of stone (cf. 31:18; 32:15–19; 34:1–4, 27 f.) for Paul's argument in 2 Cor. 3:3, 6–7, see chapters two and four.

Law and the people's rebellious nature (cf. כִּי in 34:9b).[90] The Law is now being given to Israel *in spite of* her obstinate condition. But again, this serves to highlight Moses' role as the one who now stands between the people and YHWH. The covenant will be restored, but Israel's nature demands that the restoration now take place under Moses' auspices as mediator. Childs is therefore right when he emphasizes that

"... the covenant pattern which emerges in Exod 34 is distinct from that found in chs. 19–24 and appears to reflect a different form of the Mosaic office ... Whereas in chs. 19–24 Moses acts as covenant mediator who seals the covenant between God and the people in a ritual of ratification, in ch. 34 God makes his covenant alone with Moses without any covenant ceremony. Moreover, it is indicative that the chapter concludes with the tradition of Moses' ongoing function of communicating to the people God's will (34:29–34; cf. 33:7 ff.)." [91]

For as the key to the meaning of the reestablishment of the covenant, Exod. 34:9 makes it clear that, as far as Israel is concerned, nothing has changed. Moses alone must experience the theophany and receive the Law both *because of* and *in spite of* Israel's sinful state, the former as an act of divine judgment, the latter of divine mercy. God's presence among Israel will be restored, but as an expression of YHWH's grace *and* righteous judgment it must remain a *mediated* presence.

This same dual nature of YHWH's renewed relationship with Israel, which is presented implicitly by the development of the narrative (cf. 32:30–35; 33:1–6, 7–11), is now made explicit by YHWH's proclamation in 34:6–7. As his dealings with Israel after the golden calf illustrate, God is both compassionate and patient with his people, yet he will not compromise his own righteousness by disregarding their sin. Moreover, the renewal of the covenant demonstrates that it is YHWH's mercy which prevails over judgment when it encounters those who have "found favor in his sight" (cf. again 34:9). Indeed, YHWH's mercy cannot be compared to his judgment in terms of its scope and impact, as the comparison between the "thousands" and the "third and fourth generation" in 34:7 illustrates.[92] This may explain why YHWH's compassion is mentioned first in 34:6 f., in contrast to the parallel passage in Exod. 20:5 f. where God's jealousy and judgment are given pride of place. In any case, the

---

[90] See too Moberly, *Mountain of God*, pp. 89 f., who interprets כִּי in 34:9 as an "emphatic concessive," although it is not clear why he then equates this with a causative function over against a concessive one; concessive and "emphatic concessive" should together be distinguished from a causative force. For this same divine expression of mercy in spite of the continuing rebellious nature of mankind, cf. Gen. 6:5; 8:21, and Moberly's insightful discussion of the parallels between Exod. 32–34 and the flood narratives, especially in regard to the parallel roles of Noah and Moses (pp. 91–93).

[91] *Exodus*, p. 607.

[92] For this point and an insightful analysis of 34:6–7, see J. Scharbert, "Formgeschichte und Exegese von Exod 34:6 f. und seiner Parallelen," *Biblica* 38 (1957) 130–150, esp. pp. 140–144.

text is clear that the second giving of the Law can only take place because in his sovereign freedom YHWH has deemed it glorious to bestow his mercy on Israel as an expression of his character (cf. 33:19). For Israel's continued existence under the covenant and her enjoyment of his mediated presence can only take place as a result of his forgiveness (34:9). God thus reveals his glory not only in the theophany proper, but also in the very act of renewing the covenant. This becomes even more evident in the nature of the covenant stipulations now given.

c) Exodus 34:10–28: The "Cultic Commands"

As 34:1 declares by way of introduction and 34:27 f. repeats in conclusion, the stipulations recorded in 34:10–26 are part of a second giving of the Law which is identical with the first. Moreover, the same indicative/imperative relationship which forms the heart of the Sinai covenant in the transition from Exod. 20:2 to 20:3 ff. is now repeated in the movement from 34:10 f. to 34:12–26. But whereas the former declaration of God's salvation focused on Israel's deliverance from Egypt, the present indicatives describe Israel's future deliverance in the promised land. This change reflects the fact that the restoration of the covenant is now taking place after the breaking of the former covenant with its previous basis in YHWH's acts in Egypt. The new beginning stated in 34:10a is given a new foundation as a sign of YHWH's continuing commitment to save his people, despite their sin.

The same tension between YHWH's mercy and judgment, which has been a unifying thread throughout the text (cf. 32:30–35; 33:1–6, 7–11; 34:9), is again present, however, at this point in the narrative. On the one hand, God's judgment is evident in the description in 34:10a of Israel as "Moses' people" rather than YHWH's. On the other hand, as Horn has observed, the order of the laws in 34:10 ff. is the reverse of that found in the parallel passage in Exod. 23:10 ff. Whereas in Exod. 23 the laws concerning the feasts precede the promise of the land, now the promise of the land (34:10–17) is given before the laws concerning the festivals (34:18–26).[93] This reversal serves to highlight that the reestablishment of the covenant is solely a result of God's grace. The covenant announced in 34:10a has the same structure and content as the covenant earlier established at Mt. Sinai, but the priority of the divine deliverance and promise is emphasized even more than before.

The reader is certainly surprised, therefore, when it immediately becomes clear that the laws which follow are not a repetition of the "ten words" written on the first set of tablets! Ever since the work of Goethe,[94] modern scholars

---

[93] P.H. Horn, "Traditionsschichten in Ex 23:10–33 und Ex 34:10–26," *BZ N.F.* 15 (1971) 203–222, pp. 209, 220.

[94] See his 1773 essay, "Zwo wichtige bisher unerörterte biblische Fragen, zum erstenmal gründlich beantwortet, von einem Landgeistlichen in Schwaben," *Goethes Sämtliche Werke*

have tried to reconcile this fact by suggesting that the stipulations in 34:12–26 are a "cultic decalogue," in contrast to the ethical commands of the former "tablets of the testimony" (31:18).[95] The tablets referred to in 34:1, 27 f. are then said to contain not the "Ten Commandments" of Exod. 20:3–17, but the laws of chapter 34. Within the present context, however, the explicit identification of the content of the present tablets with the original "words" of the covenant Law in 34:1, 28 will not allow such an interpretation. Moreover, although the content of the commands in 34:12 ff. is certainly cultic, the attempts to discover some sort of decalogue pattern within these laws have repeatedly failed.[96] Finally, the commands themselves are for the most part not new, but find parallels in earlier injunctions.[97] In fact, Moberly has observed that all of the commands derive logically from the first two commandments of the Decalogue.[98] There is no evidence then that Exod. 34:10–26 is meant to be

---

36: Schriften zur Literatur 1, 1902, pp. 95–105. Goethe's point was that the Ten Commandments were not written on the tablets of the covenant with Israel, but rather the cultic commands of Exod. 34:17 ff., as a demonstration of the particularistic nature of Israel's religion over against the universal relevance of the moral commands found in Exod. 20 (cf. pp. 98, 101). Goethe's goal in drawing this (faulty) conclusion concerning the nature of Israel's religion was not to criticize Israel or Judaism *per se*, but to offer a critique of contemporary church regulations as equally particularistic! For an analysis of Goethe's work, see Kurt Galling, "Goethe als theologischer Schriftsteller," *EvTh* 8 (1948/49) 529–545.

[95] Goethe's observation was introduced into modern scholarship by Wellhausen's, *Die Composition des Hexateuchs und der historischen Bücher des Alten Testaments*, 1889[2], 1899[3], pp. 84, 330–334, in which he assigned the "cultic" decalogue of Exod 34:11–26 to "J" as the earliest tradition, in contrast to the "ethical" decalogue in Exod. 20:1–17, which he attributed to "E". Since that time, 23 different source analyses of Exod. 34:10 ff. in relationship to Exod. 20 ff. have been offered! For a detailed survey see Franz Elmer Wilms, *Das Jahwistische Bundesbuch in Ex 34*, SANT 32, 1973, pp. 15–135. For the scholarly consensus that Goethe was right in making a distinction between the ethical and cultic commandments as part of two different covenant traditions (though not his view that there was originally only one set of tablets containing the cultic decalogue), see O. Eissfeldt, "Goethes Beurteilung des kultischen Dekalogs von Ex 34 im Lichte der Pentateuchkritik," now in his *Kleine Schriften, IV*, 1968, pp. 221–230.

[96] For this point, see already A. Eberharter, "Besitzen wir in Ex 23 und 34 zwei Rezensionen eines zweiten Dekalogs und in welchem Verhältnis stehen sie zueinander?" *BZ* 20 (1932) 157–162, esp. p. 161. For an analysis of Exod. 34:14 ff. as an ancient feast calender (vv. 18–24) with an appendix of four commands concerning Passover (vv. 25–26), i.e. as a series of cultic commands, see H. Kosmala, "The So-Called Ritual Decalogue," *Annual of the Swedish Theological Institute* 1 (1962) 31–61, esp. pp. 39–44, 56.

[97] All but two or three of the commands, 34:14 (cf. Exod. 20:3), 34:17 (cf. Exod. 20:4, 23), and 34:19 f. (cf. Exod. 13:13 f.), are found in Exod. 23:12–33; for the possible parallels see Brichto, "Golden Calf," pp. 32–35, and P.H. Horn, "Traditionsschichten," pp. 210–220. Childs, *Exodus*, pp. 607 f., observes that Exod. 34 picks up both the decalogue and the "Book of the Covenant" as the two collections of Law upon which the covenant was to be renewed. Similarly, M.H. Segal, *The Pentateuch. Its Composition and Its Authorship and other Biblical Studies*, 1967, p. 42, sees 34:10–26 as based on the threefold legislation of the Sinai covenant, with extracts chosen "because of their appropriateness to the condition of Israel after the sin of the golden calf, and with some important additions also occasioned by the sin."

[98] *Mountain of God*, p. 96.

read as an alteration of the original Sinai covenant. Hence, in 34:27 Moses is instructed to write down "these words," which is a clear reference to the preceding commandments, in *contrast* to v. 28, in which YHWH inscribes the tablets of stone with the "Ten Words" in fulfillment of 34:1. The two bodies of covenantal law are thus also distinguished within Exodus 34:1–28 itself.[99]

But why then the emphasis on these particular cultic laws in chapter 34:10 ff. instead of the commands of Exod. 20:3 ff.? Again, Moberly's answer to this question is particularly insightful. As he has pointed out, within their present context the point of the laws in chapter 34 is not to renew the covenant on conditions different from Exod. 20–24. Rather, the intention is "to select and emphasize those particular aspects which are relevant to the sinful tendencies which Israel has displayed."[100] This explains their specifically cultic character. In Moberly's words,

"The first two commandments are cultic commandments and Israel's sin with the calf was a cultic sin. As Yahweh renews the covenant he does so by demanding obedience in the area where Israel has already failed and where it will be under continual temptation in the promised land to sin again."[101]

Here too, therefore, the narrative is built squarely upon the theological problem of the relationship between a holy God and his sinful people. Hence, if the covenant is to be renewed, it must be established with specific consideration for the weakness of Israel. Israel is thereby warned of the indispensable and essential requirement of faithfulness to YHWH in the future.

Exodus 34:1–28 thus leaves no doubt that the covenant relationship between YHWH and his people has been restored. But there can also be no doubt that the context of the relationship between YHWH and his people within which the covenant now exists has been significantly altered. The idolatry with the golden calf has not only revealed the hardened condition of Israel, but also brought about serious consequences for the ongoing nature of the Sinai covenant. This becomes clear yet again in the conclusion of the second giving of the Law within Moses' private theophany in 34:27. The covenant is reestablished, but a distinction is now explicitly made between Moses and the people. Unlike the prior establishment of the covenant, the renewed covenant is not made solely or directly with the people (cf. Exod. 19:8; 20:22; 24:3, 7 f.). Instead, God declares that he has made the covenant "with Moses and with Israel," that is, directly with Moses on the mountain, and *through* Moses with the

---

[99] On the distinct referents of vv. 27 and 28, see Moberly, *Mountain of God*, pp. 101–105. This interpretation of 34:27 f. is also reflected in *Tg. Ps.-Jon.* 34:27–28, in which, in contrast to the writing of the commands from vv. 10–28 referred to in v. 27, it is said in v. 28 that Moses "wrote upon the *other* tables the words of the covenant, the Ten Words which had been written upon the former tables;" translation, J.W. Etheridge, *The Targums of Onkelos and Jonathan ben Uzziel on the Pentateuch*, Vol. 1, 1968, p. 561.

[100] *Mountain of God*, p. 96. See too, Davis, "Rebellion," pp. 82 f.

[101] *Mountain of God*, p. 96. For this same point, see Childs, *Exodus*, p. 615, and Cassuto, *Exodus*, p. 443.

people. "So," to quote Moberly once more, "the position of Israel in the restored covenant is not identical to what it would have been had the people never sinned. Henceforth their life as a people depends not only upon the mercy of God but also upon the intercession of God's chosen mediator."[102] Indeed, Moberly is correct in asserting that "the renewed covenant (is) not only mediated through, but in some sense necessarily dependent upon, Moses."[103] This becomes the main point of the climax of the narrative in 34:29–35.

d) Exodus 34:29–35: The Veil of Moses

The turning point of the narrative, which was reached with the granting of Moses' petition in 33:19–23, finds its fulfillment in Moses' descent from the mountain. As 34:29 makes clear, Moses returns as the "answer to his own prayers" in that he not only brings the reestablishment of the covenant, but also unknowingly becomes the *means* of its continuation.[104] The former is stressed by the emphasis on Moses as the one who brings the two tablets with him "in his hand" (בְּיַד־מֹשֶׁה, v. 29a), an allusion to the fact that Moses was the one who earlier broke the tablets by throwing them "from his hand" (מִיָּדוֹ, 32:19). The one who mediated the breaking of the covenant is the one who mediates its restoration. The latter, and now more important theme, is expressed in the reference to Moses not knowing that his face was "shining" (קָרַן) because he had been speaking with YHWH (34:29b). The translation of קָרַן is a matter of much debate. But regardless of its etymology or use elsewhere, the present context, with its emphasis on Moses' role as the mediator of YHWH's presence among the people and on their response, together with the explicit reference to the "skin of (Moses') face" (עוֹר פָּנָיו) as its subject, require that it be rendered "shine."[105] The point of 34:29 is thus made by way

---

[102] *Mountain of God*, p. 106.

[103] *Mountain of God*, p. 105.

[104] Brichto, "Golden Calf," p. 36, suggests that the role of Moses as the one who will mediate God's presence in the midst of the people is already expressed in 34:10 with YHWH's statement that he will perform his wonders for the people "in whose midst Moses is." Brichto interprets this to mean that YHWH will be present in Moses "and will thereby be present in the midst of the people." But Brichto's further attempt to identify Moses with the angel promised in Exod. 23:20–24 remains unconvincing.

[105] So too Moberly, *Mountain of God*, p. 107; Childs, *Exodus*, p. 609. The attempt to render it as a reference to "having horns" (of a priestly mask) is based on the verbal form מַקְרִן in Ps. 69:32 and the corresponding noun form throughout the OT. For an insightful study of the issue in support of the position taken here, see Karl Jaros, "Des Mose 'Strahlende Haut': Eine Notiz zu Ex 34:29; 30:35," *ZAW* 88 (1976) 275–280, and Menahem Haran, "The Shining of Moses' Face: A Case Study in Biblical and Ancient Near Eastern Iconography," in *In the Shelter of Elyon, Essays on Ancient Palestinian Life and Literature, FS G.W. Ahlström*, JSOT Supplement Series 31, ed. W. Boyd Barrick and John R. Spencer, 1984, pp. 159–173, pp. 159 f., 163–165; for the opposing view, see esp. Anton Jirku, "Die Gesichtsmaske des Mose," in his *Von Jerusalem nach Ugarit, Gesammelte Schriften*, 1966, pp. 347–349. The article by William H. Propp, "The Skin of Moses' Face – Transfigured or

of contrast. Never before, although Moses had been in the presence of God on several occasions, did his face shine as a result. Now, however, as a consequence of the unique experience of God's glory in 34:1–9, Moses bears the glory of God with him back into the camp. This is the means by which YHWH will place his presence in the midst of his people. Moses becomes not only the mediator of the covenant Law, but also of God's covenantal presence.[106]

The fact that Moses mediates the very glory of God itself in the midst of the people becomes the key, therefore, to explaining both the reason for the people's fear in 34:30 and the purpose of the veil in 34:33–35. At the first theophany and giving of the Law in Exod. 19:16–20:18a the people also responded with fear at seeing the revelation of YHWH on the mountain (cf. 20:18b–21). But this fear is interpreted *positively* as the sanctifying means employed by YHWH to keep the people from sinning (20:20).[107] Greenberg has shown that, according to Exod. 20:20, the purpose of the original Sinai revelation was not only to legitimize Moses' authority (cf. Exod. 19:9), but to accomplish this sanctifying purpose by giving Israel a "direct palpable experience of God."[108] Moses thus commands the people not to be afraid because of

---

Disfigured?" *CBQ* 49 (1987) 375–386, pp. 375–383, provides an extensive bibliography of sources and literature from antiquity to the present and a helpful analysis of the Hebrew text and its reception in the LXX and other early Jewish literature. Propp's own thesis is that Exod. 34:29 should be translated "the skin of his face was burnt to the hardness of horn" (p. 386), so that the text refers to an injury or disfigurement suffered by Moses (i.e. "some kind of light or heat burn," p. 385). For Propp, the Israelites fled from Moses because of his disfigured face, while the veil functioned "to spare the people the gruesome sight" (following B.D. Eerdmans, p. 384). Moreover, according to Propp, Moses' glimpse of YHWH's back not only disfigured him by hardening his skin, but also rendered him "invulnerable to divine radiance" (p. 386). Moses can therefore take the veil off in YHWH's presence to "renew ... his immunity" (p. 386). Hence, Exod. 34:29 ff. "has no ritual significance," rather, "the story honors Moses as the human most intimate with Yahweh, but it also specifies the price he paid" (p. 386). But just as Propp accuses those who advocate that Moses was wearing a horned ritual mask with a "disregard for the present form of the biblical text" that "diminishes the plausibility" of their theory (p. 383), so may it be said of Propp's own suggestion. For in addition to the fact that there is no direct evidence of קרן being used metaphorically of a skin disease, Propp's view fails to do justice to the cultic role of Moses in the larger context of Exod. 32–34, where in addition to Moses' role as mediator of God's presence in 34:29 ff., the narrative stresses in 33:18–23 that YHWH hid Moses to protect him, not to disfigure him. And, as we shall see, Israel's fear in 34:29 ff. is to be understood not as a response to Moses himself, but against the backdrop of 33:3,5.

[106] Contra Coats, "Loyal Opposition," p. 105, who interprets the glory on Moses' face as a symbolic expression of the authority of Moses. Although Moses' speaking with the glory of God on his face certainly substantiates his authority, against the backdrop of the problem of God's presence in 33:1 ff., this is a secondary motif.

[107] So too Childs, *Exodus*, on Exod. 20:18–21.

[108] Moshe Greenberg, "נסה in Exodus 20:20 and the Purpose of the Sinaitic Theophany," *JBL* 79 (1960) 273–276, p. 275. His argument is based on the structural parallels between Exod. 20:20 and Deut. 4:10 and 5:29 and the use of נסה elsewhere to mean "to have/cause to have an experience" (cf. 1 Sam. 17:39; Deut. 28:56; 2 Chron. 32:31; Jud. 3:1–3). Israel is thus not being "tested" at Mt. Sinai, but being brought into the presence of God (p. 276).

God's terrifying presence, but to accept it as part of the ratification of the covenant itself (20:22; cf. Exod. 24:9–11). Hence, the people are encouraged to remain as close as possible to the theophany and to hear YHWH's voice directly as an integral part of their new covenant relationship with him (20:22). In stark contrast, the people's fear in response to Moses' shining face in 34:30 ff. must be interpreted against the backdrop of YHWH's earlier statements concerning the impact of his presence after their idolatry with the golden calf. Rather than sanctification, God's presence in the midst of his people will now mean judgment for the people (cf. 33:3, 5). The people's response in 34:30 testifies to their altered relationship to YHWH. YHWH now comes to the people mediated through Moses, but even this is still too much for them to bear in their hardened condition.

Moses therefore responds with an act of grace in compensation for the people's sinful nature. He first calls the leaders (34:31a) and then the people (34:32a) to him in order to deliver YHWH's covenant commands to them. In this way, the legitimacy of the message and the authority of the messenger are again authenticated through a "tangible confirmation of the fact that it is God's word that is being spoken to them when they see the light radiating from Moses' face"[109] (cf. 34:31 f. with Exod. 19:9). But after speaking the words of YHWH to the people, Moses veils himself. *Against the backdrop of the explicit statements of Exod. 32:9, 22 and 33:3, 5 and the function of the tent of meeting in 33:7–11, Moses' veiling himself should be seen as an act of mercy to keep the people from being destroyed by the reflected presence of God.*[110] The veil of Moses makes it possible for the glory of God to be in the midst of the people, albeit now mediated through Moses, without destroying them. As such, the veil (מסוה) functions in the same way as the fence around the bottom of Mt. Sinai in Exod. 19:12 and the curtain (פרכת) before the "holy of holies" in the tabernacle as that which both separates and protects the people from the glory of God.[111] The veil does not represent YHWH, but in-

---

Even if Childs, *Exodus*, p. 344 n. 20, is correct that this factitive use of the verb has not been demonstrated, Greenberg's basic view of v. 20 seems to hold inasmuch as the giving of the Law and the theophany, by "testing" Israel, would lead to their obedience. Childs is thus right in emphasizing that there is no need to separate the giving of the Law from the theophany, as Greenberg seems to do (p. 372).

[109] M. Haran, "The Shining of Moses," p. 162. Haran is correct in emphasizing that it is not the veil *per se* which is the main point of the text, but that the glory of God can once again be seen. Coats, *Moses*, p. 131, misses this point when he suggests that the veil itself functions, like Moses' rod, as "a visible and concrete symbol of Mosaic authority derived from his intimacy with God" (cf. too pp. 138, 190). It is the shining, not the veil, which results from Moses' experience of the theophany. The veil results from Israel's hardened condition.

[110] Thus, though Moberly, *Mountain of God*, p. 108, is correct that "no reason is given" for the purpose of the veil in the text, the context indicates its function clearly enough that we need not "but speculate" concerning its function.

[111] For the veil which hung before the ark of the testimony and the mercy seat within the holy of holies, cf. Exod. 26:31–34; 27:21; 30:6; 35:12; 40:3, 21 f., 26; Lev. 4:6, 17; 16:12, 15; 21:23; 24:3; Num. 4:5, and esp. Lev. 16:2, 13 and Num. 18:7 for the warning of death for

stead keeps the people from being directly encountered by him.[112] In view of the people's "stiff-neck" and idolatry with the golden calf, Moses' veil is the final expression of YHWH's judgment and mercy, which runs throughout this narrative and ties it together theológically. The fact that the glory must be veiled is an expression of Israel's sinful state and God's consequent judgment; the fact that the glory *is* veiled is an expression of God's unexpected mercy.

Once again, however, it is YHWH's mercy which is predominant, since the veil makes possible what could not happen otherwise, namely, the presence of God dwelling in the midst of his people. The veil of Moses is thus the theological corollary to the sinful nature of Israel and the demonstration of the character of YHWH as declared in 34:6 f. Moreover, the switch to the frequentative nature of the action regarding the veil in 34:34 f. indicates that its protective function continued from this point on as the people progressed in their wilderness wanderings. Moses does not veil himself to make up for some deficiency in the glory or in himself,[113] nor as an expression of his humility and modesty,[114] nor to keep the glory of God from being wasted,[115] nor even to keep it from being profaned.[116] Rather, the veil makes it possible to bring the glory of God into the midst of the rebellious people. From the perspective of the narrative, the eventual filling of the tabernacle with the glory of God in Exod. 40:34, behind the curtain (!), is seen as the logical extension and fulfillment of Moses' experience in the tent of meeting and of his role as mediator between YHWH and Israel.[117] But as long as he lives, Moses remains the one

---

those who inappropriately violate the veil. Cf. 2 Sam. 6:6 f.par.1 Chron. 13:9 f. for an illustration of this principle and 1 Sam. 4:21 f. for the parallel between the ark and the glory of God. For the idea of the presence of God behind the veil, cf. Exod. 25:22; 30:6; Num. 7:89.

[112] For the view of the veil as a priestly mask, see e.g. Noth, *Exodus*, p. 220, and Clements, *Exodus*, p. 225. As is often pointed out, the key contextual criticism of the attempt to understand the veil as part of a priestly mask intended to reveal YHWH is that Moses wears the veil precisely when he is *not* speaking on behalf of YHWH; see e.g. Childs, *Exodus*, p. 609, and already, J. Morgenstern, "Moses with the Shining Face," *HUCA* 2 (1925) 1–27, pp. 4 f. Morgenstern also argues that Moses is here seen as "Jahwe's substitute on earth," (p. 5), but fails to see the link between the people's fear and their prior sin, suggesting rather that they were afraid because of the intensity of the brilliance (p. 11). For the other contextual arguments against the idea of Moses wearing a priestly mask with horns, see F. Dumermuth, "Moses strahlendes Gesicht," *TZ* 17 (1961) 241–248, p. 243, and Cassuto, *Exodus*, p. 449.

[113] Contra Brichto, "Golden Calf," p. 37. There is no indication that the veil exists to hide the fact that the glory was fading or to compensate for Moses' own human "concerns and aspirations." On the permanent nature of the glory on Moses' face, see Morgenstern, "Moses with the Shining Face," pp. 4 f.

[114] Contra Cassuto, *Exodus*, p. 450.

[115] Contra Haran, "The Shining of Moses' Face," p. 162.

[116] Contra O. Eissfeldt, "Das Gesetz ist zwischeneingekommen. Ein Beitrag zur Analyse der Sinai-Erzählung Ex 19–34," now in his *Kleine Schriften IV*, 1968, pp. 209–214, p. 210.

[117] The historical relationship between the tent of meeting and the tabernacle is a matter of much dispute; but for their identification in the final redaction of the text, see M. Haran, *Temple and Temple Service*, pp. 271 f. In support of this he points to Exod. 38:21; Num. 1:50, 53; 9:15; 10:11; 17:23; 18:2; and esp. Exod. 39:32, 40; 40:2, 6, 29.

who mediates God's presence in the midst of his people and who, not only as an act of divine judgment, but even more so of divine mercy, veils himself in their midst. The restoration of the covenant in Exod. 32–34 finds its climax, possibility, and means of fulfillment in Moses as the mediator of both the Law and the glory of God. It is not saying too much, therefore, to conclude with Wilms, that the theology of the "Mittleramt" of Moses determines the main points of chapter 34,[118] and, as our own study has shown, of chapters 32–33 as well.

5. The Theological Significance of Exodus 32–34

As we have seen, Moses' role as mediator provides the structural framework of Exodus 32–34 not only in terms of its plot, but also in terms of its theological significance. The central role of Moses is clear throughout the narrative as the only active counterpart to YHWH. No one besides Moses is ever directly addressed or directly addresses YHWH in these chapters. In terms of the events themselves, Moses too is the decisive figure from beginning to end. Israel's sin with the golden calf involves the desire to have a substitute for Moses as the representative of God's presence (32:1–6). Moses is the one who receives the message of the judgment of God against Israel and the invitation to intercede on Israel's behalf (32:7–10). It is again Moses who then executes this divine judgment in 32:21–33 and instigates the bestowal of divine mercy through his series of three intercessions (32:11–14, 31–34; 33:12–23). Moses is the one who is given audiences with YHWH (32:7–14, 31–34; 33:12–23; 34:1–28), receives divine revelation in the tent of meeting (33:7–11), and experiences the theophany of God's presence (34:5–8). As a result, Moses becomes the answer to his own prayers and is left alone as the sole and central character in the closing, climactic scene of the narrative (34:29–35). For this reason, Israel's position as God's covenant people (33:17) and the renewal of the covenant itself (34:27) are both dependent upon and mediated through him. Theologically, Exod. 32–34 can thus be seen as the crowning affirmation of Moses' authority and intermediary role as pictured in Exod. 19:9 and 20:19 and developed throughout the Pentateuch.[119]

But equally significant is the fact that this affirmation takes place after Israel's sin with the golden calf. Moses' activities before YHWH, as the one who has "found favor in YHWH's eyes" (33:12, 16 f.; 34:9), find their antithesis in the actions of the people. What is most striking at this point is the way in which the narrative moves from the description of what Israel has done in

---

[118] *Das Jahwistische Bundesbuch*, p. 183.

[119] On this point, see now Coats, *Moses*, p. 135: "Both the heroic man with his own personal authority calling for belief of the people in him and the mediator for God with the authority of God to call for obedience from the people to God constitute the shape of the Moses image in the Pentateuch."

32:1–6, to her sinful, "stiff-necked" *condition* in 32:9, 22; 33:3, 5; 34:9. What becomes clear as the narrative develops, therefore, is that the problem with the people, even after the establishment of the Sinai covenant, is that they cannot keep the covenant despite their original declaration of willingness to do so (cf. Exod. 19:8; 24:3). The problem with Israel is not their occasional disobedience, but their moral turpitude.[120] The gross idolatry with the golden calf serves primarily to reveal this fact.

a) The Problem of God's Presence

The antithetical roles played by Moses and Israel in Exod. 32–34 and their interrelationship demonstrate that the fundamental theological problem throughout the narrative is the possibility of God's presence abiding in the midst of a people who do not merely sin, but are by nature sinful. It has long been recognized that the theme of the divine presence is central to chapter 33, which provides the most extended treatment of this issue in the Old Testament.[121] But already in 32:9 f. YHWH declares that due to their "stiff-necks" he will destroy Israel. Moreover, the transition from 32:14 to 32:15–20 makes clear that the covenant has been broken, even though Moses' first intercession has secured the promise that the people as a whole will not be physically destroyed. The original intent of the Sinai covenant, that God would dwell in the midst of his people (Exod. 19:5 f.; 24:9 f.; 25:8; 29:45 f.; cf. Lev. 26:9, 11–13),[122] is thus already shown to be aborted before the tablets of testimony to the covenant can be delivered. From now on, the unmediated presence of God will mean only judgment. When YHWH comes to "visit," his "visit" will no longer be to bless (cf. Exod. 3:16; 4:31; 13:19), but to judge Israel (32:34; cf. 33:3, 5).[123] The theological tension within the text consequently becomes how God's presence can continue in Israel's midst without destroying the nation.

The solution to the theological problem posed by the text corresponds to the structure of the plot itself. Just as Moses is the one around whom the plot revolves, so too Moses himself becomes the final resolution of the tension within the narrative. Moses not only brings about the renewal of the covenant through his intercessions, but also becomes the mediator of God's presence in fulfillment of the covenant promises. As this solution itself indicates, Israel's position before YHWH after the renewal of the covenant in 34:1 ff. is not identical with what it was prior to the golden calf. From now on, Israel's experience of God's presence and mercy must be mediated through Moses on their behalf (33:7–11, 17; 34:34 f.).[124]

---

[120] See too Moberly, *Mountain of God*, pp. 67, 73.

[121] See Brueggemann, "Crisis and Promise," p. 48.

[122] This point has been developed at length by Cross, *Canaanite Myth and Hebrew Epic*, pp. 295–298, 313 f., 318 f., 323, and Clements, *God and Temple*, pp. 113–117.

[123] For this word play on פקד in 32:34, see Moberly, *Mountain of God*, p. 58.

This is the key to understanding the theological significance of the veil. The Israelites must be veiled from God's presence because of their sinful state (34:33–35). Due to her "stiff-neck," Israel cannot bear the radiance of God's glory (cf. 32: 9, 22; 33:3, 5 with 34:30).[125] Whereas Moses experiences protection from God's direct presence as an act of mercy in response to the favor he has found before YHWH, Israel is kept from continually seeing the glory of God as an act of both mercy and judgment in response to her sinful nature.[126] The problem of God's presence is finally solved, however, as a result of the fact that God's mercy overshadows his judgment. The answer to the problem of God's presence in the midst of a sinful people is Moses as the mediator of the will and splendor of God in anticipation of the establishment of the tabernacle. This is reflected in Exod. 39:33–43 when the articles for the tabernacle are first presented to Moses, who then inspects them and blesses the people prior to its establishment (39:42–43).[127]

b) The "Fall of Israel"

The themes of sin, judgment, and restoration thus provide the theological structure for the narrative in Exod. 32–34 as a whole, and for its climax in Exod. 34:29–35 in particular. But since Israel's sin with the golden calf be-

---

[124] So too Moberly, *Mountain of God*, pp. 75, 106.

[125] Dumbrell, "Paul's Use of Exodus 34," p. 181, is therefore right in emphasizing that the usual assumption that the purpose of the veil was simply "to allay Israelite fears, overawed as they are by the shining face of Moses ... finds no basis in the account." The key is to see that their fear was a reflection of their hardened sinful nature on the one hand, and that the shining of Moses' face was, in Dumbrell's words, "a communicated theophany" (p. 181) on the other hand.

[126] Contra Dumbrell, "Paul's Use of Exodus 34," who, in effect, draws a contrast between these two functions by concluding that "the shining face was primarily a sign more than it was a threat," pointing to the fact that Moses does speak to Israel with an unveiled face (p. 181). But the repeated need for the veil itself, within the narrative logic of Exod. 32–34, demonstrates that the veil is both a sign *and* a threat, and that what is threatening is, in fact, the presence of God. Dumbrell's argument that the veil is put on by Moses only when he is not in the divine presence or when he is *not* communicating with Israel draws an artificial distinction between Moses as covenant mediator immediately after his emergence from the tent of meeting and his subsequent teaching and leading among the people. Dumbrell is correct, however, that Moses' practice of keeping his face unveiled immediately after being in the presence of God does authenticate his message (cf. p. 181). He thus rightly concludes that "Israel's consequent inability to understand and thus to participate fully in covenant blessings, though addressed by Moses and his successors, is underscored by the veiled face of Moses after they had been addressed. Additionally, the veil was a reminder of the real character of the national relationship and it underscores the dangers now inherent for Israel in the covenant relationship. In short Exod. 34:29–35 confirms our suspicions that the implementation of the Sinai covenant for *national* Israel had never been a possibility" (p. 185).

[127] For this point and the chiastic relationship between Exod. 25–31 and 35–40, as well as the loss of the structural role of the creation motifs in chs. 35–40, facts which can only be explained by the influence of chapters 32–34, see Peter J. Kearney, "Creation and Liturgy: The P Redaction of Ex 25–40," *ZAW* 89 (1977) 375–387, esp. pp. 380 f.

comes a window to the sinful state of the people, the restoration of the covenant includes an emphasis on the implications of the fact that the Sinai covenant has not brought about the alteration of Israel's disposition toward her Lord.[128] Moses' final descent from Mt. Sinai makes clear that the covenant is indeed restored in Exod. 34, but not without serious regard for the ongoing problem of Israel's sinfulness. Although the implications that Ferdinand Weber drew from this for his understanding of the nature of Judaism *per se* must be rejected, his observation in 1880 that Israel's idolatry with the golden calf functions within the Exodus narrative as the "fall" (or in Moberly's words, "first sin"[129]) after the "creation" of the people at Sinai is therefore correct.[130]

---

[128] Cf. Brueggemann, "Crisis and Promise," p. 48: "There is not fidelity even at the mountain. And therefore there is not unmitigated well-being in the covenant from the first moment."

[129] Moberly, *Mountain of God*, p. 84.

[130] For Weber's view of the golden calf and his use of it to support an idea of Judaism as legalistic works-righteousness, see his *Jüdische Theologie auf Grund des Talmud und verwandter Schriften, System der altsynagogalen palästinischen Theologie aus Targum, Midrasch und Talmud*, 1897², pp. 274–277, and its recapitulation in E.P. Sanders, *Paul and Palestinian Judaism, A Comparison of Patterns of Religion*, 1977, pp. 36–39. For Sanders' critique of this view, see above, Introduction. Though his critique of Weber's view of Judaism is well taken in part, Sanders, p. 38, wrongly rejects the interpretation of Exod. 32:1–6 as a "fall." Moreover, Weber himself, *like* Sanders, also emphasized that in rabbinic literature repentance was always to be combined with the doing of the Law in view of one's continual transgression of its commandments. In his words, "Der Mensch sollte durch Buße und Gesetz zur Gemeinschaft mit Gott zurückkehren können" (p. 259; cf. too pp. 276 f.). The problem with Weber's view of Exod. 32 is not his understanding of the golden calf, but his view of the Law as demanding absolute and unattainable perfection and his failure to take into consideration the restoration of the covenant in ch. 34. On the parallel to the blessing of creation (Gen. 1:22, 28), pointing to its fulfillment in the promise of the land (Exod. 3:8; 23:23–33; Lev. 26:9; cf. Ezek. 36:11 f.; Jer. 3:16; 23:3), and the link between the sabbath "hidden in creation" (Gen. 2:2 f.) and the sabbath as the sign of the Sinai covenant (Exod. 31:13–17), see again Cross, *Canaanite Myth and Hebrew Epic*, pp. 295–298. Cross points to the foreshadowing and progression from the blessings of creation, to the covenants with Noah and Abraham, to the Mosaic covenant as the culmination of God's revelation to his people: "On the one hand, each pointed forward as the genealogies and the scope of the recipients of the covenants funnelled down; on the other hand, in each the divine self-disclosure and promises expanded. While both the Noahic and Abrahamic covenants remained valid, each was provisional, a stage on the way to God's ultimate covenant and ultimate self-disclosure" (p. 297). On the links between the glory-cloud in the wilderness as the expression of God's presence and the Spirit of God in Gen. 1:2, see Meredith G. Kline, *Images of the Spirit*, 1986, pp. 13–34. For the parallels between the seven speeches of Exod. 25–31 (each introduced with "the Lord said to Moses ..." cf. Exod. 25:1; 30:11, 17, 22, 34; 31:1, 12) and the seven days of creation, so that the structure of Exod. 25–40 becomes "creation (25–31) – fall (32–33) – restoration (34–40)," see Kearney, "Creation and Liturgy," pp. 375–378, 382–384. This association of the golden calf with the fall of Adam is commonly recognized in rabbinic literature (though almost always with an apologetic defense of Israel's actions); cf. e.g. *b*.Sanh. 38b; 102a; *Mek. Bahodesh* 9; *Exod. Rab.* 21.1; 30.7; 32.1, 7, 11; 43.2; 45:2; 46:1; 47:72; *Lev. Rab.* 11.3; *Num. Rab.* 16.24; *Qoh. Rab.* 8.1.3; 9.11.1; *Lam. Rab.* 1.3.28; *Pesiq. Rab.* 14.10; *Pesiq. Kah.* 37a. Cf. too *Tg. Neofiti*, where the gravity of Israel's sin with the golden calf is highlighted by the consistent refusal to translate every

Like the original creation narrative, the re-creation of a people to enjoy God's presence at Sinai is followed by a "fall" which separates them from the glory of God. As such, like Adam and Eve, Israel's sin with the golden calf becomes

mention of Israel's reference to the calf as the "gods who shall go before us," as well as those references to the calf itself (cf. *Tg. Neof.* 32:1, 4, 8, 19 f., 23 f., 31, 35), thus treating the golden calf as one of those passages which is to be read but not translated (cf. *t.* Meg. 4:31, 36; *y.* Mig. 4:11, 75c; *m.* Meg. 4:10). For these texts and others, see too Callan, "Paul and the Golden Calf," pp. 5, 14 f., and esp. the listing by Samuel Vollenweider, *Freiheit als neue Schöpfung*, FRLANT 147, 1989, p. 258, with his emphasis on the fact that not only did the sin with the golden calf reproduce that of Adam, robbing Israel of her glory, but that this was shown in particular in Israel's relationship to Moses by his need to veil himself (p. 257). As Vollenweider, p. 257 n. 299, points out, this becomes explicit in the Samaritan *Memar Marqah* 5:4 (3/4th. cent.) where we read that Moses "was vested with the Form which Adam cast off in the Garden of Eden; and his face shone up to the day of his death" (quoted according to the edition of J. McDonald). It is beyond the scope of this study to trace the golden calf tradition in the wider rabbinic literature and early Christian apologists in which the conflict between the early Church and the synagogue over the continuing validity of the Sinai covenant and Israel's election as the people of God was often played out around the significance of the golden calf in Israel's history. For a helpful survey of this tradition, see L. Smolar and M. Aberbach, "The Golden Calf Episode in Post Biblical Literature," *HUCA* 39 (1968) 91–116, and the literature they cite, esp. the studies of M. Simon and Marmorstein. As their study demonstrates, on the one hand the early Church drew the extreme conclusion that the sin with the golden calf abrogated Israel's place altogether as God's people, so that she was eventually replaced by the Church and left with only an invalid (and for some a punitive!) ceremonial law (cf. e.g., Epistle of Barnabas 14; Justin, *Dial.* 20:3; 21:1; 22:1; Irenaeus, *Against Heresies* IV.3; Tertullian, *On Fasting* 6; *On Patience* 5; *Against Marcion* II.18; *Comment. on Romans* 2:14; cf. too Tertullian, *Against the Jews* 1; Origen, *Contra Celsum* II.74). On the other hand, rabbinic literature offered a defense of Israel's continuing status as God's people by minimizing or even denying Israel's and/or Aaron's guilt with regard to the golden calf as well as the idea that the golden calf impaired Israel's relationship to YHWH (cf. pp. 107–116 and e.g. *b.*Pes. 87b; *b.*Yev. 49b; *Gen.Rab.* 94:5; *Exod.Rab.* 3:12, 41:1,7; 43:1; *Cant.Rab.* 1:6, 2:3, 3:4, 8:2; *Lev.Rab.* 27:3; *Pesiq. Rab. Kah.* 9, 78; *t.*Meg. 4:10; *b.*Shab. 88b, 89a; *b.*Sanh. 7a; *Num.Rab.* 15:7; *Pirqe R. El.* 45; *Lev. Rab.* 1:3, 10:3; *Deut.Rab.* 3:2; *Mek.* II, 223, 212; etc.). As they emphasize, "the undeniable fact" that the Scriptures make no attempt to defend Israel at the golden calf or to mitigate her guilt, "created a severe tension in the rabbinic mind, which, on the one hand, could not expunge what the Hebrew Scriptures had indelibly impressed; while on the other hand, it could not permit the fair name of the Jewish people to be dragged in the mud. Whatever the cost in terms of theological inconsistency, Israel had to be defended against its detractors" (p. 101). For the inconsistency of much of the rabbinic tradition, see too Childs, *Exodus*, p. 576. As 2 Cor. 3 demonstrates, contra Smolar and Aberbach, pp. 94, 96, Paul's view, however, does not support the later Christian polemic against Judaism as such; but neither does it support the other extreme position found in the rabbinic counter-polemic. Yet cf. pp. 102–107 in which they list 19 tradition-complexes that do make the "damaging admission" of Israel's sin with the calf. For further developments in rabbinic literature of Moses' role in Exod. 32, see Nahum M. Waldman, "Breaking of the Tablets," *Jud* 27 (1978) 442–447, pp. 443, 446, on *Ex.Rab.* 41:1; *Abot R. Nat.* A, ch.2; *Ex. Rab.* 43:1 (Moses sins by breaking the tablets in order to identify with the people and to save the covenant, since they could not receive them due to their sin); the various traditions discussed by Nehama Leibowitz, *Studies in Shemot (Exodus)*, Part II, 1981, pp. 549–553, 570–572, 603 f., 609, esp. pp. 459–470 on *Exod. Rab.* 33:3 and *Tanhuma* Terumah 8, which reject the biblical chronology in order to assert that the tabernacle was built after the sin with the golden calf as evidence of the fact that Israel's sin had

both determinative and paradigmatic for Israel's future history as God's people,[131] since it was a denial of the covenant promises at their essential point,
i.e. the revelation of YHWH's character as revealed through his deliverance of
Israel from Egypt as the means for granting the promised land (cf. Exod. 6:6–
8 and 19:4–6 with 32:1, 4, 8). Within the overall structure of the Pentateuch,
this rebellion in the wilderness, decisively revealed in their idolatry with the
golden calf, forms the negative counterpoint to God's gracious acts of election
and deliverance (cf. Exod. 32:8; 34:10–12; Num. 11:18–20; 14:11, 22; Deut.
11:1–8; 26:16–19; 31:20 f.).[132] As R.P. Carroll has observed, "In the overall
pattern of the Pentateuch the rebellion motif functioned in relation to the Exodus in the same way as the disobedience of Adam in the garden of Eden which
ruined the goodness of the divine creation."[133]

But this too is part of YHWH's sovereign plan. In Deut. 29:2–8 this contrast
between YHWH's great acts of redemption and Israel's "stiff-neck" is attributed to YHWH's divine prerogative. In spite of the Lord's great acts of deliverance, "Yet to this day the Lord has not given (Israel) a heart to know, nor
eyes to see, nor ears to hear" (Deut. 29:4; Hebrew: 29:3). Hence, the people
are specifically warned of the those who will flagrantly worship idols in spite
of the curses of the covenant, saying "'I have peace though I walk in the stubbornness of my heart (בשררות לבי) in order to destroy the watered land with
the dry'" (Deut. 29:19; Hebrew: 29:18). Such persons will not escape the
judgment of the Lord (Deut. 29:20 f.). Nor will the nation be spared when they
forsake the covenant, which the Lord declares will certainly happen (Deut.
31:16–18, 20). The "Song of Moses" in Deut. 32, together with the book of

---

been atoned for (cf. Rashi to Exod. 31:14 and 33:11); and E. Mihaly, "A Rabbinic Defense
of the Election of Israel," *HUCA* 35 (1964) 103–143 on *Sifre* Deut. 32:19 and *Pisqa* 312 as
a response, based ultimately on Deut. 14:2 and Jer. 10:16, to the Christian assertion that the
Church completely replaces Israel due to her rejection of her election with the golden calf
and confirmed by the destruction of the temple and Jerusalem (cf. pp. 119 f. and Justin, *Dialogue against Trypho* 18, 20 f., 119, 122, 135; Epistle of Barnabas 13–16, of which Mihaly
sees *Sifre* Deut. 32 to be a point by point refutation, p. 129). And for the history of the
Church's evaluation and use of the golden calf, see now Bori, *Golden Calf*, esp. his conclusion on p. 73, and Ilona Opelt, *Die Polemik in der christlichen lateinischen Literatur von
Tertullian bis Augustin*, BkAW N.F. 2. Reihe 63, 1980, esp. pp. 190 f, 201.

[131] So similarly Childs, *Exodus*, p. 565, on 32:1–6: the author "is reporting the events of
the great apostasy, but in a manner which makes it representative of all subsequent idolatry."
Thus, "one can say that the whole subsequent history of Israel's unfaithfulness ... has been
reflected in the request" (p. 564). "Embedded at the heart of the sacred tradition lies Israel's
disobedience and rebellion. The Old Testament understood this episode of flagrant disobedience, not as an accidental straying, but as representative in its character" (p. 579). See too
Moberly, *Mountain of God*, p. 46.

[132] So too Coats, *Rebellion*, p. 253, who points to the deuteronomistic theological structure in which "The events of rebellion and Yahweh's aid and patience are now ordered in a
temporal sequence. Yahweh gives his aid *in spite of* Israel's rebellion, and Israel continues
to rebel *in spite of* the aid."

[133] "Rebellion and Dissent in Ancient Israelite Society," *ZAW* 89 (1977) 176–204, p. 199.

Deuteronomy itself, are to serve as a witness against Israel when she falls into this idolatry (Deut. 31:21, 26; cf. 32:5, 15–18, 20). And as M. Zipor has observed based on the verbal parallels between Moses' speech in Deut. 31 and the motif of Israel's "stiff-neck" from Exod. 32–34 and Deut. 9:6, 13, "Diese Worte, wie die ganze Rede vv. 24–29, weisen offenbar auf die Episode mit dem Goldenen Kalb zurück."[134] For as Moses poignantly observes in conclusion to his speech and as an introduction to his song,

"... I know your rebellion (מֶרְיְךָ[135]) and your stiff neck (עָרְפְּךָ הַקָּשֶׁה[136]); behold, while I am still alive with you today, you have been rebellious against the Lord; how much more, then, after my death? ... For I know that after my death you will act corruptly and turn from the way which I commanded you; and evil will befall you in the latter days, for you will do that which is evil in the sight of the Lord, provoking Him to anger with the work of your hands." (Deut. 31:27, 29)

Conversely, the restoration of the covenant through Moses is equivalent to the expression of judgment and provisions of grace in Genesis 3:21–24. Moreover, it is specifically in the veil of Moses that these twin-motifs of judgment and mercy are brought together. Moses wears the veil in recognition that the covenant has been restored *in spite of* their sinful state. In her "stiff-necked" condition Israel cannot encounter the glory of God without being destroyed. But Moses also wears the veil as a result of the fact that, *because of* Israel's sinful state, the covenant cannot be restored completely. The glory of God cannot encounter Israel's "stiff-neck" without destroying her. The presence of God demands and is inextricably linked to the obedience of his people.[137] Although the glory of God is once again present among the people, it must now remain veiled from their view.

---

[134] ערף, *ThWAT, Bd. VI, Lieferung 3–5,* 1987, pp. 392–397, p. 394.

[135] For the theme of Israel as "rebellious" (מרי), see besides Num. 17:10 and 20:10, 1 Sam. 15:23 (concerning Saul) and 1 Kgs. 13:26; Ps. 78:8; Is. 30:9; Ezek. 2:3–8; 3:9, 26 f.; 12:2 f., 9, 25; 17:12; 24:3; 44:6. For the corresponding use of סרר ("to rebel"), see Ps. 78:8; Hos. 4:16; Is. 65:2; Jer. 5:23.

[136] Besides the texts already referred to, see also 2 Kings 17:14; 2 Chron. 30:8; 36:13; Jer. 7:26; 17:23; 19:15; and Neh. 9:16 f., 29 for the theme of Israel's "stiffening her neck."

[137] Similarly, Brueggemann, "Crisis and Promise," p. 74 n. 10, who observes that the Mosaic tradition "insists" on "the link of *presence* and *obedience*" (emphasis his). For this same point concerning Exod. 34 as a "midrash" on the Sinai covenant, see Lothar Perlitt, *Bundestheologie im Alten Testament,* WMANT 36, 1969, pp. 216–232, esp. his conclusion on p. 232: "Verheißung und Verpflichtung korrespondieren unlösbar miteinander bis in die theologisch reflektierte Namenklatur hinein (Exod. 34:10, 27)."

6. Habakkuk 3:3, Isaiah 25:7, and the Themes of Exod. 32–34 in Canonical Tradition

In surveying the canonical traditions, we will focus our attention on the three related motifs which came to the fore in our exegesis of Exod. 32–34 and which also appear explicitly in Paul's interpretation in 2 Cor. 3:7 ff.: the role of Moses as mediator and his association with the Law (cf. 2 Cor. 3:7, 12–13a, 16),[138] the golden calf as a paradigmatic illustration of Israel's "stiff-neck" (cf. 2 Cor. 3:14–15), and the veil of Moses in relationship to the glory of God and the second giving of the Law (cf. 2 Cor. 3:6 f., 13b).[139] In this last regard, attention can then be given to the themes of Exod. 32–34 in Habakkuk 3:3 and Isaiah 25:7 and their implications for understanding Paul's argument in 2 Cor. 3:7–18.

First, a survey of the Old Testament traditions illustrates that throughout the biblical material Moses' role as the authoritative mediator is everywhere affirmed.[140] This is the natural complement to the legitimizing function of the

---

[138] The history of scholarship on Moses in the Pentateuch is immense, though in the modern period it has focused almost entirely on historical and literary critical questions, both of which do not concern us here. For reviews of the history of the debate, see Rudolf Smend, *Das Mosebild von Heinrich Ewald bis Martin Noth, Beiträge zur Geschichte der biblischen Exegese, Bd. 3,* 1959, and Eva Osswald, *Das Bild des Mose in der kritischen alttestamentlichen Wissenschaft seit Julius Wellhausen,* 1962; for 1960–1984, see now Herbert Schmid, *Die Gestalt des Mose, Probleme alttestamentliche Forschung unter Berücksichtigung der Pentateuchkrise,* Erträge der Forschung Bd. 237, 1986. For a study of the traditions concerning Moses outside of Jewish and Christian literature, see John G. Gager, *Moses in Greco-Roman Paganism,* JBL Monograph Series 16, 1972.

[139] On the dominance of the position since the work of W.D. Davies that "the most pertinent 'background' to study in order to understand Paul is Judaism" and the value (and limitations) of motif research, see E.P. Sanders, *Paul and Palestinian Religion,* pp. 7 f., 10 f., 13 (quote from p. 7). Sanders is certainly right in cautioning that "Parallels *are* often illuminating, as long as one does not jump from 'parallel' to 'influence' to 'identity of thought'" (p. 11), and in drawing a distinction in purpose between motif research focusing on Paul's "background" and a thorough comparison of "a whole religion with a whole religion" (cf. pp. 10, 12).

[140] On the appropriateness of "mediator" as a summary designation for Moses' function in the OT, see Albert Gelin, "Moses im Alten Testament," in *Moses in Schrift und Überlieferung,* ed. R. Bloch and G. Vermes, 1963, pp. 31–57, pp. 31–32; this choice is confirmed by the later post-biblical and rabbinic development of Moses under this aspect; cf. my "Moses in the Apocrypha and Pseudepigrapha: A Survey," *Journal for the Study of the Pseudepigrapha* 7 (1990) 79–104, in which it becomes clear that next to Moses' personal authority, the motif of greatest significance is his role as Israel's intercessor; and Renee Bloch, "Die Gestalt des Mose in der rabbinischen Tradition," in *Moses in Schrift und Überlieferung,* 1963, pp. 95–171, who concludes that "Als Mittler zwischen Gott und Israel steht Moses am Ausgangspunkt aller göttlichen Institutionen in Israel" (p. 95; cf. pp. 124, 142). It is of course impossible to find one description which is adequate to encompass the views of Moses in the biblical tradition. On this difficulty, see esp. Rudolf Smend, *Das Mosebild ,* pp. 48–61, who surveys attempts to place Moses in ten different categories, from "Religionsstifter" and "Reformator," to "Prophet" and "Priester." For the more recent at-

Mosaic call-tradition outlined in chapter one. But even more important for the present study is that in his role as intercessor and Law-giver, Moses is portrayed as the positive counterpart to Israel's unfaithfulness and rebellion. From Numbers through Nehemiah the Scriptures affirm that it is Moses who, in the words of Hosea 12:14, "kept" Israel from destruction throughout her sojourn in the desert.[141] This tradition is given its most poignant formulation in Jer. 15:1, where Moses as mediator and Israel as God's unfaithful people are once again directly brought together. But now Israel's rebellion against the covenant has reached such proportions that the role of intercessor has been abolished. Indeed, not even Moses could prevent the ensuing judgment of God. Moses' effective role as intercessor becomes not only a symbol for God's mercy to Israel in the past, but also an *a fortiori* argument for the irrevocable nature of Israel's sin in the present. If even Moses' efforts would now be in vain, how much more those of Jeremiah! Though Jeremiah is called like Moses, and even speaks as the prophet like Moses, the Mosaic role of intercessor is nevertheless forbidden him in the strongest terms by a reference to the acknowledged effectiveness of Moses' own intercessions (cf. Jer. 7:16; 11:14; 14:11, where Jeremiah is told not to pray for the people). Israel thus stands as the counterpart to Moses as those who, like their "fathers," have "stiffened their neck" and now walk in the "stubbornness of their own evil heart" (Jer. 7:26; 16:12 17:23; 19:15,[142] cf. Ps. 106:6–39, where this is the central theme of the recapitulation of Israel's history). On the other hand, in the Servant Songs of Isaiah 42 ff., Israel's future redemption is tied to a Moses-like figure who will fulfill the calling to the nations which the people have failed.[143]

---

tempts, see now H. Schmid, *Die Gestalt des Mose*, pp. 66–83, who lists 9 different categories still remaining. Schmid opts for the general description of Moses as mediator and representative (p. 96).

[141] For the most important examples of this theme, see Num. 7:89; 9:18–23; 10:13; 11:2 f., 8 ff.; esp. 12:7 f., 13 and 14:12–20; 15:22 f.; 16:22, 45; 27:20; 30:1; Deut. 1:3; 4:1 f., 10–13, 32–36; 5:4 f., 22–27, 30 f.; 9:18 f., 20, 25–29; 10:1–3, 10; 18:15–18; 34:10–12; Ps. 106:23, 28–31 (where Phinehas' role as an intercessor parallels Moses); Is. 63:11 f., 15–19; Micah 6:4; Neh. 8:14; 9:14; 10:30.

[142] For this same motif of the "stubbornness" (שְׁרִרוּת) of an evil heart in relationship to the disobedience of the people, see Jer. 3:17; 7:24; 9:13; 13:10; 18:12; 23:17. Cf. Jer. 31:32.

[143] See e.g. Albert Gelin, "Moses im Alten Testament," in *Moses in Schrift und Überlieferung*, ed. R. Bloch and G. Vermes, 1963, pp. 31–57, p. 55, who points to the parallels between Is. 49:6; 53:12 and Exod. 32:32; Is. 42:6; 49:8 and Exod. 24:8; Is. 50:4; 42:4 and Exod. 21:1; 24:3; Deut. 4:1, 13; 7:11 f.; 10:4; Is. 50:7 f. and Exod. 32. Similarly, Geza Vermes, "Die Gestalt des Moses an der Wende der beiden Testamente," in *Moses in Schrift und Überlieferung*, pp. 61–93, p. 80, argues that the Servant in 49:5 f., 8–12 is to be identified with the "new Moses" of Deut. 18:15–18. For the "servant" of Is. 53 as a "new Moses," see too John Goldingay, *God's Prophet, God's Servant, A Study in Jeremiah and Isaiah 40–55*, 1984, pp. 147 f., and for a survey of recent scholarship on the parallels, see H. Schmid, *Die Gestalt des Mose*, pp. 64 f. Schmid himself appropriately concludes concerning the relationship between Moses and the servant that "... möglicherweise kann Mose archtypisch verstanden werden. Eine direkte Gleichsetzung scheidet aus" (p. 65). For the Mosaic im-

Second, it is self-evident that throughout this literature Moses is naturally associated with the giving of the Law.[144] But for our study the significance of this observation is that the Law of Moses not only provides the criterion for explaining why Israel was finally judged for her rebellion in the exile (cf. esp. Deut. 4:25–28; 28:58–68; Neh. 9:34), but also provides the only hope for her restoration (see esp. Deut. 30:1–3; Neh. 10:30). From a canonical perspective, and certainly from Paul's, this role of the Law on both sides of Israel's judgment, i.e. as the basis for her exile and restoration, finds its classic presentation in Exod. 32–34. Not only does Israel's later "stiff-necked" disobedience find its paradigmatic expression in the sin with the golden calf, but also the promise and hope of YHWH's future compassion and mercy are given their formulaic expression in Exod. 32–34, both in word (33:19; 34:6 f.) and deed (Exod. 34:10 ff.).[145] The Law of the covenant is not left broken with the golden calf, it too is restored to Israel as a sign of the restoration of the covenant. And as we have seen in chapter two, the eschatological hope for Israel is that she would one day keep the Law which she broke in the desert and in the promised land (Jer. 31:33; Ezek. 11:19 f.; 36:26 f.). The "negative" picture of Israel's history which can be traced throughout the biblical tradition is therefore the fitting corollary and foundation to the "new covenant" hope found most prominently in Jeremiah and Ezekiel. The proclamation and demonstration of God's "gracious lovingkindness" (חסד) in Exod. 32–34 thus becomes the theological basis for the hope of restoration after the exile.[146] YHWH's willingness to restore the covenant after the sin with the golden calf supports the hope for a future renewal after Israel's subsequent idolatry in the

---

agery in Is. 53, see P. Miller, "Moses My Servant," *Int* 41 (1987) 245–255, pp. 251, 253 f. For Moses as YHWH's "servant" (עבד) in the Pentateuch, cf. Exod. 4:10; 14:31; Num. 11:11; 12:7,8; Deut. 34:5. Moses as the "servant of the Lord" then becomes a virtual title in the biblical tradition; see Josh. 1:1,2,7,13,15; 8:31,33; 9:24; 11:12,15; 12:6; 13:8; 14:7; 18:7; 22:2,4,5; 1 Kgs. 8:53,56; 2 Kgs. 18:12; 21:8; Mal. 3:22; Ps. 105:26; Dan. 9:11; Neh. 1:7,8; 9:14; 10:30; 1 Chron. 6:34; 2 Chron. 1:3; 24:6,9. Cf. Karl Theodor Kleinknecht, *Der leidende Gerechtfertigte, Die alttestamentlich-jüdische Tradition vom 'leidenden Gerechten' und ihre Rezeption bei Paulus,* WUNT 2 Reihe 13, 1984, p. 47, and the literature cited there for the עבד-YHWH tradition associated with Moses behind passages such as Is. 41:8 f.; 44:1 f.; 45:4, etc. Kleinknecht points out, however, that of the various motifs which can be associated with Mose in the songs, that of the Servant's suffering finds no direct parallel. But in the later rabbinic tradition, see *b.*Sotah 14a, which interprets Is. 53:12 in terms of Exod. 32:32.

[144] See e.g. Num. 14:41 f.; Deut. 1:5, 42 f.; 2:1 f.; 4:1 f., 5, 14, 44 f.; 31:9, 12, 46; Mal. 4:4; Dan. 9:11, 13; Ezra 7:6; Neh. 1:7 f.; 8:1; etc.

[145] For this same point as developed in the interpretations of Exod. 32–34, esp. 32:12, 14 and 34:6 in Joel 2:1–17 and Jonah 3:1–4:11 (see esp. Joel 2:13, 17 ; Jonah 4:2, 11), see Thomas B. Dozeman, "Inner-biblical Interpretation of Yahweh's Gracious and Compassionate Character," *JBL* 108 (1989) 207–223, pp. 217–222.

[146] For the development of this theme, see Num. 11:18–20; 14:18–22; Deut. 4:29–31; 11:1–8; 26:16–19; 30:1–16; 31:20 f.; Ps. 78:38; 106:4–6, 27, 44–47; Ezek. 20:9, 14, 22, 37; Neh. 9:1 f., 32–38.

land. Exodus 32–34 provides a vivid backdrop for Isaiah's eschatological expectation of a "second exodus" and Ezekiel's corresponding hope for the manifestation of the glory of God in the new temple.[147] Moreover, Israel's "stiff-neck," paradigmatically manifested in Israel's sin with the golden calf, makes it evident that only on the basis of a change in the hearts of God's people will that obedience be created which is necessary for the continuing relationship between God and his people. Indeed, in Isaiah 2:2–4, even the redemption of the nations is tied to their learning and obeying the Law.

Third, an overview of the canonical traditions confirms that there is no attempt to play down or explain away Israel's sinful state as reflected in the narrative of the golden calf. The biblical tradition is consistent in its emphasis on the hard-hearted nature of Israel as a people and on her history of rebellion.[148] As unpopular as this view may be in modern scholarship, it cannot be denied that this is certainly one of the foundational perspectives of canonical literature. As Carroll has reminded us concerning the view of Israel's history in the biblical tradition, "rebellion was endemic in ancient Israel at the level of theological interpretation of history."[149] And nowhere is this "theological interpretation of history" more apparent than in Exodus 32–34, where the nation's sin with the golden calf functions as a paradigmatic expression and evidence of Israel's "stiff-neck." For as we have seen, an essential implication of the Exodus narrative is that Israel's heart was hardened against YHWH in spite of the redemption brought about in the Exodus and Sinai covenant.[150] Since the idolatry with the golden calf is seen as a "fall" within Israel's history parallel to that within the history of mankind in Gen. 3, the canonical tradition repeat-

---

[147] For the former, see Is. 11:15 f.; 42:16; 43:16–19; 49:6–11; 51:10; for the latter, esp. Ezek. 20:40, 43; 43:5; 44:4; 48:35.

[148] Jer. 2:2 f. and Hos. 2:17 are usually given as exceptions to this rule in that here Israel's time in the wilderness is said to be portrayed as a period of faithfulness, though scholarship has now rejected the earlier theory of the wilderness itself as a pristine place. But Jer. 2:2 f. may be a reference to YHWH's faithfulness, not Israel's; or to Israel's earlier brief period of faithfulness prior to her sin with the golden calf. And Hos. 2:17 is better read as a reference to her brief "honeymoon" prior to the rebellion at Mt. Sinai. On the former text, see Michael V. Fox, "Jeremiah 2:2 and the 'Desert Ideal,'" *CBQ* 35 (1973) 441–450 and Willy Schottroff, "Jeremia 2:1–3. Erwägungen zur Methode der Prophetenexegese," *ZThK* 67 (1970) 263–294; on the latter, Gale A. Yee, *Composition and Tradition in the Book of Hosea, A Redaction Critical Investigation*, SBL Dissertation Series 102, 1987, p. 81.

[149] "Rebellion and Dissent," p. 197, in reference to Deut. 9:7; Jer. 7:25 f.; Ezek. 16; 20; 23.

[150] For this theme and the corresponding emphasis on Israel's hardened nature, see besides the texts from Jer. listed above, n. 142, Num. 11:4 ff.; 12:1–15; 14:4–45, esp. vv. 9–11, 35, where it becomes clear that Exod. 32–34 provides the theological and conceptual foundation for the turning point in the Numbers narrative; 16:1 ff.; 25:1–4; Deut. 1:3, 19–33; 2:14–16; 3:26; 4:21, 27 f.; 5:29; 9:1–29; esp. 9:6–8, 13, 17 f., 21–23; 10:16; 28:62–68; esp. 29:2–4, 18, 22–28; 31:16–21, 26–29; 32:5, 15–18, 20; 1 Kgs. 11:1–4, 15, 24; 12:28–30; 2 Kgs. 17:14; 2 Chron. 30:8; 36:13; Ps. 78:5–8, 17 f., 22, 32, 36, 40 f. in view of vv. 9–11, 54–64; 81:12 f.; 95:7 f., 10; 106:6–46; Hos. 8:5 f.; 9:10; 10:5; 13:1–3; Is. 6:9 f.; 30:9; 48:4; 63:17; 65:1–7; Ezek. 2:3–6; 3:7; 12:2; 16, 23, 20, esp. vv. 5, 8, 10, 18, 21, 23 f., 27 f., 30 f.; Dan. 9:9–11; Neh. 9:2, 16–18, 26, 29.

edly attributes Israel's later rebellion and hard-heartedness to the "sins of the fathers" before her. Coats can consequently conclude that in the post-exilic period "a significant new interpretation of the consequences of the murmuring appears ... Why had Yahweh allowed such an event (as the Exile) to happen? The answer lay not only in the sins of the current generation but also in the rebellion of the fathers throughout Israel's history, especially the fathers of the wilderness period."[151] And as Nehemiah 9 makes clear, at the center of Israel's rebellion in the wilderness stood Israel's sin with the golden calf.

Finally, although the veil of Moses *per se* is nowhere explicitly mentioned in the canonical literature outside of Exod. 34:29–35, there are two close parallels conceptually to its function. In both cases they appear in eschatological contexts, on the one hand as a description of YHWH's coming judgment on the enemies of his people, and on the other hand as an expression of his redemption. The first is found in Habakkuk 3:3 f., a notoriously difficult text due to its condensed imagery, rare vocabulary, and opaque syntax.[152] Within the context of the theophany of vv. 3–15 and following the MT, the best sense seems to be as follows: When God comes to reveal himself in response to the prophet's prayer for deliverance (3:2),

"His radiance (הודו) covers the heavens, and the earth is full of his praise (or 'splendor').[153] His brightness (or 'lightning,' ונגה[154]) is like the light, he has twin rays from his hand (קרנים מידו לו), there is the 'covering' (חביון) of his power." (3:3 f.)

The meaning of קרנים and the hapax legomena חביון are both in question. The form חביון appears to be from the root חביוה and can be rendered literally, "the hidden hiding."[155] On the other hand, the parallels between "brightness" (נגה) and "light" (אור) and the need for the "covering" itself both support the rendering of קרנים as the rays of light which shine forth from YHWH's glory, rather than twin horns in or from his hand.[156] This latter translation seems

---

[151] *Rebellion*, p. 253. For this same point, see Carroll, "Rebellion and Dissent," p. 189.

[152] Baruch Margulis, "The Psalm of Habakkuk: A Reconstruction and Interpretation," *ZAW* 82 (1970) 409–442, therefore emends the text drastically. In verse 3 f. this includes transposing words and substituting part of verse 6 for 4b (p. 414). But as J.H. Easton, "The Origin and Meaning of Habakkuk 3," *ZAW* 76 (1964) 144–171, pp. 144 f., 148, has shown, such serious measures need not be taken since the MT of vv. 3 f. can be read as it stands.

[153] תהלתו in 3:3b can be translated either his "praise," or "splendor," cf. *BDB*, p. 237.

[154] So Easton, "Origin," p. 148, pointing to the parallels in Job 36:32; 37:3, 11, 15 and esp. Hab. 3:11. For the view that נגה refers to a glow comparable to sunlight at sunrise, see Theodor H. Gaster, "On Habakkuk 3:4," *JBL* 62 (1943) 345 f. He also opts for the translation "rays" for קרנים and points to the parallel in Deut. 33:2 to support the present form of the text.

[155] So Margulis, "Psalm," p. 414. But due to his reconstruction of the text on the basis of v. 6, Margulis takes this to be a reference to a cultic procession, with the hiding referring to the ark as that which is hidden or covered. But without his emendations this reading cannot be maintained.

[156] For the translation "rays", see e.g. also Ralph L. Smith, *Micah-Malachi*, WBC 32, 1984, pp. 112, 116 and Margulis, "Psalm," p. 414.

even more difficult contextually, while the former finds support in the parallel theophanic scene portrayed in Deut. 33:2. There too YHWH "shines forth" (הוֹפִיעַ) from Mount Paran, which is explicitly identified with Sinai. And like Hab. 3:4, when YHWH appears there is "at his right hand a burning fire (lightning)," though this phrase is notoriously difficult to translate.[157] Yet regardless of how one reads Deut. 33:2b, the first half of the verse makes it clear that this theophany from Sinai "is described as having been a time of brilliant light with the brightness emanating from the presence of God on the mountain."[158] Moreover, an understanding of Hab. 3:4 in terms of the protruding radiance of God's glory, here pictured in terms of rays of lightning,[159] is supported by the context of Hab. 3. The imagery of the Sinai theophany colors this passage (cf. 3:3, where God comes from the south, Teman and Mount Paran, rather than from the Temple) and the meaning of 3:11 seems to be that even though the sun and moon no longer shine, "the lightning flashes from God's presence furnish enough light for the battle."[160] Interpreting this verse against the backdrop of the Sinai-type theophany, Smith therefore concludes concerning Hab. 3:4 that "the lightning flashes from the cloud are symbols of his power, but his real essence or power is covered or hidden (v. 4)."[161] The link between the use of the dual form קַרְנַיִם ("rays") in this passage and the reference to Moses' face "shining" (קָרַן) is thus striking. As with the function of the veil in Exod. 34:29 ff., God's power is here spoken of as revealed and yet hidden in order "to emphasize the glory of God while rendering the glory of God, otherwise

---

[157] Reading the MT אֵשְׁדָּת, following S.R. Driver, *Deuteronomy*, ICC, 1902[2], who rightly argues that the reading אֵשׁ דָּת ("fiery law," "fire was a law") cannot be followed. Besides Hab. 3:4, Driver points to Exod. 20:18 and Ps. 50:3 as parallels. For the relevant literature, see P. Craigie, *The Book of Deuteronomy*, NICOT, 1976, p. 392 n. 1. Craigie follows those who render it, "warriors of God," but this is based on a reconstruction of the text. M. Fishbane, *Biblical Interpretation in Ancient Israel*, 1985, p. 76, translates this difficult word "fiery stream," taking the rabbinic view that it refers to the Law as a "torahistic" interpretation of the text (cf. *Sifre* Deut. 33:4). Though the attempt to read this as a reference to the Law appears to be supported by the reference to Moses giving the Law in Deut. 33:4, in the context YHWH is pictured as coming "from Sinai," not to it. Hence, Deut. 33:2 need not be a direct reference to the Law, especially since Moses and not YHWH is said to give the Law in this passage.

[158] Craige, *Deuteronomy*, p. 393.

[159] In an attempt to steer a middle course, Easton, "Origin," p. 144, translates 3:4b: "Twin prongs which project from his hand," with the prior phrase a direct reference to lightning: "and a glitter as of lightning appears."

[160] R. Smith, *Micah-Malachi*, p. 116. Smith points to Jud. 5:4–5; Ps. 18:7–15; 50:2 f.; 69:1 f.; 77:16–19; 97:3–5 as other examples of the Sinai-type theophany. For the opposing view that since this text is "hopelessly corrupt" it cannot be translated "rays" with any confidence, see Propp, "The Skin of Moses' Face," pp. 380 f. But the textual difficulties with the text he raises (the gender of תִּהְיֶה, the apparently tautological nature of the statement "brightness was like light," the meaning of "from his hand to him," and the hapax חֶבְיוֹן) do not support the alternative interpretation anymore than they disqualify taking קַרְנַיִם to mean "rays."

[161] *Micah-Malachi*, p. 116.

so completely awesome, tolerable."[162] When God reveals himself in the eschatological theophany of his judgment, even then his glory must be veiled.

As a counterpart to this veiling of God's glory in his coming theophany, Isaiah 25:7 develops the veiling of God's glory in relationship to the eschatological redemption of the nations. But in contrast to Hab. 3:3 f., the image is now reversed. Instead of emphasizing the hiding of God's glory when he comes to judge his enemies, Is. 25:6–8 stresses the uncovering of the veil which exists between God and the nations at the time of final restoration. Within the so-called Isaiah Apocalypse (Is. 24–27), the close connection between Is. 25:6–8 and 24:21–23 has long been recognized.[163] At the climax of the vision of YHWH's judgment begun in 24:1, Is. 24:21–23 pictures the destruction and punishment of all those who have rebelled against the Lord. Of importance for our study is that this judgment takes place as the result of the inbreaking of the future reign of God "on Mount Zion and in Jerusalem" (24:23a) in which YHWH's rule from Mt. Zion is pictured in terms of a display of his *glory* before his *elders* (ונגד זקניו כבוד, 24:23b). The defeat and punishment of YHWH's enemies thus results in the final establishment of the kingship of God over the world. But unlike Is. 40:5, where the future revelation of God's glory takes place before the whole world, here the glory of YHWH's reign from Mount Zion manifests itself specifically before the elders. For this reason, Wildberger has convincingly suggested that Is. 24:23 is picturing the return of YHWH's glory to the Temple in a way similar to that found in Ezek. 43:2; 44:4.[164] Against this backdrop, the reference to the elders in Is. 24:23 recalls the establishment of the Sinai covenant in Exod. 24:9–11, where the elders accompanied Moses into the presence of the Lord as the representatives of Israel.[165] The typology is clear. The future establishment of the "kingdom of God" on Mt. Zion is portrayed as the reestablishment of the covenantal presence earlier enjoyed by Israel at Sinai. At the heart of what it

---

[162] Coats, "Loyal Opposition," p. 104. Whether קרן in Hab. 3:4 means "horns" or "rays," Coats is right that the issue lies in the evaluation of the term in a metaphorical sense (p. 104 n. 25).

[163] See Hans Wilderger, *Jesaja, 2 Teilband, Jesaja 13–27*, BKAT Bd. X/2, 1989², pp. 904, 961. For the massive amount of secondary literature to Is. 24–27 and the relationship of this section to the Isaianic corpus as a whole, see now Marvin A. Sweeney, "Textual Citations in Isaiah 24–27: Toward An Understanding of the Redactional Function of Chapters 24–27 in the Book of Isaiah," *JBL* 107 (1988) 39–52, pp. 39 f.nn. 3–5. Sweeney's thesis that one cannot limit the redactional relationship of Is. 24–27 merely to the oracles against the nations in chs. 13–23, but that the themes of chs. 24–27 pick up traditions from throughout Isaiah (from Is. 2:9–17 in 25:11b–12 and 2:6–21 in 26:5 to 66:7–9 in 26:17 f.) is persuasive.

[164] *Jesaja*, p. 949. Wildberger points to Exod. 24:16 f.; 40:34 f.; Lev. 9:6, 23 as the conceptual parallels for this expectation.

[165] So too Wildberger, *Jesaja*, p. 949, though he points out that the elders in 24:23 may already point forward to the world at large in 25:6–8. For the same recognition of the parallel between 24:23 and Exod. 24:9,11, see John N. Oswalt, *The Book of Isaiah*, NICOT, 1986, p. 456 n. 58, who sees the Sinai experience to be "an earnest of the one being described here ..."

means for YHWH to reign over the world from Mt. Zion, therefore, is that his glory will be manifest before his people.

But what is even more striking is that this revelation of God's glory before his people in 24:23 is then developed in 25:6–8 in relationship to the salvation of all nations (25:6 f.). The glory of God manifested on Mt. Zion now becomes the source of redemption for all the world. For in a second allusion to the original covenant banquet on Mt. Sinai in Exod. 24:9–11, Is. 25:6 pictures the future salvation of the nations in terms of "a lavish banquet for all peoples on this mountain," which the Lord himself will prepare.[166] At this banquet, YHWH "will swallow up death for all time ... wipe tears away from all faces, and ... remove the reproach of His people from all the earth" (Is. 25:8).[167] "This mountain" (הר הזה) in Is. 25:6 is thus a reference back to Mt. Zion in Is. 24:23. Conversely, in 25:6 the elders of 24:23 are now seen to represent not merely Israel, but the entire world. Of special significance for our study is that this salvation is then depicted in verse 7 as taking place as a result of the lifting of a "covering" or "veil" which separates the nations from the Lord:

"And on this mountain He will swallow up the the face of the covering which is covering (פני-הלוט הלוט)[168] over all peoples, and the veil which is woven (הנסוכה המסכה) over all nations."

Though it is not explicitly stated, the natural implication is that the result of removing this barrier which lies over the nations is that they will be given access to the presence of God, even as Moses and the elders were in his presence on Mt. Sinai. Indeed, as Wildberger points out, the emphasis of the text is that the veil is "... nicht nur weggezogen, sondern total vernichtet, so daß keine

---

[166] For the tradition of the nations making a pilgrimage to Zion, see Is. 2:2 ff.; 18:7; 45:14; 60:3 ff.; Ps. 96:7 f.; 72:10; Zeph. 3:9 f.; Zech. 14:16.

[167] For the parallel between Is. 25:6–8 and Exod. 24, see Hartmut Gese, "Das Gesetz," *Zur biblischen Theologie, Alttestamentliche Vorträge*, 1989³, pp. 55–84, p. 76. In view of Wildberger's and Oswalt's understanding of 24:23 against the backdrop of Exod. 24, it is not clear why they ignore this background to 25:6–8. See Wildberger, *Jesaja*, pp. 961–963, where he interprets the meal of 25:6 f. in the general terms of YHWH's final victory and establishment of his kingdom in which, as attested in other ancient Near Eastern literature, a "Krönungsmahl" is celebrated. Oswalt, *Isaiah*, pp. 463 f., does not treat the question of the background at all. Even less convincing is the non-eschatological interpretation of John D.W. Watts, *Isaiah 1–33*, WBC 24, 1985, pp. 330–332, who argues that the elders of 24:23 are heavenly beings surrounding the throne and that the meal in 25:6 is a feast to announce the heroic deed that YHWH is about to do for the people, i.e. removing the curse of death and revenge from the land.

[168] Taking the verbal form הלוט to be an active participle as in *BDB*, p. 532, where the phrase is rendered, "the surface of covering which covereth over all the peoples." For the attempt to read it as a passive on the basis of 1 Sam. 21:10, see Wildberger, *Jesaja*, p. 960. But Wildberger's reading depends on emending the text so that פני is read with the following phrase. He thus suggests the translation: "Und er vernichtet auf diesem Berg die Hülle, mit der das Angesicht aller Völker umhüllt ist, und die Decke, die gedeckt ist über die Nationen allesamt" (p. 888). But in either case, the function of the "covering" or "veil" remains the same.

Gefahr mehr besteht, daß sie noch einmal über die Völker gelegt werden könnte."[169] YHWH's banquet with the peoples in Is. 25:6 ff. is pictured as a covenant with the nations in which they will be brought into the intimate fellowship with him earlier enjoyed by Moses and the elders.[170] But to do so, the barrier which now separates God and the peoples must be removed.[171] In this regard, it is striking that the word used as the synonym for הלוט ("covering") in 25:7b, מסכה ("veil"), is a homograph of the word employed exclusively in the MT to describe the process of metal-working employed to produce idols in general, and the golden calf in particular (cf. Exod. 32:4,8; 34:17; Neh. 9:18; Ps. 106:19).[172] It is possible, therefore, that in referring to the veil which lies over the people, the prophet was alluding, by way of a subtle play on words, to Israel's sin with the golden calf which stands as the exemplar *par excellence* of the idolatry which has caused the separation from YHWH not only of the nations, but also of his chosen people.[173] This implicit link between the problem of the nations and that of Israel herself is confirmed by the fact that the restoration of Israel in 24:23 prefaces the redemption of the nations in Is. 25:6–8 and becomes the climax of God's universal judgment and restoration in Is. 27:1, 12–13 (cf. Is. 11:10–16).[174] Thus, the redemption of the nations in Is. 25:6–8 is part and parcel of the redemption of Israel as the climax of God's eschatological vindication.[175] The final redemption of the nations is in itself a vindication of the faithfulness of God's covenant people (Is. 25:8c). H. Gese

---

[169] *Jesaja*, p. 966. Wildberger interprets the veil to be a sign of mourning as in 2 Sam. 15:30; 19:5; Jer. 14:3 f.; Esth. 6:12, in contrast to those who have seen it to represent the spiritual blindness of the nations.

[170] So too Gese, "Das Gesetz," p. 76: "Die Hülle, mit der sich Mose und Elia umhöllen mußten, um der Offenbarung der Transzendenz standhalten zu können, ist jetzt von allen hinweggenommen, und die Gottesschau ist von Angesicht zu Angesicht."

[171] See again Gese, "Das Gesetz," p. 76 n. 17: "Daß das den Sinn von *lot* (V. 7) ist, ergibt sich aus dem technischen Begriff *lut* 1 Kön 19:13 im Zusammenhang mit den zahlreichen Erwähnungen eines Verhüllens bei der Sinaitheophanie (Ex. 3:6; 33:20; 34:29 ff.)."

[172] It is unclear whether מסכה (from נסך , "to weave," as in the following הנסוכה in 25:7b) refers to a process of casting metal or to plating it over a form. Of its 28 occurrences in the OT, 25 refer to idols, and it is never used in a non-religious context, perhaps because of this association (see e.g. Deut. 9:16; Lev. 19:4; Num. 33:52; Jud. 17:3 f.; Hab. 2:18; 1 Kgs. 14:9; 2 Kgs. 17:6, Is. 30:22; 42:17; etc). The only other occurrences are found in Is. 25:7; 28:20 and questionably 2 Chron. 28:2. For these points concerning the meaning of מסכה, see Ch. Dohmen, art. מסכה, ThWAT, Bd. IV, Lieferung 8/9, 1984, pp. 1009–1015, esp. pp. 1010 f., 1013. But Dohmen does not point out the possible significance of the homograph in Is. 25:7.

[173] Cf. again Rom. 1:23, where Paul too seems to make this same link between the idolatry of the nations and that of Israel with the golden calf by using the imagery of the sin with the golden calf from Ps. 106:20 to describe the sin of the Gentiles. See above, n. 65.

[174] For this latter point, see M.A. Sweeney, "Textual Citations," pp. 50 f., where he points out that in both Is. 27 and 11, the defeat of the seven-headed chaos monster Leviathan (27:1; 11:15) is a prelude to the gathering of the outcasts of Israel (27:12 f.; 11:15 f.).

[175] So too Wildberger, *Jesaja*, p. 950: "Heil für die Völker bedeutet nicht, daß Israel nicht seine Sonderstellung behält."

is therefore right in emphasizing that in Is. 25:6–8, just as all the nations partake in the salvation of Israel, so too Sinai is replaced by Zion as the eschatological "cosmic mountain of the world."[176] And at the heart of this salvation is the unmediated revelation of the glory of God, first before Israel, and then among all the nations. Hence, to enjoy the salvation of the Lord (Is. 25:9 f.) is to have the veil removed which now separates both Israel and the nations from His presence.

It is this same image which is developed in Is. 60:1–5, where the eschatological appearance of YHWH's light and glory before Israel (60:1 f.) first brings about her own transformation into the radiance of the Lord (60:5). But the final result is the gathering of the nations and kings of the world to Israel's "light" and the "brightness of (her) shining" (60:3; cf. 60:5b–14). The revelation of YHWH's glory thus creates a glorified Israel (60:7b, 9). In turn, a glorified Israel attracts the attention, submission, and support of the nations, who make a pilgrimage with their wealth to Jerusalem as "the city of the Lord, the Zion of the Holy One of Israel" (60:14). The salvation of the people of God is brought about by the manifestation of the glory of God in their midst (60:13) and "upon them" (60:1 f.). Once again, therefore, the redemption of God's people, as well as the nations, comes about when YHWH reveals his glory to a people covered by darkness, a glory which transforms them into the very glory of God itself.

Of special significance for our study is that this transformation is explicitly pictured in Is. 60:5 in terms of the shining of the people's faces as a result of having encountered the glory of God on Mount Zion, just as Moses' face shone when he descended from Mount Sinai.[177] But unlike Exod. 32–34, the theophany of the glory of God on Mt. Zion in Is. 60:1–14 no longer means judgment, but rather redemption and vindication. For according to Is. 60:5, at that time the people's hearts will no longer be hardened, so that they must fear the presence of God. Instead, their hearts will "tremble" and "rejoice" in his midst as the nations come to join them on Mt. Zion in the worship of YHWH (cf. Is. 2:2–4; 56:6–8).[178] In this way, Israel's ultimate redemption and vindication are portrayed as a reversal of the cause and effects of the sin of the golden calf at Mt. Sinai. Moreover, her final restoration, brought about by the revelation of the glory of God in her midst, is the fulfillment of God's initial

---

[176] "Das Gesetz," p. 76.

[177] Cf. Propp, "The Skin of Moses' Face," p. 381 n. 27, who called my attention to the parallel between Is. 60:5 and Exod. 34:29–35. He also points to Ps. 34:6 for the same concept of the shining of faces after beholding YHWH. But Propp denies the support of these texts for the traditional view of Exod. 34:29 ff. because of the positive connotation of the shining in Is. 60 and Ps. 34 as "a blessing rather than a fearsome phenomenon." But this is precisely the point being made by the metaphorical adaptation of this motif in Is. 60:1 ff.

[178] Cf. Ezek. 20:35 f., where the eschatological revelation of the presence of God again signifies judgment against those within Israel whose hearts remain hard, and 28:22; 39:21, where it also brings judgment upon the rebellious nations.

intention for Israel as expressed in Exod. 19:5–6, which in turn is a restatement of the purpose of the Abrahamic covenant, beginning in Genesis 12:1–3: the descendants of Abraham are to be a kingdom of priests who mediate God's presence to the nations, since all the earth belongs to the Lord.[179] Rather than needing a veil to protect and separate the people from the glory of God because of their hard hearts, Is. 25 and 60 point forward to a time when the hearts of the faithful remnant will rejoice in his presence and the nations will be drawn to his glory.[180] Most astonishing of all, however, is that the glory of God will not only be revealed on Mt. Zion, but also be reflected by the glorified people themselves (Is. 60:2–5, 13 f.). With this eschatological vision from Isaiah 24:21–23, 25:6–9, and 60:1–14, together with the promise of Jeremiah 31:31 ff., the restoration pictured in Ezekiel 11:17–20, 36:21–36, and 40–48, and the overarching role of Moses in canonical literature, the essential biblical background to Paul's understanding of the letter/Spirit contrast against the backdrop of Exod. 32–34 has been established. With this in view, we can turn our attention to the way in which Exod. 32–34 was translated, and hence interpreted, in the Septuagint.

7. The Exodus 32–34 Tradition in the Septuagint

The first and most important observation to be made is that the Septuagint version of Exod. 32–34 preserves the theological points and function which have become evident in our study of the Hebrew tradition. Both the overall flow of the narrative and the specific word order of the Hebrew textual tradition are followed closely by the LXX, so that not only the story line remains unimpaired, but also the syntax itself preserves characteristic semitisms.[181] Nevertheless, there are a number of differences between the LXX and the Hebrew tradition that together indicate the direction in which the tradition is moving, and at several points are of direct significance for Paul's own interpretation of Exod. 32–34. Moreover, the links between Exod. 32–34 and the eschatological expectations from Isaiah, Jeremiah, and Ezekiel outlined

---

[179] For the link between Exod. 34, Exod. 19:5–6, and Gen. 12, and its development in detail, see Dumbrell, "Paul's Use of Exodus 34," pp. 181 f., and his *Covenant and Creation, A Theology of Old Testament Covenants*, 1984, pp. 80 ff. Moreover, cf. Dumbrell's helpful insight that Exod. 34:29–35 makes it clear "that the realization of the idealization of 19:3b–6 will have to be in some sense a matter of eschatological fulfillment if they are to be fulfilled at all. This is in fact the question which the OT will take up later under its new covenant doctrine (cf. Jer. 31:31–34)" (p. 185).

[180] For the point that the redemption in Is. 56–66 concerns only the faithful remnant, i.e. "my people," in contrast to those who "forget my holy mountain" (cf. 60:11, 19), see William J. Dumbrell, *The End of the Beginning, Revelation 21–22 and the Old Testament*, 1985, pp. 18 f.

[181] See e.g. the position of ἰδών and the repetition of ὁ λαός in 32:1, the repetitive use of βάδιζε and κατάβηθι in 32:7 for לֶךְ־רֵד, and τινι ὑπάρχει for the possessive in 32:24.

above are confirmed and undergirded in the LXX tradition. Having already studied Exod. 32–34 in some detail, it will be easiest simply to list in the order of their appearance the distinctions between the LXX and the Hebrew tradition of Exod. 32–34 of import for this study before drawing out their implications.

1. The idolatry of the golden calf is highlighted in 32:4 by the choice of γραφίδι ("engraving tool") for the difficult construction בחרט and of the literal plural translation οὗτοι οἱ θεοί σου ("these are your gods," cf. 32:8) for אלהיך.

2. In 32:6a the LXX uses singular verbs rather than plural as in the MT to emphasize that, as the priest, Aaron, rather than the people, is the only one who offers the sacrifices. This change is most likely motivated by a concern for appropriate cultic practice.[182] The striking character of this alteration is attested to by the fact that Aquila, Symmachus, and the tradition associated with Theodotion all revert to a plural form.[183]

3. In 32:7 the Piel form שחת ("destroy," "corrupt") is rendered by ἠνόμησεν ("act lawlessly"[184]), which corresponds to Moses' prayer in 34:9 that God forgive the people's ἀνομίας ("lawlessness"). The LXX thus reads Israel's sin with the golden calf in terms of an explicit rejection of the Torah. Moreover, in 34:9, where the MT tradition links Moses' request that the Lord himself accompany the people with their "stiff-necked" condition by the use of an ambiguous כי, the LXX reads γάρ. The people's "stiff-neck" (σκληροτράχηλος) is thus explicitly interpreted in 34:9 as the ground for Moses' request for the Lord's presence. Moses pleads for God's presence precisely because he knows that the people's rebellious nature requires it for the future success of their journey through the desert and possession of the land.

4. 32:9 is omitted completely in the LXX, although 33:3, 5 and 34:9 all refer to the people as σκληροτράχηλος ("stiff-necked").[185] The omission of 32:9 thus does not diminish the picture of Israel's hardened condition in the LXX. On the contrary! By postponing the declaration until the problem of YHWH's presence is explicitly expressed, the LXX actually heightens the theological problem posed by Israel's rebellious nature.

5. The theological problem of YHWH's "evil" (רעה) and "repentance" (הנחם, שוב) in 32:12 is erased with the translation παῦσαι τῆς ὀργῆς τοῦ θυμοῦ σου καὶ ἵλεως γενοῦ ἐπὶ τῇ κακίᾳ τοῦ λαοῦ σου ("Stop the wrath of your anger and show mercy upon the evil of your people"). YHWH is no longer asked to repent or change his mind and the "evil" attributed to YHWH in the Hebrew tradition is now attributed to the people. In the same way, the statement in 32:14 that the Lord changed his mind concerning the

---

[182] So too Moberly, *Mountain of God,* p. 196 n. 10.

[183] See Frederick Field, ed., *Origenis Hexaplorum,* 1875, p. 140, to Exod. 32:6.

[184] So Friedrich Rehkopf, *Septuaginta-Vokabular,* 1989, p. 25. Hahn, *Goldene Kalb,* p. 31 n. 74, renders it "hat gesetzwidrig gehandelt."

[185] As would be expected, σκληροτράχηλος is also found in the parallel passage Deut. 9:6,13. Elsewhere in the LXX it is found in Prov. 29:1 and Bar. 2:30 (on the significance of these passages, see below). This is the same word used in Acts 7:51 to describe Stephen's contemporaries, who in being "stiff-necked and uncircumcised in heart and ears" are "resisting the Holy Spirit" and thus doing "just as your fathers did." Again, Symmachus and the Theodotion tradition correct the LXX reading by adding the verse; *Hexaplorum,* p. 141 to Exod. 32:9.

evil he was going to do is now rendered, "and the Lord was reconciled (ἱλάσθη) concerning the evil which he said he would do to his people" (cf. 32:30 LXX).

6. In 32:15b the undesignated tablets (לחת) are now explicitly said to be "stone tablets" (πλάκες λίθιναι), while the fact that they were written on both sides is translated as καταγεγραμμέναι ... ἦσαν γεγραμμέναι. In 32:16, these tablets are then described as the work of God, while the writing which is said to have been "engraved on the tablets" (ἐστιν κεκολαμμένη ἐν ταῖς πλαξίν) is identified as the "writing of God" (γραφὴ θεοῦ).

7. Aaron's reference to the "evil" nature of the people (ברע) in 32:22 is now rendered τὸ ὅρμημα ("assault," "charge," "onset"[186]), so that Aaron's plea now centers on the way in which the people forced him to comply with their wishes.

8. The immediate result and punishment for the sin with the golden calf in 32:27 was that the sons of Levi "killed" (ἀποκτείνατε) their brothers.

9. In a way more consistent with the problem of YHWH's presence in the midst of his people, in 33:2 it is an angel, not YHWH himself as in the MT, which drives out the people from the promised land. This emphasis is continued in 33:3, where the LXX supplies εἰσάξω σε ("I will lead you") in order to stress that YHWH will go before the people, not in their midst. For the LXX goes on to stress that the Lord cannot go with the people due to their stiff-necked condition, lest he "consume you on the way" (ἵνα μὴ ἐξαναλώσω σε ἐν τῇ ὁδῷ). Conversely, after the restoration of the covenant in 34:10, it is once again YHWH, not the angel, who will cast out the inhabitants of the land in 34:11 (cf. ἐκβάλλω in 34:11 with ἐκβαλεῖ in 33:2). This alteration reflects in an unmistakable way the theological significance of the restoration of the covenant after the sin with the golden calf. Once again YHWH himself will lead and provide for his people in full recognition of the fact that their hearts are still hardened against him (34:9).

10. In 33:5 this emphasis on the people's rebellious nature is highlighted by the fact that the Lord pronounces that the people are stiff-necked *directly* to the people, rather than to the people through Moses as in the MT. Furthermore, the repeated warning that the people will be destroyed by the presence of God in their midst is now preceded by the threat of a plague as the means of this destruction. Finally, whereas in the MT the people respond on their own by stripping off their jewelry as an act of sorrow, in the LXX the people are commanded to remove "the garments of your glory" (τὰς στολὰς τῶν δοξῶν ὑμῶν) and their jewelry. The imagery points explicitly to the fact that they have lost the glory of God's presence in their midst.

11. The LXX attempts to solve the tension between the fact that Moses speaks to the Lord "face to face" (פנים אל־פנים) in 33:11, in spite of the fact that in 33:20, 23 Moses is not allowed to see YHWH's "face" (פני), since no one can see the Lord's face and live. By using different words for Moses' encounter in 33:11 (ἐνώπιος ἐνωπίῳ), and the prohibition in 33:20, 23 against seeing YHWH's face (τὸ πρόσωπον), a distinction between the two statements is introduced.[187] Nevertheless, the emphasis on the intimate relationship between Moses and YHWH is maintained throughout the text. Moreover,

---

[186] Rehkopf, *Septuaginta-Vokabular*, p. 211 translates it "Ansturm." J. Hahn, *Das Goldene Kalb*, p. 62, attributes this rendering to reading עברה ("arrogance," "presumption," "fit of anger"), pointing to its use in Hos. 5:10; Amos 1:11. Cf. also Deut. 28:49; Ps. 45:4; I Macc. 4:8, 30; 6:33, 47.

[187] So too Moberly, *Mountain of God*, p. 65, who suggests that this change in vocabulary "probably reflects an attempt to resolve the contradiction." But Moberly is correct in emphasizing the tension between the immanence and transcendence of God present in the MT (see p. 66). The LXX may simply reflect this tension, as 34:6 seems to indicate.

in describing the theophany in 34:6, YHWH is explicitly said to pass by the "face" of Moses, once again using πρόσωπον as in 33:20, 23, but this time in the general sense of "presence" similar to that found in 33:11. Hence, in 33:2 the angel can be said to go "before the face" (πρὸ προσώπου) of the people, while in 33:15 the LXX can refer to YHWH himself where the MT reads YHWH's "face" (פָּנֶיךָ). Hence, the difference in vocabulary does not create a semantic distinction of great significance.

12. The superiority and authority of Moses are stressed in 33:12, 17 by the assertion that the Lord knows Moses "above all" (παρὰ πάντας), where the MT reads that Moses is known "by name" (בְּשֵׁם).[188]

13. In the MT version of 33:13 Moses requests that he might know YHWH's "ways" in order that he might know YHWH. In the LXX, Moses asks, already at this point in the narrative, for a revelation of YHWH himself (ἐμφάνισόν μοι σεαυτόν) so that, having been known, Moses might see YHWH (γνωστῶς ἴδω σε). In addition, where the MT expresses the conviction that Israel *is* YHWH's people as the basis for Moses' request, in the LXX this conviction becomes Moses' desire. Moses now wants a revelation of YHWH not only to know that he himself has found favor in God's sight, but also *in order that* he might know that Israel is God's people (ἵνα γνῶ ὅτι λαός σου τὸ ἔθνος τὸ μέγα τοῦτο). Israel's precarious plight before YHWH is thus again highlighted in the LXX in a way not found in the MT.

14. In 33:14–16 God's renewed commitment to go before Moses and the people (προπορεύσομαί σου) and to go with them (συμπορευομένου σου μεθ' ἡμῶν) is interpreted in 33:16b in terms of Moses and the people being "glorified above all the nations which are upon the earth" (ἐνδοξασθήσομαι ἐγώ τε καὶ ὁ λαός σου παρὰ πάντα τὰ ἔθνη ὅσα ἐπὶ τῆς γῆς ἐστιν). That which "distinguishes" or "separates" (וְנִפְלִינוּ) Israel from the nations in the MT tradition is now explicitly said to be their participation in the glory of God. In line with this emphasis, the theophany of YHWH's "goodness" (טוּבִי) in 33:19 is explicitly interpreted in terms of God's "glory" (ἐγὼ παρελεύσομαι πρότερός σου τῇ δόξῃ μου), just as it is in 33:22. The theme of the revelation of God's glory, which becomes so predominant in 34:29 ff., is thus already brought to the fore in the promise and theophany of 33:14 ff. in a way not found in the MT.

15. Finally, at the conclusion of the restoration of the covenant stipulations in 34:10 ff., the LXX distinguishes the "words" upon which YHWH has made his "covenant" in 34:27 (ἐπὶ γὰρ τῶν λόγων τούτων τέθειμαί σοι διαθήκην) from the tablets themselves. For in 34:28, as part of the overall summary statement concerning Moses' sojourn on Mt. Sinai, Moses is instructed to write "these words" (τὰ ῥήματα ταῦτα) upon the "tablets of the covenant" (ἐπὶ τῶν πλακῶν τῆς διαθήκης), which, as in the MT, are explicitly equated with the "Ten Words." As in 32:19, here too the stone tablets become a symbol of the covenant itself and are associated specifically with their former content.

At this point in the LXX tradition, several general observations can be made. First, although the flow and main points of the narrative as found in the Hebrew tradition are clearly maintained, the LXX emphasizes the theme of the presence of God in the midst of his sinful people even more dramatically than the MT. The people's idolatry with the golden calf is now explicitly tied to the

---

[188] Aquila, Symmachus, and the Theodotion tradition all bring this alteration back into line with the MT; *Hexaplorum*, p. 143, to Exod. 33:12.

problem of keeping the Law on the one hand (32:7; 34:9), and to the enjoyment of the glory of God on the other (33:14–16, 18). Indeed, God's glory in
the midst of his people and their participation in it are what distinguishes Israel from the nations (33:16). But their lawless behavior with the golden calf
demands that they be stripped of their "garments of glory" (33:5). The LXX's
concern for the keeping of the Law also shows itself in 32:6 in its subtle concern for proper cultic practice (even in the midst of an idolatrous sacrifice!),
and in 34:28 by its identification of the tablets themselves with the covenant.
The corresponding problem of how God's glory can continue to dwell in the
midst of his sinful people is therefore central to the LXX in a way even more
pronounced than in the MT, as illustrated by Moses' prayer in 33:13 and the
unambiguous logic of 34:9. God himself now declares directly to the people
that they are "stiff-necked" (33:5). As a corollary, Moses' role is highlighted
in the LXX. In 32:8 it is Moses, not YHWH as in the MT, who is said to have
commanded the Law to the people.[189] And in response to the problem of God's
presence amidst his people, it is Moses who now asks for a revelation of God's
glory from the beginning (33:13). Conversely, YHWH addresses Moses alone
in 33:14 f., so that the people's future glorification is consistently shown to be
dependent upon Moses as mediator. Finally, Moses' requests are granted because he is the one who is "above all" (33:12, 17). In response to Moses' peti-
tions, YHWH will lead the people, and he himself will drive out the inhabitants of the land. But in view of the continuing rebellious nature of the people
the question of how this will be possible is not yet answered. Nevertheless, it
is clear in the LXX tradition that the resolution of the problem once again
centers on Moses as intercessor and recipient of the divine theophany, a
theophany now explicitly portrayed in terms of the revelation of God's glory.

This resolution of the central problem of Exod. 32–34 finds its consummation in Moses' descent from Mt. Sinai in 34:29–35. Since the significance of
this passage is best seen when it is read as a whole, it will be most helpful to
present a translation of the text before commenting on its specific features.

(29): But when Moses came down from the mountain – and the two tablets were in
the hands of Moses – and while he was coming down from the mountain, Moses did
not know that the appearance of the color (χρώματος[190]) of his face had been glorified (δεδόξασται) while he (God) was speaking to him.

---

[189] This was called to my attention by J. Hahn, *Das Goldene Kalb*, p. 33, who also points
to the parallel in Deut. 33:4.

[190] Propp, "The Skin of Moses' Face," pp. 376 f., argues that the original reading was
"skin" (χρωτός) as found in the Alexandrinus, Ambrosianus, and Coislinianus codices, as
well as Origen, Eusebius, and Cyril of Alexandria (cf. A.E. Brooke and N. McLean, *The Old
Testament in Greek, Vol. I, Part II*, 1909, p. 274). Yet the reading supported by Vaticanus and
the Old Latin here and in v. 30 is clearly the more difficult due to its deviation from the MT.
Propp's main argument is that the rendering "color" is an assimilation "to the notion that
Moses' face was radiant" (p. 376 n. 3). But this is merely an indication that the more difficult reading is not too difficult to fit its context.

(30): And Aaron and all the elders of Israel (πρεσβύτεροι Ισραηλ[191]) saw Moses and the appearance of the color of his face was glorified (ἦν δεδοξασμένη), and they feared to come near him.

(31): And Moses called them and they turned to him, Aaron and all the rulers of the synagogue (οἱ ἄρχοντες τῆς συναγωγῆς), and Moses spoke to them.

(32): And after these things all the sons of Israel came to him and he commanded to them all things whatsoever the Lord spoke to him on Mt. Sinai.

(33): And after he (Moses) ceased speaking to them, he placed a veil (κάλυμμα) upon his face.

(34): But whenever Moses entered before the Lord to speak to him,[192] he would remove the veil until he came out. And having come out, he was speaking to all the sons of Israel whatsoever the Lord commanded him, (35) and the sons of Israel saw the face of Moses, that it was glorified (δεδόξασται), and Moses placed a veil (κάλυμμα) upon his face, until whenever he would enter to speak with him.

16. The first thing that strikes one in reading this text is the emphasis throughout on the glory of God. The difficult verb קרן in 34:29 f., 35 (MT) is rendered by δεδόξασται, ἦν δεδοξασμένη, and δεδόξασται respectively. This is highlighted in the LXX by its use of ἡ ὄψις ("the appearance") and χρώματος ("color"), which have no equivalents in the MT, but call attention to the fact that Moses now appeared glorified. Some image of a radiance upon his face thus lies close at hand, as indicated by the direct reference to the glorification of Moses' face in 34:35 rather than to the "skin of the face of Moses" (עור פני משה) as in the MT.[193] The use of the perfect tenses and periphrastic construction in 34:29 f., 35 to describe the glorification of Moses' face as a permanent condition, and the explicit reference in 34:34 f. to the repeated action of removing and replacing the veil (cf. ἡνίκα δ᾿ ἄν, ἕως ἄν, and the use of the imperfect tense in vv. 34 f.) further highlights the glorification of Moses' face. Finally, the choice of δοξάζειν throughout 34:29–35 naturally recalls the theme of the glory of God introduced earlier in 33:5, 16b, 19, and the thematic parallel in 33:13. Hence, Moses becomes the vehicle through which the glory of God lost by the people as a result of the golden calf is restored, albeit in a mediated manner. The attempts of Hofius and P. Vielhauer to avoid the link between Moses' experience in 34:29 ff. and the glory of God are therefore not

---

[191] υἱοὶ Ισραηλ is read by AFM etc., but here is clearly the less difficult text and is probably an assimilation either to 34:32 or to the MT. Cf. Brooke and McLean, *The Old Testament in Greek*, p. 274.

[192] Taking the most natural reading of the infinitive phrase λαλεῖν αὐτῷ here and συλλαλεῖν αὐτῷ in v. 35 to pick up Moses as their subject; though in the MT it is YHWH.

[193] Contra Propp, "The Skin of Moses' Face," p. 377, who takes the lack of an explicit reference to radiance and the wide semantic range of δοξάζω/δόξα to be a sign of a lack of clarity concerning this point. But the context alleviates this ambiguity. For his explanation of the origin of the LXX rendering of 34:30a as the result of reading the MT עור ("skin") as אור ("light") and a possible redivision of קרן כי, see his pp. 379 f. But the simplest solution is to see the LXX as an interpretation of the MT in terms of Moses' skin shining, which is confirmed by the renderings found in the various targumic traditions (see below, chapter four) and the Peshitta. Thus, as Propp himself points out, "the majority view, that *qaran* describes a radiant phenomenon, is supported by the Peshitta, LXX, and targums" (p. 376).

supported by an analysis of this text in its context.[194] The shining on Moses' face in 34:29 ff. is the shining of the glory of God itself, which Moses reflects as a result of his theophanic experience in Exod. 34:5–8 (cf. 33:19).

17. The second striking feature is the rendering πρεσβύτεροι Ισραηλ in 34:30. In the MT, "all the sons of Israel" (כל־בני ישראל), together with Aaron, first see the glory of God on the face of Moses and are afraid to approach him. But in v. 31, it is Aaron and the "rulers in the congregation" who are summoned to return to Moses before the "sons of Israel" come near in v. 32. The LXX smooths out this apparent inconsistency in chronology by interpreting the sons of Israel in v. 30 in terms of the elders so that the sequence from the elders to the people is maintained.

18. In 34:31 this reference to the elders of Israel is further interpreted in terms of "the rulers of the synagogue" (οἱ ἄρχοντες τῆς συναγωγῆς), where the MT reads "the rulers in the assembly" (הנשאים בעדה). In the LXX, therefore, the elders of Israel, as representatives of the people, first encounter the glory of God mediated through Moses alone. But as a resolution to the problem of the presence of God in the midst of his people, this repeated encounter with the glory of God is then extended to include the people themselves (cf. 34:32, 34).

The impact of these alterations in the LXX tradition is twofold. First, the LXX leaves no doubt that in descending from Mt. Sinai Moses' face shines forth with the glory of God as a result of his experience of the theophany of 34:5 ff. and that it is this experience which brings the narrative to its climax. What causes fear among the people is the presence of the glory of God in their midst. As in the MT, Moses' experience of the glory of God is the context within which he receives the reinstitution of the covenant Law on Mount Sinai in 34:8–28, and in which he proclaims it to the people in 34:32–35. In both cases, Moses' encounter with God's glory is prior to and determinative for his acquisition of the Torah, whether on Mt. Sinai or in the tent of meeting. The Law which Moses receives and mediates derives its character from God's glory; the glory of God which Moses experienced does not derive its character from the Law. In addition, there is no uncertainty in the LXX that the glory on Moses' face was a lasting presence that necessitated his continual use of the

---

[194] O. Hofius, "Gesetz und Evangelium nach 2. Korinther 3," *Paulusstudien*, WUNT 51, 1989, pp. 75–120, argues that in the LXX of Exod. 34:29, 30, 35, δοξάζειν picks up the Hebrew קרן (understood as "shine forth") and therefore ought to be rendered not as a direct reference to the glory of God, but merely as a reference to the "strahlenden Glänzen des Angesichts Moses" (p. 88). In turn, in 3:7, when Paul picks up these texts "directly," "Das Substantiv δόξα hat hier die Bedeutung 'Lichtglanz,' 'strahlende Helligkeit,' 'machtvoller Glanz' o.ä." (p. 88). For Hofius' agreement with Vielhauer on this point, see p. 88 n. 86. For P. Vielhauer's view, see his "Paulus und das alte Testament," in his *Oikodome, Aufsätze zum Neuen Testament Bd. 2*, ed. G. Klein, 1979, pp. 196–228, pp. 210 f., where he renders the verb in 34:29 f., 35, "strahlend geworden sein." Vielhauer also makes a distinction between the δόξα of Moses and that of Christ in 3:7 ff. (cf. p. 212). Equally puzzling is A.T. Hanson's rendering of the verb throughout as "transfigured," cf. his *Jesus Christ in the Old Testament*, 1965, pp. 26 f. In contrast, the 1851 Bagster ET of the LXX appropriately renders the verb "was glorified" in 34:29, 35 and "was made glorious" in 34:30; cf. *The Septuagint Version of the Old Testament with an English Translation*, Zondervan ed., 1970, p. 118.

veil. As in the MT, the solution to the problem of the presence of God in the midst of his "stiff-necked" people thus becomes the repeated mediation and veiling of the glory of God on the face of Moses. But now this solution is made explicit by the development of the motif of the veil in connection with the δοξάζω terminology in 34:29, 30, 35.

Second, the interpretation of the "sons of Israel" in v. 30 as the "elders of Israel" (πρεσβύτεροι Ισραηλ) creates a possible allusion to the prior establishment of the covenant in Exod. 19–24. Of the seven other uses of πρεσβύτεροι in Exodus, all but one refer to the leaders of Israel (cf. Exod. 10:9 LXX). Of these six occurrences, four are found within the covenant context of chapters 19–24, where the "πρεσβύτεροι Ισραηλ" represent the people before YHWH,[195] with a fifth referring to Aaron and the "elders of Israel" eating a (covenant?) meal with Jethro in the presence of God (LXX 18:12).[196] The LXX of 34:30 may thus provide an intentional allusion not found in the MT to the prior experience of the "elders of Israel" who received the covenant stipulations in Exod. 19:7 and later joined Moses on Mt. Sinai for the "covenant meal" in Exod. 24:9–11. If so, the LXX of Exod. 34:29–35 becomes the expressed counterpart to Israel's prior covenant experience before the sin with the golden calf. The covenant has now been renewed, and with it the elders of Israel are once again brought into the presence of God's glory. But whereas in Exod. 19–24 the elders and the people experienced the presence of God directly, in Exod. 34:29–35 it is mediated through Moses who takes the place of YHWH in the theophany of God's glory. Hence, the parallel and distinction between Exod. 19–24 and Exod. 34 reflects the continuing reality of the people's rebellious nature (cf. 34:9).

In a similar way, the introduction of the πρεσβύτεροι terminology in 34:30 forges an explicit verbal link between Exod. 19–24 and Exod. 34:29–35 on the one hand, and Is. 24:21–23; 25:6–9 on the other, in addition to the thematic link already established in the MT. For in the LXX of Is. 24:23, the result of God's eschatological judgment is that "the Lord will reign from Zion and in Jerusalem, and he will be glorified before the elders" (καὶ ἐνώπιον τῶν πρεσβυτέρων[197] δοξασθήσεται). In a way not found in the MT, the terminological equivalence between these texts supports the interpretation of Is. 24:21–23 and 25:6–9 as the eschatological reversal of the consequences of the Israel's rebellion in the wilderness (see below, chapter five). In Isaiah 24–25 the me-

[195] LXX 19:7, where the equivalent πρεσβύτεροι τοῦ λαοῦ is found; 24:1; 24:9 in the variant supported by A; and 24:14 as a clear reference back to 24:1, 9.

[196] Even the rendering πρεσβύτεροι τοῦ λαοῦ in 17:5 is a clear reference to Israel's leaders. For the development of the πρεσβύτεροι terminology as a reference to Israel's representative leaders in the Pentateuch, cf. Num. 11:16, 24, 25, 30; Deut. 28:50; 31:9, 28; 32:7, 25.

[197] Sinaiticus, 88, the Lucian recension, 233, 449, 770, add αὐτοῦ; cf. Joseph Ziegler, *Isaias, Septuaginta Auctoritate Academiae Litterarum Gottingensis editum, Vol. XIV*, 1967, p. 207. Due to the probable influence of the MT on this variant, the shorter reading is to be preferred.

diation of God's presence made necessary by the people's sin at Mount Sinai is now done away with, as symbolized by the elders once again being able to encounter the glory of God directly on Mount Zion. Moreover, the revelation of the glory of God before the elders now extends not just to the people of Israel, as in Exod. 19:9–20:20 and 34:32, but "to all the nations on this mountain" (πᾶσι τοῖς ἔθνεσιν ἐπὶ τὸ ὄρος τοῦτο, Is. 25:6). The Gentiles share in the revelation of the glory of God in the midst of his people Israel. It is significant, therefore, that in Is. 56:3–11 the faithful among the nations are brought with Israel to the "holy mountain" (56:7) as a "synagogue" (συναγωγή) of those who "attach themselves to the Lord" (56:3, 6) and keep the covenant (56:6) by the Lord "who gathers the dispersed of Israel" (ὁ συνάγων τοὺς διεσπαρμένους Ισραηλ, 56:8).

Finally, the subsequent equation in 34:31 of the "elders of Israel" with οἱ ἄρχοντες τῆς συναγωγῆς as the translation equivalent of "the rulers in the assembly" (הנשׂיאים בעדה) makes it possible, by association, to interpret the synagogue practice of Paul's day as a direct extension and consequence of the chain of mediation pictured in Exod. 34:29–35,[198] though such an association and extension cannot be established with certainty. For although they overlapped semantically in the LXX,[199] already by Paul's day ἐκκλησία and συναγωγή were being distinguished as the gathering (not building!) of those who did and did not follow Christ as Messiah.[200] This is reflected in that although ἐκκλησία occurs 61 times in the Pauline corpus to refer to the gathering of Christians, Paul never uses συναγωγή in any context. Of the 56 occurrences of συναγωγή in the New Testament, only 5 are found outside of the Synoptics and Acts, and of these only James 2:2 uses it in reference to Chris-

---

[198] This same association between the "elders of Israel" and the "rulers of the synagogue" can be seen in Lev. 4:15 and Jud. 21:16, where the two concepts are combined (οἱ πρεσβύτεροι τῆς συναγωγῆς); 2 Esd. 10:8; 1 Macc. 1:26; 14:28 have "rulers and elders" (οἱ ἄρχοντες καὶ οἱ πρεσβύτεροι). For the other occurrences of the designation οἱ ἄρχοντες τῆς συναγωγῆς in the LXX, see Exod. 16:22; Num. 31:13, 26; 32:2; Josh. 9:15, 18, 19; 22:30.

[199] Though συναγωγή is most often used (i.e. 130 xs) to render עדה ("community"), it also occurs 36 xs for קהל (Hatch-Redpath, pp. 1309 f.). Cf. the use of συναγωγή to translate both קהל and עדה in Num. 20:1 f.; 4, 6, 8, 10–12, 22, the epexegetical use of συναγωγή and ἐκκλησία in Prov. 5:14; and the use of (ἐξ)εκκλησιάζω with συναγωγή in Lev. 8:3 f.; Num. 20:10; Jud. 20:1; 3 Kgs. 12:21.

[200] For this point and the relationship between συναγωγή and ἐκκλησία in the LXX, see Israel Peri, "Ecclesia und synagoga in der lateinischen Übersetzung des Alten Testamentes," BZ N.F. 33 (1989) 245–251, pp. 245 f., who also points to the fact that both terms can be used to translate קהל and related words. It is anachronistic, however, to refer to this distinction during the first century as that between "Christianity" and "Judaism," as Peri suggests. For a very helpful survey of the thorny historical and terminological issues surrounding the synagoge and proseuche in the pre- and post-70 periods, including an analysis of Hengel's important work and a survey of the evidence for the distinction between the "church" and the "synagogue" in the Gospel of Matthew, see Howard Clark Kee, "The Transformation of the Synagogue After 70 C.E.: Its Import for Early Christianity," NTS 36 (1990) 1–24.

tians.[201] Given this semantic distinction, it may have been natural for both Christians and Jews to view the first century synagogue as the continuation of the experience of the "rulers of the synagogue" and their people in Exod. 34:29 ff. Certainly within Exodus itself, the characteristic use of ἡ συναγωγή υἱῶν Ἰσραηλ ("the synagogue of the sons of Israel") for the people of Israel supports the representative identity implied between the "rulers of the synagogue" and the "sons of Israel" in Exod. 34:31 f.[202] Of special significance in this regard is Exod. 16:1–22, where the "rulers of the synagogue" (οἱ ἄρχοντες τῆς συναγωγῆς, v. 22) represent "the synagogue of the sons of Israel" (ἡ συναγωγή υἱῶν Ἰσραηλ, vv. 1 f., 6, 9 f.) before Moses as he delivers the commands of YHWH concerning the Sabbath. In the same way, in Exod. 34:29–35 (LXX), the "rulers of the synagogue" become the link between Moses and the people as their representatives. Only after Moses summons the elders to come near to the glory of God do the people themselves approach to hear what YHWH has commanded. As in Exod. 16:22, when Moses then assembles "all the synagogue of the sons of Israel" (πᾶσαν συναγωγὴν υἱῶν Ἰσραηλ) to declare to them YHWH's commands, the first subject is again the Sabbath (cf. 35:1–3). Although not identified with the beginning of the synagogue in Jewish tradition, the themes of Exod. 34:29–35:1 nevertheless form a vivid image of later synagogue practice in which the law of Moses is read on the Sabbath in the synagogue.

Such an image is reinforced by *m*. Aboth 1.1, where a direct line of tradition concerning the oral Torah is established from Moses on Mount Sinai to Joshua, from Joshua to the elders (!), from the elders to the prophets, and from the prophets to the "men of the Great Synagogue" (לאנשי כנסת הגדולה) who returned with Ezra from the exile and are said to form the beginning of the rabbinic tradition. [203] In later rabbinic tradition, not only Ezra and Nehemiah, but even sayings from the book of Nehemiah can be attributed directly to the Great Synagogue, while Liebreich has argued that the recital of the Shema and accompanying benedictions in *m*. Ber. 1:4 is patterned after the prayer of the Levites in Neh. 9:5, while the three benedictions of the Morning Service fol-

---

[201] But this may merely reflect the origin of James as a synagogue sermon. For the other uses, cf. John 6:59; 18:20; Rev. 2:9; 3:9. And as Peri, "Ecclesia," p. 245, points out, the uses in Rev. 2:9 and 3:9 also support this distinction, since "eine 'Ekklesia des Satans' wäre in jenen Zeiten schlechterdings unmöglich zu denken gewesen."

[202] Of the 20 occurrences of συναγωγή in Exodus, 12 are found in this phrase; cf. Exod. 12:3, 6, 47; 16:1, 2, 6, 9, 10; 17:1; 35:1, 4, 20; for this same phrase, see too Lev. 16:5, 17; 19:2; 22:18; Num. 8:9, 20; 13:27; 14:5, 7; 15:25, 33; 19:9; 20:22; 25:6; 26:2; Josh. 18:1. By contrast, ἐκκλησία occurs only 6 times in the Pentateuch, all in Deut. (cf. Deut. 4:10; 9:10; 18:16; 23:1,2; 31:30).

[203] Cf. Aboth 1.2, where Simon the Just is mentioned as one of the last of this Great Assembly, which is a reference either to Simon ben Onias I (High Priest from 310–291 BC) or to Simon II (High Priest from 219–199 BC), and the rest of the chapter in which the chain of tradition continues into the first three centuries AD. Text and note from Philip Blackman, *Mishnayoth, Vol. IV, Oder Nezikin*, 1954, p. 490.

low the same order as in Neh. 9:6–11.[204] But according to both the MT and the
LXX, Moses is *veiled* as he initiates this tradition by declaring the words of
the Lord to the people (cf. 35:1: οἱ λόγοι, οὓς εἶπεν κύριος ποιῆσαι αὐτούς)!
Reinforcement for reading Exod. 34:29 ff. as a symbolic prototype of later
synagogue practice can be found in later tradition as well. L.I. Rabinowitz
suggests that the first mention of a synagogue community may be found in the
mention of the "elders" (οἱ πρεσβύτεροι) of the people who gathered before
the prophet throughout Ezekiel (cf. 8:1; 14:1; 20:1), especially if the "little
sanctuary" in Ezek. 11:16 is an allusion to the synagogue itself.[205] The historical question of the actual existence of the synagogue in Ezekiel's day raised
by this observation, or of the actual link between Ezra-Nehemiah and later
synagogue practice, need not concern us. What is important is that the terminology of the "elders" found in Ezekiel and their role as representative of the
community can be taken as a parallel to the later synagogue institution. In the
same way, the demarcation in Exod. 34:29 ff. between the elders/rulers and the
people in approaching Moses as the mediator of the glory of God, as well as its
portrayal of the "synagogue community," may foreshadow the way in which
the "rulers" and "elders" represent the people in 2 Esdras 7–10 (Ezra 7–10MT)
and then extend their role in relationship to the Law of Moses as the prototype
of later synagogue practice in 2 Esdras18–19 (Nehemiah 8–9MT).[206]

---

[204] See *Gen. Rab.* 46.8; 78.3 in regard to Neh. 9:7 and *Exod. Rab.* 41.1 for Neh. 9:18. *Gen.
Rab.* 36.8, *b.* Meg. 3a, and *b.* Ned. 37b use Neh. 8:8 as grounds for the appropriate use of
"translation" (תרגום), and in the former even the LXX (!), in synagogue worship. Daniel
Sperber, "The Great Synagogue," *Encyclopaedia Judaica*, Vol. 15, 1971, pp. 629–631,
p. 629, points to the parallel between *Lev. Rab.* 2.11 and *Song of Songs Rab.* to 7:14 and the
Tg. Song of Songs 7:3 as further support for Ezra and Nehemiah's membership in the Great
Synagogue and the traditional view of its origin with Neh. 8–10. For the traditional view
that "... the beginnings of the liturgy of the post-Ezra synagogue are directly traceable to
Neh. 9:5–37, which ... determined to a large extent the structural and ideological pattern of
Jewish worship," and the parallels to Neh., see Leon J. Liebreich, "The Impact of Nehemiah
9:5–37 on the Liturgy of the Synagogue," *HUCA* 32 (1961) 227–237, pp. 228 f., 231, quote
from p. 228.
[205] See "Synagogue, Origins and History," *Encyclopaedia Judaica*, Vol. 15, 1971,
pp. 579–584, pp. 580 f.
[206] As illustrations of this representation, in 2 Esd. 7:28–8:1 Ezra expressly gathered "the
rulers" (οἱ ἄρχοντες) to go up with him to Jerusalem as representatives of the people. In 9:1
these rulers subsequently inform Ezra of the continuing transgression of intermarriage of
the people, priests, and Levites. In turn, in 10:8 these same rulers, with the "elders"
(πρεσβύτεροι) summon the people to assemble in Jerusalem in order to repent, and then in
10:14, 16 represent the people in separating from their pagan wives. Moreover, if in 10:14
the reading found in Vaticanus and Sinaiticus is followed against Alexandrinus, the people
are summoned to come to Jerusalem with their elders "from (their) synagogues" (ἀπὸ
συναγωγῶν). Similarly, together with the Levites and priests, it is "the rulers of the fami-
lies" (οἱ ἄρχοντες τῶν πατριῶν) who remain to study the Law in 2 Esdras18:13, represent
the people in setting their seal on the pledge to keep the covenant in 19:38; 20:14, and as a
result of having remained in Jerusalem to represent the people partake on their behalf in the
dedication of the wall in 22:31 (cf. 21:1). The association between Exod. 34:29 ff. and the

Solid evidence that the use of συναγωγή in Exod. 34:31 could be understood as a proleptic picture of the Jewish synagogue is found in Sirach 24:23, where in quoting Deut. 33:4 ("Moses commanded to us the law, a possession for the congregation of Jacob"), קְהִלַּת יַעֲקֹב is rendered συναγωγαῖς Ιακωβ. As M. Fishbane has pointed out concerning those responsible for the Greek version of Sirach, "In this way they brought the ancient tribal 'congregation' – which inherited the Mosaic Torah – into line with the 'synagogue of Jacob', established many centuries later."[207] It is noteworthy that in this same text the Law is identified in 24:23a as the "book of the covenant" (βίβλος διαθήκης), which in turn is equated with wisdom (cf. 24:1–22; cf. 15:1). But in contrast to the Law or "book of the covenant" now given to the synagogue on earth, wisdom is said to dwell in the midst of God's heavenly presence "in the ἐκκλησία ("assembly") of the most High" (Sir. 24:2). This distinction in terminology may reflect the fact that in Sirach συναγωγή can be used to designate the gathering of the wicked (cf. Sir. 21:9; 41:18; 45:18).[208] In contrast, ἐκκλησία is used in Sirach only to describe the gathered people of God in positive contexts.[209] Thus, in Sirach a possible negative connotation can be carried by συναγωγή which is not found with ἐκκλησία. Hence, in 16:6 we read that "In the synagogue of the sinners (ἐν συναγωγῇ ἁμαρτωλῶν) a fire is kindled, And in an apostate nation wrath burns." If Charles is right that Is. 10:6 provides a parallel to this latter phrase,[210] then 16:6 describes Gods' judgment on the

---

tradition in 2 Esdras at the level of language convention, however, is not consistent. The gathered people of God are here referred to as ἡ ἐκκλησία (θεοῦ) in 2 Esd. 18:2, 17; 23:1, and there is no use of the terminology of "the rulers of the synagogue." Nevertheless, the thematic parallels between Exod. 32–34 and Neh. 8–10 in the MT also hold true in the LXX. The common use of ἄρξοντες and πρεσβύτεροι in both contexts is therefore striking and may have cemented the two passages together for later readers by way of association. For as Jonathan Goldstein has observed, *1 Maccabees*, AB 41, 1976, pp. 502 f., the "great assembly" (συναγωγὴ μεγάλη) of priests, people, rulers of the nation (ἀρχόντων ἔθνους), and elders of the land (πρεσβυτέρων τῆς χώρας) in 1 Maccabees 14:28 recalls parallel assemblies in Exod. 19:1–9; 24:1–9; 1 Kgs. 20:7 f.; Ezra 10:9–14; and Neh. 9:1; 10:1–29. And in the Mishnaic tradition, "elders" (הַזְּקֵנִים) rule over practices in the Synagogue *(m.* Erubin 10.10), appoint R. Eliezer ben Azariah head of the academy *(m.* Zevachim 1.3), and on "the same day" even make a declaration concerning the Scriptural status of Ecclesiastes and Song of Songs *(m.* Yadayim 3.5). For the role of the "head" of the Synagogue, see *m.* Yoma 7.1; Sot. 7.7; and for that of the "minister" or "superintendent," besides these texts, *m.* Mak. 3.12. Again, although there is no direct allusion to Exod. 34:29 ff. in these passages, the constellation of terminology that was later associated with the synagogue creates an environment in which a link between the events of Exod. 34:29 ff. and later synagogue practice could possibly be conceived.

[207] *Biblical Interpretation*, p. 77. This same move is made in the LXX of Deut. 33:4.

[208] For the other positive uses of συναγωγή in Sirach to describe the gathered people of God, cf. 1:30; 4:7; 46:14. For its use outside of this context, cf. 31:3; 43:20.

[209] See Sir. 15:5; 21:17; 23:24; 31 (34):11; 33:19 (30:27); 38:33; 39:10; 44:15; 50:3, 20. The use in 26:5 is not clear.

[210] *The Apocrypha and Pseudepigrapha of the Old Testament, Vol. 1, Apocrypha*, 1913, p. 372 n. 6.

wicked of his own people and not upon the pagan nations. Moreover, this judgment against such a "synagogue" is an expression of the principle stated in 16:11 f. (cf. 16:14): "if there be one who is stiff-necked, a marvel it would be were he not punished," for God "judges a man according to his works (κατὰ τὰ ἔργα αὐτοῦ)," which, as we have seen above, is one of the few places in the LXX where σκληροτράχηλος appears outside of Exod. 33:3, 5 and 34:9! Moreover, in Prov. 29:1 we find the same association of the "stiff-necked man" (ἀνδρὸς σκληροτραχήλου) and the fire of God's judgment. Hence, God's judgment of the wilderness generation because of their "stiff-neck" can be associated by way of allusion with God's eschatological judgment of all those who manifest their "stiff-necked" condition by their works of disobedience to the Law as the embodiment of the wisdom of God.

Against this extensive backdrop of associated themes, and with Exodus 32–34 itself clearly in view, we now turn attention to Paul's argument in 2 Cor. 3:7–18. For as Dietrich-Alex Koch has recently observed, "Je stärker Paulus sich veranlaßt sieht, seine eigene Position theologisch zu klären, desto intensiver wird zugleich auch die Beschäftigung mit der Schrift und ihre Verwendung in seinen Briefen."[211] Nowhere is this more true than in 2 Cor. 3:7 ff., where Paul's purpose is to support the authority of his apostolic ministry on the basis of the Scriptures themselves.

---

[211] *Schrift als Zeuge*, p. 101.

Chapter Four

Paul's Ministry of the Spirit and Moses' Ministry of Death (2 Cor. 3:7–11)

The first and most obvious observation usually made concerning Paul's discussion in 2 Cor. 3:7–18, after its difficulty has been recognized, is that Paul builds his argument on the basis of the biblical tradition of the glory and veil of Moses from Exodus 34. Almost all interpreters assent to this fact.[1] But on the meaning and purpose of 3:7–18 itself, W.C. Van Unnik is still correct over 30 years later that "there is hardly a single point on which expositors agree."[2] The primary reason for this impasse can be traced back to the ramifications of the programmatic commentary of Hans Windisch.[3] Not surprisingly then, the way out of this impasse is to return to Windisch's original insight, but to take it in the opposite direction than has previously been the norm.

1. 2 Cor. 3:7–18 in Modern Research: The Legacy of Hans Windisch and the Deadlock in Recent Scholarship

The dominance of Windisch's work becomes evident when we compare it to J. Goettsberger's article, "Die Hülle des Moses nach Exod 34 und 2 Kor 3," which appeared in the same year as Windisch's commentary, but whose thesis

---

[1] For recent exceptions to this rule, see Carol Kern Stockhausen, *Moses' Veil and the Glory of the New Covenant, The Exegetical Substructure of II Cor. 3:1–4:6,* AB 116, 1989, pp. 113–116, who recognizes the Exod. 34 background, but sees Paul's argument in 3:7 ff. determined throughout by the prophetic texts behind 3:1–6; and O. Hofius, "Gesetz und Evangelium nach 2. Korinther 3," *Paulusstudien*, WUNT 51, 1989, pp. 75–120 (now also found in *"Gesetz" als Thema Biblischer Theologie*, Jahrbuch für Biblische Theologie Bd. 4, 1989, pp. 105–149), pp. 88 ff., for a similar view. Most recently, David Renwick, *Paul, the Temple, and the Presence of God*, Brown Judaic Studies 224, 1991, pp. 53 f., 109–121, has argued that the key to Paul's thought in 3:7–11 is the allusion to Haggai 2 in 3:10. See below for responses to these positions.
[2] "'With Unveiled Face,' An Exegesis of 2 Corinthians 3:12–18," *NovT* 6 (1963) 153–169 (now in his *Sparsa Collecta, Part One* , 1973, pp. 194–210). Van Unnik's comment follows the customary declaration of the exegetical difficulty of this passage.
[3] Windisch's work appeared in 1924 as the 9th edition of *Der Zweite Korintherbrief,* Kritisch-Exegetischer Kommentar über das Neue Testament, Begründet von H.A.W. Meyer, 6. Abteilung. It was reissued in 1970, edited by G. Strecker. The tremendous influence of Windisch's treatment of 2 Cor. 3 becomes clear when compared to its counterpart in the English-speaking world, Alfred Plummer's *A Critical and Exegetical Commentary on*

was lost in the shadow of Windisch's massive contribution.[4] Goettsberger's concern was to answer the question concerning the relationship between 2 Cor. 3:7–18 and Exod. 34:29 ff. For on the one hand, Goettsberger's exegesis of Exod. 34:29 ff. led him to the conclusion that in its original context the glory on Moses' face remained and did not vanish or fade (p. 9). But at the same time, he held firmly to the conviction that, "Der Apostel stützt sich *genau* auf das, was im alt. Texte ausgesprochen ist" (p. 13, emphasis mine). How then could Paul's apparent emphasis in 3:7, 11 and 13 that the glory *faded* (καταργουμένην, καταργούμενον, καταργουμένου) and came to an *end* (τέλος) be squared with the original intention of Exod. 34:29 ff., which clearly stressed the permanence of the glory on Moses' face? As Goettsberger realized, if these two aspects could not be reconciled, then Paul's interpretation of Exod. 34 was not merely an extension of the text, but a straightforward alteration of it (p. 7).

Goettsberger's solution was to argue that the problem itself was a false dilemma, since it was based upon a misreading of Paul's intention. In Goettsberger's opinion, the subject of the καταργέω-sayings in vv. 7, 11, and 13 was not the glory on Moses' face, but the old covenant (pp. 11 f.). As for τέλος in 3:13, Goettsberger argued that it meant "fully" or "completely" in the sense of ἕως τέλους, as in 2 Cor. 1:13 and Philo's *Vita Mosis* II, 70, and in contrast to ἀπὸ μέρους in 2 Cor. 1:14. Read in this way, 3:13 referred not to the glory coming to an end, but to Israel not seeing the "fulness" of what was fading, i.e. of the old covenant. By this Paul meant that Israel was not allowed to see the glory *at all times*, but as Exod. 34:29 ff. itself suggested, only when Moses spoke God's word. This was the deficiency of the old covenant. Unlike the new, the Mosaic covenant permitted only periodic rather than continuous access to God's glory (cf. pp. 13, 16). Once 2 Cor. 3 was better understood, the difficulties thus fell away and Paul's OT hermeneutic of faithfully relying on the OT text was vindicated.

Needless to say, Goettsberger's attempt to substantiate Paul's interpretation in 2 Cor. 3 as an accurate reflection of what Exod. 34 originally intended has not been accepted. There are serious problems with it lexically and exegetically. But his work did pinpoint the crucial hermeneutical issue at stake. Moreover, it provided a clear methodological alternative to the work of his contemporary, Hans Windisch. Nevertheless, the questionable exegesis produced by Goettsberger's desire to find continuity between Paul and his OT source[5] seemed to stand in bold contrast to what appeared to be Windisch's

---

the Second Epistle of St. Paul to the Corinthians, ICC, 1925 (last printing, 1978). Plummer's work, though filled with detailed linguistic observations, lacked Windisch's overall conception of a "midrash," which proved so determinative for future studies.

[4] Goettsberger's article appeared in *Biblische Zeitschrift* 16 (1924) 1–17. Hereafter, references to the works of Windisch and Goettsberger will be indicated in the body of the text.

[5] Besides his view of the referent of the καταργέω-sayings, Goettsberger concluded that the letter/Spirit contrast referred to the contrast between the old covenant as written on tab-

more objective and honest approach to the text. Goettsberger's attempt to reconcile Exod. 34 and 2 Cor. 3 helped to establish the very position he opposed. Where Goettsberger had worked hard to demonstrate continuity, though with little success, Windisch was content simply to acknowledge what seemed apparent to most, i.e. that Paul had radically reinterpreted his tradition.

Like Goettsberger, Windisch recognized that the καταργέω-sayings were determinative for Paul's adaptation of the Exod. 34 tradition. But unlike Goettsberger, Windisch concluded that they were "targumic like entries" which contradicted the very essence of Exod. 34 and could in no way be explained away (cf. pp. 113 f., 119–120). This conclusion, together with his admission that they referred directly to the glory on Moses' face, led Windisch to the interpretation which subsequently became exegetical orthodoxy among scholars:

"Der Glanz auf dem Angesicht des Moses war nur Abglanz von der Glorie, den Moses auf dem Berge erschienen war (Exod. 24:16 f.), und mußte *darum* erlöschen." (p. 114)

In the same way, τέλος in v. 13 must refer to the fact that the glory on Moses' face was coming to an end, so that Paul later interpreted the purpose of the veil to be Moses' attempt to hide this fact from the Israelites (p. 120).

But even more determinative was Windisch's understanding of the implications of Paul's apparently drastic reinterpretation of Exod. 34 for the question of Paul's OT hermeneutic. Windisch was not content merely to draw the conclusion that Paul simply *mis*-used or misinterpreted the OT. Rather, Windisch concluded that Paul's reading of Exod. 34 was a freely composed "midrash" motivated by the polemical situation in Corinth, and controlled by his own Christian presuppositions. In other words, Paul intentionally reinterpreted the OT text not only to support his own dogmatic assertions, but also to "slay his opponents with their own weapons" (p. 120).

These first two pillars of Windisch's position, i.e. that vv. 7, 11, and 13 radically reinterpret the original intent of Exod. 34 and that this reinterpretation can be characterized as a Christian midrash, soon became unchallenged commonplaces among exegetes. But it was the third aspect of Windisch's classic treatment of 2 Cor. 3 that came to exercise the most pervasive influence in the next 50 years of scholarship. For if 2 Cor. 3:7–18 were in fact such a "Christian midrash," then it stood out from its immediate context both in regard to its style and purpose. According to Windisch, Paul completely withdrew the polemical contrast between "Paulinismus und Judaismus" in 2:16b–3:6 and replaced it in 3:7 ff. with a more general contrast between "Christentum" and "Judentum" (p. 112).[6] Thus, although 3:7 ff. functioned to support the axiomatic statement of 3:6, it was only loosely connected with it (p. 112). In fact,

---

lets of stone and the new covenant written on the human spirit (cf. "Die Hülle des Moses," p. 10).

[6] 35 years later, J. Munck, *Paul and the Salvation of Mankind*, 1959, pp. 58, 171–187, could take this insight from Windisch to support his own thesis that, contrary to the position

according to Windisch, vv. 7–18 could be removed from the passage altogether without doing harm to its context (cf. pp. 112 f.). But if this were true, then suddenly a new question emerged. Where did this midrash come from if it was not originally part of Paul's argument in 2 Cor. 3? Since as a result of Windisch's commentary the nature of Paul's reinterpretation now seemed settled, it was this question, and not the meaning of 2 Cor. 3 itself, which provided the impulse for the next decades as scholars began to search for and reconstruct a pre-Pauline tradition (and the theology of those who created it) as the basis for Paul's argument.[7]

Ironically, then, the legacy of Hans Windisch's exegetical labor was to divert the attention of scholars away from the text he had so carefully analyzed and to plunge them into a debate concerning its pre-history.[8] Along the way, Goettsberger's exegetical question concerning the relationship between 2 Cor. 3 and Exod. 34 was lost in the shuffle. In its place came a source criticism of 2 Cor. 3 based upon the criteria of vocabulary and theological *Tendenz*. When such an approach was combined with Windisch's conception of the isolated nature

---

of the Tübingen school, 2 Cor. 3 does not contain any allusions to the position of the Judaizers. But this is certainly not what Windisch intended to imply; cf. *Zweite Korintherbrief*, pp. 112 ff. For a recent example of the influence of Windisch's position, see Jan Lambrecht, "Structure and Line of Thought in 2 Cor. 2:14–4:6," *Biblica* 64 (1983) 344–380, p. 346, who takes as his starting point the distinctive nature of 3:7–18 as a contrast between "Christentum und Judentum," so that, unlike 2:14–3:6 and 4:1–6, "Paul is no longer defending himself ... rather he gives us a theoretical comparison between the old and new dispensations."

[7] Cf. e.g. the next major commentary to appear on 2 Cor., H. Lietzmann's *An die Korinther I–II, Handbuch zum Neuen Testament, Bd. 9*, 1969[5], p. 111, where Windisch's definition of 3:7 ff. as a "Christian midrash" is quoted and then used as the basis for postulating that Paul had developed the midrash earlier and in another context in order to demonstrate the superiority of Christianity over Judaism. For the continuation of this view, see now Dietrich-Alex Koch, *Die Schrift als Zeuge des Evangeliums: Untersuchungen zur Verwendung und zum Verständnis der Schrift bei Paulus*, BHT Bd. 69, 1986, p. 322, who argues that 3:7–18 was written by Paul, though earlier and independently of the present context.

[8] The new question raised by Windisch's programmatic study received its first detailed answer in Siegfried Schulz's essay, "Die Decke des Moses, Untersuchungen zu einer vorpaulinischen Überlieferung," *ZNW* 49 (1958) 1–30. Schulz explicitly based his study on Windisch's understanding of the independent nature of 3:7–18, but took the additional step of arguing that, due to the concentration of *hapax legomena* in this section and what appeared to him to be the non-Jewish, mystery religion character of 3:18, the basis of this pericope originated in a pre-Pauline tradition (pp. 1–3, where Schulz quotes extensively from Windisch, *Zweite Korintherbrief*, pp. 112, 123.). The first step therefore was to isolate this tradition, which provided the key to the discontinuity between 2 Cor. 3 and Exod. 34. Schulz's own source analysis of the text led him to the conclusion that Paul's purpose in 3:7–18 was to oppose a Jewish Christian tradition, rooted in the OT itself and reflected in 3:7b, 13a, and 14b, that Moses wore the veil to *protect* Israel from the glory which caused them to fear because of their inability to endure its brilliance (p. 14), since for them there was an essential continuity between the experience of Moses and that of the Christian under the new covenant (p. 21). To counter this view in support of his position that Christ was the end of the Law, Paul *reinterpreted* the meaning of the veil to be Moses' attempt to *prevent* Israel from realizing that the glory was fading (p. 14).

and purpose of 3:7–18, it produced a confident dissection of Paul's argument into its pre-Pauline and Pauline elements as the key to Paul's argument.[9] The exegetical question concerning the meaning of Paul's argument itself was then soon eclipsed by the larger historical debate over the nature of Paul's opposition. But the modern debate concerning the identity and theology of Paul's opponents would grind to a halt, mired in an impasse caused by the faulty methodology upon which it was based.[10] And with its demise, the at-

---

[9] This approach reached its most thorough presentation in the work of Dieter Georgi, *Die Gegner des Paulus im 2. Korintherbrief, Studien zur Religiösen Propaganda in der Spätantike*, WMANT, Bd.11, 1964. According to Georgi, in 2 Cor. 3:7 ff. Paul confronts his opponents' adoption of the tradition that interpreted Moses to be a θεῖος ἀνήρ (cf. pp. 220–300). In order to counter this position, Paul provided his own interpretation of Exod. 33–34. But in reacting to the view of his opponents, Paul completely inverted and reversed the original intention of the OT texts (p. 259). Whereas Paul's opponents had emphasized the glory of Moses as the model θεῖος ἀνήρ, Paul de-emphasized it. To do so, Paul picked up the key terminology and themes of his opponents' midrash of Exod. 33–34 and, by quoting them in the context of his own exposition, effectively used their own ideas against them (cf. pp. 258–273). To demonstrate this, Georgi is able to separate out the genuine Pauline additions from the pre-Pauline tradition of his opponents in a detailed source-critical analysis of 3:7–18 (cf. pp. 274–282). For in Georgi's view, the critical assessments of Moses must belong to Paul, while the positive statements can be traced back to Paul's opponents. Georgi's method at this point is again reminiscent of Schulz' earlier study, although he applies it with much greater fervor. For the most recent development of Georgi's thesis, based upon a careful treatment of 3:7–18 itself, see Michael Theobald, *Die überströmende Gnade, Studien zu einem paulinischen Motivfeld*, 1982, pp. 177–211, esp. pp. 189 f., 192 f., 202–211, for his literary reconstructions and their impact on his interpretation of the text.

[10] The last serious attempt to argue from a *Religionsgeschichte* model that Paul's opponents in 2 Corinthians were gnostics was R. Bultmann's 1947 response to E. Käsemann's influential essay, "Die Legitimität des Apostels, Eine Untersuchung zu II Korinther 10–13," originally published in *ZNW* 41 (1942) 33–71, in his essay *Exegetische Probleme des Zweiten Korintherbriefes zu 2 Kor 5:1–5; 5:11–6:10; 10–13; 12:21* in *Symbolae Biblical Upsalienses, Vol.9*, 1947. By analyzing the "Stichworte" used in Paul's reply in 2 Cor. 10–13, especially τὰ σημεῖα τοῦ ἀποστόλου in 12:12 (see "Legitimität," pp. 34–36, 52–71), Käsemann had concluded that Paul's opponents were simply pneumatics who belonged to an association of Palestinians in the diaspora and had emphasized themselves in their preaching (pp. 37–49). In Käsemann's view, to say anything more than this could not be supported from the text (cf. pp. 37, 41). For the most extensive treatment of 2 Corinthians from the standpoint of the identity and theology of Paul's opponents since Baur, which once again seeks to challenge Baur's fundamental thesis, see Dieter Georgi, *Die Gegner des Paulus*. Georgi once again (!) takes as his starting point those "Stichworte" from 2 Cor. 10–13 which he feels represent the characteristics of Paul's opponents. Georgi's study leads him to the conclusion that Paul's opponents were Jewish-Christian missionaries and apostles of Palestinian origin who, as "Jewish pneumatics," utilized the propaganda methods of the Hellenistic Jewish apologists and modelled their activity and self-conception on the θεῖος ἀνήρ tradition within Hellenistic Judaism (cf. pp. 60, 145–167). With the publication of Georgi's work, Baur's thesis concerning Paul's opponents was finally presented with an equally systematic and comprehensive antithesis. But despite its widespread acceptance, Georgi's work has been severely criticized. See E. Güttgemann's review of Georgi's work in *Zeitschrift für Kirchengeschichte IV*, 77 (1966) 126–131 for one of the most severe criticisms of Georgi to date. For two additional and telling criticisms of Georgi's methodology and use of the sources, cf. John N. Collins, "Georgi's 'Envoys' in 2 Cor. 11:23," *JBL* 93

tempts to understand 2 Cor. 3 in the light of an *a priori* decision concerning the nature of Paul's opposition has also collapsed.[11] The only thing apparently left to do is to pick sides and then try to rearrange the existing data in some novel way.[12]

(1974) 88–96, and Paul Bowers, "Paul and Religious Propaganda in the First Century," *NovT* 22 (1980) 316–323. Hence, the new surge of optimism created by Georgi's work was premature. The position of F.C. Baur was, in fact, still very much alive. But in an ironic reversal of roles, it was now two scholars from outside Germany who rose up to defend Baur's classic thesis against the attack put forward by Georgi, Derk Oostendorp, *Another Jesus, A Gospel of Jewish-Christian Superiority in 2 Corinthians*, 1967, and the many works and commentaries on 1 and 2 Corinthians by C.K. Barrett from 1953–1973. Cf. now R.P. Martin, "The Opponents of Paul in 2 Corinthians: An Old Issue Revisited," *Tradition and Interpretation in the New Testament, FS E. Earle Ellis* , ed. G.F. Hawthorne and Otto Betz, 1987, p. 281, who also adduces Oostendorp and Barrett as the two central contemporary representatives of Baur's basic position. Moreover, by 1973 it had become clear to Barrett that the basic alternative was between the Bornkamm-Georgi hypothesis on the one hand, and his own position on the other. Thus, in the introduction to his commentary on 2 Corinthians, Barrett's main concern is to argue against those who hold that Paul's opponents were Hellenistic Jews who imitated the style of propaganda used by the θεῖος ἀνήρ of the Hellenistic world. For an example of the ongoing influence of the work of Schulz and Georgi as paradigmatic for understanding 2 Cor. 3, see now John Koenig, "The Knowing of Glory and its Consequences (2 Corinthians 3–5)," in *The Conversation Continues, Studies in Paul and John in Honor of J. Louis Martyn*, ed. Robert T. Fortna and Beverly R. Gaventa, 1990, pp. 158–169, pp. 159 f.

[11] Hence, the recent proposal of Jerry L. Sumney, *Identifying Paul's Opponents, The Question of Method in 2 Corinthians*, JSNT Supplement Series 40, 1990, of a methodology based upon a "minimalist approach" to identifying Paul's opponents is to be welcomed for its emphasis on the priority of exegesis in a "text-focused method," for its insistence upon a sound evaluation and use of proper sources, together with a "stringently" limited application of the "mirror technique," and for its rejection of the attempt to approach the text with a previously determined, externally based, reconstruction. For his conclusion concerning the goal and focus of this method, see pp. 115–119, 187–190 (quotes from pp. 119, 187, 189) and my review of Sumney's work in *JBL* 111 (1992) 347–350. However, when applied to 2 Corinthians, Sumney's own method offers no new insights into the identity of Paul's opponents. Cf. his pp. 145–147, 162 f., 169–172, and his final conclusion concerning their identity on pp. 177–179, 184 f., in which he agrees with the previous proposal of Käsemann concerning the opponents behind 2 Cor. 10–13 as pneumatics, rather than Judaizers, Gnostics, or Georgi's "divine men." He then argues that, although they may not be the same persons and that change and development may have taken place between the letters, Paul is nevertheless facing the same "kind of opponent" in 2 Cor. 1–9, while the short time span between these letter fragments leads one to "reasonably conclude" that they are part of the same group (p. 183).

[12] Cf. e.g. the recent study of Renwick, *Temple*, who moves his argument forward by positing at every key transition a reconstruction of what would be needed to convince Paul's opponents or make his assertions acceptable to them (cf. pp. 47 f., 52 f., 81 f., 87 f., 89 f., 95 f., 105–109, 112, 121, 150). In Renwick's view, 3:7 is an explicit reference to the Mosaic paradigm being used by Paul's opponents to illustrate the valid characteristics of those who were experiencing the presence of God, i.e., like Moses, their face would shine (pp. 48, 52). For Paul's opponents, Moses thus represented "the paradigmatic example of the appearance of a person who had been where δόξα was …" (p. 106), while Paul's suffering indicated that he was a person who did not stand in God's presence and therefore could not impart the salvation of God's presence to others (pp. 44, 47 f.). Hence, though representing Paul's own

But such a reshuffling of the evidence has been called into question by the serious doubt being raised concerning the historical reality which is said to undergird each of the two major positions being advocated today. On the one hand, Güttgemann early on questioned Georgi's evidence for the very existence of a θεῖος ἀνήρ concept in Judaism,[13] while Collins has sharply criticized Georgi's attempt to interpret διάκονοι Χριστοῦ in 2 Cor. 11:23 in the sense of "envoys," thus questioning his many parallels to Greek literature.[14] And Paul Bowers has called Georgi's entire enterprise into question by following Sandmel in maintaining that we do not have any Jewish parallels to the missionary motives and methods of Paul.[15] On the other hand, those who want to maintain that Paul's opponents were in some sense "Judaizers" must now contend with the challenge of E.P. Sanders, *et al.* and the "new perspective on Paul" which it has produced.[16] Indeed, many from this perspective doubt if Paul's polemics have anything to do with the real position of his opponents at all! But if Paul's opponents were in fact Jews who were somehow connected to Jerusalem, and if Paul did in fact understand them correctly, rather than having erected a "straw man," then the nature of this Judaistic opposition can no longer simply be *assumed* to be legalistic.[17] This is especially the case in 2 Corinthians, where it has long been observed that the issue of circumcision never appears and the Law as such is never explicitly mentioned.

The deadlock in recent scholarship illustrates how easily Paul's discussion can be made to fit into two competing pictures of Paul's opponents, neither one of which has won any kind of general acceptance. Furthermore, like the gnostic-hypothesis of a previous generation, both of these competing hypotheses stand under the shadow of serious questions concerning their historical reliability. The way out of this impasse is *not*, therefore, to construct yet another *religionsgeschichtliche* theory about the identity and theology of Paul's opponents, as needful as such a theory apparently is. The temptation to reconstruct some grand hypothesis based on isolated fragments from Paul's epistles, which are then filled out by recourse to distant parallels, must be resisted.

---

theological interpretation of Exod. 32–34, 2 Cor. 3 is Paul's response to the fundamental critique of his opponents, who *first* used the view of Moses in Exod. 32–34 and introduced the concept of "glory" into the debate (cf. pp. 48, 99, 105 f.). According to his opponents, Paul's "face did not 'shine' (presumably with the figurative light of a charismatic and dynamic personality) as it ought to have done were he truly ordained by God to the task of proclamation, as was Moses" (p. 106). Sumney's work is also characteristic of this basic approach in that it offers so little exegesis of even the most important texts.

[13] "Review," p. 129.

[14] See his entire article, "Georgi's 'Envoys'," pp. 88–96.

[15] "Paul and Religious Propaganda," pp. 321 f.

[16] See the Introduction.

[17] See e.g. E.P Sanders' own response to the views of Käsemann and Leander Keck on the nature of what Paul opposed in Romans and Galatians in his *Paul, the Law, and the Jewish People*, 1983, pp. 154–160, in which he argues that the issue was the question of the appropriate "central membership requirement" *per se* (p. 159) and not a quantitative or qualitative critique of the Law.

The history of the debate ought to make us highly suspicious of all such *a priori* approaches to Paul's letters, especially a passage like 2 Cor. 3:7 ff., with its interpretive character and polemical purpose. Rather, C.K. Barrett's advice is well taken. He advocated that we "take a number of vital and difficult passages, and establish for them, as firmly as possible, exegetical results," in the conviction that "a picture will emerge with reasonably clear outlines, however vague some of the details may remain."[18]

2 Cor. 3:7 ff. is, of course, a leading example of just such a "vital and difficult passage." But this means we must first interpret 2 Cor. 3:7–18 *on its own terms* as *Paul's perspective*, as free as possible from any preconceived notion concerning the nature of Paul's opposition in Corinth.[19] Although inextricable partners, the historical task of reconstruction must be subservient to the exegetical task of description. Only in this way will we minimize the dangers of an uncontrollable circularity. Klaus Berger's conclusion concerning the needed refinements in approaching the question of Paul's opponents is thus my starting point: "Hypothesen sind nur insoweit zulässig, als sie für die Interpretation *unabdingbar* sind."[20] Indeed, W.C. Van Unnik set the agenda and tone of the following work when he declared,

"... there is not a shred of evidence that the apostle is commenting upon a previously existing document or teaching nor is it clear why Paul himself should have been unable to make this application of the Exodus story. Before setting out on hypothetical reconstructions behind the given text, we should first try to understand the text as it stands."[21]

---

[18] "Paul's Opponents in 2 Corinthians," *NTS* 17 (1970/1971) 233–254, p. 237.

[19] See already the observations on the circularity of reasoning in current scholarship and the call back to the text by C.J.A. Hickling, "The Sequence of Thought in 2 Corinthians, Chapter Three," *NTS* 21 (1975) 380–395, p. 380, and now most extensively by Sumney, *Paul's Opponents*, esp. pp. 17 ff., 34–42, 46–55, 71, 77–83. Most recently, this need to return to the text "in its own terms and in its own literary context" provided the stimulus for Stockhausen's study, cf. her *Moses' Veil*, p. 13, and her discussion of the debate concerning 2 Cor. 3 on pp. 8–14. Though we share many of the same concerns about how to approach this text, our conclusions differ significantly (see above, chapter two and below, chapter five).

[20] "Die impliziten Gegner. Zur Methode des Erschließens von 'Gegnern' in neutestamentlichen Texten," in *Kirche, FS Günther Bornkamm zum 75. Geburtstag*, ed. Dieter Lührmann and Georg Strecker, 1980, pp. 373–400, p. 394 (emphasis mine). See too O. Hofius, "Gesetz und Evangelium," p. 107 n. 203, for a rejection of the possibility of painting a "präzises und profiliertes Bild" of Paul's opponents in 2 Cor. 3. The most that can be said is that Paul's opponents not only challenged his apostolic authority, but also represented a synthesis of the Law and Gospel, and in so doing maintained the "*Heils*relevanz" of the Torah in renunciation of the "solus Christus" of the Gospel. It is this synthesis which Paul fights against.

[21] "'With Unveiled Face'," p. 156. Cf. too Oostendorp, *Another Jesus*, p. 31, who rejects the hypothesis that in 2 Cor. 3:7 ff. Paul was merely reworking a midrash inherited from his opponents as "incredible." In Oostendorp's opinion, there is "no reason to doubt that Paul was capable of independently working out the exegetical arguments of 3:7–18" (p. 31). See now Linda L. Belleville, *Reflections of Glory, Paul's Polemical Use of the Moses-Doxa Tra-*

The ground swell of interest in 2 Cor. 3:7–18 in the past 15 years from precisely this standpoint,[22] not to mention the serious questions posed concerning the letter/Spirit contrast, indicate that the time has come to let the question of Paul's opponents lie fallow until new insights into Paul's argument itself can be harvested. But inasmuch as the interpretations of Paul's use of the tradition concerning Moses' veil currently being offered are widely divergent, the only way forward is to reopen the age-old question of the meaning and method of Paul's argument from Exodus 34 in 2 Cor. 3:7–18.

2. The Starting Point for Interpreting 2 Cor. 3

The question before us is thus the same question originally raised and answered in such distinct ways by J. Goettsberger and Hans Windisch in 1924. If Paul indeed builds his argument in 2 Cor. 3:7–18 on the basis of the glory and veil of Moses from Exod. 34:29–35, then how in fact does he interpret his

---

dition in 2 Corinthians 3.1–18, JSNT Supplement Series 52, 1991, pp. 20–23, 142–151, who argues extensively that vv. 7–18 were composed by Paul himself and play an integral role in Paul's polemic against his opponents. See her discussion for the literature of those who argue that 3:7–18 are not immediately connected to their surrounding context, lack a polemical focus, are a reworking of a non-Pauline midrash, or were originally composed by Paul for a different context; and pp. 250–257 for a refutation of these views. Belleville's conclusion, p. 144, that 3:7–18 fits into Paul's larger apologetic by making the point "that his competence as a minister lies in the competence of the ministry that he represents" (pointing to 2 Cor. 1:15–22 as well), supports the basic position taken in this work. For Belleville, however, the nature of this competence is different than that argued here.

[22] See in addition to the works of Stockhausen and Belleville, A.T. Hanson, "The Midrash in 2 Corinthians 3: A Reconsideration," *JSNT* 9 (1980) 2–28; Joseph A. Fitzmyer, "Glory Reflected on the Face of Christ (2 Cor. 3:7–4:6) and a Palestinian Jewish Motif," *Theological Studies* 42 (1981) 630–644; Morna D. Hooker, "Beyond the Things that are Written? St. Paul's Use of Scripture," *NTS* 27 (1981) 295–309; Seyoon Kim, "Excursus: The Antithetical Typology between the Sinai Theophany and the Damascus Christophany (2 Cor. 3:1–4:6)," in his *The Origin of Paul's Gospel*, WUNT 2. Reihe 4, 1981, pp. 233–239; Earl Richard, "Polemics, Old Testament, and Theology. A Study of 2 Cor. 3:1–4:6," *Revue Biblique* 88 (1981) 340–367; J. Lambrecht, "Structure and Line of Thought in 2 Cor. 2:14–4:6," *Biblica* 64 (1983) 344–380; Jost Eckert, "Die geistliche Schriftauslegung des Apostels Paulus nach 2 Kor 3:4–18," *Dynamik im Wort, Lehre von der Bibel, Leben aus der Bibel*, ed. Katholischen Bibelwerk, 1983, pp. 241–256; William J. Dumbrell, "Paul's Use of Exodus 34 in 2 Corinthians 3," in *God Who is Rich in Mercy, FS D.B. Knox* , ed. Peter T. O'Brien and David G. Peterson, 1986, pp. 179–194; Ekkehard Stegemann, "Der Neue Bund im Alten, Zum Schriftverständnis des Paulus in II Kor 3," *ThZ* 42 (1986) 97–114; Reinhold Liebers, *Das Gesetz als Evangelium, Untersuchungen zur Gesetzeskritik des Paulus*, AThANT 75, 1989, pp. 96–123; and the recent commentaries of Victor Paul Furnish, *II Corinthians*, AB Vol. 32A, 1984, pp. 201–245; Ralph P. Martin, *2 Corinthians*, WBC Vol. 40, 1986, pp. 58–74 (though see his view, p. 64, that in 3:10 Paul is responding to some Jewish or Jewish Christian apologetic on Moses' behalf, and p. 66, that there existed a "Moses-midrash" from which Paul drew certain items); and Friedrich Lang, *Die Briefe an die Korinther*, NTD Bd. 7, 1986, pp. 272 f.

Scriptural tradition and in what way does it contribute to his own presentation of the nature of his apostolic ministry? The history of the interpretation of 2 Cor. 3:7 ff. makes clear that the key to answering this question is twofold. First, the meaning of Paul's statement in 3:7, "the sons of Israel were not able to gaze into the face of Moses διὰ τὴν δόξαν τοῦ προσώπου αὐτοῦ τὴν καταργουμένην," must be determined and related to the καταργέω-terminology in 3:11, 13, 14. Second, Paul's understanding of the purpose of Moses' veil as presupposed in 3:7 and then explicitly developed (or altered[23]) in 3:13–16 must be ascertained. These issues are, of course, not distinct. Paul's perspective on the δόξα from 3:7–11 is directly linked with the purpose of Moses' veil in 3:13 and with καταργέω in 3:14b, which then supports the significance of the "veil" for his own day in 3:14–18.

This conclusion has found much support in recent literature on 2 Cor. 3, though the attempt to read Paul's interpretation of Exod. 34:29–35 against the backdrop of its OT context and later development in canonical tradition has surprisingly not been pursued in detail.[24] The reason for this is again the influence of Windisch, even among those who have rejected the history of tradition which he created. Windisch argued that Paul's "midrashic" use of this Scriptural tradition could be explained in tandem with the practices which surrounded him as a coherent and understandable exegetical enterprise, despite what for Windisch was its obvious discontinuity with the original meaning of Exod. 34:29 ff. The only difference between Paul's use of the OT and the midrashic interpretations of his Jewish contemporaries was his distinctively Christian presuppositions and the polemical purposes of his writing.[25] Under

---

[23] As paradigmatically argued by S. Schultz, "Die Decke des Moses, pp. 7–11.

[24] The glaring exception to this rule is the brief but extremely helpful essay by Dumbrell, "Paul's Use of Exodus 34," in which he argues that "the detailed application of Exod. 34:29–35 ... within 2 Cor. 3:7–18 ... virtually structures the argument of that important section" (p. 179, pointing to the use of Exod. 34:29 ff. in vv. 7, 9, 10, 13–16, and 18). In his words, "The argument from 2 Cor. 3:7–18 remains directly within the range of Moses' experience on Sinai and appears to appeal consciously to it. It would thus seem that that is the point at which an examination of the context must begin" (p. 180). For the almost total lack of regard for the OT backdrop to 3:7–18, see e.g. Theobald, *Gnade*, pp. 168 ff., in which, despite his detailed exegesis, he merely observes that Paul is building his argument on his opponents' reading of the biblical text, so that the meaning of the key terms and assertions in the passage is determined apart from and in contrast to their OT backdrop (cf. e.g. pp. 178, 185 f., 188–190, 195, 202 ff.). Even Stockhausen's major study, *Moses' Veil* , though to be applauded for its return to the text and for taking the OT backdrop to 2 Cor 3 seriously, is characterized by reading 3:7–18 in the light of her previous understanding of 3:1–6 and its background, with the latter (together with Is. 6 and 29), not Exod. 32–34, providing the insights needed to understand 3:7–18. But as we will see below, once Exod. 34 is put back within its context, not only does Paul's argument in 3:7–18 make sense in itself, but its apologetic force can be more adequately appreciated.

[25] *Der Zweite Korintherbrief*, pp. 112, 120. As other examples of such "Christian midrash" Windisch listed 1 Cor. 10:1 ff.; Gal. 3:6 ff.; 4:21 ff.; Rom. 4:9 ff.; Heb. 4:7–11; 6:20–7:28; Barn. 6:8–19; 12:5–7; 11:6–11, 13.

the power of this paradigm, still dominant among modern exegetes, Paul's interpretation of Exod. 34 in 2 Cor. 3:7–18 is merely the arena in which his prior convictions as expressed in the letter/Spirit contrast of 3:6 are played out.[26] Hence, even among those who refuse to look behind the text of 3:7–18 to Paul's opponents as the key to Paul's thinking, the apparent "midrashic" nature of Paul's Christian "rereading" of Exod. 34 has consistently directed scholars' attention away from 3:7–18 itself and its OT background in favor of Paul's controlling convictions as expressed in 3:6bc.

In returning to the questions posed by Windisch and Goettsberger, the integrated nature of 2 Cor. 3:4–4:6 requires that we do so with an eye toward Paul's previous argument in 2 Cor. 2:14–3:6. But the interpretive nature of 3:7–18 also demands that we examine this text with Exod. 32–34 firmly in view as a self-sustaining argument in support of 3:6. In this sense, those who argued that 3:7–18 is in some sense independent of its surrounding context were right in what they affirmed, though wrong in their subsequent denial of the integral contribution that Paul's argument from Scripture makes to its surrounding context. It is to this argument, considered on its own terms, that we now turn our attention.

3. The Ministry of Death and the Ministry of the Spirit (2 Cor. 3:7–8)

It has often been observed that Paul's argument in 3:7–18 falls naturally into two parts, 3:7–11 and 3:12–18. This is indicated by the inference drawn in 3:12 (cf. οὖν) on the basis of the point established in 3:7–11, which is summarized in v. 12 in the causal participial phrase ἔχοντες τοιαύτην ἐλπίδα. Verse 12 thus provides a turning point in Paul's argument in which he begins to draw the conclusion from his line of thought in vv. 7–11.[27] This logical transition is supported thematically by the switch in focus from the "glory" of the two ministries in 3:7–11, to the veil of Moses and its implications in 3:13–18. Δόξα and the related verb δοξάζω clearly dominate vv. 7–11, occurring eight and

---

[26] So recently Peter von der Osten-Sacken, "Die Decke des Mose," in his *Die Heiligkeit der Tora*, 1989, pp. 87–115, p. 101, who sees 3:6 as providing the hermeneutical key which makes Paul's understanding of the Exodus tradition possible. In von der Osten-Sacken's view, this understanding is based on the position of the opponents, who preach Christ and Moses, while Paul preaches that the glory of God is to be found only in Christ (p. 101). Hence, for von der Osten-Sacken, Paul's antithesis between the ministry of Moses and his own contradicts the positive nature of Paul's own attribution of glory to Moses, which makes his comparison work in the first place (p. 102)!

[27] See Theobald, *Gnade*, p. 170, who argues in detail that 3:12, like 3:4 before it and 4:1 after it, is a "pivot" or "joint" *(Gelenk)* in Paul's argument, summing up what Paul has just said and providing a transition to what follows. He argues further that 3:12 ties 3:7–18 together, uniting the two themes of "hope" and "boldness," while 4:1 reaches back to 3:4.

two times respectively,[28] whereas the theme is not explicitly mentioned again until v. 18. Moreover, Paul consistently places the word δόξα at the end of each of the comparative statements throughout vv. 7–11 so that the pattern established becomes striking.[29] In contrast, Paul's assertion concerning his own ministry in v. 12, the hardness of Israel's minds in v. 14a, their current relationship to the παλαιὰ διαθήκη and Moses in vv. 14b–15, and the contrast to Israel's situation in vv. 16–18 are all based upon the meaning and significance of the veil. Finally, vv. 7–11 are set off from 12–18 by their distinctive *qal wahomer* (i.e., *a minore ad maius*, or *a fortiori*) mode of argumentation, while Paul's argument in vv. 12–18 is sustained by an extended application of the interpretation of Exod. 34:29–35 first introduced in 3:7 and then developed in 3:13–14a, 16. Logically, thematically, and structurally, therefore, an interpretation of 3:7–18 must treat this section as a two step argument in which the glory of the respective ministries in vv. 7–11 becomes the basis for the conclusions drawn concerning the ministry of Paul in vv. 12–18. But, as we will now see, the structure of the argument of 3:7–8 indicates that 3:7–11 also provides the basis for the conclusions Paul has *already* drawn in 3:4–6.

a) The Argument of 2 Cor. 3:7–8

The first of Paul's three comparisons in 3:7–11 is established by the rhetorical and conditional question of 3:7–8. The comparison is based on the conditional link εἰ ... πῶς μᾶλλον ("if ... how much more"), while the negative particle οὐχί in v. 8a indicates that the question expects a positive answer. The condition is therefore a real one. But there is no question, from Paul's perspective, that the fulfillment of the condition *(protasis)*, and hence the reality of the conclusion to be drawn from it *(apodosis)*, are beyond doubt. For Paul, "the ministry of the Spirit exists in glory" (3:8). The purpose of 3:9–11 is to support this conclusion further by explaining in what way Israel's experience, as recounted in 3:7, actually leads to the conclusion of 3:8.[30]

Yet the implications of the rhetorical *form* of Paul's opening comparison in vv. 7–8 for the *function* of Paul's argument in 3:7–11 have not been taken seriously enough by commentators. Just as Paul began the previous section of his argument in 3:1–6 with the rhetorical questions of 3:1, and then supported their expected answer in 3:2 f., here too Paul introduces his discussion with a similar unanswered question and then goes on to support its intended answer in vv. 9–11 (cf. the γάρ of 3:9). An analysis of 3:1 indicates, moreover, that its

---

[28] This is often observed. See too now Hofius, "Gesetz und Evangelium," p. 107.

[29] For this observation, see Theobald, *Gnade*, p. 178, and Stockhausen, *Moses' Veil*, p. 111.

[30] So too Theobald, *Gnade*, p. 178, who argues that 3:7 f. is the "Leitsatz" for 3:9–11 and thus occupies an "übergeordnete Stellung" in the argument, with the latter verses of 3:9–10 functioning to "explicate" 3:7 f., and 3:11 drawing the summarizing conclusion.

rhetorical questions are a direct support for Paul's previous assertion in 2:17.[31] In the same way, the terminological and conceptual links between 3:6 and 3:7 ff. confirm that here too Paul continues his argument from 3:6bc in support of his sufficiency as an apostle (3:5–6a), even as 3:1–3 functioned as a continuation of 2:17.[32] This means that 3:7–11 functions not only to support what follows in 3:12–18, but also to support what precedes in 3:4–6. Rather than offering a detached, abstract reflection on the nature of the new covenant ministry originally determined for a different context, in 3:7–11 Paul is directly supporting the previous assertion of his confidence as an apostle in 3:4 as undergirded by his prior argument for his sufficiency in 3:5–6.[33]

Moreover, like 3:1, the use of a rhetorical question in 3:7–8 indicates that the *apologetic* purpose of Paul's earlier argument continues in 3:7 ff. In view of this apologetic context, we ought to be alert for the way in which Paul continues to offer *evidence* for his sufficiency.[34] It should not be surprising, therefore, that in both cases Paul argues for his sufficiency on the basis of his "ministry of the Spirit" in Corinth, buttressed by his interpretation of the Scriptures (cf. 3:7–11 with 3:3). In this sense, 3:7–11 is to the assertion of Paul's sufficiency in 3:5–6a *structurally*, what 3:1–3 is to the same assertion in 2:16b:[35]

2:16b: Paul's Sufficiency	3:5–6a: Paul's Sufficiency
2:17: First Support	3:6bc: First Support
(Paul's Suffering)	(Letter/Spirit Contrast)
3:1–3: Subsequent Support	3:7–11: Subsequent Support
(Paul's Ministry of the Spirit in view of the Scriptures)	(Paul's Ministry of the Spirit in view of the Scriptures)

But unlike 3:1, Paul's question in 3:7–8 is not a diatribal "false conclusion" introduced to stave off an objection or accusation which Paul anticipates from

---

[31] For a summary of my understanding of the function of 3:1–3 in relationship to 2:17, see *Suffering and the Spirit*, pp. 174–176, 219 f.

[32] Cf. γράμματος + γράμμα ἀποκτέννει (3:6bc) / ἡ διακονία τοῦ θανάτου ἐν γράμμασιν (3:7a); λιθίναις (3:3) / λίθοις (3:7); πνεύματι θεοῦ ζῶντος (3:3) + πνεύματος + πνεῦμα ζωοποιεῖ (3:6bc) / ἡ διακονία τοῦ πνεύματος (3:8); διακονηθεῖσα (3:3) + διακόνους (3:6) / διακονία (3:7–8).

[33] See too Theobald, *Gnade*, pp. 174 f., 178 f., who argues on the basis of the theme of *Superabundantia* throughout the context for the integral place of 3:7–18 in the argument of 3:4–4:1 and against the common conception of its function as an excursus on the general theme of the relationship between synagogue and church, letter and Spirit, or the Law and Christ.

[34] So too F. Lang, *Die Briefe an die Korinther*, NTD 7, 1986[16], p. 272, who observes that in 3:7 ff. Paul goes on, "seine Zuverlässigkeit und Aufrichtigkeit als Apostel aus der Eigenart des ihm verliehenen Amtes zu erweisen" by comparing the office of Moses under the old covenant with that of the Christian apostle under the new. Lang, however, understands the nature of this contrast to be significantly different than that proposed in this study, seeing the Mosaic ministry of death having to do with the Law as incapable of being fulfilled and as perverted into a death-producing letter used to justify oneself (cf. pp. 271, 273).

[35] For the relationship between 2:16b and 3:4–6a, see chapter two.

the Corinthians or his opponents.[36] In 3:7 f. Paul does not introduce a new theme, as he did in 3:1 in turning from the evidence of his suffering in 2:14–17 to the evidence of his ministry of the Spirit in 3:1–3. Instead, the themes introduced in 3:6bc are now *further* explained and defended. Unlike 3:1 and the use of this diatribal style elsewhere in Paul, the rhetorical question of 3:7 f. is not transitional, but indicates a *continuation* of the argument of 3:6bc.[37] Hence, by introducing his discussion of the glory of the ministry of the Spirit with a rhetorical question, Paul begins his argument in 3:7–18 by exhibiting his own confidence in the persuasive strength of the opening assertion of v. 8. Paul's question in 3:7 f. sets up between Paul and the Corinthians a common ground basis of support from which he can then draw his conclusion in 3:12–18. By using the rhetorical question Paul wins the advantage of forcing his hearers to join him in acknowledging that, given the validity of the premise from v. 7, the point of verses 8 is "obviously" true.

This is reflected in the mode of argumentation itself. It is now a commonplace among students of Paul to recognize the *qal wahomer* nature of Paul's arguments in 3:7–11 in which, according to the "seven rules" attributed to Hillel, "what applies in a less important case will certainly apply in a more important case."[38] This style of argument was, of course, not confined to Judaism, and it has been suggested that Hellenistic influence played the decisive role in the formulation of this practice now preserved in rabbinic tradition.[39] What is decisive for understanding Paul in 2 Cor. 3:7–11, however, is not where Paul learned this type of argumentation, but wherein the force of the argument itself lies. For as Carol Kern Stockhausen has recently pointed out concerning the nature of such an argument,

"This is simply an example of reasoning *a fortiori*. This rule of syllogism is familiar in Greek rhetoric of the New Testament period as an argument *a minore ad maius*. Both the similarity which is the ground of comparison and the dissimilarity on the basis of which the argument functions are presupposed and not proven by the inference. The purpose of the inference itself is only to indicate the presence of a characteristic in the superior on the basis of its known presence in the inferior."[40]

---

[36] For the development of this understanding of the form and function of 3:1, see my *Suffering and the Spirit*, pp. 177–179.

[37] Cf. the transitional use of the diatribal "false conclusion" in Rom. 3:9; 6:2; 6:15; 7:7, 13; 9:14; 11:1; 11:11. For an example of the relevance of recognizing this and other types of rhetorical questions illustrated from Rom. 9–11, see my "The Salvation of Israel in Romans 11:25–32, A Response to Krister Stendahl," *Ex Auditu* 4 (1988) 38–58, pp. 45 f.

[38] As found in Abot R. Nat. 37; Sifra 3a; *t.* San. 7.11, here quoted from the convenient listing and discussion in John Bowker, *The Targums and Rabbinic Literature, An Introduction to Jewish Interpretations of Scripture*, 1969, pp. 315–318.

[39] See already David Daube, "Rabbinic Methods of Interpretation and Hellenistic Rhetoric," *HUCA* 22 (1949) 239–264, pp. 251–257.

[40] *Moses' Veil*, p. 28. Cf. p. 28 n. 81, for a representative list of 15 recent scholars who point out the *qal wahomer* nature of Paul's argument; and p. 110, for her other formulation of the argument.

At first glance, Paul's argument in 3:7–8 thus looks surprisingly simple and straightforward once transposed from its rhetorical form into the declaration it represents: "If the ministry of *death* came *in glory*" (εἰ δὲ ἡ διακονία τοῦ θανάτου ... ἐγενήθη ἐν δόξῃ), "then the ministry of the *Spirit* will more surely[41] exist *in glory*" (πῶς οὐχὶ μᾶλλον ἡ διακονία τοῦ πνεύματος ἔσται ἐν δόξῃ;). This is especially the case if one reads vv. 7–8 (and then by implication vv. 9–11) as conceptually derived from and dependent upon 3:6c.[42] Paul's "argument" in 3:7 f. then becomes, in reality, merely a repetition of his prior Christian understanding of Jer. 31 and Ezek. 11:19, with its resultant declaration that "the letter kills, but the Spirit makes alive." In 3:7 f. Paul simply *asserts* that Moses' ministry possessed the δόξα needed to provide the *similarity* between the two ministries, *and* that it was nevertheless a ministry "of death," the point of *dissimilarity* upon which the argument turns.

This position has been argued in some detail by Stockhausen in her monograph *Moses' Veil*. Stockhausen's thesis concerning the *qal wahomer* arguments in 3:7–11 is that, "although Exodus 34:29–35 sets the scene, the section is conceptually determined by the Jeremiah/Ezekiel covenant complex and implications drawn from it" in 3:1–6 (p. 113).[43] Stockhausen points to Exod. 34:29–30 as that which "introduces the concept of glory into Paul's composition" (p. 113). But Moses is not called a διάκονος in Exod. 34:29–35. Furthermore, Paul's description of Moses' ministry of glory as a ministry of death cannot be drawn from Exod. 34; it "stems directly from the 'ἀποκτέννω' of II Cor. 3:6c" (p. 114). Indeed, such a description of Moses' ministry in Exod. 34:29–35 "is certainly *contradictory* to the view-point not only of Exodus 34, but of the Book of Exodus as a whole" (p. 113, emphasis mine). Hence, not Exod. 34, but Paul's earlier argument in 3:2–6 "supplies the information which explains these peculiarities," while the close connection between 3:6+7 "is responsible for this shockingly negative assessment" (pp. 113, 114). For Stockhausen, Paul's prior judgment that the Mosaic covenant is "inferior to the new covenant" in 3:2–6 is "the hidden premise of all three of the *kal va-homer* inferences contained in verses 7–11 ... The negativity of that ancient covenant has been transferred to Moses' ministry of it as well. Paul's final editorial addition to the verse – τὴν καταργουμένην – indicates this clearly. Therefore, the Mosaic ministry is known to be the *inferior* member of the pair of ministries which the *kal va-homer* arguments themselves explicitly compare" (p. 114). In the same way,

---

[41] Rendering εἰ ... μᾶλλον in the sense of surety rather than quantity ("to a greater degree"), cf. BAGD, *A Greek-English Lexicon*, p. 489, and BAA, *Griechisch-deutsches Wörterbuch*, p. 991. Contra, e.g. Lietzmann, *An die Korinther*, p. 11, and Theobald, *Gnade*, p. 179, who see the logic to imply both surety and a higher degree of glory, though Theobald stresses that the sense of surety, i.e. the "logical plus," is constitutive for Paul's thinking. For the significance of this point, see below.

[42] As e.g. Hofius, "Gesetz und Evangelium," see above.

[43] Cf. pp. 115 f., 120, 122, and p. 41 n. 19, where Stockhausen agrees with Richard, "Polemics," pp. 352, 362, that Jer. 31:31–34 is "the most important biblical text for the understanding of II Cor. 3:1–4:6," but contra Richard maintains that Jer. 31 is used to interpret Exod. 34:29–35, not vice versa. Indeed, for Stockhausen, "II Cor. 3:1–6 and the scriptural background discovered for it are *absolutely determinative* for Paul's interpretation of Exodus 34 and, therefore, for the meaning of II Cor. 3:7–18 as well" (p. 93, emphasis mine).

Paul's description of his ministry as "the ministry of the Spirit" is "also directly tied to II Cor. 3:6bc" (p. 114). Given Paul's previous arguments and their underlying Scriptural basis in 3:2–6, Paul's argument in 3:7–8 merely becomes a matter of plugging in the appropriate terms: "If this inferior ministry of an inferior covenant possessed such glory, then surely the superior Pauline ministry of the spiritual covenant must also possess glory. *It's as simple as that, if you will grant Paul his premises*" (p. 115, emphasis mine). For in Stockhausen's view, "Only δόξα is taken from Exodus 34 in this series of inferences. None of the descriptions of the inferior or the superior ministries are drawn from Exodus. All prove to be derived either positively or negatively from the pool of covenant characteristics described on the basis of II Cor. 3:1–6 and its scriptural background" (p. 116).

But Paul's argument is not quite as simple as it first appears. This becomes evident once the exact contours of what is and is not being proven in 3:7 f. are carefully delineated. First, it must be kept in mind that in a *qal wahomer* argument the validity of the comparison is only as strong as the persuasive force of the "minor premise" of dissimilarity upon which the comparison is built.[44] In our case, the validity of Paul's assertion that "the ministry of the Spirit exists in glory" rests entirely on the fact that Moses' ministry, to which it is compared, was a διακονία τοῦ θανάτου. But it is equally important to realize that the point of such an argument is not to *establish* the inferior nature of the "less important case." As Stockhausen herself points out, "the dissimilarity on the basis of which the argument functions" is "presupposed and not proven by the inference."[45] Third, the premise of such an argument, or in the case of 3:7–11 the *protasis* of Paul's conditional statement ("if the ministry of death came in glory …"), is only an "inferior" member *in comparison* to the conclusion drawn from it *by virtue of their distinctiveness*, just as the "superior" member derives its superiority only by the same comparison. No assumed ontological inferiority or superiority concerning the δόξα predicated about each of the ministries is therefore implied by the use of such an argument. Stockhausen's ontologically loaded language is therefore easily misleading. The same is true of those who, like Renwick, argue that the point of the comparison is quantitative, rather than qualitative, i.e. that "there should be more 'δόξα' in the new covenant than in the old."[46] Indeed, the foundation of the argument is the *simi-*

---

[44] Cf. again Stockhausen, *Moses' Veil*, p. 110, who summarizes the function of the argument to be: "if A, which lacks y, has x, then B, which has y, certainly must have x as well."

[45] *Moses' Veil*, p. 28.

[46] *Temple*, p. 53; cf. pp. 107, 109 f. Renwick will go on to argue that the point of 3:10 is that "… in the present the visible evidence of God's presence, at least as portrayed in the appearance of Moses, is of no worth at all" and that the Mosaic conception of δόξα "was worthless in the present" (p. 53). In a variation of this view, R.P. Martin, *2 Corinthians*, p. 62, asserts that 3:8 makes it clear that the weakness of the glory on Moses' face is due not only to its temporary nature, but also to the fact that the "degree of δόξα in the new covenant is superior"; and Terrance Callan, "Paul and the Golden Calf," *Proceedings* 10 (1990) 1–17, p. 8, takes Paul's main point to be "the inferiority of the old covenant to the new, as a matter of its having less glory than the new covenant, and as a matter of its being veiled while the new covenant is not veiled."

larity between the δόξα of the "ministry of death" and that of "the ministry of the Spirit."[47]

This becomes immediately apparent in Paul's other uses of the *qal wahomer* argument in Rom. 5:8–10 and 11:12, 24. In the former, the subject of the comparison in both cases is God's saving love for his people, expressed in the "inferior" member by the death of Christ on the cross on our behalf and in the "superior" member by our future salvation! Certainly Paul is here arguing that the nature of God's love toward us past and future is the same. In fact, if any ontological comparison were to be made, the greater display of this love is now in the "lesser member" of the comparison! In the same way, the point of comparison in Rom. 11:12 and 24 is the "riches" to be derived from Israel's transgression and fulfillment and the grafting in of the Gentiles and Jews respectively. Again, the point is the identity of the two experiences. It is therefore misleading to describe the basis of Paul's argument in 3:7 f. to be a comparison between the inferior and superior *natures* of the ministries of Moses and Paul.[48] Nor is there any basis for the common interpretation of this comparison as one of degrees or "amounts" of glory, which, as Morna Hooker has observed, only makes matters worse for Paul.[49] The sole basis of comparison

---

[47] With Stockhausen, *Moses' Veil*, p. 28, and contra Hofius, "Gesetz und Evangelium," pp. 110, 112 f., for whose entire argument a distinction between the two "glories" is crucial (see above).

[48] Contra Stockhausen, *Moses' Veil*, pp. 110–115, and Hofius, "Gesetz und Evangelium," pp. 108, 110 ff. At this point, Stockhausen appears to contradict her own helpful understanding of the nature of the *qal wahomer* argument. For clear examples of *qal wahomer* arguments in which the similarity of that which is asserted concerning the lesser and greater elements is the basis of the comparison, see the extensive use of this argumentation throughout the Mekilta; cf. Pisha I, 35–42 to Exod. 12:1; Pisha III, 35–42 to Exod. 12:3–4; Pisha IV, 5–10; 11–19 to Exod. 12:5; Pisha IV, 71–75 to Exod. 12:7–10; Pisha VII, 48–50 to Exod. 12:11–14 (abbreviated form); Pisha VII, 60–63 to Exod. 12:11–14 (abbreviated form); Pisha VII, 114–121 to Exod. 12:11–14 (cf. Pisha IX, 14–22 to Exod. 12:16–170); Pisha IX, 45–47, 50–52 to Exod. 12:16–17 (now used on the basis of from greater to lesser); Pisha X, 35–42 to Exod. 12:18–20 (where it is clear that if the point of dissimilarity is contested, the argument falls); Pisha XI, 70–73 to Exod. 12:21–24; Pisha XIV, 1–7 to Exod. 12:37–42; Beshallah I, 53–55, 98–102, 144–145 to Exod. 13:17–22; Beshallah II, 73–75 to Exod. 14:1–9; esp. Beshallah VII, 124–130 to Exod. 14:26–31 (where it is used to establish an identity between Moses and God so that to believe in Moses is to believe in God, etc.); Shirata I, 66–72 to Exod. 15:1; Bahodesh V, 90–92 to Exod. 20:2; Bahodesh VII, 103–111 to Exod. 20:7–11; Bahodesh IX, 137–140 to Exod. 20:15–19; Bahodesh XI, 85–91, 109–112 to Exod. 20:21–23; Nezikin I, 102–104 to Exod. 21:1–3 (cf. III, 56–79 to Exod. 21:7–11); Nezikin II, 83–86 to Exod. 21:4–6 to Exod. 21:4–6; Nezikin IV, 74–86 to Exod. 21:12–14; Kaspa II, 26–30 to Exod. 22:30–23:5; Kaspa V, 49–56 to Exod. 23:19; etc. In *every* case, the argument is based on the *identity* of the assertions made in the two elements because of a *distinction* between the elements at some other point. Moreover, in every case, the decisive element in the argument is an *external factor* brought in to establish the dissimilarity. In our case, this factor is not a difference in the two glories, but a difference in their two effects.

[49] As she puts it, "Beyond," p. 298: "If the new glory is so much greater than the old, surely this, too, will be too dazzling for human eyes to bear? If Moses was forced to cover

is, as Stockhausen has emphasized, the point of dissimilarity between the two ministries ("death" vs. the "Spirit").

But once it is recognized that the *force* of Paul's assertion in 3:8 concerning the presence of δόξα in the "superior" element of the comparison rests on the strength of "its known presence in the inferior," Paul's argument appears to fall apart. Everything depends on the validity of Paul's assertion that the ministry of Moses which came ἐν δόξῃ was *nevertheless* a ministry that can be characterized as τοῦ θανάτου. Yet this point seems to self-destruct in the contradiction which appears to exist between Paul's pronouncement that Moses' ministry came in glory *and* that it brought death. Its participation in glory apparently negates the attempt to associate it with death. Moreover, in making this assertion Paul appears to destroy the power of his apologetic, since the majority of interpreters assume that his readers would not agree with this apparently negative and distinctively Pauline evaluation of Moses' ministry.[50]

Richard Hays is therefore rightly troubled, but misses the direction and weight of Paul's argument, when he observes concerning the *qal wahomer* comparisons in vv. 7–11 that "the rhetorical effect of this ambiguous presentation is an unsettling one, because it simultaneously posits and undercuts the glory of Moses' ministry ..."[51] What is unsettling is not that Paul attempts to

---

his face with a veil, will not the Christian minister also need to cover his face – since now the irradiation hazard must be infinitely greater?" Lloyd Gaston, "Paul and the Torah in 2 Corinthians 3," *Paul and the Torah*, 1987, pp. 151–168, p. 159, also recognizes this problem, as pointed out by Hooker, suggesting that if Paul really intended to say he had that much more glory than Moses, then he would have to wear ten veils! In order to avoid this apparent problem, Gaston posits that the point of Paul's argument is to reserve Christian participation in glory until the future consummation, taking ἔσται in v. 8 to be a real future and reading v. 10 as denying glory to the present expression of the ministry of righteousness (p. 160). For the contrary positions, see below. Moreover, in addition to misreading the nature of the *a fortiori* argument in vv. 7–11, this view of the nature of the comparison as one of degree fails to recognize that according to Exod. 32–34 the veil was not needed because of the intensity of the glory, but because of the hard-heartedness of the people (see below).

[50] Cf. e.g. Theobald, *Gnade*, pp. 179 f., who sees the "Tragweite" of what he views as Paul's "presupposition" in 3:7, but argues that at this point Paul interjects the exclusive claims of the Gospel into his adaptation of the tradition which he shared with his readers. Nevertheless, contra e.g. Luz, who argues from this same evaluation that 3:7–18 is non-polemical in nature (!), Theobald still maintains that Paul is engaged in a polemic against his opponents, since Paul presupposes agreement only from the church, not his opponents, and since the issue is how God's glory is being manifest in the new covenant, not its function in the old (cf. p. 180 n. 60). But Theobald's response to Luz begs the question once the force of Paul's argument is seen to rest on the comparison with Moses' ministry. If the Corinthians readily agreed with Paul that Moses' ministry of glory brought death, then the opponents' position, if linked to Moses, would have found no hearing from the beginning.

[51] *Echoes of Scripture in the Letters of Paul*, 1989, p. 132. Hays thus asserts that Paul's argument "reaches its sharpest pitch" in the "dialectical paradox" of v. 10 (p. 133). Contra Hays, it will be argued below that it is not the case that "since Paul is arguing that the ministry of the new covenant outshines the ministry of the old in glory, it serves his purpose to exalt the glory of Moses; at the same time, the grand claims that he wants to make for his own ministry require that the old be denigrated" (pp. 132 f.). Paul's statements about the

"undercut" the glory of the Mosaic ministry in 3:7–11. Nowhere does he do so. Indeed, Paul's *qal wahomer* arguments depend on the *similarity* between the glory of the two ministries. Rather, what is unsettling is that the glory of Moses' ministry is associated with death (v. 7) and condemnation (v. 9).

Moreover, as we have seen in chapter two, Paul's conclusion that the "letter kills" in 3:6 is an inference from Jer. 31 and Ezek. 11; 36 which stands in need of support, precisely in view of the glorious nature of the Law and Moses' ministry, which Paul presupposed in 3:4–6a, but now explicitly affirms in 3:7. *The letter/Spirit contrast and its Old Testament background do not solve the problem, they create it!* Neither Paul's statement in 3:6c that the "letter kills," nor his description of Moses' ministry as a "ministry of death" in 3:7, lead *naturally* to the assertion that this ministry still participated, without a doubt, ἐν δόξῃ. Indeed, as the diatribal "false conclusion" in Romans 7:7 illustrates, the "natural" (but false) implication of Paul's assertion of the letter/Spirit contrast (cf. Rom. 7:6) seemed to be that, far from being glorious, the Law is sin! As in Romans 7:7–8:39, here too Paul must therefore defend the legitimacy of this contrast in view of the "holiness, righteousness, and goodness" of the Law (Rom. 7:12), that is, in view of the fact that Moses' ministry τοῦ θανάτου came ἐν δόξῃ (3:7). Any attempt to add this "positive" affirmation based on Exodus 34:29 ff., without defending its compatibility with the "negative" assertions of 3:6c and 3:7, would simply accentuate the problem already posed by Paul's argument. As C.K. Barrett has rightly observed, for Paul to assert that Moses' ministry was a "ministry of death" would have struck many of his contemporaries as "a resounding contradiction" of the purpose of the Law as a gift of life![52]

Hence, Paul cannot simply *assume* the validity of his central assertion in verse 7. Nor can he fall back on his prior assertion in 3:6c and its Old Testament backdrop. The apologetic context of his argument will not allow it. If left undefended, those who would resist Paul's letter/Spirit contrast in 3:6c could certainly find in v. 7 itself all the ammunition they needed to demonstrate the inconsistency of Paul's position concerning the Law. Either the "letter kills," in which case its glory must seemingly be denied;[53] or its glorious nature as

---

glory of Moses derive from Exod. 34:29 ff., not his "own purpose," and nowhere does Paul "denigrate" the "old" ministry.

[52] *A Commentary on the Second Epistle to the Corinthians*, HNTC, 1973, p. 115, who points to rabbinic sources. But one also thinks, e.g., of passages such as Deut. 28:1–14; 30:1–20; the love of the Law expressed in Pss. 1 and 119; and the explicit association of the Law with life in texts such as Sirach 17:1–14; 45:5; Ep. Arist. 31, 127; 2 Bar. 38:2; 46:4 f.; 48:22; Pss. Sol. 14:2, Pseudo Philo, LAB 23:10, etc.!

[53] That such a conclusion lies close at hand is evidenced in the programmatic works of Windisch, *Der zweite Korintherbrief*, p. 113, and following him, S. Schulz, "Die Decke des Moses," p. 3, who argued that Paul ascribed glory to the Law only because it was in his holy Scripture and therefore he was forced to do so as a "concession" (*das Zugeständnis*); what is striking about Paul's argument is that he makes this concession at all! Schulz thus concluded that the point of vv. 7–11 was to weaken the OT reference to the glory on Moses face. As we

the very writing of God himself, given within the context of the great Sinai theophany, makes it equally impossible to describe it as a "ministry of death." For his opponents, Paul cannot have it both ways. Paul's burden is to show that both must be true in order to explain why and how the new covenant ministry surpasses the old in its display of δόξα.[54] For from Paul's perspective, the apparent contradiction within the old covenant ministry is the very *basis* for his affirmation of the glory of the new covenant ministry. Thus, Paul must now *defend* how it is that the ministry of Moses was at once one of "death" *and* one of "glory."

The exegetical support for this understanding of the apologetic force of 3:7 ff. is found in 3:7 itself. Clearly, the themes of 3:7 f. are taken over from 3:3, 6bc, as indicated by their parallel terminology. However, the very presence of the interior argument of v. 7 indicates that Paul recognizes that he cannot presume that his readers "will grant ... his premises" or accept his "presuppositions."[55] Paul is not content in v. 7 merely to assert the basis of comparison, which one would expect if his argument was based on and determined by the points made in 3:6c. Instead, he elaborates the basic *qal wahomer* comparison in two ways. First, he adds the participial clause ἐν γράμμασιν ἐντετυπωμένη λίθοις.[56] Second, he expands the assertion that "the ministry of death came in glory" by indicating the *result* of its appearance with the clause

---

have seen, much of subsequent interpretation of this text is based on this negative evaluation of the Law in 2 Cor. 3 in line with the prevailing consensus concerning the letter/Spirit contrast.

[54] Contra now Theobald, *Gnade*, pp. 180, 184, 188–90, 208–211, who follows Georgi in arguing that the issue is the *manner* in which the glory is revealed in the new covenant, i.e. whether through exceptional, visible, and external charismatic experiences, as the opponents supposedly argued, or through the hidden, internal work of the Spirit on the heart, as Paul is said to have maintained. Theobald supports this position by defining the references to "face" and the visual element in 3:7, 13, and 18, not against the backdrop of the Old Testament tradition, but abstractly as that which is external (related to the "outer man" in 4:16, the "body" in 4:10 and the "mortal flesh" in 4:11), versus the internal nature of the "heart" from 2 Cor. 5:12, which he sees lying beneath 3:13–18 as well (cf. p. 185). On the misinterpretation of "heart" as that which is internal, versus that which is external, see *Suffering and the Spirit*, pp. 187–192, and now my "'Self-Commendation' and Apostolic Legitimacy in 2 Corinthians: a Pauline Dialectic?" *NTS* 36 (1990) 66–88.

[55] As argued by Stockhausen, see above. This view was also represented earlier in the massive work of K. Prümm, *Diakonia Pneumatos. Der Zweite Korintherbrief als Zugang zur Apostolischen Botschaft, Bd I: Theologische Auslegung des Zweiten Korintherbriefes,* 1967, pp. 125., who posited that in 3:7 Paul merely asserted the "Unwertbegriffe ... als anerkannte Tatsache in Erinnerung."

[56] Following NA[26]. The clear superiority of external attestation for both γράμμασιν on the one hand, and the absence of ἐν on the other, is supported by the fact that in both cases the textual variant represents the more difficult reading internally. The singular form of γράμμα in 3:7 (B, D*, F, G, etc.) appears influenced by 3:6, while the fuller reading with ἐν (א², D¹, etc.) occurs in 3:3 and follows the tendency toward pleonastic readings. For the decision to take ἐν γράμμασιν with ἐντετυπωμένη rather than with διακονία, see H. Windisch, *Der zweite Korintherbrief,* p. 113.

ὥστε μὴ δύνασθαι ἀτενίσαι τοὺς υἱοὺς Ἰσραὴλ εἰς τὸ πρόσωπον Μωϋσέως διὰ τὴν δόξαν τοῦ προσώπου αὐτοῦ τὴν καταργουμένην. When placed within the overall structure of vv. 7–11, the importance of these two alterations of the standard *a fortiori* argument, marked in the diagram below with an asterisk (*), becomes manifest:

The Basis of Comparison

v. 7: εἰ ἡ διακονία	τοῦ θανάτου (*)	ἐγενήθη	ἐν δόξῃ (*)
v. 9: εἰ τῇ διακονίᾳ	τῆς κατακρίσεως		δόξα
v. 11: εἰ τὸ ...	καταργούμενον		διὰ δόξης

The Comparison Itself

v. 8: πῶς ... μᾶλλον	ἡ διακονία	τοῦ πνεύματος	ἔσται	ἐν δόξῃ
v. 9: πολλῷ μᾶλλον	ἡ διακονία	τῆς δικαιοσύνης	περισσεύει	δόξῃ
v. 11: πολλῷ μᾶλλον	τὸ ...	μένον		ἐν δόξῃ

By disrupting the close parallels between the three comparisons, Paul's two additions call attention to themselves as the crux upon which the rest of his argument rests. It is to the content of these additions that we now turn our attention.

b) The Argument from Exod. 32–34 in 2 Cor. 3:7a: The Glory of the Law

We have already seen that the purpose of Paul's assertion that the Law of Moses can be characterized as γράμμα (3:6bc) was not to assert a deficiency in the nature of the Law itself. The Old Testament backdrop to Paul's contrast between the letter and the Spirit will not support such an interpretation. The "letter" is a description of the *function* of the Law under the old covenant without the accompanying power of the Spirit, not of its content or original intention. We have also seen that Paul's reminder that the Law of Moses was "written on stone tablets" in 3:3 prepared the way for the statement "the letter kills" by emphasizing the divine authority of the Law itself, not its deficiency, a point even more apparent in the LXX (cf. Exod. 24:12; 31:18; and esp. 32:15 f.[see chapter two]). His repetition of γράμμα from 3:6bc in 3:7 indicates, therefore, that Paul is continuing to refer to the Law's *function* within the old covenant as introduced in the letter/Spirit contrast.[57] That Paul would again express that the "ministry of death" had been "engraved in letters" (ἐν γράμμασιν ἐντετυπωμένη[58]) indicates his desire to stress this function before moving on to defend it.

---

[57] For these points, see above, chapter two, and Barrett, *Second Epistle to the Corinthians*, p. 115, who points out the causal function of ἐν γράμμασιν ἐντετυπωμένη in view of 3:6.

[58] The only use of ἐντυποῦν in the LXX is found in Exod. 36:37 (39), where it occurs modifying γράμμα as a description of the letters which were engraved on the gold plate worn by the high priest. The relationship between its use here and 2 Cor. 3 is, in my opinion,

It is this point which Paul makes explicit in his depiction of the "ministry of death" as "having been engraved on stones" (ἐντετυπωμένη λίθοις). This description derives most directly from 3:3, where the full designation ἐν πλαξὶν λιθίναις is used as a reference from Exod. 24:12 and 31:18 (cf. Deut. 4:13; 5:22; 9:9–11) to the giving of the Law as written by YHWH himself. Paul uses the shorthand reference to "λίθοις" in 3:7 as a footnote to this point.[59] Inasmuch as the description of the Law as the stone tablets of God carries with it such an immediate implication of its divine authority and nature, Paul has *already* established the assertion of v. 7a that the ministry of death came ἐν δόξῃ in a very terse and theologically loaded fashion.[60] This is confirmed by the syntax of v. 7b, in which the reference to the δόξα on Moses' face is not asserted, but assumed as the ground (cf. διὰ τὴν + accusative) for Israel's inability to gaze into Moses' face. In moving from his thesis statement concerning the new covenant in 3:6 to its support from the establishment of the old covenant in 3:7, Paul thus begins by again emphasizing the common ground assumption of the glorious nature of the Law given to Moses on Mt. Sinai.[61]

But Paul's use of the "stone" imagery within the context of the direct reference to Exod. 34:29 ff. in v. 7b also calls attention to the source of his present argument in support of the letter/Spirit contrast: Exod. 34:29–35 within the context of Exod. 32–34.[62] In using the shortened form of the description from

---

too remote to carry any exegetical weight, though it does establish the plausibility of the expression (see above, chapter two).

[59] Contra Jacob Kremer, "'Denn der Buchstabe tötet, der Geist aber macht lebendig,' Methodologische und hermeneutische Erwägungen zu 2 Kor 3:6b," in *Begegnung mit dem Wort, FS H. Zimmermann*, ed. J. Zmijewski and E. Nellessen, BBB 53, 1980, pp. 219–250, p. 224, who suggests that the reference to 3:3 in 3:7 is "unintentional" (*unwillkürlich*). But the proximity of context and verbal identity make such an assumption unlikely.

[60] For a similar point, see Joseph A. Fitzmyer, "Glory Reflected on the Face of Christ (2 Cor 3:7–4:6) and a Palestinian Jewish Motif," *Theological Studies* 42 (1981) 630–644, p. 636, who observes that this glory was "something sacred or divine which was associated with the giving of the Mosaic law in letters on tablets of stone ..." But his further assertion that Paul's reference to "splendor" in 3:7 has "nothing to do with a letter of recommendation or even with the letter/Spirit contrast ..." misses the apologetic force of 3:7 f. (see below).

[61] That the Law was associated with the glory of God and "came in glory" was, of course, a common theological maxim in post-biblical Judaism. Of special significance in this regard is the tradition found in 4 Ezra 3:19 that God's glory is that which, in a great theophany on Mt. Sinai, "passed through the four gates of fire and earthquake and wind and ice, to give the Law to the descendants of Jacob ..." (trans. from B.M. Metzger, "The Fourth Book of Ezra," *OTP, Vol. 1*, 1983, p. 529). Thus, even though Israel disobeys the Law due to her evil heart, the Law itself "remains in its glory," so that it is through the Law that those who are saved "shall be glorified ... forever" (4 Ezra 9:31, 36 f.).

[62] Contra C.J. A. Hickling, "The Sequence of Thought in II Corinthians, Chapter Three," *NTS* 21 (1975) 380–395, pp. 389 f., who unlike the vast majority does not simply *assume* that Paul read this text atomistically, but suggests that Paul's use of ἐγενήθη and ἀτενίσαι in view of Exod. 34:29 f. "makes it possible to think that in v. 7 Paul had in mind not the whole incident, but the single moment of Moses' arrival at the foot of Mount Sinai." Though this is certainly central, Paul's use of the "stone" imagery in 7a already points beyond this isolated

3:3 in 3:7, Paul has called attention specifically to the "stone" nature of the tablets. The only other specific mention of the *stone* tablets of the Law within the Pentateuch is found in Exod. 34:1, 4, where it is pointed out three times.[63] This emphasis on the stone nature of the tablets serves to underscore that the second giving of the Law is like the first (cf. 34:1), since, as we have seen in chapter three, YHWH's instruction to Moses to make the tablets out of stone also functions to introduce the *theophany* of God's glory in 34:5 ff. (cf. Deut. 10:1, 3). Moses receives the new copy of the Law within the context of the self-revelation of YHWH, just as he received the original stone tablets within the theophanic cloud of God's glory (cf. Exod. 24:15–18).[64] Conversely, the reference in 34:28 to YHWH writing the "ten words" (τοὺς δέκα λόγους) "upon the tablets of the covenant" (ἐπὶ τῶν πλακῶν τῆς διαθήκης) picks up the reference from 34:1 in order to frame the theophany within the giving of the Law.[65] Moses' experience of the glory of God in Exod. 34:5–9 consequently begins and ends with a reference to the second giving of the Law. Both in the MT and the LXX the structure of Exod. 34:1–28 therefore demonstrates that the second giving of the Law, like the first, derives its character from God's glory. Moreover, from now on, whenever Moses declares the commands of YHWH to the people, this same glory will accompany his proclamation (cf. Exod. 34:34 f.). In this sense, the Law not only "came in glory" on Mt. Sinai, it continued to come in glory throughout Moses' subsequent ministry.

Against the background of Paul's reference to Exod. 34:29 ff. in 3:7b, Paul's move from the "tablets of stone" in 3:3 to the description of the Law being engraved on "stones" in 3:7a becomes a direct allusion to the theophany of 34:1 ff. But such an allusion is anything but serendipitous. For as we have seen, the reference to the stone tablets provides the backdrop to Moses' descent from Mt. Sinai in 34:29 ff. as the climax of the narrative. In so doing, it calls to mind that in 32:15–19 the stone tablets and theophany of 34:1 ff. were made necessary by Moses' destruction of the first "tablets of stone" (πλάκες

---

incident, as does his choice of the language of inability and his reference to the function of the veil in 7bc (see below).

[63] For the other reference to the "stone tablets," cf. 1 Kgs. 8:9.

[64] Cf. already J. Goettsberger, "Die Hülle des Moses," p. 8, who concluded not only "daß Exod 34 in der Hauptsache von dem gleichen Abschluß des Sinaibundes wie Exod 19–24 berichtet," but also that "Damit stimmt Paulus überein (2 Kor 3:7)." As we have seen, however, Goettsberger's attempt to take Paul's interpretation seriously, because of its own flaws, did not win a hearing in subsequent scholarship.

[65] See Hickling, "Sequence of Thought," pp. 386 f., who also relates 3:7 to 34:1 as picked up in 34:29. Contra Stockhausen, *Moses' Veil*, pp. 106 f., who attempts to take 3:7 as a direct reference to Exod. 34:27–28. But Stockhausen fails to see the distinction between "these words" from 34:27 as a reference to the "cultic" laws of 34:10 ff. and the "ten words" of 34:28 as a summary statement referring back to 34:1. Moreover, the imagery of "stone" does not occur in either vv. 27 or 28. Stockhausen is led to this conclusion by her attempt to see 3:1–6 as determinative for 3:7 ff., and is thus drawn to the διαθήκη terminology in 34:27 f. as the link between 3:6 and 7. But Paul does not refer to the "covenant" in 3:7, though he is moving from a discussion of the "new covenant" to the "old" in 3:7 ff.

λίθιναι) in response to Israel's transgression. The imagery of the tablets of *stone* thus provides a thread which ties the narrative of Exod. 32–34 together, as well as pointing to its climax in 34:29–35. The stone tablets are given to Moses at the climax of his sojourn on Mt. Sinai in 31:18, they are again explicitly mentioned in the LXX when Moses carries them down from Mt. Sinai in 32:15–16, they are broken by Moses in judgment upon the people in 32:19, and then restored by YHWH on Mt. Sinai in 34:1–4.

But our study of Exod. 32–34 has shown that although the covenant is renewed, the theophany in 34:5 ff. and the reestablishment of the presence of God among his people which it secures are not identical with the first giving of the Law in Exod. 19–24. Paul's description in v. 7a establishes the glorious nature of the Law by pointing back to the theophany within which the Law was given,[66] but this time specifically to its "second giving" after the sin with the golden calf. In pointing to the theophany of Exod. 34:1 ff., Paul thus points toward the inherent problem encountered by Moses' ministry, a problem so great that the Law which was meant for life can be described as a "ministry of death." Why this is the case is Paul's next point. And his support for it also comes from a close reading of Exod. 34:29–35 within its larger context.

c) The Argument from Exodus 32–34 in 2 Cor. 3:7b: Moses' "Ministry of Death"

In 3:7b Paul extends his point that Moses' "ministry of death came in glory" by indicating the *actual result* of its arrival: "the sons of Israel were not able to *gaze intently* into the face of Moses because of the glory of his face" (ὥστε μὴ δύνασθαι ἀτενίσαι τοὺς υἱοὺς Ἰσραὴλ εἰς τὸ πρόσωπον Μωϋσέως διὰ τὴν

---

[66] The failure to see this significance of the "stone" imagery in 3:3 and 7, the corresponding attempt to read the references to "ink," "stone," and "letter" in contrast to the Spirit and "heart" in 3:1–11 as an external/internal or material/spiritual contrast, combined with taking καταργέω in v. 11 to mean "fade" in contrast to that which remains, lead Belleville, *Reflections of Glory*, pp. 145 f., 148 f., to establish regarding the theme of "apostolic credibility" in 2:14–4:15 that the issue is "appropriate credentials for a gospel minister" (p. 145) and "that the proper criteria for ascertaining credibility are ones that focus on the inward, spiritual dimension as opposed to some outward, material dimension" (p. 146). For Belleville, the link between the letters of recommendation and the tablets of the Law and γράμμα is that both are "types of material accreditation" (p. 148). Hence, in her view, Paul "appears to be contrasting written documents – which are able to impart an initial glory and credibility to the bearer, but because of their material nature had no lasting effects – with the permanent and lasting credibility that an inward change of heart and the internal work of the Spirit impart to the believer. So Paul introduces the old covenant and the figure of Moses to show that even the highest forms of documentary certification can only impart a limited credibility to the bearer because of their external character (γράμμα)" (pp. 148 f.). But as the present study argues, this understanding of the contrasts in 3:3–11, and hence this common thesis, do not hold up once Paul's thought is studied against its Scriptural backdrop (for the meaning of the stone and heart imagery against their biblical and Jewish backdrop, see above, chapter two).

δόξαν τοῦ προσώπου αὐτοῦ).[67] As we have seen, the addition of this clause breaks the parallel structure of the comparison, and in so doing calls attention to its strategic importance. Here Paul details the exact nature of the dissimilarity between the two ministries as reflected in their respective descriptions as ministries of "death" and "the Spirit."

Paul's reference to the events of Exod. 34:29–35 is clear. In moving from the glory of the Law as established in the theophany and second giving of the tablets in Exod. 34:1–34:28 in 3:7a to Moses' subsequent descent from Mt. Sinai in 3:7b Paul is simply following the flow of the OT narrative. Against this backdrop, Paul asserts that the *consequence* of the δόξα which shone forth from Moses' face was that the Israelites were not able to gaze intently into it. As the choice of μὴ δύνασθαι with ὥστε indicates, Paul's intention is to interpret the reaction of the Israelites in Exod. 34:29 ff. in terms of an *inability brought about by the δόξα itself.*

It has often been pointed out, however, that neither the MT nor the LXX speak explicitly of such an inability. Instead, the reaction to Moses' descent in both cases is one of "fear" (Exod. 34:30), while the people do in fact see the glory of God during those periods when Moses removes the veil to convey the words of YHWH (Exod. 34:34 f). Moreover, the history of interpretation, ancient and modern, has demonstrated that the reason for the Israelites' fear, together with Moses' subsequent and repeated veiling after speaking the words of the Lord, is not immediately obvious within Exod. 34:29–35. The most common interpretation, based on reading Exod. 34:29–35 in isolation from its surrounding context, is that the overwhelming brilliance of Moses' face caused the Israelites to fear for the well-being of their eyes. Such an interpretation is derived from the assumption that encountering such a δόξα would naturally be blinding.[68] Paul's interpretation of Exod. 34:30 in v. 7b, while not impossible, is therefore usually seen to be going beyond the explicit meaning of the OT text.

But as our study of the MT and LXX traditions has shown, the reason for Israel's fear in Exod. 34:30 becomes clear within the larger context of Exod. 32–34. The LXX's explicit interpretation of the lexically ambiguous קרן in Exod. 34:29 f., 35 as a reference to the shining forth of Moses' face with the glory of God indicates that more is at stake in Exod. 34:29 ff. than the condition of Israel's eyes. Within the context of Exod. 32–34 LXX, this glory can be nothing less than a mediation of the glory of God as the manifestation of YHWH's presence (see chapter three). Once placed within its overall context,

---

[67] The use of ὥστε + acc. with the inf. to indicate a result clause is well attested in general and in Paul. Cf. BAGD, *A Greek-English Lexicon*, p. 900; F. Blass, A. Debrunner, R.W. Funk, *A Greek Grammar of the New Testament*, 1961, § 391.

[68] See now e.g. John Koenig, "The Knowing of Glory," pp. 160 f., who follows the 1929 work of George Boobyer in viewing the reference of "glory" to be to a "light-substance" or "radiant emanation from God" (pointing to e.g. Exod. 24:16–17; Ezek. 10:3–4; Is. 60:1 ff.; Wis. 7:25–26; 1 Cor. 15:43; Phil. 3:21; 2 Cor. 4:17; 5:1 ff.; and Rom. 8:21–23).

Israel's fear is thus the natural response to YHWH's prior warning in Exod. 33:3, 5 that due to their sin/fall with the golden calf his presence among them "for one moment" would mean their destruction. As a "stiff-necked people," Israel *cannot* endure the glory of God (cf. 32:9 f., 22; 34:9). What causes fear among the people is the presence of the glory of God in their midst.[69] This becomes especially evident in the LXX, where in Exod. 33:5 the hardened nature of Israel is not only highlighted in a way not found in the MT, but YHWH's warning is also explicitly interpreted in terms of Israel's loss of their "garments of glory" (see chapter three).[70] Yet the covenant has been renewed, despite Israel's hardened condition, so that the relationship between Israel and Moses in Exod. 34:29 ff. parallels Israel's prior response in Exod. 20:19 f., with the crucial difference that the people are now right: they will die if exposed to God's presence in an unmediated manner. Hence, Moses removes the veil not only to authenticate his message, but also to indicate that the covenant has been renewed as an expression of the mercy of God. He must then replace the veil, however, as an expression of the continuing judgment of God upon his people, who remain "stiff-necked."

The choice of δόξα in v. 7b, therefore, follows the LXX's (in my view, proper) interpretation of the MT as a reference to the glory of God on the face of Moses. And as Renwick has recently pointed out in his survey of the use of δόξα in the LXX and in Paul, "... the one abiding element in each use of δόξα concerns the presence of God," entrance into which Paul conceived as the goal and essence of salvation, since, for him, the glory of God was both an (eschatological) "blessing" and a "realm."[71] Nevertheless, as the varied quo-

---

[69] This was seen already by Windisch, *Der zweite Korintherbrief*, p. 114, and now F. Lang, *Korinther*, p. 272, who states in regard to v. 7 that the Israelites could not gaze into the face of Moses, "weil sündige Menschen nicht einmal den Abglanz der Herrlichkeit Gottes ertragen können." Lang, however, follows the traditional view that Paul declares this glory to be passing away *(vergänglich)*, since for Paul the Law belongs to the old age which is passing away (Gal. 3:21–25) (p. 272). On the positive side, Paul can still refer to the glory of the Law to the degree that, as Scripture, it still contains the promise (pp. 272 f.).

[70] This interpretation is confirmed conceptually by the targumic tradition. In *Tg. Neof.* 32:5 f. Israel is told to put off their ornaments, "on which the Distinguished Name was engraved from Mount Horeb," which picks up the addition to the MT found in 32:25 in which the gold taken from the people to make the calf is said to be the gold from their crowns on which the name was engraved. For this same idea, cf. *Frg. Tgs. P* and *V* Exod. 32:25. Hence, in the targumic tradition, the result of Israel's sin is the loss of God's name, i.e. his presence in their midst and their identity as his people. Cf. too *Frg. Tg. P* Exod. 33:6, where it is Israel's weapons which bore the name.

[71] *Temple*, pp. 100 f., 103. Renwick rightly points to Paul's 58 references to δόξα outside of 2 Cor. as indication that even if its treatment here was occasioned by his opponents' use of it, the theme of God's glory/presence was of interest to Paul because of its own significance. As Renwick points out, Paul's contribution to this theme in biblical and post-biblical tradition was to explain the tension between the present inheritance of God's glory and the future, arguing that δόξα as a blessing of salvation "must be conceived of primarily as 'hope' (Rom. 5:4, 5)," with suffering as the necessary (Rom. 8:17) process before that hope becomes a re-

tations throughout his letters demonstrate, Paul's adoption of Septuagintal textual traditions is not uncritical, or merely a matter of a general quotation from memory, but reflects his own careful interpretive evaluations of fixed textual traditions.[72] As such, Paul's understanding of Moses' role as mediating God's presence in the midst of the people consciously conforms to the further development of this theme throughout the rest of the Pentateuch (see chapter three). Moreover, it stands squarely within the trajectory of tradition evidenced in post-biblical literature and the targumic traditions, where Moses is consistently seen as mediating the glory of God in Exod. 34:29–35.[73] Even the atomistic reading of Exod. 34:29 ff. in terms of the brightness of the glory no doubt presupposes this understanding. For Paul, therefore, the δόξα on Moses' face is a reflection of the very glory of God within which the Law has been reestablished in Exod. 34:10 ff., and together with which Moses' future declarations of the Lord's commands will also be given (cf. 34:34 f.).[74]

What makes Paul's interpretation distinctive, however, is his equally intentional attempt to read Exod. 34:29 ff. within its larger context.[75] Paul's own reference to the theme of the "stone tablets" in 3:7a already directed our attention to the wider context of Exod. 32–34 (cf. Exod. 31:18; 32:15 f., 19; 34:1–4, 27 f.). Paul's subsequent interpretation of Israel's fear in 3:7 in terms of Israel's inability (μὴ δύνασθαι) to endure the divine glory on Moses' face likewise corresponds to the significance of Israel's fear in Exod. 34:29–35 when read within the context of Exod. 32–34, especially in view of the LXX tradition. Paul's contextual reading also explains the use of the vivid verb ἀτενίζω ("to look intently at") to describe Israel's action, rather than the more common and neutral εἶδον ("to see") found in the LXX (cf. Exod. 34:30,

---

ality (p. 101). See his helpful survey on pp. 99–105. Renwick's emphasis on the presence of God as a key thematic element in Paul's argument is certainly correct and helpful.

[72] This has now been demonstrated by the detailed study of D.-A. Koch, *Die Schrift als Zeuge*, pp. 11–91; cf. his helpful summary on pp. 92–101.

[73] Cf. Martin McNamara, *The New Testament and the Palestinian Targum to the Pentateuch*, 1966, p. 173, whose survey of the LXX, Pseudo-Philo, and the targums leads him to conclude that "this particular text of 2 Cor, then, presents no difficulty. The Apostle is clearly dependent on a widely attested Palestinian understanding of Exod. 34:29."

[74] See the still immensely valuable study of the "glory" motif in the OT and Judaism by Helmuth Kittel, *Die Herrlichkeit Gottes: Studien zu Geschichte und Wesen eines neutestamentlichen Begriffs*, BZNW 16, 1934, pp. 1–58, in which he establishes the use of כבוד as a term of revelation for YHWH himself in the OT and its influence on the meaning of δόξα in the LXX (cf. pp. 62, 67 f.). In the Pentateuch, Kittel demonstrates that its meaning in both the MT and LXX is the "visible manifestation of the power of God" shown through its effects and present in itself (pp. 138 f., 141, 160). But his insistence on a contrast of nature between the glory experienced by Moses and that which belongs to Paul's ministry in 2 Cor. 3 (cf. pp. 203 f.) cannot be maintained.

[75] See now Renwick, *Temple*, p. 48 n. 2, who emphasizes that "... Paul's use of Exod. 34 can be understood only by affirming Paul's familiarity with Exod. 32–33." Renwick, however, does not develop this crucial OT backdrop in any detail, focusing instead on Haggai 2 as the backdrop to 3:10 (see below).

35).[76] As its use elsewhere in the NT illustrates, ἀτενίζω refers specifically to the continual and direct gaze toward something or someone, often with the expectation of receiving something.[77] In Acts 1:10 and 7:55 it is even used with reference to the glory of God (now in the form of the glorified Christ!),[78] while in Acts 10:4 it describes Cornelius' gaze at an angel of God.[79] In using this word, Paul takes cognizance of the fact that despite Israel's initial fear, the renewal of the covenant meant YHWH's glory could once again be in Israel's midst, albeit only in a *mediated and veiled* fashion. Against this background, Paul's choice of vocabulary in v. 7b is a careful attempt not only to indicate Israel's "inability" to enjoy the continual presence of God because of her sin with the golden calf, but also to reflect that this inability specifically referred to gazing *directly and continuously* into the glory of God in a way that would affect them, in this case with the judgment of God. For as the narrative makes clear, Israel did in fact see the glory of God without being destroyed in 34:30–32, and after that continued to do so whenever Moses delivered the commands of the Lord to the people (34:34b–35a). But now, rather than being continuously and immediately revealed in Israel's midst, the view of the glory of God is brief, periodic, and mediated on Moses' face, only visible when he proclaims to them the Law. Instead of guiding and protecting the people directly, the glory of God now functions to undergird the continuing revelation of the Lord's commands, and, by implication, the authority of Moses as mediator. Israel, due to her hardened condition, may no longer "gaze directly and intently" (ἀτενίσαι) at the glory of God.[80] Far from going beyond the meaning of the text, Paul's understanding of Exod. 34:29–35 derives directly from his

---

[76] Cf. BAGD, *A Greek-English Lexicon*, p. 119 with p. 220 for a comparison of the two meanings. BAA, *Griechisch-deutsches Wörterbuch*, p. 240, offers the nuance "gespannt auf etw. order jmdn. hinsehen" as that which colors ἀτενίζω.

[77] Outside of 2 Cor. 3:7, 13 it is found only in Luke's writings; cf. Luke 4:20; 22:56; Acts 3:4, 12; 6:15; 11:6; 13:9; 14:9; 23:1. Cf. 1 Esdr. 6:28; 3 Macc. 2:26 and Hofius, "Gesetz und Evangelium," p. 92. I find no explicit support for Stockhausen's suggestion, *Moses' Veil*, p. 87, that the verb also carries with it the idea of "straining the eyes."

[78] Taking the reference to the cloud which received Christ in Acts 1:9 to represent the glory-cloud of God, so that 1:11 becomes a statement of Christ's return "in glory" as in Mk 14:62 par. Matt. 26:64.

[79] One cannot help but wonder if the fact that in Acts 10:4 Cornelius was *afraid* (ἔμφοβος γενόμενος) while he gazed (ἀτενίσας) at the angel, in contrast to the lack of fear by the disciples in Acts 1:10; 7:55, could also indicate the same association of ideas as found in 2 Cor. 3:7 ff.

[80] See already Josef M. Kastner, *Moses im Neuen Testament, Eine Untersuchung der Mosestradition in den neutestamentlichen Schriften*, Diss. München, 1967, p. 193, who argued that Paul's choice of ἀτενίζειν in 3:7 showed he recognized the Israelites could in fact see the glory on Moses' face (cf. Exod. 34:30, 35), but not in the manner of the "Gespannt-Hinsehen" which this verb carries. But contra the view argued here, Kastner followed the standard interpretation that the goal of Paul's use of this verb was to point out the "Minderwertigkeit" of the glory of the old covenant (p. 193), together with his use of καταργέω (interpreted to mean "fade") as an "obvious polemic" against the old covenant in which he engages in a "Gewaltsamkeit der Auslegung" of the OT (pp. 193, 195). This con-

OT tradition.[81] It was precisely because Moses' ministry "came in glory" (cf. διὰ τὴν δόξαν τοῦ προσώπου αὐτοῦ) that the Israelites were not able to gaze intently at his face, since the result of the glory of God in the midst of a "stiff-necked" people would be destruction.[82]

Paul's understanding of Exod. 34:29–35 within its larger context thus supports his earlier description of the Law as τὸ γράμμα ἀποκτέννει in 3:6c. As we have seen, Paul's statement in 3:6c that "the letter kills" is intended to express the *function* of the Law under the administration of the old covenant whenever it encountered Israel's hardened hearts. In 3:7 Paul turns his attention to the "second giving of the Law" in order to demonstrate from the climax of the Sinai covenant itself that this is the case. For Israel's sin with the golden calf clearly revealed that, even after the establishment of the covenant at Sinai, the majority of the people remained "stiff-necked" and therefore were unable to keep the covenant stipulations in response to YHWH's gracious election. They had received the Law intended for life, but not the Spirit needed to keep it. Rather than the blessings of the covenant, from the beginning Israel is consequently placed under its curses, as Paul explicitly recognized in Galatians 3:10 in view of Deut. 27:26.[83] Indeed, the first expression of God's judgment against Israel for having broken the covenant is the slaugh-

---

forms to Kastner's view of the Law in Paul as "meaningless in regard to salvation history," "second rate," and without any role at all in regard to salvation (p. 187).

[81] See too Hofius, "Gesetz und Evangelium," p. 92, who sees Paul's use of ἀτενίζειν to derive from Exod. 34:30b and the reference to the veil in 34:33, 35b, but who still sees Paul's statement as going beyond Exod. 34:29–35 and in some tension with Exod. 34:30, 35. For Hofius does not link Israel's fear in 34:29 ff. to God's judgment from 33:3, 5, but to the distinctive nature of the glory associated with the Law (pp. 95 f.). In my view it is precisely the tension in Exod. 34:29–35 between what Israel could and could not do that leads to Paul's use of this verb. For the usual view that Paul is going beyond the OT at this point because Exod. 34:29 ff. never explicitly states that Israel could not look at Moses' face, only that they were afraid to do so, see most recently Stockhausen, *Moses' Veil*, pp. 98 f.

[82] Seen clearly by Thomas E. Provence, "'Who is Sufficient for These Things?' An Exegesis of 2 Corinthians 2:15–3:18," *NovT* 24 (1982) 54–81, p. 71 n. 47, who saw the fear of Israel in Exod. 34 to be a reference to their hard hearts and the fact that "sinful men are unable to face the revelation of God's character as a righteous and holy God." But Provence appeared to accept the traditional view of καταργέω, so that for him the glory of God on Moses' face is "limited and temporary" (p. 71); nor is it clear from Exod. 34 that the glory of God itself is that which functions to harden Israel's hearts, as Provence maintained (p. 71).

[83] Thus, the curses of the covenant law can be seen to have been operative from the beginning, eventuating in the exiles of 722 and 587 BC, which, as James Scott has argued in his insightful work, "'For as Many as are of Works of the Law are Under a Curse' (Galatians 3:10)," *Paul and the Scriptures of Israel, Studies in Scripture in Early Judaism and Christianity 1*, JSNT Suppl. Series 83, 1993, pp. 187–221, pp. 206 ff., is the decisive backdrop of Gal. 3:10. Scott's argument that Deut. 27:26, once read within the context of the blessing and curse section of Deut. 27–32 (cf. the γεγραμμένα ἐν τῷ βιβλίῳ τοῦ νόμου τούτου in Deut. 28:58, 61; 29:19, 20, 26; 30:10, which Paul cites in Gal. 3:10), including its promise of restoration after the curse (cf. Deut. 30:1–8), points to a Sin – Exile – Restoration pattern as the interpretive key for Gal. 3:10 is essential for understanding Paul's view of the Law.

ter of the guilty by the sons of Levi in Exod. 32:27–29 (cf. Exod. 32:34 f.). From its inception, therefore, the Law under the Sinai covenant killed, not because the Law was somehow deficient, but because, in God's sovereign purposes, Israel was granted the Law without the transforming work of the Spirit. Deuteronomy 29:2–4 thus provides a fitting summary of the theological point being made concerning the rebellious nature of Israel in Exod. 32–34:

"And Moses summoned all Israel and said to them, 'You have seen all that the Lord did before your eyes in the land of Egypt to Pharaoh and all his servants and all his land; the great trials which your eyes have seen, those great signs and wonders. Yet to this day the Lord has not given you a heart to know, nor eyes to see, nor ears to hear.'"

The Scriptural account of the giving of the Law supports Paul's point concerning the function of the Law in 3:6bc by illustrating vividly that the deficiency within the old covenant was not the Law, but the continuing hardened hearts of the people. As a result, Paul's move from the prophetic background of his argument in 3:6 to Exodus 32–34 in 3:7 ff. is not only a natural one thematically, but also an effective one apologetically.

Viewed in this light, the switch in terminology from the depiction of the Law in 3:6c as τὸ γράμμα because of its function as that which kills (ἀποκτέννει), to the depiction of the Law as ἡ διακονία τοῦ θανάτου in 3:7a, is motivated by Paul's desire to express carefully the exact locus of comparison between the old and new covenants. Paul avoids the direct designation ὁ νόμος in order to avoid giving the impression that the contrast between the old and the new covenants is a contrast between the Law and the Gospel understood as two qualitatively distinct means of salvation. For as Paul has reminded the Corinthians in 3:6c, it is not the Law or the Gospel which kill or make alive, but the Spirit. Apart from the Spirit, the Gospel too brings *death* to those whose hearts are hardened (cf. 2 Cor. 2:16; 4:1–6). Paul undergirds this assertion in 3:7 by introducing the διακονία-terminology in reference back to its cognates in 3:3 and 6, where it reflected the language of Paul's opponents (cf. 2 Cor. 11:13–15, 23)[84] and called attention to the effects of Paul's apostolic work. As this terminology indicates, the issue at stake is the nature and effects of the respective *ministries* of Moses and Paul.[85] In stark contrast to the

---

[84] Following D. Georgi, *Die Gegner des Paulus*, pp. 31–51, in his development of the διάκονος-terminology as part of the self-designation of Paul's opponents (see chapter two).

[85] Contra those who, like J. Christiaan Beker, *Paul The Apostle, The Triumph of God in Life and Thought*, 1980, pp. 295 f., view the contrast in 3:7 ff. to be between Christ and Moses, and in contrast to those who, like V.P. Furnish, *II Corinthians*, AB 32A, 1984, p. 202, see a material rather than functional view of 2 Cor. 3:6 continued on in 3:7, so that "the reference here is first of all to the whole system of law (the 'old covenant,' v. 14), represented by the stone tablets (v. 3) with their death-dealing commandments (cf. v. 6), and only secondarily to the agents of that ministry." For the development of this latter view, see esp. the position of Hofius, "Gesetz und Evangelium."

view of Hans Windisch and the history of interpretation dependent upon him, Paul's Gospel does not imply a quantitative or qualitative denigration of the Law of Moses or its glory, any more than his defense of his apostolic ministry involves an attack on the stature of Moses himself or his ministry.[86] Just the opposite! The authority of Moses and the glory of the Law are the necessary foundation upon which the *qal wahomer* argument is built. The force of Paul's apologetic for the glory of the διακονία τοῦ πνεύματος in v. 8 comes instead from its distinctive *function* over against that of the διακονία τοῦ θανάτου.[87]

It is thus Moses' *ministry* which can appropriately be associated with "death," not the Law *per se*, since it was Moses' mediation of the glory of God on his face that brought with it the judgment of God upon a rebellious people.[88] This becomes evident against the backdrop of Exod. 32–34, where Israel's inability to gaze into the face of Moses calls attention not only to the glory which Moses mediated, but also to the death which encountering such a glory would have entailed.[89] As we have seen in chapter three, because of Israel's

---

[86] Thus, despite his many helpful insights, Samuel Vollenweider's basic point, "2 Kor 3: Der transzendente Schein des Gesetzes," *Freiheit als neue Schöpfung*, FRLANT 147, 1989, pp. 247–284, pp. 249, 272, that Paul's *a minore ad maius* logic points to a "new understanding of glory" in which not only a qualitative, but also a "quantitative" jump from the old to the new covenant ministry must be posited, remains unconvincing. In Vollenweider's opinion, Paul's view that the ministry of Moses is to be associated with death and condemnation goes far beyond and contrary to his Jewish Christian tradition and thus can only be seen from the perspective of the new ministry of the Spirit. Hence, from his perspective, "Paulus verzeitlicht die Doxa des Mose und mit ihr das Gesetz" (p. 273). Nor is R.P. Martin's suggestion, *2 Corinthians*, p. 62, that Paul's use of πρόσωπον in 3:7 "stands in antithetic relation to 'heart,'" referring to 2 Cor. 5:12, warranted. See too Windisch, *Der zweite Korintherbrief*, p. 112, who argued that the purpose of 3:7 ff. was to establish "die Minderwertigkeit des alten Bundes ..." At this point I agree with A.T. Hanson, *Jesus Christ in the Old Testament*, 1965, p. 34, that "... Paul nowhere suggests that Moses as such was inferior to himself, only that the dispensation that Christ gave him to administer was inferior" (p. 34) since it was a dispensation in which "the Spirit was deliberately withheld" (p. 33). But I am not convinced, as is Hanson, that the pre-existent Christ is the object of Moses' vision and the giver of the Law in Exodus 32–34, as reflected in this quote (see below).

[87] Cf. Belleville, *Reflections of Glory*, p. 22 n. 3, who rightly emphasizes regarding this passage that "it is important to observe that Paul distinguishes between the positive nature of the old covenant ('came in glory') and its negative effects ('death,' 'condemnation') – a distinction not sufficiently noted."

[88] So too Dumbrell, "Paul's use of Exodus 34," pp. 185 f.: "The 'ministry of death' to which 2 Cor. 3:7 refers is not the law itself, but the circumstances surrounding the ministry of Moses in its effects on Israel, a ministry which can be summarized by St Paul by reference to the covenant statutes. Law in isolation is not the issue with which Paul is dealing here, but rather law within a covenant relationship ... The law had been given to be a means by which life might be expressed and had been meant ideally to give point to the covenant by flowing from a sanctified national heart (a note to which Deuteronomy continually refers cf. Deut. 6:4–6, 11:18). In Israel's Sinai experience, however, it had already become 'externalized.'"

[89] Contra most recently Stockhausen, *Moses' Veil*, p. 113 (see above). See too R.P. Martin, *2 Corinthians*, p. 61, who rightly emphasizes the counter-point to this, i.e. "the trouble lay with 'man' as σάρξ ('flesh') ..." But contra Martin, p. 61, Paul is not simply writing

sin with the golden calf, the original intent of the Sinai covenant, that God would dwell in the midst of his people (Exod. 19:5 f.; 24:9 f.; 25:8; 29:45 f.; cf. Lev. 26:9, 11–13), was aborted before the tablets of testimony to the covenant could be delivered. From now on, the unmediated presence of God among those in this rebellious state would only mean judgment. When YHWH comes to "visit," his "visit" will no longer be to bless Israel (cf. Exod. 3:16; 4:31; 13:19), but to judge her (32:34; cf. 33:3, 5). It is this realization that leads Paul to his final point concerning the δόξα of the ministry of death in 3:7.

d) The Consensus Concerning 2 Cor. 3:7c and Recent Challenges

Paul concludes his treatment of the glorious nature and fatal impact of Moses' "ministry of death" in 3:7 with the attributive present passive participle τὴν καταργουμένην. The participle clearly modifies Paul's reference to "the glory" (τὴν δόξαν) on Moses' face. Ever since the programmatic works of Windisch and Schultz, the almost universal decision to translate καταργέω in this context to mean "fading" has led the overwhelming majority of scholars and translators to render Paul's point to be that the glory on Moses' face was slowly passing away. In contrast to that which "remains" (τὸ μένον) from 3:11 as a description of the Gospel and/or Paul's ministry, this participle is seen to convey Paul's negative critique of the Law and/or Moses. Indeed, following this exegetical tradition R.P. Martin can refer to "the derogatory addition of τὴν καταργουμένην ..."[90] Moreover, in anticipation of Paul's point in 3:13, the fact that the glory on Moses' face was actually fading is taken to explain Moses' purpose in veiling himself, i.e. to hide this truth and/or its implications from Israel.

But inasmuch as there is no explicit mention in Exod. 34:29–35 of the glory on Moses' face fading, or of this corresponding understanding of Moses' veil, here too Paul is said to go beyond the biblical text.[91] In fact, at this point Paul's apologetic needs and Christian presuppositions are so overwhelming that he even appears to go directly *against* the expressed intention of the biblical text, whether intentionally for polemical reasons, or, as Gerd Theißen has now ar-

---

"phenomenologically ... based on what he knows of human experience, that the law produces 'a διακονία (an administration) that leads to death' ... due to their hardness (πώρωσις) of heart'" (quoting Eph. 2:2; 4:18). Paul is writing "exegetically" as well, based on Exod. 32–34.

[90] *2 Corinthians*, p. 62.

[91] The attempt by Otto Betz, "Der fleischliche Mensch und das geistliche Gesetz, Zum biblischen Hintergrund der paulinischen Gesetzeslehre," in his *Jesus, Der Herr der Kirche, Aufsätze zur biblischen Theologie II*, WUNT 52, 1990, pp. 129–196, p. 189, to suggest a possible allusion to a fading glory in Exod. 34:33 remains unconvincing. In 34:33 it is Moses' speaking that ends, not the glory, and in the text Moses' speaking is not identified with the strength of the shining glory.

gued, subconsciously in order to meet his own psychological needs.[92] For according to the virtually unanimous opinion of post-biblical Jewish tradition, the glory on Moses' face as he descended from Mt. Sinai after the second giving of the Law was not only brilliant, but also permanent.[93] This is certainly the most natural reading of Exod. 34:29 ff. itself, and the one that makes most sense within the larger context of Exod. 32–34 in view of Moses' role as the "answer to his own prayers" (see chapter three).[94]

Excursus: The Glory and Veil of Moses in Post-Biblical Judaism[95]

The only possible divergence in post-biblical Jewish tradition from the view that the glory on Moses' face was permanent, and that this glory caused the Israelites to fear

---

[92] See his "Die Hülle des Mose und die unbewußten Aspekte des Gesetzes," in his *Psychologische Aspekte paulinischer Theologie*, FRLANT 131, 1983, pp. 121–161. For Theißen, Paul was such an intelligent exegete of the Scriptures that a "conscious manipulation" (p. 157) of the OT tradition *had* to be an expression of Paul's own subconscious psychological motivations in which, in order to overcome his own cognitive dissonance created by his current rejection of his past allegiances to Moses and the Law and yet his ongoing esteem for the OT, Paul *subconsciously* reinterprets and does violence to the OT text by reading "between the lines" (cf. pp. 132, 134 f., 147, 153, 156 f.). For in Theißen's view, "Psychologie und Traditionsgeschichte sind aufeinander angewiesen" (p. 132). By subconsciously projecting his own theology into the OT in 3:7–18, Paul is not countering positions and opinions of his opponents, but his own prior convictions concerning Moses and the old covenant (cf. p. 142). However, even if Theißen's reading of 2 Cor. 3 were correct, and this particular psychoanalysis of Paul's motivations happened to be true, it would be impossible to ascertain from this passage that they were. We simply do not know enough about Paul's psyche from 2 Cor. 3 to draw such a portrait. But even more importantly, one of the fundamental points of this study is to argue that Paul did not misread or reinterpret the OT text and tradition in the first place, whether consciously or subconsciously, so that, despite his insightful observations on some of the individual aspects of the text, the basis for Theißen's overall psychological reconstruction and central thesis is flawed from the beginning!

[93] Because he accepted the view that for Paul the glory was fading, McNamara, *New Testament and Palestinian Targum*, p. 175, could thus only conclude that "Paul is dependent on some other tradition unknown to us or is drawing his own symbolism directly from the Biblical text." So too Theobald, *Gnade*, pp. 179 f., who assumed that Paul's readers must have been acquainted with this tradition, though we find no evidence of it today. Most recently, O. Hofius, "Gesetz und Evangelium," p. 101, also finds no explicit tradition to support this point but agrees with Childs, who, like McNamara, suggested that the possibility must be left open that Paul is following an interpretation shared by other Jewish interpreters unknown to us, though Hofius suggests that we must be equally open to the idea that Paul himself developed this reading. It is the burden of Belleville's work, *Reflections of Glory*, pp. 24–79, to discover this previously unknown Jewish tradition under the assuption that if Paul declares the glory to be fading then such a tradition must have existed.

[94] Contra those who suggest that Paul has rightly interpreted Exod. 34:29 ff. as inferring that the glory on Moses' face was renewed each time he returned to the tent of meeting; cf. already H.A.W. Meyer, *Critical and Exegetical Hand-Book to the Epistles to the Corinthians*, ET from 5th German ed., 1869, pp. 467 f., and R.V.G. Tasker, *The Second Epistle of Paul to the Corinthians*, Tyndale New Testament Commentaries, 1969 (1958), p. 63.

[95] The main lines of this tradition have been surveyed and need not be repeated in detail here. For a discussion of the various traditions and the relevant sources, see O. Hofius,

Moses, is found in Pseudo-Philo's first century A.D. work *Biblical Antiquities* (LAB) 19:16, though even this text in all likelihood also supports the overwhelming consensus.[96] In contrast to the biblical narrative, in LAB 12:1 Moses' face is already "bathed with invisible light ...," so that "his face surpassed the splendor of the sun and the moon, and he did not even know this," in conjunction with his *first* descent with the Law in Exod. 32:15 ff. *before* Israel's sin with the golden calf.[97] Moreover, rather than fearing Moses, the people fail to recognize him due to his transfiguration until after he speaks to them, just as with Joseph in Gen. 42:8 (12:1b). Moses then veils himself, but without explanation (12:1c). After the second giving of the Law in 12:10, Moses again descends, this time to build the tent of meeting (!), which is identified with the tabernacle (13:1–2). But at this point there is no mention of the face of Moses or the veil. Instead, the Lord himself declares the laws concerning the altar and the festivals to Moses within the tent, having covered it with the glory-cloud (13:1 f.).

The next reference to the glory on Moses' face comes at the time of his death (19:2–16) when Moses declares to the people not only that they will continue to forsake the Law and the covenant and be judged for it (19:2, 4), but that they will also "lament the day of (his) death and say in their heart, 'Who will give us another shepherd like Moses ... to pray always for our sins and to be heard for our iniquities?'" (19:3). After a reference to the blessing of Moses on the tribes (19:5), the text describes God's last revelation to Moses concerning the people's future sin, Moses' final intercession on behalf of the people, the divine revelation of the promised land, and God's promise that Moses' rod will remind him of his covenant promises (19:6–11). God then announces Moses' death with the traditional formulation "Now I will take you from here and glo-

---

"Gesetz und Evangelium," pp. 99–101 (esp. for the rabbinic texts) and the extensive survey of the traditions in Belleville, *Reflections of Glory*, pp. 24–79, now summarized in her "Tradition or Creation? Paul's Use of the Exodus 34 Tradition in 2 Corinthians 3:7–18," in *Paul and the Scriptures of Israel*, ed. Craig A. Evans and James A. Sanders, JSNT Suppl. 83, 1993, pp. 165–186.

[96] See now Vollenweider, "2 Kor 3," pp. 255 f., whose own analysis of LAB 12:1 in comparison to 12:7 and 19:16 also leads him to conclude that it was not fading, though it was weakened as a result of Israel's fall with the golden calf. Nevertheless, even in its weakened state, the glory on Moses' face necessitated the use of the veil. In support of this, Vollenweider points to the parallel traditions in *Tg. Song of Solomon* 1:5; *Pesiq. Rab Kah.* 5:3; *Deut. Rab.* 3:12; *Exod. Rab.* 11:3; *Eccl. Rab.* 9:11 f.; and esp. *Song of Songs Rab.* 3,7:5 (p. 256). In stark contrast to the position being argued here, however, Vollenweider goes on to conclude that Paul, under the impulse of the Christ-event, "radikalisiert zudem die Schwächung zum Dahinschwinden" (p. 273). See too Hofius, "Gesetz und Evangelium," pp. 100, who states concerning LAB 19:16 that it "could" (*könnte*) presuppose that the glory was fading, citing the cautious view of M. McNamara and the more certain conclusion to this effect by Ch. Perrot and P.-M. Bogaert in their *Pseudo-Philon. Les Antiquities Bibliques II: Introduction litteraire, Commentaire et Index, Tome 2*, SC 230, 1976, p. 135. But he himself carefully concludes that "Daß sich die von McNamara erwogene und von Perrot und Bogaert zuversichtlich vertretene Deutung zwingend aus dem Wortlaut von AntBibl 19:16 ergibt, wird m.E. nicht sagen können. Auszuschließen ist diese Deutung jedoch nicht" (p. 101). See too now Stockhausen, *Moses' Veil*, p. 119 n. 59: "Jewish tradition is unanimous in stressing the lasting character of Moses' glorification" (referring too to LAB 19:16 in this regard).

[97] English translations follow those of D.J. Harrington, "Pseudo-Philo," *OTP*, Vol. 2, 1985, pp. 304 ff. Latin text from Daniel J. Harrington, Cazeaux, *et al.*, *Pseudo-Philon. Les Antiquities Bibliques, Tome 1*, SC Nr. 229, 1976, pp. 60 ff.

rify you with your fathers …," predicts the ensuing mourning which it will bring, and that Moses' burial will be secret until the consummation (19:12–13). Upon hearing of the end of the age, Moses makes one final request to know how long it will be until it takes place, to which God gives a cryptic answer (19:14–15). The narrative closes with the following account of Moses' death itself, after which come references to the mourning of the angels:

> "And when Moses heard this, he was filled with understanding and his appearance *became glorious*; and he died in glory according to the word of the Lord, and he buried him as he had promised him." (19:6, emphasis mine)

> "Et audiens Moyses, repletus est sensu, et *mutata est* effigies eius *in gloria*, et mortuus est *in gloria* secundum os Domini, et sepelivit eum iuxta quod promiserat ei."

Those who argue that this text points to the fact that the glory of Moses' face was understood in LAB 12:1 to be fading do so on several grounds, as illustrated in Linda Belleville's treatment of this text. First, the reference that Moses' face "became" glorious or more literally "was changed into glory" (mutata est effigies eius in gloria) in 19:6 is taken to be a "renewal of Moses' facial splendor at death" which "suggests that the initial glory was a passing phenomenon."[98] Second, and stronger, is Belleville's observation that "Pseudo-Philo's placement of the shining face tradition prior to the golden calf episode indicates that the passing of Moses' glory was thought to be a direct consequence of the sin of the people."[99] Third, since in LAB Moses' glory is associated with his office of covenant mediator, when he smashed the tablets in LAB 12:5 because their writing had disappeared Moses was "thereby severing his link with the heavenly communication and fellowship he had experienced for 40 days …"[100] This is confirmed in that "it is only at the point when God once again communicates heavenly mysteries and realities to him that Moses' glory is restored to him (19:10–16)."[101]

But the reference to the transformation of Moses' face into glory (in gloria) in 19:6 most naturally refers back not to the need to renew the light on Moses' face mentioned in 12:1, but to the promise from the immediate context in 19:12 that God would glorify Moses with his fathers, just as the mention of the angels' mourning in 19:16 refers back to the prediction of their mourning in 19:12. That Moses is thus "glorified" is not explicitly related to the prior account of his descent in 12:1, and no inference as to the nature of the glory on Moses' face should be drawn from it. Indeed, the terminology in 12:1 and 19:6, though conceptually related, is distinct. Moreover, that LAB is not consistent in this regard is reflected by the fact that in LAB 9:7–8, 16 the promise of the glorification of Moses is extended back even to his childhood, as it is in other Jewish tradition, and can refer to his reputation and character among other men, as well as the

---

[98] Belleville, *Reflections of Glory*, p. 41, who exhibits no hesitation about drawing this conclusion. This is also the argument employed by M. McNamara, *New Testament and Palestinian Targum*, p. 174, though he is more cautious in his formulation. In his words, "This text may imply that the glory Moses received at Sinai … was passing and returned to him just before his death."

[99] *Reflections of Glory*, p. 41, following Perrot and Bogaert, *Pseudo-Philon, Tomne 2*, SC 230, 1976, p. 114. Belleville, p. 42, is correct in emphasizing that in LAB 12:1 the function of the veil is "to prevent a sinful people from gazing on the divine glory."

[100] *Reflections of Glory*, p. 42.

[101] *Reflections of Glory*, p. 42.

signs and wonders which he performs.[102] As a result, Moses "became glorious above other all other men" in his childhood and through the Exodus, although he is also glorified on Mt. Sinai, and then again later glorified at his death. Belleville's conclusion based on 19:16, that "the initial glory was a passing phenomenon"[103] thus goes beyond the explicit evidence, and, if the logic of this argument is carried on, would also mean that he lost his glory after the Exodus and before his ascent up Mt. Sinai.

The transposition of the account from Exod. 34:29 ff. to before the sin with the golden calf can be read in two ways. Rather than referring to the source of the passing away of the glory, this juxtaposition of Moses and the people may simply be part of the author's overall strategy in which he draws out the contrast between Moses, as Israel's greatest leader, and the sinful nation for whom he is to be an implied role model, even as Moses' father Amram and the other leaders of Israel function throughout the narrative as the positive counterparts to a disobedient nation.[104] Again, there is no direct reference in the narrative to any connection between the glory or the purpose of Moses' veil and Israel's sin with the golden calf. The motif of Israel's fear is omitted in LAB 12:1 ff. All that is said is that Moses' recognition that his face was shining led him to veil it. But if the glory on Moses' face is *not* fading in LAB 12:1, then this juxtaposition would make the same point implicitly that Paul does explicitly, and that the biblical account does by its reference to Israel's fear. For the most natural reading of the purpose of the veil in LAB 12:1–2 is that Israel does not recognize Moses due to the brilliance of the glory on his face, which he then veils because of Israel's sin with the golden calf. Surprisingly, Belleville herself points this out and states that "the suggestion is that Moses covered his face to prevent a sinful people from gazing on the divine glory."[105] Belleville must thus conclude that Ps-Philo, "does not link Moses' veiling with the need to cover a fading glory, as Paul does ...," even though both Paul and LAB "share the concept of a passing glory."[106] The easier and more natural interpretation of 12:1 f., however, is that LAB 12:1 f., like the rest of Jewish tradition and Paul, simply assumes that the glory was not fading and that the veil functioned to protect Israel in their sin.

Similarly, the account of Moses' breaking of the tablets in 12:5–7 makes no reference to the glory on his face, but only to the disappearance of the letters from the tablets, which is the immediate cause of their destruction.[107] And while it is certainly true

---

[102] Cf. e.g. Josephus, *Ant.* II. 231; Philo, *Vit. Mos.* I. 9:7; *b.* Sota 12a.

[103] *Reflections of Glory*, p. 41.

[104] Cf. LAB 15:5–6, where the glory of God again appears to Moses, this time to denounce the wickedness of the people. For the role of Israel's leaders in LAB in relationship to the people, see George W.E. Nickelsburg, "Good and Bad Leaders in Pseudo-Philo's *Liber Antiquitatum Biblicarum*," in *Ideal Figures in Ancient Judaism, Profiles and Paradigms*, ed. J. J. Collins and George W.E. Nickelsburg, Septuagint Cognate Studies Nr. 12, 1980, pp. 49–65, esp. pp. 53 f., on Moses, and pp. 60 f., on the function of the good and bad leaders in LAB in the context of the people's recurring idolatry.

[105] *Reflections of Glory*, p. 42.

[106] *Reflections of Glory*, pp. 42 f.

[107] Cf. the later rabbinic tradition in *Pirqe R. El.* 45, where the tablets take on a life of their own and are able to see Israel's sin with the golden calf. Hence, as a reflection of the holiness of God, the letters fly off the tablets so that, without them, the tablets become so heavy that Moses is forced to cast them to the ground. For this same tradition of the writing flying off in response to the golden calf, see *Num.Rab.* 9:48.

that Moses' glory is linked both to the Law and to divine communications,[108] in the absence of any textual indications there is no support for the conclusion that the smashing of the tablets somehow worked to diminish Moses' glory, or that the revelations in 19:10–15 renew it. Once the other more direct arguments for interpreting the glory on Moses' face as fading are judged inconclusive, these too lose their value. Hence, although it is possible to read LAB 12:1 f. and 19:16 as implying that the glory on Moses' face was fading, it seems to be a slight possibility at best, and in view of the lack of any direct support ought to be rejected.

The events of Exod. 34:29 ff. are not taken up elsewhere in the Apocrypha and Pseudepigrapha, although the related themes of Israel's hardened nature and its consequences, which provide the conceptual foundation for this passage, find ample expression in this literature (see chapter five).[109] Nor do they receive attention in the extant literature of the Jewish apologists from this period, apart from Philo and a possible allusion in Josephus, *Ant.* III. 82–88. In the latter case, we read concerning the theophany of Exod. 19 that on the third day of Moses' sojourn on the mountain the thunder and lightening led the people to believe that Moses had been killed by the storm and that they should expect the same death for themselves (III. 82).[110] In a tradition without parallel in the biblical account, we then read that "Such was their mood when suddenly Moses appeared, radiant and high-hearted" (γαῦρός τε καὶ μέγα φρονῶν), after which Moses declares to the people that God himself is going to come into their camp to recount to them his past acts of blessing and deliverance as a prelude to declaring the Law about to be given through Moses as God's "interpreter" (δι᾽ ἑρμηνέως ἐμοῦ; III. 83–88). The word translated "radiant" (γαῦρος) does not occur elsewhere in Josephus, but is better rendered "full of joy," as the corresponding use of the verb γαυρόομαι ("to be jubilant") in *Ant.* IX. 198 illustrates. Nevertheless, there is some sense of Moses' sharing in God's presence in this text, since in *Ant.* III. 388 we read that the authority of the Law which Moses interprets to the people is based on the fact that Moses has been "admitted to a sight of God." Hence, Moses' "joy" in this text might be seen as a result of being in God's presence on analogy to his experience in Exod. 34:29 ff. Although, in contrast to the targumic and rabbinic tradition (see below), they are not explicitly related in Josephus' account, it is thus striking that in *Ant.* IV. 325–326, Moses is said to disappear at his "death" into a ravine clothed in a cloud which suddenly descends upon him, reflecting typical biblical terminology for the clothing of the divine theophany of glory. Josephus therefore points out that Moses himself wrote that he died (cf. Deut. 34:5 f.) in order to avoid the impression that he

---

[108] Cf. in addition to the above texts, LAB 9:8, where the Law is interpreted in terms of God's "lamp" and "eternal light" which will be given to Moses, and 11:1, where the Law is again identified with the "eternal light," which this time is given to Israel and glorifies them.

[109] Cf. the related theme of the glory of God on the face of Enoch in 2 Enoch 37, and Methusalam's radiant face in 2 En. 69:10.

[110] Trans. and text of Josephus are taken from H. St. J. Thackeray, Ralph Marcus, Allen Wikgren, and Louis H. Feldman, *Josephus, Vol. I–IX*, LCL, 1966–1969. For the tradition of the death of Moses (cf. *Ant.* 4.326, where he seems to be offering a polemic against the exaltation and divinization of Moses found, e.g., in Philo) and a treatment of the person of Moses in general in Josephus, where the emphasis is on Moses as legislator (after the Hellenistic model of the ideal founder of a Greek city; cf. *Ant.* 1.6; 3.322) and, in a restrained fashion, as a "divine man" (θεῖος ἀνήρ) (cf. *Ant.* 4.194; 3.180), see still Wayne A. Meeks, *The Prophet-King: Moses Traditions and the Johannine Christology,* NovTSup 14, 1967, pp. 131–146.

has been translated to God! The permanence of the glory (joy!) on Moses' face might thus be presupposed in Josephus' account, though its brevity makes such a conclusion speculative. What *is* clear is that there is no indication at all of its fading.

Due to his apologetic purposes, Philo, like Josephus, does not recount the events of Exod. 32–34 in his non-allegorical, narrative account of Moses' life (see *Vit. Mos.* I. 214–236). Nevertheless, he does refer to Moses' descent from Sinai in *Vit. Mos.* II. 69–70 as part of his thematic discussion of Moses' virtues as a priest (cf. *Vit. Mos.* II. 66). Here we read that Moses' work as a prophet was based on the fact that he was possessed by the divine spirit (lit. he "bore God"; θεοφορεῖσθαι) and that because he had the inspiration of the "better food of contemplation" sent from heaven above, "he grew in grace to such an extent that those who saw him afterward could not believe their eyes" *(Vit. Mos.* II. 69).[111] Consequently,

> "... after the said forty days had passed, he descended with a countenance far more beautiful than when he ascended, so that those who saw him were filled with awe and amazement, nor even could their eyes continue to stand the dazzling brightness that flashed from him like rays of the sun" (καὶ μηδ' ἐπὶ πλέον ἀντέχειν τοῖς ὀφθαλμοῖς δύνασθαι κατὰ τὴν προσβολὴν ἡλιοειδοῦς φέγγους ἀπαστράπτοντος; *Vit. Mos.* II. 70).

As this text makes clear, the people's inability to look at Moses' face comes about because of its "dazzling brightness" acquired as a result of Moses' sojourn on Mount Sinai. But for Philo this inability is not merely a matter of being overwhelmed by the intensity of the light. According to *Fug.* 165, mortal humans are not able to study divine causation, but merely those effects which God's initiation brings about, since "the man that wishes to set his gaze upon the Supreme Essence, before he sees Him will be blinded by the rays that beam forth all around Him." Thus, for Philo, mankind cannot bear the rays of light that pour from God as the one who is truly existent in himself, even as we cannot bear the rays of the sun (cf. *De Abr.* 76; *Praem. Poen.* 36–40). For mortals, only a Platonic "copy" of God's powers at work in the world can be known *(De Spec. Leg.* I. 41–50). Hence, in spite of his semi-divine nature and unrelenting desire to do so, not even Moses is able to perceive God as he is, but must be content with viewing God's "back" (Exod. 33:18 f.), i.e. the effects of God's power in the world (cf. *De Post. Caini* 13–21, 169; *De Spec. Leg.* I. 49; *De Fug.* 165; *De Mut.* 9). On the basis of this parallel it seems probable to assume that in *Vit. Mos.* II. 70 the people cannot look upon Moses because he now mediates the divine presence itself in line with the principle stated by Philo in *Som.* II. 228 that "that which draws near to God enters into affinity with what is ..."[112] Thus, in line with his overall allegorical scheme,

---

[111] Trans. and texts from F. H. Colson and G.H. Whitaker, *Philo, Vols. VI, VII,* LCL, 1950 and F.H. Colson and G.H. Whitaker, *Philo, Vol. V,* LCL, 1949.

[112] For this same point based on these texts, see Belleville, *Reflections of Glory,* p. 33. She points to the Samaritan texts M.M. 2.12 (p. 50); LAB 12:1 (p. 41); and *Sifre Num.* 140 (p. 65 n. 6) for this same tradition of Moses' glory paralleling or exceeding that of the sun; and on pp. 50 f., 66 n. 2, to M.M. 6.3,11; *Cant. Rab.* III. 7.5; *Pesiq. R.* 10:6, *Sifre Num.* 1, and *Midr. Hagadol* חשׁא כי 30 for the tradition of the Israelites' fear and consequent inability to gaze at Moses due to the brilliance of the light. For the few rabbinic traditions concerning the veiling of Moses, Belleville points to *Pesiq. Rab.* 10.6; *Midr. Hagadol* חשׁא כי 33; and by implication *Midr. Hagadol* חשׁא כי 34 and *Mishnath Rab Eliezer,* pp. 150–151, which attributes the veiling to the fear of the angels (pp. 69 f.).

Moses comes down off the mountain bearing the divine presence of causation, which mortals may not see (= understand).[113]

At this point the adaptation of the biblical narrative ends, with no mention of Moses' veil or other tie to the overall context. Moreover, there are no other references to Moses' veil in Philo's writings, though Belleville is right in pointing to *Spec. Leg.* I. 270 as a possible allusion to Moses' entering into the divine presence.[114] There we read that the one who is cleansed by wisdom and the practice of virtue (I. 269) may come into the Sanctuary "with boldness" (θαρρῶν), but that "anyone whose heart is the seat of lurking covetousness and wrongful cravings should remain still and hide his face in confusion," though the terminology of the veil is missing here as well and no direct mention of Moses is made. Instead, the general principle is adduced that "the holy place of the truly existent is closed ground to the unholy" (I. 270). Yet, as *Rer. Div. Her.* 21 makes clear, Moses is clearly the example of the enlightened "wise one" *par excellence*.[115] Moreover, as Belleville has rightly observed in her dissertation, Philo makes no mention anywhere of Moses renewing the splendor of his face upon entering the sanctuary.[116] But, although Belleville is right in also pointing out that "there is nothing in Philo's account to suggest the notion of permanent possession found in the Targumim,"[117] Philo certainly offers no indication in his non-allegorical treatment of Moses' life that the brightness on Moses' face faded.

Indeed, in view of Philo's otherwise allegorical understanding of this splendor as Moses' participation in the divine reality of what truly exists apart from the body and its passions, if any speculation were to be offered concerning this point it would be more natural to assume that Moses' splendor remained, even as his status as the enlightened one certainly does.[118] This is supported by *Vit. Mos.* I. 158, where we read

---

[113] For this same point, see *De Post. Caini* 168–169, where it is said that not even Moses could see God, i.e. perceive divine causation, though in *Vit. Mos.* I. 158 it says that Moses "beheld what is hidden from the sight of mortal nature."

[114] *Reflections of Glory*, p. 34. Belleville points to the veiling of Tamar's face in *Mut. Nom.* 134 (with its parallel to Moses hiding his face in Exod. 3:6) and *Congr.* 124 as places where one might have expected such a reference. She offers two possible explanations for this absence: the negative connotations surrounding being veiled in Philo and its possible contradiction to Moses' boldness of speech (παρρησία), which is emphasized by Philo (p. 34 n. 1). But the former would hold only if what was hidden were in fact negative (which it is not); the latter would be true only if the issue in view were Moses' speech to the people and not the presence of God which he mediates, and if Moses were then said to be bold in speech in reference to the people, neither of which Philo asserts. What *would* be veiled in this context both for the biblical account and for Philo is not Moses' boldness of speech toward Israel, but the presence of God which he mediates. Philo's reason for not mentioning Moses' veil must thus be left open.

[115] So too Erwin R. Goodenough, *An Introduction to Philo Judaeus*, 2nd. ed., 1962, p. 145: "Moses was the one to whom Philo most usually looked for the pattern of the ideal man and saviour." See e.g. *Vit. Mos.* I. 1, 27; *De Virt.* 51–101, *Conf. Ling.* 95; *De Sacr.* 9; and Goodenough's summary of Philo's treatment of Moses on pp. 145–153.

[116] *Paul's Polemical Use of the Moses-Doxa Traditions in 2 Corinthians 3:12–18*, Diss. University of St. Michael's College, 1986 (UMI, 1987), p. 26. This observation is omitted in the published form (cf. *Reflections of Glory*, p. 33).

[117] *Reflections of Glory*, p. 33.

[118] For a treatment of Philo's view of Moses in general as the true legislator, king, prophet, priest, philosopher, and θεῖος ἀνήρ, see Meeks, *Prophet-King*, pp. 100–131, and esp. pp. 107–117, for the basic theme of *Vit. Mos.* Book I, in which, in contrast to Philo's other

that as the "friend of God" (Exod. 33:11) Moses shared in God's possessions (cf. I. 156), including even the titles and functions of "god and king" over the nation. Here too Moses shares God's possessions because he entered into "the darkness where God was, that is into the unseen, invisible, incorporeal and archetypal essence of existing things" (in reference to Exod. 20:21), and "beheld what is hidden from the sight of mortal nature" *(Vit. Mos.* I. 158). In *Quod. Om. Prob.* 43–44 we therefore read that Moses was possessed by the love of the divine and passed from man into a god, though he was not of divine rank in himself.[119] Similarly, in *QE* II. 46 Philo tells us that Moses was called up to Mount Sinai on the seventh day and experienced a "new birth" which put him beyond the bodily nature of the descendents of Adam, who was created on the sixth day. Unlike humanity, after his ascent Moses now has no mother, but only God as his divine father in a new divine birth. At this point Moses becomes deified, or perhaps even equated with God himself (cf. *QE* II. 29). In *De Fug.* 109 Moses' father is thus said to be God, while his mother is wisdom. At his death, though clothed in his mortal body, Moses therefore continues to sing the perfect "song" in tune with his divine status as the perfect "hierophant" (cf. *De Virt.* 73–75, in reference to Deut. 31:28 f.). Similarly, in *Vit. Mos.* II. 288–291 Moses' twofold nature of divine soul and human body is completely transformed at his death into pure light, like God. This perfection on Moses' part is the logical extension of the fact that in *De Virt.* 52 Philo offers two proofs of "the continual and unbroken virtue which, unmixed, he impressed as a final seal, clear and distinct, upon his soul, which had been shaped by the divine Image." It also correlates with the fact that Moses was a "divine man" who stood between God and humanity in nature and function so that, from his birth, people wondered if Moses was human or divine or a combination of the two (cf. *Vit. Mos.* I. 27). In reality, Moses is the "purest spirit" of those "angels" (ἀγγέλους) or souls which do not become mingled with the body and are sent on journeys as ambassadors (πρεσβευομένας) "bearing tidings (διαγγελλούσας) from the great Ruler to His subjects of the boons (ἀγαθὰ) which He sends them, and reporting to the Monarch what His subjects are in need of" *(De Plant.* 14). In *De Gig.* 16 and *De Abr.* 115 this definition of "angels" as souls which do not inhabit bodies and whose role is that of "ambassadors" (πρεσβευτάς) between God and mankind and mankind and God is then made explicit. Moreover, the latter text makes it clear that these angels are "holy and divine beings" (ἱεραὶ καὶ θεῖαι φύσεις). As the supreme mediator between God and mankind, Moses "holds eldership among the angels, their ruler (ἀρχάγγελον) as it were" *(De Conf. Ling.* 146). In *Rer. Div. Her.* 201 he can be identified with the sacred Word (ἱερὸν λόγον) itself, which in Num. 16:47 f. stood between God and the people in order to stop the divine judg-

---

writings, Moses is portrayed above all as the "most excellent king," the "most perfect ruler" (p. 107; cf. e.g. *Vit. Mos.* I.162, 334; II.1–7, 187). As Meeks concludes, "Moses' essential importance for Philo is as the prototypical mystic and the guide for those of his 'disciples' who, like Philo himself, long to participate in the true 'Exodus', an escape from the 'Egypt' of the senses and passions" (p. 130).

[119] Cf. Meeks, *Prophet-King*, p. 123, who argues on the basis of *Post.* 28–31; *Sac.* 9; *QE* II. 29, 40, that Moses' ascent becomes "virtually a deification." Hence, Moses does not die, but is translated (cf. *QE* I. 86; *Sac.* 8–10; *Vit. Mos.* II. 288–292; *Virt.* 53, 72–79, pp. 124 f.). Thus, as Meeks points out, pp. 121 f., the vision of God itself may be unattainable, but Moses achieved a position closer to God than anyone else (cf. *Post.* 16, 173; *Spec.leg.* I.41; *Gig.* 53 f.). Consequently, "Philo interprets Moses' ascent on Sinai as a mystical translation; the incident becomes the persistent symbol in his allegory of the experience which he sees as the goal of every σοφός, every φιλόθεος" (p. 122).

ment.[120] In this same context, Moses, as the Word, is again identified as God's "chief messenger" (ἀρχαγγέλῳ) to whom God has given "the special prerogative, to stand on the border and separate the creature from the Creator" *(Rer. Div. Her.* 205). Based on his declaration in Deut. 5:5, Moses, like the angels, is then said to have the role of pleading on behalf of the mortal to God, and to act "as ambassador of the ruler to the subject" (πρεσβευτὴς δὲ τοῦ ἡγεμόνος πρὸς τὸ ὑπήκοον; *Rer. Div. Her.* 205). This can only mean that Moses is neither "uncreated as God, nor created as you, but midway between the two extremes ..." *(Rer. Div. Her.* 206). In this role and with this identity, Moses' task in representing God is to be "the harbinger of peace to creation from that God whose will is to bring wars to an end, who is ever the guardian of peace" *(Rer. Div. Her.* 206).

There is thus no intimation in Philo's portrayal that the splendor on Moses' face, as the representation of his newly acquired divine status as the one ordained to lead humanity into the mysteries of what truly exists (cf. *De Som.* I. 164–165), ever diminished or faded. Although to draw any firm conclusion one way or the other would be to push the evidence beyond what it can bear, Belleville's conclusion that "Philo's treatment of Moses' shining face can admit the possibility of fading and termination"[121] goes against the overall tenor of Philo's interpretation of Moses' identity and role.

Finally, the tradition concerning the glory on Moses' face in rabbinic and Samaritan literature also corresponds to the emphasis in the biblical account that Moses mediated the very glory of God. Moreover, the rabbinic and Samaritan traditions agree in assuming and/or stressing the permanent character of this glory, though various theological implications are drawn from this fact throughout the rabbinic writings.[122]

---

[120] For an overview of Moses' qualities as the supreme king, lawgiver, high priest, and prophet (cf. *Vit. Mos.* II. 292), and his apparent identification with the divine logos in Philo, see now Ronald Williamson, *Jews in the Hellenistic World: Philo,* Cambridge Commentaries on Writings of the Jewish and Christian World 200 BC to AD 200 Vol. 1/2, 1989, pp. 54–59, 115–119. On Moses' semi-divine status, cf. *Vit. Mos.* I.158 with *Som.* II.189; *De Conf. Ling.* 192; etc. In examining the relevant texts Williamson concludes that "If ever a man was God it was surely in the case of Moses" (p. 58), though strictly speaking Moses was inspired and inhabited by the Spirit of God and the divine logos (p. 116).

[121] *Reflections of Glory,* p. 35. It is difficult to see how Philo's understanding of Moses' transfiguration (cf. *Vit. Mos.* II. 271, 280) and its tie to his office as lawgiver "consequently admit the possibility of the impermanence of this glory" (p. 35). Moreover, Belleville links this to the contrast between Philo and Paul, in that Paul speaks of the "paling of the Law's glory" in 2 Cor. 3:13–14, where Philo stresses its permanence (p. 35). But as we will see, Paul too does not speak of the fading of the Law, just as he does not speak of the fading of Moses' glory.

[122] The theme of Moses' veil appears not to have been significantly developed in rabbinic literature (cf. *Pesiq. Rab.* 10 § 6). Indeed, according to P. Demann, "Moses und das Gesetz bei Paulus," in *Moses in Schrift und Überlieferung,* 1963, pp. 205–264, p. 215 n. 25, the "Nüchternheit" of the midrashic tradition concerning Exod. 34:29–35 makes it difficult to determine if Paul relied on any such traditions at all. He concludes that Exod. 34:29–35 is sufficient to explain Paul's presentation. For the theme of the shining of Moses' face, see e.g. *Sifre Num.* 140; *Midrash P^etirat Mosae* (Paris 710 folio) 123–124 (in which the angel of death cannot take Moses' soul due to the shining of Moses' face like the sun, to which the angel reacts in fear!); *Gen. Rab.* 19:7; *Num. Rab.* 6:12; 13:2 (where sin is said to drive the Shekinah away, while seven righteous men bring it back and Moses is the one who brings it to earth); *Exod. Rab.* 1:18; 22:1 (where Moses' mother Jochebed also mirrors the glory of

Of special significance in this regard because of its commentary-like tie to the biblical text, and in the case of *Neofiti* its early, perhaps even pre-Christian origin, is the targumic tradition. It is therefore striking that the targums are unanimous in their emphasis that it was the glory of God which Moses experienced in the theophany and which was reflected on his face.[123] *Tg. Neofiti I* is especially instructive. In *Tg. Neof.* 33:15 f. Moses pleads for the "glory of (YHWH's) Shekinah" (שכינתך א`יקר) to accompany the people, and in 33:18 that YHWH's "glory" (א`יקרך) be revealed to

---

God on her face and is herself therefore called "the divine Glory"!); 47:5–6; *Deut. Rab.* 11.3 (where Moses retains the luster of his face which Adam lost at the fall as one of the six things Adam lost, cf. *Gen.Rab.* 12.6; *Memar Marqah* 6.3; 5.4 to Deut 34:7, where in this connection to Adam the latter text stresses that Moses' face shone until the day he died); *Deut. Rab.* 11.3 (where the lost image of Adam at the fall is identified with the light of Moses' face acquired in his first ascent up Mt. Sinai); *Tanhuma to Num.* 10:1–2; *Exod. Rab.* 15.13 (in which God's sharing his glory with those who fear him is illustrated by his making Moses "god" and "king"; cf, *Tg. Song of Sol.* 5.10, where God's glory is visualized as the shining of his face); and for the extension of these traditions to the point of Moses as "god," see *Pesiq. Rab Kah.*, Supplement I, 9 and the *Exagoge*, 66–89. For these and other texts and the related themes of Moses as visionary, high priest, prophet, king, and mediator in rabbinic literature, see the studies of H. Strack and P. Billerbeck, *Kommentar zum Neuen Testament aus Talmud und Midrasch*, Bd, II, 1924, pp. 665 f.; Bd. III, 1926, pp. 513–516; Howard M. Teeple, *The Mosaic Eschatological Prophet*, JBL Monograph Series Vol. 10, 1957, p. 39; Meeks, *Prophet-King*, 1967, pp. 176–200; and his "Moses as God and King," in *Religions in Antiquity, FS E.R. Goodenough*, ed. J. Neusner, 1968, pp. 354–371, pp. 357, 359–365; K. Haacker and P. Schäfer, "Nachbiblische Traditionen vom Tod des Mose," in *Josephus-Studien: Untersuchungen zu Josephus, dem antiken Judentum und dem Neuen Testament, FS Otto Michel zum 70. Geburtstag*, ed. Otto Betz, et al.,1974, pp. 147–174, pp. 168 ff.; Pieter W. van der Horst, "Moses' Throne Vision in Ezekiel the Dramatist," *JJS* 34 (1983) 21–29; Kim, *Origin*, p. 261; Hofius, "Gesetz und Evangelium," pp. 94 f.; 99 f.; and R. P. Martin, *2 Corinthians*, pp. 63 f.; and for the medieval Jewish commentary tradition, see N. Leibowitz, *Studies in Shemot (Exodus), Part II*, 1981, pp. 631–639. A survey of these texts, together with the overall picture of Moses developed in later rabbinic literature, leads to the conclusion of J. Jeremias, art. Μωϋσῆς, *TDNT* 4 (1967) 848–873, p. 849, that "As distinct from the basic OT approach to Moses, especially in the prophets, his person is now panegyrically magnified ...."

[123] Cf. *Tg. Onq.* 34:29, *Frg. Tgs. P* and *V* Exod. 34:29, *Tg. Ps.-Jon.* 34:29, and the helpful summaries by Martin McNamara, *New Testament and Palestinian Targum*, pp. 171–173, and William H. Propp, "The Skin of Moses' Face – Transfigured or Disfigured?" *CBQ* 49 (1987) 375–386, pp. 377 f. As Propp observes, p. 377, "It is noteworthy that the targums do not translate the Hebrew עור, 'skin,' while the nouns for 'splendor' and 'glory' have no equivalent in the MT. This is reminiscent of Gen. 3:21, where ... 'garments of skin,' is rendered in Aramaic as ... 'garments of glory.' As the midrashic tradition indicates, this interpretation stems from a wordplay, reading אור, 'light,' for עור, 'skin.'" It may, of course, also represent a different underlying Hebrew tradition, or simply reflect the widespread notion in rabbinic tradition that the skin of Moses shone with the glory of God (cf. e.g. *Exod. Rab.* 47:6; *Deut. Rab.* 3:12). In this case, as B. Grossfeld, *The Targum Onqelos to Exodus*, The Aramaic Bible Vol. 7, 1988, p. 99 n. 20, concludes concerning *Tg. Onq.* 34:29, "the Targum rendered 'skin' as 'glory,' since Moses' skin had by now, as a result of contact with the Glory of God's Divine Presence, turned into something more than just human skin and increased in radiance, hence the Targum's insertion 'increased' also present in the *Frg. Tg.* (P, V) which reads 'the radiance of his face increased.'"

him.[124] In *Tg. Neof.* 34:5 f. (cf. 33:22) it is explicitly this "glory of the Shekinah of the Lord" (אִיקָר שְׁכִינְתֵיהּ דַיְיָ) which is revealed in the theophanic cloud and passes beside Moses (cf. *Frg. Tg. P* and *Tg. Onq.* to Exod. 34:6), though the targum is careful to emphasize that Moses cannot see the face of God's glory directly.[125] Unlike the MT and LXX, here too *Tg. Neof.* follows the common targumic practice of establishing a reverential distance in speaking of God.[126] It is thus the angels and "the word" (דִּבְרָא) of God's glory which he actually sees (cf. 33:22 f.; cf. *Frg. Tgs. P* and *V* Exod. 33:23).[127] Nevertheless, after Moses descends, the "splendour of the glory" "shines" on his face (Exod. 34:29 f.). This link between Moses' experience of God's glory in the theophany and his reflection of it is made explicit in *Tg. Ps.-Jon.* 34:29, where we read concerning Moses that "the radiance of his facial features shone brightly from the radiance of the Glory of the Lord's Presence [i.e. Shekinah]."[128] Moreover, there is no indication in the text that this glory faded or diminished as time went on (cf. 34:35).

---

[124] Text and translation taken from Alejandro Diez Macho, *Neophyti I, Vol. II: Exodus*, Textos y Estudios Vol. 8, 1970, pp. 209–233, 503–516.

[125] Cf. *Tg. Neof.* Exod. 33:11, where like the LXX this problem is also avoided, this time by interpreting the text to mean that the Lord speaks to Moses "speech to speech," rather than "face to face" as in the MT. *Tg. Onq.* Exod. 33:11 renders it in terms of the Lord speaking with Moses "literally." Translation here and elsewhere according to B. Grossfeld, *Targum Onqelos*, pp. 88–98. In the same way, in *Tg. Ps.-Jon.* Exod. 33:11, we read that "the Lord spake with Mosheh word for word – the voice of the word was heard, but the Majesty of the Presence was not seen – in the way that a man converseth with his companion." Translation according to J.W. Etheridge, *The Targums of Onkelos and Jonathan ben Uzziel on the Pentateuch*, Vol. 1, 1968, p. 555. For the LXX's attempt to avoid this tension in the text, see above, chapter three.

[126] For this practice and the corresponding targumic practice of removing anthropomorphisms, cf. Martin McNamara, *Targum and Testament, Aramaic Paraphrases of the Hebrew Bible: A Light on the New Testament*, 1972, pp. 93–106, who points especially to the use of the "word" (memra), "glory," and "Presence" (Shekinah, Shekinta) in speaking of God's relations with the world. For the synonymous use of the "glory of the Lord," and the "word of the Lord," cf. *Tg. Neof.* Gen. 1:16 f., 27; 2:2 f.

[127] For this same careful distancing of God from mankind, while at the same time emphasizing the revelation of God's glory, cf. the *Tg. Genizah* MS III B to Gen. 35:10–13, where the "memra" (מֵמְרָה) of the Lord is that which is revealed and speaks to Jacob (cf. v. 9), while it is the "glory of the Shekinah" (יְקַר שְׁכִינְתֵּהּ) which is apparently in view in 35:13. In the same way, in *Tg. Genizah* MS 605 to Exod. 19:4, it is the "glory of the Shekinah" which is said to have brought Israel out in the Exodus, while in MS e 43 to Exod. 19:18, 20 it is this same "glory of the Shekinah" which is revealed to Israel on Mt. Sinai, where it is the "word" (דִּבִּירֵהּ) of the Lord which calls to Moses from the theophany. In the same MS to Exod. 20:19, the people fear the "memra" of the Lord, which is again paralleled to the revelation of the "glory of the shekinah" in the verses 20–21. For the revelation of this same "glory of the shekinah" before Moses and Aaron at the opening of the tent of meeting, cf. *Tg.* Mss. 1080 to Num. 20:6. For these texts and translations, see Michael L. Klein, *Genizah Manuscripts of Palestinian Targum to the Pentateuch, Vol. One*, 1986, pp. 74 f., 256 f., 262 f., 270 f., 324 f. This same tension and solution is found in *Tg. Onq.* 32:13; 33:14–23; 34:6, 9, where the Lord's "memra" and "presence" are revealed, while the "face of God's presence" cannot be seen. The anthropomorphic references to God's "face" (33:11) and "hand" (33:23) are thus also avoided by the use of "literally" and "the Word of My Glory" respectively; cf. too *Tg. Ps.-J.* 33:19–23.

[128] Quotation following Grossfeld, *Targum Onqelos*, p. 99 n. 20.

Indeed, the targumic tradition is unanimous that the glory persisted on Moses' face until he died.[129]

As this targumic tradition illustrates, the rabbinic trajectory confirms the amazing uniformity of opinion in the post-biblical tradition concerning the abiding nature of the glory of God reflected on Moses' face. If Paul did maintain that the glory on Moses' face was fading, he was unique in doing so. This of course in no way precludes the possibility that Paul did in fact go his own way in interpreting Exod. 34:29 ff. But from the perspective of the biblical text and its history of interpretation, it does place the burden of proof on those who argue this position. And as we have seen, this burden rests on the understanding of καταργέω in this context.

Viewed against the backdrop not only of Exod. 32–34, but also of this unified trajectory of tradition,[130] Paul's "interpretation" of Exod. 34:29 ff., understood to refer to the fading glory on Moses' face, is almost always portrayed

---

[129] See *Tgs. Neof., Frg. Tg.*, and *Onq.* to Deut. 34:7, and esp. the latter in which the same expression used to describe Moses' face shining with the glory of God in Exod. 34:29 ff. is used to describe Moses at his death in Deut. 34:7. For this point, see McNamara, *New Testament and Palestinian Targum*, pp. 174 f. For the ways in which Moses' death was taken up in later tradition, especially in view of the fact that he died outside the land and in secret, and that he had to die at all (!), see Samuel E. Loewenstamm, "The Death of Moses," in *Studies on the Testament of Abraham*, ed. George W.E. Nickelsburg, Jr., SBL Septuagint and Cognate Studies 6, 1976, pp. 185–217. Of special significance is the tradition in *Sifre* 305 and *Deut. Rab.* 10, in which the angel of death cannot prevail over Moses and fears Moses since his countenance shines like the sun. Thus God himself must come and take Moses away.

[130] So too Gaston, "2 Corinthians 3," p. 161, who observed concerning the idea of a fading glory on Moses' face that "not only is there nothing in the Exodus text to suggest such a strange conception, but what little exegetical tradition there is directly contradicts it," though it is questionable that Luke 9:32 can be taken to mean that Moses' glory persisted into the first century A.D., as Gaston, p. 238 n. 50, maintains, since this refers to Moses in his exalted glory. But Gaston's view, p. 161, that Paul is not referring to the glory on Moses' face *per se*, but to "the glory on the face of Moses' imitators or, more generally, (to) any glory of any Christian ministry" misses the explicit point and force of Paul's argument. Contra too the conclusion of Belleville, *Reflections of Glory*, p. 77, "that most of the literary materials examined include one line of interpretation that suggests that Moses' glory experienced some deterioration, or that it was lost either during his lifetime or at death." Her strongest text for this tradition is the *Zohar* 3.58 (compiled in its present form in the middle ages!), though even this text can be read to mean that due to Israel's sin with the golden calf Moses' glory was not as bright as it would have been otherwise, not that it was fading or deteriorating. And even after Israel's sin, the glory is so bright that Israel cannot bear it, but fears Moses' mediation of the glory of God (1.52a–b) (cf. Belleville, p. 75). As Belleville points out, p. 75, *Zohar* 1.31b declares that Moses' glory was with him until the end of his life. According to Belleville, what is distinct in regard to the glory on Moses' face in Paul's thought is not that the glory was fading, but that "Paul alone links the fading of Moses' glory with the waning of the covenant" (p. 78); and that "he is the only one to specify that the veil was put in place to prevent the Israelites from gazing right down to the end of this fading glory" (p. 78). Therefore, for Belleville, "there is no real uniqueness to the Moses-*Doxa* material in 2 Cor. 3:7, 12–18," though Paul's application of this material to the Mosaic covenant and his own situation is distinctively his own (p. 78). Hence, even if Belleville's analysis of the various Jewish traditions had proved to be persuasive, her conclusion is wholly dependent upon the traditional, but untenable way of reading καταργέω in 2 Cor. 3:7–13.

as an intentional *mis*-reading of the text.[131] But as Childs and Hays have realized, given the polemical situation in which Paul found himself, this traditional view would have been singularly unpersuasive.[132] As Hays has put it, "... Paul would be putting himself in an extraordinarily weak position if he based his argument on his own fictional embellishment of the text."[133]

Recently there have been several attempts to avoid such a conclusion by suggesting that καταργουμένην in v. 7 can be read to refer not to Moses' day, but to Paul's own, or even to some future point in time.[134] Taken in this way, Paul is not commenting about the glory on Moses' face after his descent from Mt. Sinai at all. Rather, Paul is asserting that since the coming of Christ it is *now* the case that the glory of the Law or ministry of Moses "is fading away" or will some day "be done away with" when the new age is consummated.

---

[131] The representatives of this position are legion (see ch. five, nn. 38–42); cf. e.g. the confident assertion of Erich Gräßer, *Der Alte Bund im Neuen*, WUNT 35, 1985, p. 86: "Es ist gar keine Frage, daß Paulus in 2 Kor 3:7 ff. diesen Text nicht das sagen läßt, was er von sich aus zu sagen hat," pointing as his first example to the fact that in vv. 7, 11 Paul says that Moses' glory was fading in spite of the opposing Jewish tradition. But of particular importance because of their work in comparing Paul to Jewish tradition is the support for this conclusion found among scholars such as H. Kittel, *Herrlichkeit*, p. 203; Paul Démann, "Moses und das Gesetz bei Paulus," in *Moses in Schrift und Überlieferung*, 1963, pp. 205–264, pp. 211 f., 214; H.J. Schoeps, *Paul: The Theology of the Apostle in the Light of Jewish Religious History*, 1961, p. 42, who on the basis of the principle in *b.* Sabb. 63a that "no verse of scripture can ever lose its original meaning," concluded that Paul "overstepped" even the limits established in rabbinic tradition; W.G. Kümmel, additions to Hans Lietzmann, *An die Korinther I–II* , HNT Bd. 9, 1969⁵, p. 199; and now Koch, *Schrift*, pp. 333 f., for whom this is another example of the way in which Paul reinterprets and selectively chooses Scriptures.

[132] Brevard S. Childs, *The Book of Exodus, A Critical, Theological Commentary*, 1974, p. 621. Childs' answer is to posit, without evidence, the existence of a generally accepted interpretive tradition in which the glory of Moses did in fact fade, since Paul makes such substantial use of this concept in his argument. But as we have seen above, Belleville's subsequent attempt to discover such a tradition is not convincing. Hays, *Echoes*, p. 133, (rightly) rejects Childs' positing such a hypothetical tradition.

[133] *Echoes*, p. 218 n. 39. This would be true regardless of whether or not Paul's opponents were making use of the Exodus tradition in some way. For this same point, see Dumbrell, "Paul's use of Exodus 34," pp. 179 f.

[134] For the view that the "passing away," is taking place at the time of Paul's writing and not at the time of Moses, see e.g. Peter von der Osten-Sacken, "Geist im Buchstaben, Vom Glanz des Mose und des Paulus," now in his *Evangelium und Tora, Aufsätze zu Paulus*, 1987, pp. 150–155 (originally in *EvTh* 41 (1981) 230–235), p. 150; and now Stockhausen, *Moses' Veil*, p. 87 n. 3, following J.F. Collange, *Enigmes de la Deuxieme Epitre de Paul aux Corinthiens. Etude Exegetique de 2 Cor 2:14–7:4*, SNTS Monograph Series 18, 1972, p. 76. Hence, Paul "is not in contradiction to, but in agreement with, his religious tradition and the text of Exodus on this point," since for Paul the glory did not fade in Moses' day, but in his own (p. 87 n. 3). For Stockhausen, Paul's insight that the glory was fading in his day came from the Prophets, as alluded to in 3:1–6, and from his own experience, not from the Exodus narrative (cf. pp. 119 f.). Recently, the view that the participle refers to Paul's own day in view of its attributive function has also been accepted by Hays, *Echoes*, pp. 134, 219 n. 43, without elaboration, though Hays rejects the meaning "fading" for καταργέω in 3:7 ff. In spite of Hays' helpful insights concerning the meaning of this verb, he therefore misses the point of 3:7, 13 itself (see below).

But the time reference of the ὥστε-clause is determined by the clause to which it belongs. The main verb of that clause, ἐγενήθη, clearly signifies that the entire protasis is referring to the time of Moses.[135] Even if it be granted that its position in the sentence may suggest that it be read independently of its clause as a predicative participle (with an article?), this is certainly not the most natural rendering here.[136] It is most easily read attributively as a simple modification of the glory in Moses' day. This is confirmed by the fact that in 3:14b and 15, when Paul does change his focus from the events of Exod. 34:29 ff. to the present, he indicates so *explicitly*. Equally improbable, if not impossible, therefore, is Stegemann's accompanying suggestion that καταργέω in 3:7 refers to "das Zeitliche" and "ein Aufhören ... mit dem die Zeit selbst aufhört," so that it points to a future eschatological time in which the glory on Moses' face will come to an end.[137] As we will see below, although καταργέω certainly carries an eschatological connotation for Paul, its significance is that those things which have already been abolished (1 Cor. 2:6), or ought to be considered to be abolished (1 Cor. 6:13), are a foretaste of the future eschatological consummation (1 Cor. 15:24–26).

---

[135] See now Furnish, *II Corinthians*, p. 203.

[136] At this point Stockhausen's argument is misleading. She refers to Blass, A. Debrunner, R.W. Funk, *A Greek Grammar of the New Testament*, p. 212, to support her assertion that the participle is related to the noun phrase "and *as such* future to the main verb" (p. 87 n. 3, emphasis mine). But the discussion on this page merely concerns the anarthrous and articular forms of attributive participles and their function as equivalent to a relative clause. Nothing in the attributive participle's relationship to its noun would indicate that it is "future to the main verb." If such an unusual use were the case, contextual indicators would have to determine it. In this regard, other examples of such a use would be helpful. In the same way, Stockhausen's reference, p. 120 n. 60, to J.H. Moulton, *A Grammar of New Testament Greek, Vol. III: Syntax*, by Nigel Turner, 1963, p. 79, in support of her position is equally puzzling. At this point Turner is discussing the time reference of *adverbial* participles to their main verbs, with the attributive use discussed on pp. 151–153. Of significance for the use of the participle in 2 Cor. 3:7 is Turner's discussion of the predicative use on pp. 158–162, in which he gives various examples (without the article). The closest examples to 3:7 are found in Mk. 5:36; Lk. 4:23; Acts 7:12; 2 Thess. 3:11; 3 John 4 (all with ἀκούω) and Mtt. 15:31; 24:30; Mk. 5:31; John 1:32; and esp. Mtt. 22:1; Mk. 11:13, where the participle modifying the direct object "is more plainly separate from the object of the main verb, and becomes in effect a distinctive complement ..." (p. 161). But in every case, the participle is used without the article and corresponds to the time reference of the main verb!

[137] "Neue Bund," p. 111, who asserts that the traditional translation of καταργέω as referring to the past time of Moses cannot be maintained, although the concept it represents is correct. Instead, as an "apocalyptic term," Paul is using καταργέω to refer to the doing away of that which belongs to the "dying-earthly-sinful sphere of this age." He thus translates 3:11, "Wenn schon das Zeitliche (τὸ καταργούμενον) durch Herrlichkeit, um wieviel mehr das Bleibende (τὸ μένον) in Herrlichkeit" (p. 111). Besides the grammatical unlikelihood of this reading for both 3:7 and 11, the conceptual problem with this view is that contextually it would mean that Paul asserts the coming to an end of God's glory! Stegemann can only avoid this conclusion by drawing a distinction between the glory of Moses and the heavenly glory of God already reflected in Christ (p. 111), a distinction that is not supported by the text or its OT backdrop.

The recognition of the improbability of Paul's having offered such an unfounded interpretation of the glory in Exod. 34:29 ff. as "fading," which lies behind these proposals, is welcome. But neither the attempt to divorce τὴν καταργουμένην from the temporal context within its clause, nor the suggestion that καταργέω itself can point to the future, are convincing. Nevertheless, the attention recently given to the meaning of καταργέω does point us in the right direction, since a reexamination of its semantic range makes clear that the consensus concerning the meaning of the verb in 2 Cor. 3:7 must be rejected.

e) The Range of Meaning of Καταργέω Outside of 2 Cor. 3:7–14

The use of καταργέω in the ancient world apart from the New Testament and the literature dependent upon it is rare. A search of the stem καταργ. in the literature from the 4th cent. BC to 4th cent. AD provided by the Thesaurus Linguae Graecae Project at the University of California, Irvine, produced over 1300 occurrences of the verb.[138] Of these occurrences, only 16 are found in literature outside the NT and its circle of influence.[139] Within a narrower scope, our own survey of *all* forms of the stem in the 156 authors contained in the TLG data base which can be dated with some certainty from the second century B.C. to the second century A.D. produced 270 occurrences.[140] Of these, only six appear outside the NT and the literature it influenced, four of which are in the LXX.[141] The vast majority of the other references are dependent either by allusion or quotation on Paul's writings, especially his statements in Rom. 3:3, 31; 6:6; 1 Cor. 1:28; 2:6; 15:24, 26; Eph. 2:15, and 2 Thess. 2:8. This is not surprising in that of the 27 times the verb appears in the NT, 25 are found in the Pauline corpus.[142] The only exceptions are Luke 13:7 and Hebrews 2:14. Hence, as

---

[138] Because of the focus on the present passive form of the verb, the Aorist and Perfect Indicative forms were not included in this broader spectrum. The papyri have not been surveyed.

[139] Besides the texts explicitly referred to below, see *Scholia in Homerum* 19.157–8.3 (no canon yet available) and the *Cyranides* (ante 1st/2nd cent. AD) 10.101 (designations, dates, and references to editions given according to Luci Berkowitz and Karl A. Squitier, *Thesaurus Linguae Graecae, Canon of Greek Authors and Works*, 1986²).

[140] This included καταργητέον ("one must abolish"), which occurs once, and ἡ κατάργησις ("making null, abolishing"), which occurs 50xs. The vast majority of these uses are found in Origen's writings (over 195 xs!). My special thanks go to my teaching assistant Mr. Craig Torell for his assistance in culling out these authors from the data base and running the appropriate searches.

[141] The other two are found in Polybius, *Fragmenta* 176 (2xs of the same form, κατηργηκέναι) (see below). The one other possible occurrence is found in an anonymous and undated commentary on Aristotle's *Rhetorica* (cf. *In Aristotelis artem rhetoricam commentarium*, ed. H. Rabe, *Anonymi et Stephani in artem rhetoricam commentaria*, 1896, p. 163.17), but due to its uncertainty need not be considered.

[142] 6xs in Romans, 9xs in 1 Cor., 4xs in 2 Cor., 3 xs in Gal., and 1x in Eph., 2 Thess., and 2 Tim. See *Vollständige Konkordanz zum Griechischen Neuen Testament, Bd. II Spezial-übersichten*, ed. K. Aland, 1978, pp. 148 f.

the lexicons testify and the TLG search confirms, our evidence for the meaning of καταργέω in 2 Cor. 3 must be drawn largely from Paul's use itself.[143]

There is little, if any, doubt concerning the semantic field encompassed by the *active* forms of the verb καταργέω in these non-Christian sources. In Euripides (5th cent. BC), *The Phoenician Maidens* 753, the verb occurs metaphorically in the phrase ὅπως ἂν μὴ καταργῶμεν χέρα with the meaning "that (my) hands might not loiter."[144] Ctesias (5th.–4th. cent. BC) also uses the active form metaphorically to refer to the easy way in which one walks a path, i.e. "abolishes the way" (καταργεῖς πρὸς τὴν ὁδόν) in *Fragmenta* 688. F. 69.7.[145] Polybius, *Fragmenta* 176, employs κατηργηκέναι in tandem with καταπροΐεσθαι ("to throw away," or "to abandon"), clearly indicating its semantic value. The lexicographer Julius Pollux (2nd cent. AD) lists it as related to ἀργέω ("to be unemployed," "do nothing," "be idle," etc.) and within the same semantic range as ὑπερβάλλεσθαι ("to put off," "to postpone") and ἐκλελύσθαι ("to set free," "to relax," "to make an end of").[146] In the same way, Apollonius (1st.–2nd. cent. AD), in his lexicon to Homer, uses the active participle form of the verb in his identification of Hermes as the one who destroys or abolishes (καταργοῦντα) the monster Argos.[147] And finally, in Porphyry's (3rd. cent. AD) *De antro nympharum* 35.9, σπουδάσαντα καταργῆσαι is used as a parallel description for the attempt to "blind" (τυφλώσαντα) the senses of this life in an attempt to free oneself. The phrase can thus be rendered, "earnestly endeavoring to abolish" in a way that also points forward to the on-going effects of such an act.[148] The use of καταργέω in these ways is confirmed by its use in non-literary sources.[149] And within the LXX, the verb occurs four

---

[143] Including the LXX, BAGD, *A Greek-English Lexicon of the New Testament*, p. 417, list the same 3 non-Christian literary sources found in Liddell, Scott, and Jones, *A Greek-English Lexicon*, 1958 (1940[9]), p. 908; W. Bauer, K. Aland, and B. Aland, *Griechisch-deutsches Wörterbuch*, 1988[6], pp. 848 f., add the Ascension of Isaiah 3:31 (which, however, is part of the Christian addition to the composite work sometimes called the Testament of Hezekiah found in Ascen. Is. 3:13–4:22; cf. M.A. Knibb, "Martyrdom and Ascension of Isaiah," *OTP*, p. 143).

[144] Trans. according to Arthur S. Way, *Euripides*, Vol. III, LCL, 1962 (1912), p. 408.

[145] Text according to F. Jacoby, *Die Fragmenta der Griechischen Historiker, Dritter Teil C*, 1958, p. 516.

[146] Cf. the *Onomasticon* 3.123.1 in Eric Bethe, *Pollucis Onomasticon*, Lexicographi Graeci Vol. 9, 1900, p. 193. For the later lexicon tradition of Hesychius (5th cent. AD), in which καταργέω is used to define ἀκυρόω ("to cancel," "to set aside,"), see his *Lexicon* alpha 2702.1 in Kurt Latte, *Hesychii Alexandrini Lexicon*, Vol. 1, 1953, p. 96; and for its use to define σκεδάζω ("to scatter," "disperse"), see *Lexicon* sigma 882.1, in Mauricius Schmidt, *Hesychii Alexandrini, Lexicon*, Vol. IV, 1862, p. 40.

[147] See *Lexicon Homericum* 42.11 in Immanuel Bekker, *Apolloni Sophistae*, 1833, p. 42. This same tradition is found in Hesychius (5th cent. AD), *Lexicon* alpha 7037.2; cf. Kurt Latte, *Hesychii Alexandrini Lexicon*, Vol. 1, 1953, p. 238.

[148] Cf. Seminar Classics 609, *Porphyry, The Cave of the Nymphs in the Odyssey*, Arethusa Monographs, 1969, p. 32.

[149] Cf. J.H. Moulton and G. Milligan, *The Vocabulary of the Greek Testament*, Part IV, 1920, p. 331, who translate it "hinder" (P.Oxy I.38.17) and "render idle or inactive" (P.Flor. II. 176.7; 218.13; P.Strass. I. 32.7) on the basis of this evidence.

times, three of which are active (2 Esdras 4:21, 23; 5:5; for the passive use, cf. 2 Esdras 6:8). In each case it refers to "rendering inactive" those men who were engaged in rebuilding the temple in Jerusalem, as evidenced by its parallel use with ἀργέω ("to be/make idle") in 2 Esdras 4:24 to describe the effect of this cessation: τότε ἤργησεν τὸ ἔργον οἴκου τοῦ θεοῦ τοῦ ἐν Ιερουσαλημ καὶ ἦν ἀργοῦν ἕως δευτέρου ἔτους τῆς βασιλείας Δαρείου τοῦ βασιλέως Περσῶν.[150] The few ancient sources that we do have outside the Christian sphere, including the LXX, thus all testify to the meanings "put to an end," "abolish," or "destroy" as adequate equivalents for καταργέω.

This same lack of uncertainty is true for Paul's writings. Paul uses the active forms of καταργέω figuratively in the sense of "to make (something) ineffective, powerless, idle," or "to nullify (something)" (Rom. 3:3, 31; 1 Cor. 1:28; Gal. 3:17; Eph. 2:15; cf. Luke 13:7). In the related sense it can mean "to abolish, wipe out, set aside something" (1 Cor. 6:13; 13:11) or "bring (something) to an end" (1 Cor. 15:24; 2 Thess. 2:8; 2 Tim. 1:10; cf. Heb. 2:14).[151] There is, of course, disagreement over the way in which the faithfulness of God and the Law are not "nullified" in Rom. 3:3, 31, and concerning the manner in which the Law does not "nullify" the promise in Gal. 3:17. Nor is it immediately clear what Christ "made ineffective" in Eph. 2:15 when καταργέω is used in reference to "the Law of commandments in ordinances" (τὸν νόμον τῶν ἐντολῶν ἐν δόγμασιν). But in these texts, as well as in the rest of the active uses of the verb, it is beyond dispute that Paul uses καταργέω to refer to the decisive act of abolishing or bringing something to an end. This is confirmed not only by the larger contexts in which these occurrences are found, but also by the specific verbs which are used in parallel constructions in several of the passages.[152]

---

[150] "Then the work of the house of God in Jerusalem *was idle* and it was *idle* until the second year of the reign of Darius, king of the Persians."

[151] So accurately BAGD, *A Greek-English Lexicon,* p. 417. BAA, *Griechisch-deutsches Wörterbuch,* pp. 848 f., give the same three meanings: "außer Wirksamkeit, Geltung setzen, entkräften" and from this "wirkungslos machen, zunichte machen"; "vernichten, vertilgen, beseitigen," and "aus d. Verbindung mit jmdm. oder mit etw. gelöst werden ...." LSJ, *A Greek-English Lexicon,* p. 908, supplies the meaning: "leave unemployed or idle." Significant in this regard is that in surveying the later Patristic evidence, the same active meanings are deduced, according to G.W.H. Lampe, *A Patristic Greek Lexicon,* 1982 (1961), p. 716: "bring to nought," "render impotent," "render unnecessary," "set at nought." Gerhard Delling, art. ἀργός κτλ., *TDNT* 1 (1964) 452–454, pp. 452 f., likewise suggests "to render inactive," "to condemn to inactivity," or in the religious sense, "to make completely inoperative," or "to put out of use" for the active uses. Cf. J.I. Packer, art. καταργέω ("Abolish, Nullify, Reject"), *NIDNTT* Vol. 1, rev. ed., 1980, p. 73, "Though *katargeō* is elusive in translation (AV renders it in 17 different ways, RV in 13), its basic meaning of rendering something inoperative is clear and constant."

[152] Cf. the contrast between καταργοῦμεν and ἱστάνομεν in Rom. 3:31; the parallel between οὐχ ... κληρονομήσουσιν and ὁ θεὸς καταργήσει in 1 Cor. 6:10, 13; the use of παύσονται as a parallel to καταργέω in 1 Cor. 13:8, 10, 11; the parallel between ἀκυροῖ and καταργῆσαι in Gal. 3:17; the synonymous use of λύσας and καταργήσας in Eph. 2:14 f. and

Furthermore, in the case of Rom. 3:3, 1 Cor. 1:28, 13:11, 15:24, Gal. 3:17, Eph. 2:15, and 2 Thess. 2:8, this act of nullification is explicitly linked to the consequent abolishment of the *consequences* of that which has been brought to an end. In Rom. 3:3 the fact that the faithfulness of God is not nullified results in the continuation of the truthfulness and justice of God (cf. Rom. 3:4–8). In 1 Cor. 1:28 God nullifies the things that are "so that (ὅπως + subjunctive) no one may boast before God" (1 Cor. 1:29). The abolishment of "childish things" in 1 Cor. 13:11 results in the putting away of speaking, thinking, and reasoning as a child. According to 1 Cor. 15:24 f., Christ abolishes every rule, authority, and power in order to eliminate the rebellion that still remains against the Father so that he can turn the kingdom over to God. The fact that in Gal. 3:17 the Law does not "nullify" the promise means that the effects of the promise remain valid, i.e. that the inheritance of God still comes "from the promise" (ἐξ ἐπαγγελίας, 3:18).[153] As the modal use of the participle καταργήσας indicates, the point of Eph. 2:15 is that Christ establishes peace *by means of* abolishing in his death the enmity which existed between Jew and Gentile. The result of this destruction is the creation of Jews and Gentiles into "one new man," which in turn establishes peace on the basis of their mutual reconciliation to God through the cross (Eph. 2:15b–16). Finally, in 2 Thess. 2:8 the Lord will bring to an end "the Lawless One," which in the context means bringing to an end his false power, signs, and wonders, together with the deception which these things caused among those who are perishing (2 Thess. 2:9 f.). It is important to see, therefore, that in developing his use of καταργέω Paul intends not simply to call attention to the fact that something has been definitively abolished, but also to raise the issue of the consequences of these acts of nullification.

In those texts where no explicit result is mentioned, it is thus consistent with Pauline usage, and confirmed by the surrounding context, that there too Paul is directing his attention to the ramification of the act of abolishing. The fact that Paul's Gospel does not "nullify" (καταργοῦμεν) the Law in Rom. 3:31 carries significant implications not only for the continuing development of his argument in Romans, but also for the implicit apologetic force of the letter as a whole. In stating against the critique of his opponents that his Gospel does not nullify the Law, Paul is implying that its past failure among the Jews, as well as its continuing validity among both Jews and Christians, can

---

of ἀνελεῖ and καταργήσει in 2 Thess. 2:8; and finally, the antithetical use of καταργήσαντος and φωτίσαντος in 2 Tim. 1:10. For the same point outside the NT, see T. Benj. 3.8, where Christ is said to "abolish" (καταργήσει) Beliar and those serving him, and where the alternative reading καταλύσει is also attested; cf. M. de Jonge, *The Testaments of the Twelve Patriarchs, A Critical Edition of the Greek Test,* Pseudepigrapha Veteris Testamenti Graece, Vol. 1, Part 2, 1978, p. 417.

[153] Cf. H. Hübner, art. καταργέω, *EWNT,* Bd. 2, 1981, pp. 659–661, who thus renders 3:17, "rechtlich außer Kraft setzen."

(and must!) be explained (cf. Rom. 2:12–16; 7:1–8:4; 9:30–10:4; 13:8–10).[154] Similarly, the implications of Paul's statement in 1 Cor. 6:13 that God will "abolish" (καταργήσει) food and the stomach are not explicitly stated in the surrounding context, but they are nevertheless clear. Christians are to act already in the present as if the lure of appetite has already been destroyed (cf. 6:9–20). This is also the point of 2 Tim. 1:9–10, though now applied to the willingness to suffer with Paul for the sake of the Gospel (2 Tim. 1:8). Hence, when Paul speaks of "abolishing," "nullifying," or "bringing something to an end," he consistently speaks, either explicitly or implicitly, of the corresponding *effects of* that which has or has not been made *in*effective. The active sense "rendering something inoperative" thus captures both the act and the result expressed by the verb καταργέω.[155] In *no* case is it appropriate to translate καταργέω with the sense of a gradual "fading away" of that which is said to be brought to an end. The action described by καταργέω is decisive and clear-cut.

But of most significance for our study is that these same three observations also hold true for the *passive* use of καταργέω in Paul's writings outside of 2 Cor. 3.[156] In each case a simple passive rendering of the active sense best fits the context: "to be made ineffective, powerless, idle," "to be nullified," or "to be abolished, brought to an end."[157] Moreover, as in the active uses, the passive forms are employed with special reference to the consequent *effects* of being abolished. Again, therefore, the passive denotation "to be rendered inoperative" captures both the meaning and significance conveyed by this verb. This can be clearly seen in 1 Cor. 15:26 (ἔσχατος ἐχθρὸς καταργεῖται ὁ θάνατος), which is merely the specific interpretation of the same point made with the *active* form of καταργέω in 15:24. The result of the final destruction of death is stated in 15:25: Christ must reign until he has put all his enemies under his feet. In the same way, Rom. 4:14 (κατήργηται ἡ ἐπαγγελία) simply presents the passive form of the corresponding *active* expression found in Gal. 3:17 (εἰς τὸ καταργῆσαι τὴν ἐπαγγελίαν). The effect of the promise (not) be-

---

[154] See now P. Stuhlmacher, *Der Brief an die Römer*, NTD Bd. 6, 1989[14], p. 64, who points to the various ways in which Rom. 3:31 is established throughout Romans in response to Paul's opponents.

[155] Cf. Kenneth Willis Clark, "The Meaning of ἘΝΕΡΓΕΩ and ΚΑΤΑΡΓΕΩ in the New Testament," now in his *The Gentile Bias and Other Essays*, selected by John L. Sharpe III, Supplements to Novum Testamentum Vol. 54, 1980, 183–191, pp. 190 f., who suggests that it ought to be translated "render powerless" as the antonym of ἐνεργέω.

[156] Of the 25 appearances of the verb in Paul, 15 are passive, including the four occurrences in 2 Cor. 3:7, 11, 13, 14; cf. Rom. 4:14; 6:6; 7:2, 6; 1 Cor. 2:6; 13:8 (2xs), 10; 15:26; Gal. 5:4, 11.

[157] This is supported by the passive use of the verb in 2 Esdras 6:8; by the passive use in *Anonymi in Aristotelis Rhetorica* 163.17 (f.51v. 29) as found in Hugo Rabe, *Anonymi et Stephani In Artem Rhetoricam Commentaria*, Commentaria in Aristotelem Graeca, Vol. 21/2, 1896, p. 163, and by its use in Athenaeus, *De Machinis* 4.6 in Rudolf Schneider, *Griechische Poliorketiker Bd. III*, Abhandlungen der königlichen Gesellschaft der Wissenschaften zu Göttingen, Philologisch-historische Klasse, N.F. Bd. 12, Nr.5, 1912, p. 8.

ing abolished in Rom. 4:14 is explicitly in view in 4:16, i.e. that the inheritance of Abraham might be certain for all those who are of the faith of Abraham. In Rom. 6:6, the crucifixion of the "old man" with Christ brings about the fact that "the body of sin" (τὸ σῶμα τῆς ἁμαρτίας) is "rendered inoperative" (καταργηθῇ), again with explicit reference to the effects of it having been abolished: τοῦ μηκέτι δουλεύειν ἡμᾶς τῇ ἁμαρτίᾳ. In the same way, in Gal. 5:11 Paul has his eye on what would be the eventual consequence of preaching circumcision when he concludes, ἄρα κατήργηται τὸ σκάνδαλον τοῦ σταυροῦ. If he were in fact doing so, he would no longer be persecuted.

This reference to the *effects* that are brought about as a result of something being rendered inoperative finds special emphasis in Rom. 7:2, 6 and Gal. 5:4, where the passive is used with the preposition ἀπό to indicate the consequence of being "rendered inoperative." In these cases the idiomatic translation "to be set free from" for καταργέω ἀπό may even be used to express this focus on the consequent effects of the action, or as Delling suggests, "to take from the sphere of operation."[158] In Rom. 7:2 the woman is "set free from the law of the husband" (κατήργηται ἀπὸ τοῦ νόμου τοῦ ἀνδρός), with reference to the effects thereof for her future marriage relations in 7:3; in Rom. 7:6a we are "set free from the Law" (κατηργήθημεν ἀπὸ τοῦ νόμου), with reference to the consequences for our resultant service in the Spirit in 7:6b (cf. ὥστε + inf.); and in Gal. 5:4 those seeking to be justified in the Law are "set free from," or "taken from the sphere of operation of Christ" (κατηργήθητε ἀπὸ Χριστοῦ), with its consequence for their relationship to grace (τῆς χάριτος ἐξεπέσατε).[159] For as Gundry Volf has pointed out, one must retain "the element of ineffectiveness or ceasing to operate which καταργεῖν is recognized to have in the active voice but which interpreters generally ignore in passive usage."[160]

Of special significance is Paul's use of the present passive participial form of καταργέω in 1 Cor. 2:6, in which he states that he does not speak a wisdom τοῦ αἰῶνος τούτου οὐδὲ τῶν ἀρχόντων τοῦ αἰῶνος τούτου τῶν καταργουμένων. Hans Conzelmann renders this participle "fading," or "transient" ("*Vergänglich*") as a parallel use to that found in 2 Cor. 3:11, 13, and in contrast to its

---

[158] *TDNT* 1 (1964), p. 454.

[159] Cf. now the helpful discussion of καταργεῖν in Gal. 5:4 and Rom. 7:2, 6 in Judith Gundry Volf, *Paul and Perseverance. Staying in and Falling Away*, WUNT 2.Reihe, 1990, pp. 210–212, who points to the word play with the active and passive voices of καταργεῖν in *Acts John* 84 (where the passive is also used with ἀπό) and insightfully renders the verb in Rom. 7:2, 6, "free from" or "become inactive in relation to the law," and in Gal. 5:4, to be "reduced to inactivity." She points out that in Rom. 7:1–6, the focus is "on the effect of this severance on a person's activity," while in Gal. 5:4 the point is the Galatians' "inactivity" in relation to Christ (p. 211). I am not convinced, however, that what Paul pictures in Rom 7:2, 6 is "the complete end of the law for Christians ..." (p. 210, following Käsemann), or that in Gal. 5:4, "Paul sees the law and faith as incompatible" not only in relation to justification, but also in regard to Christian behavior (p. 211; for my position, see above, chapter two).

[160] *Paul and Perseverance*, pp. 212.

meaning in 1 Cor. 15:24, 26.[161] Conzelmann's view is based on his conviction that the background to Paul's statement in 1 Cor. 2:6 is the mythical conception of maturity found among the mystery religions, and that the "rulers" in view are the demonic forces of this world. Hence, Paul's point is that these powers are now in the process of passing away.[162] But both of these assumptions have been seriously called into question in favor of the proleptic eschatological judgment of Christ over the political, earthly rulers and leaders of this age.[163] Paul's statement in 1 Cor. 2:6 picks up his prior use of καταργήσῃ in 1 Cor. 1:28, which Fee appropriately refers to as an "eschatological" verb.[164] Since God has chosen "the things of low birth of the world and the things that are despised, i.e. the things that do not exist, in order to render inoperative in regard to their effects the things that do exist" (1 Cor. 1:28), Paul does not speak a wisdom that derives from this age, "which is in the process of being rendered inoperative as to its effects" (1 Cor. 2:6). Here too the meaning of καταργέω is the same, but the present tense of the participle indicates that the process of abolishing this age is ongoing. In other words, Paul's use of καταργέω in 1 Cor. 1:28 and 2:6 reflects his understanding of the dialectic which now exists between this age and the age to come, in which the eschatological victory of Christ is both here and yet to come (cf. Gal. 1:4; Rom. 1:4; 1 Cor. 15:12–28).[165] As the present tense indicates, the rulers of this age still exist, but their influence and wisdom, i.e. their boast (cf. 1 Cor. 1:29), is continually being rendered ineffective by Christ. They are not fading away gradually, but have already been decisively defeated by Christ and "nullified" before God (1 Cor. 1:27–29; 2:6), even though their final destruction awaits the coming eschatological judgment in which Christ will "destroy" their very existence (1 Cor. 15:24).[166] The attempt to take 1 Cor. 2:6 to refer to a gradual

---

[161] *Der erste Brief an die Korinther*, KEK Bd. 5, 1981², p. 85 n. 46.

[162] Conzelmann, *Der erste Brief an die Korinther*, p. 85.

[163] See esp. now the arguments of Gordon D. Fee, *The First Epistle to the Corinthians*, NICNT, 1987, p. 104, and the parallel use of ἄρχοντες for earthly rulers in Rom. 13:3, and their role in the crucifixion in 1 Cor. 2:8.

[164] *The First Epistle to the Corinthians*, p. 103.

[165] Cf. most recently, Hays, *Echoes*, p. 134, "… Paul means not only that the wisdom of the rulers of this age is impermanent, but also that it is being doomed, being rendered void and done away, eschatologically, through God's act in Christ."

[166] This point has been argued in the context of Paul's theology as a whole by Martinus C. de Boer, *The Defeat of Death, Apocalyptic Eschatology in 1 Cor. 15 and Romans 5*, JSNT Supplement Series 22, 1988, pp. 121 f., in which he points out concerning καταργεῖν that throughout 1 Cor. "the basic meaning of the verb everywhere is 'to render powerless, ineffective, or invalid'" (p. 121). He emphasizes that "it is pertinent to observe that elsewhere in 1 Corinthians, as in 15:24–26, Paul always employs the verb in connection with realities that are robbed of their power and efficacy *eschatologically*, i.e., that belong to the age that is doomed and passing away …" (p. 121). He opts for the translation "destroy" or "annihilate" as best representing this eschatological act of Christ. For this same understanding of the eschatological implications of καταργέω in 1 Cor. 13:8–13, 15:24–26, Rom. 6:6, and Gal. 5:24, especially in terms of its relationship to its proleptic realization in Christ, see

fading away of the demons or rulers of this age fails to take into account Paul's conviction that Christ has already inaugurated the age to come, though its consummation still lies in the future (cf. e.g. 1 Cor. 6:9–14).[167]

The remaining three occurrences of καταργεῖν in the passive are all also found in 1 Corinthians, in 13:8 (2xs) and 10. Moreover, all three are future passive forms referring, as in 1 Cor. 15:24–26, to the eschatological abolishment (by God) of the realities of this world, this time of prophecies, knowledge, and "the partial" (τὸ ἐκ μέρους). The parallel use of παύσονται ("to cease, be at an end") in 13:8 provides a close commentary on its meaning in this passage. And again, the ensuing effects of this coming eschatological abolishment are outlined briefly, in metaphorical dress, in 13:11 f., where the corresponding active form of καταργέω is again employed. It therefore becomes evident that of the 25 uses of the verb in the Pauline corpus, 9 are found in 1 Corinthians, and that in each case, whether active or passive, the context is clearly eschatological, with reference either to the work of Christ or to the purpose of God in bringing this age to an end, either proleptically (1 Cor. 1:28; 2:6) or in the final consummation of the reign of Christ (1 Cor. 6:13; 13:8–11; 15:24–26).

As in 1 Corinthians, καταργεῖν is used throughout the rest of the Pauline literature either in reference to the inbreaking of the new age through the gospel (Rom. 3:31; 6:6; 7:6; Gal. 3:17; Eph. 2:15; 2 Tim. 1:10), or to the future consummation of Christ's kingdom at the resurrection and final judgment (Rom. 3:3; 2 Thess. 2:8). Viewed from this perspective, even Paul's statement in Rom. 7:2 can be seen to reflect Paul's eschatological perspective concerning the present dawning of the new age. The analogy from marriage law in Rom. 7:1–3 is intended to represent the reality of being set free from the Law as a result of "having died to that by which we were bound" in 7:6. But as Paul's argument in 7:4 makes clear, this "death" to the Law takes place "through the body of Christ" as the one who has already been "raised from the dead." That is to say, it is an eschatological occurrence. This is confirmed by Paul's contrast in Rom. 7:4 between being dead to the Law and joined to Christ in terms of the letter(flesh)/Spirit contrast in 7:5, 6b, which, as we have seen, is a thoroughly eschatological contrast.[168] On the other hand, Gal. 5:4, 11 reflect Paul's understanding of the interrelationship between the present and the future in the establishment of the eschatological rule of Christ. In the context, for others "to be set free from Christ" or for Paul "to abolish" in his preaching the stumbling block of the cross would have clear eschatological implications for both the present and the future (cf. Gal. 5:2, 5, 21; cf. 1:10).

Peter von der Osten-Sacken, "Die paulinische theologia crucis als Form apokalyptischer Theologie," *EvTh* 39 (1979) 477–496, pp. 480–483, 488 n. 34.

[167] With Hübner, *EWNT*, p. 660, who against Conzelmann interprets 1 Cor. 2:6 to read "die feindlichen Mächte *entmachtet*" (emphasis his).

[168] See above, chapter two, and P. Stuhlmacher, *Der Brief an die Römer*, pp. 94–97.

Moreover, to remove the stumbling block of the cross by preaching circumcision in an attempt to avoid suffering for the sake of the Gospel would be to deny the reality of the present work of Christ in inaugurating the new age and to forfeit "sharing in Christ's eschatological life" (cf. Gal. 1:4; 2:16–21; 3:1–5; 3:22–25; 4:4–11; 6:11–17).[169]

A study of καταργεῖν throughout the Pauline corpus, apart from 2 Cor. 3, thus presents a narrow semantic field for its meaning and a uniform context for its use.[170] The consistency of this usage is striking. Indeed, Paul's frequent and consistent use of καταργέω warrants its consideration as a Pauline *terminus technicus* to express the meaning of the coming and return of Christ in relationship to the structures of this world on the one hand, and its significance for the effects of those structures on the other. Καταργέω becomes for Paul a *theological* designation in which the turn of the ages is expressed in terms of what the gospel does and does not abolish and what does and does not continue to be effective or operate as a result. Paul's characteristic use of the term therefore poses in itself the question of the continuity and discontinuity between this age and the age to come.

But again, in *no* case does it refer to the gradual "fading away" of some aspect of reality. The inbreaking of the kingdom does not bring that which it abolishes to a gradual end, but is decisive in its destruction. The ages may be overlapping for Paul, but the distinction between the power of Christ and the power of this world is clear wherever and whenever the former is manifest. In returning to the argument of 2 Cor. 3:7–11, the question before us is whether this consistent Pauline use of καταργέω is also found in 2 Cor. 3:7 ff., or whether Paul has in fact, as past students of Paul have assumed, introduced a distinctive meaning for the verb in this one context. If so, it would be an anomaly. The lexica and scholars who adopt this reading can rely only on this one context for such a rendering.[171] Clearly, therefore, the burden of proof is on those who render καταργέω in 2 Cor. 3 in any way different than the range of meaning established by Paul in the rest of his writings or understand the context in any way other than eschatological.

---

[169] For a treatment of Galatians that takes the eschatological nature of the Spirit and Gospel seriously as the key to Paul's argument, see the important study of Charles H. Cosgrove, *The Cross and the Spirit, A Study in the Argument and Theology of Galatians*, 1988, esp. pp. 149–154, on 5:2–6, and 186–188, on Paul's suffering and the nature of the cross in Galatians as "epochal" and "cosmic"; the quote is from p. 187; and now the significant work on the second-Exodus restoration context of Gal. 4 by James Scott, *Adoption as Sons of God, An Exegetical Investigation into the Background of ΥΙΟΘΕΣΙΑ in the Pauline Corpus*, WUNT 2.Reihe 48, 1992, pp. 121–186.

[170] Cf. now Hays, *Echoes*, p. 134, who concludes that for Paul "it always means to nullify, to abrogate, to invalidate, or to render ineffectual."

[171] Cf. BAGD, *A Greek-English Lexicon*, p. 417, which translates it "what is transitory" in 3:11, 13 and "doomed to perish" in 3:7; BAA, *Griechisch-deutsches Wörterbuch*, pp. 848, which renders both 1 Cor. 2:6 and 2 Cor. 3:7, "vergänglich," and "das Vergängliche" in 3:11, 13; J.I. Packer, art. καταργέω, p. 73, who, despite his stress on the clear meaning of "render-

f) The Argument from Exod. 32–34 in 2 Cor. 3:7c: The Function of Moses' Veil

When 2 Cor. 3:7 is read against the backdrop of Exod. 32–34, such an idiosyncratic meaning for the verb need not be suggested. If the universally attested referent of καταργέω is assigned to 3:7c as well, the meaning of Paul's result clause becomes, "so that the sons of Israel were not able to gaze intently into the face of Moses because of the glory of his face, *which was being rendered inoperative* (with special regard for the effects of such an action)."[172] Like Paul's other use of the passive participle of καταργέω in 1 Cor. 2:6, here too that which is being rendered inoperative still exists (i.e. the glory on Moses' face), but that which it would otherwise affect has been abolished. Within the context of Exod. 32–34 already relied upon throughout verse 7, this points naturally to the fact that, if left unattended, the glory on Moses' face would have destroyed Israel due to their "stiff-necked" condition. In 3:7c Paul indicates precisely the point of Exod. 34:29–35, i.e. that although the glory of God was once again in the midst of Israel, it was now kept from destroying the people.

The most important point to be made about Paul's use of the participle καταργουμένην is therefore not its attributive function or its position in the sentence, but the fact that it is *passive*.[173] As such, the most natural question to

---

ing something inoperative," speaks of the glory, "such as it was" as "transient" in 3:7 ff.; Delling, *TDNT* 1 (1964), p. 454, remarks that 2 Cor. 3 "causes difficulty," and in spite of his own suggestion that the verb in 3:7, 13 refers to a "complete destruction" as in 1 Cor. 15:24, etc., especially in terms of its effects, nevertheless translates it "transitory" (orig. "vergänglich") in reference to the face of Moses; and H. Hübner, *EWNT*, p. 661, who suggests that it refers to "die Vergänglichkeit der mosaischen Heilsordnung." For numerous other examples, see the commentaries.

[172] See already Derk William Oostendorp, *Another Jesus, A Gospel of Jewish Christian Superiority in II Corinthians*, 1967, p. 37 n. 24, who emphasizes the passive view of καταργέω in 3:7–14 and suggests it be translated "put out of action," not "fading." In his words, "There is no reason to think that Paul thought that the glory on Moses' face faded" (p. 38 n. 24). But Oostendorp does not see the implications of this insight in terms of Exod. 32–34, but in terms of the coming to an end of "God's entire revelation in the Old Testament" (p. 38 n. 24). Earlier, Hanson, *Jesus Christ in the Old Testament*, p. 27, also rejected the meaning "fade" and suggested as well "render ineffective," since "it never carries any suggestion of fading away" elsewhere. Hanson's view, however, is based on his theory that, according to Paul, Moses saw the pre-existent Christ in the tabernacle and on Mt. Sinai, so that it was Christ himself who gave the Law (p. 27, cf. p. 34; Hanson points to this same interpretation in modern times by Hodge, and by Irenaeus and Tertullian among the fathers). But as we will see in chapter five, this is nowhere made explicit in 2 Cor. 3 (he reads 2 Cor. 3 in light of 1 Cor. 10:4) and is not supported by the context.

[173] See Dumbrell, "Paul's use of Exodus 34," p. 192 n. 13, who also stresses that the verb must be taken to be passive. But contra the view argued here, Dumbrell agrees with those who see the meaning to be that the glory of God *itself* was being abolished, and hence takes this as an indication that "the glory associated with the face of Moses pointed beyond itself to a possibility which under changed circumstances others might certainly share" (p. 186). But it is hard to see how *abolishing* the glory of God signifies that others will be able to

ask is the identity of the unexpressed subject of the action. Who or what is bringing about the action described by καταργέω in v. 7c? Again, the answer is clear, both within the context of Exod. 32–34 as referred to in 3:7, and within the larger context of 2 Cor. 3:7–14. It must be Moses' veil.[174] In v. 7c, Paul is *already* referring to the fact that the veil of Moses brought the glory of God to an end in terms of that which it would accomplish if not veiled, i.e. the judgment and destruction of Israel. Paul's statement in 3:7c merely reflects the point of Exod. 34:29 ff. concerning the fear of the Israelites and Moses' response.

Far from going beyond the text, and by no means against it, Paul's interpretation of Exod. 34:29 ff. therefore remains faithful to its original context, including his interpretation of the glory of Moses' face "being rendered inoperative" (τὴν καταργουμένην) by the repeated veiling of Moses (cf. Exod. 34:34 f.). There is no indication that Paul is leaving the time frame of the original narrative, or that the glory in view represents Christ. The glory in view is the glory of God as mediated on the face of Moses. Much less can it be argued that it is a "symbol" for the old covenant as a whole, so that it should be read "in light of verses 10–11, as Paul's retrospective judgment on that which the radiance on Moses' face symbolized."[175] Moreover, Paul's interpretation of Exod. 34:29 ff. in 3:7 is a whole cloth which gives no evidence of an attempt to insert negative evaluations into an otherwise positive evaluation of the OT account.[176] Understood against Paul's OT backdrop, the implied reference to the function of the veil in 7c further underscores the premise upon which Paul's argument is built, i.e. that the "ministry of *death* came in *glory*," a premise supported by Exod. 32–34. Rather than calling the nature of the glory of Moses' ministry into question, the need for the "continual bringing to

---

share in it. Moreover, the significance of the passive nature of the verb is missed once καταργέω is rendered as a verbal adjective and translated "fading," since this requires no implied subject for the passive action.

[174] Contra Belleville, *Reflections of Glory*, p. 22 n. 3, who rightly affirms that the attempt to see in vv. 7–18 contradictory motives for the veiling of Moses' face "involves reading into the text something that is plainly not there," but then solves this apparent difficulty by stressing that "all v. 7 explicitly states is that the Israelites were unable to gaze intently at the face of Moses for the brilliance" (p. 22 n. 3), and that there is no "explicit connection ... either in the Exodus narrative or in any extra-biblical traditions" between Moses' veiling himself and Israel's inability to gaze at the glory on Moses' face (contra Oostendorp, Barrett, and Wendland, p. 206 n. 1). But both Exod. 34 read in its wider context and the use of καταργέω in 3:7–13 point to precisely the opposite conclusion. Hence, the apparent tension between vv. 7 and 13 is resolved once one views the function of the veil in the two passages against their OT backdrop.

[175] So Hays, *Echoes*, pp. 134 f., 219 n. 43, quote from p. 135. Hays can argue this only because he takes the participle to refer to the present and because he reads 3:7 in view of 3:11 and under the influence of his interpretation of 3:10. But as we will see in chapter five, 3:11 must be read in view of 3:7–10, not vice versa, if the logic of Paul's argument is to be followed.

[176] Contra Windisch, Schulz, Georgi, and the tradition of interpretation they represent.

an end" of that glory is yet another attestation of its reality. Moreover, as our study of Exod. 32–34 has shown, Moses' act of veiling his face in 34:29 ff. is a further manifestation of the grace and mercy of God declared in Exod. 34:6 f. In response to their fear of Moses, the veil keeps Israel from "gazing" into the face of Moses and thus from being destroyed.[177] At the same time, the fact that the glory on Moses' face had to be veiled underscores the point of both Exod. 32–34 and 2 Cor. 3:7 that, due to Israel's hardened nature as manifested in her sin/fall with the golden calf, Moses' mediation of the glory of God is now a ministry of *death*.[178] As such, the veil of Moses is also a manifes-

---

[177] For an independent confirmation of this, see now Vollenweider, "2 Kor 3," p. 258, who observes that what is most striking about the narrative in Exod. 32–34 and the evaluation of it in Jewish tradition is that "*erst die Sünde Israels die Hülle des Mose notwendig zu machen scheint*," so that "Die oft als gekünstelt empfundene Übertragung der Hülle von Mose auf das Herz in 2 Kor 3,14 f. entspricht völlig der in den Sinaitraditionen angelegten Logik: *Sünde verunmöglicht die Schau göttlichen Lichts*" (emphasis his). The point to be made here is that this logic is also at work in 3:7–11. Hence, Vollenweider insightfully concludes concerning 3:7 that for Paul the veil of Moses, like the tablets of stone, is a result of the hardheartedness of Israel (p. 262). But over against the position being argued here, Vollenweider takes this to mean that Paul's own adaptation of this tradition is in *contrast* to the positive evaluation of the veil within Jewish tradition, so that for Paul the veil too takes on a negative character as part of Paul's critique of the Law as stone tablets (cf. p. 262). As we have seen, though Israel's sinful state necessitates the veil, neither the veil nor the fact that the Law is written on stone tablets are to be taken as a critique of the Law or of the Mosaic ministry *per se*. Hickling, "Sequence of Thought," p. 390, is therefore correct when he observes that Paul's use of μὴ δύνασθαι refers to Israel's fear and anticipates "part of the motive for Moses' donning the veil," but his subsequent point that "the text of Exodus, of course, does not connect the people's fear with the later action of Moses" cannot be sustained. In a similar way, N.T. Wright, "Reflected Glory: 2 Corinthians 3," in his *The Climax of the Covenant, Christ and the Law in Pauline Theology*, 1992, pp. 175–192, p. 178, is correct in his observation that "the reason why the Israelites could not look at Moses was not, here, because the glory was passing away, but because it was at present so bright." But because he too takes καταργέω to mean "passing away" as a reference to the impermanence of the glory itself, as part of the old covenant, he must then add that Paul's use of καταργέω in v. 7 is not a reference to the Exodus narrative, but "is simply introduced as a foretaste of Paul's third *a fortiori* (v. 11), much as his reference to the 'ministry of death' (v. 7) is a foretaste of the second *a fortiori* (v. 9)" (p. 178). But as we will argue, this misses the force of the logic within vv. 7–11, as well as the meaning of v. 11 itself. Despite Wright's insightful recognition that the problem being addressed in 2 Cor. 3 is fundamentally that of Israel's hardened condition under the old covenant (cf. pp. 180–183), he does not carry this insight through consistently in his exegesis of the text. Hence, Wright's view of 3:7 is necessitated not by the text itself, but by his equation of God's glory with the old covenant and the Law, and by his view of the temporary role of both the old covenant and the Law in salvation history, both of which have now been fulfilled and terminated by and in Christ (see *Climax*, pp. 39 f. 196, 198, 241–244; and below, ch. 5).

[178] Thus, because he adopts the traditional understanding of the function of the veil in Exod. 34:29 ff. as concealing the fact that the glory of the old covenant was being annulled, Callan, "Paul and the Golden Calf," pp. 8, must conclude that "Paul's view that the old covenant was one of condemnation and death does not seem to derive from Exod. 34:29–35, but does seem to relate to the larger context of which it is a part, namely, the story of the golden calf." Callan rightly attributes Paul's statements in 3:6, 7, 9 to the impact of the Law on

tation of YHWH's judgment against his rebellious people. As an explication of this judgment, Paul's interpretation of Exod. 32–34 in the result clause of 3:7bc provides the point of comparison upon which his argument turns in 3:8. But this interpretation is not merely a "theological afterthought" derived from Paul's own peculiarly Christian reading of the text.[179] As we have seen in chapter three, although the veil of Moses itself is not picked up in later biblical tradition, such a reading of Exod. 34:29 ff. stands at the end of a long line of canonical interpretations of Exod. 32–34 in which Moses' ministry was interpreted not only as an act of divine mercy and grace, but also as a ministry of judgment upon a rebellious people.[180]

g) The Glory of the Ministry of the Spirit (2 Cor. 3:8)

As established by the *qal wahomer* mode of argumentation, the point of *similarity* between the ministry of death and the ministry of the Spirit is their respective glory. This is the presuppositional foundation upon which Paul's argument rests. But for the argument to work, the *glory* of Moses' ministry cannot be the main point of verse 7, but rather its function as that which brought *death*. This is reflected in the syntax of verse 7 itself, in which the ὥστε-clause is logically the main point. The assertion of v. 8 is based not on the fact that Moses' ministry came in glory, but on the *result* of that ministry, i.e. that the sons of Israel could not gaze into the glory of Moses face, which due to their hardened condition had to be continuously veiled to prevent them from being destroyed. For the result clause of v. 7 provides the *evidence* needed to support the propriety of Paul's description of Moses' ministry as a ministry of death, which is the point of *dissimilarity* between the two covenants that gives the argument its force.

Once the structure of Paul's argument is clearly in view, the compelling nature of Paul's conclusion in v. 8 becomes manifest. Unlike Moses' ministry of death, Paul's ministry of the Spirit makes it possible to encounter the glory

---

Israel's sin in view of Exod. 22:19; 32:19 and 34:17, but fails to see that Exod. 34 in and of itself also supports the conclusion that the ministry of the old covenant was one of death (cf. p. 9). Instead, Callan argues that Paul may have been making the connection between Exod. 34 and the Law's condemnation of idolatry in accordance with the tradition now found in *Abot R. Nat.* 2, in which Moses is said to have broken the tablets in order to keep from having to condemn Israel as transgressors of their law. Hence, Paul could be thinking that, "if the law would condemn Israel to death for its worship of the golden calf, breaking the first set of tablets only delays this condemnation; and restoring the tables sets it in motion once again" (p. 9). But as Callan himself recognizes, such reconstructions are speculative.

[179] Contra Hays, *Echoes*, p. 135.

[180] Cf. e.g. Num. 14:26–35; Deut. 1:3, 34–46; 2:14–16; 9:6–8; 29:4; Ps. 78:21 f.; 95:10; 106:23, 26; Jer. 7:24–26; Ezek. 20:21–26. For this point, see too the work of William J. Dumbrell, *The End of the Beginning, Revelation 21–22 and the Old Testament*, 1985, p. 109, who in noting the dual significance of Moses' veil writes, "... the unveiled face of Moses in reception and communication of the divine word ... continues to express to Israel the poten-

of God without being destroyed.[181] If the old covenant ministry which consequently brought *death* came in glory, so that Israel could not endure it but had to have it repeatedly veiled, "then certainly the ministry of the Spirit will exist that much more in glory" (3:8), since it brings *life* and thus must not continually "veil" its mediation of God's glory.

The comparison in 3:7–8 is therefore established on the basis of the contrast between Moses' ministry of death and Paul's ministry of life. But where one would expect ἡ διακονία τῆς ζωῆς, in continuation of ζῳοποιεῖ in 3:6c, as the natural counterpart to ἡ διακονία τοῦ θανάτου as the continuation of ἀποκτέννει, Paul returns to the Spirit. Instead of focusing on the *result* of the ministry of the new covenant, as he did with that of the old, he returns to its *source*. In doing so, Paul does not make the basis of comparison explicit in verse 8, but waits until later in his argument to fill it out in detail (cf. 3:9, 14–18). For the moment he is content to leave the point of comparison undeveloped, though it is evident in the contrast between τοῦ θανάτου and τοῦ πνεύματος. Instead, as this contrast indicates, Paul calls attention at this juncture to the apologetic force of his argument by unexpectedly switching terminology. The reason for this switch is best explained by the polemical situation in Corinth.[182]

---

tial of the Sinai covenant while the veiled face of Moses proclaims the Israelite inability to receive the covenant blessings in which Moses still shares (cf. Exod. 33:12–17 where the blessing of Exod. 3:14–15, the giving of the name and the promise of the presence, are virtually transferred to Moses from that point onwards). The veil thus speaks of lost opportunities and yet also of the glory to be associated with divine revelation." Dumbrell thus insightfully concludes that "as a summary of what Sinai both could have been but yet had become for Israel, this closing episode of Exod. 34:29–35 is an eloquent commentary upon the history of Israel in the OT" (p. 109). As Dumbrell observes, "The ministry of death under the old order was exemplified by the fact that the Israelites could not gaze on the face of Moses (v. 7). Because of national sin the glory associated with Moses' experience could not be Israel's" (p. 110). But in contrast to the view argued above, Dumbrell takes καταργέω to mean that the old covenant was therefore "'about to be abolished' or was 'in the process of being abolished,' i.e. it refers to the gradual replacement of the old covenant with something new," which for Dumbrell is eventually brought about by the work of Christ (p. 110). Yet the further work on the semantic field of καταργέω presented above supports Dumbrell's position even more forcefully.

[181] See too Dumbrell, "Paul's use of Exodus 34," p. 186, who argues that the increased glory in v. 8 is not one of quantity or quality, but that the comparison points "to the inferiority of the old covenant (certainly as it was renewed in Exod. 34), *in its power to provide full access*, and *thus* to its deficiency in glory" (emphasis mine).

[182] Contra Provence, "Sufficient," pp. 71–73, who argued that the switch in terminology reflects that in 3:7–11 Paul is thinking of the negative aspect of his own ministry, i.e. that the ministry of the new covenant, with its greater glory, also causes those with hardened hearts to be unable to accept the gospel. But the *contrast* between the two ministries throughout 3:7–11, upon which the *qal wahomer* argument turns, speaks against this interpretation. Moreover, the Spirit referred to in 3:8 is clearly associated with life, not hardening, as is "righteousness" in 3:9 (see below). Provence's argument depends on his view of the contrast as between two distinct natures of the glory of God itself, i.e. a "lesser" and "greater" glory, rather than their respective functions within the two covenant ministries (p. 73). Provence's

In view of the recent attacks on his apostolic authority, Paul cannot merely describe his ministry as one that brings "life." For the strength of his assertion that his ministry exists in glory is based on the implied *contrast* between the results of death and life produced by the respective ministries in view.[183] Yet this is precisely the point of contention between Paul and his opponents, who question whether Paul's "ministry of suffering" indeed brings about life among others as he asserts (1 Cor. 2:3–5; 4:6–15; 2 Cor. 1:3–11; 2:14–17; 4:10 f.; 6:1–10[184]), especially when the "life produced by the Spirit" which Paul experiences and preaches is set over against the "death produced by the Law" as in 3:6 (cf. Gal. 2:19 f.; 3:10–14; Rom. 8:1).[185] Hence, Paul's assertion in verse 8 cannot simply be offered as a logical deduction drawn from the *qal wahomer* argument alone.[186] Just as he had to defend his assertion that Moses' ministry of glory was a ministry of *death*, so too Paul must demonstrate that his own ministry is one of "life." By stressing in v. 8 that his implied ministry of life is a διαϰονία τοῦ πνεύματος, Paul does so by recalling his prior *evidential* arguments for the legitimacy of his apostolic ministry from 3:1–6. Paul's evidence for his assertion that the ministry of the Spirit exists in glory, i.e. that unlike Moses his διαϰονία is one which brings life, is once again the very existence of the Corinthian church. As a result, the Corinthians cannot deny the truth of Paul's assertion in 3:8 without denying their own standing in Christ.[187] The Corinthians themselves are Paul's evidence that his ministry of

---

conclusion concerning 3:7–11 that "nowhere in this section does Paul emphasize the life-giving character of the new covenant" (p. 72) thus goes against the main point of Paul's argument!

[183] See too Seyoon Kim's "Excursus: The Antithetical Typology between the Sinai Theophany and the Damascus Christophany (2 Cor. 3:1–4:6)," in his *The Origin of Paul's Gospel*, WUNT 2 Reihe, Bd. 4, 1981, pp. 233–239, p. 234, who stresses that the comparison in 3:7–18 is between the two ministries of the old and new covenants and their effects upon Israel and the church respectively. He thus rightly points out that J. Munck's emphasis on Moses and Paul as personifications of Judaism and Christianity is an "exaggeration of a valid point," though anachronistic if we keep in mind that what is being contrasted here are the respective effects of their ministries and not two religious systems (pp. 236 f.). Hence, "Paul establishes an antithetical typology between Moses the minister of the old covenant and Paul himself the minister of the new" (p. 236, emphasis his; cf.p. 238).

[184] For the development of this criticism of Paul and his response, see my *Suffering and the Spirit*, pp. 51–87. For an understanding of the non-reciprocal nature of Paul's apostolic "sentence of death" in 2 Cor. 1:3–11, in which he suffers in order that the Corinthians may be comforted, see now my "The Comfort and Power of the Gospel: The Argument of 2 Corinthians 1–3," *Review and Expositor* 86 (1989) 325–344, pp. 327–330. Paul's subsequent apologetic is merely a development of this basic theme.

[185] See chapter two for the development of this contrast.

[186] Contra e.g. Stockhausen, *Moses' Veil*, pp. 111, 115 (see above).

[187] See above, chapter two and my *Suffering and the Spirit*, pp. 195–203, 220 f. For Paul's corresponding use in 2 Cor. 10:12–18 of the existence of the Corinthian church as the "canon" for establishing his apostolic authority in Corinth, see my "'Self-Commendation' and Apostolic Legitimacy in 2 Corinthians: A Pauline Dialectic?" *NTS* 36 (1990) 66–88, pp. 76–84.

the Spirit certainly exists in glory, inasmuch as their new life in the Spirit testifies to the distinction between Paul's ministry and the ministry of Moses.[188]

It is now apparent that in support of his assertions in 3:7–8 Paul appeals to two sources of uncontested validity. For his description of the ministry of death he rests his case on the Scriptural account of *Israel's experience* in response to Moses. For his corresponding description of the ministry of the Spirit, he points to the *Corinthians' own experience* in response to Paul's apostolic ministry in their midst. The force of Paul's argument for the past is the OT account; for the present it is the reality being experienced in his own apostolic ministry.[189] In both cases his focus is on his audience, who cannot deny either one of these presuppositions.[190] Paul's point is not to demonstrate the superiority of the new covenant over the old *per se*, though this is the implied basis of his argument, but to demonstrate his own qualifications to be a minister of the

---

[188] Not only the use of the present tense in 3:9, 18 and the specific reference to the experience of the Christian in 3:18, but also the structure of Paul's argument itself makes it impossible to follow J. Munck's suggestion, *Paul and the Salvation of Mankind*, 1977 (1959), pp. 58 f., that ἔσται in 3:8 is a real future, not a logical one. For Munck, 3:7–18 speaks throughout of Israel's future salvation and experience of the glory of God; but as we will see below, Israel's future conversion is not referred to in this text at all. In 3:14 ff. Paul has in view only Israel's *present* condition and experience in contrast to that of the Church. Contra too Lloyd Gaston, "2 Corinthians 3," pp. 160 f., who opts for the future because of his view that the contrast in 3:7–11 is between the ministries of Paul and his opponents, rather than Paul and Moses, because he sees the nature of the contrast to be one of degree or amount, and because he fails to see that Paul affirms the presence and revelation of the glory of God in and through his own ministry, as argued as the central thesis of my *Suffering and the Spirit*. Hence, for him, "what is being contrasted is the present glory of Christian ministry, which exists in the case of the opponents and perhaps even of Paul, with the future glory of God which puts all other glory to shame." Gaston thus misses the eschatological tension between the "now" and the "not yet" in Paul's thought when he concludes that "what (Paul) does not say, in 2 Corinthians or anywhere else, is that his apostolate is a ministry of glory" (p. 161).

[189] So too Richard, "Polemics," p. 354, though he describes Paul's argument from the present in terms of "concepts of the Christian dispensation," which misses the argumentative force of Paul's statements, rather than the *experience* of the Christian dispensation.

[190] Contra e.g. Vollenweider, "2 Kor 3," pp. 273 f., who misses the apologetic and logical function of the comparison. He thus plays down the need for the common ground basis of the *qal wahomer* argument in favor of the general Christian "Umgang mit der Vergangenheit" (p. 273), in which the present understanding of the significance of the work of Christ can be seen primarily by negative contrast with the past. Stockhausen, *Moses' Veil*, p. 111, also misses the apologetic force and focus of Paul's argument because she attributes *both* points to Paul's reliance on "the reliability of the Old Testament text, coupled with the reliability of the exegetical procedure applied to it" as that which "provided an assurance to Paul that glory must indeed be a characteristic of his superior ministry." Those who miss the apologetic nature of Paul's argument here often do so because, like Stockhausen, p. 107, they view the emphasis on the ministries of Moses and Paul merely as a surface expression of the real issue at stake, i.e. the contrast between the two covenants they represent; cf. too Hofius, "Gesetz und Evangelium," pp. 107–110.

new covenant.[191] Seen in this light, Paul's argument in 3:7 f. does not focus on a comparison of two covenants expressed in terms of their respective ministries, but of two ministries based on their respective covenants. The ministries and their results are themselves the issue, since what is at stake is Paul's legitimacy as an apostle. Stripped of its rhetorical nature and its conditional, *qal wahomer* mode of argumentation, the flow of thought in 3:7–8 may therefore be represented as follows, with the logical relationships between the various propositions indicated in italics and the unexpressed premises in parenthesis:

7a: *Since* the ministry of death came in glory,

7a: *as evidenced by the fact that* it was engraved with letters on stones (= its glory),

7b: *so that as a result* the sons of Israel were not able to gaze into the face of Moses (= its glory *and* its character of death)

7c: *because* of the glory of his face which was being cut off and rendered inoperative (by the veil; again as an expression both of its glory and of its character of death),

8: *Therefore* the ministry of the Spirit must certainly exist that much more in glory (since your status in Christ testifies to the life that it brings).

4. The Ministry of Judgment and the Ministry of Righteousness (2 Cor. 3:9–11)

The main point of Paul's argument in 3:7–8 is that the ministry of the Spirit certainly exists in glory as evidenced by the life it creates (v. 8). In verse 9, Paul introduces the second of his three *qal wahomer* rhetorical arguments in which he again compares the glory (δόξα) of the two ministries. Moreover, the continuation of the same verb (now implied) and the reference to the "condemnation" brought about by the first ministry (τῇ διακονίᾳ[192] τῆς κατακρίσεως) indicate that here too Paul is thinking of the events of Exod. 34:29–35 within their larger context. For the natural candidate for the elided verb of 9a is ἐγενήθη from v. 7a, while the motif of "condemnation" supplies the theological counterpart to the effect of "death" already described in v. 7b. This is confirmed by the fact that, as Paul's other use of κατάκρισις in 2 Cor. 7:3 illustrates, its referent is to the pronouncement of the sentence of judg-

---

[191] So too Provence, "Sufficient," pp. 68–70, who rightly points out that to read 3:7–11 as a contrast between the two covenants provides no direct support for Paul's assertion of his sufficiency and forces the section to be seen as a parenthesis in Paul's argument.

[192] Following NA, 26th ed., because of the strong witnesses in favor of the textual variant and, decisively here, because the variant ἡ διακονία (B, D², etc.) is clearly a later attempt to smooth out the text's style. See too Theobald, *Gnade*, p. 181 n. 64. Surprisingly, R.P. Martin, *2 Corinthians*, pp. 57 f.n.a, opts for the nominative (as do Barrett and Collange), seeing it as the more difficult reading. But the nominative form in v. 8 makes this judgment doubtful.

ment itself, in contrast to κατάκριμα, which focuses on the punishment following the sentence.[193] In 2 Cor. 7:3, Paul wants to make sure that the Corinthians do not misunderstand the nature of Paul's admonitions. He is "not speaking to condemn" the Corinthians (πρὸς κατάκρισιν οὐ λέγω), since they are bound to him as his spiritual children. Paul's point in 2 Cor. 3:9a in the genitive of reference τῆς κατακρίσεως, therefore, is that Moses' ministry as pictured in Exod. 34:29–35 embodied the declaration of YHWH's sentence of judgment upon Israel as manifested in the fact that Moses veiled himself. Hence, as we have seen in chapter three, Moses' act of condemnation in Exod. 34:29–35 (cf. Exod. 32:34 f.) is declared explicitly in the curses of the Sinai covenant (cf. Deut. 11:26–28; 27:14–26; 28:15–68; 30:15–20) and in the prophecy that Israel will suffer under them (Deut. 4:27 f.; 29:22–28; 31:16–21). Paul's awareness of this tradition is signaled not only here, but in Gal. 3:10, where he explicitly quotes Deut. 27:26.[194] But again, "glory" came in this ministry of condemnation. What Moses veiled was the glory of God.

The assertion of the lesser element within the *qal wahomer* argument in v. 9a provides the theological foundation for the results of Moses' ministry among the people of Israel as pictured in v. 7a–b. Moses' ministry was a ministry of death (v. 7a–b) *because* it was the extension of divine condemnation upon Israel (cf. the γάρ in v. 9a). In the same way, the point of comparison in v. 9b supplies the theological support for the *consequence* of the ministry of Paul which was implied in v. 8. Whereas Moses' ministry brought about death (v. 7a–b) because it embodied God's sentence of condemnation (v. 9a), Paul's ministry brings about life as a result of the work of the Spirit (v. 8) *because* it embodies God's "righteousness" (δικαιοσύνη) (v. 9b). Moreover, Paul's transition from the Spirit in v. 8, with its implied life-giving task, to its foundation in a ministry of righteousness in v. 9b, follows a typical Pauline pattern.

In Gal. 2:20 f. Paul's "life to God" is now the life of Christ in him, which he carries out by faith in the Son of God on the basis of his prior experience of justification by faith (cf. 2:16). But as Gal. 3:1 f. makes clear, this life by faith is a life in the Spirit, which is also said to result from justification in Christ, i.e. from "the hearing of faith" (ἐξ ἀκοῆς πίστεως, 3:2). Paul's point is that the Galatians first received the Spirit as a result of having been justified by faith in Christ, and continue to do so (cf. 3:5)! Here too, Paul moves theologically from the experience of the Spirit to its foundation in the righteousness of God received through justification in Christ. This same structure is evident in Rom. 1:16b–17, where Paul supports the assertion that "the gospel is the power of God unto salvation" by the fact that in it the "righteousness of God" (δικαιοσύνη θεοῦ) is being revealed (cf. the γάρ in v. 17a). In Rom. 1:17b, this salvation based on God's righteousness is then equated with "life" (cf. ζήσεται). Similarly, in Rom. 5:1 our peace with God is predicated upon our experience of having been rendered righteous

---

[193] This is the only other use of κατάκρισις in the NT; for κατάκριμα see Rom. 5:16, 18; 8:1. For the difference between these two nouns, see BAGD, *A Greek-English Lexicon*, p. 412.

[194] See note 83.

or justified (δικαιωθέντες). In the context, this justification results in the believers' experience of the love of God in their hearts "through the Holy Spirit" (5:5). When Paul picks up this theme again in Rom. 8:2–3, he explicitly grounds the Christian's experience of the Law under the power of "the Spirit of life" (τοῦ πνεύματος τῆς ζωῆς) on the basis of the condemning of sin as a result of the sending of Christ as a sacrifice for sin (cf. the γάρ in v. 3a). Against the backdrop of Rom 3:21–26, this is the revelation of the righteousness of God toward those who believe. In Rom. 8:5–9 Paul can thus identify belonging to Christ with possessing the Spirit, so that Christian experience becomes a contrast between living in the body (σῶμα), which is "dead because of sin" (νεκρὸν διὰ ἁμαρτίαν), and experiencing the Spirit (τὸ πνεῦμα), which is "life because of righteousness" (ζωὴ διὰ δικαιοσύνην; Rom. 8:10). As in 2 Cor. 3:6, 7, and 9, here too the Spirit of the one who raised Jesus from the dead makes alive, both in the present (cf. 8:10; and 8:6: τὸ φρόνημα τοῦ πνεύματος ζωή) and in the future (cf. 8:11: ζῳοποιήσει ... διὰ τοῦ ἐνοικοῦντος αὐτοῦ πνεύματος ἐν ὑμῖν). In short, the kingdom of God can thus be described as "righteousness ... in the (Holy) Spirit" (δικαιοσύνη ... ἐν πνεύματι, Rom. 14:17). For as in Galatians and 2 Cor., the experience of the life of the Spirit, present and future, is based upon the manifestation of the righteousness of God in Christ.[195]

The grounding of the Christian experience of the Spirit in the righteousness of God thus formed an essential aspect of Paul's apostolic preaching of the cross.[196] For to Paul, the dynamic presence of the righteousness of God in the life of the believer, secured and manifested in the death of Christ for the ungodly (cf. Rom. 3:21–26; 2 Cor. 5:16–21), was *expressed and evidenced* by his/her new life in and through the Spirit. Paul can thus move theologically from faith in Christ to the experience of the Spirit, as he does in Gal. 2:16–3:6 or Romans 5:1–5. But because of this integral link between the manifestation of the righteousness of God and the subsequent life in the Spirit which it produces, Paul can also move from the life-giving experience of the Spirit to the righteousness of God upon which it is based, as he does in Romans 1:17 f. and 8:2 f., and here in 2 Cor. 3:8 f. The presence of the one supports and leads *inextricably* to the presence of the other. Of most significance for our study is the way he makes this same move in 2 Cor. 5:14–21, where Paul's διακονία of

---

[195] For this same theological structure in Phil. 1:6–11, see chapter five, where its relevance to 2 Cor. 3:12 is discussed.

[196] For this same view and the corresponding point that although in 3:9 the "forensic" view of God's righteousness is accented, the association of God's righteousness with his power and the Spirit points to its inextricable link with the divine work of "actual" righteousness in the lives of God's people, see Walter Klaiber, *Rechtfertigung und Gemeinde, Eine Untersuchung zum paulinischen Kirchenverständnis*, FRLANT Bd. 127, 1982, pp. 161 f. and esp. 162 n. 452. For a helpful survey of the current debate over the meaning of the righteousness of God in Paul's thought and for the growing emphasis on the inextricable link between God's righteousness as a divine gift *and* as the effectual divine power of the new creation, bridging the positions of R. Bultmann and E. Käsemann, see now Hans Hübner, "Paulusforschung seit 1945. Ein kritischer Literaturbericht," in *ANRW* II.25.4., 1987, pp. 2649–2840, pp. 2694–2709, esp. pp. 2700–2704, 2707–2709, on the work of Bultmann, Käsemann, Ziesler, Watson, and Kertelge. For Stuhlmacher's contribution, see below, n. 199.

preaching the reconciliation found in the cross is again in view.[197] As in 2 Cor. 3:8–9, here too the righteousness of God manifested in Christ's death for all as stated in 5:14–15a supports the purpose clause of 5:15b, "that they who live (οἱ ζῶντες) should no longer live (ζῶσιν) for themselves, but for Him who died and rose again on their behalf." The equivalence between the Spirit and the life which it produces is evident. Moreover, as 2 Cor. 5:17 makes explicit, the theological foundation for this new way of life of the Spirit, grounded in the cross, is the "new creation" (καινὴ κτίσις) which comes about "in Christ," a theme to which Paul will return in 2 Cor. 3:18.

Paul's theological move in 2 Cor. 3:8–9, therefore, is yet another example of the essential unity in Paul's thinking and preaching between his doctrine of justification by faith (the "indicative" of the gospel) and his emphasis on its evidential attestation, with a corresponding emphasis on an eschatological judgment by means of works (the "imperative" of the gospel).[198] Although Paul's immediate referents in 3:8 and 9 are distinct theologically for the sake of his argument, any attempt to divorce them is impossible.[199] As with his own apostleship and the genuine nature of his gospel in 2 Cor. 3:8–9, Paul consistently argues throughout his epistles from the external evidence of the Spirit to the legitimacy of one's standing in faith.[200]

---

[197] Following O. Hofius, "'Gott hat unter uns aufgerichtet das Wort von der Versöhnung' (2 Kor 5:19)," *ZNW* 71 (1980) 3–20, p. 5, who demonstrates that Paul's reference is to his preaching of the cross alone as the "ministry of reconciliation" in 2 Cor. 5:19 and in the parallels in 2 Cor. 8 f. For this view of 2 Cor. 3:9, see too Lietzmann, *An die Korinther*, p. 111.

[198] Cf. Gal. 6:4 f.; Rom. 2:6–13, 25–29; 1 Cor. 3:13–15; 4:3–5; 2 Cor. 5:10. For a development of this relationship in terms of the evidence Paul offers for his own apostleship, see my *Suffering and the Spirit*, esp. pp. 188–194, and "Self-Commendation," pp. 80–88; and for its implications for understanding Paul's use of the language of justification itself, see Charles H. Cosgrove's important study, "Justification in Paul: A Linguistic and Theological Reflection," *JBL* 106 (1987) 653–670.

[199] See already P. Stuhlmacher, *Gerechtigkeit bei Paulus*, FRLANT Bd. 87, 1966², pp. 76, 158, 224, for the essential connection of righteousness and the Spirit in Paul and the parallel between the conception in 2 Cor. 3:9 and that found in 1QH 6:19 and 1QH 4:9. Hence, in 2 Cor. 3:9 Paul conceives of the church as "die eschatologische Kampftruppe des Christus" (p. 205) in which "Paulus stellt die Menschen auf Grund des Ereignisses der Gottestreue in Jesus Christus vor Gott und damit in den Dienst dieser Treue (2 Kor. 3:9)" (p. 248). See now his summary "Exkurs III: Gottes Gerechtigkeit bei Paulus," *Der Brief an die Römer*, pp. 30–33, where he points out, on the basis of the OT background and parallels in post-biblical Judaism, that the history of Israel is "von Heil und Rettung schaffenden 'Erweisen der Gerechtigkeit Gottes' erfüllt" (p. 31); and that God's righteousness can at the same time refer to God's own work of salvation (Rom. 3:25 f.) and "ihre Auswirkung in Gestalt der Gerechtigkeit ..., die denen zuteil wird, die sich zu Christus glaubend bekennen (2 Kor. 5:21)" (pp. 31 f.; cf. esp. Is. 54:17 and its targum). For the opposite view in response to Stuhlmacher, see Barrett, *Commentary*, p. 117.

[200] For this same argument from the evidence of God's work in one's life to the genuine nature of faith, see Gal. 5:16–26; 1 Thess. 1:3–6; Phil. 1:6; 2:12 f.; Rom. 1:5; 8:3 f.; 15:18; 2 Cor. 13:5; and maybe 1 Cor. 3:13–15.

Both the point and force of the *qal wahomer* comparison in v. 9 are now clear. If Moses' ministry of mediating a veiled glory as an expression of God's decreed judgment against Israel nevertheless still came in glory, then Paul's ministry must "abound" (περισσεύει) that much more in glory, since it is an expression of God's *saving* righteousness in Christ (cf. 2 Cor. 5:18–21). For again, the presence of the Spirit among the Corinthians is ample testimony to the fact that *Paul's* gospel of the cross must be the valid gospel of God's righteousness. Since this is true, Paul can turn this argument around and *support* his assertion concerning the glory of his ministry in v. 8 with the assertion of v. 9b (cf. the γάρ in v. 9a).[201] Inasmuch as the purpose of Paul's ministry is to reveal God's righteousness in a way that need not bring about the destruction of the wicked (cf. Rom. 1:18 ff.), this "ministry of righteousness" must excel in glory over that of the ministry of condemnation as the final desire of God's work in the world.[202] For God's ultimate purpose in revealing his glory is not judgment, but salvation, with the former being a means to the latter in God's economy (cf. Rom. 9:22–29; 11:11–15, 25–32).[203] Moreover, inasmuch as Paul's opponents "disguise themselves as servants of righteousness" (μετασχηματίζονται ὡς διάκονοι δικαιοσύνης, 11:15), Paul's introduction of this theme at this point in his discussion clearly continues the apologetic force of his argument.[204]

a) The Surpassing Glory of the New Covenant (2 Cor. 3:10)

Verse 10 begins with γάρ, though its force is usually ignored because of the significance of the content of the verse and the intensification indicated by καί, which together have led commentators to consider it the climax or crux of

---

[201] Contra R.P. Martin, *2 Corinthians*, p. 59, who follows Plummer in seeing the three uses of γάρ in 3:9, 10, 11 all to be explicative in force because of his understanding of this passage as a midrash (but cf. p. 63 in reference to v. 10, where he sees it as establishing "the foundation on which the previous deductions have been made," only to offer the translation "thus it is quite true that" [following Collange and Godet], or "indeed," cf. pp. 57, 63, while on p. 64 he renders it "for" in 3:11, yet takes the verse as a "summary conclusion"), and Prümm, *Diakonia Pneumatos*, pp. 127–129, who correctly points out that 3:7–11 anticipate Paul's argument in Rom. 7:7–25 and 8, but concludes concerning 3:9 that "Demgemäß stellt er die beiden Bünde ... vorwiegend unter einem Gesichtspunkt gegenüber, d.h. hinsichtlich der Befähigung oder Nichtbefähigung zum sittlichen *Tun*, die die beiden Bünde vermitteln" (cf. p. 130). This same view was argued already by Emil Sokolowski, *Die Begriffe Geist und Leben bei Paulus in ihren Beziehungen zu einander, Eine exegetisch-religionsgeschichtliche Untersuchung*, 1903, cf. esp. pp. 43 f. This is certainly the point of 3:8, but not of 3:9 as its support. For although the two are inextricably linked, it is important for Paul's argument that they be differentiated.

[202] Contra the many who, like Theobald, *Gnade*, p. 181, take the verb περισσεύειν in 3:9 to indicate a qualitative difference in the degree or manifestation of the glory itself.

[203] For the development of this relationship between God's purpose in condemnation and in salvation as set forth in Rom. 9:22 f., see John Piper, *The Justification of God, An Exegetical and Theological Study of Romans 9:1–23*, 1983, pp. 186–199.

[204] I owe this insight to Furnish, *II Corinthians*, p. 204.

Paul's argument in 3:7–11.[205] In reality it is neither. Just as in the parallel uses of καὶ γάρ elsewhere in Paul, in which the γάρ conveys a causal sense as the *conjunction*, while the καί is used *adverbially* as an intensification,[206] here too Paul's purpose in verse 10 is to offer a *ground* for the point he has just made in v. 9b, i.e. that the ministry characterized by its declaration of the righteousness of God certainly "is extremely rich" (περισσεύει) in glory.[207] For in v. 9b Paul breaks the pattern established in 3:7–9a by supplying a new verb in his comparison, switching from ἔσται to περισσεύει. In doing so, he adds to the comparison between the two ministries the nuance of "greater degree" or "intensity." The glory of the new covenant ministry *certainly exists* in glory (v. 8) precisely because its glory *abounds* in comparison to that of the old covenant (v. 9b). It is this extension of his argument in v. 9b that Paul now undergirds in v. 10. As such, rather than being the high point of Paul's argument, v. 10 is subordinate logically to the point made in v. 9b.

In v. 10 Paul supports why the ministry of righteousness abounds in glory in comparison to the ministry of condemnation by explaining in what sense he means "abound". In turning our attention to this statement we must keep in mind that for Paul the glory of God revealed in the ministry of Moses was and remains the glory of God.[208] The Law was and is "holy, righteous, and good" (Rom. 7:12). That the Law's function, when revealed apart from the Spirit, was to kill does not diminish this fact, nor does it diminish the glory of God

---

[205] See e.g. already Schulz, "Die Decke des Moses," pp. 3, 6; Lietzmann, *An die Korinther*, p. 112, who takes the γάρ of v. 10 to be an intensification; Theobald, *Gnade*, p. 182, who sees it as the high point of Paul's argument; and most recently Renwick, *Temple*, pp. 110 f., who rightly observes that v. 10 is "prominent" within the structure of Paul's argument and that it "stands apart from the surrounding verses," but wrongly concludes from this that the γάρ is "indicating the addition of another remark (a further conclusion)" (p. 110 n. 33).

[206] Contra Norbert Baumert, *Täglich Sterben und Auferstehen. Der Literalsinn von 2 Kor 4:12–5:10*, SANT Bd. 34, 1973, pp. 370, 380, who points to 1 Cor. 11:9; 12:14; 14:8; 2 Cor. 5:2; Phil. 2:27; and 1 Thess. 3:4; 4:10 to support his view that in 3:10 καὶ γάρ *together* function as an intensification, since he can see no support given in vv. 9–10. But in each of these cases the γάρ functions as the conjunction (with a causal force), while the καί carries the intensification. For the other uses of καὶ γάρ in Paul, in which in every case this is also true, cf. Rom. 11:1; 13:6; 15:3, 27; 16:2; 1 Cor. 5:7; 8:5; 11:19; 12:13; 2 Cor. 2:9 f.; 5:4; 7:5; 10:14; 13:4; Col. 2:5; 3:3; 2 Thess. 3:10.

[207] Following BAGD, *A Greek-English Lexicon*, p. 651; see now Furnish, *II Corinthians*, p. 204, on the meaning of καὶ γάρ: "In the present case, the expression introduces a comment intended to clarify and thus further support the argument to which it is added." R.P. Martin, *2 Corinthians*, p. 63, translates περισσεύει as "excels" and, following Collange, points out that this verb is often used "to set apart the new age of salvation in contrast to the old order," thus furthering the emphasis on "the element of 'already begun' which is to be seen in ἔσται ... though not without remainder."

[208] Contra e.g. Theobald, *Gnade*, p. 182, who argues that the contrast in 3:10 leads to the conclusion that *by comparison* Paul is now denying the reality of the "glory" of the old covenant ministry in view of the "new content" given it in the new covenant: "Der Glanz auf dem Antlitz des Mose kann nur noch *uneigentlich* mit δόξα bezeichnet werden" (emphasis his).

itself from which the Law derives its divine nature and authority. On the contrary, as we have seen in 3:7, it establishes it. Moreover, God *continues* to reveal his glory in judgment upon those who suppress the truth of the Gospel because of their hardened hearts or blinded eyes (2 Cor. 2:15–16a; 4:1–6; cf. Rom. 1:18 ff.). God's glory remains God's glory, whether revealed in connection with the Law or with the Gospel. Hence, the glory of the ministry of the new covenant cannot be so much "more" glorious than the ministry of condemnation because the latter glory is of an inferior quality or quantity.[209] It is not as if the glory of God in the new covenant is better or stronger, or more brilliant than the revelation of the glory of God on Mt. Sinai or that associated with the Law through the ministry of Moses.[210]

Rather, the key to Paul's thinking is the summarizing *neuter* designation τὸ δεδοξασμένον, together with the perfect form of the same verb, δεδόξασται. This use of the substantival participle denotes that Paul is now referring not to the Law (the masculine ὁ νόμος), or to the glory of the old covenant itself (the feminine δόξα), or even to the ministry of the glory as such (the feminine ἡ διακονία). As the abstract or collective use of the neuter indicates, at this point Paul's reference is to the ministry of the old covenant *as a whole*, especially its theological purpose (v. 9a) and results (v. 7).[211] Within the context, this use of the neuter picks up Paul's earlier designation of the purpose of the old covenant encompassed in his description of the function of the Law under the old covenant as τὸ γράμμα in 3:6 and/or the fact that it was the face of Moses (τὸ πρόσωπον) which was in fact glorified (cf. 3:7). Read from this perspective, Paul's point in v. 10 is that when one compares the results and purposes of the two covenants, *in this respect* (ἐν τούτῳ τῷ μέρει[212]) the former has not been

---

[209] Contra recently, e.g. Hofius, "Gesetz und Evangelium," pp. 112 f., who understands v. 10 to represent a comparison of the Law and Gospel in terms of their "Qualität." Yet Hofius' insight (following Schlatter) that the distinction between the two ministries concerns their respective functions, since Moses was not granted a ministry of the Spirit and righteousness for salvation, is certainly correct. My objection is that he carries this distinction concerning the ministries of Moses and Paul over to that of the Law and Gospel themselves (cf. pp. 102, 113).

[210] See e.g. Furnish, *II Corinthians*, p. 203, who even translates δόξα as "splendor" throughout this passage "because the thought is especially of the relative brilliance with which the ministries of the old and new covenants are endowed."

[211] So too most clearly M. Rissi, *Studien zum zweiten Korintherbrief: Der alte Bund – Der Prediger – Der Tod*, AThANT Bd. 56, 1969, pp. 28–29, and most recently O. Hofius, "Gesetz und Evangelium," p. 89. The view taken here is close to that of Theobald, *Gnade*, p. 184, who relates it to the face of Moses (τὸ πρόσωπον) in v. 7 (though with very different exegetical consequences), since it is the glorification of Moses' face that brings about the results in view.

[212] For the use of μέρος to refer to the part or component part in contrast to the whole, cf. BAGD, *A Greek-English Lexicon*, pp. 505 f. When used with the preposition ἐν it means "in the matter of," "with regard to" (p. 506). Here it is to be taken with the majority as modifying δεδόξασται rather than τὸ δεδοξασμένον (i.e. "glorified in part," so Bachmann, Héring, Allo); moreover, the referent of τὸ δεδοξασμένον is clearly not the glory of the new

glorified *at all* (οὐ δεδόξασται)![213] Paul's careful choice of the perfect tense in v. 10 indicates that the old covenant, with its purpose and results, does not carry forward into the present.[214] In regard to God's *purposes and effects* in redemptive history (3:7–9), the dawn of the new covenant indicates that the eschatological era of salvation has now begun. God's primary purpose of condemnation under the old covenant has now been replaced by the purpose of manifesting his righteousness for salvation as evidenced by the pouring out of the Spirit. *In this respect* it is not merely *as if* the old covenant and its effects have no glory; Paul's point is that in view of the new covenant they *in reality* do not![215] The *old covenant* is no longer the locus of the revelation of God's glory in the world; the new covenant of the new age has arrived. And as the prophets promised, the cross of Christ reveals, and the pouring out of the Spirit through Paul's apostolic ministry confirms, God's purpose in the new covenant is no longer to reveal his glory in the judgment of death, as in the old covenant, but in the life of the Spirit. Paul's point is not, therefore, that "that which has been glorified" is now finally seen to be less glorious in view of the greater glory that has arrived, as so often represented in the application of the

---

covenant (contra Hill, Baumet, and now Gaston). For these points and the relevant literature, see Theobald, *Gnade*, p. 182 n. 68. For the other opposing reading of this phrase to refer "in a general way to the whole preceding remark" because of the conviction that Paul is contrasting the two covenants materially, see now Furnish, *II Corinthians*, pp. 203, 205, and the scholars on both sides of the issue listed there. R.P. Martin's suggestion, *2 Corinthians*, p. 64, following Bachmann and Héring, that μέρος carries a restrictive nuance as in 2 Cor. 1:14 and 2:5 (thus meaning that it has been glorified "partially," as a reference to the transient nature of its glory), fails to take into account that in 1:14 and 2:5 the idiomatic expression is ἀπὸ μέρους rather than ἐν τούτῳ τῷ μέρει as found here.

[213] Contra Dumbrell, "Paul's use of Exodus 34," pp. 186 f., who takes v. 10 to refer to the glory of the old covenant (missing the force of the neuter). Hence, because he *rightly* sees that the glory of the old covenant does not come to an end or lose its merit with the dawning of the new covenant, Dumbrell must argue that the perfect tenses in v. 10 indicate "that Paul sees the old covenant not as having been abolished but as having been subsumed or built upon, and that the essence of the Sinai covenant had been retained, as Jeremiah had argued that it would be (cf. Jer. 31:31–34)" (p. 187). But in reading 3:7–18 one must distinguish between the old covenant and its ministry on the one hand (which *has been* abolished in Christ), and the glory of God revealed in that covenant and ministry (which has not been abolished, but, indeed, is *retained* in the new covenant).

[214] Cf. e.g. Blass, Debrunner, Funk, *Greek Grammar*, § 340, for the meaning of the perfect tense as that which "combines in itself ... the present and the aorist in that it denotes *continuance* of *completed action* ..." and § 342, for its use "to denote continuing effect on subject or object." As pointed out there, "the effect need not always be expressed even though it is present ...."

[215] Though this force of the perfect has not been picked up in more recent studies of the text, for this same point see Oostendorp's insightful discussion, *Another Jesus*, p. 37, and H.A.W. Meyer, *Epistles to the Corinthians*, p. 470, though he seems to contradict his point by introducing the analogy of the sun and moon. On the other hand, those who miss the force of the comparison must end up concluding, with Windisch, *Der zweite Korintherbrief*, pp. 116 f., and Schulz, "Die Decke des Moses," p. 6, that in v. 10 Paul contradicts what he has just asserted in 3:7–9!

sun and moon analogy to this text.[216] Instead, as in 2 Cor. 3:3 and 6, the point of v. 10 is an *eschatological* one.[217] The comparison in v. 10 is one of divine purpose and result, not of quality or quantity.[218] Paul grounds his assertion concerning the glory of the ministry of the new covenant (v. 8) by referring to its purpose and results as the eschatological manifestation of the righteousness of God (v. 9b), which as such *surpasses* the purpose and results of the old (v. 10). The meaning of v. 10 can thus be paraphrased as follows:

10b: *Because* of the "surpassing glory" of the new covenant ministry (εἵνεκεν τῆς ὑπερβαλλούσης δόξης) (i.e. because God's purpose and its results in the new covenant are a fulfilment of his ultimate purpose in redemptive history and in that sense greater than what he has accomplished thus far in the old covenant),[219]

10a: *therefore* that which *formerly* was the vehicle of the revelation of God's glory (τὸ δεδοξασμένον, i.e., the old covenant) is indeed (καί) in this respect (ἐν τούτῳ τῷ μέρει) no longer the means through which God is revealing his glory (οὐ δεδόξασται).

Based on this analysis of the text, the main point of Renwick's study of 3:7–11 must be called into question (cf. *Temple*, pp. 109–121). Renwick argues that in 3:10 Paul is asserting that the glory of the new covenant is so great that it renders that of the old covenant to be of "no consequence" *(Temple*, p. 112). In his words, the old covenant "had been 'de-δόξαfied' by the exceeding δόξα of the New Covenant, invisible though this new δόξα appears to be" (p. 112). In addition, Renwick does not see v. 10 to be the *ground* for 3:7–9, but yet a further inference and conclusion. Nor does he think that Paul's emphasis throughout 3:7–18 is on the *present* reality and experience of God's glory, but takes the time reference of 3:8–9 to be future (cf. p. 118). As a result,

---

[216] For this analogy and examples of its application, see already J. Calvin, *The Second Epistle of Paul the Apostle to the Corinthians and the Epistles to Timothy, Titus and Philemon,* Calvin's Commentaries Vol. 10, trans. T.A. Smail, 1964, p. 46; for other examples and a recent application, see P.E. Hughes, *Paul's Second Epistle to the Corinthians,* NICNT, 1962, p. 105 n. 33, and F. Lang, *Korinther,* p. 273.

[217] See too H.-D. Wendland, *Die Briefe an die Korinther,* NTD Bd. 7, 1972[13], p. 180, who emphasizes that Paul's point in v. 10 is that the coming of the new order has abolished the old order.

[218] Contra Theobald, *Gnade,* p. 186, who argues that this eschatological reality of the glory of God leads to the conclusion that that which "abounds" in the new covenant has "hardly anything to do" with the fading glory on Moses' face, which he characterizes finally as an "an der Oberfläche liegende Wirklichkeit." In support of this conclusion, he points to Eph. 1:18 and 2 Cor. 4:6 (see below for my own interpretation of these texts). See too E.P. Sanders, *Paul, the Law, and the Jewish People,* 1983, p. 138, who rightly sees that in 3:10 "it is only the new dispensation that devalues the old," and that the force of the contrast is to make the point that the dispensation of death "now has no glory at all (3:10 f.)." But Sanders goes on to evaluate this "black-and-white contrast" as "between *degrees* of whiteness: what was glorious and what is *more* glorious" (emphasis mine), the latter of which is not part of Paul's assertion.

[219] For this meaning of ὑπερβάλλω as "to go beyond," "surpass," "outdo," cf. BAGD, *A Greek-English Lexicon,* p. 840, and 2 Cor. 11:23; Eph. 1:19; 3:19. For its relationship to the adverbial and noun forms, all of which occur only in the Pauline corpus, see G. Delling, art. ὑπερβάλλω κτλ., *TDNT* 8 (1972) 520–522.

Renwick evaluates the burden of Paul's argument to be to redefine the *nature* of the *present* experience of God's glory/presence in the new covenant (no longer to be expected to be visible as "light"), and to refocus the *occasion* of the experience of the visible, eschatological glory (to be experienced in the future, not in the present). Hence, in 3:7–11, especially in 3:10, "... Paul has both laid the groundwork for redefining the present expression of δόξα (by annulling the value of the present appearance of the traditional manifestation of δόξα) and has placed in the future, in the eschaton, the ultimate appearance of δόξα (in its traditional manifestation)" (p. 121). But Paul's point in 2 Cor. 3:7–11 is not that the nature of God's glory has now changed from a visible to invisible presence, but that the effects of the *same* glory of God are now distinctively different, precisely because the new age *has dawned*. The fact that Paul's face (and that of other Christians) did not shine posed no problem for either Paul or his opponents, since throughout the old covenant Moses' experience was seen to be unique. God's glory/presence can thus be affirmed to be present among his people even without such a display. In 2 Cor. 3 Paul therefore nowhere refers to a contrast between visible and invisible manifestations of the glory of God. Rather, the issue was whether the glory/presence of God was present *at all* in and through Paul's ministry. Moreover, because Renwick takes 3:10 to be drawing yet another controversial conclusion, this time "without rationale" and with "no good reason" (since in his reading Exod. 32–34 would not support his interpretation of the meaning of 3:10) (p. 112), Renwick must look elsewhere for "some known tradition or text" implied or alluded to in 3:10 that "was recognized both to lie behind the argument and to be regarded as authoritative by the opponents" (p. 112). His answer to this need is Haggai 2 (cf. pp. 113–120). But in the absence of any clear linguistic tie between these texts, the general thematic parallels which Renwick draws between 3:10 and Haggai 2 (Paul's interest in the cult, temple, and presence of God, the use of δόξα three times in Hag. 2 in connection with the temple, and the fact that in Hag. 2:9 LXX Haggai compares the glory of the two temples) are not enough to be convincing (cf. p. 114). Nor is his argument from the link between 3:7–11 and the comparisons between the present and future forms of "a certain kind of temple" in 2 Cor. 4:16–5:10, though the latter is now confirmed by Pate's study,[220] determinative for 3:10, given their distinct subject matter (cf. pp. 116 f., 119 f.).[221] If Renwick is correct, Paul would be equating the present experience of the glory of God in the new covenant with the glory of the temple after the exile, while the future glory of the temple corresponds to the future experience of God's glory in the eschaton. But given Paul's conviction that the age to come has *already* arrived, the glory of the new covenant is to be equated with the glory of the future, eschatological temple anticipated in Haggai 2! Indeed, for Renwick it is only the future manifestation of the glory of God which is greater than that of the old (cf. p. 118)! Finally, it is doubtful that Haggai 2 supports Renwick's view that the contrast between the present and future experience of the glory of God in the new covenant is between that which is invisible and visible. But even if Renwick *is* correct in his as-

---

[220] See C. Marvin Pate, *Adam Christology as the Exegetical and Theological Substructure of 2 Corinthians 4:7–5:21*, 1991, pp. 48–50, 52–55, 121–124. Pate too emphasizes that, for Paul, the restoration of Adam's lost glory, which Judaism anticipated in the eschaton, has *now* become a reality through the suffering and resurrection of Christ (cf. pp. 22, 77, 89 f., 96, 107, 111, 137 f., 141).

[221] 2 Cor. 3:10 is comparing the old and new covenants, 4:16–5:10 is comparing the present and future state of believers within the new covenant.

sessment of an allusion to Hag. 2 in 2 Cor. 3:10, it is only of the most general kind, and thus his conclusion to take Hag. 2 as "the authoritative and logical rationale for (Paul's) exposition of Exodus 34" in 3:7–11 is unwise exegetically (p. 118). As this study attempts to demonstrate, there is no need to look outside of Exod. 32–34 for the key to Paul's interpretation of it. Rather, Exod. 32–34 ought to be seen as the key to Paul's interpretation of Exod. 32–34.

This eschatological interpretation of v. 10 as a reference to the coming of the new covenant manifestation of the glory of God is confirmed by Paul's use of the related noun ὑπερβολή in 2 Cor. 4:6 f. to describe the *present* "light of the knowledge of the *glory* of God on the face of Christ" (φωτισμὸν τῆς γνώσεως τῆς δόξης τοῦ θεοῦ ἐν προσώπῳ Ἰησοῦ Χριστοῦ) and in 2 Cor. 4:17 to refer to the *future* "eternal weight of *glory*" (αἰώνιον βάρος δόξης).[222] As in 2 Cor. 3:10, here too the present and future revelation of the glory of God is not only "*surpassing*," but also explicitly tied to Paul's *ministry* (διακονία) of suffering and the Spirit (cf. 4:1, 7, 13). Moreover, this ministry both reveals this glory, and causes others to glorify God with their thanksgiving in response to the fact that through Paul's ministry the grace of God is "*abounding*" (cf. 4:15b: ἵνα ἡ χάρις πλεονάσασα διὰ τῶν πλειόνων τὴν εὐχαριστίαν περισσεύσῃ εἰς τὴν δόξαν τοῦ θεοῦ)![223] These same themes are again developed in 2 Cor. 9:12–15, this time in direct relationship to the ministry of the Corinthians. In 2 Cor. 9:14 Paul uses ὑπερβάλλω to refer to the grace of God which has been given to the Corinthians. But as its parallel in 9:13 demonstrates, this "surpassing grace of God" (cf. τὴν ὑπερβάλλουσαν χάριν τοῦ θεοῦ) is a reference to the Corinthians' "obedience to (their) confession of the gospel of Christ" as manifested in their generous giving, since, as 9:8–11a and 15 make clear, both are a gift from God. Moreover, in 2 Cor. 9:12 this "surpassing grace" toward the Corinthians is further described in terms of the Corinthians' own "*ministry* of service" (ἡ διακονία τῆς λειτουργίας), which not only meets the needs of the saints, but is also the vehicle through which "many thanksgivings are *abounding* to God" (περισσεύουσα διὰ πολλῶν εὐχαριστιῶν τῷ θεῷ). "Because of the proof of this *ministry*" (διὰ τῆς δοκιμῆς τῆς διακονίας ταύτης), others will *glorify* God (δοξάζοντες, 9:13). As in 2 Cor. 3:10, here too the διακονία of the gospel, both in its acceptance by the Corinthians and in its embodiment in their own lives of service to the saints, is pictured in terms of its *function* as that which "abounds" (περισσεύω) in its manifestation of the "glory of God" (δοξάζω τὸν θεόν) because the grace of God which it reveals is "surpassing" (ὑπερβάλλω) in its *character*.[224] To describe something as "surpassing" is thus, for Paul, tantamount to describing it as part of the new covenant reality.

---

[222] For the other uses of the noun in Paul, cf. Rom. 7:13; 1 Cor. 12:31; 2 Cor. 1:8; 12:7; Gal. 1:13.

[223] For a study of the structure and meaning of 2 Cor. 4:7–16a, see my *Suffering and the Spirit*, pp. 65–76.

[224] This same complex of ideas in an eschatological context is represented in Eph. 2:7, where God's purpose in granting mercy to his people (2:4) is to display in the ages to come

b) The Eternal Nature of the New Covenant (2 Cor. 3:11)

In verse 11 Paul brings this section of his argument to a close by introducing a third *qal wahomer* comparison. The point of the comparison is the same as in vv. 7–8, since the elided verbs are most naturally those from Paul's initial argument. When Paul wanted to deviate from them in v. 9, he did so explicitly. For this reason, the present participle καταργούμενον should be taken as contemporaneous with the past time instituted in v. 7 and reflected in v. 10, while the participle μένον agrees with the present time established in the logical future of v. 8 and picked up with περισσεύει in v. 9. In addition, in v. 11 Paul continues his use of the *neuter* substantival participle introduced in verse 10. Paul's focus is still on the purpose and results of the old and new covenants respectively,[225] with the neuter form referring in a broad, encompassing sense[226] to "that which was being rendered inoperative" (τὸ καταργούμενον) over against "that which is remaining" (τὸ μένον).

Hence, in v. 11 Paul maintains the same basis of comparison (i.e. the similarity between the δόξα of the respective ministries[227]), as well as the same

"the surpassing riches of His grace" (τὸ ὑπερβάλλον πλοῦτος τῆς χάριτος αὐτοῦ) in kindness toward us in Christ Jesus. In view of Eph. 1:6, 12, 14, this purpose is clearly the manifestation of the glory of God.

[225] Contra Sanders, *Paul and the Law*, p. 139, who takes the reference of the neuter participles in v. 11, based on v. 10, to refer to the Law itself, though he is correct in arguing against Morna Hooker's view, "Beyond the Things," pp. 303 f., that what is being abolished and what remains in v. 11 are two different aspects of the Law, i.e. the Law as a way of salvation based on obedience is passing way, while the Law as a witness to Christ remains. Sanders' identification of the neuter referent of the participles with the Law itself leads him, however, to posit that Hooker was merely attempting to solve "a true ambiguity in Paul's position" and "two sides of a dilemma" in Paul's argument (p. 139). For in Sanders' view, "on the one hand (since the law does not save) the law is a law of condemnation and death, and it (not just an aspect of it) is passing away; on the other hand only its splendor has passed away while it still remains and testifies to Christ ... and it can still be correctly read by Christians" (p. 139). But this dilemma dissipates once the force of καταργέω is recognized and the problem in view is seen not to be the Law itself, but Israel's hard-heartedness. Paul is not moving in his thinking, as Sanders posits, from "what is surpassingly valuable" to "what is exclusively valuable," so that Paul is led "to give the law a purely negative role: it kills (2 Cor. 3:6)" (pp. 140 f.).

[226] Cf. Theobald, *Gnade*, p. 184, who sees even an "*umfassenderes* Verständnis" of the participles in 3:11, over against 3:10 (emphasis his). But his attempt to read τὸ καταργούμενον as a further, amplified reference to τὸ δεδοξασμένον in 3:10 leads to confusion. The "face" of Moses, which in his view is said to have been glorified in 3:10, can hardly be said to pass away in v. 11 (!), without reading "face" as an abstract reference to that which is external and visible (cf. pp. 185 f., 188), for which there is no indication in the passage, nor in Paul's thought overall. Theobald's thesis only works, therefore, when the text is read apart from the text's own references to its conceptual framework in the OT tradition.

[227] Paul's switch in terminology from διὰ δόξης to ἐν δόξῃ in v. 11 is best understood as a stylistic variation, as found also in 1 Cor. 15:21–22, contra Theobald, *Gnade*, pp. 182 f., who sees the change as indicating two distinctive relationships of the glory to the two ministries, i.e. an accompanying circumstance over against a close connection. This leads to his central thesis in which he posits a distinct meaning for "glory" in the two ministries, indi-

distinctive point around which the comparison is formed (i.e. the dissimilarity between their respective functions). The introduction of v. 11 with yet another γάϱ follows a common Pauline stylistic tendency to string together grounding assertions, which are all introduced by γάϱ, in order to undergird his main point with a step by step series of supports.[228] Verse 11 is therefore not merely a restatement of vv. 7–8 and 9–10, but functions to support the point just made in v. 10.[229] But how does v. 11 support Paul's assertion that his ministry is a vehicle through which the surpassing glory of the new covenant is now being revealed (3:10)?

The answer is found in the two new, interrelated elements in v. 11, upon which the force of the *qal wahomer* argument is again built. First, Paul transfers the καταϱγέω-terminology from its restricted use in v. 7 as a direct reference to the glory on Moses' face, to the old covenant ministry conceived as a whole. But although the referent has been changed, there is no contextual reason to interpret καταϱγέω in v. 11 differently than it was understood in v. 7, i.e. as denoting the act of being rendered inoperative or ineffective. What *is* changed, however, is that Paul now applies this verb to the old covenant *as a whole*, including not only its glory, but also its results and theological purpose. The Sinai covenant's mediation of the glory of God, which due to the hard hearts of Israel had to be continually rendered inoperative by the veil (τὴν καταϱγουμένην, 3:7), is now *itself* described as that which "was continually being rendered inoperative" (τὸ καταϱγούμενον, 3:11). In doing so, Paul creates a play on the use of καταϱγέω in which what happened to Moses' glory in Exod. 34:29 ff. becomes a metonomy for the old covenant which it represented. For Paul, the veiling of Moses' face in order to bring the *glory* to an end in terms of its effects in 3:7 is a demonstration of the fact that the *Sinai*

---

cated by the motif of "overabundance" in relationship to the new covenant, so that the parallel between the glory of the two covenants is not one of identity, but of analogy. Indeed, this distinction leads to positing a "new nature" *(Wesen)* for the glory of the new covenant as that which is unseen and eternal, over against that which is seen and transitory (pp. 183 f.). His thesis finds no support in the interpretation argued in this work. For the syntactical position taken here, see Lietzmann, *An die Korinther*, p. 112, Furnish, *II Corinthians*, pp. 205 f. (contra e.g. Plummer, Hughes, Collange, who see it reflecting a theological contrast between the impermanent and the permanent); and Hofius, "Gesetz und Evangelium," p. 90 n. 103, who point to Rom. 3:30; 5:10; 1 Cor. 12:8 f.; Gal. 2:16; Phm. 5 as examples of similar alterations. In both cases, as Hofius argues, the phrases mean "to be filled, determined, characterized by glory" (p. 91 n. 103).

[228] Cf. e.g. the chains of γάϱ in Rom. 1:16–21; 2:11–14; 4:1–3, 13–15; 5:6–7; 7:14–15, 18–19; 8:1–6, 12–15, 18–24; etc.; 1 Cor. 1:18–21; 3:2–4; 9:16–17; 12:12–14 (with καὶ γάϱ); etc.; 2 Cor. 5:1–4; 13:4 (with καὶ γάϱ); etc.

[229] Contra e.g. Windisch, *Der zweite Korintherbrief*, p. 116, Prümm, *Diakonia Pneumatos*, p. 127, Barrett, *Commentary*, pp. 117–118, who do not give the γάϱs in vv. 9–11 their logical force at all; and Hofius, "Gesetz und Evangelium," p. 90, who takes it to be an inference; but cf. Lietzmann, *An die Korinther*, p. 112, who takes the γάϱ of v. 10 to be an intensification, but does take v. 11 to ground v. 10.

covenant, from its very beginning, was continually being hindered from accomplishing its desired results.

Against the background of Exod. 32–34, we have seen that this is true in both its positive and negative sense. The first establishment of the Sinai covenant was broken before it could be fully inaugurated. It consequently never brought about its positive purpose of establishing God's immediate and abiding presence among his people, nor could it, given Israel's hardened condition. As a result, although the renewed covenant made it possible for God's glory to accompany Israel, it had to be veiled as an act of mercy and as an expression of judgment (cf. Exod. 34:6–7). For given her "stiff-necked" condition as revealed in Israel's sin with the golden calf, the revelation of the glory of God, which was originally intended to *sanctify* Israel (cf. Exod. 19:5, 9; 20:20), would now mean her destruction (cf. Exod. 33:3, 5; 34:9). But at the same time, the veiling of God's glory was an act of judgment inasmuch as it pointed to God's eventual judgment against his people (cf. Exod. 32:34 f.), as well as being a constant expression of the fact that they were being kept separated from his sanctifying presence. As such, Moses' veiled mediation of the glory of God was, from the very beginning, destined to be replaced by a "new" covenant ministry.

Paul's support for his assertion that the old covenant ministry was not to endure and has now been brought to an end (3:10) is thus contained in his interpretation in 3:11a of the old covenant itself as evidenced in Exod. 32–34.[230] The fact that Paul's argument in 3:11 is rooted in Exod. 32–34 is confirmed by the way in which Israel's history of disobedience was understood throughout the canonical tradition. As we have seen in chapter three, Israel's history of rebellion from the conquest to the exile is consistently attributed to her hardened condition and traced back to her wilderness experience, which itself is anchored in her sin with the golden calf. The canonical tradition also emphasized that, from its very beginning, the Sinai covenant ran shipwreck against Israel's hardened condition, so that the promise of the new covenant found in Jeremiah and Ezekiel was based historically and theologically upon Israel's persistent repetition of the "sins of her fathers" in the wilderness. Paul's assertion in 3:11 that the covenant mediated by Moses was being rendered inopera-

---

[230] Contra Renwick, *Temple*, p. 54, who maintains that no explanation or proof is offered in 3:7–11 to substantiate Paul's claim that the old covenant was one of death and condemnation, but that the explanation and biblical example justifying this claim first comes in 3:12–18. But as the following discussion attempts to highlight, 3:7–11 is, in reality, one long biblical support for these very assertions. Renwick comes to his position because he does not take Exod. 32–34 seriously as the backdrop of 3:7–11, but looks instead to Haggai 2 (see above), and because, pp. 123, 125 f., he wrongly sees two sets of comparisons operating in 3:7–11, a "primary" one between the glory of the old and new covenants, and a "secondary" one between the ministries of the two covenants (death, condemnation, abolition vs. the Holy Spirit, righteousness, and permanence), where only the latter one, in *relationship* to the *one* glory of God, is in view.

tive, as indicated by the need for the veiling of the glory on Moses' face, thus functions to ground the abolishment of the "old" covenant in 3:10 in the same way that its continual ineffectiveness in reforming Israel grounded the eventual need for the "new" covenant throughout the canonical tradition. The difference, of course, is that for Paul, unlike the Deuteronomistic historian, the psalmists, and the prophets, the new covenant of righteousness has *now* been inaugurated. As an apostle of the Gospel, Paul ministers on the other side of the eschatological divide.

But rather than leaving this point implicit, Paul explicitly describes the new covenant ministry of glory as that which "remains," "lasts," or "persists" (μένω[231]). Paul's choice of this terminology is not coincidental. His return to this verb recalls its earlier use in 1 Cor. 3:14 to refer to that work which "remains" beyond the eschatological judgment; and in 1 Cor. 13:13 to refer to faith, hope, and love as the three things which "remain" in the future eschatological era when the "perfect" has come. In this latter context, as in 2 Cor. 3:11, καταργέω forms the counterpart to μένω as a description of those things which are abolished, or do not "remain" eschatologically (cf. 1 Cor. 13:8, 10, 11). Moreover, as the quote from Ps. 111:9 (LXX) in 2 Cor. 9:9 indicates, this connotation for the verb μένω in reference to those things which last eschatologically finds its explicit theological foundation for Paul in the psalmist's declaration that the Lord's "righteousness remains forever" (ἡ δικαιοσύνη αὐτοῦ μένει εἰς τὸν αἰῶνα), even as Paul's own new covenant ministry of God's righteousness (2 Cor. 3:9) is said to remain in 3:11. For only those things which are based upon and produced by God's own δικαιοσύνη can stand the test of his "righteous judgment" (δικαιοκρισία, Rom. 2:5; cf. 2 Thess. 1:5; Rom. 3:4 f.; 2 Cor. 5:10). Hence, that which lasts *eschatologically* is described in 1 Cor. 3 and 13 as that which "remains" precisely because it corresponds to God's "righteousness" which "remains." This same correlation between God's δικαιοσύνη and that which "remains" (μένω) is borne out in Rom. 9:11 as well, Paul's only other use of the verb with a non-personal referent.[232] Here we read that God's election of Jacob over Esau is carried out "in order that God's purpose according to election might remain" (μένῃ). As Rom. 9:14 goes on to conclude, this election does not render God unrighteous (ἀδικία), since "the most fundamental characteristic of God's righteousness is his allegiance to his own name, that is, to his honor and glory," which his sovereign election clearly reveals.[233] Consequently, since God's glory consists in his sovereign freedom to bestow mercy upon and harden whomever he will (cf. 9:15–18), God's purpose of election "remains" as that which corresponds to his righteousness.

---

[231] BAGD, *A Greek-English Lexicon*, p. 504.

[232] Cf. 1 Cor. 7:11, 20, 24; 15:6; Phil. 1:25; 2 Tim. 2:13; 3:14 for its use in reference to persons, where it conveys the meaning of the verb without eschatological connotations.

[233] John Piper, *The Justification of God*, p. 90. For an interpretation of the context and the relevant OT background in support of this point, see his pp. 34–101.

As a description of the purpose and results of the new covenant and its ministry, τὸ μένον in 2 Cor. 3:11 thus carries with it a pronounced eschatological connotation consistent with Paul's use throughout the Corinthian correspondence and in continuation of the eschatological referent of v. 10. Moreover, as seen in 2 Cor. 9:9 and illustrated in Rom. 9:11–18, it is the natural theological corollary to the presence of God's righteousness displayed in the ministry of the Spirit (3:9). In the context of 3:7–11 it provides the antonym to καταργέω by calling attention to the persisting validity of the new covenant and its ministry as the beginning of the *eschatological* fulfillment of God's purposes. Unlike the covenant under which Moses ministered the veiled glory of God, the new covenant under which Paul ministers does not announce its own eventual replacement by having to be continually rendered inoperative in its mediation of the glory of God. In stark contrast to Moses' own experience under the "old" covenant, Paul's ministry of glory need not be "cut off" from those to whom he preaches because the Spirit is now at work transforming "hard hearts of stone" into "receptive hearts of flesh" (cf. 3:6b, 8) as a result of the fact that in the Gospel the righteousness of God is now being revealed "unto salvation" (3:9; cf. Rom. 1:16f.). In other words, the new covenant "remains" in force (τὸ μένον) since it reveals the righteousness of God in the way which will last forever.[234] Viewed from this perspective, Paul's description of the ministry of the Spirit as that which "remains" corresponds to the everlasting eschatological reality of the new covenant, which is presupposed in Ezek. 11, 36, and Jer. 31, and made explicit in Jer. 32:37–40 (39:38–40 LXX).[235] In the comparison established in v. 11 Paul moves from the past of Exodus 32–34 to the present of his own ministry as a fulfillment of the prophetic promises of Jeremiah and Ezekiel.

This is the second way in which 3:11 provides the ground to 3:10. Paul's assertion that that which "remains" certainly exists "ἐν δόξῃ" (3:11b) supports his prior assertion concerning the abolishment of the old covenant by drawing specific attention to the new covenant as the beginning of the eschatological consummation. Indeed, as Peter Stuhlmacher already pointed out and C. Marvin Pate has now surveyed in detail, the expectation that the righteous

---

[234] Cf. F. Hauck, art. μένω κτλ., *TDNT* 4 (1967) 574–588, pp. 574–576, for the use of the verb in Jewish and non-Jewish religious texts, where in both cases "μένειν is a mark of God and what is commensurate with Him ..." (p. 574). Hauck also outlines the key OT background of the word in eschatological contexts (cf. Is. 40:8; 66:22; Ps. 101:12; Dan. 4:26; 11:6; Zech. 14:10; Wis. 7:27; Sir. 44:13; 4 Esdr. 9:37) and points out how in John the eschatological promise of that which remains is realized in that God "remains" in Christ, Christ "remains" in believers, and believers "remain" in Christ (cf. John 6:56; 8:35; 15:4–7, 9f.; 14:10; 1 John 2:26–28; 3:6, 24; 4:16; etc.).

[235] So too Stockhausen, *Moses' Veil*, pp. 65f., 121, who emphasizes that Jer. 39:38–40 LXX is behind 3:11, though due to the constraints of her reliance on the principle of analogy she does not see this text as also playing a role in the constellation of ideas behind 3:6, nor does she see the meaning of the "fear of the Lord" in this passage as a reference to obedience to the Law (see above, chapter two).

would experience the glory of God in the eschaton was widespread within post-biblical Judaism.[236] What is striking, therefore, is that the eschatological reality which is pictured as "remaining" in the *future* in 1 Cor. 3 and 13 is pictured as *already* "remaining" in the *present* in 2 Cor. 3:11. It is this proleptic eschatological fulfillment taking place in the apostolic ministry of the Spirit, as a result of the establishment of the new covenant in Christ, which supports Paul's point that the Sinai covenant established through Moses is now over. If the "new" has come, the former is now "old." This eschatological transformation from the old to the new covenants, with the permanent validity and significance of the latter, provides the final and most foundational step in Paul's argument in 2 Cor. 3:7–11.

5. Conclusion: The Main Point of 2 Cor. 3:7–11

As our structural analysis has shown, the main point of 3:7–11 remains the assertion of v. 8 that the "ministry of the Spirit certainly exists in glory." Having already argued for this point in v. 7 on the basis of Exod. 32–34, in verses 9–11 Paul supports it by a stair-step series of three further assertions, each of which is introduced by γάρ (cf. 9a, 10a, 11a) and is itself supported either by its own *qal wahomer* argument, or, in the case of verse 10, by the ground clause introduced with εἵνεκεν. The structure of verses 8–11 can thus be represented as follows:

Verse 8 (Main point of 7–11)

– Supported by Verse 9b
　　　　　　(which is supported by Verse 9a)

　　– Supported by Verse 10a
　　　　　　(which is supported by Verse 10b)

　　　　– Supported by Verse 11b
　　　　　　(which is supported by Verse 11a)

Our study has also shown that at the base of Paul's argument is the contrast between τὸ καταργούμενον and τὸ μένον in 3:11, which simply restates the well-known "two age" conception common to the Old Testament and early Judaism. But Paul's argument here demonstrates that he has brought to this conception the distinctive Christian modification of its proleptic inauguration

---

[236] Cf. his "Erwägungen zum ontologischen Charakter der καινὴ κτίσις bei Paulus," *EvTh* 27 (1967) 1–35, p. 28. He points to Paul's view of baptism as picturing the same proleptic fulfillment of the apocalyptic conception (cf. its reflection in Rom. 8:29 f. and Gal. 3:28a and explanation in Phil. 2:12–18) that I am arguing Paul presents in 2 Cor. 3:7–11. For Pate's detailed development of this expectation in the OT and post-biblical Judaism, see his *Adam Christology*, pp. 33–76.

in Christ as a fulfillment of the new covenant promises of Jeremiah and Ezekiel, to which he alluded in 3:6. Throughout 3:7–11 this perspective is simply repeated without further development in the descriptions of his ministry as a "ministry of the Spirit" (3:8), "of righteousness" (3:9), "of surpassing glory" (3:10), and as "that which remains" (3:11). Paul's evidence for the validity of this conviction in 3:6 and 8 and its theological underpinnings in 3:9–11 is once again the new eschatological life of the Corinthians themselves, also first introduced in 3:1–6. What is distinctive about 3:7–11, therefore, is not its positive affirmations concerning the ministry of the new covenant as an extension of his thesis-like statement in 3:6 that "the Spirit makes alive."

What *is* new in 3:7–11 is the way in which Paul supports his prior statement that the "letter kills," which becomes the crux of the *qal wahomer* arguments in 3:7–11. In 3:7–11, Paul turns from his present apostolic experience of suffering and ministry of the Spirit to the Scriptural account of the second giving of the Law in Exod. 32–34. In doing so, Paul offers an argument *from the events surrounding the giving of the Law itself* for his prior assertion that "the letter kills" and its corollary that, with the dawning of the new covenant, the old is brought to an end.[237] Paul's argument in 3:7–11 thus provides biblical support from the history of God's dealing with Israel for Paul's apostolic self-understanding as a διάχονος of the new covenant whose ministry is to reveal through his own suffering the glory of God as manifested in Christ (cf. 2:14–17; 4:6–15).

It must nevertheless be kept in mind that in spite of the ways in which 3:7–11 supports 3:6, we observed at the beginning of this chapter that this is not its only function. An examination of the continuation of Paul's argument will demonstrate that 3:7–11 also provides the foundation for his subsequent discussion concerning the nature of his ministry of the Spirit in 3:12–18, to which we now turn our attention.

---

[237] Stockhausen's central thesis, *Moses' Veil*, p. 122, that "the promises of the prophets are the interpretive key to the Pentateuchal narrative" in 3:7–11, so that throughout 3:7–11 "Paul's use of Exodus 34:29–35 itself has so far proved to be very slight," while the influence of 3:1–6 and its prophetic "new covenant conceptual pool" is "immense" is therefore not convincing. Cf. now Hays, *Echoes*, p. 132, who in speaking of 3:7–18 in general concludes, "In this passage, in contrast to verses 1–6, there is no complex interplay of subtexts; the single obvious subtext is Exodus 34."

Chapter Five

The Boldness of Paul and the Veil of Moses
(2 Cor. 3:12–18)

The comparison between the ministries of Paul and Moses begun in 3:7–11 reaches its high point in 3:12–18. In 3:12–18 Paul draws the conclusion prepared for in 3:7–11, where he was also supporting his prior argument in 3:4–6. Thus, Paul's points concerning his own call and ministry in comparison to the call and ministry of Moses from 3:4–6 and 3:7–11 are still clearly in focus[1] and provide the presuppositions for understanding Paul's continuing defense of the validity of his apostolic διακονία in 3:12–18.[2]

This integral link between vv. 7–11 and 12–18 becomes even more clear once it is recognized that not only 3:12 f., but also Paul's assertions concerning the hardness of Israel's minds in v. 14a, their current relationship to the παλαιὰ διαθήκη and Moses in vv. 14b–15, and the contrast to Israel's situation in vv. 16–18, are all based upon the significance of Moses' veil from Exod. 34:29–35 as referred to in 3:7–11.[3] That Paul is basing his argument on Exod. 34:29–35 has now been confirmed by Belleville's extensive study of

---

[1] Cf. Michael Theobald, *Die überströmende Gnade, Studien zu einem paulinischen Motivfeld*, 1982, p. 192, who points out that the comparisons of the "Überbietungsschemas" in 3:7–11 give way to direct contrasts in 3:12–18. But Theobald's understanding of the structure, focus, and nature of these contrasts is very different from that which is argued here.

[2] In support of this point, see Linda L. Belleville, *Reflections of Glory, Paul's Polemical Use of the Moses-Doxa Tradition in 2 Corinthians 3.1–18*, JSNT Supplement Series 52, 1991, p. 165, who concludes on the basis of her study of the themes and structure of 2 Cor. 1–7 (cf. pp. 84–164) and specifically of 3:4–4:18 (pp. 142–151) that 3:12–18 are part of Paul's "offensive polemic against an itinerant group of outsiders in 2:12–5:21 ..."

[3] Contra Dietrich-Alex Koch, *Die Schrift als Zeuge des Evangeliums: Untersuchungen zur Verwendung und zum Verständnis der Schrift bei Paulus*, BHT Bd. 69, 1986, p. 332, who argues that 3:12–18 represents an independent train of thought. Koch rightly sees that the focus of 3:12–18 is now on the remaining or removal of the veil (cf. 3:14 f.), and that the reference to the veil binds 3:12–18 with 3:7–11, but he misses the conceptual link between the veil and the sufficiency of Paul as an apostle. He can thus conclude that "ab V 13 das Problem des Apostelamtes überhaupt nicht mehr präsent ist" (p. 332). For the structural parallels between Paul's use of the motif of "glory" in 3:7–11 and that of the veil in vv. 12–18, see Erich Gräßer, *Der Alte Bund im Neuen, Exegetische Studien zur Israelfrage im Neuen Testament*, WUNT 35, 1985, pp. 89 f., though Gräßer sees the purpose in both sections to be to demonstrate the inferiority of the old covenant and Law as such. Gräßer, p. 90, supports this latter view by following those who, like R. Bultmann and P. Vielhauer, wrongly see the contrast in 3:7–18 to be between Moses and Christ, based on the identification of the glory of the new covenant with that of Christ in 2 Cor. 4:4, 6, the equation of the "letter" with the

the structure of 3:12–18 in which she argues that vv. 12–18 evidence the discernable pattern of "(1) opening statement, (2) text + commentary, and (3) textual summary."[4] Her basic outline of vv. 12–18 is as follows:[5]

opening statement	v. 12
text	vv. 13–14a: Exod. 34:33[6]
commentary	vv. 14b–15
text	v. 16: Exod. 34:34
commentary	v. 17
text and commentary combined	Exod. 34:35/v. 18

1. The Essential Contrast between the Ministries of Moses and Paul (2 Cor. 3:12–13)

Verse 12a indicates explicitly that what Paul is about to say is built squarely on what he has just said. Paul begins his conclusion concerning his apostolic ministry by directing his hearers' attention to the main point of 3:7–11 with the adverbial participial phrase ἔχοντες τοιαύτην ἐλπίδα. Rather than a general reference to all that Paul has just said, the careful logical structure in 3:7–11 clearly supports 3:8 as the main point from which his present argument begins.[7] The "hope" to which Paul refers in 3:12, therefore, is that his ministry

---

Law, and the (false) identification of the Spirit with Christ in 3:17, rather than viewing the contrast throughout 3:7–18 to be between the ministries of Moses and Paul.

[4] Belleville, *Reflections of Glory*, p. 179. The "textual summary" (here in v. 18) acts as a commentary on the implied text (in this case Exod. 34:35) and as a summary of Paul's thought in 3:12–17 (p. 179). Belleville argues that this pattern is not unique to Paul, but can be found in "both the biblical and extra-biblical literature of Paul's day" (p. 179), so that Paul's argument has an "essentially haggadic character," with "certain midrashic features," though not formally a "midrash" (pp. 177, 186). In support of this larger thesis, an examination of which is beyond the scope of this work, she points to John 6:31–59; Philo, *Leg. all.* I.97–98; *Fug.* 137–39; *Mek.*, Shirata 5.1 ff.; 6.141–159; 8.95–105; LAB 17:1–4; M.M. 1.9; Josephus, *Ant.* 3.26 ff. (pp. 179–186). She also points to the common practice of a phrase-by-phrase commentary in Jewish, Samaritan, and Nag Hammadi literature, as in vv. 13–15 and 16–17; to the "contemporizing haggadah" in which "the biblical text is interpreted in light of the situation contemporary with the author" (p. 188), as in vv. 14b–15; and to the "haggadic expansion of a biblical text without explicit citation of that text," as in v. 18 (p. 189; see pp. 186–191).

[5] Belleville, *Reflections of Glory*, p. 177. As the following discussion will make clear, however, at key points the present study understands Paul's thought to be very different than that proposed by Belleville, albeit within the same overall structure which she has ably presented. The basic disagreements stem from our distinct understandings of Paul's point concerning the glory of the old covenant as reflected on the face of Moses (see above, ch. four).

[6] In contrast to Belleville, however, we will argue below that Paul's commentary on the text actually begins in v. 13b!

[7] Contra the majority of scholars who try to relate it to some abstract summary distilled from 3:7–11 or to v. 11; cf. e.g. David A. Renwick, *Paul, The Temple, and the Presence of God*, Brown Judaic Studies 224, 1991, pp. 124 f., Carol Kern Stockhausen, *Moses' Veil and*

certainly "exists in glory" (3:8).[8] It is important to keep in mind that for Paul "hope" (ἐλπίς) refers to a solid confidence concerning the *future* because of the promises and acts of God in the *past*.[9] By introducing this concept at this juncture in his argument, Paul is implicitly reminding the Corinthians of the *basis* of his hope in 3:8 as set forth in 3:7–11. Paul's assertion in 3:8 is certain due to the surpassing glory of the righteousness of God being revealed in his ministry, as demonstrated both from the OT and from his own experience as an apostle. Paul's hope is that as he embodies and proclaims the gospel of Christ the glory of God will continue to be manifest through his ministry as the initial proleptic experience of the believer's future.[10]

---

the Glory of the New Covenant, The Exegetical Substructure of II Cor. 3:1–4:6, AB 116, 1989, p. 124, 124 n. 63, following Plummer, Barrett, Bultmann, Allo, Collange, van Unnik, Prümm, and Thomas E. Provence, "'Who is Sufficient for These Things?' An Exegesis of 2 Corinthians 2:15–3:18," *NovT* 24 (1982) 54–81, p. 74 n. 53, who also followed the commentaries of Bultmann, Barrett, Collange, and the influential article by W.C. van Unnik, "'With unveiled face.' An Exegesis of 2 Corinthians 3:12–18," *NovT* 6 (1963) 153–169, p. 159. Provence was led to his view by his understanding of 3:7–11 as a reference to the negative condemning function of Paul's ministry over against vv. 12–18 as its positive function in salvation. Hence, for Provence, Paul is bold in spite of the fact that his message may bring pain and death (p. 74). Yet the connection between 3:7–11 and 12–18 is not concessive, but inferential. For a critique of this view, see chapter four. Even less convincing is the attempt to treat vv. 12–18 separately from vv. 7–11 as a "'tangent of thought which would neither convince nor conciliate' his opponents" (Strachan), or as "'a passage like a cock-and-bull story'" with little meaning or relevance (Collange); cf. R.P. Martin, *2 Corinthians,* WBC Vol. 40, 1986, pp. 65–67, for these views and his own argument for the "integral" relationship between the two sections based on their verbal and thematic links. Martin himself, however, also opts for v. 11 as the referent to the "hope" of v. 12 (cf. p. 67). The essential connection between vv. 7–11 and 12–18 was already argued by Hans Windisch, *Der zweite Korintherbrief,* KEK Bd. 6, 1970[9], p. 117, based on the parallel transitions in 1 Cor. 10:1–5 and 6–13; Rom. 1:18–4:25 and 5:1 ff.; and Heb. 10:1–18 and 19 ff.

[8] For a listing of the five different possibilities that have been suggested as the referent for this hope, see P.E. Hughes, *Paul's Second Epistle to the Corinthians,* NICNT, 1962, p. 107, who points to the work of Alford in support of the position taken here. Hughes follows the majority view. For the relationship between 3:12 and 3:8, see too H.-D. Wendland, *Die Briefe an die Korinther,* NTD Bd. 7, 1972[13], p. 181.

[9] So too O. Hofius, "Gesetz und Evangelium nach 2. Korinther 3," *Paulusstudien,* WUNT 51, 1989, pp. 75–120 (now also found in *"Gesetz" als Thema Biblischer Theologie,* Jahrbuch für Biblische Theologie Bd. 4, 1989, pp. 105–149), p. 115 n. 230, though Hofius views the referent of Paul's "hope" to be everything from 3:4 on.

[10] So too N.T. Wright, "Reflected Glory: 2 Corinthians 3," in his *The Climax of the Covenant, Christ and the Law in Pauline Theology,* 1992, pp. 175–192, pp. 176 f., 179 n. 16, who sees Paul's emphasis on the surety of the future eschatological glory due to the present experience of the Spirit in his ministry. He thus rightly contrasts Paul's point here with that in Rom. 8:30. Contra Belleville, *Reflections of Glory,* pp. 192 f., who stresses that Paul's hope itself is in the process of unfolding. But it is not clear how Belleville derives this emphasis from the word ἐλπίς, since the Pauline use of "hope" does not carry such a connotation. If such a connotation were there, it would have to come from the object of ἐλπίς or from the use of ἐλπίς as the object of what is hoped for, if that object is an unfolding reality. In and of itself, ἐλπίς in Paul simply means "absolute confidence in a future reality." In this case, Paul's confidence is that the glory of God will continue to be manifest, not that his

It is clear that the force of this phrase is causal, providing the ground for his following assertion πολλῇ παρρησίᾳ χρώμεθα. Here, as well as throughout 2:14–4:6 (except for 3:18!), the plural forms of the verbs are all "apostolic plurals" referring to Paul himself in his authority and role as an apostle.[11] Paul's point in 12a is that "because he has the certain confidence (ἐλπίς) that his ministry mediates the glory of God, therefore (οὖν) he behaves with much *boldness*" (πολλῇ παρρησίᾳ χρώμεθα).[12] Within this apologetic context, Paul's use of παρρησία carries with it the connotation of shamelessness in one's behavior and the consequent "freedom of speech" and "openness or plainness of

---

hope itself is unfolding. Contra too Renwick, *Temple*, p. 125, who sees the focus of Paul's hope in 2 Cor. 3 to be solely on the future because of what he argues is the future eschatological orientation of 3:7–11. As such, he reads 3:12 as parallel to Rom. 5:2 (the hope of sharing in the glory of God in the future). But while the theological parallels he adduces between Rom. 5:1–5, 16–17 and 2 Cor. 3 are very helpful, he fails to note their distinct subject matter. Romans 5:1–5 concerns the believer's present hope for future glory in the midst of suffering, whereas 2 Cor. 3 concerns Paul's present hope for the genuine effectiveness of his ministry in mediating the first fruits or down payment of that glory in the Spirit (cf. 2 Cor. 1:22). For as 2 Cor. 2:14–3:3, 3:18 (ἀπὸ δόξης εἰς δόξαν), and 4:4–6 demonstrate, what Paul has in view here is the *present* experience of the glory of God in anticipation of its final eschatological realization. This is confirmed by the parallels between 3:4, 12, and 4:1, in which Paul's hope is equated with his confidence and his ministry (see below). Moreover, since Paul can use ἐλπίς to refer to objects or expectations prior to the eschaton (cf. Rom. 4:18; 1 Cor. 9:10; 2 Cor. 1:7; and esp. 2 Cor. 10:15; Phil. 1:20; and the verbal form in 1 Cor. 16:7; 2 Cor. 1:10, 13; 5:11; 8:5; 13:6; Phil. 2:19, 23; 1 Tim. 3:14; 6:17; Phlm. 22), Renwick's reading of "hope" as in itself a reference to the future eschaton, and hence his future reading of 3:7–12, are not persuasive. For the attempt to read vv. 12 ff. as an exclusive reference to the future (including v. 18!), see already J. Munck, *Paul and the Salvation of Mankind*, 1959, pp. 58–60.

[11] For the contextual arguments in support of this point, see my *Suffering and the Spirit, An Exegetical Study of II Cor. 2:14–3:3 within the Context of the Corinthian Correspondence*, WUNT 2. Reihe 19, 1986, pp. 12–18. Hence, Belleville, *Reflections of Glory*, p. 193, is correct in arguing that there has been no shift in subject since 2:17 ff, but 2:14–17 also refer to Paul himself.

[12] Contra those who, like Renwick, *Temple*, pp. 129–131, and Peter von der Osten-Sacken, "Geist im Buchstaben, Vom Glanz des Mose und des Paulus," now in his *Evangelium und Tora, Aufsätze zu Paulus*, 1987, pp. 150–155 (originally in *EvTh* 41 (1981) 230–235), p. 152, follow Bultmann in seeing the boldness in view to be over against God, i.e. the right to openness before God. But it is Paul's *assumed* acceptance by God and legitimacy as an apostle which undergirds, but is not the subject of, his boldness toward others. For a helpful overview of the use of παρρησία in religious contexts, see Windisch, *Der zweite Korintherbrief*, pp. 118 f., where he (surprisingly!) argues against those who take it to be a contrast to the deceitful actions of Moses. Instead, he too takes it to be an example of its common use in religious contexts to refer to one's confidence before God, which supports one's speaking out in prayer (cf. Heb. 4:16; 1 John 5:14). Windisch sees that this confidence derives from Paul's experience of the glory of God. For the view that Paul's reference must be to his confidence toward others, see Samuel Vollenweider, "2 Kor 3: Der transzendente Schein des Gesetzes," in his *Freihet als neue Schöpfung, Eine Untersuchung zur Eleutheria bei Paulus und in seiner Umwelt*, FRLANT 147, 1989, pp. 247–284, p. 250, 250 n. 251. And for the arguments against taking v. 12a as a hortatory subjunctive ("let us act"), see V.P. Furnish, *II Corinthians*, AB 32A, 1984, p. 206.

speech" that it produces.[13] As Erik Peterson observed in 1929, παρρησία derived from the political arena where it was used to characterize the shameless freedom of speech associated with the absolute right within a democracy to say anything, a privilege granted, however, only to those within the class of the "freedmen."[14] As such it carried a *polemical* nuance which separated the slave from those who were free, as well as being repeatedly associated with freedom (ἐλευθερία) and truth (ἀλήθεια).[15] As time went on, it was transferred from the political to the moral realm, where it characterized the relationship of friends as part of the φιλία they shared, and was used to describe one of the central characteristics of cynics such as Diogenes.[16] Hence, as Peterson concludes, "Mit dem Begriff der παρρησία verbindet sich für den Griechen stets die

---

[13] Cf. W. Bauer, F.W. Gingrich, and F. Danker, *A Greek-English Lexicon of the New Testament*, 1979², p. 630, and the common use of παρρησία in Philo, where it is predominantly associated with boldness and plainness of speech (see *De Sac.* 35; *De Ag.* 64; *De Plan.* 8; *De Io.* 107, 222; *De Eb.* 149; *De Conf.* 165; *Rer.Div.Her.* 5–6, 14; *De Spec. Leg.* III.138; *De Cong.Ling.* 151; *De Som.* II.83, 85; see below, p. 346, for its use in relationship to Moses). For a discussion of the relevant background, together with the secondary literature, see Belleville, *Reflections of Glory*, pp. 194–198. She too concludes that the emphasis in Paul's use is on a certain kind of behavior, not a certain kind of speech. She thus opts for a reference to "open/public" behavior in contrast to that which is "obscure/hidden" (p. 197), though with a different application of this insight to Paul's argument. For the denotation and connotation of χρᾶσθαι παρρησία as "to exercise boldness," especially in relationship to one's freedom of speech, see W.C. van Unnik, "With unveiled face," pp. 158 f. But van Unnik's attempt to explain Paul's reference to the veil of Moses in support of this assertion, based on the Aramaic equivalent to παρρησία, "to uncover the face" or "head" (אפין גלה or ראש גלה) as a reference to confidence and freedom, so that Mose's practice signifies the opposite (pp. 160 f.), is questionable. As van Unnik himself points out, παρρησία was used as a loan word in Aramaic (p. 160), so that the allusion to the Aramaic equivalent is distant at best. Moreover, in 3:13 Paul is not referring to the general custom of covering one's face, but to the specific action of Moses in Exod. 34:29 ff., in which there is no indication of any sense of shame; nor did later Jewish tradition understand it this way. Van Unnik's view is based on his inability to see any immediate coherence between 3:12 and 3:13 due to his failure to interpret 3:13 against the backdrop of Exod. 32–34 (cf. pp. 159, 161). For in his opinion, v. 13 "is not in the OT" (p. 161)! But once v. 13 is read against its OT background, the logic of Paul's contrast can be followed without resort to some linguistic missing link. Paul's lack of shame concerns his own ministry, because of its "unveiled" nature, *in spite of* his suffering; it is not a reference to the ministry of Moses.

[14] See his "Zur Bedeutungsgeschichte von Παρρησία," in *Reinhold-Seeberg-Festschrift, I: Zur Theorie des Christentums*, ed. Wilhelm Koepp, 1929, pp. 283–297, pp. 283, 285.

[15] Peterson, Παρρησία, p. 284. Peterson points out that it is used primarily by political authors, with Demosthenes becoming the Greek model of such freedom of speech, along with Cato the Roman (cf. Plutarch, *Demosthenes* 12, 14 and *Cato*, 33, 35, and the other sources reviewed on pp. 284–288).

[16] See Peterson, Παρρησία, pp. 286–288, and the sources there. The parallel between its use in these two realms is striking: "Wie in der politischen Sphäre nur derjenige ein Recht auf παρρησία hat, der 'frei' ist, so kann auch in der moralischen Welt der hellenistischen Popularphilosophie nur derjenige ein Recht auf παρρησία haben, der – im moralischen Sinne – frei ist" (p. 288).

Vorstellung des Öffentlichen und einer öffentlichen Lebensführung."[17] Its use here thus calls to mind Paul's "self-commendation" statements throughout 2 Corinthians and the function of the letter itself as an apologetic self-commendation, as well as corresponding to his assurance in exercising his apostolic ministry despite the accusations of his opponents.[18]

This meaning of παρρησία as a reference to Paul's courage and openness in proclaiming the Gospel parallels its frequent use elsewhere in the NT to describe a forthright manner of speaking, especially in the preaching of the Gospel, and its attestation in Jewish literature in reference to speaking boldly.[19] Within the immediate context it is confirmed by the parallel between 3:12 and Paul's earlier statement in 3:4 on the one hand, and by its parallel to his subsequent summary statement in 4:1 f. on the other:[20]

3:4: ἔχομεν   τοιαύτην   πεποίθησιν

3:12: ἔχοντες   τοιαύτην   ἐλπίδα

4:1: ἔχοντες   ταύτην   διακονίαν

In 3:4 Paul's "confidence" is that God is indeed revealing the knowledge of himself in Christ through Paul's ministry of suffering and the Spirit (2:14–3:3).[21] In

---

[17] Peterson, Παρρησία, p. 288. He traces these same connections in the Hellenistic Jewish literature, cf. pp. 289 f.

[18] For the self-commendation statements, cf. 4:1–2; 6:4; 12:11 and my study of their central role in the apologetic of the epistle and the evidential basis for these assertions as a "boast in the Lord" (2 Cor. 10:17 f.), "'Self-Commendation' and Apostolic Legitimacy in 2 Corinthians: A Pauline Dialectic?" *NTS* 36 (1990) 66–88; for the genre of 2 Cor. as a letter of self-commendation, see Linda L. Belleville, "A Letter of Apologetic Self-Commendation: 2 Cor. 1:8–7:16," *NovT* 31 (1989) 142–163. For similar statements, cf. 2 Cor. 1:12; 2:14–17; 4:13; 5:11; 7:2; 10:7; 11:23; 13:6; and elsewhere esp. Rom. 1:16 f.; 9:1 f.; 15:15 f., 29; 1 Cor. 4:15–21; 9:1 f.; 11:1; 15:10; Gal. 1:1, 11 f.; 6:17.

[19] Cf. Mk. 8:32; John 7:13, 26; 10:24; 11:14; 16:25, 29; 18:20; Acts 2:29; 4:13, 29, 31; 18:26; and esp. Eph. 6:19 f.; Acts 9:28; 13:46; 14:3 (of Paul in the synagogue!); 26:26 (of Paul before Festus); and 28:31 (of Paul's continual practice in Rome). For its use in Jewish literature of the period to refer to speaking with boldness, see Ep. Arist. 125; Joseph and Aseneth 17:9; 23:10; and 3 Apoc. Bar. 9:8. Of special interest in this regard is T. Reub. 4:2, where the patriarch declares that because of his disgraceful act with Bilhah, he "did not have the boldness to gaze (!) into the face of Jacob or to speak to any of his brothers" (οὐκ εἶχον παρρησίαν ἀτενίσαι εἰς πρόσωπον Ἰακὼβ ἢ λαλῆσαί τινι τῶν ἀδελφῶν) and that his "conscience" (ἡ συνείδησίς μου) continues to bother him because of his sin (cf. 2 Cor. 3:12 with 2 Cor. 1:12). Text from M. De Jonge, *The Testaments of the Twelve Patriarchs, A Critical Edition of the Greek Text*, PVTG 1,2, 1978, p. 7.

[20] For the meaning and reference of 3:4 see chapter two. Belleville's rejection of the equation of 3:4 and 3:12 is not convincing, being based on a false distinction between Paul's hope in 3:12, as a reference to the fact that the gospel ministry is in the process of unfolding, and Paul's confidence in 3:4, which is viewed as based on "an accomplished fact" (*Reflections of Glory*, pp. 192 f. and 193 n. 1) (see above, n. 10). But Paul's hope is based on the same accomplished facts as his confidence, and is no less sure.

[21] Though Renwick, *Temple*, pp. 126 f., sees the antecedent of τοιαύτην in 3:12 to be the various characteristics of the new covenant from 3:7–11, he too sees the parallel between

view of Paul's similar statement in 4:6, this "knowledge" is specifically "the glory of God" as manifest "on the face of Jesus Christ." In the same way, Paul's "hope" in 3:12 is the revelation of the glory of God in his ministry of the Spirit (3:8).[22] In 4:1 both Paul's confidence and hope are then summarized in terms of his διακονία itself, which picks up the introduction of this terminology in 3:3, 6, and 7–11. In view of these same parallels, Paul's "shameless boldness" (παρρησία) in 3:12 corresponds to Paul's preaching with the sincere motives that *result* from God's elective call (ὡς ἐξ εἰλικρινείας ... ὡς ἐκ θεοῦ), and from the knowledge that one stands before the presence of God in judgment (ὡς ἐξ εἰλικρινείας ... κατέναντι θεοῦ ἐν Χριστῷ; 2:17b)[23] on the one hand; and to his determination not to lose heart but to renounce the hidden things of shame (οὐκ ἐγκακοῦμεν ἀλλὰ ἀπειπάμεθα τὰ κρυπτὰ τῆς αἰσχύνης; 4:1 f.) on the other.[24]

In this light, the use of παρρησία in Wisdom 5:1 for the boldness of the righteous before *others*, in view of the judgment of God, is striking[25] and pro-

---

3:12 and 3:4 to mean that Paul is pointing back to 3:3, i.e. that the basis for Paul's ministry is the establishment of a new covenant characterized by the presence of the Spirit. Vollenweider, "2 Kor 3," p. 271, 271 n. 376, takes exception to this emphasis on Paul as a mediator of the knowledge of Christ through the Spirit, now being substantiated in this present work, explicitly rejecting my earlier thesis from *Suffering and the Spirit*, p. 221, that Paul pictures himself as "a revelatory agent of the Spirit in the role of a Moses-like intermediary between God and his people." Vollenweider argues instead that the stress is on a transparency and immediacy of revelation which Paul merely "assists" (cf. p. 271). But when Vollenweider, p. 283, goes on to argue that Paul is "*transparent* für seine Botschaft und beansprucht keinen Platz mehr zwischen Gott und den Herzen," so that "Gerade so kommt aber *durch ihn* der schöpferische Geist Gottes im Evangelium zur Welt" (emphasis his), the difference between his position and my own becomes moot. Unlike that of a medieval priest, Paul's role as mediator is eschatological and "prophetic/apostolic," and not personal or individual.

[22] Cf. Gerd Theißen, "Die Hülle des Mose und die unbewußten Aspekte des Gesetzes," in his *Psychologische Aspekte paulinischer Theologie*, FRLANT 131, 1983, pp. 121–161, pp. 123–125, who sees Paul moving from a comparison of the relative degrees of glory in the two ministries in vv. 7–11 to a comparison of the old and new covenants based on the function of the veil in vv. 12 ff. In doing so, Paul moves from a comparison in terms of increase (from a lesser to a greater glory) to a direct contrast. But in addition to taking the contrast in vv. 7–11 to be one of degree (for the contrary view, see ch. 4), Theißen fails to take into account the content of Paul's hope in v. 12, as well as the integral links between 3:12 ff. and 3:7–11.

[23] Following Renwick's helpful emphasis on the centrality of the presence of God in these phrases, though he does not point out the specific reference to judgment; cf. *Temple*, pp. 61–74.

[24] Cf. 1 Cor. 5:8; 2 Cor. 1:12. For this interpretation of 2:17 and its relationship to 4:1 f., see my *Suffering and the Spirit*, pp. 163–174.

[25] Peterson, Παρρησία, pp. 289–291, points to this use of the word in relationship to God (the freedom of the slave/friend of God over against his Lord, expressed in prayer), and in connection with the conscience (συνείδησις), as something new within Jewish literature in distinction to non-Jewish Greek literature. He traces this use primarily to Philo, who points to Moses (and secondarily Abraham) as his model (see below). Peterson also points to the use of παρρησία in Eph. 3:12; Heb. 4:16; 1 John 2:28; 4:17 as examples of the word used to describe one's freedom of speech and access to God before his throne as King and in the context of eschatological judgment (pp. 292, 294).

vides a conceptual parallel to Paul's thought in 2 Cor. 2:17 and 3:12. There we read concerning the final judgment of the wicked that,

"They shall come, when their sins are reckoned up, with coward fear; and their lawless deeds shall convict them to their face. Then shall the righteous man (ὁ δίκαιος) stand in great boldness (ἐν παρρησίᾳ πολλῇ). Before the face of them that afflicted him, and them that make his labours of no account." (Wis. 4:20–5:1)[26]

As in Paul's argument, here too the "righteous" person is vindicated by his/her deeds on the day of judgment in which "salvation" is granted (σωτηρία; cf. Wis. 5:2), while the wicked are judged on the basis of their lawless deeds. As such, the day of judgment is a reversal of the fortunes of the righteous on earth, where the wicked derided their life as madness and without honor (Wis. 5:4), when in reality it was the wicked upon whom "the light of righteousness" (τὸ τῆς δικαιοσύνης φῶς) did not shine (Wis. 5:6). Hence, the righteous may now act with "great boldness" in the face of those who formerly afflicted them. In the same way, since Paul is confident that the righteousness of God is now being revealed in his Gospel, he is *already* exercising the "boldness" that characterizes the righteous at the final judgment in proleptic anticipation of the eschatological cosummation. Moreover, for Paul, as in Wis. 4:20–5:7, the evidence of this righteousness is the fulfillment of the Law, now brought about, however, by the power of the Spirit in the new covenant inaugurated by Christ (see chapters two and four).

Although the underlying Greek text is lost, this same constellation of ideas is most likely found in the discussion of the wicked and righteous before the judgment of God in 4 Ezra 7:75–101 (late first cent. A.D.), which provides a confirmation of the underlying theological construct presupposed by Paul in 2 Cor. 2:17 ff.[27] Here too the wicked and righteous are characterized by their respective attitudes and actions in regard to the Law (cf. 7:79, 81, 89, 94). Moreover, the worst of the seven judgments to befall the wicked is that they will "be consumed with shame" and "wither with fear at seeing the glory of the Most High before whom they sinned while they were alive, and before whom they are to be judged in the last times" (4 Ezra 7:87).[28] In contrast, the

---

[26] Translation from R.H. Charles, *The Apocrypha and Pseudepigrapha of the Old Testament, Vol. 1, Apocrypha*, 1963 (1913), p. 542.

[27] Derk William Oostendorp, *Another Jesus, A Gospel of Jewish Christian Superiority in II Corinthians*, 1967, p. 39, also points to the parallels between 3:12 and Wis. 5:1; 4 Ezra 7:89 ff., but argues that this association with the Law was the view that Paul opposed! This has been confirmed by E.P. Sanders, for whom 4 Ezra is an exceptional example of legalistic self-righteousness and perfectionism within post-biblical Judaism, cf. his *Paul and Palestinian Judaism, A Comparison of Patterns of Religion*, 1977, pp. 409 ff. But once the import of Jer. 31 and Ezek. 36 is kept in mind, as well as the integral link in Paul's thinking between the righteousness of God and the sanctifying work of the Spirit, such a contrast need not be supposed.

[28] Translations again from B.M. Metzger, "The Fourth Book of Ezra," *OTP, Vol, 1*, 1983, p. 540.

righteous "shall see with great joy the glory of him who receives them" as a result of having kept "the Law of the Lawgiver perfectly" (7:89, 91; cf. v. 94 f. and 4 Ezra 3:20; 9:32).[29] Hence, rather than shame and fear, the seventh and greatest reward for the righteous is that "they shall rejoice with boldness, and shall be confident without confusion, and shall be glad without fear, for they hasten to behold the face of him whom they served in life and from whom they are to receive their reward when glorified" (7:98).

But again, in 4 Ezra 7:75 ff. what takes place in the future judgment is for Paul *already* taking place in the new covenant ministry of the Spirit. The glory of God is now being revealed on the "face of Christ" (2 Cor. 3:8; 4:6), and the future boldness of the righteous is presently being realized in Paul's own boldness and, as we will see below, in the experience of all Christians (cf. 3:18). For the new covenant of the future has already been inaugurated in Christ, and the final salvation and judgment have already begun (cf. 2 Cor. 2:15–16a). Moreover, whereas in 4 Ezra the preparation for the future judgment may possibly be construed as "legalistic," or, more precisely, "Law-centered," with its emphasis on performing the requirements of the Law in preparation for the consummation of the age, Paul's point is exactly the opposite! It is the proleptic dawning of the new age *itself*, with its gift of forgiveness and justification in Christ and the subsequent empowerment of the Spirit, that now *enables* the ungodly to begin keeping the Law. Rather than "Law-centered" in anticipation of the coming kingdom of God, Paul's thought is "Christ-centered" as a result of the arrival of God's kingdom. The decisive difference, therefore, is not their theological structures, since both Paul and this Jewish tradition point to the necessity of obedience in anticipation of the coming judgment. What distinguishes Paul's thought is his conviction that the new age has already begun in Christ as the Messiah, and that the ungodly are being invited to participate in it! In short, what sets Paul apart is his conviction that the new covenant promised in Jeremiah 31 and Ezekiel 36 has *already* been established and that this new covenant work of God in Christ through the Spirit is the way in which God is gathering his people and fitting them for the day of judgment. It is for *this* reason, and not because of some theological inadequacy in the Law itself, either qualitatively or quantitatively, that the Sinai covenant can no longer be the means of preparing for the final consummation.

---

[29] See too the early second cent. A.D. work 2 Bar. 32:1, where this same point concerning keeping the Law perfectly as a basis of salvation may be made, though in 2 Bar. 38:1 we read that the Lord is the one "who has always enlightened those who conduct themselves with understanding," so that here too obedience to the Law in preparation for the coming judgment may be conceived of as a response to God's prior work within those who "proved to be righteous on account of my law" (2 Bar. 51:3; cf. 2 Bar. 46:4 f.; 48:22–24). It is thus difficult to determine whether, in speaking of the eschatological salvation, the statement in 2 Bar. 51:7 that the righteous "are saved because of their works and for whom the Law is now a hope" is legalistic in the theological sense of the word. In any case, in contrast to Paul, it is certainly "law-centered," rather than "messiah-centered."

If the new covenant has indeed arrived, then any return to the "old" as the basis of one's relationship to God would be a fundamental denial of the validity of God's present activity in Christ.

Although it is beyond the scope of this study to develop these in detail, Paul's understanding of his apostolic ministry as the vehicle through which the glory of God is now being revealed "unveiled" finds striking and extensive parallels in the Thanksgiving Hymns from Qumran.[30] The significance of these parallels is enhanced if these hymns represent the personality and self-understanding of the Teacher of Righteousness, through whom the community received her authoritative interpretation of the Law and the Prophets. But in any case, it is evident that the role of the individual who speaks in the psalms was conceived in much the same terms as Paul portrays his own ministry in 2 Cor. 3:12 f. In view of these affinities, the moves Paul is making conceptually in 2 Cor. 3 cohere with the kind of conclusions made by others who have a similar conviction concerning the dawning of the "new covenant" and its implications (see chapter two).

Hence, the same eschatological convictions which supported the nature of his ministry in 3:3–6 and 7–11 also provide the pillars for Paul's boldness in 3:12. Such an understanding of the eschatological connotations of Paul's παρρησία in our present passage is confirmed by Paul's parallel use of the word in Philippians 1:20. Here too Paul's hope is Christ's glorification through his "boldness" in preaching the Gospel in the midst of his apostolic suffering (cf. Phil. 1:12 f.), in contrast to the possibility of experiencing shame on behalf of Christ (ἐν οὐδενὶ αἰσχυνθήσομαι). As in 2 Cor. 3:6, 8, this "boldness" is based in his ministry of the Gospel and brought about by the power of the Spirit (cf. Phil. 1:19). In the same way, as in 2 Cor. 2:17 and 3:10 f., God's "good work" begun among the Philippians in the Gospel is interpreted in Phil. 1:6, 10–11 in terms of the sincerity and blamelessness produced by love that will last until the day of judgment, since the Philippians' "work" of love is, in reality, "the fruit of righteousness (καρπὸς δικαιοσύνης) which comes

---

[30] Cf. e.g., 1QH 4:5, where the psalmist thanks God that, unlike those who "walk in stubbornness of heart," the Lord "has illumined my face by Thy Covenant" as a result of the fact that God appears to him "as [perfect Light]." More specifically, the psalmist testifies in 1QH 4:23, that God "hast revealed Thyself to me in Thy power as perfect Light, and Thou has not covered my face with shame." As we have seen in chapter two, the consequence of this illumination is that the Law has been engraved on the psalmist's heart (1QH 4:10; cf. 1QH 2:17–18; 5:11), which has made him and his message a source of instruction to the faithful. To the community of the faithful, the psalmist, as one who has been enlightened by the Light of God, becomes a mediator of this same "Light." In the words of 1QH 4:27, "Through me Thou hast illumined the face of the Congregation and hast shown Thine infinite power." For the sake of consistency the translations for the various writings are all taken from G. Vermes, *The Dead Sea Scrolls in English*, 3rd. ed., 1987. Cf. esp. for these same motifs, which will be presented in detail in a subsequent study, 1QH 5:32–35; 6:17–19; 7:24–27; 9:26–32; 11:6; 16:8–9; 18:27–30; and the related passages in 1QM 13:9–12; 14:7–8; 4QAmram; 1QSb 3:22–4:28; 4Q184; 4Q510–511; 4Q511 Fr. 1; and 4Q511 Fr. 18.

through Jesus Christ to the glory and praise of God" (1:11). This imagery immediately calls to mind Paul's description of the "fruit of the *Spirit*" (καρπὸς τοῦ πνεύματος) in Gal. 5:22 f. The same theological move expressed in 2 Cor. 3:8–9, from the eschatological work of Christ in revealing the righteousness of God on the cross, to the eschatological work of the Spirit in revealing the righteousness of God in the sanctification of his people expressed, is thus apparent in Phil. 1:6–11 concerning the Philippians, as it is in 1:19–25 concerning Paul. For as Schütz has pointed out concerning Paul's use of παρρησία and its counterpart αἰσχύνεσθαι, Phil. 1:20 "shows the sharp eschatological flavor which both words can have in Paul's vocabulary ... Together they present a picture of religious, eschatological freedom ... Paul is referring to eschatological freedom grounded in the new covenant."[31] Hence, as in the parallel between 2 Cor. 3:4 and 12, here too Paul's "boldness" in reference to his own ministry (Phil. 1:20) corresponds theologically, both in terms of its foundation in the Gospel of Christ and in its goal of glorifying God, to his "confidence" in reference to the Philippians (Phil. 1:6).

It is striking, therefore, that in 2 Cor. 3, where the same themes are developed, Paul cannot make a similar comparison between his own ministry and the lives of the Corinthians, but must apply *both* concepts to himself! For although Paul is confident concerning many, if not most of the Corinthians (cf. 2 Cor. 2:5–8; 7:4–16), the polemic situation in Corinth requires that he "test" the genuineness of their faith (cf. 2 Cor. 13:1–5). And the test is how they will respond to Paul's assertions in 3:4, 12, and 4:1 f. concerning his boldness and confidence as a minister of the new covenant. Whether those in Corinth accept or reject Paul's final defense of his ministry in this letter will determine whether or not they too have been brought into this new covenant relationship with God, and thus, whether they too will be able to stand before the judgment of God (cf. 2 Cor. 5:10–12). Given the unity between Paul's person and his proclamation of the Gospel, to reject the former is to be excluded from the latter.

Indeed, at this point Paul's argument in support of his apostolic ministry is, in a real sense, already complete, since in 3:12 Paul returns to where he began in 3:4 and anticipates the point he will make in 4:1 f.[32] Because it is based squarely on his Moses-like prophetic call to the ministry of the Spirit, not the

---

[31] John H. Schütz, *Paul and the Anatomy of Apostolic Authority*, SNTS Monograph Series 26, 1975, p. 223.

[32] For this same point, see R.P. Martin's insightful observations, *2 Corinthians*, p. 65: "In one sense, Paul's argument can rest here, for to his own satisfaction and given his premises, he has proved his point. This is that the ministry of the new covenant is God's way of offering life ... and it has no rivals with such credentials (cf. Gal. 2:21). If the issue is whether Paul's own claim to be 'a minister of the new covenant' (3:6) is central, then his case rests on the indisputable logic he has drawn – partly using exegetical details from Exod 34, and partly making an appeal to his apostolic service which centers on a 'writing of the Spirit' that places its mark on the human lives at Corinth."

letter (3:5–6bc), Paul's ministry is not an exercise in self-recommendation or self-delusion, nor is it an elaborate attempt to swindle his churches. In his "boldness" Paul is therefore confident before the judgment of God (2 Cor. 2:17) precisely because he too, like Moses, has been chosen to speak on God's behalf.

In this respect, rather than presenting a contrast, Paul's παρρησία before God is parallel to the "boldness" associated with Moses in Philo's writings. In *Rer. Div. Her.* 20 Moses is described as having such "boldness" (παρρησία) before God that he not only speaks to God, but also cries out with true emotion (pointing to Exod. 5:22; 32:32; Num. 11:12 f, 22).[33] Paul too exhibits such emotion in Rom. 9:1–3, again concerning Israel's rebellion against God, and in 1 Cor. 15:31; 2 Cor. 1:8; 12:8; etc. concerning his own sufferings. In answer to why Moses could be so bold before God, Philo points to Exod. 33:11 to argue that, as the wise one, Moses is the "friend of God," and "frankness of speech (παρρησία) is akin to friendship" *(Rer. Div. Her.* 21). "For to whom should a man speak with frankness (παρρησιάσαιτο) but to his friend?" *(Rer. Div. Her.* 21). In *Rer. Div. Her.* 27 Moses thus confesses in view of his calling in Ex. 4:12, in which he is given his speech, that God is his παρρησία and tells God "frankly" (παρρησίας) that he has no gift of speech or eloquence *(De Sac.* 12). In the same way, in 2 Cor. 3:4–12 Paul moves from his own call, patterned on that of Moses, to his παρρησία. And like Moses, Paul too was apparently known for his lack of eloquence (2 Cor. 10:10). Like Moses in *Rer. Div. Her.* 27, Paul is confident before God, but his confidence comes from God (2 Cor. 3:4 f.) and not from his own superiority.[34] Finally, for Philo the apologetic point of Moses' παρρησία is to contrast him with those pseudo-mystics of his day who hide their secret rules from the people (cf. *De Spec. Leg.* I.321). Such workers of mischief are admonished to "feel shame" and to hide themselves for concealing their message *(De Spec. Leg.* I.321). In contrast, if the message is of value, "Let those who serve the common good use παρρησία and walk in daylight in the marketplace with their message" (I.321). Against this backdrop, Paul is not ashamed of his gospel (Rom. 1:16), preaches it openly with παρρησία (2 Cor. 3:12), and rejects the hidden ways of deception which are based on a message which has been adulterated (2 Cor. 4:1 f.). Thus, if Philo's description of Moses' "boldness" represented a more widespread tradition, then Paul's use of this concept at this point certainly carried with it several important allusions and implications.

In addition, for Paul it is the work of the Spirit, in making alive those who have accepted Paul's Gospel, which testifies to the genuine nature of his apostleship and of his claim that the new covenant of the new age has now

---

[33] Texts and trans. for these passages from F.H. Colson and G.H. Whitaker, *Philo, Vol. IV,* LCL, 1949 and F.H. Colson, *Philo, Vol. VII,* LCL, 1950.

[34] The basis of Paul's comparison between his ministry and that of Moses thus stands in contrast to Philo's evaluation of Moses' lack of boldness in *Quod Deterius Potiori insidiari solet* 38 and *De Sacrificiis Abelis et Caini* 12, where Philo argues that Moses' lack of eloquence in Exod. 4:10 was his rejection of sophistic rhetoric so that his boldness consisted in his frank declaration of this fact (see above, chapter one, pp. 76–79). Moreover, instead of his own shortcomings, Philo argues that Moses' lack of sufficiency was related to Israel's desire to believe that which was merely plausible (τοῖς εὐλόγοις) or probable *(Vit. Mos.* I, 174), rather than God's "unfailing truthfulness" *(Vit. Mos.* I, 196; cf. II, 261).

arrived among God's people (3:6c). The fact that Paul's apostolic ministry mediates the Spirit is evidence that his διακονία mediates the glory of God among the people of God, not for their condemnation and destruction, but to bring about their life as an expression of the righteousness of God (3:7–11). Therefore, Paul is confident (3:4) and bold (3:12) because he knows that he is a mediator of the glory of God as revealed in and through the ministry of the new covenant in the new age. In turn, this boldness supports his legitimacy as an apostle, since it points directly to God's approval of his life and message. For Paul's free and open behavior as an apostle (3:4, 12) derives not from his own "sufficiency" (3:5–6a), but from his confidence that God has called him and is therefore at work through his suffering and ministry of the Spirit to reveal his own glory through the knowledge of Jesus Christ (3:6bc, 7–11; cf. 2 Cor. 2:14–3:3; 4:6–15).

2. Τέλος and the Use of Exodus 32–34 in 2 Cor. 3:13

But Paul does not stop here. Instead, as v. 13 indicates, he returns once again to Exod. 34:29–35 in order to illustrate the difference between his own boldness in mediating the glory of God through the Gospel and Moses' veiling himself.[35] This verse has been the subject of much debate, concerning both its meaning and its ensuing implications for the comparison now introduced. The reason for this, as Stegemann has pointed out, is that 3:13 is the verse "which must carry the entire load of the dominant exegesis" of this passage.[36] Moreover, at the center of the debate has been the meaning of τέλος, concerning which, as Renwick has pointed out, "to date ... no solution ... has proven satisfactory."[37] Beginning with Windisch and Shulz, the dominant approach has been to take Paul's statement to refer to Moses' practice of hiding from Israel the fact that the glory on his face was coming to an end (τὸ τέλος) because of its fading nature (τοῦ καταργουμένου).[38] Viewed as a parallel to Romans 10:4,

---

[35] Although not a direct quotation of a single text from Exod. 34:29–35, Koch, *Schrift*, pp. 16 f., classifies 3:13 as an "(extended) paraphrase" of a larger paragraph, though he observes that it stands on the border of being a citation which is not explicitly introduced as such, since it has close affinities to both Exod. 34:33b and 34:35b. As such, 3:13 refers to the entire paragraph of Exod. 34:29–35, which reaches its climax in Moses' veiling himself.

[36] E. Stegemann, "Der Neue Bund im Alten, Zum Schriftverständnis des Paulus in II Kor 3," *ThZ* 42 (1986) 97–114, p. 112.

[37] *Temple*, p. 136.

[38] Besides the various commentaries, see chapter three and the influence of this "exegetical orthodoxy" on the views of e.g. van Unnik, "With Unveiled face," p. 162; Kurt Stalder, *Das Werk des Geistes in der Heiligung bei Paulus*, 1962, p. 52; J. Jeremias, art. Μωϋσῆς, *TDNT* 4 (1967) 848–873, p. 869; K. Prümm, *Diakonia Pneumatos. Der Zweite Korintherbrief als Zugang zur Apostolischen Botschaft, Bd I: Theologische Auslegung des Zweiten Korintherbriefes*, 1967, pp. 134–137; Heikki Räisänen, *Paul and the Law*, 1986 (1983), pp. 56 f.; and C.J.A. Hickling, "The Sequence of Thought in II Corinthians, Chapter Three,"

Moses' use of the veil was his attempt to keep the transitoriness of his ministry and authority, and thus the "end" (in the sense of "termination") of the old covenant itself, from the people.[39] Put in its best light, Moses did so because of the rebellious nature of the people, or because of the divine purpose to harden Israel (of which Moses was or was not aware),[40] or as a reference to the eventual end of the old covenant with the coming of Christ and the Gospel.[41] But other commentators have not stopped short of understanding Paul to be accusing Moses of duplicitous actions because of deceitful motives.[42] In con-

---

NTS 21 (1975) 380–395, p. 390, who attributes Moses' actions to the reverential motive of protecting the sacred character of the glory as it faded, since in Exod. 34:29 ff. the glory was "a kind of phosphorescence" that was bound to fade when away from its source. Hence, "no one was likely to have been surprised at this gradual dimming of the light" (p. 391); and Koch, *Schrift*, pp. 334 f., who accepts the standard view that Paul interprets the function of the veil negatively as the means of hiding the end of that which was "fading." Paul thus deliberately goes beyond the textual basis of Exod. 34:30–35 (p. 334). This view has again been championed by Belleville, *Reflections of Glory*, pp. 201 f.

[39] So already H.A.W. Meyer, *Critical and Exegetical Hand-Book to the Epistles to the Corinthians*, ET from 5th German ed., reprint 1979 (1883), pp. 472 f., and recently, Hofius, "Gesetz und Evangelium," pp. 96, 102 (following the commentaries of Weiss, Bachmann, Plummer, Furnish, Lietzmann, Kümmel, Wendland, Bultmann). As an unusual variation on this position, Prümm, *Diakonia Pneumatos*, pp. 138 f., argues that τέλος in 3:13 means "end," but in Rom. 10:4 means "goal," since in the latter text Paul is referring only to the "non-legalistic" sections of the OT, not to the Law itself. In contrast, 2 Cor. 3:13 has the "legalistic" view of the old covenant in mind. But as we have seen in chapter two, Prümm's distinction between the promise and the legal aspects of the OT, with "letter" referring to the Law itself, cannot be supported from 3:6.

[40] So Hofius, "Gesetz und Evangelium," p. 105, who points to the parallel use of πρὸς τό in Matt. 26:12, where the woman did not know the real significance of her actions. Thus, in 2 Cor. 3:13 Moses veils himself so that *God's* intention to keep Israel from seeing the fading of the glory and its deeper significance for the end of the Law might be fulfilled. But unlike Matt. 26:12, there is no explanation in the present text of the "real" significance of the action from a third party. The most natural reading of the text is to take the purpose clause to refer directly back to Moses; it is his intention which is in view.

[41] See e.g. Morna D. Hooker, "Beyond the Things that are written? St. Paul's Use of Scripture," *NTS* 27 (1981) 295–309, p. 304, who argues that Paul's point was that the Law's true role was to witness to Christ, so that when Christ comes, the Mosaic ministry is superseded; for this same view, see recently Stockhausen, *Moses' Veil*, pp. 120, 126, who views the point of καταργέω in vv. 7, 10, 13 to be that "Moses' veiling himself had to do with the eventual ending of his own service and the passing away of the covenant he brought in the inauguration of that which replaced and surpassed it." Stockhausen thus suggests that τέλος here is "deliberately ambiguous" and means both temporal end and completion or fulfillment (pp. 126 f.). She can conclude this, however, only because of her understanding of the syntactical function of καταργέω in vv. 7,13 as a reference to what is taking place in Paul's day (for a critique of this view, see chapter four).

[42] Cf. e.g. C.K. Barrett, *A Commentary on the Second Epistle to the Corinthians*, HNTC, 1973, p. 119, who sees the point to be that "Moses did not act towards the children of Israel with the same complete frankness that Paul employed ..."; J. S. Vos, *Traditionsgeschichtliche Untersuchungen zur Paulinischen Pneumatologie*, Van Gorcum's Theologische Bibliotheek, Nr. 47, 1973, p. 139, who sees Paul accusing Moses of "Heimlichkeit und Verfälschung der Wahrheit"; Gerd Theißen, "Die Hülle des Mose," pp. 125, 142, who sees Paul attributing to the veil a "betrügerische Funktion" in which it becomes a "Symbol des

trast, whatever the case may be concerning Moses, Paul is both forthright and honest.[43]

As a critique of this traditional view, other scholars have argued that τέλος in 3:13, as in Rom. 10:4, does not mean "end" in the sense of termination, but in the sense of "goal" or "purpose." Paul's point then becomes that Moses veiled himself to keep Israel from seeing the true meaning, or ultimate fulfillment of the (fading or abolished) glory on his face, either as a direct reflection of the pre-existent Christ,[44] or as a pointer to the consummation of the old covenant and/or Law (correctly understood) in Christ or the gospel.[45] On the basis of his

---

Betrugs und der Täuschung"; J. Munck, *Paul and the Salvation of Mankind*, p. 180; Prümm, *Diakonia Pneumatos*, p. 139; and the views of Schulz, Ulonska, Luz, and Klauck referred to by Hofius, "Gesetz und Evangelium," p. 104 and 104 n. 188. To this list, Belleville, *Reflections of Glory*, p. 207 n. 4 adds Menzies, Thrall, Sickenberger, Kuss, and Jervell. Kent and Godet think that Moses was embarrassed (!), cf. Belleville, p. 207 n. 5.

[43] So e.g. Belleville, *Reflections of Glory*, p. 197, who contrasts Paul's "open" and "public" behavior referred to in 3:12 to "Moses' action of veiling (which) serves to prevent public scrutiny of the fading splendor (13b)." For a typical example of the common way in which this same misunderstanding of 3:7, 13 leads to a reading of v. 12 in terms of a contrast between Paul's boldness and Moses' *shame*, see Hans Lietzmann, *An die Korinther I–II*, HNT Bd. 9. 1969⁵, p. 112.

[44] So A.T. Hanson, *Jesus Christ in the Old Testament*, 1965, pp. 27–29, 34, and his *Studies in Paul's Technique and Theology*, 1975, p. 190.

[45] See e.g. R.V.G. Tasker, *The Second Epistle of Paul to the Corinthians*, Tyndale NT Commentaries, 1969 (1958), p. 64; R.P.C. Hanson, *The Second Epistle to the Corinthians*, 1967³, pp. 38, 40; J. Héring, *The Second Epistle of Saint Paul to the Corinthians*, 1968 (ET of 1958 original), pp. 24 f; R.P. Martin, *2 Corinthians*, p. 68 (following Collange), who sees the problem to be that Israel "persisted in looking at a face that symbolized a 'ministration' ... which in turn was on the way out"; W.D. Davies, "Paul and the People of Israel," *NTS* 24 (1978) 4–39, p. 11, and Wright, *Climax*, p. 181. More distinct theologically in relationship to the Law itself is the view of M. Rissi, *Studien zum zweiten Korintherbrief: Der alte Bund – Der Prediger – Der Tod*, AThANT Bd. 56, 1969, pp. 32 f., who follows R. Bring and F. Flückiger in arguing that τέλος in Rom. 10:4 refers to the goal of the Law properly understood as teaching faith, so that in 2 Cor. 3:13 Paul is saying that Israel was kept from seeing the real goal or meaning of the entire old covenant, i.e. Christ (cf. pp. 37). For Rissi, therefore, the glory on Moses' face was, in reality, the glory of the pre-existent Christ, who was already experienced in a hidden sense by those within Israel who believed (p. 41). For the most persuasive presentation of this view, in support of Paul's view of the Law as understood by C.E.B. Cranfield and D.P. Fuller (see Introduction), see T. Provence, "Who is Sufficient," pp. 74–77. Provence sees the meaning of τέλος as "goal" to be the key to understanding 3:13 (p. 75), in parallel to this same meaning in Rom. 10:4 and throughout the Pauline corpus (p. 75 n. 60). As in Rom. 10:4, here too the "goal" is Christ (p. 76), so that Moses' veil kept the Israelites from seeing that the goal of the glory of God revealed by Moses was faith in Christ as the source of salvation (pp. 76 f.). As a result, Israel sought to establish her own righteousness, rather than trusting in God (Rom. 10:3) (p. 77). Provence's basic view is also followed by William J. Dumbrell, "Paul's Use of Exodus 34 in 2 Corinthians 3," in *God Who is Rich in Mercy, FS D.B. Knox*, ed. Peter T. O'Brien and David G. Peterson, 1986, pp. 179–194, pp. 187, 192 n. 12. But despite Provence's insights concerning the function of the Spirit in relationship to the Law and the centrality of Israel's hard hearts in Paul's argument in 2 Cor. 3 (see chapter two and below), this view suffers under its acceptance of the traditional meaning of καταργέω as "to fade away," so that Provence is

understanding of κατασγέω as referring to this age in contrast to the eschatological age to come, Stegemann has even suggested that τέλος refers both to the "Ende des Endlichen" or the "Aufhören des Zeitlichen" and to the goal of that which comes after this abolishment of time.[46] He thus suggests the translation "Ausgang" in the double sense of "Ende" and "Anfang."[47] Yet whatever the case, in all these views it remains the Law or the old covenant[48] (or Israel's

---

forced to make an artificial distinction between the "trappings of the Old Covenant" which are "passing away" (p. 76) and the Law, properly understood, which remains, while Dumbrell's view is based on taking κατασγέω to mean that the glory itself was in the process of being abolished. Moreover, Provence must see v. 14a to be a restatement of the point of v. 13, which loses sight of the fact that it was the glory on Moses' face which was veiled in v. 13 and not Israel, thereby missing the force of the ἀλλά in v. 14a. This view has also been argued by Richard B. Hays, *Echoes of Scripture in the Letters of Paul*, 1989, pp. 137–139, though he rejects the idea that the glory was fading (see chapter four). For Hays, however, the τέλος is Moses himself as "the person transfigured in the image of God, who is the true aim of the old covenant," which can then be identified with Christ, as in Rom. 10:4 (p. 137), with the Gospel itself (cf. p. 144), and then ultimately with the church as the eschatological covenant community being transformed by the Spirit (cf. pp. 151 f.). Hays can make these associations because, for him, Moses in 3:13 becomes "a complex parable, figuring forth the tension between ignorance and knowledge, hiddenness and revelation" (p. 144; cf. p. 151). Finally, Peter Jones, *La Deuxieme Epitre de Paul aux Corinthiens*, CEB 14, 1992, pp. 77 f., takes τέλος to mean "goal" and attempts to overcome the difficulty inherent in positing that Moses concealed the Christological context of the old covenant from Israel by arguing that the opportune moment had not yet come within the history of redemption for making this truth known (pointing esp. to Rom. 16:25 and Eph. 3:5 as parallel notions). But, against all these attempts, it must be emphasized that, unlike Rom. 10:4, τέλος in 2 Cor. 3:13 is explicitly *not* interpreted in terms of Christ, nor any other reality beyond the old covenant itself, which would have been an easy move had this been Paul's intention. These attempts all see symbols and metaphors where Paul is continuing to describe a historical occurrence.

[46] "Neue Bund," p. 112.

[47] "Neue Bund," p. 112. Hence, for Stegemann, Moses' goal is to keep Israel from seeing the exit of the temporal and the fading, as well as that which comes when time and history give way to the eternal (p. 112). Stegemann's interpretation thus substitutes an abstract interpretation of Paul's thought for the context of Exod. 34.

[48] In addition to the sources listed above (nn. 38, 39), see now Hofius, "Gesetz und Evangelium," p. 106, in support of his consistent application of the traditional law/Gospel contrast throughout 3:6–18 (cf. pp. 80–86, 107–113). For its classic presentations, see the positions of Windisch and Schulz outlined in chapter four, and that of Adolf Deissmann's *Paul, A Study in Social and Religious History*, trans. W.E. Wilson, 1926[2], p. 180, who sees Paul's "polemic against Moses" in 3:13 ff. as probably "the strongest instance" of the fact that Paul was "often a harsh opponent of the Law." For more recent examples of this move, see Lietzmann, *An die Korinther*, p. 113; A.T. Hanson, *Studies*, p. 152, who can speak of Moses' role as mediator as indicating "the inferior nature of the relationship between God and Israel established by the Torah"; and Seyoon Kim, *The Origin of Paul's Gospel*, WUNT 2 Reihe, Bd. 4, 1981, p. 239, who concludes that Moses "has something to hide because of the defective nature of his ministry, and that it is not his gospel, but the Mosaic law that is veiled." But as we have seen, Moses' role as mediator is not established by the Law, but by Israel's hardened hearts and sin; while what is veiled in v. 13 is not the Law, but the glory of God!

perverted understanding of it as teaching legalism,[49] or her fixation on the text as an end in itself[50]) that becomes devalued and rejected in comparison to the Gospel.[51] Moreover, inasmuch as there is no mention in Exod. 34:29ff. of either motive for Moses' act of veiling himself, much less that the glory was fading, it is common fare to conclude that Paul willfully goes beyond, or even against, the OT text[52] and in doing so, in the words of R.H. Strachan, "cannot be acquitted of a clever attempt to score off his opponents ...."[53]

---

[49] So Provence, "Who is Sufficient," pp. 76 f.

[50] So Hays, *Echoes*, p. 137

[51] For Stegemann, "Neue Bund," pp. 112 f., the glory of Moses is "eine nur irdische und dem Vergänglichen zugehörende Herrlichkeit." Moreover, the veil on their hearts in 3:15 means that they cannot see that Christ is the "Ausgang" of the Law (p. 113). See now Renwick's study, whose central point concerning 3:13–18 is that a "fundamental shift" has taken place in Paul's use of δόξα from that of 3:7–11 *(Temple*, p. 133). In his view, rather than referring to God's glory as a symbol of apostolic authority, in contrast to the "undesirable" glory of the Mosaic covenant, in 3:13–18 it refers to the more desirable "religious 'blessing' given to God's people in general" in the new covenant (pp. 158, 135, cf. pp. 112, 121, 124). Thus, he must end up agreeing with Furnish that, by implication, Paul is speaking pejoratively and unflatteringly of the old covenant and the Law themselves (p. 134 n. 21). Hence, although Renwick recognizes that the major issue in Exod. 33:1–17 was the problem of God's presence dwelling in the midst of a sinful people (cf. pp. 54, 142–144), and that *this* was the reason for Moses' use of the veil (cf. pp. 54, 142–144 and below), he does not apply this insight consistently to his exegesis of the passage. In the end, the contrast for Renwick ends up being between two distinct natures of the glory of God revealed in the old and new covenants respectfully, and thus between the nature of the covenants *themselves*, rather than between the two conditions of the people to whom God's glory is manifest.

[52] Besides those scholars listed in ch. four, nn. 92–93, 131, cf. e.g. H.J. Schoeps, *Paul: The Theology of the Apostle in the Light of Jewish Religious History*, 1961, p. 183 n. 2, who calls Paul's interpretation "fantastic"; Lietzmann, *An die Korinther*, p. 112, who concludes that Paul's interpretation "unquestionably contradicts" the OT text; Josef M. Kastner, *Moses im Neuen Testament, Eine Untersuchung der Mosetradition in den neutestamentlichen Schriften*, Diss. München, 1967, p. 199, who declares that it is "astounding how Paul, without giving it a thought, springs beyond the meaning of the Scripture for the sake of his train of argument"; E. Richard, "Polemics, Old Testament, and Theology, A Study of II Cor. 3:1–4:6," *RB* 88 (1981) 340–367, p. 344, who asserts concerning Paul in 3:13, 16, "that he reads more into the text than was intended ... is not in doubt ..."; Theobald, *Gnade*, pp. 195 f., who sees Paul going beyond the OT text in that Paul asserts by implication that Moses creates the "illusion" that the glory remains when it does not, while in fact the OT text speaks of its brilliance as that which made it impossible for Israel to endure the glory; Peter von der Osten-Sacken, "Die Decke des Mose, Zur Exegese und Hermeneutik von Geist und Buchstabe in 2 Korinther 3," in his *Die Heiligkeit der Tora*, 1989, pp. 87–115, p. 102, who argues that Paul takes the text against its original meaning in which it was intended to protect Israel from the shine of Moses' face; and Hofius, "Gesetz und Evangelium," p. 104, who sees 3:13 to be "in erheblicher Spannung" to Exod. 34:29–35 so that Paul's view becomes an "eigentümlichen Interpretation." For in Hofius' view, "Mit dieser Interpretation von Exod. 34:33–35 trägt Paulus eine theologische Erkenntnis in den biblischen Bericht ein, die er zunächst ganz unabhängig von diesem Text und im Blick auf das Israel seiner Zeit und Gegenwart gewonnen hat" (p. 106). But Hofius' view is based on his interpretation of 3:13 as a reference to Moses' being veiled when he *spoke* to Israel, which Exod. 34:33; 34:3

(Footnote n. 53 see below page 352)

Although none of these interpretations of Paul's statement in 3:13 are to be accepted, their common recognition of its apologetic force is certainly correct.[54] That Paul is again building an argument for the legitimacy of his apostleship in 3:12 ff. is beyond doubt. For although the main clause of v. 13 is elided, the negative particle οὐ clearly relates to the unexpressed thought of Paul's bold preaching referred to in v. 12. The point is that Paul is *not ministering* καθάπερ Μωϋσῆς ἐτίθει κάλυμμα ἐπὶ τὸ πρόσωπον αὐτοῦ.[55] Moreover,

---

clearly denies, and his acceptance of the usual understanding of καταργέω. The latter point has been taken up in chapter four; in regard to the former, it need merely be observed that in 3:13 there is no mention of Moses' speaking to Israel when veiled, but merely of his veiling himself as a general practice. Moreover, the quote of Exod. 34:34 in 3:16 indicates that Paul was clearly aware that Moses did in fact remove the veil during the periods of theophanic activity, which included the deliverance of YHWH's message. Finally, see Stockhausen, *Moses' Veil*, pp. 124 f., who calls Paul's use of Exod. 34:29 ff. here an "unabashed interpretation" since "There is absolutely no way to justify such a conclusion about Moses' veil from the text of Exodus 34:29-35 alone, but II Cor. 3:13a states Paul's viewpoint very clearly. Paul's interpretation of Exodus 34:33-34 is guided by a simple presupposition – we are not like Moses." Stockhausen's view is based on her conviction that Paul himself supplies the motive for Moses' action, which is not present, "even implicitly" in the original narrative (p. 97). But in Stockhausen's view, Paul was not "'reading into' the text of Exodus a perspective of his own ..." (p. 120). Instead, his interpretation is derived from the prophetic promises behind 3:6, which led him to conclude that the glory on Moses' face must be fading in his own day (cf. p. 120). For a critique of this view, see chapter four. At this point it may be pointed out that in spite of her own emphasis on the narrative nature of Exod. 34:29 ff. and the consequent need to read "the whole story" (cf. pp. 96, 101 n. 30), Stockhausen fails to put this text into its larger context and thus misses the motive for Moses' action supplied by the Exodus narrative itself.

[53] *The Second Epistle of Paul to the Corinthians*, MNTC Vol. 8, 1948[5], p. 87.

[54] So too E. Stegemann, "Neue Bund," p. 103, who rightly opposes Theißen's view, "Die Hülle des Mose," p. 136, that Paul's supposed transformation of the OT text indicates that Paul did not have his opponents in view (since they would never be convinced by his violent reinterpretation of the text!), but only the Corinthians, since the Corinthians too knew themselves to be "distanced" from the OT! Stegemann rightly points out, p. 104, that this entire approach is based on the view that the glory is fading in 3:7 and 3:13, for which there is no support in the OT or Jewish tradition. On the other hand, Stegemann also emphasizes that Paul's argument is not dependent upon that of his opponents (p. 105). For Stegemann's own solution to the problem of the meaning of καταργέω, which differs from that which is argued here, see chapter four, n.137.

[55] Contra Theobald, *Gnade*, pp. 192 ff., whose exposition of this text is built on the unusual and unconvincing attempt to read οὐ καθάπερ Μωϋσῆς as a contrast to 3:18, with 3:13b-17 being one long parenthesis in Paul's argument. Rather, this is an example of an abbreviation of a main clause in a comparison; cf. the discussion of aposiopesis in F. Blass, A. Debrunner, and R. W. Funk, *A Greek Grammar of the New Testament*, 1961, § 482, though 3:13 is not an aposiopesis in the strict sense, which does not occur in the NT; cf. Hofius, "Gesetz und Evangelium," p. 115 n. 232. So too now Belleville, *Reflections of Glory*, p. 177, who rejects M. Theobald's structural analysis of 3:12-18 because, among other problems, "it overlooks the basic conceptual and grammatical contrast between 'we are very bold' in v. 12 and 'not as Moses' in v. 13." Belleville, p. 177, also rightly rejects Theobald's attempt to play down the significance of v. 16 in Paul's argument and to regard v. 17 as merely transitive in function based on his attempt to read vv. 14c and 16 as conceptually parallel (see below).

when interpreted against the background of Exod. 32–34 already picked up in 3:7–11, and with a more appropriate view of the meaning of καταργέω (see chapter four), Paul's point is quite different than usually portrayed, regardless of how τέλος has been construed. For as in 3:7, Paul's use of the imperfect ἐτίθει in v. 13 refers to Moses' repeated practice of having to veil his face *due to the hard hearts of the people*.[56] Here too, the time frame throughout 3:13 is the past of Moses' day.[57] At this point, however, Paul turns his attention from the *consequences* of Moses' ministry in the midst of the rebellious people, which formed the heart of the comparison in 3:7–11, to the distinction in *purpose* between Moses' veiling himself and his own ministry of preaching the gospel openly. Whereas in 3:7–11 Paul based his comparison between the ministries of the old and new covenants upon their different *results*, in 3:13 he bases his comparison on the corresponding difference in the *goals* of the two ministries. But in both cases it is the same glory of God which is being mediated through the respective ministries of Paul and Moses.

This change in focus is reflected in the move from the result clause of v. 7b (ὥστε + inf.), with its emphasis on Israel's inability to gaze into Moses' face, to the purpose clause of v. 13b (πρὸς τό + inf.).[58] When the two clauses are compared directly it becomes clear that the purpose clause of v. 13b is merely the corresponding response to the reality already described in v. 7b:

---

[56] Hughes, *Second Epistle to the Corinthians*, p. 108, has also argued that the purpose of the veil was to keep Israel from seeing the glory of God, since it was "entirely incompatible with the wickedness of a rebellious and stiff-necked people (cf. Exod. 32) …," though he continues to view the glory itself as impermanent. But Hughes rightly understands the veiling of Moses to be "a kind of enacted parable" pointing to Israel's iniquities and "a condemnation of the people." Against the traditional view, Hughes points out that it "confuses the issue at this stage in Paul's argument by proposing that it was not the glory but the *fading* of the glory which Moses was intent on hiding from the people," which can only be interpreted ultimately as attributing to Moses the practice of a "subterfuge, and this to Paul would have been unthinkable" (p. 109). Yet because Hughes accepts the idea that the glory was fading, he must argue that Israel also knew this fact, and that when the glory had fully faded away, Moses would remove the veil until he returned to the tent of meeting to have the glory "renewed" (p. 109). For Hughes, therefore, τέλος must refer to "duration," meaning here "right on to the end," "so that the people might not gaze right to the end of the glory which was passing away" (p. 109). But there is no evidence either in Exod. 34 or in 2 Cor. 3 that Moses did not continue to veil himself, for as we have seen, the point of the text is that the glory did not fade away at all.

[57] So too Koch, *Schrift*, p. 334.

[58] For 13b as a purpose clause, see Windisch, *Der zweite Korintherbrief*, p. 120, Provence, "Who is Sufficient," p. 74, 74 f. n. 55, Stegemann, "Neue Bund," p. 112, Hofius, "Gesetz und Evangelium," p. 103, Vollenweider, "2 Kor 3," p. 250 n. 252, and with substantial argumentation, Belleville, *Reflections of Glory*, p. 200. It is not clear, however, how seeing 3:13b as a purpose clause rather than result will solve the difficulty of the transition to the ἀλλά of v. 14b, as Belleville maintains, since both purpose and result clauses are final, main points of arguments, so that she too must try to relate v. 14b directly to v. 13b. A different reading of the logic in 3:12–14 is needed (see below).

3:7ba: ὥστε   μὴ δύνασθαι   ἀτενίσαι   τοὺς υἱοὺς Ἰσραήλ

3:13ba: πρὸς τὸ   μὴ   ἀτενίσαι   τοὺς υἱοὺς Ἰσραήλ

3:7bb: εἰς τὸ πρόσωπον ... δόξαν τ. προσώπου αὐτοῦ τὴν καταργουμένην

3:13bb: εἰς τὸ τέλος   τοῦ καταργουμένου

As this comparison reveals, in v. 7b Paul pointed to the effects of the *glory* mediated by Moses among the "stiff-necked" people, which necessitated his use of the veil: On the one hand, because of her hardened condition, Israel was not able to gaze continuously into the glory on the face of Moses because it would destroy the rebellious people; on the other hand, because of Israel's hardened condition, Moses wore the veil both to embody this judgment and to grant the accompanying mercy of the renewed covenant. For as we have seen in chapter three, since the covenant had been renewed, the people could encounter God's glory during those periods in which Moses spoke the words of the Lord to Israel, but they could no longer enjoy his uninterrupted presence in their midst. In v. 13b Paul makes this purpose of the veil explicit by calling attention to *Moses'* corresponding intention *itself* in veiling the glory of God: he veiled himself *in order that* in their "stiff-necked" state Israel could not gaze εἰς τὸ τέλος τοῦ καταργουμένου.[59]

---

[59] To my knowledge, the only other persons to suggest this position in our century have been Oostendorp, *Another Jesus*, p. 39, and now, independently of this study, Renwick, *Temple*, pp. 54, 138–144. On the one hand, Oostendorp recognized not only that "there is no hint at all in the Old Testament account that the brightness on Moses' face faded," but also that "above all, Paul has just forcefully argued that the insufficiency of Moses' ministry and glory is found in its very essence, namely, that it brings only condemnation and death, so that it is inconceivable that in v. 13 he must resort to the exegetical trick of deducing from the fact that Moses wore a veil that Moses' glory faded." Oostendorp pointed out that, in view of v. 7, it is the inability of the Israelites to look at the glory of Moses' face which provides the purpose for Moses' veil in v. 13. For "if Moses had allowed the full glory of the Lord to shine forth, it would have meant the destruction of the children of Israel because his ministry was incapable of conferring the righteousness needed to stand in the presence of the holy God" (pp. 39 f.; cf. p. 40 n. 34 where he supports this perspective by referring to Exod. 33:3,5!). "Therefore, this veil at the high point of the Old Testament revelation does not only conceal part of God's glory, but it is also a sign of God's grace, for it shows that he is unwilling to reveal His glory if it means the total destruction of His people. And then the ministry of Moses and of the precepts of the law point beyond themselves to the time when God will confer righteousness on man and take this veil away" (p. 40). On the other hand, Renwick too asserts that there is no evidence to support those who take τέλος to mean termination based on the fading nature of Moses' glory, and thus argues that it must mean "goal" or "outcome" (p. 138). Moreover, he too argues that the key to Paul's thought is reading Exod. 34:29 ff. within the context of Exod. 32–34 (cf. p. 142–144). The goal of the old covenant manifestation of the glory of God, as exemplified by the γράμμα in 3:6, can thereby be seen to be to effect the death and condemnation of those who gaze upon it (pp. 139, 142), so that, "more precisely, the Mosaic experience of God (as represented by the δόξα on Moses' face) ... leads to death and condemnation" (p. 140). Hence, what is being abolished in 3:13 is the "outcome" of old covenant, i.e. its *goal* of condemnation (p. 141). Τέλος therefore

In the context, the parallel between 3:7b and 13b makes it evident that here too the passive meaning of καταργέω conveys the action of being rendered inoperative or ineffective. As such, it assumes that Moses' veil is the agent of this action, as now confirmed by 3:13a itself. Moses continually placed a veil upon his face (3:13a), in order that the sons of Israel might not gaze εἰς τὸ τέλος of that which was continually (present tense participle) being rendered ineffective (τοῦ καταργουμένου, 3:13b) by the veil.[60] The repetition of the neuter form of the participle in 3:13 recalls its earlier inclusive referent to the old covenant *as a whole*, with its results and underlying theological purpose (3:9–10), rather than referring solely to the glory of God on Moses' face as in 3:7b.[61] In 3:13b, Paul once again intends to assert that Moses' veil kept the old covenant ministry from accomplishing what it would have had it not been stopped by this covering.

---

refers to the effect on the old covenant members of gazing on the glory of Moses' face, since to continue to gaze at Moses would kill them; it was this outcome of the old covenant that Moses brought to an end with the veil (pp. 141–142). As Renwick himself recognizes, this is close to the view represented here (cf. p. 140, where he refers to my work as the only other in support of this position). But since Renwick equates the outcome of the old covenant glory with the old covenant itself, the γράμμα with the Law, and the condemnation which the old covenant brings with the "Mosaic experience of God," he ends up with a different conclusion concerning the contrasts between Paul and Moses being made in 2 Cor. 3. In his view, an encounter with the Mosaic appearance of glory "is not merely not necessary in the present (the point of 3:7–11 in Renwick's view), but that it is in fact quite undesirable – because this δόξα, at least as made manifest in the old covenant ... will literarily kill you if you fix your gaze upon it (ἀτενίζω, 3:13): if you allow yourselves to desire it intensely, as if, for example, salvation depended upon it" (p. 144; cf. p. 156). Indeed, in Renwick's view, p. 158, "the Mosaic pattern of δόξα as some kind of radiance (as in Exodus 34) – literal or figurative – was demonstrated by Paul to be no longer necessary, desirable, or authoritative for Christian experience in the present age (II Cor. 3:7–16)." The point of this present study, however, is that salvation *does* depend upon encountering this very glory, the thing which Israel, in her hard-hearted state, could not do! Indeed, Renwick's view here is hard to reconcile with his own later emphasis that the point of 3:17–18 is that all Christians should be like Moses, albeit now by encountering YHWH in the Spirit (cf. p. 155).

[60] The power of the traditional view over the rendering of καταργέω in 3:7–11 and 3:13b can be seen in Belleville, *Reflections of Glory*, pp. 204 f. Though she recognizes the meaning of the verb as "to render powerless" or "useless" in Heb. 2:14 and Lk. 13:7, and even argues that its meaning is "to cause to become idle," "to render inoperative," etc., rather than "to abolish" or "to do away with" in 1 Cor. 15:56; Gal. 3:17; Rom. 4:14, etc. (p. 204 n. 3), her view of the glory as fading leads her to reject this meaning for 2 Cor. 3:13b, and to take the verb as a middle (cf. p. 205).

[61] So too Barrett, *Second Corinthians*, p. 119; Hooker, "Beyond the Things that are written?" p. 299; Furnish, *II Corinthians*, p. 207; Belleville, *Reflections of Glory*, p. 203; contra those who, like Hofius, "Gesetz und Evangelium," p. 102, relate it only to the δόξα on Moses' face as in v. 7, which is, of course, feminine in gender. Nor could it, however, be a reference to the Law in particular as Barrett suggests, which would require a masculine form, though Koch's argument against taking it to refer to the Law or old covenant, *Schrift*, p. 334 n. 16, based on the fact that in v. 14 the old covenant is still being read, misses the point of v. 14 (see below). Koch's own view that the neuter form points to the fact that the glory is no longer in the foreground of Paul's thought, but has been replaced by the "Vorgang des

Viewed from this perspective, the numerous debates over the precise meaning of the ambiguous phrase εἰς τὸ τέλος receive new light. Recent studies have shown that the range of meaning for τέλος includes the idea of "end" both in the sense of "abolishment" or "termination," and in the sense of "outcome," "consequence," "goal," or even "purpose."[62] The question becomes which of these two basic meanings is appropriate *here*. Two considerations speak in favor of the latter.

First, if τέλος in the sense of "abolishment" were Paul's meaning, then his purpose statement would revert to a useless tautology, given the denotation of καταργέω: Moses veiled himself in order that the sons of Israel might not gaze "into the abolishment of that which was being abolished (in regard to its effects)." Those who argue most cogently for this meaning for τέλος in its present context can only do so, therefore, on the basis of understanding τοῦ καταργουμένου to mean "fade away"; though even this rendering leads to a redundancy in Paul's expression.[63] But once this meaning is rejected for the

---

Verbergens selbst und dessen Resultat, die heutige Verborgenheit" (p. 334), is correct as far as it goes, but fails to offer a concrete referent for the participle and labors under the standard view of the meaning of καταργέω. Renwick, *Temple*, p. 137, takes it as a reference to γράμμα in 3:6 as that which represents the old covenant and its goals (see above, n. 59). Lloyd Gaston's suggestion, "Paul and the Torah in 2 Corinthians 3," in his *Paul and the Torah*, 1987, pp. 151–168, pp. 163 f., that it refers "to the more general statement of all charismatic phenomena as transitory in verse 11," is a result of his attempt to exonerate Israel under the old covenant. Gaston's view is based on the meaning of καταργέω as signifying something as "transitory" and his equation of the past and present situations depicted in 2 Cor. 3:11–14 with the *future* situation described in 1 Cor. 13:8–13, since he takes the glory in v. 8 and Paul's hope in v. 12 to be references to a future reality (cf. pp. 158, 161).

[62] See BAGD, *A Greek-English Lexicon*, pp. 811 f., and its confirmation in W. Bauer, K. Aland, and B. Aland, *Griechisch-deutsches Wörterbuch*, 1988⁶, pp. 1617 f. The critical response of Hofius, "Gesetz und Evangelium," pp. 110 f., to the work of R. Badenas, *Christ the End of the Law. Romans 10:4 in Pauline Perspective*, JSNT Supplement Series 10, 1985, p. 79, in which Badenas argues that "Τέλος with genitive is generally used in expressions indicating result, purpose, outcome, and fate, not termination," together with Hofius' list of instances on p. 103 n. 175 in which it means "termination," illustrates that the issue finally revolves not around which meaning is more prominent, but which meaning is called for in any given context. For this reason, the highly controversial text of Rom. 10:4 should intentionally be excluded from determining Paul's meaning in 2 Cor. 3:13.

[63] For an example of this redundancy, see the translation offered by Stockhausen, *Moses' Veil*, p. 88: "so that the sons of Israel might not continue to gaze upon the end of what is being brought to an end," and that of Furnish, *II Corinthians*, p. 201, who rejects the translation "fading" for καταργέω, but still renders the meaning, "so the Israelites could not gaze at the end of what was being annulled." The tautological nature of the common translation of τέλος as "termination" has also been recognized and stressed by Prümm, *Diakonia Pneumatos*, p. 139 (though he keeps it); Provence, "Who is Sufficient," p. 76 n. 62; and most insightfully by H. Ridderbos, *Paul, An Outline of His Theology*, 1975, pp. 219 f. n. 28. Ridderbos rejects the traditional view that the glory was fading and interprets the purpose of the veil to be to hide the glory itself as "the clear sense not only of Exod. 34, but also of the whole argument of Paul." He thus renders τέλος to mean "summit" or "fullness," as a reference to the glory on Moses' face. But Ridderbos continues to accept the usual view of καταργέω as a reference to the passing away, not of the glory, but of the old covenant as a whole.

participle, the meaning of "termination" for τέλος also becomes difficult to sustain.[64]

Second, the meaning of τέλος as "aim" is confirmed by the backdrop of Exod. 32–34.[65] For Furnish is right in objecting that "Proponents of the second view have in general not been persuasive in their explanations of *why* Paul thought Moses wanted to hide the aim of the old covenant – that is Christ – from Israel ... or *how* the veil could have done that."[66] *But the problem with past attempts to read τέλος in this way has been their assumption that its referent in this context is Christ.* Yet the parallel indicated above between τέλος in 3:13b and "the face of Moses because of the glory of his face" in 3:7b demonstrates that Paul is now simply summarizing in one word what he described at length earlier. That this is the case was already seen by those responsible for the textual variant τὸ πρόσωπον as an attempt to relieve v. 13b of its ambiguity.[67] Within the context of 2 Cor. 3:7, 13, therefore, the specific denotation of τὸ τέλος in v. 13 is "the end" in the sense of "the outcome," "consequence," or

---

[64] This latter point has been well made by Hays, *Echoes*, p. 136. He concludes that once the idea of "fading" is rejected for the participle, "there is really no other possibility" other than "aim," or "purpose" for τέλος.

[65] So too Renwick, *Temple*, pp. 138–142, though with very different results.

[66] *II Corinthians*, p. 207. Furnish's criticism also applies to Gaston's suggestion, "Paul and the Torah in 2 Corinthians 3," p. 164, that the veil keeps Paul's opponents, as representatives of Israel, from seeing "through the veil to learn that the present transitory phenomena of the Christian ministry have a *telos*, a goal." See too Vollenweider, "2 Kor 3," p. 250 n. 252, who objects against past attempts to read τέλος as "goal" that they have failed to explain Paul's negation in v. 13, which read from the traditional understanding of v. 13 as a reference to Christ is a point well taken. In his words, "Deutungen dieser Art scheiten mE daran, dass Paulus dann in V.13b etwas hätte weglassen müssen: entweder μή ['damit sie schauen auf das Ziel des Vergehenden'] oder τέλος τοῦ ['damit sie sich nicht fixieren auf das Vergehende']." But this objection falls away once the proper referent for v. 13b is recovered, as does his central thesis that Paul's point in 3:13, expanded in 3:14–18, is that "Die Hülle verdeckt die Zeitlichkeit der mosaischen Doxa" (p. 274), which he then equates with the Law itself, together with the old covenant (cf. his pp. 274–284 for the theological development of this thesis). Hence, contra the view argued here, Vollenweider follows the traditional view that "Paulus spricht dem Gesetz die *Zeitinvarianz*, die ihm von der jüdischen Tradition zugeignet worden war, ab" (p. 274, emphasis his), which he must support by falsely equating God's hardening of Israel's minds in v. 14 with sin and the Law (p. 274)! For Vollenweider, therefore, sin and the Law are an interdependent "closed system" ("ein *in sich geschlossenes System*") in such a way that they mutually define one another ("worin sie sich *gegenseitig definieren*") (p. 274, emphasis his). Indeed, in Vollenweider's view the veil becomes a symbol for Israel's blindness to the true and disappointing nature of the Law, while he can speak of "the true Doxa of God" in reference to Christ (cf. p. 275). Such a distinction between the nature of the Mosaic glory and/or Law and that of the new covenant, together with many of the theological implications he draws from it, are not supported by this study.

[67] Cf. A *pc* b f* vg (bo^mss).

"result" of a prior action,[68] and its referent is not to Christ, but to the function of the old covenant in reference to the glory on the face of Moses.[69]

The "how" and "why" of Paul's statement in 3:13 now become apparent. In turning from the glory on Moses' face to the purpose of the veil which it made necessary, Paul is calling explicit attention to the unexpressed presupposition which also undergirded his earlier statement in v. 7b. Specifically, Moses veiled himself in order that the sons of Israel might not gaze "into the outcome or result" (τὸ τέλος) of that which was being rendered inoperative, i.e. the death-dealing judgment of the glory of God upon his "stiff-necked" people as manifested in the old covenant.[70] For unlike Rom. 10:4, the τέλος in 2 Cor. 3:13b takes place within the time frame of Moses' activity, rather than referring to the future time of Christ. For this reason, in the present context Paul explicitly does *not* identify the τέλος of the old covenant with Christ, as he does in Rom. 10:4, even though the two statements are related theologically. It is precisely because Moses had to veil the purpose (τέλος) of the glory of the old covenant from Israel due to their hard hearts (2 Cor. 3:13b) that Christ must become the τέλος of the Law (Rom. 10:4).[71] Hence, within the context of Exod. 32–34 in which Paul now places it, the τέλος of 3:13b is not some divine purpose or revelation known or unknown to Moses, or some future, yet veiled, fulfillment in Christ and the Gospel. Hays' view that it signals the beginning of a complex metaphor, in which Moses embodies a series of interconnected theological constructs, also cannot be supported from the text. For although it is internally coherent within Hays' interpretation of Moses as a metaphor, such an interpretation creates a symbolism in v. 13 and a corre-

---

[68] This use of τέλος in 2 Cor. 3:13 to refer to the outcome or consequence of a given action corresponds to Paul's undisputed use of τέλος with this same meaning in Rom. 6:21 f.; 2 Cor. 11:15; Phil. 3:19. Cf. too 1 Tim. 1:5; James 5:11; 1 Pet. 1:9; 4:17.

[69] Contra Theobald, *Gnade*, p. 197, who relates this phrase to the glory on Moses' face alone, without identifying the glory and the veil with the old covenant and/or the function of the Law. But his support for doing so is his underlying assumption that Paul is combatting his opponents' emphasis on unique pneumatic experiences, rather than on the old covenant as such. He is thus forced to argue against what he admits appears to be "self-evident" from the text taken in its own right (cf. p. 197).

[70] Belleville, *Reflections of Glory*, p. 206, objects to such a reading on the grounds that if Moses' motive were to protect Israel from the splendor of a holy God, then one would have expected the use of διά + accusative or a causal conjunction like ὅτι in 3:13b, rather than πρὸς τό + infinitive. But this would only be true if v. 13 referred to Moses' motive, rather than to his purpose, which are two distinct aspects. In v. 13b Paul is not describing *why* Moses did this (motive, or causal ground), but for *what purpose* it was done. Belleville's objection confuses the use of a ground clause ("why" in the sense of motivation) with that of a purpose clause ("why" in the sense of intended outcome) (cf. her own insightful rejection of the attempt to get at the "motive behind the motive" on p. 208 with her recognition of 13b as a reference to Paul's intent on p. 211).

[71] I am purposely avoiding determining whether τέλος in Rom. 10:4 means "termination" or "goal," because in either case Paul's point would be substantiated by his understanding of the inadequacy of the old covenant as portrayed in 2 Cor. 3:6–13.

sponding tension in vv. 14 f. where neither exists. Paul's point in v. 13 is more simple and straightforward, though no less profound. The τέλος kept from Israel's view was the outcome of the glory of God itself as it encounters a rebellious people, and as such the purpose of the old covenant as a whole (cf. 3:7, 9), had it not been veiled.[72] Far from duplicity, Moses' merciful *intention* was to keep Israel from being judged by the glory on his face, which was the τέλος of that glory in response to the hardened nature of the people.[73]

Once again, Paul's meaning in 3:13 is best recaptured when read against the backdrop of Exod. 34:29–35 (esp. 34:33–35) within its larger context. For there is no compelling exegetical basis for concluding that it is the expression of a foreign, specifically "Christian" rereading of the text, whether based upon Paul's supposedly negative view of Moses and the Old Covenant, his introduction of the idea of a "fading" glory not found in the biblical account, the postulating of some hidden referent in Exod. 34:29 ff. imported into the present context on the basis of Rom. 10:4, or, in the case of those who argue for the veiling of the pre-existent Christ, on the basis of 1 Cor. 10:4.[74] Nor is there any textual support for Theißen's supposition that the veil has become for Paul a symbol of an inner threshold or limitation of one's understanding ("eine innere Verstehensgrenze") in which it functions psychologically as a symbol of the border between the conscious and the subconscious, with its unveiling signifying the "enlightenment of a darkness within us."[75] And given

---

[72] Cf. Jost Eckert, "Die geistliche Schriftauslegung des Apostels Paulus nach 2 Kor 3:4–18," *Dynamik im Wort, Lehre von der Bibel, Leben aus der Bibel*, ed. Katholischen Bebelwerk, 1983, pp. 241–256, p. 250, who also understands the veil in the OT context as the means which makes it possible for Israel to encounter Moses without fear (though without developing how or why this is the case), but follows the typical view by referring to the fading glory in 3:13.

[73] It is important to keep in mind, therefore, contra M. Rissi, *Studien*, p. 31, Hughes, *Second Epistle to the Corinthians*, pp. 110 f, and Provence, "Who is Sufficient," pp. 76 f., that the hardening of Israel is not the result of the veiling (Rissi, Hughes), nor equated with the veiling (Provence), but the *cause* of it. Most instructive is the position of Hughes, who reverses the order of the Exodus narrative when he argues that Israel's minds were hardened as a *result* of their unwillingness to listen to Moses, rather than being the cause of their unwillingness. Hughes has Israel rejecting God's glory rather than not being able to endure it. He comes to this conclusion by reading Rom. 1:21 into the events of Exod. 34, when even in Rom. 1:21 this hardening of the heart results in the idolatry of 1:22 f.

[74] The question of the adequacy of this understanding of 1 Cor. 10:4 itself need not detain us at this point.

[75] Gerd Theißen, "Die Hülle des Mose," pp. 127, 129 (translations my own). Theißen's view is based on his misreading of the significance of the "heart" in Paul's discussion as a reference to the inner (unconscious) reality of a person (p. 146; see above, ch. two) and on his assumption "daß die Bilderwelt religiöser Symbole psychische Prozesse im Menschen repräsentiert" (p. 155). As we have seen in chapter four, Theißen's view also presupposes that Paul has subconsciously reinterpreted the nature of the glory as fading and the purpose of the veil as a deceitful attempt to hide this fact, both of which have been contested in this study.

the integral role which v. 13 plays within 2 Cor. 3:7 ff., as well as its correspondence to the biblical narrative, there is no reason to suppose, as Gaston
does, that v. 13 represents the view of Paul's *opponents* rather than that of
Exodus 34:29 ff. itself as read by Paul.[76] Moreover, Paul has not ignored or
reinterpreted the fact that Israel saw the glory of God on the face of Moses
during those periods of revelation in which Moses removed the veil, as is often maintained. Rather, Paul's careful choice of ἀτενίσαι in verses 7 and 13
indicates that this periodic and limited access to the glory of God is presupposed as indicative of Israel's problem.[77] They were not able to "gaze" into the
glory of God, but could only encounter it briefly.[78] When seen in this light,
rather than being in tension with v. 7, not to mention contradicting it, v. 13 is

---

[76] "Paul and the Torah in 2 Corinthians 3," pp. 161 f. Gaston supplies the implied thought
of v. 13 to be: "and not like [they say:] 'Moses used to put a veil on his face'" (p. 161). This
is Gaston's attempt to overcome Hooker's objection that the transitions from 3:12 to 13 and
14 are a *non sequitur*. But just as in the commonly accepted reading of this text, for Gaston
v. 13 is still an expression of Moses' lack of freedom and openness. The only difference is
that, for Gaston, it was Paul's *opponents* who used the idea of a veiled Moses against *Paul*,
rather than vice versa. In an inversion of the typical reconstruction of the polemical situation
behind 2 Cor. 3, Gaston posits that Paul's opponents were not comparing *themselves* to Moses as veiled, but Paul (!) (cf. p. 163). As he puts it, "the Moses who speaks ecstatically after
his vision on the mount with glory on his face is the ideal of the rival missionaries; the Moses who says nothing because his face and his message are veiled represents the charge
made against Paul" (p. 163). Gaston thus reads v. 13 as an "ironic reprise of the language"
of his opponents (p. 163) in which "the super apostles appealed to the example of Moses in
Exod. 34:30; they accused Paul of being like the Moses of 34:33; Paul then argues that they
have not read far enough in the text. The example to be followed is the Moses of 34:34 ..."
(p. 164). Moreover, in Gaston's view, v. 14 must refer to the dulling of the thoughts and
reading of Paul's *opponents*, rather than Israel. As he construes v. 14: "They say that, but
their thoughts have been dulled" (p. 163; cf. too p. 162). But with the rejection of his hypothesis concerning v. 13, his understanding of v. 14 fails to be convincing (see below,
n. 90). It is difficult to imagine that either Paul or his opponents would build a case for their
self-understanding on Exod. 34:30 without reading through to v. 33! Moreover, for Philo,
who is usually pointed to as the exemplar of a Hellenistic Jewish exaltation of Moses as the
archetype recipient of revelation and wisdom, the veil is part of Moses' exaltation (see
above).

[77] See above, chapter four, on the meaning of ἀτενίσαι. Contra Belleville, *Reflections of
Glory*, p. 222 f., who interprets the "intent observation" signified by this verb to have a
negative nuance for Paul, indicating Israel's obstinate desire to gaze at the glory on Moses'
face when they should not have insisted on doing so! For the implications of this reading for
her view, see below, n. 103.

[78] Contra Dumbrell, "Paul's use of Exodus 34," p. 187, who rightly argues that the main
point of 3:12–13 is the question of access to God, so that there is "no warrant for the assumption generally applied to v. 13 that Moses' attitude was merely protective or designed to
'veil' a passing glory," but then concludes that Paul's use of ἀτενίσαι "seems to rule out the
notion that mere contact with the supposedly evanescent glory would destroy those who saw
it" (p. 187). This fails to take into consideration that in both 3:7 and 11 Paul negates the verb.
The point is not that Israel can have access to God's glory, but that they cannot do so.

its natural complement, just as v. 12 is Paul's equally natural response to his own ministry of the glory of God.[79]

Paul's point, therefore, is not that he is open and honest in contrast to Moses' conscious or unconscious deception. Rather, Paul is bold in preaching the Gospel in the knowledge that the glory of God now being revealed need not be veiled from those to whom he is sent, since its τέλος is life, not death. Paul has no shame in preaching the glory of God on the face of Christ (4:6) not because he is more honest than Moses, but because his suffering as an apostle is the vehicle through which the very glory of God is now being shown openly to God's people. Whereas Moses had to veil himself as an act of judgment and mercy toward a rebellious people, Paul need not "veil himself" before a people whose disposition toward God and his will has been radically changed. While Moses proclaimed the Law without the Spirit (= the letter of 3:6), Paul preaches the Gospel, through which the Spirit is now at work to change people's hearts in accordance with the promises of Jeremiah and Ezekiel.[80] Provence is thus essentially correct when he summarizes the difference between the old and new covenants in terms of "the activity, or lack of activity, of the Holy Spirit within the human heart."[81]

Paul is consequently bold in his ministry because he knows that God's glory can now reach his people without the fear of judgment. Paul must no longer keep God's people from seeing the goal (τέλος) of the glory of God, since their hearts are being transformed by the Spirit (cf. 3:3, 3:6).[82] In short, the "fulfillment" of the old covenant "promise" of "achieving a truly personal relationship between himself and his people ... and his design for accomplishing it" are now taking place through Paul's preaching of Christ.[83] Or in the

---

[79] Cf. e.g. the strong statements of Morna D. Hooker, "Beyond the Things that are written?" pp. 297 f. Because she fails to see the role played by Israel's "stiff-neck" in Exod. 32–34 as the backdrop to Moses' use of the veil in Exod. 34:29 ff., the nature of the *qal wahomer* argument in 3:7–11, and the meaning of τέλος in v. 13, she concludes that Paul is inconsistent in 3:12 ff., indeed, that his thought is a *non sequitur*. For in Hooker's view, Paul would need to veil his face with an even thicker veil (!), since the new glory is so much greater than the old.

[80] Contra Theobald, *Gnade*, p. 197, who argues that the power of the letter, through which death and condemnation are spread, has nothing to do with the glory of Moses *per se*, but comes about only through the veiling and the "Verfälschung" of the Law which this veiling brings about. But as Exod. 34 makes clear, it is the Law and the glory of God which, apart from the Spirit, kill. Theobald's view is part of his attempt to argue that the issue at stake throughout 3:12–18 is not the Law or the hermeneutical question, but the significance of the Mosaic encounter with God as represented in his experience of God's glory (cf. p. 198).

[81] "Who is Sufficient," p. 77, though he misses the force of τέλος because of his reliance on the parallel to Rom. 10:4, where he reads it to mean "purpose," rather than on the context of Exod. 34. He thus must take the reference of v. 13 to be to Christ as the hidden purpose of the Law.

[82] This understanding of v. 13 is picked up and confirmed by Paul's point in 3:18; see below.

[83] Following C.F.D. Moule, "Fulfilment-Words in the New Testament," *NTS* 14 (1968) 293–320, p. 294, who, in analyzing the "promise/fulfillment" motif in the NT, argues for the

words of our text, Paul is bold because those who belong to the new covenant people of God are able to "gaze intently at the outcome of that which must no longer be brought to an end." In view not only of the promises of Jeremiah 31 and Ezekiel 36, now read against the backdrop of Exodus 32–34, but also of the tradition preserved in 4 Ezra 7:112, in which the key distinction between this age and the age to come is that "in the present world the glory (of God) does not continuously abide in it," the eschatological nature of Paul's assertion in 3:12 f. is apparent. The amazing, even shocking nature of Paul's contrast in 2 Cor. 3:12 f. between his own ministry and the ministry of Moses, often missed today because of its familiarity and the exclusively Christian context in which it is normally read, should not be overlooked. No one has seen this more clearly than J. Munck, who in commenting on 3:12 observed that,

"Of Paul's many new and startling utterances, this is perhaps the most surprising. The greatest man in the history of Israel is put beneath the travelling tentmaker, a man who is at the same time contending for the church at Corinth, so that it may submit to him. No stronger proof can be produced that as a figure in redemptive history in the age of the Messiah Paul far surpassed even the greatest of the great figures of Israel."[84]

Paul is keenly aware of the implications of what he has just said, not only for the significance of his own ministry, but also for those who accept or reject it. The establishment of a contrast between his boldness and the ministry of Moses in terms of the unveiled glory of God can only mean that those who are now accepting the Gospel number among the people of God to whom this glory is being revealed. The unexpressed element in vv. 12–13 is Paul's corresponding boldness in making it possible for the "sons of Israel" to gaze into the glory of God which is no longer being rendered ineffective. But it is, for the most part, precisely these "sons of Israel" who are not accepting Paul's message of the glory of God on the face of Christ. At this point in his argument, therefore, he turns his attention to the vexing question of Israel's lack of response to the Gospel of Christ.[85]

---

concept of "covenant-promise" not in the sense of a single promise, but of the inclusive promise and hope for this personal relationship with YHWH. Unlike the more narrowly conceived "prediction/verification" concept in the NT, which functions to establish the competence and truthfulness of God (cf. pp. 296 f.), the "fulfillment" of this promise is "the fully achieved relationship itself" (p. 294).

[84] *Paul and the Salvation of Mankind*, p. 61; though it must be kept in mind that the contrast is not between their personalities, but between their distinct ministries.

[85] So too R.P. Martin, *2 Corinthians*, pp. 66 f., who argues that in 3:12 ff. Paul is turning to face the allegation that his ministry has had little success among the Jews. Martin, however, follows the majority in seeing Paul, in his weakness, as being confronted by his opponents with a comparison to the glory of Moses himself, for which no evidence appears in the text. As the biblical record makes clear, Moses *too* had no success among the Israelites/Jews! Nor were the Jewish people of Paul's day as a whole characterized by their faithfulness to the Law! Rather, the structure of 2 Cor. 3:1–18 corresponds to the structure of the book of Romans as a whole, in which after a presentation of the revelation of the glory of God in the

3. The Veil of Moses and the History of Israel (2 Cor. 3:14–15)

Paul's seemingly abrupt transition in v. 14a, introduced by the strong contrast ἀλλά, has caused interpreters much difficulty. The difficulty derives from the common attempt to relate the contrast of v. 14a directly back to the purpose clause in v. 13b, which renders Paul's thought hard to follow at best.[86] In this reading of the text, Moses veiled his face in order that the sons of Israel might not gaze into the goal of that which was being brought to an end, *but* their minds were hardened (v. 14a). Yet it was *because* their minds were hardened that Moses had to veil himself in order that they might not experience the judgment of God![87] On the other hand, those who take τέλος to mean "termination," or "goal" in reference to some kind of fulfillment in Christ are confronted with equally serious problems, as evidenced by having to create a negative assertion in Paul's argument where none exists to provide a counterpart to the contrast in v. 14a.[88]

Gospel, with the work of the Spirit at its center (cf. 2 Cor. 3:1–13 with Rom. 1–8, climaxing in the work of the Spirit in revealing the future glory of God, 8:6–21), Paul turns to the question of Israel's present rejection of the Gospel (cf. 2 Cor. 3:14–15 with Rom. 9–11).

[86] An example of this difficulty is Koch's conclusion, *Schrift*, p. 334, that the relationship between v. 13b and 14a is merely one of a general "correspondence" in which the veil corresponds to the hardening of Israel. Koch comes to this conclusion because he recognizes that Israel's hardening is not pictured as the result of the veiling, and yet there is a clear conceptual relationship between the two clauses. But this interpretation, though generally correct, ignores the actual force of the ἀλλά altogether.

[87] For this reason Prümm, *Diakonia Pneumatos*, p. 140, takes v. 14 to be a fulfillment of an implied prophecy in 3:13 in which Moses' action becomes a type of the later hardening of Israel. But this is difficult to maintain in view of the aorist of v. 14a, and requires that he translate the ἀλλά as "certainly" ("doch"). For this unusual translation, see too F. Lang, *Die Briefe an die Korinther*, NTD 7, 1986[16], p. 273. The only other option, as Prümm points out, is to supply a missing idea, i.e. that in reality Israel did not see the end of that which was being abolished, but rather ... (p. 141 n. 1).

[88] See e.g. Gerd Theißen, "Die Hülle des Mose," p. 144, who must suppose that behind Paul's text stands the conviction, "Eigentlich soll der Strahlenglanz bis ins Innere hineinwirken," and Furnish, *II Corinthians*, p. 207, who, following Schildenberger and Barrett, must read Paul to be saying, "not that Moses sought to deceive, rather, their own minds were hardened." But this assertion is neither stated nor implied in the text. In a similar way, Rissi, *Studien*, p. 31, must supply the missing idea of "the Scripture says" before the reference to Moses, taking the phrase "and not as" to be an introductory formula so that v. 14a can then function as an explanation for Israel's inability in 3:13. But again, no such idea is expressed in 3:13 as it now stands. The same can be said for Theobald's attempt, *Gnade*, p. 192, to add the intensifying negative assertion, "and not only this, but ..." Stockhausen, *Moses' Veil* , p. 149, takes the ἀλλά to indicate an "interpretive reformulation" of 3:13, translating it, "but Scripture also says ..." Yet there is no direct Scriptural text in view in 3:14a, but rather a summary statement of the significance of Israel's experience in view of later prophetic developments of this theme (see below). Hofius, "Gesetz und Evangelium," p. 105, adds the idea "und nicht nur dies, sondern ..." to make sense of Paul's transition. For this same view, see van Unnik, "With unveiled face," p. 162. Dumbrell, "Paul's use of Exodus 34," p. 187, supplies the idea that the veil "might, however, have suggested to the participating Israelites that there was a covenant dimension in which they were not sharing,"

But before we posit a missing link in Paul's argument, or conclude that Paul's thought is simply a *non sequitur*, [89] the possibility of reading the contrast against the counterpart which Paul *does* supply in v. 13 should be attempted.[90] And in this case, the apparent difficulty in Paul's thought is erased once the structure of Paul's argument and the common use of ἀλλά are both kept in mind. For the syntax of vv. 12–13 indicates that v. 13 *taken as a whole*, including its main point concerning Moses' purpose in 13b, is *all* intended to support Paul's boldness as asserted in v. 12. In 3:13 Paul merely picks up and restates his assertion from 3:12, this time in a negated form. Hence, the reason for the unusual and awkward expression in v. 14a is that ἀλλά is commonly used after the negative οὐ to introduce a positive contrast to what precedes, either in respect to a clause or to an entire sentence.[91] This negative/positive

---

which is contrasted to the fact that their minds were hardened so that they could not understand this function of the veil. Renwick, *Temple*, p. 147, adds the idea that the Israelites never grasped the significance of Moses' action with the veil, not seeing that it was intended to keep them from death or that death and condemnation were its ultimate consequences.

[89] As does Hooker, "Beyond the Things that are written?" p. 299. But Hooker fails to see the function of Moses' veil in relationship to the hard hearts of Israel and thus misses the point of vv. 13 f. Since she sees Paul's "whole argument" in 3:7–18 to be based on the fading of the glory on Moses' face (p. 300), her understanding of Paul's thought runs aground. For in Hooker's view, the main problem with Paul's thought is that in Exod. 34 Moses does not wear the veil when revealing the Law, whereas in 3:14 it is the Law which is now veiled. She thus sees a contradiction between Paul's point and Exod. 34, where in fact none exists. The point in both texts is the abiding presence of God with his people, not the accreditation of Moses and the Law which he mediates.

[90] Indeed, Gaston, "2 Corinthians 3," p. 162, sees the transfer of the motif of the veil from the Exodus narrative to the hearts of Israel to be "completely without precedent," so that "one can either conclude that this is 'one of the most unusual exegetical arguments ever contrived' (quoting C. Buck and G. Taylor, *Saint Paul: A Study of the Development of his Thought*, 1969, p. 63) and despair of following its logic or try a completely new tack." As we have seen, his tack is to read Paul's statements in vv. 13–14 to refer to Paul's opponents, rather than to Israel (pp. 162 f.; see above, n. 76). Verses 13–14 are thus construed to mean: "Paul speaks with *parresia* and not with a veiled gospel, as they accuse him of doing, following the example of the veiled Moses. They say that, but their thoughts have been dulled … those who say that I do have dulled thoughts" (p. 163). His support for this is to read 3:13–18 in terms of 4:1–6, rather than taking 4:1–6 to be an *application* of the perspective developed in 3:13–18. Gaston's view does violence to the flow of Paul's argument, though his recognition of the difficulty of Paul's attributing to Moses the motivation of covering up the fact that the glory on his face was fading is to be welcomed (cf. p. 163). Gaston's attempt to exonerate Israel and to read 2 Cor. 3 exclusively in terms of the Corinthian Christians (cf. pp. 164 f.) leads him to fail to recognize that the problem being addressed in 3:13–17 is, in fact, primarily Israel's history of hard-heartedness and subsequent rejection of the gospel, as indicated by the significance of the veil within the OT backdrop to Paul's argument. It is the function of the veil in vv. 13–14, properly understood, that provides the contrast to Paul's "openness," which, as Gaston rightly observes, is otherwise difficult to explain (cf. p. 163).

[91] See BAGD, *A Greek-English Lexicon*, p. 38. Contra Belleville, *Reflections of Glory*, p. 219, who concludes that "there is no cogent reason why ἀλλά should not be taken in its normal, adversative sense," not taking its use in negative/positive contrasts into consideration. She points to Allo, Howard, Héring, and Lias as all supporting this reading. Belleville

c ntrast between distinct clauses or sentences, indicated by the syntactical construction οὐ ... ἀλλά, is common in Paul's epistles.[92] Once v. 14 is recognized to relate directly back to the main point of vv. 12–13 as expressed in v. 13a,[93] Paul's argument in 3:12–14a follows a typical Pauline pattern and works as follows:

   3:12a: *Because* we have this hope,

3:12b: *Therefore* we behave with boldness.

(-) 3:13a: *That is to say,* we do *not* behave as Moses

     3:13b: *who* was placing a veil upon his face

     3:13bb: *in order that* the sons of Israel might not gaze into the outcome of that which was being rendered inoperative.

(+) 3:14a: *But* their minds were hardened.

Hence, the contrast established is not between Moses' intention and the "hardened minds" of Israel,[94] but between Paul's boldness and the fact that Israel's "minds were hardened" (ἐπωρώθη τὰ νοήματα αὐτῶν).[95]

Paul's statement in v. 14a is yet another reference to the events of Exod. 32–34 as part of Paul's continuing commentary on Exod. 34:29–35.[96] The seman-

---

too recognizes that once ἀλλά is given its adversative meaning, "it is impossible to establish a reasonable sequence of thought, since the content of both clauses is negative: v. 13b, hindrance of sight; v. 14a, hindrance of understanding" (pp. 219 f.). Her solution is to take 14a as an adversative to the entire preceding thought in v. 13, so that v. 14a "would introduce a reaction on the part of Israel that is opposite to the action and intent of Moses" (p. 220). But this positing of an adversative relationship between vv. 12–13 and 14 is too general, since it cannot incorporate the fact that the use of the veil in v. 13 is *occasioned* by Israel's hardness, not contrasted to it. Cf. Windisch, *Der zweite Korintherbrief*, p. 119, who sees that καὶ οὐ (v. 13) expects a positive contrasting sentence, but fails to pick up the significance of ἀλλά in this regard, since he views Paul's discussion of the Jews in 3:14–17 to be an aside. Windisch therefore points to v. 18 as the necessary contrast. But this misses the function of both vv. 14–17 and v. 18 in Paul's argument.

[92] Cf. Rom. 1:32; 4:4, 13; 6:14; 7:19 f.; 8:15, 26, 32; 9:8; 1 Cor. 1:17; 9:12; 11:8; 12:24; 14:34; 15:10; 2 Cor. 1:19; 2:13; 5:12; 10:12, 18; 12:16; Gal. 4:14, etc.

[93] See Belleville, *Reflections of Glory*, p. 176, who also concludes that "both v. 13a and v. 13b are closely tied to v. 14 by means of the contrast οὐ καθάπερ Μωϋσῆς ἀλλά, and vv. 13b–14 share a common subject and historical setting (the Israelites of Moses' generation)." This is part of Belleville's convincing refutation of Lambrecht's chiastic understanding of the structure of 3:12–18 (cf. pp. 175 f.).

[94] Contra Windisch, *Der zweite Korintherbrief*, p. 120, and the history of interpretation dependent upon him.

[95] This point was arrived at independently of Wright, *Climax*, p. 181, who also relates the ἀλλά of v. 14a to οὐ καθάπερ Μωϋσῆς, so that he too argues that Paul's point becomes: "*We* use great boldness in relation to you, unlike Moses before the Israelites, because your hearts are not like those of the Israelites, in whose presence Moses had to veil the glory" (emphasis his).

[96] See too Koch, *Schrift*, p. 334, who argues that v. 14a still refers to the past, but by virtue of its content provides a necessary transition to what follows in v. 14b; and Belleville,

tic parallels between the motif of Israel's "stiff-neck" and the other expressions used throughout the canonical literature (see chapter three) and post-biblical Judaism (see below) to describe her hardened condition make Paul's equivalent here readily recognizable. But that Paul does not use a direct equivalent to the MT of his own choosing, or σκληροτράχηλος ("stiff-necked") from the LXX of Exod. 33:3,5; 34:9 (cf. Acts 7:51), is in its own right significant. In choosing the verb πωρόω ("to harden") in v. 14a Paul is interpreting Israel's character as revealed in her sin with the golden calf in the same terms associated in early Christian tradition with Israel's hardened condition as depicted in Isaiah 6:9 f., Jeremiah 5:21–24, and Ezekiel 12:2.[97] This is reflected in Mark 8:17 f.'s mixed citation of Jeremiah 5:21 and Ezekiel 12:2 as a parallel to the earlier reference to Is. 6:9 f. in Mark 4:12 (cf. Mk. 3:5; 6:52; 10:5).[98] Since there is no direct use of πωρόω for the hardening motif in either Jer. 5:21, Ezek. 12:2, or Is. 6:9, its introduction in Mk. 8:17 most likely derives from Is. 6:10 as the continuation of the text explicitly quoted in Mk. 4:12, from its parallels in Jer. 5:22–24 as the continuation of Jer. 5:21, and from the references in Ezek. 12:2, 3, 9 to Israel as a "house of provocations" (οἶκος παραπικραίνων) as the equivalent to their earlier description as a rebellious "house of provocations" (LXX: οἶκος παραπικραίνων; MT: "stiff-faced

---

Reflections of Glory, pp. 177 f., who limits the textual basis to Exod. 34:33. Belleville, however, posits that in 13b Paul expands Exod. 34:33 by incorporating two Jewish traditions (one which links the veiling to the intent to prevent Israel's gazing at the glory and one concerning the impermanent character of the glory itself) and in 14a further expands the text by adding his own "interpretive addition" to Exod. 34:33, so that, in her view, Paul is modifying the text substantially in a way similar to a Targum (pp. 209–211). But there is no need to view vv. 13b–14a as the addition of any subsequent traditions once Paul's comments are seen to be interpretations warranted by the biblical text. In Belleville's view, Paul's commentary on Exod. 34 first begins in vv. 14b, when in reality it begins back in 13b.

[97] Cf. Stockhausen, *Moses' Veil*, pp. 135–146, for Is. 6:9–10 (and 29:10–12) as the background to 3:14 on the basis of the parallels in John 12:39–41 and Rom. 11:7–8. She is certainly correct that Paul "has used Is. 6:9–10 and 29:10–12 to interpret and contemporize Exodus 34:33–35 ..." (p. 148) based on his own experience of rejection by the Jews (p. 33), though my understanding of the significance of Is. 29:10–12 as a background to Paul's thought is significantly different (see below).

[98] The fact that in Mk. 8:17 Jesus asks the disciples whether they do not yet "perceive or understand," or whether they have a "hardened heart" (πεπωρωμένην τὴν καρδίαν) as his introduction to the quote from Jer. 5:21 in 8:18 clearly recalls Jesus' earlier reference to the same motifs of "seeing" and "understanding" from Is. 6:9 in 4:12 and their application to the disciples' "hardened hearts" (ἡ καρδία πεπωρωμένη) in Mk. 6:52, to the Pharisees in 3:5 (ἐπὶ τῇ πωρώσει τῆς καρδίας), and to the Jews in general in 10:5 (σκληροκαρδία). The point of the narrative is to raise the question of whether the disciples themselves lack the same faith that characterizes those who are outside of the kingdom, even though they have been given its "mystery" (cf. Mk. 4:11). For the description of the Pharisee's "hard hearts" in Mk. 3:5 and 10:5 as a reference to Israel's "fall from the Law" into the idolatry first seen in the golden calf, see R. Pesch, *Das Markusevangelium, II. Teil*, HThKNT Bd. 2,2, 1977, pp. 123, 193 f., and the extensive literature cited there, though I do not share Pesch's acceptance of Berger's view, based on Ezek. 20:25 f., that the cultic Laws are given as a compromise to Israel's idolatry and are thus of lesser value.

and hard-hearted") in Ezek. 2:3–8 (see chapter three). For although our recensions of Is. 6:10 (LXX) use the verb παχύνειν (fig. "to make impervious, dull") to describe Israel's resistant heart (cf. Matt. 13:15; Acts 28:27),[99] the adaptation of Is. 6:10 in John 12:40 illustrates the equivalence between the concepts of Israel's "dull" and "hardened heart" on the one hand (cf. ἐπώρωσεν αὐτῶν τὴν καρδίαν), and her "blinded eyes" on the other (cf. τετύφλωκεν αὐτῶν τοὺς ὀφθαλμούς).[100] In addition, the implicit divine passive in 3:14a is made explicit in John 12:40. As a particularly clear illustration of these same conceptual equivalents, the description of the people in Jer. 5:21 as those who have eyes but do not see and ears but do not hear is supported by their subsequent depiction in 5:23 as a people who have "a disobedient and rebellious heart" (καρδία ἀνήκοος καὶ ἀπειθής). Moreover, as we have seen in chapters two and three, it is this hardened condition (as a parallel to Is. 6:9 f. and Ezek. 2:3–8, 12:2–9), with its resultant transgressions against the Law because of the refusal to "fear the Lord," that God promises to overcome forever in the new covenant (cf. Jer. 38:31–37 with 39:37–41 LXX).

Paul's move from his present bold behavior to Israel's gnomic[101] condition as reflected in her sin with the golden calf is therefore an essential step in his apologetic for his calling as an apostle. Israel's rejection of his Gospel is no argument against the validity of Paul's message, or the legitimacy of his min-

---

[99] For the other uses of παχύνειν in the LXX, all with its literal meaning, see Deut. 32:15; 2 Kgs. 22:12; Eccl. 12:5; Is. 34:6.

[100] On the use of πωρόω in John 12:40, see the helpful survey by J.M. Lieu, "Blindness in the Johannine Tradition," *NTS* 34 (1988) 83–95, pp. 85–88, who points out that the quotation from Is. 6:10 in John 12:40 continues the allusion to Is. 6:9 in John 9:39 (p. 85), and that John's use of πωρόω in 12:40 parallels that found in Mark 6:52; 8:17; Rom. 11:7 (also standing "within the Isa 6:10 tradition"); and 2 Cor. 3:14 (p. 87). She thus concludes that "the choice of πωρόω to express 'hardening' in John's quotation ... has no clear precedent in the LXX, other Jewish literature or in Greek writers. Yet the evidence of Mark and Paul also relates the term to Isa 6:10 and suggests that it is not a Johannine peculiarity. Rather, John is part of a wider tradition of interpreting Isa 6:9–10 in terms of blinding (τυφλόω) and hardening (πωρόω), a tradition which could speak of judgement and of healing, through word or through miracle-sign" (p. 88). Moreover, Lieu argues that in John it was not the experience of being excluded from the synagogue which led to the development of the theology of blindness, but that "the verbal links John shares with Mark and Paul point to the origin of that [i.e. a theological understanding of unbelief as blindness as a result of a "direct exegesis of Isa 6:9–10 ..."] working out in the wider exegetical traditions of the early church with their background in Jewish exegetical patterns" (p. 90). The only other uses of πωρόω in the LXX are found in Job 17:7, Prov. 10:20, both in contexts unrelated to the motifs of Is. 6:9 f., and Jer. 5:21–24. Thus, Belleville's suggestion that in 3:14 πωρόω refers to the "dulling" of Israel's perceptions rather than "hardening" (*Reflections of Glory*, pp. 220 f.) draws a conceptual distinction where none is intended. Nor, against the biblical backdrop to 3:13–14, must its aorist form be taken as ingressive (p. 221). Rather, Paul's choice of words is determined by the biblical traditions to which he is alluding (which Belleville also notes, p. 222, but does not develop in detail).

[101] Taking the aorist ἐπωρώθη to be "gnomic," i.e. representing "an act which is valid for all time ... because (originally at least) the author had a specific case in mind in which the act had been realized," Blass, Debrunner, and Funk, *Greek Grammar*, § 333.

istry as a revelation of the glory of God, as his opponents apparently maintained.[102] For Exod. 32–34 clearly demonstrates that according to God's sovereign action the majority of Israel was unable to respond to the redemptive work of God on her behalf in the Sinai covenant (cf. Exod. 20:1 ff.; Deut. 29:1–6). This is the point of the transition from 13b to 14a.[103] Paul's experience in regard to "Israel according to the flesh" is no different than that of Moses and the prophets before him, just as his call is patterned after theirs. Since the nation of Israel, apart from the remnant, "was hardened,"[104] it is not surprising that Israel continues to reject the message of repentance and restoration initiated by Moses, picked up by the prophets, and, from Paul's perspective, realized in Christ.[105] What is true in Paul's day has been true throughout Israel's history. Only those whose hearts have been changed by the Spirit will accept the (new) covenant redemption (in Christ) and be enabled by the Spirit to keep its stipulations as revealed in the Law (see above and chapter two).[106] Following the example set down by Moses and the prophets, Paul therefore remains bold in spite of Israel's rejection of his message.

---

[102] Cf. Morna D. Hooker, "Johannine prologue and the Messianic Secret," *NTS* 21 (1975) 40–58, p. 58, who emphasizes that in reconstructing the possible background and opponents of 2 Cor. and Romans it is easy to overlook that the obvious and most pressing problem which confronted these early Christians was their relationship to their Jewish heritage. For she observes that "In both II Corinthians and Romans we see Paul wrestling with the problem of reconciling faith in Jesus as Christ not only with his conviction that God had spoken through the Old Testament, but also with the failure of the Jews to recognize this truth" (p. 58). See too Hickling, "Sequence of Thought," p. 393, who recognizes Paul's failure to convert many Jews as part of the opponents' attack and thus as an important aspect behind Paul's argument in 3:14 ff.

[103] Contra Belleville's reading of the sequence of thought in vv. 13b–14a, *Reflections of Glory*, pp. 223 f.: "Moses veiled his face so that the Israelites' gazing should not become so obstinately riveted that they fail to understand the significance of the fading splendor (i.e. so that they do not stare intently right down to the last glimmer). However, the drama had been played out so many times (ἐτίθει) that their perceptions had become dulled to the point of incomprehension." Besides viewing the glory on Moses' face to be fading, Belleville's unique reading is based on taking v. 13b to refer to Israel's obstinate desire to gaze at the glory of Moses' face and on an ingressive reading of ἐπωρώθη in 14b, all of which have failed to be supported by this study. The problem with Israel was not her *desire* to see the glory on Moses' face, but her *inability* to do so due to her hardened condition.

[104] On the parallel between καρδία and νοῦς in the LXX as renderings for לב ("heart") as a "Bezeichnung des Ich als eines Wollenden, planenden, trachtenden," and their parallel use in Paul, see e.g. R. Bultmann, *Theologie des Neuen Testaments*, UTB 630, 1980[8], p. 221. The parallels within 2 Cor. 3:14 f. itself establish this point; see too Phil. 4:7. Bultmann points out that for Paul, both the "mind" (cf. Rom. 1:28; 2 Cor. 3:14; 4:4; 11:13) and the "heart" (cf. Rom. 1:21; 2:5; 16:18) can be pictured as hardened and blinded. In the same way, both the mind (Rom. 12:2) and the heart (2 Cor. 4:6) must be renewed.

[105] For the canonical link between Moses' message of repentance and restoration and that of the prophets, see chapter three.

[106] As E. Sokolowski emphasized almost a century ago, in Paul's conception the "mind" (νοῦς) and the "thought" which it produces (νόημα) are more than mere intellectual ability, but refer to that facility and recognition which regulate one's behavior. The "mind" is that organ from which one's religious and ethical life derives. See his *Die Begriffe Geist und*

Paul's use of νόημα in 3:14 thus provides an essential link in the development of the motif of the hardened and renewed "mind" throughout 2 Corinthians. Its parallel use in 2 Cor. 4:4 demonstrates that whether or not one's "mind" has been "blinded" by Satan is yet another way to draw a distinction between those who do and do not have the Spirit. Hence, by means of a clever play on words, the believers in Corinth who are described in 2:11 as not ignorant of Satan's "evil designs" (τὰ νοήματα) provide the counterpoint to those unbelievers in 4:4 whose "minds" (τὰ νοήματα) Satan has deceived. In the context of 2:14–4:6, "the Spirit makes alive" (3:6c), therefore, by working on the heart (3:3) to remove the hardness, which, according to God's sovereign will (cf. the divine passive in 3:14), accompanied Israel under the old covenant (3:7, 13) and continues to be inflicted by Satan on all those who reject the Gospel under the new (4:6; cf. 2:16).[107] Within this theological framework it becomes clear why in 2 Cor. 10:5 Paul can picture his apostolic ministry in terms of a war against spiritual powers in which his goal is to destroy "every high defense being raised up against the knowledge of God" and to take captive "every thought (πᾶν νόημα) to the obedience of Christ." As the parallel to 2 Cor. 4:6 demonstrates, the knowledge (γνῶσις) opposed by God's enemies, who have been blinded by Satan, is that God's glory is now being revealed on the face of Christ. Conversely, the close parallel between 2 Cor. 10:5 and 2 Cor. 2:14–17 (cf. 4:7 ff.) makes it evident that the "thought" which must be "captured" and made obedient to Christ is the rejection of Paul's ministry of suffering as the vehicle through which this divine glory in Christ is now being made known![108] For given the attack on Paul's ministry in Corinth, Paul fears for the Satanic influence on the Corinthians' own "minds" (τὰ νοήματα ὑμῶν), through which Satan is attempting to lead them astray as he did Eve (2 Cor. 11:3).[109] Hence,

---

Leben bei Paulus in ihren Beziehungen zu einander. Eine exegetisch-religionsgeschichtliche Untersuchung, 1903, pp. 131–134. Belleville, *Reflections of Glory*, p. 220, points out that τὰ νοήματα is used in the NT only by Paul (besides Phil. 4:7, all in 2 Cor., cf. 2:11; 4:4; 10:5; 11:3) and that "within a religious context, the term denotes the faculty of perception of the revelation of God."

[107] Cf. Eph. 4:18, where the same motif of the "hardness of heart" (πώρωσις τῆς καρδίας) is applied to Gentiles as the root cause for their "being excluded from the life of God" (ἀπηλλοτριωμένοι τῆς ζωῆς τοῦ θεοῦ). Here too, this is the counterpart to the work of the Spirit among believers, who makes them alive with Christ in spite of their prior imprisonment by Satan and empowers them to obey (cf. Eph. 1:13, 17f.; 2:1–7, 22; 3:16, 20; 4:30; 5:18).

[108] I owe this point to the insightful work of Abraham J. Malherbe, "Antisthenes and Odysseus, and Paul at War," *HTR* 76 (1983) 143–173, pp. 168, 172, who has shown that what is at stake in 2 Cor. 10:1–6 is not an "intellectual confrontation" between Paul and his opponents, but their opposition to his "voluntary self-humiliation" as a result of his decision to support himself in Corinth. Malherbe also points to 2 Cor. 2:14–17 as the closest parallel; see now my *Suffering and the Spirit*, pp. 18–39, 51–64, for an interpretation of 2:14–17 in terms of Paul's suffering (see the Introduction above).

[109] The only other use of νόημα in the NT occurs in Phil. 4:7 in reference to the "minds" of believers as kept by the peace of God "in Christ." This too provides a clear contrast to the Satanic influence and hardening pictured in 2 Cor.

Paul's contrast between his own boldness (3:12–13a) and the divine hardening of Israel (3:14a) not only supports his own legitimacy as an apostle,[110] but
also contains an implicit warning to the Corinthians themselves. Despite any
claim to the contrary by the "super apostles," a rejection of Paul's message
and ministry is sure evidence of the blinding influence of Satan among those
who, like Israel, have been hardened according to God's sovereign will (cf. 2
Cor. 4:4).

In verse 14b, Paul now begins to offer support for his assertion that Israel
was hardened from the beginning (cf. the γάρ in v. 14b).[111] He does so by
moving from the *past* hardening of Israel, as manifested in Moses' need to
veil *himself* because of their idolatry with the golden calf (vv. 13–14a), to Israel's *present* (ἄχρι τῆς σήμερον ἡμέρας) veiled condition *when* reading the
"old covenant" (ἐπὶ τῇ ἀναγνώσει τῆς παλαιᾶς διαθήκης; v. 14b).[112] In this
context, ἐπί with the dative does not indicate the place *where* the veil remains
(i.e. "*on* the reading of the old covenant"), but "the occasion on which or circumstances in which something takes place," as in 2 Cor. 1:4 and 7:4.[113] Not
only the prior statement in v. 14a, but also the close parallel between v. 14b
and its reiteration in v. 15, in which ἡνίκα ἄν ("whenever") replaces ἐπί in describing the reading of Moses, support such a reading (see below). In contrast,
when Paul desires to indicate explicitly *where* the veil is now located (a point
not addressed in v. 14), he does so by using ἐπί plus the *accusative* (ἐπὶ τὴν

---

[110] See too Stegemann, "Neue Bund," p. 106, who maintains that the context of Paul's
defense is the incongruence between the glory of the apostolic office and Paul's suffering on
the one hand, and between the offer of salvation in the Gospel to all and the reception of the
message by so few on the other.

[111] Contra those who, like Barrett, *Second Corinthians*, p. 120, take the γάρ in 14b to be
explanatory. It is difficult to see how this statement "explains how and why their minds were
hardened." Hofius, "Gesetz und Evangelium," p. 117 n. 241, is correct that the γάρ here has
an "anknüpfenden und weiterführenden Sinn," but the question is, in what *way*?

[112] Only in v. 14b does Paul turn his attention to the present situation regarding Israel's
condition as manifested in her relationship to the Law in the synagogue; cf. too Hofius,
"Gesetz und Evangelium," p. 114, and Koch, *Schrift*, p. 335, for this same understanding of
v. 14b as the turning point in Paul's argument. See too Belleville, *Reflections of Glory*,
p. 227, and esp. p. 173 n. 2, who points out that the common attempt to apply the designation "pesher" to vv. 14b–15 is "to misrepresent Paul's intent, which is to provide a basis for
his scriptural claims in vv. 12–14a by turning for support to his current-day situation (see
the opening γάρ in v. 14b). This is the reverse of the Qumran pesher methodology, which
sees the scriptural texts as being fulfilled and finding their meaning in current-day events"
(for this same point, see pp. 227 f.n. 3).

[113] Contra the majority view; but following e.g. Prümm, *Diakonia Pneumatos*, p. 141, and
Furnish, *II Corinthians*, p. 208, who in turn cite Plummer and Barrett. For these two basic
meanings, cf. BAGD, *A Greek-English Lexicon*, pp. 286 f. Belleville, *Reflections of Glory*,
pp. 231 f., like the majority, rejects this reading, and supports her view by positing a conceptual "haggadic" parallel between ἐπὶ τῇ ἀναγνώσει in v. 14b and ἐπὶ τὸ πρόσωπον αὐτοῦ in
v. 13 (p. 231). But the switch from the accusative object of the preposition in v. 13 to the
dative in v. 14 signals a change in meaning for the preposition itself.

καρδίαν αὐτῶν) in v. 15. In v. 14b, as in vv. 14a and 15, it is not the old covenant which is veiled, but *Israel*.[114]

But the very fact that Paul chooses to use the *veil* as that which links the experience of *Moses* in regard to *Israel* in Exod. 34:29 ff. to *Israel* in regard to the *old covenant* (= *Moses*) in the present day synagogue indicates that, in moving from the past to the present, Paul has shifted from the concrete to the symbolic. More specifically, Paul's reference to "the same veil" in 3:14b is an example of a metonomy. As G.B. Caird has defined it, a metonomy is a figure of speech in which one thing is called

"... by the name of something typically associated with it: e.g. the Bench, the stage, the turf, the bottle may stand for magistrates, the theatrical profession, horse-racing and alcoholic liquor. In the Old Testament we find sceptre (Gen. 49:10) and key (Isa. 22:22; cf. Rev. 3:7) standing for authority, sword for war (Lev. 26:6); and in the New Testament tongues for languages (1 Cor. 12:30; 14:1–9), thrones for superhuman powers (Col. 1:16), and the Circumcision for the Jews (Gal. 2:7–9, 12; Eph. 2:11; Col. 4:11)."[115]

As Caird's examples show, such a move was common practice for Paul. Moreover, the introduction of this figure of speech at this point in his argument ought not surprise us. For as we have seen, both in Exodus 34:29 ff. and in Paul's prior treatment of this passage in 3:7, 9, the veil of Moses has been inextricably linked to Israel's hardened condition.[116] The image of the Mosaic

---

[114] Contra those who, in taking ἐπί in v. 14 to refer to the location of the veil, conclude, as does Koch, *Schrift*, p. 335, that Paul's use of the biblical tradition at this point is "äußert gewaltsam." Koch posits that Paul is making allusion to the "Torahüllen" being used in the synagogue to cover the book of the old covenant (p. 335). The search for a historical custom in which the old covenant or Law was actually veiled during its reading, such as suggested by Gerd Theißen, "Die Hülle des Mose," p. 127 (who sees a parallel in a synagogue fresco from Dura, in which the Torah-shrine or cupboard [which Theißen takes as a symbol of the old covenant] is portrayed as veiled during the reading of the Law), is wrong-headed. See too now Vollenweider, "2 Kor," p. 250 n. 256: "Allen Versuchen, die Hülle im Synagogengottesdienst wiederzufinden, stellt sich die Schwierigkeit entgegen, dass die Tora während der Lesung nicht verhüllt ist – dies gilt auch für die Freske von Dura Europas, auf die Theissen, Aspekte 126 f. und Stegemann 99 aufmerksam machen."

[115] *The Language and Imagery of the Bible*, 1980, p. 136. Caird points out that "Some linguists classify synecdoche and metonymy as metaphor, on the ground that all three consist in the transfer of a name from one referent to another. This usage, however, blurs one important distinction: in synecdoche and metonomy the link between the two referents is one of contiguity and in metaphor it is one of comparison" (p. 137). See too the helpful discussion of the use of metonomy by Herbert Chanan Brichto, "The Worship of the Golden Calf: A Literary Analysis of a Fable on Idolatry," *HUCA* 54 (1983) 1–44, p. 12, in which he points out that in Hebrew idiom there is a "regular metonymic (part for the whole, cause for the effect) use of the terms for crime, sin, and guilt to stand for their consequences; thus, respectively, punishment (for crime), expiation (for sin), indemnity (for guilt)."

[116] Contra e.g. Koch, *Schrift*, p. 335, who misses the conceptual link between Israel's hardness of heart in Exod. 32–34 and the veil, so that for him Paul's move in v. 15 is "völlig unanschaulich." Koch is correct, however, when he concludes, p. 336, that in v. 15 "Das κάλυμμα des Mose ist bei Paulus völlig aus dem ursprünglichen Erzähl- und Geschehens-

veil continuing to exist at the reading of the old covenant thus provides a powerful symbol of this same "stiff-necked" rebellion by using the effect for the cause.[117] Paul's point is that, although the "old covenant" is read weekly in the synagogue, "until this very day" Israel remains cut off from its revelation of the glory of God as an act of divine judgment because of her "stiff-necked" rebellion.[118] Just as the revelation of the Law within the Sinai covenant did not

---

zusammenhang von Exod 34 herausgelöst und zur Metapher für einen heutigen Sachverhalt geworden." However, because he misses the significance of the veil in its original context, he fails to see the way in which Paul brings it over into his own context (see below).

[117] So too F. Lang, *Korinther*, p. 274, who sees that "die Decke des Mose als Typos für das Unverständnis der Glieder der Synagoge beim Vorlesen aus dem (hier zuerst genannten) 'alten' Testament dient." In Lang's view, however, what the Jews do not recognize is that through Christ the Sinai covenant has become the "old" covenant and that the Law's perverted function as a death-producing letter first finds its end in Christ, taking Rom. 10:4 as the key to Paul's meaning and taking the subject of v. 14b not to be the veil (as argued in this study), but the old covenant itself. For a response to this view, see below. See now Belleville, *Reflections of Glory*, pp. 230 f., who, based on the parallel between Μωϋσῆς ἐτίθει κάλυμμα in v. 13a and τὸ αὐτὸ κάλυμμα μένει in v. 14b, sees the function of the veil and its continuation as that which "serves to veil the covenantal glory down even to Paul's time" (following Bultmann, Schekle, Dodd, Lietzmann, Schulz), but denies that this also entails a reference to Israel's condition of unbelief and rebellion. But see Wright, *Climax*, pp. 181 f., who independently of this study sees that Paul's point in v. 14b–15 is that the Jews are still in the "same condition of 'veiledness'" as the Israelites were in Moses' day, and that the original reason for the veil has not changed. Wright thus sees that in v. 15 it is the veil, not the Torah, which is abolished. But in contrast to the position argued in this study, Wright follows those who argue that the removal of the veil refers to the taking away of the "inability to understand Torah," which in Wright's reading of Paul means coming to "the true understanding of Torah, precisely as a God-given deliberate temporary dispensation" (p. 182; cf. pp. 191 f.). Only those in the new covenant can comprehend that to understand the Law properly is to understand that it is over. In Wright's view this answers the apparent contradiction between Gal. 3, which teaches that the Law is abolished, and 2 Cor. 3, which seemingly teaches that it is maintained (pp. 182, 191 f.). Wright thus takes his important insight in the wrong direction.

[118] See now Renwick, *Temple*, pp. 147 f., who insightfully posits that in vv. 14b–15 the veil is "... still ... a symbol of the protection needed against the penetration of δόξα into the Israelites' lives because of the power of such δόξα, at least in its Mosaic context, to bring not life, but death." But he rejects the use of the veil as a symbol of Israel's hardened hearts, missing the primary referent in favor of the implied secondary motif. He therefore concludes that in 3:14–15 the veil is "initially positive not negative, one of mercy given to those who foolishly persist in seeking for that which would kill them if they were to find it" (p. 148). Conversely, since in 3:18 Paul refers to glory as that which transforms one, Renwick turns around and argues that if the covenant should change, the same veil becomes a "hindrance to blessing," since it then prevents one from encountering this glory. The veil thus has a dual function, depending upon which covenant is in force (p. 148). But the clear implication of 3:14 is that in the new covenant something *negative*, now associated with the veil, is being abolished, not something positive. Moreover, this attempt to read the significance of the veil in two distinct ways at once leads Renwick to end up agreeing with Hanson that καταργέω in 3:14 "... can more easily be associated with covenants than veils" (p. 148 n. 54; see below, n. 143) (!), since for him what is abolished in 3:14 is explicitly the veil, but implicitly the old covenant and its decree of death (p. 148; for my view on the antecedent of καταργεῖται, see below).

bring about Israel's redemption in Moses' day, so too it continues to "kill" rather than make alive in Paul's. For then, as now, the revelation of the glory/ presence of God in the Law encounters a people who have been hardened to its salvific power.[119]

The fact that Paul refers explicitly to the "reading" of the old covenant in presenting this image does not indicate, therefore, a veiling of the "hidden" or "real" meaning of the Sinai covenant itself. The veil placed upon Israel at the reading of the old covenant is not a reference to a divine hiding of the hermeneutical key to the Scriptures, so that Israel is unable to see that the real meaning of the Law is Christ or that the old covenant was destined to be done away with in Christ.[120] Nor is 2 Cor. 3:14b Paul's justification for rereading the Law against its original intention. Even less is it an attempt to argue that the old covenant message or the Law itself is somehow misleading or inadequate. Although such interpretations attempt to do justice to the symbolic nature of the "veil" in 3:14b, they miss the point of the veil as a metonomy which derives its meaning from the original Scriptural context out of which it is taken. Instead, they look beyond Paul's argument in 3:7–14 to some more general principle or construct supposedly inherent in Paul's thinking.[121] But as we have seen in 3:6, the point is not that Israel could not and cannot under-

---

[119] A classic example of the problems encountered by those who try to understand the purpose of the veil in 3:13 in terms of hiding the fading of the old covenant, etc., and at the same time take Paul's statement in 14ab seriously, is found in Lietzmann, *An die Korinther*, p. 112, who therefore concludes that although Moses veiled himself, he really did not need to do so, since Israel's mind was so hardened that she could not have seen the truth anyway!

[120] Hence, the alternative to Windisch first given by J. Goettsberger cannot be accepted (see above, chapter four). Goettsberger too must add an entire thought to make Paul's argument work. In Goettsberger's view, "Die Hülle des Moses nach Ex 34 and 2 Kor 3," *Biblische Zeitschrift* 16 (1924) 1–17, the fact that the glory of the old covenant could only be seen periodically was an indication that it would be done away with in Christ, but the veil hid this implication from Israel (cf. pp. 13, 16).

[121] This is the weakness in Provence's otherwise insightful treatment of the meaning of the veil. Since he views τέλος to refer to Christ in 3:13, he must take the veil in 3:14 to be a reference to the function of hiding the *purpose* of the glory of God, rather than as a metonomy for Israel's hard hearts; see his "Who is Sufficient," p. 78. Provence thus speaks of a "veiling function of the old covenant" as that which can "account for the unbelief of Israel" (p. 78). In his words, "The Old Covenant ... is veiled *so that* the heart of Israel is hardened and turns away from God's will" (p. 79, emphasis mine). But the veil is not the cause of Israel's unbelief, it is the divine response to it! For a view similar to mine, see Hughes, *Second Epistle to the Corinthians*, p. 111, who concludes concerning Paul's sequence of thought in 3:14 that "Paul introduces a bold transference of thought when he affirms that *the same veil* remains when the old covenant is read; but he is fully justified in doing so because he is thinking historically: the placing by Moses of a veil over his face was in itself an action symbolical of the veil of rebellion and unbelief which curtained the hearts of the people ... During the succeeding centuries that veil has never been removed ..." But Hughes' interpretation of the function of the veil in Exod. 34 as keeping the people "from the true apprehension of God's glory," so that it has not been removed "from the understanding of the nation," fails to take the *moral* nature of Israel, which the veil represents, as the issue at stake in both Exod. 32–34 and 2 Cor. 3:13 ff.

stand the Law and its covenant intellectually, but that, as in Galatians 4:22–5:26, 6:13, and Romans 2:17–29,[122] she is not able to respond to the Law *morally* because of her "heart of stone." Apart from his subsequent psychological reinterpretation of the text, Gerd Theißen's arguments against an exclusively hermeneutical reading of 3:14 are thus compelling.[123] For against all such attempts it must be emphasized that it is not the *reading* of the old covenant which is veiled, but *Israel* when she reads it.[124]

The problem signified by the veil is thus not a *cognitive* inability due to the lack of a special spiritual endowment, but an inescapable *volitional* inability as a result of a hardened heart untouched by the Spirit's transforming power.[125] It is not that Israel cannot understand the meaning of the old covenant, as if it were an esoteric secret to be unlocked by a special gnostic revelation, but that she *will not* accept it as true for her and *cannot* submit to it.[126] In other words, what Paul says descriptively by the "letter" in 3:6, he now restates symbolically with the metonomy of the "veil" in 3:14b.[127] Israel's "stiff-necked" condition continues to cover her response to the Sinai covenant.

---

[122] Cf. Luke 16:31; Acts 7:53; John 5:46 f.; 7:19.

[123] See his "Die Hülle des Mose," p. 148. As Theißen observes: "Der Alte Bund ist für Paulus nicht nur eine 'literarische,' sondern eine sachliche Größe. Das Problem ist nicht, daß der Buchstabe unverständlich ist, sondern daß er tötet (3:6). Nicht der dunkle Sinn der Schrift, sondern die existenzgefährdende Drohung des verurteilenden und tötenden Gesetzes verbirgt sich hinter der Decke ... Die Entfernung der Decke bedeutet nicht nur Zuwachs an Erkenntnis, sondern Verwandlung des Menschen ... so gewiß sie auch ein neues Verständnis des Alten Testamentes umschließt." Contra the view argued here, however, Theißen sees the veil as hiding the subconscious aggressive and anxiety-producing power of the Law, from which one is then freed to become like Christ, who "tritt als Zielbild des wahren Menschen an die Stelle des strafenden Überichs" (p. 155, cf. pp. 152–155).

[124] Cf. already J. Calvin, *The Second Epistle of Paul the Apostle to the Corinthians and the Epistles to Timothy, Titus and Philemon*, trans. T.A. Smail, Calvin's Commentaries Vol. 10, 1964, p. 47, who stressed that Paul "lays the whole blame upon (Israel) since it was their blindness that kept them from gaining any advantage from the teaching of the Law." Calvin understands the point of v. 15 to be that "In case any blame should be attached to the Law, he again repeats that their hearts were covered with a veil" (p. 47). Moreover, in 3:13, "nothing that is said here is derogatory to Moses" (p. 47).

[125] Again, Provence, "Who is Sufficient," p. 80, is correct when he concludes that the point of the veil is "a hardening of the will rather than an obscuring of the perception," as long as one keeps in mind, contra Provence, that the veil *represents* this hardening itself and is not the cause of it.

[126] See Jürgen Roloff, *Apostolat – Verkündigung – Kirche. Ursprung, Inhalt und Funktion des kirchlichen Apostelamtes nach Paulus, Lukas und den Pastoralbriefen*, 1965, p. 101, who, though he views the veil to rest on the old covenant itself, summarized Paul's point concerning the old covenant in 3:14 well: "Israel kann also ihren wahren Inhalt nicht erkennen; nicht darum freilich, weil ... eine 'Decke' des Nichtverstehens zwischen die Schrift und Israel treten mußte, sondern weil Israel selbst nicht verstehen kann und will! Die Verantwortung für das Nichtverstehen der Schrift liegt nicht in ihr selbst, sondern in denen, die sie hören und – nicht verstehen wollen!"

[127] Contra the many who, like Koch, *Schrift*, p. 336, conclude that the veil in vv. 14 f. refers to "die Verhüllung des Sinns der Schrift für die ihrer Verlesung beiwohnenden Israeliten."

This interpretation most easily fits the structure of Paul's argument in which he indicates that the continuing presence of the "veil" (v. 14b) grounds the fact that Israel has always been hardened (v. 14a). From Paul's perspective, Israel's continuing hard-heartedness against the Sinai covenant *up until the present* is sure evidence for her hardened condition from the beginning. In making this move from 3:14a to 14b, Paul establishes through the introduction of the metonomy of the veil the same point that he makes and supports in Romans 11:7–10. There too Paul explains the fact that only a remnant of Israel has responded to the Gospel by pointing to God's elective grace (11:5 f.; cf. Rom. 9:11). Once again using the same vocabulary as in 2 Cor. 3:14a, Paul can therefore conclude that "those who were chosen obtained it, and the rest were hardened" (ἐπωρώθησαν, 11:7). As in 2 Cor. 3:14a, this gnomic characterization in Rom.11:7 is the inference to be drawn from Israel's history of rebellion, which in 2 Cor. 3:7 ff. is pictured in terms of Exod. 32–34 and in Rom. 10:21 is stated directly from Isaiah 65:2. Moreover, just as in 2 Cor. 3:14b, in Rom. 11:8–10 Paul supports this assertion by describing Israel's *continuing* hardness, this time not in symbolic terms derived from the Scriptures, but by introducing a combination of Is. 29:10 and Deut. 29:3(4), with a secondary allusion to Is. 6:9 f. (cf. the use of πωρόω in 11:7).[128] Paul's point from these texts is clear: God has given Israel "a spirit of stupor" (Is. 29:10) "*until this very day* "(ἕως τῆς σήμερον ἡμέρας, Deut. 29:3; cf. the almost direct parallel to 3:14b, 15), which can then be described as eyes which have been darkened not to see and backs which have been bent *always* (διὰ παντός, Ps. 68:23). Moreover, the inability of Israel and her prophets "to see" the things of the prophet's vision because they are "asleep" in Is. 29:10 is interpreted in Is. 29:11 in terms of their inability to read the words of a sealed book.[129] But here too, this inability is not intellectual but moral, as indicated in

---

[128] For this point, see too Lang, *Korinther*, p. 274. Contra Stockhausen, *Moses' Veil*, pp. 141, who takes the reference to "eyes which do not see and ears which do not hear" in Rom. 11:8 to be a reference to Is. 6:10. Though she sees this reference as "obvious," in Is. 6:10 the reference is rather to the people who "hear with difficulty with their ears and close their eyes (καὶ τοῖς ὠσὶν αὐτῶν βαρέως ἤκουσαν καὶ τοὺς ὀφθαλμοὺς αὐτῶν ἐκάμμυσαν), while the subsequent reference to their eyes not seeing and ears not hearing is not to their current state, as in Rom. 11:8, but to the purpose of Isaiah's ministry in keeping them hardened. But in both regards, the parallels between Rom. 11:8 and Deut. 29:3 are striking, including the reference to "eyes which do not see and ears which do not hear." Moreover, the link between Is. 29:10 and Deut. 29:3 is established on the basis of what the Lord "gave" Israel in each case (cf. ἔδωκεν in Deut. 29:3 and ἔδωκεν in Rom. 11:8 for πεπότικεν of Is. 29:10). Isaiah 6:9 f. is thus related to Is. 29:10 and Deut. 29:3 in Rom. 11:7–10 as its conceptual introduction, but is not itself in view in Rom. 11:8.

[129] The MT of Is. 29:10 speaks of the prophets and seers of Israel "being covered," which keeps them from seeing the vision, but the LXX has replaced this verb with the substantive "covered or hidden things" (τὰ κρυπτά), so that the relationship between Is. 29:10 and Exod. 34 is tenuous in the LXX; for this point, see too Stockhausen, *Moses' Veil*, p. 144. But the conceptual link between Israel's hardened condition in Exod. 32–24 and the experience of Isaiah is certainly maintained.

Is. 29:13a, where the people who cannot see the words of the book are described as those who "draw near to the Lord with their mouths and honor him with their lips, but their heart (καρδία) is far away from me."[130] For Isaiah, the people cannot respond to YHWH correctly because, *like* a book which cannot be read because it is sealed (cf. the ὡς οἱ λόγοι τοῦ βιβλίου τοῦ ἐσφραγισμένου τούτου), their hearts are hardened to the presence of God, even in their worship of him (Is. 29:13b).[131]

These verbal and conceptual parallels to 2 Cor. 3:14ab are striking and confirm our interpretation of the symbolic meaning of the veil in v. 14b.[132] The almost exact parallels between Deut. 29:3 and ἄχρι τῆς σήμερον ἡμέρας in 3:14 and ἕως σήμερον in 3:15 are therefore not coincidental, but reflect Paul's understanding of the hardening of Israel in the wilderness as the conceptual counterpart to the hardening of Israel declared in the prophets.[133] The same combination of the Law and the Prophets which is introduced explicitly in Rom. 11:7–10 in support of Paul's understanding of Israel's hardened condition is thus given implicitly in 2 Cor. 3:14f. (ἐπωρώθη ... ἄχρι τῆς σήμερον

---

[130] For the link between the "covering" and the hardening of the people in Is. 29:10, cf. too van Unnik, "With Unveiled Face," p. 162.

[131] Contra Stockhausen, *Moses' Veil*, p. 144, who argues on the basis of the occurrence of ἀναγινώσκω in Is. 29:11 f. that in 3:14 f. Paul has taken his concept of Israel's inability from Is. 29:11, which she understands as a statement of Israel's inability to read the words of the book hermeneutically (pp. 144, 145 n. 107, 149, 153). Although she rightly states that "For Isaiah 29:11–12, the phenomena of disbelief and ignorance are symbolized by Israel's inability ... to read the words of a book," she draws the wrong conclusion that, "This metaphor of Israel's disbelief is concretized by Paul in II Cor. 3:14–15 as their inability to read the 'old covenant' or 'the books of Moses,' just as Isaiah had foretold" (p. 145). Such a "hermeneutical" reading is foreign both to Isaiah and 2 Cor. 3:14 f., where the problem is not that the book is sealed *per se*, but that Israel is hardened. In Is. 29:10 the sealed book remains a metaphor. And in 2 Cor. 3:14 f. the "veil" does not exist both on Israel and upon the reading of the old covenant as Stockhausen maintains (cf. p. 149). For this same view of the double function of the veil, see Lietzmann, *An die Korinther*, p. 112.

[132] Contra Theobald, *Gnade*, p. 203, who argues that there is no parallel between 3:14–16 and Rom. 9–11, since 3:16 does not speak of the future conversion of Israel, but of the continuing possibility of turning from the hardness characteristic of Israel to faith in Christ. Though this latter point is certainly true (against Windisch, Georgi), this does not mean that Paul is not developing in short form in 2 Cor. 3:14–16 the other points concerning Israel's history and nature that he makes in Rom. 9–11.

[133] So too e.g. Furnish, *II Corinthians*, p. 208, but without seeing the implications for the development of Paul's argument against the backdrop of the Law and the Prophets, Provence, "Who is Sufficient," p. 78 (following Hickling), and Hofius, "Gesetz und Evangelium," p. 105. Contra Belleville, *Reflections of Glory*, pp. 226 f., who notes the background to Rom. 11:8 in Deut. 29:3(4) and Is. 29:10, but surprisingly denies that Is. 29:10 and Deut. 29:3(4) are also in view in 2 Cor. 3:14 since the correspondence is not exact. She takes ἄχρι τῆς σήμερον ἡμέρας merely to be a common idiomatic phrase found in all types of literature. She also rejects Deut. 29:3(4) as behind 3:15a (see below). But the structural parallels between the arguments of Rom. 11:7–10 and 2 Cor. 3:14 are too close for the same background to be denied to 2 Cor. 3:14, and the conceptual identity between Paul's choice of ἄχρι and ἕως in the LXX of Deut. 29:3, the *only* difference between the two phrases (!), is so close as to make the allusion unmistakable, esp. in view of Paul's subsequent use of in ἕως v. 15a.

ἡμέρας ... ἕως σήμερον).[134] Just as Israel was hardened to the Law in Moses' day (Deut. 29:3 f.) and in the days of the prophets (Is. 6:9 f.; Jer. 5:21–24; Ezek. 12:2, 3, 9), Israel continues to remain hardened under the old covenant in Paul's day as well.[135] Indeed, as James M. Scott has demonstrated, Paul's understanding in Galatians 3:10 of the curse of the Law under which Israel has lived derives from this same context within Deuteronomy 27–32,[136] of which Deut. 29:3 f. is a key component as the historical-theological rational for Israel's hardened state and her ensuing judgment. Moreover, as we have seen in chapter three, Paul's move from Exod. 32–34 to the summary statement in Deut. 29:3 f., together with the later prophetic traditions from Jeremiah and Ezekiel, has been prepared for by the canonical tradition itself.

But equally striking is the way that Israel's history of rebellion was repeatedly attributed to her earlier disobedience in the wilderness, beginning with the golden calf, as evidence of Israel's hardened state as a people.[137] In moving from the present to the gnomic past in 2 Cor. 3:14ab and Romans 11:7–10, Paul is therefore simply making the same theological move common throughout the Scriptures (see chapter three). Paul's thinking in 2 Cor. 3:7–14b is thus part of a long canonical tradition in which Israel's continuing rejection of the Law and the Prophets is seen as evidence of her recalcitrant condition, which in turn is traced back to her "original sin" with the golden calf in the wilderness. Moreover, we have also seen how, conceptually, later synagogue prac-

---

[134] So too Theobald, *Gnade*, p. 196, who concludes that, "so zeigt das Passiv ἐπωρώθη, mit dem die Überlagerung der Exodusszene mit dem prophetischen Konzept der Verstokkung anhebt (vgl. Jes 6; 29 und Dtn 29), daß Gott der eigentliche Urheber der Verhärtung ist." But Theobald, p. 196, in contrast to the view suggested here, argues that according to 2 Cor. 3 the hardening of Israel in Exodus, like that in Is. 6:9–13, was intended to point to the ultimate redemption to take place beyond the judgment. By covering up the fading glory, Moses was thus giving a sign of the fact that Israel was hardened and that the transitory nature of the Sinai-glory would only be seen in light of the glory of Christ.

[135] Although Hickling does not carry this insight through to his understanding of the function of the veil in Paul's argument (see above, n. 38), he insightfully points out that Moses' descent in Exod. 34 was made necessary by Israel's apostasy so that, "like the new covenant of Jeremiah 31:31, this διαχονία of Moses resulted from the people's disobedience to a former divine dispensation," "Sequence of Thought," p. 392. He thus concludes that "the thought that the sin of Israel, at the end of time as at Sinai, had made necessary a new action on God's part could well have suggested the reflection that the sin was continuing even in the face of the declaration of this new covenant" (p. 392).

[136] "'For as Many as are of Works of the Law are Under a Curse' (Galatians 3:10)," *Paul and the Scriptures of Israel, Studies in Scripture in Early Judaism and Christianity 1*, JSNT Suppl. Series 83, 1993, pp. 187–221; cf. pp. 194 f., in which he argues that Paul's combination of Deut. 27:26 with Deut. 29:19b (or 28:58), together with the formulaic expression γεγραμμένα ἐν τῷ βιβλίῳ τοῦ νόμου τούτου quoted in Gal. 3:10 (cf. Deut. 28:58, 61; 29:19, 20, 26; 30:10), shows that Paul read Deut. 27–32 as a unit, which then becomes the key to understanding Paul's point in Gal. 3:10.

[137] Cf. Hofius, "Gesetz und Evangelium," p. 106 n. 196, who refers to Exod. 32:9; 33:3, 5; 34:9 to support the idea that from Deut. 29 Paul could conclude that the Israelites were already hardened at the time of Exod. 34, but does not develop this insight either for his view of Exod. 34 itself or for Paul's argument in 2 Cor. 3.

tice could have been prefigured in the motifs concerning the "synagogue" from Exod. 34:29 ff. The introduction of the synagogue practice in 3:14b may thus have been suggested by Paul's reading of the LXX of Exod. 34:29 ff. in view of his own experiences. For given the terminology and authority structure present in Exod. 34:29 ff., Paul's association of Israel's present hardened condition while reading Moses with the events of Exod. 32–34 is a natural one.[138] Finally, Paul's ability to point to Israel's present hard-heartedness as evidence for her hardened state as a people finds its place within a continuing chain of post-biblical tradition in which Israel's rebellious nature is not only stressed, but also becomes evidence of the need for a restoration expression of the power of God among his people.[139]

Paul's specific assertion in 3:14b in support of v. 14a, as the counterpart to his own boldness, is that this veil, as a metonomy for Israel's hard heart, "*remains*" (μένει) to this very day at the reading "of the *old* covenant" (τῆς παλαιᾶς διαθήκης). Paul's vocabulary, in both cases, is once again unquestionably loaded with eschatological connotations. In the latter case, Paul can refer to the Sinai covenant as the "old" covenant only because he is convinced that the "new" covenant has been inaugurated. The designation "old" is not a pejorative evaluation of the character of the Sinai covenant, but a temporal and eschatological designation of its fulfillment.[140] As we have seen in chap-

---

[138] As also recognized by Vollenweider, "2 Kor," p. 258, who, on the basis of his own investigation of the post-biblical and rabbinic traditions surrounding Exod. 32–34, esp. the golden calf viewed as a second fall, the parallels between the glory of Adam before the fall and the glory of Israel lost with her sin with the golden calf, and the expectation that in the eschaton the righteous will once again see and be transformed into the glory of God (cf. pp. 257 and esp. his references to 1 Enoch 38:4; 62:16; 2 Bar. 51:3, 10; 4 Ezra 7:97, 127; and the many Qumran traditions), concludes that, "Bemerkenswert ist vor allem, dass *erst die Sünde Israels die Hülle des Mose notwendig zu machen scheint*: Die oft als gekünstelt empfundene Übertragung der Hülle von Mose auf das Herz in 2Kor 3:14 f. entspricht völlig der in den Sinaitraditionen angelegten Logik: *Sünde verunmöglicht die Schau göttlichen Lichts*" (emphasis his). Of course, contra Paul, these traditions often associate this transformation with the Law itself.

[139] For some of the key texts, see Pseudo-Philo, LAB 11:5 f.; 12:1–10; 13:10; 19:6 f.; 30:5 f.; 1 Esdras 1:18 f., 22, 45 f.; 8:71–74; Sir. 16:11; 33:10–15; Bar. 1:19 f.; 2:8; Jub. 1:7–25; 1 Enoch 1:4–7; 5:4–6; 38:2; 89:33–35; 99:2; 4 Ezra 3:20–27; 7:46–61; 117 f.; 9:31–33; 1QS 1:16–2:25; 5:5; CD 2:16–18; 4:15; 5:17–19; 8:7–11; 4Q504; 1Q22 1:5–8; 4Q 171 1–10; etc.; Philo, *Vit.Mos.* II.159–173, 270–272; QE 49; *De Eb.* 69–70, 98–11; *De Spec. Leg.* I.124–127; and *Tg. Neof.* to Exod. 32–34. For a very helpful study of Israel's hard-heartedness in the LXX and post-biblical literature, see Klaus Berger, "Hartherzigkeit und Gottes Gesetz. Die Vorgeschichte des antijüdischen Vorwurfs in Mc 10:5," *ZNW* 61 (1970) 1–47.

[140] Contra Gaston, "Paul and the Torah in 2 Corinthians 3," p. 164, who suggests the translation "ancient covenant" as a designation originating with Paul's opponents and reflecting "the propaganda value of representing ancient traditions." Gaston's desire to deflect criticism of the Sinai covenant is correct, but his view misses the eschatological context of Paul's statement and that the use of the veil as a metonomy makes it clear that the problem in view is not the covenant *per se*, but Israel.

ter two, the Sinai covenant is abolished and replaced by the new, not because its message was inferior, but because it was broken by Israel. We have also seen in chapter four that "to remain" in 3:11 is to endure through the inaugurated new age and its consummation at Christ's return and final judgment. In 3:11, however, it was used to describe the positive "remaining" of the ministry of the new covenant. Now, as its negative counterpart, Paul can describe the continuing hard-heartedness of Israel under the Sinai covenant, i.e. the "veil," as that which "remains" through the present overlapping of the ages and into the day of judgment inasmuch as Israel continues to look to the old covenant, rather than to the new, for her identity and salvation. Whereas the implications of "remaining" in 3:11 were altogether positive, now they speak of the present and final judgment of rebellious Israel. For Paul, the fact that Israel continues to be hardened as she relates to the Sinai covenant (v. 14b) supplies the needed evidence that Israel has been hardened from the beginning (v. 14a). Conversely, from the fact that Israel's hardened condition from the beginning is *continuing*, in spite of the coming of Christ and the pouring out of the Spirit, Paul draws the conclusion that Israel will continue to *remain* hardened until the new age is consummated with God's final judgment (v. 14b). This is, as Paul says in Rom. 11:25, the "mystery" of the new covenant. That the vast majority of Israel would reject the dawning of the *new* covenant is thus no argument against its validity, given her stiff-necked state. Paul's description of Israel's continuing "veiled" state in relationship to the Sinai covenant as the "*old* covenant" is *in itself* a statement of Israel's hardened nature toward the new.[141] The same contrast between Paul's boldness and Israel's hardness established structurally in vv. 12–13a and v. 14a is therefore confirmed by Paul's repetition of the vocabulary from 3:11. With the dawning of the new age and in anticipation of its final consummation, the new covenant ministry "remains" (3:11b), but so does Israel's hard heartedness (3:14b).

That this interpretation of v. 14b is warranted can be seen not only by the parallel use of μένω in 3:11, but also by the contrasting eschatological use of καταργέω in 3:14d as the logical counterpart to its earlier use in 3:11. Moreover, whereas in v. 14 the subject of "that which remains" has been reversed, "that which is done away with" is still associated with the ministry of the old covenant and its effects. Now, however, it is not the covenant itself which is in

---

[141] Cf. Barnabas Lindars, *New Testament Apologetic: The Doctrinal Significance of Old Testament Quotations*, 1961, pp. 162 f., who rightly saw Paul's point: "In ch. 3 Paul is saying that the Jews were guilty of *porosis* even in the time of Moses, and that this persists even now when they cling to the old Law." But his overall thesis that Paul's thought at this point is "very different" from that found in Mark or John, since it is characterized by a Hellenistic perspective in which the Jews' failure "was due to their failure to perceive the real meaning of the Law from the very beginning," i.e Christ (p. 163), cannot be sustained. Rather, for Paul, as in Mk. 4:10–13, the function of the Gospel, as with the parables of Jesus, is to "sift" out the people, since it is the elect who perceive them while those who are blind reject them (cf. Lindars, p. 159).

view, but that which determined its character of "death," namely, the "stiff-necked" nature of Israel, here portrayed in terms of the "veil." With the addition of the participial phrase μὴ ἀνακαλυπτόμενον modifying τὸ αὐτὸ κάλυμμα, Paul continues his metonymy in order to indicate the ground for the fact that Israel's hardened condition is still remaining, which he further supports with the following causal clause: "since it is being rendered inoperative or abolished in Christ" (ὅτι ἐν Χριστῷ καταργεῖται).[142] The unexpressed subject of καταργεῖται in v. 14d is the veil of v. 14b, since this is the subject of the finite verb μένει to which the participle belongs upon which the ὅτι-clause is dependent syntactically. Without an indication that a new subject has been introduced, there is no impulse to look outside the interrelationship between these clauses in order to import the more general subject of the "old covenant" or its glory.[143] The same contrast between "that which remains" (τὸ μένον) and

---

[142] For μὴ ἀνακαλυπτόμενον either as a predicate participle (e.g. AV, RSV, NASB, NIV, etc.), or as an accusative absolute (e.g. Allo, Collange, Bachmann) in reference to the veil, with ὅτι then being causal, see the persuasive arguments of Windisch, *Der zweite Korintherbrief*, p. 122; the three arguments given by S. Schulz, "Die Decke des Moses. Untersuchungen zu einer vorpaulinischen Überlieferung in II Kor. 3:7–18," *ZNW* 49 (1958) 1–30, pp. 12 f. nn. 63–64; Hughes, *Second Epistle to the Corinthians*, p. 112 n. 9; Gerd Theißen, "Die Hülle des Mose," pp. 148 f.; Furnish, *II Corinthians*, p. 209, following Barrett; Hofius, "Gesetz und Evangelium," p. 117 n. 243; and the other commentators mentioned by these authors. For the opposing view that the participle introduces an additional thought defined by a following ὅτι of content, see R.P. Martin, *2 Corinthians*, p. 69, Belleville, *Reflections of Glory*, pp. 233–235, and the 12 sources listed there. Belleville bases her view on the supposed "haggadic" parallel between πρὸς τὸ μὴ ἀτενίσαι τοὺς υἱοὺς Ἰσραήλ in v. 13 and μὴ ἀνακαλυπτόμενον in v. 14 (p. 233). But the use of the same verb to refer to the lifting of the veil in v. 18 and the reference to the abolishment of the veil itself in v. 16 are ultimately decisive in favor of the view taken here, whereas Belleville must suppose that Paul is making use of a "double meaning of the word to his advantage" (pp. 234 f.). A contextual clue for such a double meaning is lacking. Lang, *Korinther*, p. 274, and Stockhausen, *Moses' Veil*, p. 89 n. 8, take the particle μή to indicate a negative purpose clause and translate it "lest it be revealed that in Christ it [the old covenant] is being brought to an end." But in order to establish their interpretation of what was hidden from Israel, such a reading overloads the meaning of the particle and misses the reference of the participle to the veil.

[143] Contra e.g. Prümm, *Diakonia Pneumatos*, pp. 142 f.; R.P. Martin, *2 Corinthians*, p. 69; Furnish, *II Corinthians*, p. 210, who follows Lietzmann, Allo, and Bultmann in reading it this way; A.T. Hanson, "The Midrash in II Corinthians 3: A Reconsideration," *JSNT* 9 (1980) 2–28, p. 18, who takes the subject to be the old covenant because "the verb καταργεῖν cannot be appropriately used for the removal of a veil"; cf. too his *Studies*, p. 139 (but this view disregards its use in 3:14bc as a metonomy in parallel to the concept of Israel's hardened condition, which was also used in relationship to this verb in 3:7–11); Dumbrell, "Paul's use of Exodus 34," pp. 188, 193 n. 25; Belleville, *Reflections of Glory*, p. 235; and recently Liebers, *Das Gesetz als Evangelium*, p. 118, who takes it to refer to the old covenant in general and to the Law in particular, as well as taking the ὅτι to be declarative, since in his view the hardening of Israel in v. 14 is not taken away, and hence the Law in its killing function remains. But this identification of the veil with the Law cannot be sustained. Liebers is correct, however, in maintaining that according to 3:15 the problem with the old covenant is not in the Law itself, but in the hearts of the Jews (p. 119). In support of my reading, cf. Windisch, *Der zweite Korintherbrief*, p. 122; Schulz, "Decke," p. 12 n. 64 (minus his view that this is a

"that which is being rendered inoperative" (τὸ καταργούμενον) in 3:11 is therefore replayed in 3:14, but now the subject is Israel's hardened condition represented by the veil.[144] Paul's point in 3:14 is clear. Only the dawning of the new covenant of the new age in Christ can abolish the veil of Israel's hard-heartedness – there is no power to do so under the Sinai covenant.[145] And since Israel's hardened condition means that she will fall under the judgment of God, Renwick is correct in concluding that "in Christ" in 3:14 refers to "the new covenantal sphere within which ... the death penalty (integrally related to the *curse* of Gal. 3:13) is being abolished (καταργέω)."[146] Hence, even though Paul preaches the Gospel of the new covenant in the power of the Spirit, Israel's hard-heartedness is destined (by God!) to continue throughout the dawning of the new age, since the very one whom they reject is the only one who can remove their blindness. Only in Christ can the heart of stone be removed by the Spirit.[147]

Pauline addition to a non-Pauline tradition, p. 13 n. 65); Kümmel's critique of Lietzmann's view in his supplements to *An die Korinther*, p. 200; and now Hofius, "Gesetz und Evangelium," p. 117 n. 243, though with different understandings of the meaning of the veil itself.

[144] Contra the view represented by Kamlah, Käsemann, Beker, Hays, and esp. in regard to 2 Cor. 3:14, P. Stuhlmacher, *Vom Verstehen des Neuen Testaments, Eine Hermeneutik; Grundrisse zum Neuen Testament*, NTD Ergänzungsreihe 6, 1979, pp. 59–66, p. 61 (see above, Introduction) and Koch, *Schrift*, p. 337, that v. 14d refers to the removal of the veiling of the Scripture in Christ, which previously hindered its Spirit-led understanding. Moreover, Koch, p. 337, stresses that this is the only text in Paul's writings which contains this "Spitzenaussage" concerning the meaning of the Scripture – so that if it does not hold here, there remains no other statement to support this understanding of Paul's hermeneutic.

[145] Belleville's view that vv. 14b–15 are a haggadic interpretation of vv. 13–14a leads her to posit that ὅτι ἐν Χριστῷ καταργεῖται is parallel in meaning to εἰς τὸ τέλος τοῦ καταργουμένου in v. 13. As a result she concludes that in v. 14d Paul is still referring to the concept of the fading glory of the covenant, rendering Paul's thought to mean that "in Christ the covenantal glory is in the process of fading" (pp. 235 f.), so that the period from Moses until the current day is "characterized by this fact of diminution" (p. 237). In addition to taking καταργέω to refer to "fading," and to not recognizing the symbolic use of the veil in v. 14 as a metonomy, Belleville's view fails in that for Paul the old covenant has come decisively to an end. The present tense of καταργέω in v. 14 need not indicate that this has not yet taken place completely, but is only in the process of being removed, as Belleville maintains (p. 236 nn. 1, 3), but that its removal is (now) accomplished in Christ, reading it as a "gnomic present" expressing "a state or condition" in which the time element is "remote" (James A. Brooks and Carlton L. Winbery, *Syntax of New Testament Greek*, 1978, p. 79).

[146] *Temple*, pp. 148 f. Though taking a different significance for the meaning of the veil itself and the source of the problem under the old covenant, Renwick's further point is equally insightful, i.e. that for Paul the abolition of the veil is a "declaration that the 'death penalty' of the old covenant has been removed" (p. 150). But since the removal of this penalty takes place only in Christ, Paul's point in v. 15 is that any attempt to continue to look to Moses/old covenant for God's glory is misplaced (cf. pp. 150 f.). For this same point in regard to the restoration from the curse of the Law in Christ as portrayed in Gal. 3:10, see now Scott, "Works of the Law," pp. 213–221.

[147] See R.P. Martin, *2 Corinthians*, p. 46, who observed that in 3:12–18 Paul contrasts negatively the old and new covenants by making the point that "unlike Moses' ministry, his ministry takes away the veil of hard-heartedness ..."

In v. 15 Paul completes his discussion of the veil which now resides over the reading of the old covenant by *restating* the point of v. 14b, this time by using the metonomy of the veil in explicit relationship to Israel's "heart" when she reads Moses.[148] His purpose in doing so, as the adversative conjunction which introduces his statement indicates,[149] is to stress that although Christ is the one who removes the hard heart of God's people (3:14d), "*nevertheless* (ἀλλά)[150] until today, whenever[151] Moses is read, a veil is being laid upon their heart" (3:15). As the negative counterpart to the positive work of Christ in 14d, v. 15 provides an exact conceptual parallel to Paul's prior statement in v. 14b, illustrated by the verbal parallels between the two verses:

3:14b: ἄχρι τῆς   σήμερον ἡμέρας   τὸ αὐτὸ   κάλυμμα   μένει

   3:15: ἕως   ·   σήμερον   κάλυμμα   κεῖται ἐπὶ τὴν καρδίαν
                                                   αὐτῶν

3:14b: ἐπὶ τῇ   ἀναγνώσει   τῆς παλαιᾶς διαθήκης

   3:15: ἡνίκα ἂν ἀναγινώσκηται   Μωυσῆς

---

[148] So too Wright, *Climax*, p. 182, who recognizes that 3:15 is an assertion, not an argument in and of itself, and F. Lang, *Korinther*, p. 275, who insightfully comments: "In V.15 geht der Blick von der Verlesung der Mosetora hinüber auf die Seite der Hörer; hier dient die Decke als Typos für ihre verfinsterten, unverständigen Herzen." Lang also insightfully argues that what they cannot see is the glory of God on the face of Christ (2 Cor. 4:6), and thus are not open to the new order of salvation which he has established, though in his view this means the abolishment of the Law.

[149] In contrast to v. 14a, here ἀλλά is not used as the positive contrast to an expressed negative assertion, but as the contrast to a positive assertion, and as such carries an adversative meaning; cf. BAGD, *A Greek-English Lexicon*, p. 38. Contra Theobald, *Gnade*, pp. 192 f., who reads the ἀλλά of v. 15 to be a contrast to the μή of 14c as an intensification. For the same adversative reading of v. 15 taken here, see Windisch, *zweiter Korintherbrief*, pp. 122 f. and Barrett, *Second Corinthians*, p. 121, though I have argued against their reading of v. 14b as a reference to the Law, and now Belleville, *Reflections of Glory*, p. 228, although she equates the adversative meaning of v. 15a with that of 14a, because she does not see the contrast in v. 14a to be *specifically* to the action of Moses, but takes it to refer to the entirety of v. 13.

[150] So too Belleville, *Reflections of Glory*, p. 237, who argues for an adversative reading of the ἀλλά in 15a against those who take it to indicate merely an intensification or resumption of the previous thought (see, e.g. Furnish, Theobald, Osty, Kuss, etc.). Belleville does so, however, based on the parallel she sees between v. 15a and 14a which brings her to the surprising conclusion that Paul is referring to two *different* veils in v. 14b and v. 15, in which the veil in v. 15 no longer refers to the veil of Moses, but to any ordinary veil (due to the anarthrous construction) (pp. 177, 238). For her view of the parallels between vv. 13 and 14b and v. 14a and 15 leads her to conclude that the contrast in v. 15a is to *all* of v. 14bcd, rather than just to v. 14d, so that, in her view, a veil is said to lie over their hearts (parallel to the fact that their perceptions were dulled, v. 14a) *in spite of the fact* that the same veil remains over the reading of the old covenant (parallel to Moses placing a veil over his face in v. 13) (cf. p. 238). This establishes a contrast, however, between two *equivalent* ideas. But this parallel makes perfect sense once the use of the veil in v. 14 as a metonomy is recognized.

[151] See the insightful observation of R.P. Martin, *2 Corinthians*, p. 69, that ἡνίκα ἂν in 3:15, being a *hapax* in the NT, is taken directly from Exod. 34:34. But contra Martin, et al.,

The parallel between the placement of the veil on Moses' face in v. 13, its placement on Israel "at the time of (ἐπὶ) the reading of the old covenant" in v. 14b, and Paul's reference to "reading Moses" in v. 15 also clearly indicates Paul's acceptance of the common Jewish identification, first indicated in Deuteronomy itself, of the role and authority of Moses with that of the Torah which he mediated and vice versa.[152] To read Moses is to read the Sinai covenant and its Law; to read the Law is to read Moses. It can thus be said that "Moses" is "read in the synagogues every Sabbath" (Acts 15:21; cf. Acts 13:15).[153] The substitution in v. 15 of "Moses" for the "old covenant" as that which is read (ἀναγινώσκηται Μωϋσῆς) unmistakably establishes this equation, as does Paul's other references to that which Moses "says" or "writes" (cf. Rom.10:5; 10:19). Here, as elsewhere, Paul's use accords with common early Jewish and Christian practice.[154] By the designation "old covenant" Paul is not attempting, therefore, to indicate a distinction between the Law as the "old covenant," which is done away with, and the Scripture as that which remains valid.[155] This covenant and the Law given at Sinai remain for Paul an

---

there is no need to posit a polemic in 3:15 against those who glory in their appearance ("face"), rather than in their "heart" (2 Cor. 5:12), or against some reconstructed Moses typology in which Moses functions as a θεῖος ἀνήρ.

[152] For this identification in Deut. and throughout canonical literature, see above, chapter three, esp. n. 144.

[153] For the corresponding reading of the prophets in the synagogue, see Luke 4:16–19; Acts 13:27. Against this background it is significant that Paul's letters are also to be read publicly in the church; cf. the Pauline prescripts, 1 Thess. 5:27; 2 Cor. 1:13; Col. 4:16; for the reading of Scripture, cf. the general admonition in 1 Tim. 4:13; and for the revelation of John, Rev. 1:3.

[154] Contra Gaston, Paul and the Torah in 2 Corinthians 3," p. 164, who prefers to read v. 15 as a reference to "the passage under discussion and to how the person of Moses is understood as a model." His support for this view is the contrast established in v. 16 (for the nature of the contrast in v. 16, see below). For the view of v. 14 here being argued, see too Hofius, "Gesetz und Evangelium," pp. 76 f., who concludes, following Kutsch, Behm, and Windisch, that the "old covenant" refers to the Torah from Sinai as the "entire corpus of the declaration of the will of God." For the use of Moses as the one who speaks, gives, or commands the Law, see Mk. 1:44 par.; 10:3 f. par.; 12:19 par.; 7:10; 12:26 par.; Lk. 16:29, 31; 24:27; John 1:45 (cf. 5:46); 7:22; 8:5; Acts 3:22 (cf. 7:37); 6:14; 21:21; 26:22; Heb. 7:14; 9:19; Rev. 15:3. For the corresponding designation, "the Law of Moses," see from Paul 1 Cor. 9:9; and elsewhere Lk. 2:22; 24:44; John 1:17; 7:19, 23; Acts 13:39; 15:5 (cf. 15:1); 28:23; Heb. 10:28. For the substitution of Moses for the Law, see Acts 6:11; 21:21. In the same way, Belleville, *Reflections of Glory*, p. 38, in speaking of the "interchangeability of references" between the Law and Moses in Josephus "similar to what is found in 2 Cor. 3:12–18," concludes that, "Paul similarly can speak interchangeably of the veiling of Moses and the veiling of the covenant (vv. 13–14), as well as of the reading of the covenant and the reading of 'Moses' (vv. 14–15)" (cf. p. 232).

[155] Contra those who, like A.T. Hanson, *Studies*, pp. 136–138, 140, make such a distinction. For Hanson, this differentiation allows him to support the traditional view that for Paul the Torah was "old, out-dated," since, "According to Paul, the Torah had never been intended by God as anything but a temporary expedient, whose main function was to bring men to a realization of their sin and their inability to obey God by means of obedience to the Torah" (p. 137). For Hanson, therefore, Christ abolishes the old covenant, which is equated

essential part of Scripture (cf. Rom. 3:21; 4:3, 17 f.; 9:17; Gal. 3:8, 22; etc.). Moreover, the fact that in 3:14 f. Moses and the old covenant can be "read," together with the prior reference to the Law as "letter" in 3:6 f., make it clear that Paul has in view the actual reading of the Torah in the synagogue as the embodiment of the old covenant mediated by Moses.[156] Hence, although Paul's reference to the "old covenant" in 3:14b cannot be understood as a direct equivalent for the later Christian designation "Old Testament" for the Jewish Scriptures,[157] this development does reflect Paul's *theological* conviction as expressed in 3:14. For as we have seen in chapter two, Paul's point in using such terminology is eschatological. The designation "old covenant" is Paul's description of the Sinai covenant ministered by Moses *in view of the "new covenant" inaugurated by Christ and ministered by Paul*.[158] The fact that the Sinai covenant is now the "*old* covenant" stands at the very heart of Paul's understanding of the work and significance of Christ. As a consistent application of this conviction, Paul concludes that, just as Moses was veiled *due to Israel's stiff-necked condition*, so too "the same veil" (τὸ αὐτὸ κάλυμμα) can be said to exist *on Israel's heart* (v. 15b) whenever the Law (= old covenant) which Moses mediated continues to be read (v. 14b, 15a).[159] Indeed, this conclusion lies especially close at hand when it is kept in mind that in post-biblical Jewish tradition the Law, once given, continues to represent the glory of God among his people.[160] Moreover, its apologetic force be-

---

with the Pentateuch itself (pp. 140, 145). This of course depends on reading the "old covenant" rather than "the veil" as the subject of 3:14c; see below.

[156] For the corresponding concept of the "Book of the covenant" (βίβλος διαθήκης) in reference to the Law, cf. e.g. Sir. 24:23; 1 Macc. 1:57; 2 Kgs. 23:2, 21; 2 Chron. 34:30, and van Unnik, "Η καινὴ διαθήκη – A Problem in the Early History of the Canon," in *Studia Patristica*, Vol. IV/Part II, ed. F.L. Cross, TU Bd. 79, 1961, pp. 212–227, p. 220.

[157] So with the vast majority of modern commentators and scholars; see e.g. Furnish, *II Corinthians*, p. 209, and Hofius, "Gesetz und Evangelium," p. 76, who points to Paul's use of ἡ γραφή ("the Scripture") to refer to the "Old Testament Scriptures" in Rom. 4:3; 9:17; 10:11; 11:2; Gal. 3:8; 3:22; 4:30; the plural αἱ γραφαί ("the Scriptures") in Rom. 15:4; 1 Cor. 15:3 f.; and γραφαὶ ἅγιαι ("holy Scriptures") in Rom. 1:2.

[158] So too Belleville, *Reflections of Glory*, p. 232, who argues that "… Paul's focus is on the ministerial as opposed to the legal side of this covenantal relationship, as the emphasis on διακονία in 3:1 ff. indicates." Contra that exegetical tradition which sees the contrast not to be eschatological, but material, as a contrast between the Law and Moses on the one side and Christ and the Spirit on the other. For a paradigmatic example of this position, see Erich Gräßer, *Der Alte Bund im Neuen*, pp. 91–95. For Gräßer's explicit rejection of an eschatological contrast in favor of one between the present "either/or" of the Law or Christ, see p. 91.

[159] Given this widespread tradition, it is not clear to me how Hays, *Echoes*, p. 145, can consider this equation a "dreamlike transfiguration of Moses from man into text." Moreover, it is not the text which is "veiled" in v. 14, but Israel. Hays' continuing attempt to turn Moses into a metaphor for Paul thus once again runs aground on Paul's argument itself. Hays is right, however, that "the single phrase *to auto kalymma* clinches and requires a hermeneutical reading of the passage" (p. 145); see below.

[160] Cf. e.g. Hosea 4:6 f.; and Sir. 4:13 (in which "taking hold of wisdom" parallels "taking hold of the law" in 15:1, through which one finds glory from the Lord); 24:23; Bar. 4:2 f.;

comes apparent when one realizes that Moses was no doubt also being read in Christian worship services and would one day be subsumed under the reading of the Gospels and the other apostolic writings.[161] Conversely, in Sirach 1:26–30, it is "in the midst of the synagogue" (ἐν μέσῳ συναγωγῆς) that disobedience to the "fear of the Lord" as expressed in the commandments is revealed by the Lord and judged. This disobedience finds its root in approaching the fear of the Lord "in a double heart" (ἐν καρδίᾳ δισσῇ, 1:28), i.e. "the heart full of deceit" (ἡ καρδία σου πλήρης δόλου, 1:30).[162] By implication, obedience to the Law comes about as a result of being able to approach the "fear of the Lord" with a clean heart intent on keeping its commandments as the expression of the wisdom of God (cf. 1:26 f.).[163]

Thus, it is not surprising that those who have not received this "new heart" invariably reject Christ, even as they fail to respond appropriately to the old covenant itself. For as Theobald has rightly emphasized concerning Paul's point in 3:15, "Der 'Verhüllung' meint nicht nur ein faktisches Nicht-Verstehen des Gesetzes, sondern darüber hinaus ein Nicht-Verstehen-*Können*, das in der Verdunklung des menschlichen Herzens begründet ist."[164] Israel's history of rebellion, which began with the golden calf, is continuing with her rejection of Jesus as the messianic Son of God, even though his life and resurrection testify that he is the one who has fulfilled the promise of the Scriptures (cf. 1 Cor. 15:2–6; 2 Cor. 1:19 f.; Rom. 1:2–4). The contrast to the tradition represented by Baruch 2:30, 35, where Israel's return to the Lord as a result of having received a new heart is to take place in the "land of Israel's captivity," at which time God will bring them back into the promised land and make with them an "everlasting covenant," or to that of 1 Enoch 90:6–39, in which the restoration of the people is to take place after the period of the Maccabean revolt when God appears to open the eyes of his people to his glory, is striking. For from Paul's perspective, although the "new covenant" has been inaugu-

---

Letter of Aristeas 133 (for the similar conception that the "power" of God pervades the Law); 2 Apoc. Bar. 59:1; and 4 Ezra 8:29, esp. 4 Ezra 3:19, where God's glory is said to have given the Law, and 9:31, 36 f., where the glory of God remains forever and is the means to the glorification of those who are saved, as we also find expressed in LAB 9:7 f.; 11:2, 5; 22:5, 30:2, etc.; see too Lives of the Prophets 2 (Jeremiah):18; 1QH 5:29–32; 1QH 6:9,12; *Exod. Rab.* 33:1; *Pesiq. Rab.* 11:13; etc.

[161] For this point, see Martin Hengel, "Probleme des Markusevangeliums," in *Das Evangelium und die Evangelien, Vorträge vom Tübinger Symposium 1982*, ed. P. Stuhlmacher, WUNT 28, 1983, p. 264 n. 97.

[162] Cf. Sir. 23:2 for the parallel in Sirach between "mind" or "thoughts" (διανόημα) and the "heart" (καρδία).

[163] For this same equation of wisdom with the fear of the Lord and with fulfilling the Law, see Sir. 19:20; 21:11; 33:2; 37:12; 39:1. For the parallel idea of the blessing which rests upon the one who directs his heart to meditate on the ways of wisdom, cf. Sir. 14:20 f., though Sir. is ambivalent when it comes to attributing to God the ability to direct one's heart to him.

[164] *Gnade*, p. 193. Theobald also stresses the conceptual parallel between the hardening of Israel's heart and the veil on the heart.

rated in Christ, Israel's present rejection of the messiah demonstrates that such a redemption has not yet occurred. Israel remains hardened "until this very day" (2 Cor. 3:14 f.). Instead of "rejoicing in the glory of the Lord" as the regathered people of God (Bar. 4:37; cf. 5:1–4, 7, 9), Israel finds herself "veiled" from the glory of God revealed in Christ (cf. 2 Cor. 3:15; 4:4, 6).[165] The continuation of Paul's argument through v. 15 can therefore be represented as follows:

3:12a: *Because* we have this hope,

3:12b: *Therefore* we behave with boldness.

(-) 3:13a: *That is to say,* we do *not* behave

3:13b: *as* Moses (who) was placing a veil upon his face

3:13bb: *in order that* the sons of Israel might not gaze into the outcome of that which was being rendered inoperative.

(+) 3:14a: *But* their minds were hardened.

3:14b: *For* until this very day the same veil remains at the reading of the old covenant,

3:14c: *because* it is not being unveiled,

3:14d: *since* it (i.e. the veil) is being rendered inoperative in Christ,

3:15a: *nevertheless* until today a veil has been laid upon their hearts,

3:15b: *whenever* Moses is being read.

---

[165] Contra the conclusion drawn by Belleville, *Reflections of Glory*, pp. 241 f., whose view of the contrast between vv. 14bcd and 15 leads her to argue that μὴ ἀνακαλυπτόμενον in v. 14 means "not clearly disclosing," so that the veil in v. 14b does not "completely conceal or mask the gospel realities, and the diligent observer could penetrate the veiling." Hence, for Belleville, v. 15 must refer to a further hardening (p. 243). In Belleville's reading of Paul, "the Israelites should have been able to infer the truths about the new covenant in spite of the old covenant veiling, and thus should have been prepared to receive the gospel at the appointed time" (p. 245). But Israel has a "dulling of perception, which developed through the centuries into a settled condition of blindness" (p. 246). The passages from Matt. 13:16, 35, Rom. 16:25, Eph. 3:3, 9, etc. and Jesus' parables which Belleville adduces to support this view actually make the opposite point, i.e. either one is hardened to the message so that it is not understood, or one understands. There is no concept in the NT of a partially concealed reality which is open to diligent observation. The parallels drawn from Philo, Nag Hammadi, and the Corpus Hermeticum (cf. pp. 242 f.) ought to be read as *contrasts* to Paul's thinking.

4. The Promise to Israel: "Moses" and the Veil (2 Cor. 3:16)

At this point in Paul's discussion, he returns to the significance of the new covenant ministry of the Spirit. In doing so, he first takes up in v. 16 the significance of his ministry for the redemption of Israel. In vv. 17–18 Paul then turns to the ministry of the Spirit in relationship to those within the new covenant community. Paul thus begins and ends his argument in 3:7–18 by drawing a contrast between Israel's hard heartedness, first revealed in her sin with the golden calf (cf. 3:7, 13–14), and the eschatological work of the Spirit among both Jews and Gentiles (cf. 3:8, 15–18). By now, we should not be surprised that he does so at the end of his argument in the same way that he did at the beginning, i.e. by referring to the events of Exodus 34:29 ff. within the context of Exod. 32–34. What is surprising is that Paul returns to these events, not to draw a negative contrast between his ministry and the ministry of Moses as before, but to establish a positive comparison between Moses himself and the experience of those (Israelites) now within the new covenant.[166]

In v. 16 Paul paraphrases Exodus 34:34a,[167] the most explicit reference to Exod. 32–34 in our passage. The introduction of this text at this place in Paul's discussion not only displays Paul's own mastery of the Scriptural text, but also demonstrates the way his thought remains interwoven with it as a verse by verse commentary on the narrative.[168] In its original context, Exod. 34:34a

---

[166] F. Lang, *Korinther*, p. 275, who sees the subject of v. 16 to be Israel, and then by extension all those who believe in Christ. So too Wright, *Climax*, p. 183, and Renwick, *Temple*, pp. 56, 151, though Renwick takes this to mean that Paul is calling Christians to join Moses in experiencing God directly, rather than through the old covenant Scriptures as a type of "second hand" gazing at God parallel to the Israelite's gazing at Moses (pp. 55 f., 152, 154). But there is no indication that Paul is rejecting the Scriptures as a second hand mediation of God's glory! His consistent argument from Scripture indicates just the opposite! (But see below, n. 176, for Renwick's subsequent qualification of this point.) In line with the position taken here, see Koch, *Schrift*, pp. 126, 337, who argues that Paul's adaptation of the OT text at this point has as its goal making the description of Moses' practice in Exod. 34 a statement concerning the present possibility for Israel of removing her veil. Again, however, Koch's corresponding understanding of the removal of the veil as a referent to the possibility of understanding the Scriptures by turning to the "Lord" (understood Christologically) misses the direct point of the comparison. Cf. too Hays, *Echoes*, pp. 142 f., who stresses that v. 16 is the place in Paul's argument where the differences between Moses and Paul cross over (i.e. "the crossover point") to the similarity between Paul and Christians and Moses. For Hays, this becomes "the moment when the dissimile collapses into a positive metaphor" so that "... Moses becomes paradigm rather than foil" (p. 145). It must be kept in mind, however, that the contrast in 3:7–15 has not been between Moses *per se* and Paul, but between their two ministries. Nor does Moses function in Paul's argument as a metaphor with "multiple senses." Earlier it was the metonomy of the veil, not Moses, that provided the link between v. 13 and 14.

[167] For the structural clue in v. 17 (a subsequent interpretive statement) that v. 16 is a citation from Scripture, see Koch, *Schrift*, pp. 13, 126.

[168] See above, p. 336, for Belleville's understanding of the basic structure of the passage, and *Reflections of Glory*, p. 248, for its further development in regard to v. 16. Contra those

provides the concluding contrast between Moses' veiling of himself after speaking for YHWH to the people (v. 33, 34b) and his removing the veil when he speaks with the Lord. As such, it establishes the theological contrast between Israel's "stiff-necked" state and Moses as the one whose heart has been transformed by the Spirit. In the same way, Paul's citation of this text provides a clear transition in his own argument by picking up the conditional, temporal designation ἡνίκα ἄν ("whenever") from v. 15 in the parallel designation ἡνίκα (ἐ)άν found in the LXX of Exod. 34:34a. Indeed, since ἡνίκα appears nowhere else in Paul's writings as an adverb of time (or in the NT), and is rare in Hellenistic literature as a whole, it is probable that Paul introduced it in v. 15 in conscious anticipation of the transition to be made in v. 16 on the basis of this OT text.[169] Whereas a veil continues to be laid upon Israel's heart *whenever* (in the sense of "as often as") Moses is now read (v. 15), *whenever* (in the sense of "as soon as") "he" returns to the Lord, the veil is being taken away (v. 16).[170] Understood against the backdrop of Exod. 32–34, the adaptation of Exod. 34:34 in verse 16 thus establishes a contrast within Paul's argument (cf. the δέ of v. 16a) between Israel's old covenant experience (vv. 14–15), and Moses' experience in the tent of meeting as a *type* of the one whose heart has been changed by the power of the Spirit under the ministry of the new covenant (cf. 3:6 and the following interpretation of 3:16 in 3:17).[171]

---

who, like Fitzmyer, "Glory," explain the movement in Paul's thought on the basis of an element *foreign* to Exod. 34, namely, that the glory on Moses' face was fading. Thus, for Fitzmyer, p. 637, Paul moves from the veil on Moses' face to protect the frightened Israelites (3:7), to the veil as concealment of the fact that the glory is fading (3:13), to the veil which serves to hide Moses from the Israelites, to the veil over the Israelites themselves (3:14–15). Hence, although Fitzmyer is correct in observing that "what began as an instrument to conceal the glory of Yahweh from frightened Israelites has become an instrument which prevents Israelites from understanding Moses, as they read him" (p. 637), he can only conclude, like Windisch, that Paul's argument is a "Christian midrash" in which the key element in the interpretation is introduced into the text from the outside as a distinctly Christian perspective (see chapter four).

[169] Cf. Blass, Debrunner, and Funk, *Greek Grammar*, §§ 105, 455 (1), and Furnish, *II Corinthians*, p. 210.

[170] Note the switch from the present tense in v. 15 to the aorist in v. 16, which this translation attempts to reflect; see now Hofius, "Gesetz und Evangelium," p. 118.

[171] Contra e.g. Theobald, *Gnade*, p. 194, who argues against taking the original sense of Exod. 34:34 as the key to Paul's thought on the basis of his larger conviction that Moses is being contrasted to the experience of "we all" in 3:18. But Paul's use of Moses as a type in 2 Cor. 3:7 ff. parallels his use of Abraham as a type in Rom. 4; cf. E. Käsemann, "Der Glaube Abrahams in Röm. 4," in his *Paulinische Perspektiven*, 1972², pp. 140–177, p. 167. My use of "type" here follows Käsemann's distinction between typology in Paul on the one hand, and prophecy and allegory on the other, in its view of the OT text as the tradition of an event in which "das Historische (hat) jedoch eigene Realität und Bedeutung," so that this original historical event "erst freigelegt werden muß, und zwar nicht als verborgener Sinn eines Textes, sondern als Korrelation von Ereignissen, die sich entsprechen oder feindlich gegenüberstehen" (p. 170). Moreover, Paul's use of Moses as a type in 2 Cor. 3 bears out Käsemann's conclusion that, "Für paulinische Typologie ist die Entsprechung der Urgeschichte, zu der jüdisch auch die Exodus-Überlieferung gehört, zur Endzeit konstitutiv,

It is this typological use of Moses' experience before the Lord in the tent of meeting that explains the differences between Paul's adaptation of the text and its form in the LXX tradition. We have already seen that when Paul diverges from the OT text, he does so intentionally, and not as a result of a faulty memory or careless handling of the Scriptures.[172] A comparison of these two passages reveals that Paul has remained true to the sense of the original text,[173] while indicating, by means of the changes he has introduced, that he regards Moses to be the prototype of those within the remnant of Israel who follow him "to the Lord."

34:34a: ἡνίκα δ᾽ ἂν Μωυσῆς εἰσεπορεύετο ἔναντι κυρίου περιῃρεῖτο   τὸ κάλυμμα

3:16: ἡνίκα δὲ ἐὰν   ἐπιστρέψῃ   πρὸς κύριον περιαιρεῖται τὸ κάλυμμα

First, the absence of a direct reference to Moses as the subject of the verb ἐπιστρέψῃ makes it possible for Paul to establish a correlation between Moses and the indefinite person from within Israel now in view.[174] This also explains the switch from the imperfect indicative εἰσεπορεύετο (indicating an iterative

---

wobei Wiederholung und Steigerung ebenso wie Antithese eine Rolle spielen mögen" (p. 171).

[172] For this same point, see Richard, "Polemics," p. 356, and Koch, *Schrift*, pp. 346 f. (see above, Introduction). Koch concludes from this, however, that Paul is intentionally rereading the text in a way not supported by its original meaning. Koch comes to this conclusion regarding 3:16 because he understands the text to refer exclusively to the *present* reading of Moses as representing the old covenant Scriptures, rather than to Moses' *himself* and his *past* experience as a model for that of present day Jewish Christians (cf. pp. 126, 114, 337).

[173] See too van Unnik, "With unveiled face," p. 165: "Since in the context of Exod. 34 Moses' going is really a return, Paul's translation was 'ad sensum' correct." In spite of Paul's alterations of the text, the parallels to Exod. 34:34 are too close to conclude that this text is not in view as the foundation of Paul's thought. For this point, demonstrated by the five similarities she lists between the passages, see Belleville, *Reflections of Glory*, p. 250. The view argued here is contrary to that of those who, like Vollenweider, "2 Kor," pp. 250 f., maintain that "V.16 wirkt erneut wie eine Vergewaltigung des alttestamentlichen Textes ... und geht entschieden über die für Midrasch und Targum charakteristische Exegese hinaus," following Vielhauer, Käsemann, Gräßer, and D.-A. Koch (p. 251 n. 258). Part of his reason for holding to this is his misidentification of the "Lord" in v. 16 with Christ (cf. pp. 251 and 262 f., where he sees this identification as already part of the pre-Pauline interpretation of Exod. 34), as well as his view of the Law (see chapters two, four, and above, n. 66). But like the view being argued in this study, Vollenweider, p. 263, argues that the parallel in 3:17 is between Moses and true Israel, which is then equated with Christians in v. 18, an equation which for Vollenweider was also made in the pre-Pauline tradition.

[174] So too Furnish, *II Corinthians*, p. 210, who translates the subject of this verb "anyone" and points out that most commentators see it as a reference to the Israelites; Koch, *Schrift*, p. 126 (and the literature cited there), and Belleville, *Reflections of Glory*, pp. 248–250, who argues persuasively that Paul has the individual Israelite in view as the subject of ἐπιστρέψῃ, rather than Moses, Israel as a whole, the heart, the Christian believer, or humanity in general, all of which have been suggested. Stockhausen, *Moses' Veil*, p. 89, 89 n. 9 (following Collange, Richard), rightfully observes that the subject is "intentionally ambiguous," and renders it "anyone," though "the proximate reference is to the 'heart' of Israel in v. 15" (p. 89 n. 9).

action in the Exodus narrative) to the aorist subjunctive ἐπιστρέψῃ with ἡνίκα in order to indicate the constative nature of this activity as one which presents a general and repeatable possibility.[175] Whenever "he or she" (like Moses) returns to the Lord, the veil is being removed.

Furthermore, Paul's choice of ἐπιστρέφω πρὸς κύριον ("to turn," "return to the Lord") provides a conceptual parallel to εἰσπορεύομαι ἔναντι κυρίου ("to enter before the Lord") within the Exodus narrative,[176] while at the same time introducing the connotation of a "conversion" to the Lord associated with its use in religious contexts in the NT based on the LXX.[177] Moreover, we have seen that Paul's prior use of πωρόω to describe Israel's hardening in 3:14a was an allusion to Exod. 32–34 as picked up in Jeremiah 5:21 and Ezekiel 12:2 in parallel to Is. 6:9 and in association with Deut. 29:3. Viewed in this light, his use of ἐπιστρέφω in 3:16 provides its conceptual counterpart, once again in dependence upon the tradition of the Law and the Prophets. For against the background of Exod. 32–34 as it was picked up and developed in the Pentateuch, it is significant that this exact expression for conversion is used in Deut.

---

[175] Cf. Blass, Debrunner, and Funk, *Greek Grammar*, §332, "The complexive (constative) aorist ... is used (1) for linear actions which (having been completed) are regarded as a whole"; and Koch, *Schrift*, p. 114 n. 2.

[176] Contra Koch, *Schrift*, pp. 151 f., who misses the tie to the Exodus narrative and thus concludes that Paul changes the wording of the text to make it usable in the present context. Renwick, *Temple*, pp. 153 f., argues that Paul's insertion ἐπιστρέψῃ πρὸς κύριον, since it is found in the Alexandrian MS of Exod. 32:31 to describe Moses' return to the Lord on Mt. Sinai, indicates "beyond doubt" that "Paul is here joining the two texts of Exod. 32:31 and 34:34 together" (p. 153). Such a connection emphasizes that God's immediate presence was the location where the veil could be legitimately removed, whether in the tent of meeting (Exod. 34:34), or on Mt. Sinai (Exod. 32:31) (p. 154). Part of the problem with this, however, is not only the supposition that Paul was following the Alexandrian tradition, which would need confirmation from other passages, or that v. 16 is in fact a composite quote, which does not seem likely, but also the fact that in Exod. 32:31 Moses was not yet veiled, so that the two incidents allegedly combined would not be conceptually compatible, rendering Paul's thought abstruse. Hence, although possible, it is far from "beyond doubt" that Paul was combining these passages. But in either case, the motif of "turning to the Lord" as a reference to conversion cannot be denied, so that Renwick's rejection of v. 16 as a reference to Christian conversion is to be questioned. His reason for doing so is that Paul is speaking to those who claim that they were already converted, but still believed that they could encounter God's glory through the Mosaic scriptures (p. 152). But the subject in view appears to be the conversion of Israel, not converted Christians, and there is no indication that Paul is rejecting the Mosaic scriptures as a vehicle of the revelation of God's glory (see above, n. 166), although Renwick nuances this to mean that Paul's point is that reading the scriptures "untransformed by Christ" will not bring one into an intimate experience of God's presence (p. 156), which is certainly in line with Paul's intention.

[177] Cf. BAGD, *A Greek-English Lexicon*, p. 301, its only other use by Paul in 1 Thess. 1:9 (with πρὸς τὸν θεόν), its use with ἐπὶ (τὸν) κύριον in Lk. 1:16 f. (quoting Mal. 4:6); Acts 9:35; 11:21; with ἐπὶ (τὸν) θεόν in Acts 14:15; 15:19 (of the Gentiles in fulfillment of Amos 9:1 f.; Jer. 12:15; Is. 45:1); 26:18 (of Paul's ministry to the Jews and Gentiles in fulfillment of Is.42:7, 16; cf. Is. 35:5), 20; with ἐπὶ τὸν ποιμένα καὶ ἐπίσκοπον τῶν ψυχῶν ὑμῶν in 1 Pet. 2:25 (quoting Is. 53:6); and its absolute use in Acts 3:19.

4:30 to describe the future restoration of Israel from her hardened condition, when Israel will "return to the Lord her God" (ἐπιστραφήσῃ πρὸς κύριον τὸν θεόν σου) in the last days (after her judgment of exile) and listen to his voice. This is then held out as a conditional promise in Deut. 30:2, 9–10, where the almost identical phrase is again used (cf. v. 2: ἐπιστραφήσῃ ἐπὶ κύριον τὸν θεόν σου; v. 10: ἐπιστραφῇς ἐπὶ κύριον τὸν θεόν σου).[178] This same phrase is used to describe Israel's future restoration in 2 Chron. 30:9 as the time when they "turn to the Lord" (ἐπιστρέφειν ... πρὸς κύριον), which provides the counterpart to the fact that throughout Israel's history God had already sent prophets "to turn (Israel) to the Lord" (2 Chron. 24:19: ἐπιστρέψαι πρὸς κύριον), without success.[179] In the same way, in Is. 6:10b Israel's "turning" (ἐπιστρέψωσιν) is the reversal of her hardened condition described in Is. 6:9–10a (par. Jer. 5:21; Ezek. 12:2), and is quoted as such in Matt. 13:15 and Mark 4:12. In this Synoptic context, those who do not respond to Jesus' preaching of the kingdom in parables are those whose hearts still remain hardened in fulfillment of Is. 6:9 f., while those who repent are the ones being "healed" of this condition. How one responds to the parables reveals whether one is among those who are still recalcitrant, or whether one belongs to those to whom the "mystery of the kingdom" has been given (Matt. 13:11; Mk. 4:11). This juxtaposition between Israel's hardened condition (Is. 6:9–10a) and the one who "returns to the Lord" (Is. 6:10b) in 2 Cor. 3:14 and 3:16 reflects the same theological presupposition. To follow Moses into the presence of the Lord is to be converted to the Lord as a result of having one's hard heart of stone removed by the Spirit (cf. 3:6bc). Moreover, as with Paul's self-understanding as a prophet-like apostle,[180] the allusions to Is. 6:9 f. and Deut. 4:30;

---

[178] It is important to note that in these contexts, as in Ezek. 11, 36, and Jer. 31, this turning to the Lord is associated with keeping God's commandments with their hearts! See too Dumbrell, "Paul's use of Exodus 34," p. 188, who argues that Paul's use of ἐπιστρέφω, "while referring to the Mosaic position, betrays also the covenant return allusions which *epistrepho* customarily carries in the LXX. In short, the argument runs that on a different level the access which Moses enjoyed is now open to all Israel or Israelites through Christ."

[179] Belleville, *Reflections of Glory*, p. 252 n. 4, also points to this same phrase in 3 Kngdms 8:47–48; 2 Chron. 6:37 (38) as describing the condition for returning from exile, as well as the criterion for distinguishing between good and bad kings in 4 Kngdms. 23:25; 2 Chron. 19:4; 30:6; 35:19; 36:13. But because this phrase occurs so often in the OT to describe covenant faithfulness and one's approach to God, Belleville thinks it "unlikely" that it is being used to refer to "conversion" in 2 Cor. 3:16, "although the thought can by no means be completely excluded" (pp. 252 f.). She prefers to understand it in the general sense of "dependence on God" (p. 253). But in the context of their hardened state, such a dependence upon God would certainly mean a conversion back to God.

[180] For this point, see the thesis of Karl Olav Sandnes, *Paul – One of the Prophets? A Contribution to the Apostle's Self-Understanding*, WUNT 2.Reihe 43, 1991, pp. 18, 243 f. (see above, chapter two, p. 101). Sandnes, p. 136, also sees Paul's use of ἐπιστρέφω πρὸς κύριον in 3:16 to indicate that the return is a conversion, and that the subject in view in v. 16 is "multidimensional," i.e. Moses and the Jews who undergo this conversion. "By undergoing this conversion the Jews can therefore, like the Christians, permanently enjoy the same situ-

30:2, 9–10, against the backdrop of Exod. 32–34, point to a specific *post-exilic restoration context* for Paul's understanding and adaptation of Exod. 34:34 in v. 16. This confirms the eschatological context of his argument already apparent in 3:7–11 on the basis of the canonical and post-biblical understanding that Israel's exile had not come to an end in the late sixth century B.C. (see above, pp. 321 ff.). Against this backdrop, and with Exod. 34 itself clearly in view, the "Lord" in v. 16 is not Christ, in whom the veil is taken away in v. 14b, but YHWH, *to whom* one returns once the veil has been removed.[181] This corresponds to the other ten times in which κύριος in Pauline citations of Scripture reflects κύριος in the LXX and יהוה in the MT.[182] At this point, Paul is thinking theologically, not Christologically.

In this regard it is striking that in Acts 28:26 f., Isaiah 6:9 f. is again quoted as a description of those Jews who do not accept the Gospel of Christ, but this time as *Paul's* "parting word" (28:25) to those who are rejecting his preaching! Moreover, here too Paul's message is "the kingdom of God" inaugurated in Christ as "the hope of Israel" (Acts 28:20, 23), which he proclaims "from both the Law of Moses and from the Prophets" (28:23). Hence, as in 2 Cor. 3, in Acts 28:26 f. Israel's rejection of Paul's message is attributed to their hardened condition, once again using the same motifs from Is. 6:9 f. found in 2 Cor. 3:14 and 16. And again, this rejection on Israel's part provides the rationale for Paul's ministry to the Gentiles (Acts 28:28), in parallel to his argument in Rom. 11:11 ff. and as manifested in the Corinthian church itself. Although certainly Luke's adaptation, Acts 28:20 ff. thus reflects the same Pauline explanation for Israel's rejection of his message and his corresponding rationale for his ministry to the Gentiles represented in 2 Cor. 3:14 and 16.

---

ation which Moses, according to Exod 34 enjoyed only temporarily" (p. 136). But as we have argued, what is temporary in this passage is not Moses' experience, but the hardness of the hearts of those who are in fact converted.

[181] Contra the majority who take κύριος in v. 16 to refer to Christ and read the removal of the veil in v. 16 as parallel to its abolishment "in Christ" in v. 14; and those who, like Oostendorp, *Another Jesus*, pp. 41–44, Rissi, *Studien*, pp. 36 f., and Hanson, "Midrash," pp. 18 f., see the subject of v. 16 to be Moses, but the "Lord" to be Christ, so that Moses is portrayed as speaking with the pre-existent Christ. Richard, "Polemics," p. 356 n. 60, argues that Paul is deliberately ambiguous at this point, intending to include both YHWH and Christ; but this simply muddies the waters. In support of the reading followed here, see the extensive discussion of Prümm, *Diakonia Pneumatos*, pp. 148–154, the recent conclusion of Stockhausen, *Moses' Veil*, pp. 112, 130 f., who follows Dunn as "conclusive" in his argument for this position, the arguments of Belleville, *Reflections of Glory*, pp. 254 f., and those listed by her in support of this view (pp. 254 f. n. 4).

[182] These 11 uses are pointed out by Koch, *Schrift*, p. 86 (cf. besides 2 Cor. 3:16, Rom. 4:8; 9:28; 9:29; 10:13; 11:34; 14:11; 15:11; 1 Cor. 2:16; 3:20; 10:26). To these may be added 2 Cor. 8:21, in which the LXX also reads κύριος, but the MT reads אלהים (p. 86 n. 18). Of special interest is Koch's observation, p. 87, that in Rom. 11:3 (1 Kgs. 19:10) Paul can introduce κύριος, rather than θεός, as his choice to refer to God, though this may be influenced by the use of κύριος in the LXX and יהוה in the MT shortly before the cited text from 1 Kgs. 19:10 itself, or by analogy with Is. 53:1 cited in Rom. 10:26.

In turn, Paul's choice of ἐπιστρέφω in 2 Cor. 3:16 was motivated by his intention to read Moses' experience as a paradigm for those from within Israel who now provide the eschatological counterpart to Isaiah's description of Israel in Is. 6:9 f.[183] Against this backdrop, the conceptual and verbal parallel to Tobit 13:6 is striking, further confirming our eschatological, restoration interpretation of 2 Cor. 3:16. For there we read concerning Israel's relationship to the Lord in the exile that

"... when you turn to him (ἐὰν ἐπιστρέψητε πρὸς αὐτὸν) with your whole heart (ἐν ὅλῃ καρδίᾳ) and with your whole soul, to do truth before him, then he will turn to you (ἐπιστρέψει), and he will not hide his face from you."

Moreover, this turning to the Lord on the part of Israel is to take place in the midst of the nations so that they might see the greatness and mercy of the Lord (Tobit 13:3). But this manifestation of God's righteousness (cf. Tobit 13:7) merely anticipates the eschatological revelation of God in the new Jerusalem and temple, from which a "bright light will shine unto all the parts of the earth" (13:13; φῶς λαμπρὸν λάμψει εἰς πάντα τὰ πέρατα τῆς γῆς) drawing the nations to the Lord (cf. Tobit 13:3–5 with 9–13). At the center of this proleptic display of God's character, therefore, is Israel's prior "returning to the Lord" with her "whole heart," which will enable God's presence to "return" to his people, not in judgment as in the past (cf. Tobit 13:5), but in mercy (13:8).

Finally, Paul's alteration of the imperfect middle περιῃρεῖτο to the present (divine) passive περιαιρεῖται signifies not only that he is thinking typologically in regard to the present experience of those who follow in the footsteps of Moses, but also that what happens at conversion is the removal (by God!) of the hard heart which has characterized Israel throughout her history, but which was promised to be removed after her punishment in the exile.[184] For here too, the veil which *is now* being removed is the veil originally

---

[183] Contra Hofius, "Gesetz und Evangelium," p. 119, who argues that Paul's choice comes from reading Exod. 34:34a in line with Exod. 34:31 LXX, where the people turn to Moses, which Hofius takes to be a reference to turning to Moses in the synagogue. For Hofius, the point of v. 16 is that rather than turning to Moses, the people now turn to the Lord. But such a contrast between Moses and the Lord goes against the role of Moses as the mediator of the glory and Law of God on the one hand, and the parallel between Moses and the one who turns on the other. Hofius must thus argue that ἐπιστρέψῃ does not carry the connotation of conversion in this context. In the same way, Kim's view, *Origin of Paul's Gospel*, p. 231, that already in 3:16 Paul is alluding to his own experience on the Damascus Road in language taken from Exod. 34:34, so that Paul's own experience is that which becomes "typical" for all Christians, may be correct conceptually, but does not yet seem to be in view in Paul's argument. The focus is still on the experience of Moses.

[184] See Belleville, *Reflections of Glory*, pp. 253 f., who argues that a divine initiative is behind the passive. Cf. Koch, *Schrift*, p. 114, who rightly points out that with the removal of the explicit subject in 3:16, περιαιρεῖται is not to be understood as a middle, but as a passive in parallel to 3:14 f. Koch is also correct in observing that all of the changes are designed to transform the text so that it might describe a present possibility (pp. 114 f., 337). But he misses Paul's point when he concludes from this that Paul is altering the meaning of the OT

brought about by Israel's "stiff-neck" as recounted in Exod. 32–34.[185] But if the veil is being removed, this can only mean that the hard-heart of stone has also been removed. Indeed, as N.T. Wright has pointed out, this is the "basic point of the chapter," i.e. that "those who are in Christ, the new covenant people, are *unveiled* precisely because their hearts are *unhardened* (3:1–3, 4–6)."[186] Hence, like Moses, the one who "returns to the Lord" in conversion can encounter the glory of God without fear of judgment or destruction since the hard heart of rebellion has been removed, and, on the basis of the righteousness which comes from Christ (3:9), forgiveness has been received (3:6, based on Jer. 31:31 ff.). In this sense, like the interpretation of Exod. 33:7 f. given in *Tg. Ps.-J.*, those who belong to the new covenant can follow Moses into the tent of meeting.[187]

Within the canonical tradition in which the problem of Israel's hardness and the promise of her redemption are developed, Paul's thought at this point corresponds to the eschatological revelation of the glory of God as pictured in Isaiah 24:21–23 (cf. Hab. 3:3 f. and its conceptual parallels in Ezek. 43:2; 44:4). As we have seen in chapter three, there the future establishment of the "kingdom of God" on Mt. Zion is portrayed as the reestablishment of the covenantal presence earlier enjoyed by Israel at Sinai (cf. esp. Exod. 24:9–11). Paul's ministry as portrayed in 2 Cor. 3:7 ff. can thus be seen as a fulfillment of the uncovering of the veil between God and his people at the time of the inbreaking of the future reign of God "on Mount Zion and in Jerusalem" (Is. 24:23a). For as in Is. 24:23b, in which YHWH's rule from Mt. Zion is pictured in terms of a display of his *glory* before his *elders* (וְנֶגֶד זְקֵנָיו כָּבוֹד), the glory being revealed in Paul's ministry is portrayed in 2 Cor. 3:7 ff. as the reversal of the veiling which took place in Exod. 34:29 ff. At the heart of what it means for YHWH to reign over the world from Mt. Sinai, therefore, is that his glory will be manifest before his people. From Paul's perspective, this fulfillment of

---

event itself, since Koch fails to see the typological significance of the text due to his Christological interpretation of 3:16 f. and his interpretation of the veil as that which covers the Scripture's meaning, rather than as a metonomy for Israel's hard-heartedness.

[185] Taking the verb to be passive rather than middle, though the difference in meaning at this point is slight. The conceptual parallel to καταργέω in v. 14b speaks for this translation.

[186] *Climax*, p. 183, emphasis his. Wright, p. 183 n. 32, follows Le Déaut in pointing to the targum to Exod. 33:1–6 in which the penitent Israelites return to the tent of meeting to confess their sins (!), thus lending additional support to the nuance of conversion argued for in this study. Wright's point is that the absence of τις in 3:16, together with this targumic tradition, supports the idea that Paul intends a "double reference" to both the Exodus and contemporary situations.

[187] See Martin McNamara, *Targum and Testament*, 1972, p. 111, who in this later work again reaffirms Le Déaut's recognition of this same parallel. I do not want to suggest, however, any direct dependence of Paul on this targumic tradition, which may or may not be true. The evidence is simply insufficient to make such a determination. But it is instructive that here too the same exegetical and theological move can be made based on the Exod. 32–34 narrative.

the promises of Isaiah and Ezekiel is already taking place in his own ministry, albeit only among a small remnant of the people (cf. Rom. 11:1, 5)! This stress on the revelation of the glory of God in the ministry of Paul in fulfillment of the promises of the Law and the Prophets explains the fact that "while there are important Christological aspects to the discussion in this part of the letter, these are nevertheless secondary to a specifically *theo*logical emphasis which has been present since 2:14."[188]

But as we have seen, what is even more striking is that this revelation of God's glory before his people in Is. 24:23 is developed in Is. 25:6–8 in relationship to the salvation of the nations. The glory of God manifested on Mt. Zion now becomes the source of redemption for all the world, in which the "covering" over the nations is removed and they too are brought into the presence of the glory of the Lord (Is. 25:7; cf. Is. 56:6–8; 60:1–5, 13). Moreover, Liebers has pointed out that, in view of Is. 24:5, the veil in view in Is. 25:7 can represent the fact that the nations break the Law, so that their veiling consists in their disobedience. Conversely, as in Jer. 31 and Ezek. 36, here too the eternal covenant is therefore pictured as bringing about obedience to the decrees of the Law.[189] Isaiah 24:21–25:8 thus provides an important conceptual backdrop to Paul's thought in 2 Cor. 3:16,[190] as does the development in post-biblical Judaism of the prophetic tradition of the redemption of the Gentiles through their pilgrimage to the revelation of God's glory in Jerusalem (= Zion) and the temple.[191] Part of the "mystery" of the kingdom, however, is

---

[188] Furnish, *II Corinthians*, p. 211, although Furnish does not link this emphasis to the OT background as I have done. For this theological emphasis, see besides 3:16, 2:14, 15, 17; 3:3, 4, 5, the motif of glory in 3:7–11, and 3:17 f.; 4:2, 4, 6.

[189] *Das Gesetz als Evangelium*, p. 109. Liebers also points to Wisdom 17:3 as making this same point, and observes that for the Gentiles to be veiled is a punishment (p. 110 n. 63). But since he misses the point of the veiling of Moses in Exod. 34:29 ff., he draws a contrast between the experience of the nations and that of the Jews, who are said to see the glory on Moses' face so that the Law brings life (pp. 109 f.). In developing the "Jewish" view of the Law, he thus fails to take into account the emphasis within the tradition on the hardheartedness of Israel (cf. pp. 110, 112, 115).

[190] With Gaston, "Paul and the Torah in 2 Corinthians 3," p. 166 (who leaves it undeveloped), and contra Koch, *Die Schrift*, pp. 336 f., and Hofius, "Gesetz und Evangelium," p. 119 n. 253.

[191] See e.g. Tobit 13:11, 15 f. and Sir. 36:1–17; 49:12, where the rebuilding of Jerusalem (and in Sir. the filling of the temple with God's glory) is connected to the open display of God's glory, which the Gentiles will see in the last days. In Sir. 36:1 ff. this eschatological redemption in fulfillment of the promises of the prophets (cf. vv. 15 f.) is also portrayed in terms of a second Exodus (vv. 1–7) and the renewal of creation (vv. 12, 15). In Bar. 5:1–9, this restoration is pictured in terms of Is. 40, but now the people are said to be borne back to Jerusalem "with glory" and led safely back "in the glory of God" (5:6, 8). In 2 Macc. 2:4–8, Jeremiah hides the ark, etc. on the mount where Moses viewed God's glory until that future time when God's glory will be revealed again in the cloud as it was in Moses' day and at the consecration of Solomon's temple. In 2 Bar. 51:16, the future age is described as "the time which causes glory." In Sib. Or. 3:703–709, 719 (2nd cent. B.C.), after the consummation of final judgment the sons of God will live around the Temple protected by God himself, so

that from Paul's perspective this final restoration of the Gentiles is already beginning to take place, with only a small *remnant* of the Jews being saved, in fulfillment of Hosea 2:1, 25 and Isaiah 10:22 f. as quoted in Romans 9:24–27.[192] At this point, therefore, Paul turns his attention from the problem of Israel's hardness to the Gospel and the promise of her eschatological redemption as discussed in 3:14–16, to the experience of those who are *now* within the new covenant community being created from *both* the remnant of the Jews *and* the salvation of the Gentiles.

5. The Spirit and the Veil (2 Cor 3:17)

The age-old problem of the apparent identification of Jesus and the Spirit in v. 17a for the doctrine of the Trinity can now be seen to be a creation in large measure of the interpretation of this statement apart from, or in contrast to Exod. 34 in 3:16, to which it is directly related.[193] But within the argument of

---

that even the nations will not attack Israel but will want to come to the Temple "and ponder the Law of the Most High God" (3:719). This corresponds to the first cent. B.C. prayer in Pss. Sol. 7:1, 6 f. for God to continue to dwell in the midst of his people Israel as their protection against the nations, though in the Psalms there is no thought or hope that the Davidic messiah will redeem those nations who have oppressed Israel (cf. Pss. Sol. 8:23 f.; 17:22–25, 27 f.). However, there may be room for the future redemption of the other nations, since when the kingdom is established it is said that the Gentile nations will also serve the Messiah and he will "glorify the Lord in (a place) prominent (above) the whole earth and he will purge Jerusalem and make it holy ... (for) nations to come from the ends of the earth to see his glory ... and to see the glory of the Lord with which God has glorified her. And he will be a righteous king over them (Israel and the nations who come to Jerusalem to see the glory of God and his messiah?) in his days, for all shall be holy, and their king shall be the Lord Messiah" (17:30–32; trans. R.B. Wright, "Psalms of Solomon," *OTP, Vol. 2*, 1985, p. 667). For in the future messianic kingdom Israel will be regathered from the nations as a "second exodus" (cf. Pss. Sol. 11:3 with Is. 40:4) "so that Israel might proceed under the supervision of the glory of their God" and again be admonished to "put on (the) clothes of your glory" (17:6 f.; cf. Exod. 33:3, 5 LXX!). In the later development of this tradition, the goal of the end times is that "all faithful and all righteous people could see the glory of eternal God" in the holy temple which he builds of such great proportions that it is visible to all (Sib. Or. 5:424–427; from A.D. 80–132; For the translation and dating, see J.J. Collins, "Sibylline Oracles," *OTP, Vol. 1*, 1983, pp. 325, 377 f., 390, 403).

[192] But as J. Munck, *Paul and the Salvation of Mankind*, p. 58, already pointed out, Paul's view here, as in Rom. 11, is that "this condition will not be the final one," pointing to the temporal expressions in vv. 14–16.

[193] For a representative example of reading 3:17 apart from its context, being content merely to assert that 3:17 equates "in some sense" "the Spirit and the resurrected, exalted Lord," see Neill Q. Hamilton, *The Holy Spirit and Eschatology in Paul*, SJTh Occasional Papers No. 6, 1957, quote from p. 4. The view that in v. 17 Paul is radically reinterpreting his OT background has received its strongest presentation by I. Hermann, *Kyrios und Pneuma, Studien zur Christologie der paulinischen Hauptbriefe*, SANT Bd. 2, 1961, pp. 31–58. Hermann's starting point is that 3:16 is not a quote from Exod. 34:34 at all, but "ein freies Spiel mit einer bekannten Vorstellung aus dem Alten Testament. Es soll dabei

2 Cor. 3:12–18, verse 17a most easily explains the thought of v. 16, where the Lord (κύριος) to whom one turns is the Lord as experienced by Moses in the tent of meeting.[194] There is no indication that in developing the typology of v. 16 in v. 17 Paul has substituted Christ for YHWH. For as Furnish has pointed out, κύριος in Paul "generally means Christ, *except when the apostle is quoting Scripture or working closely with a scriptural text.*"[195] Although adapted for his purposes, this is certainly the case in Paul's use of Exod. 34:34 in 3:16, in which in both texts κύριος occurs without the article. Indeed, the logic of Paul's argument requires that the "Lord" in view in 3:16 be YHWH to make the link between Paul's ministry and the eschatological promises apparent. Moreover, in Paul's only other use of ἐπιστρέφω in 1 Thess. 1:9, he speaks of returning "to God" (πρὸς τὸν θεόν), so that v. 16 as a reference to "returning to YHWH" is itself not foreign to Paul's thought, even as a Christian. Although Paul often uses ὁ κύριος to refer to Jesus, in this context the article before κύριος in v. 17a is not a sudden, unprepared reference to "the Lord Jesus," but a natural reference to the Lord of v. 16. For the definite article in reference to the Lord or God is "sometimes missing" in the NT, "especially after prepositions," since the omission of definite articles after prepositions is still common in Koine Greek.[196] Yet, when this is the case, as in 3:16, it is then *supplied* in the following reference, just as we find in John 3:2.[197]

---

eine völlig neue Aussage gemacht werden, die nur durch freie Assoziation der Worte im Vorstellungsbereich der alttestamentlichen Vorlage bleibt" (p. 38). On the other hand, Hughes' attempt, *Second Epistle to the Corinthians*, pp. 115 f., to read πνεῦμα in 3:17 as a reference to life rather than to the Holy Spirit is an extreme and untenable solution to the problem, see chapter two. The attempt to read "spirit" here as a reference to something other than the Holy Spirit has also been tried by Goettsberger (see n. 194), Prat, Allo; cf. J. Héring, *Second Epistle*, pp. 25–27, who in addition also attempts to repunctuate v. 17b to read, "there where the spirit is, is the liberty of the Lord," and to conjecture this same reading for 17a. Neither proposal has any textual support. Finally, for a recent example of the predominant attempt to see the reference to the Spirit here to be eschatological, and hence to confirm the Christological identification, see Gerd Theißen, "Die Hülle des Mose," p. 135, and Peter von der Osten-Sacken, "Die Decke des Mose," in his *Die Heiligkeit der Tora*, 1989, pp. 87–115, p. 103.

[194] Supported now in detail by Belleville, *Reflections of Glory*, pp. 257–262, who rightly argues that v. 17 is Paul's commentary on v. 16 (17a interpreting 16a, 17b interpreting 16b). See too Furnish, *II Corinthians*, p. 212, who points out that δέ can be used to introduce a comment on what precedes and calls attention to 1 Cor. 10:4b and Gal. 4:25, where it is used to introduce an explanation of a scriptural text. But the force of δέ is so malleable that its sense can only be determined by the content of the sentences it introduces. For the identification of the Lord of v. 17 with YHWH from v. 16, see already Goettsberger, "Die Hülle des Moses," p. 14, though he interpreted the Spirit in v.17 to refer to the spiritual and prophetic meaning behind the letter of the OT!

[195] *II Corinthians*, p. 211 (emphasis mine). Paul's use of Exod. 34:34 in 3:16 takes precedence for determining its meaning over his prior statement in 3:14d.

[196] So Blass, Debrunner, and Funk, *Greek Grammar*, §§ 254, 255.

[197] Cf. again note 196, and for the view that the article in v. 17 is referring back to v. 16, see too Barrett, *Second Corinthians*, p. 123.

Paul's use of the article in 3:17 is thus anaphoric.[198] Moreover, as Furnish has pointed out, Paul nowhere else directly identifies Jesus and the Spirit, whereas he often speaks of the "Spirit of God" as found in the LXX and in the second half of 3:17 itself.[199] The "is" (ἐστίν) of 3:17a is thus better rendered "means"[200] as an indication that Paul is here interpreting Moses' paradigmatic

---

[198] For this point see Belleville, *Reflections of Glory*, pp. 261 f., supported by Turner, *Syntax*, p. 174, and the work of Dunn, Harris, Martin, Collange, Furnish, McNamara, etc.

[199] *II Corinthians*, pp. 212 f., where Furnish points to 1 Cor. 6:17; 12:3; Rom. 8:9–11; Phil. 1:19; and Gal. 4:6 for associations, but not identifications, between Jesus and the Spirit in Paul; and to Rom. 8:9, 11, 14; 1 Cor. 2:10–14; 3:16; 6:11; 7:40; 12:3 for Paul's use of the "Spirit of God." See his discussion for relevant passages from the LXX. Koch's argument, *Schrift*, p. 337 n. 35, that this use of the "Spirit of God" indicates a subordination of the Spirit to God, which excludes an identification in 3:17, remains unconvincing given the way in which the Spirit alone can be said to carry out God's activity and establish God's presence, being used e.g. in parallel to God in 1 Cor. 3:16 f.

[200] For this same use of ἐστίν in the sense of "means" or "implies" as an interpretation of Scripture, see 1 Cor. 10:4; Rom. 10:6–8; Gal. 3:16; 4:24. Paul's statement in 3:17 is therefore often related to and even (wrongly) identified with the pesharim of the Qumran community; cf. already J.A. Fitzmyer, "The Use of Explicit OT Quotations in Qumran Literature and in the NT," now in his *Essays on the Semitic Background of the New Testament*, 1971, p. 26, Hooker, "Beyond the Things that are written?" p. 297, "if anything may properly be described as *midrash pesher* ... 2 Corinthians 3 certainly qualifies," and Stockhausen, *Moses' Veil*, pp. 130 f., who goes so far as to conclude that pesher exegesis is the "determining structure of verses 12–18 as a whole" (pp. 91 f. n. 15) ! But such an analogy, not to mention classification, should be avoided, since not only is Paul's movement exegetically opposite to that found in such literature, but also such "pesher" approaches go beyond the original contextual meaning of the text, as Belleville, *Reflections of Glory*, rightly maintains (cf. her analysis of these approaches and conclusion on pp. 263–266). Belleville, *Reflections of Glory*, p. 172, is thus right in rejecting the designation "midrash" for 3:12–18 as "far too general to be of specific help in understanding the exegetical links of Paul's thought ..." and the designation "pesher" as "only marginally applicable to vv. 16–17 and ... really not an appropriate designation for what Paul is doing in the remainder of these verses" (p. 173). For as Belleville, p. 186, points out, Paul's exposition in vv. 12–18 cannot formally be termed a "midrash" since vv. 12–18 "do not exist for the sake of elucidating the OT text." Rather, "In vv. 12–18 the Exodus narrative is drawn in to support and develop Paul's opening statement" in v. 12 (p. 186 n. 1). For this same point in regard to the purpose of the Qumran pesher, in contrast to Paul's purpose, see above, n. 112. Belleville also rightly rejects the labels of "allegory" and "typology" as inadequate attempts to "account for all the exegetical intricacies of these verses" (p. 173). But Belleville herself, in spite of her own critique, nevertheless goes on to accept this functional equivalent as the key to Paul's use of Exod. 34:34 (pp. 266 f.) ! See below, n. 203. Apart from the general, common practice of relating Scripture to one's own situation, Timothy H. Lim, "Paul's Alteration of the Biblical Text: The Evidence of the Qumran Pesharim," SBL Annual Meeting Seminar Paper 1989, is right in emphasizing that unlike the pesharim, Paul never uses the distinctive introductory formula פשר, while the use of ἐστίν is itself not a decisive indicator of this genre. See Koch, *Schrift*, pp. 229 f., for a helpful discussion of this question and the various interpretive characteristics of the Qumran pesher, to which he also concludes that although Paul no doubt interpreted Scripture in an actualized and eschatological sense analogous to the Qumran pesher, nevertheless there is otherwise only a very limited correspondence between the two in terms of the ways in which the Scriptures themselves are handled and interpreted. He thus explicitly rejects such an identification or parallel to the pesher in Rom. 10:6–8, 1 Cor. 15:56, and 2 Cor. 3:17. For

experience in terms of the experience now being realized in the new covenant in Christ.[201]

Paul is not identifying Christ and the Spirit, but making it clear that Moses' experience of YHWH in the tent of meeting is equivalent to the current *experience of the Spirit* in Paul's ministry, even as Paul could refer in 3:3 to the Spirit unleashed in his ministry as the "Spirit of the living God."[202] Belleville has noted that any kind of personal or ontological identification of the Lord with the Spirit is excluded by v. 17b, where the two are clearly distinguished.[203] As William Dumbrell has summarized it, Paul's point is that

---

similar points and cautions, see Devorah Dimant, "Qumran Sectarian Literature," *Jewish Writings of the Second Temple Period*, CRINT Section 2, Vol. 2, ed. Michael E. Stone, 1984, pp. 483–550, p. 507, who points out that "the designation *pesharim* was given to a group of biblical interpretations of a peculiar type. They have a fixed literary structure: a biblical quotation to be expounded, followed by the commentary which is often introduced as such by the word *pesher*. It consists of an identification of certain nouns in the text with the aid of various exegetical methods, and further elaborations on one or two details. Thus the term *pesher* designates the isolated unit of interpretation, the interpretation itself, its technique and its literary form." Dimant thus argues that within the *pesharim* "the traditional exegetical devices and literary forms are employed in the service of (their) particular ideas, and only in this respect can the *Pesharim* be defined as a special genre" (p. 507). This need for precision in defining what is meant by a "pesher" as a genre designation, together with a strong caution against general comparative uses of such a designation outside of the Qumran literature, was already given in the programmatic (but neglected) essay of George Brooke, "Qumran Pesher: Towards the Redefinition of a Genre," *RevQ* 10 (1981) 483–503.

[201] Contra Theobald, *Gnade*, pp. 194 n. 137, 205, who rejects this interpretation because of his prior decision that 3:16 cannot be a quote or paraphrase from Exod. 34:34. He thus posits a break in thought between vv. 16 and 17 based on a source hypothesis in which in v. 16 Paul is reinterpreting Christologically his opponents' pre-existing interpretation of the text where YHWH was identified with the Spirit. But what Theobald attributes to Paul's opponents is actually the point of Paul's own argument (see below)!

[202] So too Renwick, *Temple*, pp. 155 f. Cf. too McNamara, *The New Testament and the Palestinian Targum to the Pentateuch*, Analecta Biblica 27, 1966, pp. 182–184, and *Targum and Testament*, p. 112, who supports this same conclusion based on the targumic parallels, esp. in *Tg. Ps.-J.* Num. 7:89 par.Exod. 33:11, 16, between Moses' hearing the "word," "voice," and "Spirit," all of which are identified with the Lord as he reveals himself to mankind. Cf. too pp. 182 ff., where McNamara points out that in the targums it is the Holy Spirit who speaks to Moses in the tent of meeting. Thus, H. Conzelmann's objection that this interpretation cannot show how Paul came to it falls away, once Exod. 34 is read within its larger context; cf. his "Current Problems in Pauline Research," *Interp* 22 (1968) 171–186, p. 184 n. 24. Conzelmann's own view that the Lord is identified not with the Spirit *per se*, but with freedom, denies the real presence of the Spirit in Paul's theology and misses the point of Paul's direct assertion in 3:17b.

[203] Belleville, *Reflections of Glory*, p. 259. But since Belleville rightly sees a problem with identifying YHWH directly with the Spirit (p. 263), but does not take into account the parallel between Moses' *experience* and the *experience* of those who now turn to the Lord, she is forced to conclude that, like a pesher approach to the Scriptures which ignores or goes beyond the original context, "... Paul need not be construing κύριος in v. 17a in any personal sense. It is merely a term in his text that finds its meaning and application in his contemporary situation" (p. 267). Though this is certainly true concerning the *application* of Exod. 34:34, the meaning of the text is still rooted in the original context. Moreover, Belleville's

"The glory in which Moses has participated is available by way of overplus through the Spirit of the new covenant. The transformation wrought in Moses by the immediacy of the divine presence comes to pass in the believer by the Spirit."[204]

In view of 3:3–6 and 3:8, this identification carries with it an apologetic purpose. Just as Moses mediated the glory of YHWH, Paul mediates the Spirit of YHWH.[205] In 3:14–16 Paul was concerned to show that the rejection of his Gospel by the vast majority of Israel is no argument against its validity or the genuine nature of his ministry. Conversely, Paul's identification of YHWH with the Spirit in 3:17a is intended to make it clear that those who are presently accepting the message of the new covenant in Christ are in direct continuity with the revelation of YHWH begun at Sinai.[206] Again, however, this assertion is not merely theological speculation on Paul's part. Paul is defending the legitimacy of his own ministry, and in doing so implicitly criticizing those who deny the validity of his ministry of the Spirit on the basis of some contrary "spiritual" experiences as perhaps documented in their letters of recommendation (cf. 3:1 f.).[207] his positive declaration concerning his own ministry in 3:17a is thus the counterpart to his denunciation of those who preach "a different spirit" ($\pi v \epsilon \tilde{v} \mu \alpha$ $\H{\epsilon} \tau \epsilon \varrho o v$) in 2 Cor. 11:4. For in Paul's conception, the true Gospel and the true Spirit are inextricably united, so that Paul can argue from the experience of the latter to the truth of the former to support the legitimacy of his message, both for justification (cf. Rom. 8:1 f.), and, more importantly in the case of the Corinthians, for their *continuing* life in Christ (2 Cor. 11:3; cf. Gal. 3:1–5).[208]

---

view forces her to take $\varkappa \acute{v} \varrho \iota o \varsigma$ as a reference to YHWH in 16a, 17b, and 18a, but not in 17a, where she posits that it is simply "a pointer to a specific term in the Exodus citation without any implication of personal significance" (p. 267), and to relate v. 17b not to 17a, but back to 16b (p. 268).

[204] "Paul's use of Exodus 34," pp. 188 f.

[205] Contra all those who, like Liebers, *Das Gesetz als Evangelium*, p. 119, identify $\varkappa \acute{v} \varrho \iota o \varsigma$ with Christ in 3:16 and conclude that Paul's apologetic claim is that the "return to the Lord" is no longer to be equated with a return to the Law, but with turning to Christ. This conclusion is built on Liebers' view that it is the glory of the Law which is now veiled and no longer operative, but fading (p. 119). Liebers, pp. 120 f., makes this same point concerning v. 18, where he argues that the issue is whether the Law or Christ is the mirror (cf. Wisd. 7:16); for the view argued here, see below.

[206] So too Hays, *Echoes*, p. 143: "the *kyrios* in the LXX of Exod. 34:34 is being read by Paul, for his present purposes, as a figure for the Spirit (i.e., the form in which God is regularly experienced in the Christian community) ..." See too Stockhausen, *Moses' Veil*, pp. 9 f., 131 f., for this same point, following Prümm, L. Cerfaux, Schneider, and Dunn, whose arguments are substantial enough that "the question should now be laid to rest" (p. 10).

[207] So already Kurt Stalder, *Das Werk des Geistes in der Heiligung bei Paulus*, 1962, p. 53, who pointed out that the emphasis in 3:17 is on the fact that Paul's ministry is a ministry of the Spirit, so that the existence of the church is a better letter of recommendation than the letters of the false apostles. Stalder, however, wrongly identified the Lord of v. 17 with Christ and the "letter" of 3:6 with the means of writing these letters of recommendation.

[208] For a corresponding understanding of the force of Gal. 3:1–5 as an argument from the Galatians' earlier reception of the Spirit by faith in response to Paul's Gospel (v. 2) to the

In v. 17b Paul further explains this statement of continuity by pointing to the "freedom" (ἐλευθερία) which comes about in response to the work of the Spirit,[209] a corollary which is *assumed* by Paul to be understood by his readers, together with its content.[210] But Paul does not further explain 17a simply for the sake of providing more information, but for the sake of advancing his argument from 3:16–17a in anticipation of 3:18. As the link between the reference to Moses' typological experience of YHWH's glory without the veil in 3:16 and the reference to the experience of the glory of the Lord without the veil in 3:18, this assertion ought not to be understood as the introduction of a Christian reinterpretation of YHWH in terms of Christ. Rather, Paul's point concerns the consequence of encountering the Spirit of the Lord (= YHWH)[211] under the new covenant. If, as Paul's entire ministry and the very existence of the Christian community presupposes, the new covenant of the Spirit is now being realized, then in fulfillment of Jer. 31:31 ff. and Ezek. 36:26 ff. (cf. 3:6) encountering God no longer means judgment and condemnation (3:6c, 7, 9), but the righteousness of justification and of life in the Spirit (3:6c, 8, 9).

In this context, and especially in view of Exod. 32–34, the "freedom" referred to in v. 17b cannot be interpreted in terms of a freedom from the old covenant in general (though of course for Paul the "old" covenant is no longer in force, 3:6), much less from the Law in particular. If taken negatively at all, its most natural reference in view of 3:7–11, and as the parallelism between 3:16b, 17b, and 18 demonstrates, is to a freedom from the veil of hard-heartedness that is the root cause of this condemnation and death and its ensuing

---

necessity of remaining in this Gospel for their continuing life in the Spirit (v. 5), see Charles H. Cosgrove, *The Cross and the Spirit, A Study in the Argument and Theology of Galatians*, 1988, pp. 39–48.

[209] Taking the second δέ in 3:17 to be explanatory and, as such, consequential in terms of its implied function.

[210] Following Vollenweider, "2 Kor," pp. 251 f., who in turn refers to Collange, Bultmann, and D.-A. Koch (cf. p. 251 n. 263). Vollenweider's helpful thesis is that the "freedom" in view in 3:17b must be understood within the context of the letter/Spirit contrast and as part of the history of traditions context which determines all of 3:7–18. Vollenweider thus rightfully takes Paul's reference to "freedom" in v. 17b to refer back to 3:6c, which then leads *against* interpreting it merely as a restatement of his παρρησία from 3:12 (p. 252), though his view of the letter/Spirit contrast as a reference to a contrast between the Law and Christ leads him to conclude that the freedom of v. 17b is a freedom from the Law and the misleading nature of the glory of the Mosaic covenant (cf. his pp. 277, 282, and n. 67 above). In contrast to Vollenweider's central thesis, however, we have seen that what produces Paul's confidence is the new covenant freedom from the hard-heartedness being brought about by the power of the Spirit, not a freedom from the glory and Law of the Sinai covenant.

[211] Paul's usual expressions, which can be used interchangeably, are the "holy Spirit" (Rom. 5:5; 14:17; 15:13, 16, 19; 1 Cor. 6:19; 12:3; 2 Cor. 6:6; 13:13; Eph. 1:13; 1 Thess. 1:5 f.; 2 Tim. 1:14; Titus 3:5) or the "Spirit of God" (Rom. 8:9, 14; 1 Cor. 2:11, 14; 3:16; 6:11; 12:3; 2 Cor. 3:3; Eph. 3:16; Phil. 3:3) (cf. Eph. 4:30; 1 Thess. 4:8, where the two are combined). Here, as in Rom. 1:4 (κατὰ πνεῦμα ἁγιωσύνης), Paul's unique departure from these forms evidences his dependence upon tradition, in this case that of the Exodus tradition.

inability to enter into the presence of the Lord.[212] Only by implication would this mean freedom from the *function* of the old covenant as it relates to those who have been so hardened, and hence, in view of the coming of the Spirit, ultimately freedom from the old covenant itself.[213] But this last implication is at least two steps removed from Paul's direct assertion. Nor should we follow the common attempt to equate the freedom spoken of in 3:17 with Paul's "boldness" in 3:12, rather than seeing v. 17 as support for this prior assertion (i.e. *because* of the freedom in view in v. 17, Paul is bold in his ministry).[214]

---

[212] For this view, see Belleville, *Reflections of Glory*, p. 270. So too already J.H. Bernard, *The Second Epistle to the Corinthians,* The Expositor's Greek Testament Vol. 3, 1903 (reprint 1979), p. 58, who interpreted the freedom as "the freedom of access to God under the New Covenant, as exemplified in the removal of the veil ...," and Stalder, *Werk des Geistes*, p. 53, who saw the freedom to be freedom from that which separates one from God so that the church "sees" God and is transformed into his image. See too Kümmel, additions to Lietzmann, *An die Korinther*, p. 200, followed by F. Lang, *Korinther*, p. 275, who interpret the freedom as a freedom from the veil, but contra the view argued here take the "Lord" in v. 16 to be the Spirit, while in v. 17b they see it to be Christ (the "Spirit of the Lord" = the Spirit of Christ). The veil thus represents the inability to understand the OT, which, as in v. 14, is taken away in Christ. For a similar view, see Koch, *Schrift*, p. 338, who takes the function of the freedom to be negative as a referent to "die Aufhebung der das Verstehen der Schrift verhindernden Verstockung, die nur in Christus möglich ist" from v. 14, which in v. 17 is tied to "einem fundamentalen inhaltlichen Wandel der Voraussetzungen ... von denen her und auf die hin jetzt die Schrift aufgrund der Hinwendung zum κύριος gelesen wird." Koch's view of v. 14, while at first glance close to the position argued here, is shown by his interpretation of v. 17 to lead to a different conclusion, namely, that the freedom in view is a freedom from the original sense of the Scriptures in favor of his Christian presuppositions. For Koch, p. 339, this leads to positing a hermeneutical circle in which the use of Exod. 34:34 in 3:17 in support of Paul's thesis that an appropriate understanding of Scripture exists only in Christ is itself only possible because Paul has *already* interpreted and altered the text's actual content "in Christ." The position argued here calls such a conclusion into question.

[213] So again Stalder, *Werk des Geistes*, p. 359, who concludes that when Paul speaks of freedom from the Law he is always thinking of freedom from the curse which the Law legitimately pronounces as the witness of the demand of God on mankind. Thus, the freedom in view in 3:17 is not freedom from a "Heilsordnung" which is now superseded, or freedom from a demand which is too hard, or from the external Law, since the divine demand always comes from "outside" (p. 491). But contra the view argued here, Stalder asserts that even in the old covenant Israel had the power to keep the Law, but did not do so due to the unexplainable mystery of sin (pp. 359 f., 490) and their own disobedience and guilt, which is true of the new covenant as well (p. 490). So for Stalder, righteousness does not consist in receiving the possibility and power given by the Spirit to keep the Law, since mankind can keep the Law on his/her own, but in being freed from one's "slavery to guilt" (pp. 360, 491). For in his view, there is for Paul no anthropological or metaphysical necessity to sin, but sin is merely the result of demonic power or our own guilt (p. 490), while the Spirit functions merely to help us understand the divine demand on our lives, which we then fulfill "with our own strength" (p. 493)! The point made here, however, is that for Paul, precisely because Israel (and all people by implication) remains hardened apart from the work of God in their hearts, both justification and sanctification take place precisely *through* the reception and power of the Spirit, rather than the Spirit being given later as the confirmation of one's liberation and sanctification (p. 491).

[214] For this equation, see Wright, *Climax*, p. 179, who nevertheless clearly sees the logic between the two texts: "Paul can use boldness not because he is different from Moses but

Although this reading of the object of freedom is possible, a negative definition of "freedom" (ἐλευθερία) as freedom *"from* something" is not in accord
with Paul's usual use of the term. When Paul does intend to stress that from
which one has been set free, he does so explicitly with the prepositions ἐκ (cf.
1 Cor. 9:19) and ἀπό (cf. Rom. 6:18). But Paul's primary use of the concept in
contexts where it does not refer to the political and social status of being
"free,"[215] along with its related verbal (ἐλευθερόω, "to free, set free") and adjectival (ἐλεύθερος) forms, is to refer to the *positive* results of having been "set
free." In Romans 6:22, Paul can therefore even reverse the image and express
this positive outcome of one's freedom in terms of "being enslaved to God"
(δουλωθέντες τῷ θεῷ), with its resultant "fruit resulting in sanctification" (τὸν
καρπὸν ὑμῶν εἰς ἁγιασμόν) and its "outcome, eternal life." In the context, this
enslavement to God is equated with presenting one's members as "slaves to
righteousness in 6:19, as indicated by their corresponding links with "sanctification" (cf. δοῦλα τῇ δικαιοσύνῃ εἰς ἁγιασμόν in 6:19 and the same description
in 6:18). Although it must imply the object from which one has been released,
even here "freedom" is thus primarily a freedom *"for* something." In this regard it is striking that the "slavery to God" or "to righteousness" in Rom. 6:19,
22 is explicitly linked with its "fruit" of "sanctification, and its outcome, eternal life," just as Paul's reference to righteousness in 2 Cor. 3:9 supports the
ministry which brings about a life of obedience by the power of the Spirit in
3:8. In Romans 6:16–23, this "sanctification" which derives from being "enslaved to God" (6:22) or "to righteousness" (6:19) is identified in 6:17 with
"becoming obedient from the heart to that form of teaching to which you were
committed" (ὑπηκούσατε ἐκ καρδίας ...).[216] Hence, as in 2 Cor. 3:8 f., here too
Paul can speak of God's righteousness leading to a life of obedience as a result
of having been freed from the power of sin.[217] On the other hand, left to itself

---

because those who belong to the new covenant are different from those who belong to the
old" (p. 180, emphasis mine), thus correctly emphasizing that the contrast is between the
Christians and the Israelites, whether in Moses' day or Paul's (cf. p. 180). His summary of
the force of Paul's affirmation in v. 17 is identical to that taken here, though he understands
the implications of the veil to be different (cf. p. 184).

[215] For its use to refer to one's social status as "free" over against being a slave, cf. 1 Cor.
7:21 f; 12:13; Eph. 6:8; Col. 3:11; Gal. 3:28; 4:22 f., 26, 30 f., though in Gal. 4:22–31 the
social status of the "free woman" is loaded with theological significance as representing the
"children of promise" down through Israel's history and into the present (cf. 4:28 f.).

[216] Cf. the close parallel in 1 Thess. 4:1–3, where the will of God is again identified with
the sanctification of the believer, which in turn is defined in terms of obedience to the commandments which were received from Paul. But here it is made explicit that these commands derive their authority from Jesus and not from the old covenant (cf. 4:2). Though
beyond the scope of this study, Paul's statements in Rom. 2:14 f., 27–29 concerning the obedience of the Gentiles as evidence of "the work of the Law written in their hearts" (2:15)
should be understood in terms of the sanctifying work of the Spirit as well.

[217] Unlike 2 Cor. 3:7–11, however, in Rom. 6:16 Paul takes the additional step of describing this life of obedience *itself* in terms of *"righteousness."* On the equation in Rom. 6:16 ff.
of being enslaved to "God" (v. 22), "obedience" (v. 16), and "righteousness" (v. 19), and its

the "fruit" of the "impurity and lawlessness" produced by the power of sin is once again "death" (Rom. 6:17, 19, 21). The same contrast found in 2 Cor. 3:7–9 between the righteousness which leads to life and the condemnation which leads to death is thus also represented in Rom. 6:18 ff., but now interpreted in terms of the obedience which derives from "the free gift of God" and the impurity and lawlessness (!) produced by the power of sin (cf. 6:16 f., 23). In Romans 6:17 ff., therefore, the power of sin as the ultimate source of death takes the place of the old covenant ministry of death as found in 2 Cor. 3:7–11. Romans 6:18–23 consequently provides a confirmation of our earlier interpretation of 3:6–11. But it also illustrates that in speaking of "freedom" Paul has in mind, above all, the results for which one is freed or able to act, rather than an abstract concept of "freedom" *per se*.[218]

In Corinth, the church has already heard Paul speak in this manner in relation to the concrete situation of remarriage after the death of one's husband in which one is "free to be married," (ἐλευθέρα γαμηθῆναι, cf. Rom. 7:3), though "only in the Lord" (1 Cor. 7:39). Moreover, in 1 Cor. 9:1 Paul characterized his own apostolic experience as one of being "free" (ἐλεύθερος), which in the context of 1 Cor. 9:19 meant "free from all" so that he might be "a slave to all" and in so doing win more to Christ. The emphasis of Paul's freedom is clearly on its result and goal, not on its source. And in both cases this goal is defined in terms of obedience to God in Christ as an expression of the love called for by the Gospel (cf. 1 Cor. 7:17, 22; and 9:16 f., 20–23 as an example of 8:1–3, 8 f. 11–13).[219] In the same way, the believer's freedom in 1 Cor. 10:29 is a

---

implications, see P. Stuhlmacher, *Der Brief an die Römer*, NTD Bd. 6, 1989, p. 88. For Paul, being "enslaved to God" (6:22) results in a life of obedience or sanctification, which, due to the inextricable link between justification by faith on the basis of the righteousness of God and sanctification by faith in God's same power and righteousness, can also be expressed in terms of becoming a "slave to righteousness" (6:19) as a result of having become "enslaved to righteousness" (6:18). Paul does not shrink, therefore, from referring to the life of obedience in Christ among those who have been freed from the power of sin as a "real" righteousness.

[218] See now F. Stanley Jones' study, *"Freiheit" in den Briefen des Apostels Paulus, Eine historische, exegetische und religionsgeshichtliche Studie*, GTA Bd. 34, 1987, p. 141, who concludes, against the influential view of Bultmann that "freedom" in Paul refers to being free from sin, the Law, and death, that in reality "Die Einheitlichkeit seines Freiheitsverständnisses liegt weniger in dem Inhalt, den er den ἐλευθερ-Wörtern jeweils zugeschrieben hat, als ... in der geistesgeschichtlichen Richtung, die seine Aussagen reflektieren ...."

[219] Cf. my *Suffering and the Spirit*, pp. 127–144, for an exposition of 1 Cor. 9 within the larger context of chs. 8–10, where Paul offers his own willingness to preach the gospel free of charge as a paradigmatic example of that ethic of love that "edifies" (8:1) by not insisting upon its own rights, but doing all things for the sake of the gospel (9:23). Paul's own life thus embodied the ethic of love he proposed as the fulfillment of the Law. For as I have tried to show, the three purpose clauses of 1 Cor. 9:12, 19, 22, in which Paul expresses his intention to do all things for the sake of the Gospel, even if this means enduring the suffering that comes from giving up his right to financial support, are all to be taken as an expression of Paul's love for the Corinthians (p. 136). Hence, the force of Paul's argument for the Corinthians not to eat meat offered to idols is, in part, an a-fortiori one, i.e., "if our apostle,

freedom to eat or not to eat meat offered to idols for the sake of the other person's faith, again as an act of obedience to God in Christ as manifested in the love (= "mutual acceptance," cf. Rom. 15:1–7) of the Gospel (cf. 1 Cor. 10:31 f. in view of 8:1–3, 8 f., 11–13).

This use of "freedom" throughout 1 Corinthians to refer to the ability to perform concrete acts of love in obedience to Christ leads one to read Paul's reference to "freedom" in 3:17b as that freedom to obey which flows from the Gospel. Such an impulse is sustained by Paul's development of the veil as a metonomy for Israel's hard heart in 3:14 f. and its removal in 3:16–17a. This means, however, that in Paul's thinking where the Spirit is experienced, there is freedom *from* the hard-heartedness characteristic of Israel's history. But more importantly, there too is the corresponding freedom *for* the obedience to the Law promised by Jeremiah and Ezekiel as the reversal of the state of affairs illustrated in Exod. 32–34. Far from being a "freedom from the Law," the freedom of v. 17b is therefore a freedom from the veil[220] in order to create a freedom *"for the Law!"* In 3:17 Paul is not polemicizing against the Law, but against those who argue that one can fulfill the Law apart from the power of the Spirit being poured out in the new covenant.[221]

Although this interpretation sounds strange to ears trained to read Paul's statements on freedom in terms of Bultmann's famous triad of "freedom from sin, the Law, and death,"[222] we must keep in mind that in building his theo-

---

to whom we owe our very lives as Christians (cf. 9:11), has given up his 'rights' (cf. 9:4, 5, 12a, 19a), how much more ought we to give up ours!" (p. 132).

[220] Cf. Peter von der Osten-Sacken, "Die Decke des Mose," p. 104, who rightly sees that the freedom here is a freedom from the veil, but wrongly interprets this to mean a freedom from the anxiety and care which flowed from participating in the passing nature of the glory associated with Moses. He therefore does not see the corresponding freedom for obedience which Paul also intends.

[221] See Otto Betz, "Der fleischliche Mensch und das geistliche Gesetz, Zum biblischen Hintergrund der paulinischen Gesetzeslehre," in his *Jesus, Der Herr der Kirche, Aufsätze zur biblischen Theologie II*, WUNT 52, 1990, pp. 129–196, p. 188, who argues that the freedom in view is not freedom from the Law, since what must be changed is the person by means of the Spirit. Contra the traditional view, as well as M. McNamara, *The New Testament and the Palestinian Targum*, p. 170, who suggested that in 3:6, 17 Paul was speaking against those who, on the basis of the tradition now found in *m.* Abot 6:2 on Exod. 32:16, associated the Law with freedom. In *m.* Abot 6:2, the Hebrew word *haruth* ("graven") in Exod. 32:16 is read *heruth* ("freedom"), with the conclusion that "thou findest no freeman excepting him that occupies himself in the study of the Law" (Danby, *The Mishnah*, 1933, p. 459). The parallel is instructive for showing the theological presupposition which is surely alive in Paul's day, and which is functioning in Paul's own argument. As our exegesis argues, Paul would not have disagreed with this statement in principle, but would have seen his ministry to be an affirmation of it! The issue was whether one could keep the Law apart from the Spirit.

[222] See his *Theologie*, §§ 38–40, pp. 331–353. For recent examples of the application of this triad to 3:17, see e.g. Erich Gräßer, *Der Alte Bund im Neuen*, p. 91, who does so following the work of P. Vielhauer, who extends it in terms of freedom from the old age and condemnation as well; Barrett, *Second Corinthians*, p. 123, who suggests that of the three, the Law is specifically in view; and now Hofius, "Gesetz und Evangelium," p. 120, who interprets it as freedom from the Law's "accusation and sentence of death."

logical foundation for dealing with the implications of the Gospel, Paul has already explicitly stated in 1 Cor. 7:19 that what is really of significance in the Christian calling is "keeping the commandments of God."[223] The freedom to obey the Gospel outlined in 1 Corinthians must therefore be seen as a concrete expression of "the commandments of God," which refers to the Mosaic Law as it is being kept in the Christian community. In the same way, in Gal. 2:4 and 5:1 the freedom in view is the freedom not to be circumcised as a direct implication of the Gospel, which then in 5:13 f. is given its corresponding positive counterpart as a freedom to love one another in *fulfillment* of the Law itself (cf. Rom. 13:8–10). Against the backdrop of this Pauline interpretation of Christian love as a fulfillment of the Mosaic Law, 1 Cor. 13 certainly speaks of this same freedom to obey (the commandments of the Law of God as the Law of Christ!) that Paul develops in 1 Cor. 7:39, 9:19, and 10:21.

The force of Paul's argument in 3:17 can now be uncovered. Paul is confident that the Spirit experienced in his ministry is the Spirit of the one true God first revealed in the Sinai covenant because the consequence is a life lived in freedom for obedience to the Law of God.[224] Just as Israel's continued harden-

---

[223] So too Jones, *Freiheit in den Briefen des Apostels Paulus*, p. 63. But Jones' attempt to read the freedom of v. 17 as a synonym for παρρησία in 3:12, understood as "Lauterkeit" (cf. pp. 64 f.), not only jumps over the immediate context of v. 17, but also depends on a cynic background to Paul's thought which is equally foreign at this point. Paul does not have his own experience of preaching in view in v. 17, but the experience of YHWH within the new covenant. Moreover, as we have seen, the contrast in v. 12 is not between Moses' lack of openness and Paul's openness, but between their respective relationships to those to whom they were sent, so that v. 17 makes no sense in any case as a statement of Paul's freedom of speech (contra Jones, following van Unnik, p. 66). Furthermore, Jones' reference, pp. 66 f., to Acts 4:29, 31 and Phil. 1:19–20 in support of the link between the Spirit and freedom of speech merely establishes a link between the Spirit and "boldness" (παρρησία), albeit in a different way than in 2 Cor. 3, and thus begs the question of the synonymous nature of freedom and boldness in 2 Cor. 3:17. Finally, such an absolute use of "freedom," with the connotation of "freedom of speech," would be unique in Paul's writings, whereas freedom to obey fits Paul's overall development of the concept.

[224] Contra Renwick, *Temple*, pp. 128, who denies that in 3:7–18 the new moral power provided by the Spirit is the basis upon which Paul argues that the new covenant brings freedom, since even "in the face of moral lapses which plagued the Christian Community at Corinth ... from time to time (see, e.g., II Cor. 2:5–11), freedom from the fear of death and condemnation ... could nevertheless be presumed – for the covenantal change instituted by Christ was not first of all a moral one (leading to a change in behavior) but a legal one (leading to a change in covenantal rules)." Renwick holds to this view because he takes the "counterpart" to καταργέω to be the death and condemnation of the old covenant itself, rather than the function of the glory of God in regard to Israel's hard-heartedness. He thus concludes that γράμμα in 3:6 refers to the old covenant *per se*, which, because of its demand for sinless perfection (i.e. "that if a person commits a single trespass the result would be condemnation ... and death [... see Rom. 5:16–17]," p. 129), has been and is being abolished (p. 128). Hence, in his view, it is the "abolition" of this "decree" that a single trespass must result in death which "functions as the crucial difference in the old covenant as compared with the new" and is the basis of Paul's confidence (p. 129, cf. p. 132). But given Paul's arguments in 1 Cor. 3:17, 6:7–11, and 2 Cor. 5:6–10, 13:1–10 (cf. Rom. 2:1 ff., Gal.

ing to the demands of the old covenant in 3:14 could be pointed to as evidence of their continuing separation from the God of the covenant, so too the "freedom" of those in the new covenant can be pointed to as evidence of their experience of YHWH in the Spirit. In 3:17b Paul is thus returning to the evidential argument for the validity of his ministry of the Spirit first introduced in 3:1–3 and then picked up in 3:6c and 8.[225] The way of life of the new covenant community in Christ proves the genuine nature of the encounter with YHWH now being experienced as a result of Paul's ministry. The argument for the truth of Paul's message is the obedience to the Law now being manifest in the love of the genuine believers in Corinth for one another and for the world, even as his own life exhibits this same obedience to the Law of Christ. It is this realization that gives Paul's admonitions throughout 1 and 2 Corinthians their gravity. Nothing less than the truth of the Gospel and the corresponding validity of one's Christian confession are ultimately at stake (cf. 1 Cor. 3:1–4; 5:7, 11–13; 6:19 f.; etc. and 2 Cor. 2:8–11; 12:19 f.; 13:1–5).

6. The Transformation of the People of God (2 Cor. 3:18)

The interpretation of 3:17 offered here is confirmed by Paul's final series of statements in 3:18 in which he draws and supports the conclusion that naturally follows from his identification of YHWH with the Spirit as the power of new life. Against the backdrop of Paul's argument in 3:12–17, the meaning of Paul's statements in 3:18, despite their complicated mode of expression, is readily apparent and can be paraphrased as follows: Since the Lord is the Spirit, as demonstrated by the freedom (from the veil) for obedience created by the Spirit (v. 17), "we all," that is, all members of the new covenant community, both Jews and Gentiles,[226] "are being transformed into the same im-

---

5:16 ff., etc.), it is difficult to maintain that the covenant rules or expectations concerning obedience have changed in the new covenant. If anything, they have intensified (cf. Matt. 5:17 ff.). Paul's expectation is that those who profess to be Christians but do not progress in obedience will be judged and condemned. For a development of this point within the Corinthian context, see my *Suffering and the Spirit*, pp. 155–157. Renwick's view is based on the widespread view that the Law and old covenant demanded sinless perfection to be saved.

[225] Contra Koch, *Schrift*, p. 338 n. 38, who asserts that the reference back to 3:6,8 is "gekünstelt" and that "Das Thema der διακονία ist mit V 11 abgeschlossen."

[226] Contra Belleville, *Reflections of Glory*, pp. 275 f., who denies that ἡμεῖς πάντες in v. 18 is a reference to all believers, taking it instead to refer to "all true gospel ministers without exception" (p. 276). She argues this because she sees no contextual evidence for a shift from the consistent reference to ministers in the plural throughout 2:14–7:2. But Belleville misses this evidence because she does not see that the plurals in 2:14 ff. are apostolic plurals in reference to Paul himself, so that πάντες cannot refer to a broader group of apostles or co-workers (see above, chapter two, pp. 97 ff.). Moreover, Belleville rightly observes that ἡμεῖς indicates an intensification rather than a broadening of the reference, but wrongly carries this

age" (μεταμορφούμεθα τὴν αὐτὴν εἰκόνα), that is to say, we are experiencing in a progressive sense this freedom to obey God in Christ in the power of the Spirit and, as a result, are being changed into God's own image.[227] It is this transformation which marks the decisive difference between the old and new covenant ministries of Moses and Paul.[228] Moreover, this transformation is taking place "from glory unto glory" (ἀπὸ δόξης εἰς δόξαν), i.e. this gradual growth in obedience takes place on the basis of God's initial revelation of his glory to us and results in our own becoming more and more like him until the final eschatological consummation and transformation.[229] As such, it is brought about by the Lord, who is the Spirit (καθάπερ ἀπὸ κυρίου πνεύματος).[230] This transformation takes place "by means of an unveiled face" (ἀνακεκαλυμμένῳ), that is to say, by means of our encountering the

over to the meaning of πάντες as well (cf. p. 275 n. 3). She thus misses the contextual evidence supplied by πάντες itself. Moreover, her view fails to note the evidential proof which v. 18 offers *for* Paul's assertion of his legitimacy as an apostle, taking it merely to be yet another affirmation *of* Paul's legitimacy (cf. p. 276). Finally, Belleville's view forces her to read v. 18 as suddenly establishing a contrast to Moses' being veiled, rather than seeing it as a parallel to Moses' being unveiled, as in vv. 16–17 (cf. p. 277), and to take κατοπτριζόμενοι as a reference to "reflecting," rather than "beholding" (see below, n. 231). On the other hand, her objection to the view taken here that "then Paul's shift from the Israelite heart veil to the Christian face veil remains inexplicable" (p. 277 n. 1) is overcome once the use of the veil in vv. 14–18 is recognized to be a metonomy for hard-heartedness and the consequences of the glory of God.

[227] Renwick, *Temple*, pp. 56 f., argues that the evidence of being in the presence of God is "transformation into the sacrificial image of Christ" as seen in Paul's own life of suffering, so that Paul is here offering a "cultic interpretation of Christian experience" (cf. p. 159). This is certainly true, but must not be affirmed apart from the moral and ethical dimensions of this Christ-like life. It is not suffering *per se*, but the obedience of faith toward God in Christ that is the parallel between Paul and believers.

[228] I owe this point to Gerd Theißen, "Die Hülle des Mose," pp. 144 f., though his subsequent psychological interpretation of this transforming enlightenment as an "Erhellung des Unbewußten," over against "das herrschende Bewußtsein" (which is Theißen's reinterpretation of the role of Satan as portrayed in 4:4) in which Christ represents "die archetypische Zielgröße des Selbst" (cf. pp. 154–156), is to be rejected.

[229] Taking the ἀπὸ ... εἰς construction to express cause or source and result in parallel to the ἐκ ... εἰς construction in 2 Cor. 2:16 and Rom. 1:17. For this meaning of 2 Cor. 2:16 and 3:18, see A. Schlatter, *Paulus Der Bote Jesus. Eine Deutung seiner Briefe an die Korinther*, 1969⁴, pp. 497, 521, and already E. Sokolowski, *Die Begriffe Geist und Leben bei Paulus in ihren Beziehungen zu einander. Eine exegetisch-religionsgeschichtliche Untersuchung*, 1903, p. 63; for this understanding of Rom. 1:17, see Stuhlmacher, *Der Brief an die Römer*, p. 30.

[230] For the six possible ways to take this phrase grammatically, see Furnish, *II Corinthians*, p. 216. Given Paul's earlier statement in 3:17, the most probable is to take the second genitive πνεύματος as epexegetical in relation to the Lord; see too Stockhausen, *Moses' Veil*, pp. 90, 151, and Belleville, *Reflections of Glory*, pp. 293 f. Here, as throughout v. 18, the reference continues to be to YHWH and not to Christ; see again Furnish, p. 214, who follows Collange in taking "Lord" in 3:18 to be YHWH and for support points to the background of the verse in Exod. 24:17 and 34, to Paul's reference to the glory of God elsewhere in 1 Cor. 11:7; 2 Cor. 8:9; Rom. 3:23; 5:2, etc., and to the common occurrence of this idea in the LXX.

glory of God itself, made possible by the Spirit's work in removing from us the barrier of our hard hearts of rebellion against him. As a result, "we behold as in a mirror" (κατοπτριζόμενοι[231]) the glory of the Lord without being destroyed by it.

The conceptual link between 3:13–17 and 18 is clear. It is the Spirit which removes the "veil" on the "faces" of those within the new covenant so that, like Moses in Exod. 34:34–35, they too may encounter the glory of God. This parallel between the experience of those in the new covenant in v. 18 and Moses in v. 16 is established by the repetition of the theme of the unveiled "face" in v. 18, which picks up the picture of Moses as unveiled in v. 16, which in turn points back to the emphasis in 3:7 and 13 on the glory upon Moses' "face" (πρόσωπον). As in v. 16, the comparison with Moses in v. 18 continues to be a positive one, in contrast to the negative comparison between Paul's ministry and the ministry of Moses in 3:12 f. For whereas in vv. 12 f.

---

[231] In the active this verb means "to show as in a mirror or by reflection," and in the passive, "to be mirrored," while the middle means "behold (something) as in a mirror," Liddell and Scott, *Greek-English Lexicon*, p. 929. As Furnish, *II Corinthians*, p. 214, has pointed out, the attempt of those like van Unnik, Knox, Dupont, Allo, etc., to read this middle participle to mean "reflecting as a mirror" clearly goes against the linguistic evidence. He points esp. to Philo, *Leg. All.* 3, 101 and 1 Clem. 36:2 as examples in favor of the meaning "beholding as in a mirror" adopted here. See too esp. Hughes, *Second Corinthians*, p. 119, for the significance of the passage from Clement, Lietzmann, *An die Korinther*, pp. 113 f., for a treatment of the text from Philo, and now Hofius, "Gesetz und Evangelium," p. 116. Most recently, the view that the verb refers to "reflecting the glory of God" has been argued in detail by Belleville, *Reflections of Glory*, pp. 273 f., 277–282. Belleville's attempt to adduce NT-era evidence for the use of the middle to mean "reflect" breaks down (cf. pp. 280 f.), since the parallels from Plutarch, *Mor.* 696A and *Mor.* 936E, the only contemporaneous source which Belleville points to as evidence, actually contain different compound forms of the verb (in the former, ἐνοπτρίσασθαι is paralleled to ἐσοπτρίζει, in the latter, only the *noun* form ἐσοπτρισμούς is found [contra Belleville's reading of this as an adjectival form of the verb, p. 280 n. 2), while *Mor.* 894 F, which she apparently also points to as evidence for the middle form meaning "to reflect," actually contains the *active* form κατοπτρίζοντος, rather than the middle. Belleville thus presents no NT-era evidence to support her conclusion that "although few in number, examples of κατοπτρίζεσθαι meaning 'to reflect' do exist" (p. 280). The examples she does have are all from the church fathers. But even if it were true that the distinction between the meaning of the middle and the active had broken down by the time of the NT, so that on occasion the middle could take on the transitive sense of "to reflect," as Belleville maintains (p. 280), the question still remains whether this meaning is in force in v. 18. Belleville argues for this reading in v. 18 because she does not see the idea of an indirect view of God's glory as signaled by the meaning "beholding with unveiled face" supported in the Exodus narrative, esp. in view of Num. 12:6–7 (pp. 277 f.), and because she sees the use of εἰκών in v. 18 as suggesting that Paul is referring to the idea of a reflected image (p. 279 n. 3). But in view of Moses' encounter with God in Exod. 33 (see above, chapter two), such an indirect encounter with God is precisely what Moses experienced on the mountain. Moreover, the "image" in v. 18 does not describe the nature of κατοπτριζόμενοι, but the *result* of this action, i.e. their transformed moral character (see below). In Belleville's view, this cause-effect relationship between κατοπτριζόμενοι and μεταμορφούμεθα becomes a tautology, which makes the relationship between reflecting and transformation in this verse difficult to explain (cf. p. 282).

Paul was comparing his apostolic *ministry* with the *ministry* of Moses, here, as in v. 16, Paul is comparing the *experience of the believer* under the new covenant to the *experience* of Moses.[232] For as Dumbrell has observed,

"Implicit in Paul's thinking is the Mosaic position to which he has referred in 2 Cor. 3:16. We are being changed in a manner analogous to the way Moses was being glorified under the circumstances of the Sinai encounter; that is, by contact with Yahweh who is now being experienced as Spirit."[233]

As such, the experience of the believer, like that of Moses in Exod. 34, is the positive counterpart to that of Israel in her hardened condition as portrayed in 3:13.[234] The very thing which led to the difference between Moses and Paul now supports the similarity between Moses and the believer, i.e. the presence and absence of the hard heart. By implication, the description of those under the new covenant in v. 18 as those who follow Moses into the tent of meeting carries with it a contrast to those Jews (and Gentiles) who, like Israel in Exod. 32–34, remain hardened due to the absence of the transforming work of the Spirit (cf. 3:14b–15).[235] This is confirmed by the contrasting parallel between καθάπερ Μωυσῆς in 3:13 and καθάπερ ἀπὸ κυρίου πνεύματος in v. 18.[236] Just

---

[232] So too Gerd Theißen, "Die Hülle des Mose," p. 128, who argues that in 3:16–18 "Mose wird hier zum Prototypen des Bekehrten." Wright, *Climax*, p. 180, rightly sees the basis of Paul's confidence in 3:12 to be the different experience of those under the new covenant from those under the old, and that the implied contrast in 3:14–15 is between the condition of Israel under the old covenant and the changed condition of the new covenant people of God. He also argues that in v. 18 Paul understands Moses to be a precursor of the new covenant people of God, since Moses alone could look at the divine glory with unveiled face. But because he takes καταργέω in 3:7 to refer to the impermanence of the glory itself as part of the old covenant, and thus ultimately to the impermanence of the Law, Wright does not follow this fundamental insight consistently in his understanding of Paul's argument. Thus, as Wright reads Paul, Moses had to veil himself because the glory, as part of the old covenant, was temporary, while the Law was given only for a specific period of time and then set aside once its purpose had been accomplished in Christ (pp. 181, cf. 39, 196, 198, etc.). See too his consequent reading of τέλος in v. 13 as referring to the final destination or goal of the glory on Moses' face as the glory of the Gospel (p. 181).

[233] "Paul's use of Exodus 34," p. 189.

[234] So too Windisch, *zweiter Korintherbrief*, pp. 127, who saw v. 18 to be the continuation of v. 12, the positive completion of v. 13, and the antithesis to vv. 13–16 and thus argued for the meaning "behold" for κατοπτρίζω (cf. his extensive listing of parallels from Jewish and Greco-Roman lit.). See too Stockhausen, *Moses' Veil*, pp. 127 f., and the literature cited there. As Stockhausen points out, Paul and the other Christians are being compared with Moses and contrasted with the sons of Israel in v. 13, but the primary parallel is with Moses himself. Yet for Stockhausen this parallel is to Moses as the one who reflected God's glory, rather than to his experience in v. 16 (see below).

[235] See Belleville, *Reflections of Glory*, p. 177 n. 4, who argues that "there are two positive stages in Paul's argument, involving two different types of veiling: (1) the removal of the veil over the heart in vv. 16–17, which is the reverse of vv. 14a and 15, and (2) the unveiling of the face in v. 18, which is parallel to v. 12 and antithetical to vv. 13 and 14b."

[236] I owe this parallel to Hays, *Echoes*, p. 144, and now Wright, *Climax*, p. 189 n. 53, who recognize the allusion to v. 13a in 18.

as Moses could not mediate the glory of the Lord to Israel due to her hardened nature, the transformation of believers under the new covenant comes about precisely by means of the mediation of this divine glory. In this regard, Paul's choice of πάντες in 3:18a to describe those who *are* encountering the glory of God may be an intentional allusion to the fact that in Exod. 34:30, 31, and 32 it is repeatedly stressed that "all" (πάντες) the elders of Israel, rulers of the synagogue, and sons of Israel were afraid of and veiled from the glory on Moses' face.[237]

On the other hand, the conceptual link between the experience of the new covenant believer in 3:18 and Paul's prior discussion of his own ministry in 3:3, 6–13 is also apparent. In contrast to Moses, who had to veil the glory of God from stiff-necked Israel, Paul ministers the glory of God boldly, i.e. in an "unveiled" fashion, because the Spirit is now at work to replace the hard heart of stone with receptive hearts of flesh. The experience of the glory of God which transforms believers in 3:18 is thus the direct result of Paul's ministry of the Spirit as the manifestation of the glory of God described in 3:8, 9b, 10b, and 11b.[238] Paul is a mediator of the glory of God in the midst of the Corinthians, who through Paul's ministry of suffering and the Spirit are being brought into the presence of the Lord himself (cf. 2:14–16a, 4:7 ff.).

This conceptual contrast between Paul's ministry and that of Moses in 3:12 f. and 18 further supports the exegetical decisions which have been made concerning these verses. The link between 3:13 and 18 makes it evident that κατοπτριζόμενοι (v. 18), as the counterpart to μὴ ἀτενίσαι (v. 13), must refer to beholding the glory of God as in a mirror, not reflecting it.[239] This is sub-

---

[237] I owe this observation to Furnish, *II Corinthians*, p. 213. Though in contrast to my view, Furnish sees this to be the central thrust of 3:18 and therefore takes the reference to the "face" in v. 18 as parallel to the "heart" of v. 15. But the use of πρόσωπον in 3:7 and 13 to refer to Moses makes its repetition in v. 18 most easily understood against the backdrop of Moses' own experience.

[238] See too Provence, "Who is Sufficient," p. 64. Contra Belleville, *Reflections of Glory*, p. 285, who takes the meaning of the glory in v. 18 to be "knowledge of the salvific work of God in the gospel" in parallel to 4:6. But in 4:6 it is also the knowledge of the glory of God which is shone in one's heart.

[239] So too R.P. Martin, *2 Corinthians*, p. 71 (pointing to the arguments of Hugedé, *La métaphore du miroir*, 17–24, 32), Furnish, *II Corinthians*, p. 221, and Dumbrell, "Paul's use of Exodus 34," p. 189. Contra Belleville, *Reflections of Glory*, pp. 277–282, and Stockhausen, *Moses' Veil*, pp. 151 f., who follows Dupont and Le Chretien in taking this verb "primarily" to mean "reflect," since she views v. 18 to refer to Paul, not to the experience of all believers. She suggests that only "secondarily" does it refer to all Christians and mean "behold" (p. 150 n. 111). For Stockhausen, then, Paul introduces "a deliberate wordplay on both possible meanings" (p. 11; cf. p. 90 n. 11). But it is doubtful that Paul is intending a double entendre here, especially given the lack of lexical support for the former meaning! Moreover, in Paul's view it is Christ who reflects God's glory (4:4, 6), not himself; he merely reveals it through his suffering. Kim, *Origin of Paul's Gospel*, p. 231, is more accurate in suggesting that in v. 18 Paul applies his own experience as "typical" for all Christians. Kim, pp. 232 f., thus also argues for the meaning "to behold as in a mirror" and points

stantiated by Paul's corresponding reference to the fact that in the case of those who are rejecting Paul's Gospel, the "God of this age has blinded the minds of those who do not believe so that they cannot *see* (αὐγάσαι) the light of the gospel of the glory of Christ" (2 Cor. 4:4). Moreover, it is striking that Philo interprets Moses' request to see God's glory in Exodus 33:13 in terms of his desire not to see God manifested (ἐμφανισθείης) in any created thing, or perceived as reflected (κατοπτρισαίμην) in anything else, but to see the form (ἰδέαν) of God himself *(Leg.All.* III, 101).[240] Furthermore, this parallel between the two outcomes in vv. 13 and 18 confirms the decision that τὸ τέλος in v. 13, like μεταμορφούμεθα in v. 18, must refer to that which the glory in each case brings about. In the former case it was the judgment of the hard-hearted, in the latter it is the transformation of those whose hearts have been changed by the Spirit.[241]

That Paul's thought in 2 Cor. 3:18 was not out of the ordinary, but part of a larger field of tradition, is apparent in view of the general parallels to the transforming and judging power of the glory of God which we have already pointed to in conjunction with Paul's argument in 3:7. But even more striking is the close conceptual parallel (and differences!) to Paul's thought found in the early second century A.D. text of 2 Baruch 51:1–12.[242] For in describing the events that will take place immediately after the eschatological day of judgment, we read there concerning the transformation of the wicked and the righteous that

---

to Ezek. 1:5 and 24:17 as the conceptual background for Paul's imagery, where the vision of God is portrayed in terms of seeing God's reflection in a mirror, and to Wis. 7:26, where the motifs of "image" and "mirror" are brought together. For this latter parallel, see too Richard, "Polemics," pp. 359 f., though there is no reason to pit this text against the creation backdrop to 3:18 and 4:6 in order to force a choice between the two as he does.

[240] I am indebted to Theobald, *Gnade*, p. 200 n. 160, for calling attention to this parallel, which he adduces to show that the verb can still mean "to see in a mirror," rather than simply meaning "to see." Text from Colson and Whitaker, *Philo, Vol. 1*, LCL, 1949 (1929), p. 368.

[241] Contra Hooker, "Beyond the Things that are written?" p. 301, who suggests that the contrast is between two kinds of glory, one derivative and the other direct, and Hofius, "Gesetz und Evangelium," p. 116, who argues that the contrast is between the "Strahlenglanz" on Moses' face, which was only a fading "reflex" of the glory in the Law, and the glory of the Lord himself in the gospel. But the contrast throughout 3:7–18 is not between two types of glory, but between two types of people! The glory in view is always the very glory of God himself, and in both cases it is mediated, either by Moses or by Paul, and not direct. Hence, in the case of Hofius, the attempt to see a Law/Gospel contrast *per se* in 3:18 fails. The problem with this attempt is ultimately made clear in that, to be consistent, Hofius must conclude that in 3:18 Christians are not like Moses, since Moses was himself not transformed! Moses remains outside the saving experience of God's presence! For unlike believers, Moses encountered only the glory of the Law, which was the manifestation of the glory of God to kill, not the "saving manifestation of the δόξα of God" (p. 117). Moses thus remains unchanged, as evidenced by the fact that the glory faded (pp. 116 f.).

[242] R.P. Martin, *2 Corinthians*, p. 72, also points to 2 Bar. 51:3, 7, 10, without developing it. See too the parallels in 1 En. 109:11–13 and 4 Ezra 7:97 pointed to by Belleville, *Reflections of Glory*, pp. 286 f., as further evidence that this concept of transformation was associated with the eschatological end times.

"... both the shape of those who are found to be guilty as also the *glory* of those who have proved to be righteous *will be changed*. For the shape of those who now act wickedly will be made more evil than it is (now) so that they shall suffer torment. Also, as for the glory of those who proved to be righteous on account of my law, those who possessed intelligence in their life, and those who planted the root of wisdom in their heart – their splendor *will then be glorified by* transformations, and the shape of their face will be changed into the light of their beauty so that they may acquire and receive the undying world which is promised *to them* ... then both these and those will be changed, these into the splendor of angels and those into startling visions and horrible shapes ... And they will be changed into any shape which they wished, from beauty to loveliness, and *from light to the splendor of glory* ... And the excellence of the righteous will then be greater than that of the angels."[243]

Like 2 Bar. 51:1 ff., in 3:18 Paul too conceives of the glory of God as that which transforms those who already perceive it into even greater glory (ἀπὸ δόξης εἰς δόξαν). Paul also understands this transformation as a prerequisite to inheriting the world to come. But as soon as these similarities are noticed, it is the differences which call attention to themselves. Unlike this tradition, for Paul it is the image of the Lord himself, as revealed in Christ (cf. 3:18 with 4:4, 6), not the glory of the angels, into which believers are being transformed. And even more importantly, for Paul this transformation is already taking place in relationship to Christ, rather than merely being a hope for the future based on one's allegiance to the Law. Since the new covenant has been inaugurated in Christ, it is not the Law which is equated with the "power" of God, to which those who "believe" must submit themselves in order to overcome Adam's curse, as in 2 Baruch 54:14–16, but the Gospel of Christ (Rom. 1:16).[244]

---

[243] Translation from A.F.J. Klijn, "2 (Syriac Apocalypse of) Baruch," *OTP Vol. 1*, 1983, pp. 615–652, p. 638.

[244] See now Wright, "Adam, Israel, and the Messiah," in his *Climax*, pp. 18–40, for the idea that in Judaism, and subsequently for Paul, Adam speculation is not applied fundamentally to humankind in general, but to Israel as the people of God, so that this tradition consistently makes the point that God's purposes for humanity have "devolved on to, and will be fulfilled in Israel" (pp. 20–21). Hence, "what God intended for Adam will be given to the seed of Abraham," and the "last Adam" becomes equated with the eschatological people of God (pp. 21–25). But in contrast to Wright, Paul's argument in 3:12–18 indicates that this *still* holds true as a promise for Israel, rather than having already reached its "climax" and come to an end as a result of having been fulfilled in Christ as the "last Adam" incorporation of Israel, as Wright maintains (cf. Wright, *Climax*, pp. 26, 28 f., 35–37, 40, and the summaries on pp. 261–264). Wright is certainly correct in seeing Christ accomplishing what God had first intended to do through Adam and then Israel, but he over-interprets the significance of Christ as "second Adam," seeing Christ to be the termination of Israel's role within salvation history, since "the role traditionally assigned to Israel had devolved on to Jesus Christ. Paul now regarded him, not Israel, as God's true humanity" (p. 26). Though this is true for Christ himself, Paul's argument in 3:12–18 is not fundamentally about Christ's *replacement* of Israel, but about the implications of Christ's representation as "last Adam" for Israel, and through Israel for the Church as the *continuation* of the people of God in the eschatological age. Indeed, Paul's concern in 2 Cor. 3:12–18 is not about Christ or the Church *per se*, but

Again, therefore, it is the existence of the Corinthians themselves as Christians that supports the validity of Paul's ministry. Indeed, Paul can expect a ready assent to the affirmations of v. 18 from the Corinthians, who do not hesitate to affirm their spiritual standing and experiences of the Spirit (!). But as the integral tie between 3:18 and 3:3, 6–12 demonstrates, one cannot approve the latter without accepting the truth of the former. The transformation of the Corinthians themselves thus points to the reality of the glory of God in the ministry of Paul. For according to 3:18, this experience of the glory of God is both the ground (ἀπὸ δόξης) and means (ἀνακεκαλυμμένῳ προσώπῳ τὴν δόξαν κυρίου κατοπτριζόμενοι) of the believers' transformation, as well as the ultimate goal or result (τὴν αὐτὴν εἰκόνα ... εἰς δόξαν) of the transformation itself.[245] The "same image" into which one is being transformed is the image or glory of God that one encounters. For as Belleville has recently pointed out, this Pauline assertion is his commentary on Exodus 34:35, in which Paul may have read concerning Moses that δεδόξασται ἡ ὄψις τοῦ χρώματος τοῦ προσώπου αὐτοῦ.[246]

---

about Israel! Wright's view thus leads to an over-realized eschatology in which the hope for Israel's future restoration is completely subsumed in Christ. In Wright's words, "The last Adam *is* the eschatological Israel, who will be raised from the dead *as* the vindicated people of God. Paul's claim is that Jesus, as Messiah, *is* the realization of Israel's hope, the focal point and source of life for the people of God" (p. 35, emphasis mine). Hence, in Wright's view of Paul, "Jesus stands in the place of Israel" (p. 40). This, of course, has a dramatic impact on Wright's reading of Rom. 9–11 (cf. *Climax*, pp. 231–257, esp. pp. 236, 242 f.). For Wright, therefore, Paul "forcibly rejected" the traditional Jewish eschatological expectations (p. 26), developing instead an eschatological and theological framework which Wright must describe as "paradoxical" (cf., e.g., pp. 236, 244) and as God's "strange covenant faithfulness and justice, in Jesus" (p. 255). But Paul's point in 3:12–18 is not that Jesus and his people are substituted for Israel as those who encounter the glory of God, but that the locus of that encounter is now in and through Christ and the new covenant he has inaugurated, rather than through the old covenant. Paul's answer to Israel's rejection of Christ in 3:12–4:6 is thus *not* that they have been subsumed in and replaced by Christ and the Church, their role in salvation history having being fulfilled (à la Wright, p. 39), but that they are still in their hardened condition. By implication, then, they are still awaiting their restoration!

[245] Hays, *Echoes*, p. 138, is therefore right in observing that for Paul "Moses becomes a metaphor for the person who 'turns to the Lord' and sees the glory of God's image, thereby undergoing transformation" (cf. p. 143, where Hays speaks of Moses' act of entering God's presence as "paradigmatic for the experience of believers"), and in his recognition of the apologetic force of Paul's statements. But he goes beyond Paul's intention when he concludes that for Paul the problem with the old covenant was that it was "veiled in script," whereas the "new covenant is manifested in the transformation of human community" (p. 138). The contrast here is not between the written nature of the old covenant and the church, but between the conditions of the heart under the respective covenants. Hays' conclusion that for Paul "revelation occurs not primarily in the sacred text but in the transformed community of readers" (p. 144) misses the point of Paul's contrast in 3:13–18. Moreover, for Paul the community witnesses to the "knowledge of the glory of God on the face of Christ" (4:6, 11), which, *like the old covenant*, is revealed in the sacred writings (like the Law and the prophets, Paul's own letters were to be read in the worship service!).

[246] Belleville, *Reflections of Glory*, p. 286. Though not all MSS of the LXX include the phrase δεδόξασται ἡ ὄψις τοῦ χρώματος τοῦ προσώπου αὐτοῦ, Belleville argues that it was

At this point, however, Paul is also speaking from his own experience. As we have seen in chapter two, Paul's call, like that of Moses and the prophets, derived from his own encounter with the glory of God, this time as revealed "on the face of Christ" (4:6).[247] Moreover, as Seyoon Kim has demonstrated, what Paul saw on the road to Damascus was a theophany of Christ as the "image (εἰκών) of God," and it is this experience that provides the foundation for his argument in 2 Cor. 3:16–4:6.[248] In the context of 3:18–4:6, "the same image" and "glory" in 3:18 is specifically the "glory of God" being revealed "in the face of [Jesus] Christ" (ἐν προσώπῳ Ἰησοῦ Χριστοῦ, 4:6), who "is the image of God" (εἰκὼν τοῦ θεοῦ) in the sense of "God's likeness" (4:4).[249]

---

part of the tradition before Paul, based on Paul's use of εἰκών in v. 18, "since εἰκών is a perfectly adequate equivalent for the expression ἡ ὄψις τοῦ χρώματος, as the rendering in *Tg. Ps.-J.* demonstrates ..." (p. 286 n. 3). As support, he points to Pseudo-Philo, LAB 19:16, and to the fact that the MT, Samaritan Pentateuch, Samaritan Targum, and the targumim all include this phrase. However, Belleville draws the unwarranted conclusion that μεταμορφούμεθα refers to the fact that the glory on Moses' face was short lived or fading (p. 286). Nor is this idea supported by Paul's reference to the fact that the glory is increasing (i.e. "from glory to glory"), as Belleville maintains (cf. p. 289). Finally, Belleville's decision to take κατοπτριζόμενοι as a reference to reflecting gospel truths, rather than to beholding the glory of God, leads her to take "the *same* image" to refer to "the gospel ministers themselves, who are being transformed into – so to speak – carbon copies of one another" (p. 290, similar to the positions of van Unnik, Dunn, and Wright). Paul's point, in Belleville's view, is that "among the reflected images of the gospel truths there should be no distinction. True gospel ministers present the same image to their audience" (p. 291). Such a view has not found support in this study.

[247] Of special relevance is the fact that Ezekiel's encounter with the glory of God is also portrayed in terms of seeing the "image" or "likeness of God" in human form in a mirror in the midst of the fire (see Ezek. 1:1, 4, 5, 10, 16, and esp. vv. 26 f.); cf. Kim, *Origin of Paul's Gospel*, pp. 205–207, 212, 214 f. Paul's use of the concept of "looking as in a mirror" at the glory of God in Christ as the image of God in v. 18 may very well derive from this backdrop; cf. Philo, *Somn.* 1:227–241.

[248] For the detailed development of this thesis, see his *Origin of Paul's Gospel*, pp. 137–268, and the statements of his thesis on pp. 137, 193, 223, 229. Specifically, Kim argues that on the road to Damascus, "Paul saw the exalted Christ as the εἰκὼν τοῦ θεοῦ and as the Son of God ... This perception led him to conceive of Christ in terms of the personified, hypostatized Wisdom of God ... on the one hand, and in terms of Adam, on the other. Thus, both Paul's Wisdom-Christology and Adam-Christology are grounded in the Damascus Christophany" (p. 267). For the Adam-Christology Kim points primarily to Gen. 1:27 and its development in Rom. 8:29; 1 Cor. 15:45 ff.; for the Wisdom-Christology he points to Wis. 7:26 and its development in Col. 1:15 (cf. pp. 137, 144). For our purposes the question of the origin of the emphasis on Christ as a "second Adam" and as the personification of wisdom may be left open, though it is doubtful whether there were distinct and separate "Adam" and "Wisdom-Christologies" as such. It is more appropriate to speak of various Christological conceptions which were integrated into a general Christological portrait, most likely around the dual aspects of Jesus as the Son of Man and Son of God. This is confirmed by 3:18–4:6 itself, for as Kim himself points out, p. 144, in this passage Paul forges together these two strands.

[249] For the meaning of εἰκών as "likeness" or "representation," see BAGD, *A Greek-English Lexicon*, p. 222; BAA, *Griechisch-deutsches Wörterbuch*, p. 448; and Paul's use in Rom. 1:23. Kim, *Origin of Paul's Gospel*, pp. 137–141, shows that the concept of transfor-

Thus, as Kim concludes, "when the δόξα of God shone in the face of Christ, Christ appeared to Paul as the εἰκών of God."[250] Paul's reference in 2 Cor. 4:6 to the "glory of God on the face of Christ" indicates that, as the "image of God," Christ is the very embodiment and revelation of God himself, even as Phil. 2:6 can speak of Christ as existing "in the form of God" (ἐν μορφῇ θεοῦ)[251] and Col. 1:15 can speak of Christ as the "image of the invisible God, the first born of all creation" (εἰκὼν τοῦ θεοῦ τοῦ ἀοράτου πρωτότοκος πάσης κτίσεως).[252] Indeed, in surveying Paul's thought Alan F. Segal can even conclude that "the center of Paul's gospel is the identification of Christ as the Glory of God."[253] The parallel between the revelation of God encountered by Moses in 3:16 and the experience of believers in 3:17–18 supports this identification. As the resurrected "Lord" (4:5) encountered by believers with "unveiled faces," Christ is not merely reflecting the glory of God as Moses did, he *is* the glory of God. Conversely, it is not Christ, but Paul who mediates God's glory in the new covenant. The comparison throughout 2 Cor. 3:7–18 is not between Moses and Christ as mediators of the glory of God, but between Moses and Paul, with Christ equated with YHWH himself as the glory of God.[254] For to Paul, as in the early Christian tradition which he adopts, Christ's resurrection declares him to be the "Son of God," who as such is "the Lord" (Rom. 1:4; cf. Phil. 2:9–11). Thus, as Furnish has observed, for Paul "Christ is God's image because he is God's Son (see Rom. 8:29) in whom God is beheld, and the image into which believers are being transformed is the same one they see mirrored there."[255] Paul's description of Christ as the "image of God" in 4:4 certainly carries with it connotations of Christ's deity.

---

mation into the image of Christ is a distinctively Pauline theological development. The question of whether or not the "image-Christology" upon which it is based is also Paul's contribution (as Kim argues, pp. 144–159), or derived from a pre-Pauline tradition, is dependent upon the origin of Phil. 2:6–11 and Col. 1:15–20 and need not detain us here. For the fact that Paul's emphasis on Christ is based in his OT heritage and Christian experience, rather than in some proto-Gnostic speculation current in Corinth (à la Brandenburger), see Kim's refinement of Wedderburn's thesis, pp. 164–179, 187–192.

[250] *Origin of Paul's Gospel*, p. 230.

[251] On Phil. 2:6 as a statement of Christ's divinity and preexistence, see Moisés Silva, *Philippians*, Wycliffe Exegetical Commentary, 1988, pp. 113–117.

[252] Cf. Kim, *Origin of Paul's Gospel*, p. 219, who concludes this same point based on his study of the motifs of צלם ("image") and דמות ("likeness") in the OT and Jewish literature (see esp. the parallel between Gen. 1:26 and 5:3, where both are rendered in the LXX by εἰκών), in which both "can never be understood without a connotation of physical representation and external likeness of form," so that Christ is here pictured as the "(visible, therefore material) manifestation of (the invisible) God ..." Yet as Kim points out, the primary referent is to a functional likeness as an agent of representation, cf. p. 199. See below, n. 268.

[253] *Paul the Convert, The Apostolate and Apostasy of Saul the Pharisee*, 1990, p. 156.

[254] Contra e.g. Gerd Theißen, "Die Hülle des Mose," pp. 142, 144–146, who sees Paul as arguing that Christ supplants Moses inasmuch as Moses himself turned to Christ, reading the references to the Lord in vv. 16–18 to be references to Christ.

[255] *II Corinthians*, p. 215.

But the reference to being transformed into "the image of God" in 3:18 and the subsequent identification of this image with Christ as the glory of God in 4:4, 6 primarily presuppose the conception of Christ in his humanity, albeit his *resurrected* humanity, as the "second Adam." Paul's description in 1 Cor. 11:7 of the man as "the image and glory of God" (εἰκὼν καὶ δόξα θεοῦ), based on the creation of Adam in Gen. 1:26–28 and 2:7, illustrates that this same description of Christ in 2 Cor. 4:4, 6 recalls for Paul the "man" created in God's image from Gen. 1–2.[256] Hence, as Segal has observed, in 2 Cor. 3:15–18,

> "Paul expresses the subject of correct faith in eschatological, future terms as the spiritual glow, radiance or splendor, the special resemblance of Adam to God before the fall, which is imparted only to those who, like Moses, have been called into the presence of God. Paul implies that converted Christians have also received this glow from the presence of God. Paul has been called into Christ's enthroned presence by his conversion, as are all in the Christian community of faith."[257]

Such a conception of the resurrected Christ as the federal "second Adam" (before the fall!) is not foreign in Corinth, being a central part of Paul's understanding of the way in which, as with the sin of the first Adam, the *effects* of the *resurrection* of the new "Adam" are experienced by those "in Christ" (1 Cor. 15:21 f., 45–49).[258] The corresponding presentation in Rom. 5:15–19 of Christ as the new Adam in relationship to the effects of the *cross* indicates that Christ's role as head of the "new humanity" also played a central part in Paul's Gospel.

In the context of 2 Cor. 3:6–18, it is therefore significant that in Paul's prior development of Christ as the second Adam in 1 Cor. 15, Christ is the one in whom "all shall be made alive" (πάντες ζῳοποιηθήσονται; cf. 2 Cor. 3:6) in the future resurrection (15:21 f.). As the resurrected, second Adam, Christ provides an example of the resurrected "body" itself, since he has already experienced the "the glory of the heavenly" (ἡ τῶν ἐπουρανίων δόξα, 15:40) or "spiritual body" (σῶμα πνευματικόν, 15:44). But as the "last Adam" Christ is more than an example of the future resurrection, he is the means through which it will be experienced. Just as the first Adam was "from the earth," and thus became the one through whom the "earthly body" was given, the second or "last" Adam, Christ, is from heaven, and has thus become "a life-giving Spirit" (εἰς πνεῦμα ζῳοποιοῦν), i.e. the one through whom the resurrection life of the Spirit, the "heavenly body," will be granted to those who belong to

---

[256] The question of Paul's conflation of Gen. 1:26 and 2:15–18 need not concern us here.

[257] *Paul the Convert*, p. 152.

[258] See now Wright, *Climax*, pp. 30–32, who also argues that the focus of 1 Cor. 15:42–49 is not Christological, but "anthropological" as part of Paul's discussion of the nature of humanity in the present and future. As such, v. 47 refers to the type of humanity rather than to the origin of the particular "man" in view (pp. 31 f.). Paul's point is that Christ is the source of the new spiritual and bodily life promised to his people and that heavenly humanity will be like the resurrected Christ (p. 32).

him (15:45, 47–48).[259] Speaking of the future resurrection of believers, Paul consequently concludes in 15:49 that "just as we have borne the *image* (τὴν εἰκόνα) of the earthly (Adam), we shall also bear the *image* (τὴν εἰκόνα) of the heavenly (Adam)."

As in 2 Cor. 3:18, here too believers will share in the "image" of the second Adam, who in his resurrected glory is the "image of God." But whereas in 1 Cor. 15:21 f. and 40 ff. Paul's focus is on the future resurrection, so tnat this participation in the glory of Christ is a "change" (πάντες ἀλλαγησόμεθα) which takes place in a "moment" (15:51 f.), in 2 Cor. 3:18 Paul's focus in on the present. Rather than a change (ἀλλάσσω) into the resurrection glory of Christ, Paul now speaks of a progressive transformation (μεταμορφόω) into the glory of God (note the present tense of the verb). But the two concepts are intricately connected, belonging to the same conceptual complex expressed by Paul's use of the related concepts μορφόω, σύμμορφος, and συμμορφίζω, all of which occur only in Paul's writings.[260] Thus, in Phil. 3:21 Paul can use the adjective σύμμορφος ("similar in form") to describe the believer's future resurrection state in comparison to "the body of Christ's glory," while in Rom. 8:29 it is used to describe our future conformity "to the image of God's son," which in 8:30 is identified with our ultimate glorification. Conversely, in Phil. 3:10 Paul can speak of "being conformed" *in the present* (συμμορφιζόμενος) to Christ's death as the basis for knowing the present power of Christ's resurrection. On the other hand, Paul can strive with the labor of child birth until Christ "is formed" (μορφωθῇ) in the Galatians (Gal. 4:19). The ultimate "change" into the glory of Christ as the last Adam at the eschatological consummation of the "kingdom of God" (1 Cor. 15:50; cf. Phil. 3:21) is merely the final step of the "transformation" into the glory of Christ as the "image of God" which has already begun in the new covenant (2 Cor. 3:18; cf. Rom. 5:17).[261] Only those who are experiencing this transformation in the present can expect, therefore, to be changed in the future. For in the words of our present text, this transformation into the "same image" of God now seen in Christ is "from glory to glory."

---

[259] So too Wright, *Climax*, p. 33: "Paul does not write, 'Christ became the last Adam, a life-giving spirit,' but 'the last Adam became a life-giving spirit.'"

[260] On the close semantic relationship between "to change" (ἀλλάσσω) and "to transform" (μεταμορφόω), cf. BAGD, *A Greek-English Lexicon*, p. 39, on the former, and p. 511, on the latter.

[261] It is striking that the only other occurrences of the verb μεταμορφόω ("to transform") in the NT outside of 2 Cor. 3:18 and Rom. 12:2 are found in Matt. 17:2 and Mk. 9:2 in reference to the transfiguration of Christ. If this specific form of the tradition was known by Paul, then his choice of this verb here and in Rom. 12:2 might reflect the conception of a transformation into Christ's resurrected glory as manifested in Christ's transfiguration.

7. Paul's Opponents and the Moral Transformation of Believers in 2 Cor. 3:18

Paul's statement in 3:18 is not, therefore, a precursor to the gnostic and mystery religion conceptions of the next century,[262] though it *is* an expression of a real participation in the presence of God in Christ mediated through the Spirit.[263] In this sense Segal is correct in calling our attention to the fact that Paul was a "mystical Jew," whose real experiences of the glory of God in Christ ought not be explained away because of modern skittishness in regard to the supernatural, and whose spiritual experiences were "apocalyptic, revealing not meditative truths of the universe but the disturbing news that God was about to bring judgment."[264] For 2 Cor. 3:18 is yet another example of

---

[262] See the helpful discussion in Wendland, *An die Korinther*, pp. 184 f., who stresses that although the terminology of transformation parallels that of the mystery cults, the idea of an apotheosis is completely foreign to Paul's thinking. As Wendland points out, Paul's conception of God from the OT and his eschatological theology make such an identification impossible. Wendland observes, however, that Paul has used such mystical language in order to develop his modification of apocalyptic theology in terms of a present experience of the future reality.

[263] For a classic presentation of this view in relationship to 2 Cor. 3:17f., see A. Deissmann, *Paul, A Study in Social and Religious History*, ET 1957 (1927²), pp. 137–140, although Deissmann's view is based on an identification of Christ and the Spirit (pp. 138, 140), and a contrast between this Hellenistic perspective and the Jewish "son of God" concept (p. 137), both of which must be rejected. Cf. Windisch, *zweiter Korintherbrief*, p. 125, for the influence of these latter two views on the exegetical tradition. For Deissmann's view of "in the Spirit" and "in Christ" as parallel "mystical formulae," which are "really the characteristic expression of his Christianity," see pp. 139f., 143. By "mysticism" Deissmann meant the most general conception of "every religious tendency that discovers the way to God direct through inner experience without the mediation of reasoning. The constitutive element in mysticism is immediacy of contact with the deity" (p. 149; cf. pp. 149–154). It is doubtful that Paul shared this dichotomy between experience and reason, yet there is no doubt that for Paul the presence of God in Christ, mediated through the Spirit, was real, with real consequences. For a helpful reassessment of Deissmann's view and its development by Schweitzer, against Bultmann's attempt to reject such a realistic conception of the Spirit, see now E.P. Sanders, *Paul and Palestinian Judaism*, pp. 453 f. For a summary of Sanders' own modified view of this mysticism in terms of Paul's "pattern of religion" as "participationist eschatology," see pp. 548 f.

[264] *Paul the Convert*, pp. 10 f., 13, 22 f., 34 [quote], 59 [quote]. Once again, by "mysticism" is not meant the modern religious pattern of (trance-like) experience in which one seeks private, immediate, and subjective experience after a "dark night of the soul." Segal's development of Paul's religious experience in terms of first century Jewish apocalyptic categories (cf. e.g. 2 Cor. 12:1–9 with 1 Enoch 39:3; 52:1; 71:1–5; 2 Enoch 3–11; 3 Baruch 2 as referred to on p. 313 n. 5 and the literature cited there, and now the Angelic Liturgy from Qumran [4QShir-Shab], the significance of which for understanding Paul is indicated on p. 40), together with a comparison to the later Jewish *merkabah* mysticism, is very helpful (cf. pp. 38 ff.). For as Segal points out, "the term (mysticism) retains its analytic power only when its first-century context has been adequately explored" (p. 34). This all-important qualification means that the use of the latter frame of reference must be done with caution, since, as Segal himself recognizes, Paul "is the only early Jewish mystic and apocalypticist

Paul's conviction concerning the present reality of the future eschatological age.[265] Those who are now experiencing God's glory in Christ are already beginning to take on "God's image" revealed in the resurrected Christ as the "last Adam" (1 Cor. 15:45) and as the "human form of God" seen in the biblical visions of God's glory.[266] But this process of transformation into "God's image" *in the present* does not entail living the resurrection mode of life on earth. The proof of this was Paul's demonstration of the Spirit and resurrection power of Christ *in the midst of and by means of* his own weakness and suffering (cf. 1 Cor. 2:1–5; 4:9–13; 2 Cor. 2:14–17; 4:7–12). The Corinthians could therefore not be "reigning" already, since their apostle, to whom they owed their very existence as Christians, was not yet experiencing the consummation of the kingdom (1 Cor. 4:8). The fact that Paul's apostolic life was still "characterized by weakness is an indication that the eschaton has not yet arrived in its fullness, but that the power of God, once displayed in the cross, is still to be found in the midst of the suffering of this world."[267] It was this over-realized

---

whose personal, confessional writing has come down to us" (p. 34). Thus, it is to be questioned how far Paul's letters can be read as "personal, confessional writing," and Segal's own suggestion, pp. 323 f. n. 94, that the use of the mirror image in 3:18 is a "magicomystical theme" which can be traced back to the use of the word עין in Ezek. 1:4, 7, 16, 22, 27 and which "possibly refers to some unexplained technique for achieving ecstasy" is unconvincing. His attempt to describe this technique based on the mystic bowls of the magical papyri is a step removed from the mirror image itself, while in 2 Cor. 3, as well as in Paul's other writings, there is no hint of any pursuit of techniques for stimulating a trance. Paul is not a "mystic" in this sense; his conversion and revelations come to him from without, they are not generated from within. Nor is Paul in 3:18 referring to a mystical journey into the heavenly presence of God as described in 2 Cor. 12:1 ff., as Segal, pp. 60 f., maintains.

[265] See F. Lang, *Korinther*, p. 276, who concludes that although Paul's expression has a formal similarity to the mysteries, "In der Sache ist die Aussage aber scharf geschieden von der hellenistischen Verwandlungsvorstellung. Die paulinische Aussage ist geschichtlich-eschatologisch bestimmt (vgl. 4:16–18)."

[266] This last identification is taken from Segal, *Paul the Convert*, p. 60. For a review of the image of God motif in early Jewish traditions, growing out of Gen. 1:26; Exod. 23:21 and 24; Ezek. 1:26 and Daniel 7 (though his reading of the son of man as an angel in Dan. 7:13 is to be questioned, cf. pp. 41, 53), in which the lost image of God enjoyed by Adam before the Fall comes to be associated with God's human appearance in the Bible or the angel of the Lord who bears God's name, likeness, and/or glory, see his pp. 40–52. Segal thus concludes, p. 60, that "Paul's phrase the Glory of the Lord must be taken both as a reference to Christ and as a technical term for the *Kavod*, the human form of God appearing in biblical visions." Cf. already Sokolowski, *Geist und Leben bei Paulus*, pp. 38 f., 62–64, who also stressed the material conception of the glory of God in this passage. Contra e.g. J. Munck, *Paul and the Salvation of Mankind*, pp. 59 f., who argued that Paul's reference to glory in this context meant that Paul could only be thinking of the final revelation of the glory of God to Israel at the end of the world. In contrast, Schoeps, *Paul*, p. 80 n. 4, following Marmorsten, has pointed out that Paul's concept of the presence of the Holy Spirit is similar to the rabbinic belief in the indwelling of the Shekinah. Hence, Paul's transition from the veil in 3:12–18 to the indwelling of the Spirit, through the link between the Lord and the Spirit in 3:17, is a natural one.

[267] *Suffering and the Spirit*, p. 62; see my discussion of 1 Cor. 4:8–13 on pp. 58–64 for the support of this point and the parallels between this passage and 2 Cor. 2:14–16a. The failure

eschatology on the part of the Corinthians against which Paul had already fought so vigorously. And it was this same fundamental theological error that made them so susceptible to the message of the "super apostles," with its emphasis on an apostolic legitimacy based upon a pseudo-charismatic experience of the Spirit.

2 Corinthians 3:18 is thus part of Paul's implied polemic against his opponents and those Corinthians who continue to fall prey to their false gospel because of their misunderstanding of the present overlapping of the ages. Though not to be denied or discouraged (cf. 1 Cor. 12:31; 14:1, 18; 2 Cor. 12:12), the experience of the resurrection power of Christ in the Spirit ultimately shows itself to be genuine not in its ecstatic or mystical manifestations, but in its ethical transformations. Morality, not the miraculous, becomes the true expression of genuine spirituality, though as Paul's argument shows, morality is not viewed as a replacement for the experience of God's glory.[268] Hence, in Rom. 12:1, which Paul wrote from Corinth (!), he can admonish the Romans to express their worship by presenting their "bodies as a living sacrifice, holy and acceptable to God." In 12:2 this command is then defined by using the same "transformation" terminology found in 3:18, although this time as an admonition (μεταμορφοῦσθε) ! Moreover, in Rom. 12:2 this command is again linked with the concept of the "mind," as in 3:14, 18, but this time with an explicit reference to the "newness" that comes about in Christ (μεταμορφοῦσθε τῇ ἀνακαινώσει τοῦ νοός). Finally, the result of such a renewed mind is the ability to approve the will of God in their lives (12:2b), which in the context is that moral lifestyle appropriate to those who are one body in Christ (cf. 12:3 ff.). As this consequence indicates, the transformation brought about by a new mind in

---

to see the "overlapping of the ages" in Paul's thought leads Gaston, "Paul and the Torah in 2 Corinthians 3," p. 165, to conclude, based on Paul's reference to suffering and tribulation in passages such as 2 Cor. 4:7, 16–17, that "Now Paul has confidence (3:4), hope (3:12), this ministry (4:1), a treasure in vessels of clay (4:7); but what he does not claim is glory. Frankness (3:12) and freedom (3:17) yes, but glory not yet." The point being argued here is that Paul would not draw this kind of either/or contrast between the present and future experiences of the glory of God.

[268] For this same point, see again Segal, *Paul the Convert*, pp. 59 f., who in commenting on 2 Cor. 3:18–4:6 observes that "The social aspect of this mysticism-apocalypticism is *equally* important to Paul. In calling him a mystical Jew, we discover a whole *social and ethical* side to first-century mystical writings normally missed in the modern separation of ethics, apocalypticism, and mysticism. Paul's writings are social and ethical; yet behind them lies a mystical experience that he calls ineffable and that is always confirmed in community" (emphasis mine). For as Segal points out, the implication of the parallel between Moses' experience and that of the Christians in 3:18 is that "the church has witnessed a theophany as important as the one vouchsafed to Moses, but the Christian theophany is greater still, as Paul himself has experienced" (p. 60). But as we have argued here, what makes it greater is not a greater degree of God's glory which has been experienced (contra Segal, p. 60, who unreflectively follows the common interpretation that Moses veiled himself to hide the "embarrassing fading splendor," p. 151), but the transforming, rather than judging, impact of God's glory on those whose hearts have been changed "in Christ."

Rom. 12:1 f., like that brought about by the mind which is not hardened in 2 Cor. 3:14–18, is a moral one empowered by the Spirit.[269]

What made Paul's opponents in Corinth so dangerous, therefore, was not merely the way they played to the Corinthians' bad theology, but the way they "disguised themselves as servants of righteousness" (2 Cor. 11:15a). Their false understanding of the Spirit was cloaked in a false understanding of its implications for a life lived in the Spirit. That this was the case is evidenced by Paul's response to their deception, i.e. that their "end will be according to their deeds" (2 Cor. 11:15b). At the final judgment, no one will be able to escape the testimony of their behavior (2 Cor. 5:9 f.; cf. Rom. 2:5–16). For to Paul, the process of "being transformed into the image and glory of God" (3:18), as revealed in Christ (4:4, 6) and as a result of the work of the Spirit in one's life (3:3, 6, 8, 17), is to take on those attitudes and actions which correspond to the way in which Christ himself lived as the "second Adam" (cf. Col. 3:8–10).

Paul, together with early Christianity as a whole, understood the indwelling of the Holy Spirit as the concrete and real presence of God himself.[270] But for Paul this reception of God's nature did not erase the distinction between deity and humanity, it accentuated it (!) by pointing to the struggle against sin being waged by those who possessed the Spirit and to the present difference between one's mortal and spiritual existence.[271] For as Paul had already argued repeatedly in 1 Corinthians, the present experience of the resurrection power and glory of Christ is being experienced proleptically in the spiritual conversion and moral sanctification of the believer (1 Cor. 1:30; 3:1–3, 17; 5:4 f. 6:9–11; 10:11), which is the goal of the gifts of the Spirit themselves (cf. 1 Cor. 12:3, 7; 13:1–13; 14:3, 12).[272] Conversely, the Corinthians' lack of growth in obedi-

---

[269] For this point see E.E. Ellis, "II Cor. 5:1–10 in Pauline Eschatology," *NTS* 6 (1959/1960) 211–224, p. 215, who writes of Rom 12:1, "There, as also in II Cor. 3:18, μεταμορφόω must be understood not as a physical-metaphysical change but as a moral and *weltanschaulich* (or psychological) transformation which the indwelling Spirit, the power of the new aeon, is effecting in the lives and minds of Christians." Ellis points out that this is in contrast to the "resurrection," which is always a "point action at conversion or parousia, never does Paul speak of it as a process which is now going on" (p. 215).

[270] Cf. 1 Thess. 4:8; Gal. 3:2, 5; 4:6; 1 Cor. 2:12; 3:16; 6:19; 2 Cor. 5:5; 11:14; Rom. 5:5; 8:16, 23; 14:17, etc., plus the treatment of the gifts of the Spirit in 1 Cor. 12–14 and Rom. 12:3–7. For the glory of God as a reference to the real presence of God in the OT, with the corresponding view "that God's nearness is prerequisite to the blessings afforded by his great power," see the helpful summary by Baruch A. Levine, "On the Presence of God in Biblical Religion," in *Religions in Antiquity, FS E.R. Goodenough*, ed. J. Neusner, Studies in the History of Religion Vol. 14, 1968, pp. 71–87, quote from pp. 75 f. Levine points to Deut. 33:2; Jud. 5:4 f.; Ps. 68:8 f.; 74:11 f.; Micah 1:34 as typical examples of this conception (pp. 73–75), and to Num. 14:13–16, 42; Jud. 6:13; 1 Sam. 4:3 f.; 7:3 f. as examples which bear out the concept of "the potent presence" of YHWH (pp. 76–78).

[271] Cf. Gal. 5:16–26; 1 Cor. 6:9–20; 15:53; 2 Cor. 4:16; 6:14–7:1; Rom. 8:9–13; Col. 3:5–17, etc.

[272] Cf. Liebers, *Das Gesetz als Evangelium*, p. 106, who points out that in Wis. 3:7; 4 Ezra 7:97; 2 Apoc. Bar. 49:2; 51:3; 1 Enoch 38:4; 51:5; 104:2; 108:13 f., the glory of God saves and is the conspicuous sign of deliverance.

ence could cause Paul to question to what extent many of the Corinthians were participating in the true work of the Spirit (cf. 1 Cor. 3:4; 5:1; 6:5–7, 9; etc.). In the same way, Paul rejects the opponents' claims based on their "deeds" (2 Cor. 11:15), supports his own legitimacy based on his behavior (2 Cor. 2:14–3:3; 4:2; 5:9 f. 6:4–10; 10:12–18; 11:23b–33; 12:5, 9 f.),[273] and fears that many of the Corinthians are not really believers because they are not repenting from their "impurity, immorality, and sensuality" (2 Cor. 12:21). Indeed, Paul calls for the Corinthians to test the genuine nature of their faith against whether or not they accept Paul's legitimacy and admonitions (cf. 2 Cor. 13:5 with 7:11).

In 2 Cor. 3:18 Paul is reminding the Corinthians that the experience of the glory of God in Christ does not lead to being spiritually "superior" because of one's gifts (1 Cor. 4:7), but rather brings about a reversal of the sinful propensity to "boast before God" because of one's attainments and status in the world (cf. 1 Cor. 1:29). Those in the new covenant find the "wisdom of God," as well as their own "righteousnes, sanctification, and redemption" in *Christ* (1 Cor. 1:30). Moreover, the very fact that one is in Christ is *God's* doing as a result of *his* call (1 Cor. 1:30, 26 f.). Hence, those who encounter the glory of God in Christ no longer boast in themselves, but in the Lord (1 Cor. 1:31), knowing that everything they have, they have received as a gift (1 Cor. 4:7). For this reason Paul stressed to the Corinthians that the result of this new orientation is a life lived in thanksgiving to God, not only for the redemption found in Christ, but also for the gifts he has given in creation (1 Cor. 3:22; 10:30). Such thanksgiving glorifies God as the appropriate response to his sovereignty and grace (1 Cor. 3:21; 10:31), and in turn manifests itself in obedience to God's commands as that which glorifies God "in one's body," since this obedience is brought about by the work of God's grace and the power of his Spirit (1 Cor. 6:11, 20).[274] In 2 Corinthians, Paul again stresses the glorification of God which comes about both through thankfulness for his gifts of creation and redemption (2 Cor. 1:20; 4:15), and through the obedience rendered in response to the cross and in the power of the Spirit (2 Cor. 8:9; 19, 23; 9:13).[275]

In view of this development in 1 Corinthians and its parallels in the present letter, "the same image" and "glory" in view in 3:18 are both spiritual *and*

---

[273] See my "Self-Commendation," pp. 84–87, for a development of this argument from the evidence in 2 Corinthians, and now the full-length study of Ulrich Heckel, *Kraft in Schwachheit, Untersuchungen zu 2. Kor 10–13*, WUNT 2. Reihe 56, 1993, esp. his conclusions on pp. 307–309, 319–325.

[274] For the root of sin as the failure to glorify God by thanking him, see Rom. 1:20–23, which then results in the lifestyle of immorality described in 1:24–32. For a conceptual parallel to Paul's thinking, see e.g. Sir. 47:8, where David is described as one who "in all his works gave praise" to God "with words of glory" and sang praises to God "with his whole heart," since "he loved the one who made him."

[275] For this same concept, see Rom. 4:20 (where one's faith is that which glorifies God by calling attention to his promises); 15:6 f., 9; Phil. 1:11; 2:11.

moral.[276] The "life" created by the Spirit in response to the commandments of God described in 3:6 (cf. 1 Cor. 7:19) is the theological corollary to the transformation created by the glory of God pictured in 3:18. For the work of the Spirit (3:6) is the removal of the heart of stone, which makes encountering the glory of God possible (3:8, 12f., 16, 18). The result is an ethical way of life which can be attributed either to the power of the Spirit or to the positive effect of the glory of God on those whose hearts have been renewed. Such an interpretation is confirmed by the background of Gen. 1:26–27, from which the concept of the "image of God" introduced in 3:18 and 4:4 no doubt derives. In its original context, the "image of God" is primarily a functional description of mankind's role in relationship to their sovereign Creator.[277] Hence, just as Adam related to God in dependence and obedience before the Fall (cf. Gen. 1:28–30 with 2:15, 19f.), Christ, as the "second Adam," was in the "image of God" in his faithful obedience to God, even to the point of his death on the cross (cf. Rom. 5:19; Phil. 2:8).[278] It is this "image of God" into which believers are being transformed as a result of encountering the glory of God on the face of Christ.[279]

---

[276] Cf. the emphasis of John Koenig, "The Knowing of Glory and its Consequences (2 Corinthians 3–5)," in *The Conversation Continues, Studies in Paul and John in Honor of J. Louis Martyn*, ed. Robert T. Fortna and Beverly R. Gaventa, 1990, pp. 158–169, pp. 160f., who stresses both the materialistic view of glory in 2 Cor. 3 and the fact that the movement in Paul's thought is from "perceiving and acquiring glory (see 3:18) to becoming righteousness," in reference to 2 Cor. 3:9 and esp. 5:21. Koenig points out the present emphasis of the transformation in view in 3:18, so that, according to Paul, "believers are being presently transformed, in some sense glorified even now, prior to their resurrection" (p. 161), though he rightly stresses in view of 2 Cor. 5:1–10 that "the somatic glory of the future, which far surpasses anything that one can presently have at one's disposal, will be distributed in varying degrees from the judgment seat of Christ according to what believers have done in their bodies on earth to please the Lord ... the glory that really counts depends on one's obedient relationship with Christ now. This naturally has moral connotations, but more basically for Paul it means sharing Christ's cross ..." (p. 163). However, Koenig too quickly leaves the moral dimension of Paul's thought behind when he presents the central thesis that "the primary consequence of knowing God's glory in the face of Christ is ... a fuller incorporation into God's reconciling work on behalf of the world" (p. 164), taking "righteousness" in 3:9 and 5:21 to consist "most fundamentally of God's reaching out to make the world right" (p. 164). He can do this only because he (in my view, wrongly) interprets the first-person plural pronouns throughout 5:16–6:2 to refer to both Paul and the Corinthians and plays down the distinction between Paul and the Corinthians in 2 Cor. 3:7–18 (cf. pp. 164f.).

[277] For a very helpful treatment of the "image of God" in Gen. 1:26f., see Anthony A. Hoekema, *Created in God's Image*, 1986, esp. pp. 66–83.

[278] On the "undeniable network of associations between Phil. 2 and Genesis 1–3 (mediated by such passages as Rom. 5:19; 8:29; 1 Cor. 15:41; 2 Cor. 3:18; 4:4; Phil. 3:21; Col. 1:15; 3:10)," see Silva, *Philippians*, p. 116, and the literature cited there.

[279] See Dumbrell, "Paul's use of Exodus 34," p. 189, who, on the basis of the fact that the transformation takes place "through Christ as the image into whom the believers are to grow," concludes on 3:18 that "it is the recovery of the prospect that Gen. 1:26 had entertained for the species which is uppermost in Paul's mind."

But where and how does this encounter with the glory of God take place for Paul? Although Paul does not deal with this question directly in the passage before us, the answer is certainly presupposed in the matter of fact way in which Paul introduces the concept in 3:18 and 4:4–6, and in his reference to his own boldness in ministry in 3:12. These texts give the most immediate answer, namely, in the preaching of the Gospel of Jesus Christ. For in addition to the implications of Jesus' life, death, and resurrection for the justification and sanctification of the believer (cf. e.g. Rom. 1:16f.; 3:21–26; 2 Cor. 5:14–21; Col. 1:13f.), Paul's proclamation of the Gospel declares the glory of God as revealed in Jesus Christ (cf. 1 Cor. 2:7f.; Col. 1:15–20). Inasmuch as the Gospel unleashes the power of the Spirit, the glory of God is also revealed through the renewed lives of those who now possess the Spirit as his "temple" (cf. esp. 1 Cor. 6:19f.).[280] Moreover, this proclamation of the Gospel is inextricably bound up with Paul's ministry of suffering. As the corollary to his preaching, Paul conceived of his experiences of suffering as the corresponding vehicle for the revelation of the glory of God in Christ. Paul's "boldness" in 3:12 thus relates directly to his willingness to preach the crucified Jesus as the Messiah and the cross as the power of God (1 Cor. 1:23f.), supported by his own suffering as the place in which this same glory and power of God continues to be manifested (2 Cor. 2:14–17; 4:7ff.). For in both cases it is through weakness and suffering that the glory of God is revealed, first in the death of the Son of God, and now in the fact that his apostle is always "being led to death" in Christ (2:14). In the first instance, Christ's death established the new covenant (cf. Mark 14:24 par.); in the second, Paul's ministry of proclamation and suffering extends it throughout the Gentile world (3:6).

---

[280] See too Wright, *Climax*, pp. 185–188, who offers a sustained argument for the fact that the "mirror" in view is not the Lord or the gospel, but Christians "when they come face to face with one another" (p. 185). Though I would not draw this conclusion as an either/or reality, Wright's emphasis on the transformation of believers in v. 18 is very helpful, as well as his recognition that v. 18 continues the implied contrast of vv. 12–17: "Unlike the Israelites, those in the new covenant can look at the glory as it is reflected in each other" (p. 185). Wright concludes that this transformation of believers under the new covenant is the final proof that the Corinthians themselves are to be Paul's letter of recommendation, and hence the crucial support for his boldness (pp. 186f.). "God shines, with the light of the gospel of Jesus Christ, into the hearts of his people, who then reflect his light, becoming mirrors in which others can see God's glory," as this is revealed in the "paradoxical pattern of Christ, that is, the pattern of suffering and vindication" (pp. 189f., 191). But Wright's view leads him to take εἰκών in v. 18 to refer to the work of the Spirit, and thus to translate it as "a reflection," denying the background to the verse in Wis. 7:26 and Gen. 1:26 (p. 188). "The same image" refers to the fact that Christians are being changed into the same image *as each other* (p. 188). To do so Wright must read Paul's mind and maintain, p. 188, that "Paul is quite well aware of the other overtones that might be heard (of Genesis 1:26, for example) in what he is saying; but his present use is simply part of the overall metaphor of this particular verse (so Barrett, Furnish)." But given the direct parallels of thought adduced above, Wright has inverted the "overtones" and undertones of the text.

It is significant in this regard that the only other reference in Paul's writings to the "new covenant" and its experience of the glory of God in Christ is found in 1 Cor. 11:23–25. For this passage clearly illustrates that for Paul the Lord himself is being encountered in the Lord's Supper (1 Cor. 11:26). Only this presupposition can account for Paul's attribution of the sickness and death that has been experienced by some to God's judgment upon those who are partaking of the "cup of the Lord in an unworthy manner" (11:27, 29, 32). Hence, for Paul, the glory of God in Christ is encountered not only in the missionary proclamation of the cross, but also in the worship of the gathered community where Christ's death is repeatedly proclaimed and embodied in the sharing of the Lord's Supper, as well as in the songs, Scriptures, teachings, and revelations that surrounded it (cf. 1 Cor. 14:26; Eph. 5:18–20). The continual transformation of the believer thus takes place as a result of a continuing fellowship with the Lord in the midst of his people, even as God's discipline is also meted out in this context. Conversely, one cannot take part in this fellowship in a worthy manner unless his or her life evidences the fact that it has begun the process of being transformed by the presence of the Lord, which in the context of the Corinthian correspondence entails nothing less than a growing obedience to the commands of God.

This is why it is in the midst of the gathered community that Paul exercises his judgment on the unrepentant sinner in 1 Cor. 5:4 f., as well as the restoration of the offender in 2 Cor. 2:6–11. For unlike the synagogue, which stood next to the Temple but did not replace it, the new covenant community stood alone as the place in which God's presence was being revealed. From early on, therefore, those gathered in the name of Christ distinguished themselves as the ἐκκλησία of God (cf.1 Cor. 1:2; 2 Cor. 1:1) over against the continuing συναγωγή within Israel.[281] To the community called by his name, the pouring out of the Spirit in the new covenant meant that those in Christ were now the redeemed eschatological community of the new age in the midst of the old. As a consequence, it is within the church, gathered as the body of Christ and as the temple of the Holy Spirit (1 Cor. 3:16; 6:19;12:12–18, 27), that the presence of God in Christ (1 Cor.14:25 f.; 2 Cor. 2:10) is now being revealed and encountered, while outside of the community of the Spirit the reign of Satan still prevails (cf. 1 Cor. 5:5; 2 Cor. 2:11).[282]

---

[281] See above, chapter three, nn. 199–200, for the linguistic evidence for this surprisingly early demarcation.

[282] If the thesis of Alan F. Segal, "2 Corinthians 3 and the *Tallit*," 1989 SBL Annual Meeting Seminar Paper (now incorporated into his *Paul the Convert*, pp. 152–154) is correct that the practice of wearing the prayer shawl extended back into the first century (he points to Mk. 12:38), then the removal of the veil by the Spirit which Paul develops theologically in 2 Cor. 3 would have a real counterpart in the distinctive practices of the church and synagogue. The absence of veils for men in the church would portray for Paul the theological reality of the encounter with the glory of God now taking place "with unveiled faces". For as Segal points out, the later rabbis regarded the wearing of the fringed prayer shawl as a "mark

8. The Argument of 2 Corinthians 3:12–18

The final stage of Paul's argument in support of his boldness as an apostle in contrast to the ministry of Moses (3:12 f.) can now be construed as follows:

3:12a: *Because* we have this hope,

3:12b: *Therefore* we behave with boldness.

(-) 3:13a: *That is to say*, we do *not* behave

3:13b:*as* Moses was placing a veil upon his face

3:13bb: *in order that* the sons of Israel might not gaze into the outcome of that which was being rendered inoperative.

(+)3:14a: *But* their minds were hardened.

3:14b: *For* until this very day the same veil remains at the reading of the old covenant,

3:14c: *because* it is not being unveiled,

3:14d: *since* it (i.e the veil) is being rendered inoperative in Christ,

3:15a: *nevertheless* until today a veil has been laid upon their hearts,

3:15b: *whenever* Moses is being read.

3:16b: *On the other hand*, the veil is being removed,

3:16a: *whenever* "he" (like Moses) returns to the Lord.

3:17a: *because* the Lord (YHWH) is the Spirit,

3:17b: *so that as a result* there is freedom (from the veil)

3:17c: *where* the Spirit of the Lord is.

3:18a:*As a result of the work of the Spirit*, we all are being transformed into the same image,

3:18b: that is to say, *to the result of* glory (εἰς δόξαν).

3:18c: *The transformation takes place by means of* an unveiled face

3:18d: *and by means* of beholding the glory of the Lord

3:18e: that is to say, *on the basis of* glory (ἀπὸ δόξης),

3:18 f: *just as this is accomplished* from the Lord who is the Spirit.

---

of reverence for the divine presence *(b.* Shab. 10a) ...," while in mystical practice "wrapping oneself in a tallit is necessary for being in the presence of the divine" (p. 153). Segal himself, however, understands the difference between the Christian and synagogue practice in this regard as primarily an issue of custom, separating Paul's Gentile believers from the Jewish Christians who brought this practice with them into the churches (cf. pp. 155 f.). Secondarily, the continued use of the Jewish *tallit* would be "a symbol of faded glory" associated with the continued reliance on the oral law, which Christians should now reject (p. 154). In sharp contrast to the position being argued in this study, Segal must therefore conclude that "no doctrinal statement inheres in Paul's change of practice," although it does, for Segal, signal a "symbolic message about the value of Torah" in that "the new Christian experience of Christ as Lord, based on a new understanding of Scripture, does not need the obfuscation that Moses inserted into Jewish rites" (pp. 154 f.).

The fact that Paul's ministry brings about the spiritual and moral transformation pictured in 3:18 is thus the final support for Paul's prior assertion that Israel continues to be hardened "until this very day" (3:14a, 15b), which in turn supports Paul's boldness by explaining its lack of success among his fellow Jews. For if they, like their "fathers" before them, had not been hardened to the revelation of God's glory in the world, they too would be able to behold the glory of God on the face of Christ and be transformed by it.

Having made this point in 3:14–16 and supported it with the revelation of the glory of God in the church in 3:17–18, Paul now restates his conclusion from 3:12 f. in 4:1 f.[283] Because of the transformation taking place through his ministry, Paul is bold (3:12), i.e. he does not lose heart (4:1 f.). For, as in 3:14–16, if Paul's Gospel is being rejected, this is not a strike against the genuine nature of his call (4:1, 6),[284] or against the Gospel of Jesus Christ as Lord which he preaches and which is embodied in his suffering as their "slave" (4:2, 5; cf. 2:17).[285] Rather, as in 3:14–15, "even if (Paul's) Gospel is being veiled, it is being veiled among those who are perishing" (4:3a). For as Paul concludes in 4:3b, a present rejection of the Gospel can only mean that "the god of this age has blinded the minds of those who are not believing so that," just like Israel in 3:13 and in contrast to those within the church as pictured in 3:18, "they might not see (εἰς τὸ μὴ αὐγάσαι[286]) the light of the Gospel of the glory of Christ, who is the image of God" (4:3 f.). For as in Gen. 1:3 and Is. 9:1, it is the knowledge of the very glory of God himself that has now been revealed to Paul in the face of Christ as the means and goal of the "new creation" (4:6).[287] Moreover, this same glory is being revealed in his ministry, not

---

[283] Cf. Bultmann, *Zweiter Korintherbrief*, p. 78, and now Furnish, *II Corinthians*, p. 217, on 4:1: "The present verse resumes the point initiated in 3;12, but now with the added support of 3:18 in particular."

[284] For the reference to the mercy received in 4:1 as an allusion to Paul's call and for the development of 4:6 as a description of Paul's experience on the Damascus road, see esp. Kim, *Origin of Paul's Gospel*, pp. 8–11, 137–145, 229–233, who supports this recognition on the part of R.P. Martin, J. Dupont, Kümmel, etc.

[285] For Paul's description of himself as the Corinthians' δοῦλος in 4:5 as a reference to his willingness to support himself in Corinth and its OT and Jewish background, see E. Ellis, "Paul and His Co-Workers," *NTS* 17 (1971) 437–452, pp. 443 f., and for the OT backdrop especially G. Saß, "Zur Bedeutung von δοῦλος bei Paulus," *ZNW* 40 (1941) 24–32. Thus, Paul's statement in 4:2, 5 recalls his prior argument from 2:17, which was based on his willingness to suffer on behalf of the Corinthians, even as Christ died for them; see my *Suffering and the Spirit*, pp. 103 ff.

[286] See again Furnish, *II Corinthians*, p. 221, on 4:4b: "The overall context, as well as the specific reference in this same verse to being blinded, requires one to interpret the verb as a synonym of *gaze* in 3:13 and of *beholding* in 3:18."

[287] For the background of 4:6 in Gen. 1:3, see e.g. J.A. Fitzmyer, "Glory Reflected in the Face of Christ (2 Cor. 3:7–4:6) and a Palestinian Jewish Motif," *TS* 72 (1981) 630–644, p. 639, and esp. Kim, *Origin of Paul's Gospel*, p. 236, and for Is. 9:1 and the servant passages, e.g. Oostendorp, *Another Jesus*, p. 48, and Richard, "Polemics," p. 360, and now Webb (see below, n. 289). But as Kim, p. 10, has pointed out, Paul's use of Gen. 1:3 is combined with the Isaiah traditions in 4:4–6. Klaiber, *Rechtfertigung*, pp. 81–82, thus refers to

in spite of his suffering, but through it (4:5, 7 ff.; cf. 2:14–17). The eschatological life being created among the Corinthians by the power of the Spirit as they encounter the glory of God revealed in Paul's ministry testifies to this reality (3:1–3, 6, 18).[288] In contrast, those among Israel who reject Paul's ministry are giving evidence by this very rejection that they continue to experience the Law of Moses as the "letter which kills" (3:6). Their condemnation under the Law is simply confirmed by Gospel, which also leads to the "death" of those who are perishing (4:3; cf. 2:15 f.).

9. Conclusion: The New Covenant as the Inauguration of the New Creation

The problem of God's presence caused by the hard-heartedness of Israel as portrayed in Exod. 32–34 functions, therefore, as the interpretive backdrop to Paul's assertion in 3:18, just as it provided the foundation for his argument in 3:7–17. The fact that in the transition to the assertions of 3:18 Moses provides a type of the church's experience (3:16–17), in contrast to the experience of Israel in her stiff-necked condition (3:14–15), demonstrates that for Paul the theological and historical problem manifested in Israel's sin with the golden calf is being overcome in the new covenant people of God as the gathered eschatological community. Though the precise language is not employed in 2 Cor. 3:12–18, the movement in Paul's argument from 3:12–17 to 3:18 thus indicates that the transformation being brought about through his ministry can be understood in terms of the eschatological "new" or "second exodus."[289]

---

the light of the knowledge of the glory of God in 4:6 as the "light of the new creation." Cf. too P. Stuhlmacher, "Erwägungen zum ontologischen Charakter der καινὴ κτίσις bei Paulus," *EvTh* 27 (1967) 1–35, pp. 32 f., who understands 4:6 to refer to the "light-creating word of the first day of creation" and thus to the fact that Paul's Gospel is "die apokalyptische Prolepse des neuschaffenden Gotteswortes."

[288] So too Theobald, *Gnade*, p. 201, who links the reference to the Spirit in 3:18 with the contrast in 3:3 and 6 and concludes that "dann ist πνεῦμα in Übereinstimmung mit 3:3 allein mit der Kategorie der Neuschöpfung zu erfassen." Theobald rightly emphasizes that ζῳοποιεῖν in 3:6 is for Paul an eschatological term, referring to Rom. 4:17; 8:11; 1 Cor. 15:22, 45; 2 Cor. 1:9; Gal. 3:21 (p. 201 n. 165). But in contrast to the view argued here, Theobald takes the letter/Spirit contrast to be a contrast between the external and the internal, hidden realm of the heart (p. 201). And yet, Theobald can rightly conclude, p. 211, that the ultimate mark of the Spirit is not pneumatic experiences, but a changed life in conformity to the image of Christ. Following Theobald, Eckert, "geistliche Schriftauslegung," p. 252, also understands the locus of the revelation of the glory of God to be the invisible realm of the heart or the "inner man" so that the transformation in view n 3:18 is an "weitgehend unsichtbaren Vorgang."

[289] Contra E.P. Sanders, *Paul and Palestinian Judaism*, pp. 468 f., 511–513, who argues that the concept of transformation belongs, for Paul, with the concept of new creation and change of Lordship/aeons, rather than a new exodus. Sanders maintains that Paul does not connect his ethical admonitions with references to a new covenant, but to receiving the

The transforming experience of the glory of God in the face of Christ within the church is the beginning of the eschatological fulfillment of the restoration of Israel promised in Isaiah, Jeremiah, and Ezekiel, in which God will once again dwell in the midst of his people. The Corinthians themselves, as the temple of the Holy Spirit, are proof that the promises of the prophets concerning the inclusion of the Gentiles in the last days in response to the revelation of the glory of God and the pouring out of his Spirit are indeed being realized in Paul's ministry. The present experience of the glory of the Lord through Paul's ministry of proclamation and suffering (2 Cor. 2:14–17; 4:7) is thus the means to the proleptic fulfillment of the "incomparable eternal weight of glory" which is now being being prepared for the people of God, who must patiently endure "the same sufferings which Paul also suffers" (2 Cor. 4:17; 1:6 ; cf. Phil. 3:11, 20f.; Col. 1:27; 3:3f.; Rom. 5:2; and esp. 8:18, 21).

As such, it is not saying too much to conclude that the transformation pictured in 3:18 is the evidence of and foundation for Paul's subsequent assertion in 2 Cor. 5:14–17 that the eschatological "new creation" has indeed been inaugurated by the death and resurrection of Christ.[290] Furthermore, Paul is convinced that this "new creation" is now taking place in response to the Gospel as embodied and proclaimed in Paul's own ministry and in the community of

---

Spirit (p. 513). Hence, for Sanders, "the exodus typology does not seem to have determined Paul's thinking" (p. 513). Sanders must therefore posit that the new covenant was not established by a "new exodus" (p. 513). Sanders is arguing against the positive assertion of W.D. Davies, *Paul and Rabbinic Judaism*, p. 108, that Paul was the herald "not of a new mystery but of a new Exodus," an interpretive perspective for understanding Paul which this study has now confirmed. Sanders is drawing a distinction between the conceptual worlds of the new exodus and the new creation where, for Paul, none exists. See too, e.g., his statement that "another way of responding to Davies' view is to argue that Paul's principal conviction was not that Jesus as the Messiah had come, but that God had appointed Jesus Christ as Lord and that he would resurrect or transform those who were members of him by virtue of believing in him" (p. 514). For Paul's understanding of the new creation and reconciliation as an extension and application of the restoration (second exodus) motif from the prophets (see esp. Is. 43:18–19; 65:17), see the very helpful article of G.K. Beale, "The Old Testament Background of Reconciliation in 2 Corinthians 5–7 and its Bearing on the Literary Problem of 2 Corinthians 6:14–7:1," *NTS* 35 (1989) 550–581, and the important work of William J. Webb, *Returning Home, New Covenant and Second Exodus as the Context for 2 Corinthians 6.14–7.1*, JSNT Suppl. Series 85, 1993, esp. pp. 72–102. Webb, p. 97, argues that Paul's quotation in 2 Cor. 4:6 "most probably" derives from Is. 9:1. In contrast to the work of Beale, Webb, p. 28, views the OT traditions behind Paul's argument in 2 Cor. 2:14–7:1 "under the broader rubric of 'new covenant and second exodus/return theology,'" which corresponds to the present work in which the "new creation" motif is viewed as an extension of the more primary and fundamental new covenant and second exodus themes.

[290] This is not to argue for any one original source for the concept of "transformation" itself. Cf. Fitzmyer, "Glory Reflected," p. 632, who argues against the view that the transformation in view should be associated with the theme of the "new creation" in Paul's theology (p. 632). Rather, he argues that this transformation is "a mythical figure taken over from Greco-Roman metamorphosis literature." Yet even Fitzmyer concludes that Paul "has suffused the Greco-Roman image with Jewish, Old Testament, and Palestinian motifs; he uses it with the aid of his midrashic development of the Moses story" (pp. 632f.)!

the Spirit which it creates.[291] For Paul, the "old" (with its covenant) has already passed away and been replaced by the "new" (with its covenant).[292] As a mediator of the glory of God on the face of Christ (3:18; 4:4, 6), Paul's "ministry of the Spirit" (3:6, 8) is the means by which the prophetic expectation is beginning to be realized.[293] For at the very center of the "new creation" as a "second Exodus" redemption is the manifestation of the glory of God in the midst of his people, both Jew and Gentile, and among his creation.[294] The ultimate result of this revelation of God's glory in the new creation is a life of faithful obedience among the people of God, in contrast to Israel's present rebellion and the wickedness of the nations, and the reign of peace throughout the newly created order.[295] In this sense, the "end" is like the "beginning," since God's people are freed from slavery to the power of sin so that they may fulfill the Law by their love for God and mutual acceptance of one another (1 Cor. 1:9 f.; 8:6;12–13; cf. Rom. 8:3 f.; 13:8–10; 14:6–23;15:5–7; Gal. 5:6, 14).

The parallel between Paul's thought at this point and the wisdom tradition found in Sirach 17 is therefore of special significance in that it illustrates fur-

---

[291] See too Stegemann, "Neue Bund," pp. 109 f., who points out that for Paul the Holy Spirit is the down payment of the resurrection, the new creation, "d.h. die eschatologische Erneuerung und Vollendung der in Adam intendierten und in Jesus Christus, freilich erst und allein in ihm, an ihr Ziel gekommenen Schöpfung."

[292] See P. Stuhlmacher, "Ontologischen Charakter," p. 8, in which he points out that Paul's view of the "new creation" embodies his understanding of the overlapping of the age to come with that of the present in the "now and the not yet" inaugurated by Christ within the eschatological community.

[293] The key OT texts concerning the eschatological "new creation" are Is. 43:16–21; 65:16b–23; and 66:22 f. For a detailed treatment of these texts and the later post-biblical expectation of a new creation in 1QH 3:19–23; 11:9–14; 13:11–12; 15:13–17; 1QS 4:23–26; 11QTemple 29:7–10; 1 En. 91:15 f.; 72:1; LAB 3:10; 32:17; Jub. 1:29; 4:26; 4 Ezra 7:75; and 2 Apoc. Bar. 32:6; 44:12; 57:2 see Ulrich Mell, *Neue Schöpfung, Eine traditionsgeschichtliche und exegetische Studie zu einem soteriologischen Grundsatz paulinischen Theologie*, BZNW 56, 1989.

[294] Cf. now Vollenweider, "2 Kor," p. 263, who argues that already at the level of the pre-Pauline interpretation of Exod. 34 the parallel between Moses and Christians and the use of the "image of God" language in 3:18 lead to the conclusion that "Die Umkehr zu Christus erscheint einmal as *Erneuerung der Schöpfung* durch den lebenspendenden Geist: In der *Metamorphose in Christi Eikon* (3:18; 4:4, 6; vgl. Röm. 8:29) kehren der göttliche Glanz und die Gottebenbildlichkeit, die Adam wie Israel einst verspielten, wieder" (emphasis his). Hence, as he concludes concerning Paul's theological framework, "Die Vexierfrage, ob 2 Kor 3:18 präsentisches oder künftiges Geschehen meine, verstellt sich mit ihrer Begrifflichkeit die Wahrnehmung, dass in Christus Gegenwart der Ort ist, wo alle Zukunft potentiell präsent ist. Die 'Hoffnung' von V.12 qualifiziert die in 2 Kor 3 stark betonte Gegenwart als eschatologische Gegenwart; Im 'Angeld des Geistes' (1:22; 5:5) ist Zukunft *als Zukunft präsent*" (p. 275, emphasis his). There is, of course, for Paul a future reality associated with the return of Christ that is not potentially present this side of his parousia (cf. 1 Cor. 15:12–57).

[295] Cf. Is. 2:2–3; 24:23; 25:6–9; 43:21; 56:6–8; 60:1–3; 65:19, 24; 66:18–21, 23, etc. for the revelation of the glory of God in the midst of Israel and among the nations and Is. 43:19 f.; 65:25, etc. for its revelation among the beasts and created order.

ther the conceptual background against which Paul's thinking took shape. For here Sirach maintains that at creation mankind's heart was filled with understanding (vv. 6 f.), inasmuch as God is said to place "his eye upon their hearts to show to them the majesty of his works" (v. 8). This act is interpreted in vv. 11–13 as God's setting before them "knowledge" (ἐπιστήμη) and giving them as an inheritance a "law of life" (νόμον ζωῆς; v. 11). In view of Sir. 45:5, where the "law of life" is equated with the Mosaic law, Sir. 17:11 signifies that already at creation before the Fall mankind was given the knowledge needed to keep the Law later given at Sinai, which now existed in a pre-Fall form. This interpretation is confirmed by the parallels in the next verse, where the "knowledge" given mankind at creation is equated with an "eternal covenant" (διαθήκη αἰῶνος) and the "law of life" is identified with the judgments of God (τὰ κρίματα αὐτοῦ; 17:12). It is striking, therefore, that the result of the establishment of this "eternal covenant," with its "law of life," is that "their eyes" are said to have "seen the greatness of his glory (δόξης) and their ears heard the glory (δόξαν) of his voice" (17:13). Hence, prior to the Fall, with hearts full of understanding in obedience to the Law, mankind is able to encounter the glory of God. Finally, the voice of God which they hear then declares in 17:14 that mankind is to flee "from all unrighteousness" (ἀπὸ παντὸς ἀδίκου) and commands them "each concerning his neighbor," which is most likely an allusion to the commands to love God above all else and one's neighbor.[296] The law of life given at creation, which stands at the center of the eternal covenant as the precursor to the Mosaic law, is thus the command to love! And before the Fall, this command is kept, since mankind's heart is still able to understand and the glory of God can still be seen and heard. In Sir. 49:16 we thus read that Adam "was glorified (ἐδοξάσθη) above every living thing in creation."[297]

In addition, given the explicit references to Moses and his experience of the glory of God throughout 2 Cor. 3:7–18, the description of Moses in Sir. 45:1–5 is also of special importance for understanding the conceptual background against which Paul's thought developed. In Sirach 45:3, 5, Moses is distinguished as the one to whom God showed his glory and caused to hear his voice at the time in which God "gave to him face to face the commandments" (ἔδωκεν αὐτῷ κατὰ πρόσωπον ἐντολάς).[298] In 45:5b these commandments are then identified with the "law of life and knowledge" (νόμον ζωῆς καὶ ἐπιστήμης). We have noted above that this description recalls the "knowledge and law of life" (ἐπιστήμην καὶ νόμον ζωῆς) originally given to mankind at

---

[296] Cf. already, R.H. Charles, *Apocrypha*, p. 376 n. 14.

[297] Cf. the late first cent. A.D. T. Abraham 11:4–12 (recension A), in which Adam, as the "first-formed," is pictured as glorified and sitting on a golden throne in heaven, alternately crying and rejoicing over the fate of the wicked and the righteous who have come from him.

[298] Cf. 4 Baruch 7:11, 20 (early second cent. A.D.), the glory of God is said to accompany the eagle sent with the message to Jeremiah, which then leads the people to say that God has appeared to them through the eagle just as he did in the wilderness "through Moses."

creation in Sir. 17:11, where once again the glory of God is encountered (cf. 17:13). As this parallel indicates, Moses' experience at Sinai is considered to be the reenactment of the original manifestation of the glory of God and the giving of the law at creation. The "covenant" (διαθήκη) and "judgments of God" (κρίματα αὐτοῦ) which Moses is then said to teach Jacob and Israel in 45:5c thus correspond directly to the "eternal covenant and judgments of God" (διαθήκη αἰῶνος ... καὶ τὸ κρίματα αὐτοῦ) which God originally established with mankind before the Fall (17:12).

In Sirach too, therefore, the glory which Moses encounters and, according to Exod. 34:29 ff. then mediates, is associated with the Law given on Sinai. Moreover, Moses' experience parallels that of mankind at creation, so that his encounter with the glory of God and reception of the Law can be seen as a "second creation," or "new creation" of the original covenant and its law. Against this backdrop, Israel's sin with the golden calf can naturally be considered a "second fall" from this "new creation" paradise enjoyed by Moses.[299] In contrast, Paul's ministry of the Gospel can be seen to be the means by which Jews and Gentiles are now being brought "back" to this experience of God's glory as the reversal of Israel's "fall" on the one hand, and as the proleptic beginning of the reversal of Adam's fall on the other hand. In and through Paul's ministry, this "unveiled" encounter with the glory of God is extending the "new creation" inaugurated by Christ in which God's new covenant and its Law will be kept.

Hence, in 1 Cor. 2:7–10 Paul reminded the Corinthians that it is this very glory which, in anticipation of the eschatological consummation, is already being revealed through his ministry of the Spirit to those now "in Christ." Paul's description of Christian experience in 2 Cor. 3:18 thus reflects a central pillar of Paul's theology, in which, through the Gospel as the "word of God," God is calling his people "into his own kingdom and glory" (1 Thess. 2:12 f.; cf. 2 Thess. 2:14; Rom. 9:23 f.). Against the backdrop of Exod. 32–34 in 2 Cor. 3:1–18, this divine call finds its negative counterpart in Israel's idolatry with the golden calf, which we have seen in chapter three becomes a paradigm for Israel's continuing history of rebellion and for the subsequent judgment of separation from God's presence (cf. 2 Thess. 1:9). Paul's contrast between the transformation taking place in the new covenant and Israel's hardened condition in 3:12–18 thus recalls his prior use of Israel's sin with the golden calf and her ensuing acts of rebellion in the wilderness in 1 Cor. 10:1–14.[300] In this context, Israel's experience provided an illustration of the kinds of responses

---

[299] This interpretation may find confirmation in the fact that in Sir. 42:17 God must make his angels strong enough to endure his glory, since according to Sir. 43:31 no one has seen God or can fathom him who is greater than the greatness of his works (cf. 43:28 f.). But it is precisely these works and the glory of God which mankind at creation and Moses at Sinai are able to understand and see (cf. 17:4–8; 45:2 f.).

[300] 1 Cor 10:7 f. refers explicitly to the idolatry with the golden calf.

to God's provision which, if copied by those "upon whom the end of the ages has come" (10:11), would call their own legitimacy as God's people into question and lead to the same kind of judgment experienced by Israel. For in 1 Cor. 10:1 ff., as in 2 Cor. 3:18, Paul's warning reflects his conviction that the result of the experience of God's glory in the new covenant is the "sanctification" of those who are "in Christ" (1 Cor. 1:2), which in view of 2 Cor. 5:17 is another way of describing their status as a "new creature in Christ," in which "new things have come."[301] In contrast, as in 2 Cor. 3:7–18, here too Paul can point to Israel's experience of "stiff-necked" rebellion in the wilderness as a clear example of the "old things" which have "passed away" (cf. 2 Cor. 5:17). The new creation brought about in Christ consequently entails the "new heart" of responsive obedience to the redemption and provision of God which, rather than discontent and the idolatry it produces, renders to God the gratitude and honor due his name (see above).[302]

As the instrument of the "new creation," it is also not concluding too much to say, therefore, that Paul understood his ministry of the Spirit to be the means by which God is reversing the effects of mankind's "fall" into sin in Gen. 3. For according to Rom. 3:23, after the Fall humanity was no longer able to encounter God's glory because it had lost its conformity to the glory (= righteousness) of God itself (cf. Rom. 5:12 in light of 5:2).[303] According to Paul's prior description of sin in Rom. 1:18–23, this "fall" results in the same lack of gratitude and idolatry typified in Israel's wilderness experience. In view of this fundamental datum of Paul's preaching, the transformation into the image of God by the glory of God in 3:18 brings about a reversal of the effects of the Fall as experienced by humanity in general (cf. Rom. 3:24 f.; 5:16–19).[304] Moreover, against the background of Exod. 32–34, the believer's

---

[301] Cf. Rom. 6:4, where this "newness of life" is being created by means of the same glory which raised Christ from the dead. Once again, this "newness of life" is a life lived in "a manner worthy of the God who calls you into his own kingdom and glory" (1 Thess. 2:12; cf. Rom. 6:4 in view of 6:6 f., 12).

[302] Cf. too Sir. 40:27, where the "fear of God is as a paradise (παράδεισος) of blessing, and he spreads it over all that is glorious" (ὑπὲρ πᾶσαν δόξαν).

[303] For the interpretation of Rom. 3:23 as a statement of the effects of the Fall, see Stuhlmacher, *Der Brief an die Römer*, p. 55 f., who points to the Apoc. Mos. 20 f. as the key conceptual background linking Paul's statement with Gen. 3. Moreover, as Stuhlmacher, "Ontologischen Charakter," p. 13, emphasized earlier, this "new creation" in Paul's thinking corresponds to the "Realistik" of the concept of the new creation found in Jewish traditions such as 1 Enoch 106:13 and 1QGen.Apoc. I/II.

[304] For this concept within Paul's overall ecclesiology, see W. Klaiber, *Rechtfertigung und Gemeinde, Eine Untersuchung zum paulinischen Kirchenverständnis*, FRLANT Bd. 127, 1982, p. 163, who points to 3:18 ff. as occupying the very center of Paul's theology in which the positive counterpart to the conception of Rom. 3:23 is presented. In addition to Apoc. Mos. 20 f., he points to 1QS 4:23; CD 3:20; and 1 QH 7:14 f. as the key conceptual background. For this expectation of a new creation in later Jewish tradition, see Test. Levi 18:10 f., in which fallen Adam and the Messiah are contrasted, *Gen. Rab.* 12:6, *Num. Rab.* 13:12, and *Exod. Rab.* 30:3, in which the six things Adam lost at the fall are restored in the

transformation as a result of the removal of the heart of stone by the Spirit (cf. 3:6, 16–18) can also be conceived of as the reversal of the effects of Israel's subsequent "fall" with the Golden Calf.

This conceptual link between the events of Exod. 32–34 (2 Cor. 3:7–18) and the Fall in Gen. 3 (Rom. 3:23, 5:12–19), which we have already noted within the canonical tradition in chapter three, is also reflected in the conception found in later Jewish tradition that Moses' experience in Exod. 34, as the culmination of the Sinai revelation, was a result of his being reclothed with the glory (light) of God lost by Adam at the Fall.[305] Moreover, in 2 (Syriac Apocalypse of) Baruch 18:1 Moses is described as the one who "lighted took from the light, and there are few who imitated him." For in the next verse we read that "many whom he illuminated took from the darkness of Adam and did not rejoice in the light of the lamp" (2 Bar. 18:2). Here too, Israel's sin in the wilderness, and perhaps even the golden calf incident itself, is depicted in terms of following Adam in his "fall," rather than Moses in his participation in the "light," which in 2 Baruch, however, is not the glory of God as such, but

---

messianic age, Kim's evaluation of these texts, *Origin of Paul's Gospel*, pp. 188–190, and now the survey of the motif of the restoration of Adam's glory by C. Marvin Pate, *Adam Christology as the Exegetical and Theological Substructure of 2 Corinthians 4:7–5:21*, 1991, pp. 33–76. Pate demonstrates that beginning in the third century B.C. speculation concerning Adam increases in Jewish literature and that much of it focuses on the restoration of Adam's lost glory in terms of an "Urzeit-Endzeit" scheme in which the primeval glory that Adam lost because of his sin will be restored in the world to come to the righteous who now suffer (cf. pp. 33–34). It is this theme which then provides the clue to Paul's thought in 2 Cor. 4:7–5:21 (p. 34), especially those texts in which the metaphors of a glorious garment and a glorious building are used to describe the eschatological future (cf. pp. 49, 52 f., 55, 58, and 1 Enoch 90:28 ff.; 2 Bar. 4:2–7; 4 Ezra 7:26; 13:36). Surprisingly, however, Pate does not develop the theme of the restoration of Adam's glory in conjunction with 2 Cor. 3:18. For the development of these themes he points to Ezek. 1:26–28; 1QS 4:22 f.; CD 3:20; 1QH 7:15; Wis. 1:23; 2:23; 3:4–7; 8:10, 13; 4 Ezra 3:4–7; 4:11; 7:11–12, 88–98; 8:51; 13:36; 1 Enoch 32:3–6; 39:9; 50:1; 58:2; 62:15 f; 90:28–36; 103:2 f.; 2 Bar. 4:2–7; 15:8; 54:15, 21; 3 Bar. 6:16; 2 Enoch 30:11; Life of Adam and Eve 13:2; 29:13; Apoc. Moses 20:1–3; *Gen. Rab.* 12:6; 21:7, etc. But as Wedderburn and Kim have pointed out, pre-fall Adam can also be used in Jewish tradition as a positive example of Israel's righteousness (cf. Wis. 7:27 [in the context of wisdom!]; 10:11; Jub. 2:20; 19:24–29; 22:13; Philo, *Vit. Mos.* 2:60, 65; *Quaest. Gen.* 2:56). Thus, the use of Adam in Jewish tradition can emphasize either this positive, pre-fall role (as Paul does in his view of Christ as the "second Adam"), or Adam's negative post-fall influence on mankind (as Paul does in his view of Adam in Rom. 5:15–19).

[305] Cf. the Samaritan texts Memar Markah 2:12; 5:4; and Pitron 9:20 (for the same idea, now related to Moses' experience of the glory of God in Exod. 3:1 ff.) pointed out by Belleville, *Reflections of Glory*, pp. 49 f., who observes that Moses' shining face was also associated with the Law in M.M. 4:6 (p. 50); and Furnish, *II Corinthians*, p. 215, who also points to M.M. 5:4 as reflecting a conceptual background to 3:18. For the corresponding idea of Sinai as a second creation in the Samaritan texts, see Meeks, *Moses*, p. 360, and for this concept in Philo, *Quaest. Exod.* 2.46, and in rabbinic texts (e.g. *Exod. Rab.* 23:15; *Lev. Rab.* 20:10, based on Num. 12:8), see Kim, *Origin of Paul's Gospel*, p. 236, and the literature cited there.

the light of the "lamp of the (eternal) Law" (cf. 2 Bar. 17:4; 59:2, reflecting Ps. 119:105). In a similar way, Paul pictures the unveiled experience of the believer in the footsteps of Moses in 3:18, as well as his own experience as reflected in 4:6, to be the "new creation" restoration of the access to the glory of God which began for Moses and the remnant in the Sinai covenant, but was lost by Israel as a nation at their sin with the golden calf.[306] Hence, to be like Moses in 3:18 is to be brought back to the experience of Adam and Eve in the "garden of Eden," which is paralleled to Israel's experience of God's glory at Mt. Sinai. But whereas Adam and Eve, and then Israel, "fell short of the glory of God," those in Christ, who is the "second Adam," are now being transformed by it into that "same image" and "glory" revealed in Christ. Christ, therefore, and not the "light of the lamp of the Law" *per se*, is the means of encountering the glory of God and experiencing the transformation it brings about.[307] And it is this transformation as the expression of the "new creation" which supports Paul's legitimacy, so that he needs no "letter of recommendation" in Corinth beyond the Corinthians themselves. As "new creatures" in Christ, the Corinthians testify that the effects of the fall for all mankind in Gen. 3, and for Israel as the called of God in Exod. 32–34, are being reversed through Paul's apostolic ministry!

---

[306] Cf. too Kim, *Origin of Paul's Gospel*, p. 236, who concludes that "This Jewish conception of the Sinai revelation as a second creation, as the restoration of the primeval glory, provides a good parallel to Paul's conception of the Damascus revelation of the gospel as a new creation, as the restoration of the primeval light of glory, in 2 Cor. 4:6," though he does not develop the implications of the sin with the golden calf for Paul's argument.

[307] For a similar development of this perspective, cf. the mid second cent. A.D. Christian interpolation in 4 Bar. 9:14, where this substitution of Christ for the Law may be reflected in Jeremiah's confession that Jesus is the one who woke him from the dead as "the *light* of all the aeons, the *inextinguishable lamp*, the life of faith!" (trans. and dating by S.E. Robinson, *OTP, Vol.* 2, 1985, pp. 414, 424; emphasis mine). In 4 Bar. 9:16–18, the end of the age is then described as a return to the garden of eden, where the tree of life will bring about life among the Gentiles in the context of the "great light of the joy of God." Similarly, in the Odes of Sol., Jesus is apparently called the "Light" which opens the heart in 10:1 and is brought before the "Lord's face" as the Son of Man and the Son of God in 36:3; following J.H. Charlesworth, "Odes of Solomon," *OTP, Vol.* 2, 1985, pp. 733, 743, 765. In 10:6 Christ declares that "traces of light were set upon (the Gentiles') heart" so that they walked according to Christ's way and were saved, becoming his people forever. Cf. Odes 11:11; 32:1 for other references to the saving function of the Lord's "light" which dwells in the hearts of believers. Conversely, in Ode 41:4, the Lord gives his glory to his people so that they are admonished in 41:6 to "shine in his light."

Conclusion

The Salvation-History Framework of Paul's Thought

"Daß Altes vergangen und Neues geworden ist
und darin das Heilsgeschehen ἐν Χριστῷ im
Horizont der καινὴ κτίσις theologisch zu
bewältigen ist, bleibt die herausfordernde, von
Paulus gestellte Aufgabe."[1]

Otto Merk

By way of summary, we have seen that the structure of Paul's argument in
2 Cor. 3:4–18 is as follows:

3:4 + 12: Paul's Confidence and Boldness as as Apostle of the Spirit (is)
  3:5–6a: *Supported by* Paul's Call like Moses (which is)
   3:6b: *Supported by* Paul's Call to Mediate God's New Covenant (which is)
   3:6c: *Supported by* the Nature of the New Covenant Itself (which is)
   3:8: *Supported by* the New Covenant Mediation of the Glory of God (which is)
  3:7–11: *Supported by* the Difference between the ministries of the old and new
    covenants
3:13–18: and their consequences.

Paul's confidence and boldness as an apostle are grounded in his understanding of the difference between the *ministries* of the old and new *covenants* as
summarized in the letter/Spirit contrast. Hence, despite the wide diversity
within the current debate concerning Paul's view of the Law, scholars have
been rightly united in their conviction that the letter/Spirit contrast in 2 Cor.
3:6 must be interpreted within an "economy-of-salvation" perspective. Within
this perspective, however, 2 Cor. 3 has continued to be viewed as one of
Paul's paradigmatic "negative" statements about the Law itself, about some
sociological or ritual and/or purity sub-set within the Law, or about the Law
perverted into legalism. In each case, Paul's "negative view" of the Law as the
γράμμα (= "letter") which "kills" (3:6) is seen to find expression in his characterization of the ministry of Moses as one of "death" (3:7) and "condemnation" (3:9). In stark contrast, Paul's own ministry of the "Spirit" (3:8) and of
"righteousness" (3:9) makes alive (3:6).

As such, together with Galatians 3–4, 2 Cor. 3 must be either reconciled,
placed in a developmental view, or branded as irreconcilable with Paul's other

---

[1] "Paulus-Forschung 1936–1985," *ThR* 53 (1988) 1–81, p. 69.

"positive" statements about the Law, such as found in Romans 3 and 7, not to mention with the "positive" affirmations within the supposedly negative passages themselves.[2] Nowhere is this more clear than in 2 Corinthians 3. Here Paul's "negative" statements are couched within the context of his own declaration that God's *glory* accompanied the giving of the Law in letters engraved on stones (3:7a), radiated forth from Moses' face, and provided the context of his ministry (3:7c, 9, 11). Hence, the two poles represented in the "lesser member" of Paul's *qal wahomer* argument in 3:7 (i.e. death and glory), left unexplained, appear to render his thought at best abstruse, and at worse, hopelessly self-defeating. It is this tension between Paul's apparently positive and negative views of the Law which presents the "problem of the Law" in Paul's writings.

1. The Covenant Context of the Letter/Spirit Contrast within the History of Redemption

The study now before us has demonstrated that such a categorization of 2 Corinthians 3 as containing both "negative" and "positive" statements about the Law can no longer be maintained. Instead, the letter/Spirit contrast and the distinct ministries of Moses and Paul which are based on it are expressions of the function of the Law within a "salvation-history" contrast between Israel, who received the Law of God without the Spirit, and the Church, which now

---

[2] In developmental views of Paul's view of the Law, 2 Cor. 3 is in the pivotal position between Galatians and Romans. See Räisänen, *Paul and the Law*, 1986 (1983), pp. 7–12, for a survey of the various developmental theories (esp. those of Drane and Hübner). But as Räisänen points out, "a severe difficulty for development theories is posed by the short time space between Galatians and Romans" (p. 8). In his view, "... the notion of a dramatic theological development within a very short period of time in the thinking of one already engaged in missionary work for some twenty years is strange enough" (p. 8). But such an objection is not a decisive criticism – people can change their views with rapidity, as seen in Paul himself in his pre- and post-Damascus-Road experience! What *is* telling, however, is that Paul apparently says both "negative" and "positive" things about the law *within* Galatians and 2 Corinthians 3 (cf. Gal. 3:13 to 3:19 and 5:14). For Räisänen, of course, these apparent inconsistencies or even contradictions cannot be reconciled. For him, "contradictions and tensions have to be *accepted* as *constant* features of Paul's theology of the law" (p. 11, emphasis his; cf. pp. 150–153). Moreover, Räisänen cites Wrede's evaluation with approval that "'Tortured attempts to reconcile these opposites are in all such cases mischievous'" (p. 11). But one gets the impression that *all* such attempts must be, for Räisänen, "tortured attempts." For Räisänen, the value of Paul's inconsistencies is the insight they give us into Paul's mind and his own personal theological problems (p. 12), thus essentially returning to the approach of the liberalism of the turn of the century! In doing so, Räisänen falls prey to the intentional fallacy and to the danger of psychologizing the text. For to him, the idea that "Paul's difficulties with the law are *in principle* explicable through psychological, sociological and historical factors should not be thrust aside lightly" (p. 11, emphasis mine). Hence, in his study, in stark contrast to the present work, "tensions will not be resolved by theological dialectic," but seen to be "indications of a personal conflict which requires a historical and psychological explanation ..." (p. 14).

lives by the power of that same Spirit in obedience to the Law.[3] In other words, 2 Cor. 3 is a thesis-like summary of Paul's understanding of the history of redemption from Adam and the Fall in the Garden, to Sinai, to the "second Fall" in the wilderness with the golden calf, through the history of Israel's hard-heartedness under the old covenant, to the inauguration of the new covenant by Christ as the "second Adam," who is the very image of the glory of God, to the transformation of the Corinthians into that same image, and beyond. This "fall-judgment-restoration" sequence in the history of Israel is the "plot" or framework of Paul's thinking.[4] What ties this history together is not

---

[3] My view is thus in the trajectory begun by the work of Leonhard Goppelt, now helpfully summarized by E. Earle Ellis, *The Old Testament in Early Christianity, Canon and Interpretation in the Light of Modern Research*, 1992, pp. 58–63. As Ellis points out, in Goppelt's work on typology he established that, in contrast to the history-of-religions approach, "the New Testament writers viewed their own time as a midline segment in the continuing historical unfolding of God's purpose that began in the Old Testament. From those events they discovered the meaning of the contemporary time of salvation, which was their primary interest" (Ellis, p. 62), referring to Goppelt's *TYPOS: The Typological Interpretation of the Old Testament in the New*, 1982 (1939), 12, 17 f., 201–205. Moreover, such typology appears not only in OT citations, "but also in the Christian community's total representation of itself and of its mission" (p. 62). Goppelt's view offers the alternative to Bultmann's argument that the origin of typology was a cyclical view of history in distinction to the salvation-history, promise-fulfillment view of OT prophecy (cf. R. Bultmann, *Exegetica*, 1967, 369–380; Ellis, p. 63). The eschatological aspect of this trajectory is carried on in the work, above all, of Peter Stuhlmacher, to whom the present work is indebted in many ways; Goppelt's emphasis on the Christian community's understanding of itself finds strong recent support in the work of N.T Wright, who emphasizes the critical importance of the narrative sub-structure concerning God's covenant with Israel which undergirds Paul's thought; cf. his *The Climax of the Covenant, Christ and the Law in Pauline Theology*, 1991. The differences between our views have become clear in the course of the discussion.

[4] For this pattern in Paul's thought, based on his own studies of Gal. 3–4 and 2 Cor. 6:14–7:1, see too the work of James Scott (see below, nn. 7,8). This pattern has long been recognized in Deuteronomy, in the so-called Deuteronomic history, and in the major prophets, but for this pattern as that which also provides the coherence for the "Book of the 12," see now Paul R. House, *The Unity of the Twelve*, JSOT Suppl.Series 27, 1990. For this framework as the "plot" behind NT theology and for this basic point as applied to the NT as a whole, see already the programmatic, but often neglected work of C.H. Dodd, *According to the Scriptures, The Sub-Structure of New Testament Theology*, 1952, esp. pp. 72 f., 88. Dodd's point was that "the crisis out of which the Christian movement arose is regarded as the realization of the prophetic vision of judgment and redemption." Hence, Dodd summarized this framework as follows: "The whole process of judgment and renewal is conceived as 'fulfilled' in the Gospel facts ... The 'hardening' of Israel, the 'stone of stumbling,' and in general the judgment of God upon His disloyal people, are conceived as already within the experience of those who witnessed the events of the life and death of Jesus; and equally the calling of the 'remnant,' the inauguration of the New Covenant, the designation of 'Lo-ammi' as 'Ammi' and the abiding presence of 'God with us' (Immanuel) are conceived as realized in the emergence of the Church, which thus figures as the new (and true) Israel of God ..." (p. 88). As is well known, however, Dodd took this to mean that the future aspect of the "plot" was already fully realized in and through Christ and the Church (cf. e.g. pp. 113 f.), something which need not necessarily follow from these insights. For this same critique of Wright's position, which seems to follow Dodd at this point, see below, n. 15.

a contrast between the Law (or some derivation of it) and the Gospel, *but the contrast between not encountering and encountering the glory of God*, or between the absence and presence of God's Spirit among and within his covenant people. This is the contrast which is represented in the respective ministries of Moses and Paul on the one hand, and in the distinct nature of Israel under the old covenant over against those Jews and Gentiles who now make up the new covenant people of God.[5]

As we have seen, it is the history of Israel and the inaugurated eschatology of Paul which determine his understanding of the Spirit and the nature of the new covenant ministry of "righteousness" and "life" in relationship to what Paul, for the first time in Christian writing, called the "old covenant," with its corresponding "ministry of condemnation" and "death." What sets Paul apart is his conviction that the new covenant promised in Jeremiah 31 and Ezekiel 36 has already been established and that it is this new covenant in Christ by which God is gathering his people and fitting them for the day of judgment. *This* is the reason, and not some theological inadequacy in the Law itself, either qualitatively or quantitatively, that the Sinai covenant can no longer be seen as the means for preparing for the final consummation. If the new covenant has indeed arrived, then any return to the "old" as the basis of one's relationship to God would be a fundamental denial of the validity of God's present activity in Christ.[6]

For Paul the key to understanding the relationship between Israel and the Church as presented in 2 Cor. 3, together with their corresponding ministries of Moses (and the prophets) and Paul, is twofold. On the one hand stands Exodus 32–34 and its development within canonical and post-biblical literature. On the other are the corresponding second-Exodus expectations within canonical and post-biblical traditions surrounding the restoration from exile and their implications for the new creation of the new covenant. As these traditions make clear, the condition of the *heart* within the covenant community, and not the structure of the covenant relationship between God and his people

---

[5] With the qualifications noted in the study concerning the meaning of "mysticism" in Paul's thought, Alan F. Segal is therefore correct in pointing out that "Paul is intent on discussing the participation of faithful Christians in the Glory of God; this is the mystical and apocalyptic core of Christianity," *Paul the Convert, The Apostolate and Apostasy of Saul the Pharisee*, 1990, p. 155.

[6] It must be emphasized, therefore, that according to Paul the "old covenant" is over, contra the view, e.g., of Peter von der Osten-Sacken, "Geist im Buchstaben, Vom Glanz des Mose und des Paulus," now in his *Evangelium und Tora, Aufsätze zu Paulus*, 1987, pp. 150–155 (originally in *EvTh* 41 (1981) 230–235), p. 151, who follows Paul Démann in arguing that in Paul's eschatology the person and work of Moses are not gone, but seen in a new perspective where they receive only a relative and temporally limited significance in comparison to the new realities of the new covenant. In addition, K. Stendahl's two covenant theory does not find support in Paul's perspective in 2 Cor. 3; for a summary of his position and my earlier evaluation of his theory in view of Rom. 9–11, see "The Salvation of Israel in Romans 11:25–32. A Response to Krister Stendahl," *Ex Auditu* 4 (1988) 38–58.

per se, has now been changed as a result of the work of Christ and the power of the Spirit. Viewed from this perspective, 2 Cor. 3, as part of the wider context of 2 Cor. 3–7,[7] like Gal. 3–4 (!),[8] presents a thoroughgoing "positive" view of the Law within both the "old" *and* "new" covenants.[9] Paul's discussion of Exod. 32–34 makes it clear that from the beginning of Israel's history the problem was not the Law which was given to Israel or the old covenant *per se*, but *the nature of the Israel* which was given to the Law and with whom the covenant was made.[10] In God's sovereignty, Moses was called to declare the

---

[7] For the "second Exodus" and "new creation" background to 2 Cor. 3–7, see now the works of G.K. Beale, "The Old Testament Background of Reconciliation in 2 Corinthians 4–7 and Its Bearing on the Literary Problem of 2 Corinthians 6:14–7:1," *NTS* 35 (1989) 550–581, William J. Webb, *Returning Home, New Covenant and Second Exodus as the Context for 2 Corinthians 6:14–7:1*, JSNT Suppl.Series 85, 1993, and the forthcoming article by James M. Scott, "The Use of Scripture in 2 Corinthians 6:16c–18 and Paul's Restoration Theology," *JSNT*, 1994.

[8] That the "second Exodus" and "restoration from Exile" expectations, together with Israel's judgment under the curse of the Law due to her hardened state, are the key to understanding Gal. 3–4 has now been shown by the works of James M. Scott, *Adoption as Sons of God, An Exegetical Investigation into the Background of* ΥΙΟΘΕΣΙΑ *in the Pauline Corpus*, WUNT 2.Reihe 48, 1992, and "'For as Many as are of Works of the Law are Under a Curse' (Galatians 3:10)," *Paul and the Scriptures of Israel, Studies in Scripture in Early Judaism and Christianity 1*, JSNT Suppl.Series 83, 1993, pp. 187–221.

[9] Against the work of Reinhold Liebers, *Das Gesetz als Evangelium, Untersuchungen zur Gesetzeskritik des Paulus*, AThANT 75, 1989, pp. 242, 2 Cor. 3 does not support the conclusion that covenant and Law and Law and promise are no longer a unity, but now oppose one another (Gal. 3:15–22; Rom. 4:13–16), or that Paul contests the belonging together of the indicative and imperative in the Law. Nor does it support his conclusion, p. 244, that Paul critiques the wisdom conception of the Law: "Die Tora ist eben nicht 'Gnade' und 'Weisung,' sie besitzt und vermittelt eben nicht den 'Geist' im 'Buchstaben.' Anders gesagt: Paulus Kritik richtet sich gegen das 'Gesetz' als 'Evangelium.'" But for Paul neither the Law nor the Gospel mediate the Spirit in and of themselves, so that without the Spirit both kill (cf. 2 Cor. 2:15 f.). Though Liebers is correct, pp. 117, 119n. 115, that for Paul the new covenant brings the old covenant to an end, rather than restoring it as a mediation of the old covenant in a new way, he is wrong in drawing from this that the Law can no longer make possible the choice of life (Deut 30:15; Prov. 3:18; 2 Bar. 46:3) and with it bring confidence (3:4) and freedom (3:12). Nor is he right, p. 117, that both Paul and Moses claim to have the ministry of the Spirit as their sign. Hence, although Liebers is correct when he concludes, pp. 119–120, that the point of contention between Paul and Judaism was to whom or what the Spirit and the freedom the Spirit brings was to be attributed, he misses the eschatological context. Liebers sees as the key problem "the soteriological claim of the Law understood as wisdom, over against the claim of Christ" (p. 121), but he follows Windisch in seeing the antithesis to be Christianity vs. Judaism (p. 122). He must therefore conclude that Paul opposes the Law itself as the "Machtbereich" in which the Jews boast and upon which they depend (pp. 238 f.). In his view, Paul is negating "das 'vertrauenswürdige' Fundament des jüdischen Gottesverständnisses, die Verläßlichkeit der (heilbringenden) göttlichen Ordnung" (p. 239). He misses the fundamental point that the problem is not the Law but the condition of Israel's heart.

[10] Contra the conclusions of two of the most influential and programmatic works on Paul's view of the Law, those of E.P. Sanders and H. Räisänen. For Sanders, Paul's problem with Judaism is with the covenant and election of Israel itself, and therefore with the works of the

saving will of God to the people without the accompanying life-giving work of the Spirit. As a result, the necessity of the veil in Exod. 34:29–35 announced the need for the ultimate replacement of the Sinai covenant. What Jeremiah and Ezekiel declared concerning the "problem" of the old covenant (cf. 2 Cor. 3:6), Exod. 34:29 ff. already demonstrates (2 Cor. 3:7–11): although the covenant was renewed, Israel's hearts remained "stiff-necked," so that the covenant could not be kept (cf. Deut. 29:2–4). From its very beginning, therefore, the old covenant of the Law without the Spirit implicitly looked forward to the time when the Law would encounter a people whose hearts had been changed and empowered to keep God's covenant.

For this reason, E.P. Sanders and those who follow him miss the point of Paul's argument when they posit that Paul's "solution" in Christ preceded and led to his understanding of its corresponding "plight." Sanders "cannot see how the development could have run the other way, from an initial conviction that the law only condemns and kills, to a search for something which gives life, to the conviction that life comes by faith in Christ, to the statement that the law lost its glory because a new dispensation surpasses it in glory."[11] But once the plight in view is not seen to be the Law *per se*, but the history of Israel's hard-heartedness, beginning with her sin with the golden calf and its consequences in Exod. 32–34, so that the glory of the Law is no longer seen to be "lost," the canonical and historical antecedents to Paul's "solution" concerning the plight of Israel and the nations become readily apparent.[12] Thus, to rephrase Sanders, the development of Paul's thought ran from an initial conviction that Israel as a people was hardened and therefore unable to encounter God's glory without being destroyed, to a search for something (as a Pharisee) to save his people, to the conviction that Israel's restoration, as well as the salvation of the Gentiles, comes by faith in Christ as the Messiah, to the statement that the old covenant is no longer the means by which the remnant will encounter God's glory because the new covenant has now been inaugurated.

Law built upon it as the corresponding covenant stipulations ("In short, this is what Paul finds wrong in Judaism: it is not Christianity," *Paul and Palestinian Judaism, A Comparison of Patterns of Religion*, 1977, pp. 551 f.); for Räisänen, Paul's problem with Judaism is that "the Jews err in imagining that they can be saved by keeping the law rather than by believing in Christ" *(Paul and the Law*, p. 176.). But since Räisänen also believes that the Judaism of Paul's day was characterized by a covenantal nomism, Räisänen "cannot avoid the strong impression that Paul actually does give his readers a distorted picture of Judaism. He comes to misrepresent Judaism by suggesting that, within it, salvation is by works and the Torah plays a role analogous to that of Christ in Paulinism" (p. 188).

[11] *Paul, the Law, and the Jewish People*, 1983, p. 138.

[12] For a similar argument that the biblical and post-biblical view of the plight of Israel and the world as a result of their sinful state in general preceded Paul's solution, see now Frank Theilman, *From Plight to Solution, A Jewish Framework for Understanding Paul's View of the Law in Galatians and Romans*, Suppl.Nov.T. 61, 1989, though it is beyond the scope of the present work to discuss Theilman's own view of the Law in Paul's thought.

But if 2 Cor. 3, a perennial pillar in the traditional Law/Gospel debate, can no longer be viewed as a Pauline critique of the Law itself, or even of its misuse as a platform for legalism, then the age-old "problem" surrounding Paul's view of the Law takes another important step toward dissipating altogether. Furthermore, all attempts within the "new perspective on Paul" to "solve" the apparent tension in his thought by viewing the "letter" as a reference to some down-sized sociological or ritual aspect or function of the Law are also found to be unnecessary. Paul may certainly envision that the Law without the Spirit (= the "letter") can produce a prideful legalistic or sociological, ritual, or ethnic perversion of its role in relationship to God and his people when it encounters hard-heartedness (cf. 2 Cor. 11:22; Rom. 2:17–24; Gal. 2:11–14; 6:11–16), but such misuses of the Law are not in view in 2 Corinthians 3. Nor must we conclude with N.T. Wright that Paul's view presents a "constant paradox" in that Paul "is consistently undermining the traditional Jewish view of election, and establishing a new view of the people of God ... without, apparently, going the whole way into (what we have come to call) a Marcionite position."[13] This study has confirmed Wright's insightful emphasis that covenant theology is "one of the main clues, usually neglected, for understanding Paul."[14] However, his corollary that Paul's theology "consists precisely in the redefinition, by means of christology and pneumatology," of the "twin heads" of Jewish theology, i.e. monotheism (God) and election (Israel), so that faith in Christ, and not the Jewish "badges" of circumcision, kosher laws, and the sabbath, becomes the "boundary markers round the community" needs refinement.[15] As 2 Cor. 3 demonstrates, the essential discontinuity between the old and new covenants does not lie in the nature of the covenants themselves or in a new definition of the "remnant" people of God (note the parallel between

---

[13] *The Climax of the Covenant*, 1992, p. 14.

[14] *The Climax of the Covenant*, p.xi. See too his conclusion, p. 203, concerning Rom. 2, 4, 8:1–11, Gal. 3, and 2 Cor. 3 that "though it is unfashionable to use covenantal categories in interpreting Paul ... they are actually central; and moreover, *they are habitually expressed in forensic language*, i.e. using the root δικ-," and his overall thesis, p. 258, that "... Paul's whole view of Christ and the law can be understood in terms of the *story* of God and the people of God ...," which for Wright is the story of the history of salvation and of its covenant (cf. p. 207). Wright too sees that the "plight" in view for Paul preceded his "solution," since "Paul, like all first-century Jews, had a 'plight' ... the 'plight' consisted of the sorry state of Israel, interpreted as a problem about the covenant faithfulness and justice of the creator God who had called her to be his chosen people" (pp. 260 f.). Indeed, "as long as Herod or Pilate ruled over her, Israel was still under the curse of 'exile'" (p. 261).

[15] *The Climax of the Covenant*, pp. 1, 13. Wright's views are based on his conviction that the notion of Jesus as the Messiah means (correctly, in my view) that he represents his people Israel, which he then takes to mean (incorrectly, in my view) that Jesus stands for and indeed comes to replace Israel within the history of salvation (cf. e.g., pp. 33–35, 40, 196, 198, 261–263, etc.). This leads Wright, like Dodd before him, to minimize the future eschatological consummation and its implications for Israel's future in Paul's thought and produces what appear to be a series of over-realized interpretations of the significance of Jesus' "first" coming within redemptive history.

Christians and Moses in 2 Cor . 3:16–18 and that, according to Gal. 3:7–9 and Rom. 11:17–20, Gentile believers are children of Abraham and have been grafted into Israel!). The contrast is solely between Israel under the old covenant and the Church under the new, and *hence* between the meaning and function of the ministries of Moses and Paul in regard to the covenant people, including the role of the Law under the old and new covenants respectively.[16] Finally, what brings force to this contrast and provides its *Sitz im Leben* in 2 Cor. 3 is not an abstract reflection on the history of salvation, but the apologetic and polemical context in which Paul found himself when writing 2 Corinthians. We now turn our attention to this context and its implications for Paul's understanding of the letter/Spirit contrast, the history of Israel, and the argument from Scripture.

2. The Role of the Letter/Spirit Contrast in Paul's Apology

Given the nature of the letter/Spirit contrast between the Law without the Spirit and the power of the Spirit under the new covenant, the key question to answer is this: how did Paul come to discuss the Law and Moses in this context, where the dominant theme has been the sufficiency of Paul's apostleship as demonstrated through his own ministry of suffering and the Spirit and by the experience of the Corinthians themselves?[17] Was the introduction of the

---

[16] Though it is beyond the scope of the present work to discuss in detail the complex question of the role of the so-called Jewish "badges" or "boundary markers" of circumcision, purity regulations, and the sabbath under the new covenant, see above, chapter two pp. 135–140. In short, the observance of these Laws in Paul's thinking is not *denied*, but rather becomes a matter of personal preference (!) *not* primarily because they present sociological barriers between Jews and Gentiles, but because their function and intention are being fulfilled in the changed hearts of *obedience* under the new covenant as a result of the work of Christ as the last sacrifice (cf. 1 Cor. 7:19!). Circumcision thus becomes "circumcision of the heart" (Rom. 2:25–29; Col. 2:11); believers are made pure before God so that they themselves become the temple of the Holy Spirit (1 Cor. 3:16 f.; 6:19; 2 Cor. 6:16; cf. Mark 7:15–23, esp. v. 19!), and the proper keeping of kosher and celebration of holy days becomes determined by the changed heart of thankfulness (Rom. 14:1–6 as the reversal of the root sin of ingratitude, cf. Rom. 1:21). In each case the mark of this obedience is that love which is a fulfillment of the Law in that it considers the needs and conscience of others more important than one's own because of the believer's acceptance and dependence on God's covenant provisions (1 Cor. 13; Rom. 13:8; Gal. 5:14; Phil. 2:1–4, etc).

[17] That this is the key question to ask was put forth already by Ulrich Luz in his "Der alte und der neue Bund bei Paulus und im Hebräerbrief," *EvT* 27 (1967) 318–336, pp. 322 f., which is programmatic in many ways. But in contrast to the present study, Luz' correct intention to counter the work of Georgi and Schulz led him to the extreme conclusion that 3:4–18 is a doctrinal section without a polemic character (cf. pp. 324 f.). But like the present study, Luz sees the basis of Paul's argument in 3:4–18 not to be a critique of Moses or the glory of the old covenant, but rather Paul's understanding of the history of salvation, albeit with a different understanding of the meaning of the "letter" than argued here (for Luz it is not to be equated with the Law or the OT, but refers to the Law now viewed *from the per-*

"letter" as a reference to the function of the Law apart from the Spirit motivated by Paul's concern with the *outside* opponents in Corinth, as many argue? Or did the question of the Law and the old covenant play a significant role within the Corinthian church itself?

Conceptually, once 2 Cor. 2:16b and 3:4–5 are seen as allusions to the call of Moses, it is not surprising *that* Paul moves from the way his own call is *like* that of the call of Moses, to the *difference* between his *ministry* of the new covenant and the Mosaic *ministry* of the old covenant. Equally as natural is the move in 3:6 from Paul's ministry of the new covenant, to his reintroduction of the Law in its function as "letter" over against the Spirit, just as Paul moved earlier in 3:3 from his ministry of the Spirit to the tablets of stone. For historically and redemptively, to speak of Moses is to speak of the divine Law which he mediated, and which can even carry his name. As we have seen in chapter one, the inextricable association of Moses with the Law characterizes the view of Moses not only in the Scriptures, but also in the Apocrypha, Pseudepigrapha, Qumran literature, Philo, and Josephus. Of significance for appreciating Paul's thought in 2 Cor. 3:6 ff. is the fact that as this tradition develops, the association of Moses with the Law comes to occupy center stage within the *call* of Moses itself in *Tg. Ps.-J.* Exod. 3:5. Here the "holy place" upon which Moses stands when confronted with the theophany of the burning bush is explicitly identified as the place where Moses is "to receive the law (אוריתא) to teach it to the sons of Israel," so that the theophanic glory of God and the purpose of Moses' life are both identified with the Law, even before it has been given at Sinai. Hence, rather than being abrupt and puzzling, *that* Paul's thought naturally moved in this direction is in itself nothing unusual. Once the contrast of 3:6 is established, its further development in 3:7–18 also seems natural, especially since the repetition in 3:7 of the themes of "ministry," the Law as written in letters, and death provide the material link between 3:6 and 3:7 ff., which makes divorcing 3:7 ff. from 3:6 forced and unnecessary.

What *is* surprising is that Paul should introduce the parallels and distinctions between his call and ministry of the Spirit in the new covenant and Moses' call and ministry of the Law as "letter" in 3:6–18 *in the first place*. Paul's prior argument for his legitimacy in 2:14–3:3 is, taken by itself, complete (cf. 2 Cor. 1:3–11 where this same argument is made without allusion or reference to Moses, his call, and/or the Law). Hence, the most probable explanation for the themes of the call of Moses and his ministry of the Law as "letter" in this context is their significance *apologetically*.[18] Their function must be to clarify

---

spective of the new covenant as a visible, objective, principle of life, over against the Spirit as the hidden work of God in the present, cf. pp. 326 f.).

[18] So too already J. Calvin, *The Second Epistle of Paul the Apostle to the Corinthians and the Epistles to Timothy, Titus and Philemon*, Calvin's Commentaries Vol. 10, 1964, p. 41: "his purpose was to show them the chief excellence of the Gospel and the chief recommen-

just how and on what basis Paul can assert that his sufficiency as an apostle in mediating the Spirit actually does "make alive." Given the apologetic context, the point of contention against which 2 Cor. 3:6–18 is to be read is that Paul's opponents question whether Paul's "ministry of suffering" indeed brings about this life of the new covenant produced by the Spirit, as he asserts (1 Cor. 2:3–5; 4:6–15; 2 Cor. 1:3–11; 2:14–17; 3:1–3; 4:10f.; 6:1–10). That the issue is the validity of Paul's *ministry*, over against that of his opponents, is confirmed by the fact that, according to 2 Cor. 11:23, Paul's opponents call themselves διάκονοι Χριστοῦ, so that Paul too employs the "servant"/"minister" terminology in 2 Corinthians to describe himself,[19] when elsewhere he prefers the prophetic title "slave of Christ" (Rom. 1:1; Gal. 1:10).

The two predominant paradigms for interpreting 3:7–18 are thus in need of revision. On the one hand, 3:7–18 has usually been taken to be an independent unit of thought reworked from Paul's opponents, or written by Paul on another occasion. On the other hand, it has often been read *completely* in view of 3:1–6, so that the key ideas of 3:7–18 are read as restatements of the letter/Spirit contrast, which itself is read in the light of one's convictions concerning "Paul's view of the Law" in general. However, given its apologetic context, 3:7–18 should be read as *additional support* for 3:4–6, which is marshalled by *Paul himself* to undergird his thesis-like affirmation that the letter kills and the Spirit makes alive. Paul's purpose in 3:7–18 is to show, through *additional argument* from Scripture (i.e. from Exodus 32–34) and experience (i.e. from the work of the Spirit and from the consequences of encountering the glory of God, cf. 3:16–18), that Paul's ministry actually does make alive in contrast to the ministry of Moses. For as we have seen, Exodus 32–34 is *the* paradigmatic text within the OT canon for demonstrating the problem with the Sinai covenant and the need for the new covenant as outlined in Jeremiah 31 and Ezekiel 36, as well as being the foundational text for these themes in the biblical and post-biblical traditions. Thus, in turning to Exodus 32–34, Paul was merely following the logic of the Scriptures themselves.[20] This is confirmed by the fact that this close conceptual link between Jeremiah 31:31–34 and

---

dation of its ministers, which is the efficacy of the Spirit. For this purpose a comparison between Law and Gospel is of great value and that seems to me to be why he goes into the question here." Though Calvin equates the "letter" with the Law and Old Testament, he sees the contrast functionally to be between "external preaching which does not reach the heart" and "lifegiving teaching which is, through the grace of the Spirit, given effective operation in men's souls," a contrast based on the prophecy of Jer. 31:31, which Paul considered to be fulfilled in his ministry (pp. 41 f.).

[19] Cf. 2 Cor. 3:6; 6:4; 11:5, 23 for διάκονοι; cf. 3:7, 8, 9; 4:1; 5:18; 6:3; 8:4; 9:1, 12, 13; 11:8 for διακονία; and 3:3; 8:14 for διακονέω, though not in each case can it be argued that these too owe their use to Paul's opponents.

[20] Contra Richard Hays, *Echoes of Scripture in the Letters of Paul*, 1989, p. 126, who argues that Paul's discourse has "its own internal metaphorical logic," so that the juxtaposition of the ministry of the new covenant with that of Moses is of Paul's "own devising spontaneously generated out of rhetorical momentum."

Exodus 32–34, introduced by Paul in 2 Cor. 3, is also made in the later Palestinian Triennial Cycle of synagogue readings, which combines Exod. 34:27–35 and Jer. 31:31–34 as seder and haftara.[21] As Wacholder has pointed out, in contrast to the Annual Cycle (where it is based on a conceptual link between the Law and any portion of the prophetic text), the connection between the Law and the Prophets in the "Triennial" haftara is usually established on a verbal connection between the first and second verses of the Torah and the first verse of the prophetic text,[22] *and* a conceptual link between the two texts, with the focus of the prophetic text being on the messianic kingdom as the corresponding development of the text from the Law![23] The parallel to Paul's thought is immediately manifest.

In addition, this reading of 3:7–18 as a subsequent argument in support of Paul's ministry is undergirded by the fact that the contrast in 3:7–18 is not between the Law and the Gospel as such, but between the *ministries* of Moses and Paul (see chapter four), even as the letter/Spirit contrast supports the sufficiency of Paul's *ministry* in 3:4–6. The switch introduced in 3:6c from Paul as "minister" to the nature of the ministry is thus *continued* in 3:7 ff. This is

---

[21] Carol Kern Stockhausen, *Moses' Veil and the Glory of the New Covenant, The Exegetical Substructure of II Cor. 3:1–4:6*, AB 116, 1989, p. 108, and Hays, *Echoes*, p. 132, both point to this traditional cycle of readings, though they do not develop the conceptual parallels. For the listing of the sources for the seder/haftara of Exod. 34:27 and Jer. 31:31, see now the "Prolegomenon" by Ben Zion Wacholder to J. Mann, *The Bible as Read and Preached in the Old Synagogue, Vol. I*, 1971 (1940), pp. XI–LXVII, pp. LVI–LVII, and the discussion of it and the homilies it produced on pp. 530–533. Mann conjectured that the prophetic reading included Jer. 32:40–41 as well (p. 530). But as Wacholder points out, although the practice of reading in the synagogue from the prophets as well as from the Law no doubt originated in the Second Temple period (cf. Lk. 4:16–19; Acts 13:15), "it is impossible to reconstruct the respective readings of the Torah and Prophets for the Sabbaths when Jesus and Paul appeared in the synagogues of Nazareth and Antioch" (p. XVI). Indeed, there is no evidence that either the Law or the Prophets were read in a set cycle during the NT period. As Wacholder points out, "during talmudic and even post-talmudic times variety rather than uniformity prevailed in the practice of the Sabbatical readings of Scripture" (p. XVII). Hence, the earliest sources from the Mishna (cf. e.g. *m*. Taan. 4:3; Meg. 3:4–6; 4:1–9; Shab. 16:1; Yoma 7:1; Sotah 7:7), though increasingly formative, "reflect merely a version of the rite as recommended and observed in tannaitic circles" (p. XVII; cf. p. XLV nn. 22–287 for these and additional sources). The crystallization of the traditions into a Palestinian "Triennial" and Babylonian Annual Cycle dates from the end of the talmudic period in the sixth century (cf. p. XXI). On this tradition, see too Martin McNamara, *Targum and Testament, Aramaic Paraphrases of the Hebrew Bible: A Light on the New Testament*, 1972, pp. 43–46.

[22] Cf. the link between Exod. 34:27, "I have cut a covenant (כרתי ... ברית) with you and with Israel," and Jer. 31:31, "I will cut a new covenant (וכרתי ... ברית חדשה) with the house of Israel ... not like the covenant which I cut (לא כברית אשר כרתי) with their fathers ..."

[23] See Wacholder, "Prolegomenon," pp. XXX–XXXI. As Wacholder has determined, "The verbal link between the beginning of the Torah lesson and that of the Prophetic selection, combined with the messianic message, accounts for more than four-fifths of the Palestinian readings" (p. XXXIII).

true not only of 3:7–11, where the διακονία-terminology is repeated, but also of 3:12–18, as 4:1 makes clear (cf. ἔχοντες τὴν διακονίαν ταύτην). This too is not surprising since, as we have seen, the purpose of 3:7–18 is not to provide a loosely connected digression on "the nature of the old and new covenants" or "Judaism and Christianity," but to support and elucidate the letter/Spirit contrast itself.

All of this leads to the conclusion that Paul's argument from Scripture in 3:7–18 in support of the letter/Spirit contrast must carry a relevance for the Corinthians themselves, instead of merely looking through them to the opponents who had arrived since the writing of canonical 1 Corinthians. If this is the case, then the opponents of Paul now at work in Corinth were not only calling Paul's apostleship into question because of his suffering and lack of impact among his fellow Jews, but also were associating the continuing work of the Spirit with the Law as part of the old covenant. The most plausible explanation is that Paul's opponents were appealing to the Corinthians' desire for spiritual experience as an expression of their over-realized or "spiritualized" eschatology[24] by linking the new covenant promise of the Spirit's work to the old covenant, and by defining their own ministry and its "success" in terms of both the Mosaic and apostolic ministries (cf. 2 Cor. 11:22 f.). Hence, the traditional dichotomy of Paul's opponents into contrasting camps, a Judaizing faction in Galatia over against a proto-Gnostic or θεῖος ἀνήρ pneumatic faction in Corinth, breaks down completely in view of Paul's argument in 2 Cor. 3 concerning the relationship between the Spirit and the Law. Although the point of entry into the community may be different, the strategy and arguments of Paul's opponents in Corinth, together with Paul's responses (!), resemble those in Galatia more than they differ from them.[25] In both cases the appeal of the "Judaizers" was to the desire for the power of the Spirit, while their corresponding promise of the Spirit was conditioned on a willingness to become "full-fledged" members of God's people by submitting to the stipulations of both the old *and* new covenants. For Paul, however, to advocate such a synthesis was to deny the significance of the life and death of Christ in inaugurating the new covenant ministry of the Spirit. In order to combat such a heresy, Paul sought to make clear that the old covenant experience of the Law was, for the vast majority of Israel,[26] devoid of the Spirit. And

---

[24] Following the reconstruction of the Corinthian "theology" now presented by Gordon D. Fee, *The First Epistle to the Corinthians*, NICNT, 1987, pp. 10–12.

[25] Cf. again 2 Cor. 3 with the covenantal, history of salvation arguments in Gal. 3:6–29 and 4:21–31, together with the parallels between Paul's argument from his suffering and ministry in the Spirit in 2 Cor. 2:14–3:3 and those same arguments in Gal. 4:12–20 and 3:1–5. For the centrality of Gal. 3:1–5 within the argument of Galatians and the corresponding link between the Spirit and the Law in the thought of Paul's opponents as addressed in Galatians, see the important work of Charles H. Cosgrove, *The Cross and the Spirit, A Study in the Argument and Theology of Galatians*, 1988.

[26] This was not true, of course, for Moses and the remnant like him (cf. 2 Cor. 3:16; Rom. 11:1–6), which is why in 2 Cor. 3:16–18 Paul must show the parallel between Moses and the

now that the Messiah has in fact come, one can experience the power of the Spirit which makes alive only by faith in Christ alone (2 Cor. 3:6; cf. Gal. 3:1–5). Rather than drawing a wedge between the opposition in Galatia and Corinth, the apologetic role of 2 Cor. 3 testifies to the essential unity of the front against which Paul had to defend himself throughout his ministry. At the center of this defense in 2 Cor. 3 was Paul's comparison between his own ministry and that of Moses, the latter being epitomized in Moses' wearing of a veil as a result of Israel's sin with the golden calf.

3. The Veil of Moses and the Legitimacy of Paul's Apostolic Ministry

Against the background of Exod. 32–34 as developed in 3:7–18, and in view of Paul's understanding of his call as a continuation of the experience of the prophets in the likeness of Moses in 3:4 f., Paul presents his ministry as the eschatological contrast to the ministry of Moses, since the people to whom he is sent are those upon whom the Spirit is now being poured out (3:6, 8). Hence, the experience of the church as the inauguration of the "new creation" in 3:18 is the ultimate ground for the corresponding contrast between the ministries of Moses and Paul in 3:12 f. Although called like Moses (3:4 f.), Paul does not minister like Moses because the people to whom he is called are not like the Israel of the old covenant. Unlike the prophets before him, who were also called like Moses, Paul's ministry is determined by the reality of the new covenant which he mediates. For Paul, therefore, the *similarity* between Moses and the Christian in 3:18 leads to the *dissimilarity* between the ministry of Moses and that of the Christian apostle in 3:7–13. As with the prophets before him, the

---

experience of Christians under the new covenant. For the work of the Spirit in the OT, see the helpful survey of Daniel I. Block, "The Prophet of the Spirit: The Use of *RWH* in the Book of Ezekiel," *JETS* 32 (1989) 27–29, pp. 40 f., who argues for the indwelling presence and work of the Spirit under the old covenant among the remnant, based on the parallels between Jer. 4:4, Deut. 10:16 and 30:6, the argument of Ps. 51:12–13 (one of the three explicit references to "Holy Spirit" in OT; cf. Ps. 51:13[11]; Is. 63:10, 11), and Jesus' rebuke of Nicodemus in John 3 in view of Ezek. 36:25–29. But Block emphasizes that the key text is Ezek. 34–39, since "It is unlikely that Ezekiel was self-consciously introducing a new notion with his promise of the transforming work of the indwelling *rwh* of Yahweh ... What concerns him, however, is the fundamental incongruity between the idealistic designation of his own people as 'the people of God' and the reality that he observed. The problem was not the absence of the Holy Spirit to transform lives, but that this was not occurring on a *national* scale. The issue was one of *scope*. The emphasis in the present text (Ezek. 36:27–28), as in the broader context of Ezekiel 34–39 in general, is on national renewal and revival, not individual regeneration. In 36:25–29 Ezekiel anticipates the day when the boundaries of the physical Israel will be coterminous with the spiritual people of God. In his day a vast gulf separated the two" (p. 41, emphasis mine).

apostle Paul has been called *like* Moses (3:4 f.), but now, in view of the dawning of the new covenant, with a ministry *dislike* that of Moses (3:7–11).

In this way, it is Paul's ministry as the *antitype* to the ministry of Moses which functions to support the legitimacy of Paul's apostleship. Just as Moses' call provided a paradigm for *establishing* Paul's authority in 2 Cor. 3:4 f., Moses' role as the authoritative mediator between God and his people continues to provide the model for *defining* Paul's apostolic function, first stated in 3:6 and then developed in 3:7–18. For Paul, as for Moses before him, it is the glory of God revealed in his ministry which authenticates the legitimacy of his message and life. Moses' central role in Israel's history and tradition as mediator thus provides part of the broad conceptual framework within which Paul develops his understanding of his own role as an apostle, even as the call of the prophets was based on Moses' prior experience.

But Paul is not a "second Moses." Nor should the Corinthians fall prey to those who call Paul's authority into question because he no longer gives allegiance to the "old" covenant. Whereas Moses' authority was demonstrated by what he could *not* do because of Israel's "stiff-necked" condition (3:13), Paul's is now authenticated by what he *can* do in view of the present work of the Spirit among those who believe (3:12, 17 f.).[27] In short, the difference between the ministries of Moses and Paul becomes the difference between the "letter" and the "Spirit," i.e. the difference between mediating the glory of God to those with or without the hardened heart of rebellion and its results in relationship to the Law, either under the old covenant of Sinai (3:6) or under the new covenant established by Christ (3:18).

As the focus in 3:14–15 on Israel's *continuing* hard-heartedness illustrates, Paul's ministry of the new covenant also entails the mystery of Israel's rejection of the Gospel in order that the Spirit might now gather the people of God from among the nations (cf. Rom. 11:25). Hence, Israel's rejection of Paul's ministry cannot be marshalled as evidence against his legitimacy as an apostle. Much less should a synthesis of the old and new covenants be created in order to attract the Jews. For as 2 Cor. 3:16–18 makes clear, the means for

---

[27] Stockhausen, *Moses' Veil*, p. 123, is certainly correct in observing that "Paul is like Moses in his status as a covenant minister (II Cor. 3:4–6) and in the glory that such a ministry entails." But the contrast between Moses and Paul in 3:12–18 does not lead Paul to say or imply that he is "even superior to Moses in glory because his covenant is superior to that of Moses in many ways (II Cor. 3:2, 3, 6, 8–11)" (p. 123). The point of contrast is not between Paul and Moses, but between their respective ministries. For this same reason, Kim's thesis that Paul establishes an "antithetical typology" between the Sinai theophany and the Damascus Christophany, *Origin of Paul's Gospel*, WUNT 2. Reihe 4, 1981, pp. 233–239, esp. pp. 236 f., misses the point of the distinction between Moses and Paul, which for Kim ultimately becomes an extension of the traditional law/Gospel contrast (cf. pp. 4, 13, 47 f., 235). Again, the point of contrast revolves around the work of the Spirit in the ministry of the new covenant, not around two distinct experiences of the glory of God, or some difference in nature between the Law and the Gospel.

removing the heart which is hardened under the old covenant is not the Law as given under that same covenant, but the revelation of the glory of God in the new covenant inaugurated by Christ. It is not the Law *per se* which transforms the people of God in either case, but encountering the glory of God. Israel remains blinded under the Sinai covenant and cannot therefore be saved through it. Instead, only in Christ can one now receive the Spirit, through which the work of the "god of this age" is thwarted (cf. 2 Cor. 4:4). But for those whose hearts remain "veiled" (i.e. "stiff-necked" or "blinded," cf. 3:14 f. with 2 Cor. 4:3 f.), the glory of God now being revealed in Christ must remain veiled from view, both as an act of judgment and as an expression of God's continuing mercy until their final judgment (cf. Rom. 2:4 f.). To Paul's anguish, this continues to be Israel's experience. But for those from whom the "veil" has been removed from their hearts by the Spirit, the glory of God revealed in Christ can now be encountered without fear of destruction. Instead, the glory of God once again becomes the sanctifying presence of God in the midst of his people (3:18; cf. Exod. 20:20; Gen. 1:26 f.). Paul's confidence as an apostle (3:4), his boldness in ministry (3:12), and his refusal to lose heart in spite of Israel's rejection (4:1 f.) are all confirmed by this latter sanctifying purpose now being realized through his life and message (3:18). In the end, therefore, the present work of moral transformation among those who respond to Paul's life and message is that which establishes the legitimacy of Paul's own ministry as a mediation of the glory of God on the face of Christ. Conversely, this transformation also provides the criterion for determining those who are and are not now part of God's "new creation" in Christ.[28] Yet Paul's *initial* basis for asserting his legitimacy is the argument from Scripture which he employs in 3:4–17. However, this obvious assertion raises the question of Paul's hermeneutic, the answer to which has been anything but obvious in modern scholarship.

---

[28] This becomes readily apparent when Paul's statements in 1 Cor. 7:19, Gal. 5:6, and Gal. 6:15, that neither circumcision or uncircumcision now "matter", are compared:

1 Cor. 7:19a: ἡ περιτομὴ οὐδέν ἐστιν καὶ ἡ ἀκροβυστία οὐδέν ἐστιν,
    Gal. 5:6a: οὔτε περιτομή τι ἰσχύει οὔτε ἀκροβυστία
    Gal. 6:15a: οὔτε περιτομή τί ἐστιν οὔτε ἀκροβυστία

1 Cor. 7:19b: ἀλλὰ τήρησις ἐντολῶν θεοῦ.
    Gal. 5:6b: ἀλλὰ πίστις δι' ἀγάπης ἐνεργουμένη.
    Gal. 6:15b: ἀλλὰ καινὴ κτίσις.

The parallels between these texts demonstrate that, for Paul, what now counts is the present experience of the new creation, which is primarily to be seen in the ethical transformation of the people of God in accordance with the commandments of God.

4. Paul's Eschatological Hermeneutic of the Heart

As we have seen, though "realistic" in its "meaning," the letter/Spirit contrast has increasingly been viewed to carry a hermeneutical "significance" for Paul, especially in the general contrast between γράμμα and γραφή, and in Paul's assertion in 3:14–15 that "until this very day the same veil remains at the reading of the old covenant, because it is not being unveiled, since it (i.e. the veil) is being rendered inoperative in Christ, nevertheless until today a veil has been laid upon their hearts." This present study certainly undergirds this insistence that 2 Cor. 3 manifests Paul's hermeneutic both in theory and practice, as well as his understanding of the relationship between the old and new covenants.[29] But perhaps the most startling conclusion of all to be drawn from this work concerns the *nature* of Paul's hermeneutic as demonstrated in 2 Cor. 3. For the growing consensus has been that, based on his new-found Christian presuppositions[30] and motivated by his own polemic purposes, Paul often creatively reinterpreted the Old Testament with little regard for its original context and contrary to its canonical meaning.[31] 2 Corinthians 3 has almost

---

[29] Contra the conclusion of Stephen Westerholm, "Letter and Spirit: The Foundation of Pauline *Ethics*," *NTS* 30 (1984) 229–248, pp. 233–235, 240–241 (see Introduction, nn. 69, 93).

[30] I.e., whether primarily Christological, à la Käsemann and Stuhlmacher, etc., eschatological in general, à la Koch, or ecclesiological, à la Hays; see the Introduction.

[31] To give just one of a legion of examples, see the influential work of Richard B. Hays, *Echoes of Scripture in the Letters of Paul*, 1989, who concludes that Paul's interpretations and applications of Jer. 31, Ezek. 36, and Exod. 34 in 2 Cor. 3:1–4:6 are "audacious" (p. 130), "allusive" (pp. 130, 133), "distinctive" (p. 132), "daring" (p. 129), and held together by "metaphorical moves as he evokes scriptural figurations, deforms them, and fuses them with other figurations" (p. 125). In particular, Paul's interpretation of Exod. 34 is "imaginative ... mystical and eschatological" (p. 140), "parabolic" (p. 144), and a "fanciful figurative exposition" (p. 221 n. 67). For Hays, such an approach to Scripture, as illustrated by Paul's use of the OT in 3:16, is Paul's own hermeneutical transformation of the text as the result of the Spirit within the Church, in which the words of Exod. 34:34 are "unveiled and released into a new semantic world where immediately they shine and speak on several metaphorical levels at once" (p. 147). In a surprising but consistent move, and in spite of his own disavowal of it (cf. p. 150), Hays thus reverts back to a modified Origenian approach in which he concludes, p. 149, that for Paul (and us!), "Scripture must not be read slavishly according to the *gramma*. It must be read ... under the guidance of the Spirit as a witness to the gospel. This means, ultimately, that Scripture becomes – in Paul's reading – a metaphor, a vast trope that signifies and illuminates the gospel of Jesus Christ." In direct contrast to this present study, Hays therefore ends up arguing that in Paul's apology for his ministry, "His radical proposal is to reject all text-bound criteria for discerning authenticity" (p. 149). For in Hays' view, Paul's "metaphorical fusion of Moses and Torah-text in verses 12–18 suggests that those who turn to Christ *will* be granted a transformed capacity to perceive the *telos* of Scripture, and his handling of Exodus 34 provides a paradigmatic instance of exactly this sort of transformative, Spirit-inspired reading" (p. 151). As Hays' work illustrates, although there is much in common in our understanding of the centrality of the new covenant community and its moral transformation by the Spirit for Paul's thought, this under-

always been used as a classic proof-text for this consensus. In stark contrast, it has been argued throughout this study that Paul's view of the letter/Spirit contrast and his understanding of their respective ministries in 2 Cor. 3:6–18 have been consistently derived from a careful, contextual reading of Exodus 34:29–35 in accordance with its original canonical intention. [32] Admittedly, this is an "extremely conservative" conclusion,[33] and one that is put forth on the basis of the very passage that has most often been seen to be the clearest example of Paul's distinctively Christian, non-contextual hermeneutic. But it too is based on a recognition of the covenantal and eschatological framework of Paul's thinking.[34] However, the implications of the eschatological interpretation of the veil and its removal in 2 Cor. 3:14–15 advocated here lie in a different direction than almost universally argued.

First, we have seen that the γράμμα (= "letter") of 3:6 does not refer to the Scriptures themselves, nor to a way of reading them. Second, the τέλος of v. 13 which is veiled from Israel does not refer to the "real" or Spirit-inspired meaning or goal of the old covenant and/or the Law, but to the consequences of encountering the glory of God with hardened hearts. And third, the "veil" in

---

standing leads to an alternative view of Paul's hermeneutic which is equally paradigmatic for understanding Paul, but in an entirely opposite direction.

[32] This is asserted in contrast to Carol K. Stockhausen, "2 Corinthians 3 and the Principles of Pauline Exegesis," in *Paul and the Scriptures of Israel*, ed. Craig A. Evans and James A. Sanders, JSNT Suppl.Series 83, 1993, pp. 143–164, who builds on her major study of 2 Cor 3 *(Moses' Veil)* by positing as a principle of Paul's exegesis that he pays "consistent attention to the context of cited passages" (p. 145). For although she argues that Paul takes into consideration the context of the passage, his interpretation is still not *contextual*. Rather, for Stockhausen, both in 2 Cor. 3 and Gal. 1–4 "... Christian disciples are called upon to make choices ultimately mediated by an exegetical manipulation of a narrative scriptural tradition" (pp. 152 f.). Rather than the original context of the passage, what is determinative for Paul's exegesis are "hook-word" links and associations among texts which allow Paul to interpret them in terms of one another, thus "explaining Paul's otherwise illogical jumps in 2 Cor. 3:1–6" (pp. 155 f., quote from p. 156, based on the results of her full-length study of 2 Cor. 3). But "contextual" here means Paul's interpretations themselves are *controlled* by the original context of the passage.

[33] See H. Räisänen, *Paul and the Law*, p. 72, commenting on 2 Cor. 3:15: "As everyone except for the extreme conservatives admits, Paul's actual reinterpretations of the Old Testament are rather ingenious; no one will today seriously suggest that we should follow Paul in his exegesis." The question, however, is not whether such a conclusion is "conservative," but whether it best fits the evidence.

[34] Again, see already C.H. Dodd, *According to the Scriptures*, p. 128, who argued that in the main the NT writers "interpret and apply the prophecies of the Old Testament upon the basis of a certain understanding of history, which is substantially that of the prophets themselves," which Dodd went on to relate to the specific history of God's people. Dodd, however, argued that although the NT writers remained faithful to the original intention of the OT in general, what made the NT great was its ability to go beyond that intention so that "it perpetuates itself by unfolding ever new richness of unsuspected meaning as time goes on," albeit for the most part as "an organic outgrowth or ripening of the original thought ..." rather than "an arbitrary reading into a passage of a meaning essentially foreign to it" (pp. 131, 133).

3:14b does not exist "over" the reading of the old covenant, but *at* its reading, while the veil itself is a metonomy for Israel's hard-heartedness. Hence, in view of the letter/Spirit as a history of salvation, eschatological contrast between the role of the Law without the Spirit and the power of the Spirit to make alive under the new covenant, the hermeneutical implications of 3:13–14b do not derive from the use of the veil as a code-word for the lack of a Spirit-led or Christological reading of the Scriptures (see Introduction). Instead, the hermeneutical significance of 3:13–14 for Paul's understanding of how one reads the Scriptures derives from his ability to explain Israel's present rejection of the *new covenant* on the basis of Israel's continuing hardened nature against God, as *already* revealed in her rejection of the *old*! Israel's continuing rebellion under the Sinai covenant demonstrates, for Paul, that she does not have the *moral* ability to accept the Gospel. In other words, Israel continues to be outside the realm of the Spirit's renewing work, so that the Law still remains for Israel the "letter that kills."

The implication of this argument is that, in Paul's view, had Israel as a nation been redeemed from her "stiff-necked" state, the evidence for such a renewal as promised by Jeremiah and Ezekiel would certainly be her acceptance of the new covenant in Christ as the fulfillment of the old! And as we have seen, both in the canonical tradition and in its development in post-biblical Jewish literature, this renewal consistently included a renewed obedience to the Law itself. This Paul does not deny. Indeed, his argument from the prophets in 3:6 and the transformation language of 3:18, not to mention the Pauline understanding of "righteousness" (cf. 3:9), give every reason to conclude that he affirms it. Hence, those for whom the Law has now been "written on the heart" by the power of the Spirit are those who have also come to Christ as the glory and image of God (3:6bc; 4:4, 6). In Paul's view, one cannot be experienced without the other. The Spirit-filled remnant of the old covenant will thus readily become followers of Christ in the new (cf. Rom. 11:1–5; Phil. 3:2–9), while Israel "according to the flesh" (Rom. 9:8; cf. Phil. 3:2) will continue to be hardened to the present creation of the "Israel of God" in Christ (cf. Gal. 6:16 and Rom. 10:18–21 with 11:7–10). Although Paul wished deeply that his fellow Israelites would come to Christ (Rom. 9:1–3; 10:1), and most likely believed that in the eschatological consummation the nation would be converted to Christ in fulfillment of the promises to the fathers (Rom. 11:26–29), the present rejection of the Gospel by the vast majority of Jews led him to the conclusion that "a partial hardening has happened to Israel until the fulness of the Gentiles has come in" (Rom. 11:25). Indeed, Paul's own mission strategy seems to have been determined by his awareness that Israel would deny the witness of the Scriptures and reject the Gospel, not because they could not *understand* the coherence and propriety of Paul's message due to its supposedly in-house and distinctively Christian hermeneutic, but because in God's sovereignty they had not been "appointed to eternal life" (Acts 13:48; cf. Acts 13:45–48; 17:1–13).

Hermeneutically, then, the majority of Israel rejects the Gospel because in its hardened condition it refuses to submit to the Law (3:14) and the prophets (3:6) themselves, both of which "witness" to the Gospel as the revelation of God's righteousness and as the power of God unto salvation (2 Cor. 3:9; cf. Rom. 1:16 f.; 3:21). But they do so not by providing secret eschatological codes and prophecies which can only be understood by Christians who have the Spirit. What is transformed by the Spirit is not the *text*, but the *people* who read it! Rather than providing the Christological or ecclesiological secret for unlocking the "true meaning" of the old covenant Scriptures, Paul's argument throughout 2 Cor. 3:7–15 has been based on common ground understandings of Exodus 34:29–35 as derived from its larger context and in line with its subsequent development in canonical tradition. Moreover, we have seen that Paul's interpretations find significant parallels in post-biblical Jewish tradition. Paul can therefore simply allude or refer to Exod. 32–34 and the tradition based on it as the "subtext" for his argument, without detailed support, *even though he is defending his legitimacy as an apostle within a highly charged polemic context!* In such a situation, Paul cannot afford to pull rank on his readers based on some Spiritual reading possessed only by the enlightened.

Paul's argument from Scripture in 2 Cor. 3:7–15 is surprisingly straightforward. From his perspective, the "old covenant" Scriptures unmistakably witness to the validity of his Gospel and new covenant ministry in two ways. First, the Scriptures demonstrate that the need for the new covenant outlined in Jer. 31 and Ezek. 36 was manifest from the very beginning of Israel's history. Paul can thus move from his own ministry as the fulfillment of the promises of the prophets in 3:6, to the very beginning of the Sinai covenant in Exod. 32–34 in 3:7–11. Conversely, Paul can proclaim the new covenant established through the Gospel of Christ as the answer to that need, since the revelation of the righteousness of God on the cross makes it possible for the Spirit to be poured out on the ungodly (3:8–9; cf. Rom. 3:21–26 in light of 3:9–20 as the witness of the Law and the Prophets, 3:21). Second, the Law and the Prophets testify that the evidence of this new covenant would be a people redeemed from the hard-hearted reality so clearly revealed in the sin of the golden calf and repeatedly manifested in Israel's history of rebellion against the Sinai covenant.[35] This too finds ready support in the theological thinking

---

[35] See too Terrance Callan, "Paul and the Golden Calf," *Proceedings* 10 (1990) 1–17, for a brief survey of the four references to the golden calf in Paul (1 Cor. 10:1–22; Rom. 1:23, which focus on the incident of idolatry; and 2 Cor. 3:7–18; Gal. 3:19–4:11, which focus on its implications for understanding the Sinai covenant). His programmatic thesis is that Paul "uses it as a focal point for re-interpretation of the situation of Israel and the meaning of the Sinai covenant" (p. 2). In his words, "Paul clearly sees Israel as God's people, and the Sinai covenant as the work of God and as serving God's salvific purposes. But Paul regards Israel as in need of the messiah, and the Sinai covenant as a 'negative' preparation for the coming of the messiah. Paul says this in order to argue that Gentile Christians should not enter into the Sinai covenant or become part of the people of Israel" (p. 2). This, however, is not a

of Paul's day. Once again, Paul can thus move from the beginning of Israel's rebellion against the covenant in Exod. 32–34 in 3:7–11 and 13–14a, to his present experience with Israel as a rebellious people in 3:14b–15, in contrast to those from within Israel and among the Gentiles who are now fulfilling the Law in the power of the Spirit (3:3; 6bc; cf. Rom. 2:14 f., 26; 8:3 f.; 13:8–10; Gal. 5:6,13–26).

In view of this "plain" witness of the Scriptures and the manifestation of the Spirit through the Gospel, Paul can only conclude that those who reject the Gospel do so not because they cannot accept it as a valid interpretation of the Scriptures, nor because there is no evidence of it in the lives of Christ's followers. Rather, they refuse the message of the cross and Spirit because they remain hardened to God's will as revealed in both the old and new covenants and cannot accept the message of Christ morally,[36] which in turn leads to alternative "readings" of the Scriptures. In Paul's view, their continuing "stiff-necked" response to the old covenant in the midst of the dawning of the new age in Christ is clear evidence that they belong to the majority of Israel whose minds have been hardened from the beginning of the Sinai covenant. Hence, in sharp contrast to the later rabbinic tradition, there is no attempt on Paul's part to ameliorate Israel's sin with the golden calf and its implications for her subsequent history of rebellion against the Sinai covenant. On the other hand, the unexpected mystery of Israel's continuing hardness to the Sinai covenant, and in turn her rejection of its fulfillment in the new covenant of Christ, in no way calls into question the validity of God's present work in the Gospel.

Thus, it is important that we reopen the question originally posed by the difference between the studies of Goettsberger and Windisch (see chapter four, pp. 255 ff.). Windisch's position that Paul radically reinterpreted the original intention of Exod. 34 and that this reinterpretation was nevertheless legitimized by its "midrashic" character, though often considered exegetical orthodoxy, cannot be sustained. Paul's epistles certainly do not belong within the genre of the midrashim, nor is his method midrashic. For the same reason, *gezera shawa* should be avoided. In 2 Cor. 3 Paul does associate texts, but his association is based on close thematic links, which naturally manifest some verbal "hook-word" associations, and not on mere verbal ties. Moreover, Paul's

---

reinterpretation of the history of Israel, but is derived from the testimony of the Scriptures themselves.

[36] Contra Dietrich-Alex Koch, *Die Schrift als Zeuge des Evangeliums: Untersuchungen zur Verwendung und zum Verständnis der Schrift bei Paulus*, BHT Bd. 69, 1986, p. 351, who concludes that the Scripture remains for Paul the word of God and witness to the Gospel "natürlich in einer notwendigerweise nur selektiven Aufnahme und mit z.T. massiven Eingriffen in den Wortlaut einzelner Schriftaussagen ..." This study removes one of the central pillars of his thesis that Paul deliberately reinterpreted and altered the OT text in view of his new, decisively Christian hermeneutic. Koch and those who share his view are right that 3:14–16 lead to the conclusion that the possibility of understanding the Scripture is only given to those who turn to the Lord (p. 337). But they miss the reason why!

argument does not move forward solely on the basis of these associations, but is built on a series of careful, logical supports and inferences. Paul's OT texts in 2 Cor. 3 belong together naturally and not merely because they share a common pool of terminology. In stark contrast, the later rabbinic practice of building analogies based on common terminology *(gezera shawa)* is marked by its conspicuous *lack* of such thematic correlation and logical structure.

Finally, it is questionable whether Paul's interpretation of the OT in 2 Cor. 3 can be called a "pesher." It neither follows the format of a pesher style of exegesis, nor exhibits the distinctive features of pesher exegesis.[37] Paul's interpretation is not guided by a specific historical link between the OT texts he treats and his own situation, as if Paul understood Jer. 31, Ezek. 11, 36, Exod. 32–34, etc. to be referring directly to his ministry. Paul does not interpret his texts as explicit prophecies of himself or of the Corinthians in the way in which the Qumran community read the OT to refer directly to their own leader and history. Paul's interpretation is not esoteric in the sense of the Qumran community's understanding of the mysteries now being revealed to them. Paul's use of the Old Testament is conspicuously free of an appeal to some hidden meaning in the text which has now been revealed to him, to his community, or even to Jesus, which can only be accepted if one first accepts the authority of this hidden and private revelation.[38] Paul's interpretation of Exod. 34 is not presented from his pen as a Christian "Teacher of Righteousness."

The tendency to appropriate such descriptions for Paul's exegetical practice has also been motivated, however, by an apologetic purpose. Scholars have sought to redeem Paul's practice by associating it with common exegetical practices of his day and in this way legitimizing it. Paul is seen to handle his Scriptures violently, but his violence is justified by its common existence in his tradition.[39] We have therefore also not used these designations because

---

[37] See above, ch. 5, n. 200.

[38] Cf. the important work of William J. Dumbrell, "Paul's Use of Exodus 34 in 2 Corinthians 3," in *God Who is Rich in Mercy, FS D.B. Knox*, ed. Peter T. O'Brien and David G. Peterson, 1986, pp. 179–194, p. 190, who concludes that "the initial step in the interpretive process of St. Paul is a proper understanding of the respective OT passage within its own literary context." He too therefore argues that there are no grounds for appealing to 2 Cor. 3 as a Christian "midrash" or "pesher"; "Paul is not only being fair to the Exod 34 context but is basing his arguments with his interlocutors entirely upon it" (p. 190). Dumbrell concludes, however, that the key to Paul's interpretive process "is the christological fulfillment to which Paul points," which would not have been shared by his opponents who therefore interpreted and applied the text differently. But in contrast to Dumbrell, the point made here is that although non-Christian Jews may have applied the Scriptures differently, Paul's interpretation was intended to be viewed as common ground. As with the majority, Dumbrell must draw this conclusion because he (incorrectly) takes καταργέω in 3:7, 11, and 13 to refer to the abolishment of the glory itself as an indication of the coming of the new covenant in Christ.

[39] Besides the Introduction, see e.g. the conclusion of the major study by Linda L. Belleville, *Reflections of Glory, Paul's Polemical Use of the Moses-Doxa Tradition in 2 Corinthians 3.1–18*, JSNT Supplement Series 52, 1991, p. 297, whose interpretation of this pas-

our study of this text has shown how sober and careful Paul's handling of the OT tradition within its original context has been. Moreover, the widespread assumption that the Jewish interpretive practices of Paul's day were largely atomistic and non-contextual has now been seriously called into question by the ground-breaking work of David Instone Brewer.[40] Like many of his contemporaries, therefore, Paul has not ripped his texts out of context and then misread them according to his own theological presuppositions, so that it takes a modern scholar to discover what they originally really meant. Rather, in 2 Cor. 3:4–18 Paul has presented an interpretation of the Scriptures which is based on their original intention.

5. A Paradigm for Paul?

This study has focused on only one text within the Pauline corpus. But given the fact that in 2 Cor. 3 Paul develops his understanding of the relationship between the old and new covenants on the basis of the canonical account of

---

sage leads her to conclude that Paul is not providing a "wholly creative interpretation of Exod. 34:28–35," nor depending on any "existing, single unit of tradition ... The evidence indicates, rather, that Paul is drawing on a wide range of Moses-Δόξα traditions, which he utilizes in accordance with the accepted exegetical methodologies of his day." Paul's creativity, therefore, "is to be found not in the traditions themselves but in how Paul employs these various traditions to support his overall argument" and in his "own haggadic expansions of the text" (p. 297). Paul's purpose in doing so is not "to elucidate the biblical text" or to provide "a running commentary on Exod. 34:29–35," but to "forward his polemic" (297). Hence, Paul's use of the biblical text is "selective" – "He introduces only those features of the text that meet his purpose and adapts them to fit his particular situation. So the fact that Paul makes sustained use of Exod. 34:28–35 says nothing about the primary importance of this text; it merely indicates that various aspects of Moses' behavior and the Israelites' response provide a good foil for what Paul wants his readers to understand. Paul's primary intent in 2 Cor. 3:12–18, then, is not to interpret a biblical text, but rather ... to interpret his own current situation" by using this text, traditions, haggadah, and "whatever else was at hand" (pp. 297 f.). For Belleville, therefore, Paul's use of the OT, like much of the exegetical literature of his day, does not use Scripture *per se* in his polemic, but "rather Scripture and tradition filtered first through the lens of salvation history; that is, Scripture that has been, so to speak, 'allegorized' in the light of God's salvific work in Christ" (pp. 299 f.). Moses' act of veiling is read in light of new covenant truths (p. 300). Hence, Paul's content and links of thought in 3:12–18 "are supplied from a base of 'Christianized' δόξα traditions" (p. 300). She thus concludes that 3:12–18 is composed of "Jewish-Hellenistic exegetical traditions, as filtered through the lens of salvation history, being applied to the problems at hand by means of midrashic methods of text interpretation" (p. 301). Hence, for Belleville, this "salvation history" grid through which Paul reads the OT derives from his own Christian experience, and not from the Scriptures themselves.

[40] See his *Techniques and Assumptions in Jewish Exegesis before 70 CE*, Texte und Studien zum Antiken Judentum 30, 1992, in which he demonstrates that "the predecessors of the rabbis before 70 CE did not interpret Scripture out of context, did not look for any meaning in Scripture other than the plain sense, and did not change the text to fit their interpretation, though the later rabbis did all these things" (p. 1).

the (second!) giving of the Law itself, and inasmuch as 2 Corinthians is closely related chronologically (and we would add conceptually as well!) to both
Galatians and Romans,[41] the latter having even been written from Corinth (!),
this one text is particularly significant for determining Paul's view of the Law.
This is especially the case since 2 Cor. 3 is usually viewed as poignantly presenting the "problem" of the Law for Paul.[42] At the same time, 2 Cor. 3
presents one of the most sustained examples of Paul's OT hermeneutic, in the
course of which he also explicitly reflects on the role of the Scriptures within
the Judaism of his day. Here too 2 Cor. 3 takes on special importance, since it
is usually viewed as a classic example of Paul's non-contextual reinterpretation of the Old Testament.[43] Moreover, it is the only text in which Paul's
hermeneutical reflection on reading the old covenant comes to the fore.[44] Any
attempt to describe Paul's interpretive approach must therefore grant this passage pride of place. But we have sought to demonstrate that Paul had no
"problem" with the Law, nor did he reread the Scriptures with a distinctively
Christian presupposition in order to make his case concerning Christ and the
new covenant ministry of the Spirit. Hence, if this study can be sustained, the
salvation-history paradigm presented here for understanding Paul's view of
the Law and his OT hermeneutic may be considered an essential key to a coherent and positive reading of Paul, the Law, and the history of Israel. In turn,
Paul may be recovered as a model for us as well. For from the vantage point of
2 Cor. 3, the other "problem" passages in Paul concerning the Law and his OT
hermeneutic take on a decidedly different perspective. After all, in remarking
concerning the fact that exegesis is more important than rhetoric, Josephus
observed that the Jews of his day

"... do not favour those persons who have mastered the speech of many nations or who
adorn their style with smoothness of diction ... But they give credit for wisdom
(σοφία) to those alone who have an exact knowledge of the law and who are capable of
interpreting the meaning of the Holy Scriptures." *(Ant.* 20:264–265)

---

[41] Regardless of where one places Galatians within Paul's ministry, the chronological
proximity of the letters cannot be denied, see W.G. Kümmel, *Introduction to the New Testament*, 1975[17], p. 303.

[42] To give one final and influential example, see again E.P. Sanders, *Paul, the Law, and
the Jewish People*, pp. 138 f., where he points to 2 Cor. 3:10 f. as verses which "reveal the
dilemma about the law which constantly plagues Paul's discussions of it," and 3:7, 14–16 as
an expression of "Paul's difficulty in dealing with the law." Sanders concludes this because
he does not see Paul offering any explanation for the fact "that something which condemns
and kills can be glorious" (p. 138). In Sanders' view, therefore, Paul "is caught here as elsewhere between two convictions, but here there is no struggle to resolve them; he states them
both as facts" (p. 138). The present study offers no support for such a perspective.

[43] See the forthcoming *Right Doctrine from Wrong Text? Collected Essays on the Use of
the Old Testament in the New*, ed. G.K. Beale, 1994. As Hays, *Echoes of Scripture*, p. 125,
has pointed out, "If the text does offer a hermeneutic, it is reasonable to expect Paul's practice to exemplify – and therefore to illuminate – the theory he espouses." Nowhere is this
more true than in 2 Cor. 3.

[44] As emphasized by Koch, *Schrift als Zeuge*, p. 337.

Index of Selected Passages

III. Old Testament Pseudepigrapha

IV. Qumran Writings

VI. Jewish Hellenistic Writings

A. Exagogue

B. Josephus

Antiquitates

VII. Rabbinic Writings

A. Mishnah

B. Babylonian Talmud

C. Tosefta

D. Midrashim

Genesis Rab.

Exodus Rab.

Leviticus Rab.

Numbers Rab.

Deuteronomy Rab.

Index of Modern Authors

Aalen, S. 112, 113
Aberbach, M. 229
Ackroyd, P.R. 4
Aland, B. 302, 356
Aland, K. 302, 356
Alford, H. 337
Allo, E.B. 323, 397, 409
Alter, R. 193
Anderson, B. 193, 193, 194
Aurelius, E. 190

Badenas, R. 356
Bachmann, P. 323, 324
Bailey, L.R. 198
Baird, W. 114
Baltzer, K. 60
Banks, R. 103, 103, 137, 162
Barr, J. 7, 124
Barrett, C.K. 94, 260, 262, 273, 275, 311,
    317, 329, 337, 348, 355, 370, 382, 397,
    405, 425
Barth, G. 9
Barth, K. 128
Bauer, W. 259, 260, 302, 356
Baumet, N. 322, 324
Beale, G.K. ii, 108, 122, 430, 441, 459
Behm, J. 124, 128
Beker, J.Chr. 21, 22, 22, 27, 28, 109,284
Bekker, I. 302
Belleville, L. ii, 29, 94, 96, 262, 263, 278,
    285, 287, 288, 289, 290, 292, 293, 295,
    298, 311, 335, 336, 337, 338, 339, 340,
    348, 349, 352, 353, 355, 358, 360, 364,
    365, 366, 367, 368, 370, 372, 376, 380,
    381, 382, 383, 384, 385, 387, 389, 391,
    392, 393, 397, 398, 399, 402, 407, 408,
    409, 410, 411, 412, 414, 415, 435, 458
Berger, K. 262, 378
Berkowitz, L. 301
Bernard, J.H. 402
Berquist, J.L. 41, 60, 60, 61
Bethe, E. 302
Betz, O. 21, 80, 86, 110, 133, 168, 173,
    179, 180, 286, 405
Beyerlin, W. 51, 51, 207

Bietenhard, H. 85, 87
Blackman, P. 251
Bloch, R. 81, 232
Block, D.I. 58, 139, 147, 149, 181, 182,
    449
Bogaert, P.M. 63, 98, 288, 289
Boobyer, G. 279
Bori, P.C. 194, 198, 216, 230
Bornkamm, G. 260
Bowers, P. 260, 261
Brandenburger, E. 72, 416
Braulik, G. 132
Braun, H. 154, 155, 162
Brewer, Instone, D. 138, 139, 468
Breytenbach, C. 117
Brichto, H.C. 194, 195, 197, 198, 199,
    200, 202, 204, 205, 206, 208, 210, 216,
    219, 221, 224, 371
Bring, R. 10, 349
Brooke, A.E. 246, 247
Brooke, G. 399
Brueggemann, W. 212, 214, 215, 216, 226,
    228, 231
Buhner, Jan-A. 45, 86, 87, 88
Bultmann, R. 2, 8, 10, 18, 39, 97, 127,
    139, 177, 259, 319, 335, 337, 338, 348,
    368, 401, 404, 405, 419, 428, 439
Burrows, M. 162
Buss, M.J. 59

Caird, G.B. 371
Callan, T. 208, 229, 270, 312, 313, 455
Calvin, J. 6, 325, 374, 445, 446
Carroll, R.P. 132, 230, 235, 236
Cassuto, U. 46, 195, 196, 198, 199, 205,
    207, 220, 224
Cazeaux, J. 63
Cerfaux, L. 400
Charles, R.H. 63, 65, 71, 72, 253, 342,
    432
Charlesworth, J.H. 436
Chevallier, M.-A. 182
Childs, B.M. 42, 61, 101, 195, 197, 198,
    210, 216, 217, 219, 220, 221, 222, 223,
    224, 229, 230, 299

Paternoster Biblical Monographs

(All titles uniform with this volume)
Dates in bold are of projected publication

Joseph Abraham
Eve: Accused or Acquitted?
*A Reconsideration of Feminist Readings of the Creation Narrative Texts in
Genesis 1–3*
Two contrary views dominate contemporary feminist biblical scholarship. One
finds in the Bible an unequivocal equality between the sexes from the very
creation of humanity, whilst the other sees the biblical text as irredeemably
patriarchal and androcentric. Dr Abraham enters into dialogue with both camps
as well as introducing his own method of approach. An invaluable tool for any
one who is interested in this contemporary debate.
2002 / 0-85364-971-5 / xxiv + 272pp

Octavian D. Baban
Mimesis and Luke's On the Road Encounters in Luke-Acts
Luke's Theology of the Way and its Literary Representation
The book argues on theological and literary (mimetic) grounds that Luke's on-
the-road encounters, especially those belonging to the post-Easter period, are
part of his complex theology of the Way. Jesus' teaching and that of the apostles
is presented by Luke as a challenging answer to the Hellenistic reader's thirst for
adventure, good literature, and existential paradigms.
2005 / 1-84227253-5 / approx. 374pp

Paul Barker
The Triumph of Grace in Deuteronomy
This book is a textual and theological analysis of the interaction between the sin
and faithlessness of Israel and the grace of Yahweh in response, looking
especially at Deuteronomy chapters 1–3, 8–10 and 29–30. The author argues
that the grace of Yahweh is determinative for the ongoing relationship between
Yahweh and Israel and that Deuteronomy anticipates and fully expects Israel to
be faithless.
2004 / 1-84227-226-8 / xxii + 270pp

Jonathan F. Bayes
The Weakness of the Law
God's Law and the Christian in New Testament Perspective
A study of the four New Testament books which refer to the law as weak (Acts,
Romans, Galatians, Hebrews) leads to a defence of the third use in the
Reformed debate about the law in the life of the believer.
2000 / 0-85364-957-X / xii + 244pp

Mark Bonnington
The Antioch Episode of Galatians 2:11-14 in Historical and Cultural Context
The Galatians 2 'incident' in Antioch over table-fellowship suggests significant disagreement between the leading apostles. This book analyses the background to the disagreement by locating the incident within the dynamics of social interaction between Jews and Gentiles. It proposes a new way of understanding the relationship between the individuals and issues involved.
2005 / 1-84227-050-8 / approx. 350pp

David Bostock
A Portrayal of Trust
The Theme of Faith in the Hezekiah Narratives
This study provides detailed and sensitive readings of the Hezekiah narratives (2 Kings 18–20 and Isaiah 36–39) from a theological perspective. It concentrates on the theme of faith, using narrative criticism as its methodology. Attention is paid especially to setting, plot, point of view and characterization within the narratives. A largely positive portrayal of Hezekiah emerges that underlines the importance and relevance of scripture.
2005 / 1-84227-314-0 / approx. 300pp

Mark Bredin
Jesus, Revolutionary of Peace
A Non-violent Christology in the Book of Revelation
This book aims to demonstrate that the figure of Jesus in the Book of Revelation can best be understood as an active non-violent revolutionary.
2003 / 1-84227-153-9 / xviii + 262pp

Robinson Butarbutar
Resolving a Dispute, Past and Present
An Exegetical Study of Paul's Apostolic Paradigm in 1 Corinthians 9
The author sees the apostolic paradigm in 1 Corinthians 9 as part of Paul's unified arguments in 1 Corinthians 8–10 in which he seeks to mediate in the dispute over the issue of food offered to idols. The book also sees its relevance for dispute-resolution today, taking the conflict within the author's church as an example.
2005 / 1-84227315-9 / approx. 280pp

Daniel J-S Chae
Paul as Apostle to the Gentiles
His Apostolic Self-awareness and its Influence on the Soteriological
Argument in Romans
Opposing 'the post-Holocaust interpretation of Romans', Daniel Chae competently demonstrates that Paul argues for the equality of Jew and Gentile in Romans. Chae's fresh exegetical interpretation is academically outstanding and spiritually encouraging.
1997 / 0-85364-829-8 / xiv + 378pp

Luke L. Cheung
The Genre, Composition and Hermeneutics of the Epistle of James
The present work examines the employment of the wisdom genre with a certain compositional structure and the interpretation of the law through the Jesus tradition of the double love command by the author of the Epistle of James to serve his purpose in promoting perfection and warning against doubleness among the eschatologically renewed people of God in the Diaspora.
2003 / 1-84227-062-1 / xvi + 372pp

Youngmo Cho
Spirit and Kingdom in the Writings of Luke and Paul
The relationship between Spirit and Kingdom is a relatively unexplored area in Lukan and Pauline studies. This book offers a fresh perspective of two biblical writers on the subject. It explores the difference between Luke's and Paul's understanding of the Spirit by examining the specific question of the relationship of the concept of the Spirit to the concept of the Kingdom of God in each writer.
2005 / 1-84227-316-7 / approx. 270pp

Andrew C. Clark
Parallel Lives
The Relation of Paul to the Apostles in the Lucan Perspective
This study of the Peter-Paul parallels in Acts argues that their purpose was to emphasize the themes of continuity in salvation history and the unity of the Jewish and Gentile missions. New light is shed on Luke's literary techniques, partly through a comparison with Plutarch.
2001 / 1-84227-035-4 / xviii + 386pp

Andrew D. Clarke
Secular and Christian Leadership in Corinth
A Socio-Historical and Exegetical Study of 1 Corinthians 1–6
This volume is an investigation into the leadership structures and dynamics of
first-century Roman Corinth. These are compared with the practice of leadership
in the Corinthian Christian community which are reflected in 1 Corinthians 1–6,
and contrasted with Paul's own principles of Christian leadership
2005 / 1-84227-229-2 / 200pp

Stephen Finamore
God, Order and Chaos
René Girard and the Apocalypse
Readers are often disturbed by the images of destruction in the book of
Revelation and unsure why they are unleashed after the exaltation of Jesus. This
book examines past approaches to these texts and uses René Girard's theories to
revive some old ideas and propose some new ones.
2005 / 1-84227-197-0 / approx. 344pp

Scott J. Hafemann
Suffering and Ministry in the Spirit
Paul's Defence of His Ministry in II Corinthians 2:14–3:3
Shedding new light on the way Paul defended his apostleship, the author offers
a careful, detailed study of 2 Corinthians 2:14–3:3 linked with other key
passages throughout 1 and 2 Corinthians. Demonstrating the unity and
coherence of Paul's argument in this passage, the author shows that Paul's
suffering served as the vehicle for revealing God's power and glory through the
Spirit.
2000 / 0-85364-967-7 / xiv + 262pp

Scott J. Hafemann
Paul, Moses and the History of Israel
The Letter/Spirit Contrast and the Argument from Scripture in 2 Corinthians 3
An exegetical study of the call of Moses, the second giving of the Law (Exodus
32–34), the new covenant, and the prophetic understanding of the history of
Israel in 2 Corinthians 3. Hafemann's work demonstrates Paul's contextual use
of the Old Testament and the essential unity between the Law and the Gospel
within the context of the distinctive ministries of Moses and Paul.
2005 / 1-84227-317-5 / 498pp

Douglas S. McComiskey
Lukan Theology in the Light of the Gospel's Literary Structure
Luke's Gospel was purposefully written with theology embedded in its patterned literary structure. A critical analysis of this cyclical structure provides new windows into Luke's interpretation of the individual pericopes comprising the Gospel and illuminates several of his theological interests.
2004 / 1-84227-148-2 / approx. 400pp

Stephen Motyer
Your Father the Devil?
A New Approach to John and 'The Jews'
Who are 'the Jews' in John's Gospel? Defending John against the charge of antisemitism, Motyer argues that, far from demonising the Jews, the Gospel seeks to present Jesus as 'Good News for Jews' in a late first century setting.
1997 / 0-85364-832-8 / xiv + 260pp

Esther Ng
Reconstructing Christian Origins?
The Feminist Theology of Elizabeth Schüssler Fiorenza: An Evaluation
In a detailed evaluation, the author challenges Elizabeth Schüssler Fiorenza's reconstruction of early Christian origins and her underlying presuppositions. The author also presents her own views on women's roles both then and now.
2002 / 1-84227-055-9 / xxiv + 468pp

Robin Parry
Old Testament Story and Christian Ethics
The Rape of Dinah as a Case Study
What is the role of story in ethics and, more particularly, what is the role of Old Testament story in Christian ethics? This book, drawing on the work of contemporary philosophers, argues that narrative is crucial in the ethical shaping of people and, drawing on the work of contemporary Old Testament scholars, that story plays a key role in Old Testament ethics. Parry then argues that when situated in canonical context Old Testament stories can be reappropriated by Christian readers in their own ethical formation. The shocking story of the rape of Dinah and the massacre of the Shechemites provides a fascinating case study for exploring the parameters within which Christian ethical appropriations of Old Testament stories can live.
2004 / 1-84227-210-1 / xx + 350pp

Ian Paul
Power to See the World Anew
The Value of Paul Ricoeur's Hermeneutic of Metaphor in Interpreting the Symbolism of Revelation 12 and 13
This book is a study of the hermeneutics of metaphor of Paul Ricoeur, one of the most important writers on hermeneutics and metaphor of the last century. It sets out the key points of his theory, important criticisms of his work, and how his approach, modified in the light of these criticisms, offers a methodological framework for reading apocalyptic texts.
2005 / 1-84227-056-7 / approx. 350pp

Robert L. Plummer
Paul's Understanding of the Church's Mission
Did the Apostle Paul Expect the Early Christian Communities to Evangelize?
This book engages in a careful study of Paul's letters to determine if the apostle expected the communities to which he wrote to engage in missionary activity. It helpfully summarizes the discussion on this debated issue, judiciously handling contested texts, and provides a way forward in addressing this critical question. While admitting that Paul rarely explicitly commands the communities he founded to evangelize, Plummer amasses significant incidental data to provide a convincing case that Paul did indeed expect his churches to engage in mission activity. Throughout the study, Plummer progressively builds a theological basis for the church's mission that is both distinctively Pauline and compelling.
2005 / 0-85364-333-7 / approx. 324pp

David Powys
'Hell': A Hard Look at a Hard Question
The Fate of the Unrighteous in New Testament Thought
This comprehensive treatment seeks to unlock the original meaning of terms and phrases long thought to support the traditional doctrine of hell. It concludes that there is an alternative—one which is more biblical, and which can positively revive the rationale for Christian mission.
1997 / 0-85364-831-X / xxii + 478pp

Sorin Sabou
Between Horror and Hope
Paul's Metaphorical Language of Death in Romans 6.1-11
This book argues that Paul's metaphorical language of death in Romans 6.1-11 conveys two aspects: horror and hope. The 'horror' aspect is conveyed by the 'crucifixion' language, and the 'hope' aspect by 'burial' language. The life of the Christian believer is understood, as relationship with sin is concerned ('death to sin'), between these two realities: horror and hope.
2005 / 1-84227-322-1 / approx. 224pp

Rosalind Selby
The Comical Doctrine
Mark and Hermeneutics
This book argues that the gospel breaks through postmodernity's critique of truth and the referential possibilities of textuality with its gift of grace. With a rigorous, philosophical challenge to modernist and postmodernist assumptions, Selby offers an alternative epistemology to all who would still read with faith *and* with academic credibility.
2005 / 1-84227-212-8 / approx. 350pp

Kevin Walton
Thou Traveller Unknown
The Presence and Absence of God in the Jacob Narrative
The author offers a fresh reading of the story of Jacob in the book of Genesis through the paradox of divine presence and absence. The work also seeks to make a contribution to Pentateuchal studies by bringing together a close reading of the final text with historical critical insights, doing justice to the text's historical depth, final form and canonical status.
2003 / 1-84227-059-1 / xvi + 238pp

George M. Wieland
The Significance of Salvation
A Study of Salvation Language in the Pastoral Epistles
The language and ideas of salvation pervade the three Pastoral Epistles. This study offers a close examination of their soteriological statements. In all three letters the idea of salvation is found to play a vital paraenetic role, but each also exhibits distinctive soteriological emphases. The results challenge common assumptions about the Pastoral Epistles as a corpus.
2005 / 1-84227257-8 / approx. 324pp

Alistair Wilson
When Will These Things Happen?
A Study of Jesus as Judge in Matthew 21–25
This study seeks to allow Matthew's carefully constructed presentation of Jesus to be given full weight in the modern evaluation of Jesus' eschatology. Careful analysis of the text of Matthew 21–25 reveals Jesus to be standing firmly in the Jewish prophetic and wisdom traditions as he proclaims and enacts imminent judgement on the Jewish authorities then boldly claims the central role in the final and universal judgement.
2004 / 1-84227-146-6 / xxii + 272pp

Lindsay Wilson
Joseph Wise and Otherwise
The Intersection of Covenant and Wisdom in Genesis 37–50
This book offers a careful literary reading of Genesis 37–50 that argues that the Joseph story contains both strong covenant themes and many wisdom-like elements. The connections between the two helps to explore how covenant and wisdom might intersect in an integrated biblical theology.
2004 / 1-84227-140-7 / xvi + 340pp

Stephen I. Wright
The Voice of Jesus
Studies in the Interpretation of Six Gospel Parables
This literary study considers how the 'voice' of Jesus has been heard in different periods of parable interpretation, and how the categories of figure and trope may help us towards a sensitive reading of the parables today.
2000 / 0-85364-975-8 / xiv + 280pp

Paternoster
9 Holdom Avenue
Bletchley
Milton Keynes MK1 1QR
United Kingdom

Web: www.authenticmedia.co.uk/paternoster

November 2004

Paternoster Theological Monographs
(All titles uniform with this volume)
Dates in bold are of projected publication

Emil Bartos
Deification in Eastern Orthodox Theology
An Evaluation and Critique of the Theology of Dumitru Staniloae
Bartos studies a fundamental yet neglected aspect of Orthodox theology: deification. By examining the doctrines of anthropology, christology, soteriology and ecclesiology as they relate to deification, he provides an important contribution to contemporary dialogue between Eastern and Western theologians.

1999 / 0-85364-956-1 / xii + 370pp

Iain D. Campbell
Fixing the Indemnity
The Life and Work of George Adam Smith
When Old Testament scholar George Adam Smith (1856–1942) delivered the Lyman Beecher lectures at Yale University in 1899, he confidently declared that 'modern criticism has won its war against traditional theories. It only remains to fix the amount of the indemnity.' In this biography, Iain D. Campbell assesses Smith's critical approach to the Old Testament and evaluates its consequences, showing that Smith's life and work still raises questions about the relationship between biblical scholarship and evangelical faith.

2004 / 1-84227-228-4 / xx + 256pp

Tim Chester
Mission and the Coming of God
Eschatology, the Trinity and Mission in the Theology of Jürgen Moltmann
This book explores the theology and missiology of the influential contemporary theologian, Jürgen Moltmann. It highlights the important contribution Moltmann has made while offering a critique of his thought from an evangelical perspective. In so doing, it touches on pertinent issues for evangelical missiology. The conclusion takes Calvin as a starting point, proposing 'an eschatology of the cross' which offers a critique of the over-realised eschatologies in liberation theology and certain forms of evangelicalism.

2005 */ 1-84227-320-5 / approx. 224pp*

November 2004

Sylvia Wilkey Collinson
Making Disciples
The Significance of Jesus' Educational Strategy for Today's Church
This study examines the biblical practice of discipling, formulates a definition,
and makes comparisons with modern models of education. A recommendation is
made for greater attention to its practice today.
2004 / 1-84227-116-4 / xiv + 278pp

Darrell Cosden
A Theology of Work
Work and the New Creation
Through dialogue with Moltmann, Pope John Paul II and others, this book
develops a genitive 'theology of work', presenting a theological definition of
work and a model for a theological ethics of work that shows work's nature,
value and meaning now and eschatologically. Work is shown to be a
transformative activity consisting of three dynamically inter-related dimensions:
the instrumental, relational and ontological.
2004 / 1-84227-332-9 / xvi + 208pp

Stephen M. Dunning
The Crisis and the Quest
A Kierkegaardian Reading of Charles Williams
Employing Kierkegaardian categories and analysis, this study investigates both
the central crisis in Charles Williams's authorship between hermetism and
Christianity (Kierkegaard's Religions A and B), and the quest to resolve this
crisis, a quest that ultimately presses the bounds of orthodoxy.
2000 / 0-85364-985-5 / xxiv + 254pp

Keith Ferdinando
The Triumph of Christ in African Perspective
A Study of Demonology and Redemption in the African Context
The book explores the implications of the gospel for traditional African fears of
occult aggression. It analyses such traditional approaches to suffering and
biblical responses to fears of demonic evil, concluding with an evaluation of
African beliefs from the perspective of the gospel.
1999 / 0-85364-830-1 / xviii + 450pp

Andrew Goddard
Living the Word, Resisting the World
The Life and Thought of Jacques Ellul
This work offers a definitive study of both the life and thought of the French
Reformed thinker Jacques Ellul (1912-1994). It will prove an indispensable
resource for those interested in this influential theologian and sociologist and for
Christian ethics and political thought generally.
2002 / 1-84227-053-2 / xxiv + 378pp

David Hilborn
The Words of our Lips
Language-Use in Free Church Worship
Studies of liturgical language have tended to focus on the written canons of
Roman Catholic and Anglican communities. By contrast, David Hilborn
analyses the more extemporary approach of English Nonconformity. Drawing
on recent developments in linguistic pragmatics, he explores similarities and
differences between 'fixed' and 'free' worship, and argues for the
interdependence of each.
2005 / 0-85364-977-4

Roger Hitching
The Church and Deaf People
A Study of Identity, Communication and Relationships with Special Reference to
the Ecclesiology of Jürgen Moltmann
In *The Church and Deaf People* Roger Hitching sensitively examines the history
and present experience of deaf people and finds similarities between aspects of
sign language and Moltmann's theological method that 'open up' new ways of
understanding theological concepts.
2003 / 1-84227-222-5 / xxii + 236pp

John G. Kelly
One God, One People
The Differentiated Unity of the People of God in the Theology of Jürgen
Moltmann
The author expounds and critiques Moltmann's doctrine of God and highlights
the systematic connections between it and Moltmann's influential discussion of
Israel. He then proposes a fresh approach to Jewish-Christian relations building
on Moltmann's work using insights from Habermas and Rawls.
2005 / 0-85346-969-3 / approx. 350pp

Mark F.W. Lovatt
Confronting the Will-to-Power
A Reconsideration of the Theology of Reinhold Niebuhr
Confronting the Will-to-Power is an analysis of the theology of Reinhold Niebuhr, arguing that his work is an attempt to identify, and provide a practical theological answer to, the existence and nature of human evil.
2001 / 1-84227-054-0 / xviii + 216pp

Neil B. MacDonald
Karl Barth and the Strange New World within the Bible
Barth, Wittgenstein, and the Metadilemmas of the Enlightenment
Barth's discovery of the strange new world within the Bible is examined in the context of Kant, Hume, Overbeck, and, most importantly, Wittgenstein. MacDonald covers some fundamental issues in theology today: epistemology, the final form of the text and biblical truth-claims.
2000 / 0-85364-970-7 / xxvi + 374pp

Keith Mascord
No Challenge Unfaced
Alvin Plantinga's Contribution to Christian Apologetics
This book draws together the contributions of the philosopher, Alvin Plantinga, to the major contemporary challenges to Christian belief, highlighting in particular his ground-breaking work in epistemology and the problem of evil. Plantinga's theory that both theistic and Christian belief is warrantedly basic is explored and critiqued, and an assessment offered as to the significance of his work for apologetic theory and practice.
2005 / 1-84227-256-X / approx. 304pp

Gillian McCulloch
The Deconstruction of Dualism in Theology
With Reference to Ecofeminist Theology and New Age Spirituality
This book challenges eco-theological anti-dualism in Christian theology, arguing that dualism has a twofold function in Christian religious discourse. Firstly, it enables us to express the discontinuities and divisions that are part of the process of reality. Secondly, dualistic language allows us to express the mysteries of divine transcendence/immanence and the survival of the soul without collapsing into monism and materialism, both of which are problematic for Christian epistemology.
2002 / 1-84227-044-3 / xii + 282pp

Leslie McCurdy
Attributes and Atonement
The Holy Love of God in the Theology of P.T. Forsyth
Attributes and Atonement is an intriguing full-length study of P.T. Forsyth's doctrine of the cross as it relates particularly to God's holy love. It includes an unparalleled bibliography of both primary and secondary material relating to Forsyth.
1999 / 0-85364-833-6 / xiv + 328pp

Nozomu Miyahira
Towards a Theology of the Concord of God
A Japanese Perspective on the Trinity
This book introduces a new Japanese theology and a unique Trinitarian formula based on the Japanese intellectual climate: three betweennesses and one concord. It also presents a new interpretation of the Trinity, a co-subordinationism, which is in line with orthodox Trinitarianism; each single person of the Trinity is eternally and equally subordinate (or serviceable) to the other persons, so that they retain the mutual dynamic equality.
2000 / 0-85364-863-8 / xiv + 256pp

Eddy José Muskus
The Origins and Early Development of Liberation Theology in Latin America
With Particular Reference to Gustavo Gutiérrez
This work challenges the fundamental premise of Liberation Theology, 'opting for the poor', and its claim that Christ is found in them. It also argues that Liberation Theology emerged as a direct result of the failure of the Roman Catholic Church in Latin America.
2002 / 0-85364-974-X / xiv + 296pp

Jim Purves
The Triune God and the Charismatic Movement
A Critical Appraisal from a Scottish Perspective
All emotion and no theology? Or a fundamental challenge to reappraise and realign our trinitarian theology in the light of Christian experience? This study of charismatic renewal as it found expression within Scotland at the end of the twentieth century evaluates the use of Patristic, Reformed and contemporary models of the Trinity in explaining the workings of the Holy Spirit.
2004 / 1-84227-321-3 / xxiv + 246pp

Anna Robbins
Methods in the Madness
Diversity in Twentieth-Century Christian Social Ethics
The author compares the ethical methods of Walter Rauschenbusch, Reinhold Niebuhr and others. She argues that unless Christians are clear about the ways that theology and philosophy are expressed practically they may lose the ability to discuss social ethics across contexts, let alone reach effective agreements.
2004 / 1-84227-211-X / xx + 294pp

Ed Rybarczyk
Beyond Salvation
Eastern Orthodoxy and Classical Pentecostalism on becoming like Christ
At first glance eastern Orthodoxy and classical Pentecostalism seem quite distinct. This ground-breaking study shows they share much in common, especially as it concerns the experiential elements of following Christ. Both traditions assert that authentic Christianity transcends the wooden categories of modernism.
2004 / 1-84227-144-X / xii + 356pp

Signe Sandsmark
Is World View Neutral Education Possible and Desirable?
A Christian Response to Liberal Arguments
(Published jointly with The Stapleford Centre)
This book discusses reasons for belief in world view neutrality, and argues that 'neutral' education will have a hidden, but strong world view influence. It discusses the place for Christian education in the common school.
2000 / 0-85364-973-1 / xiv + 182pp

Hazel Sherman
Reading Zechariah
The Allegorical Tradition of Biblical Interpretation through the Commentary of Didymus the Blind and Theodore of Mopsuestia
A close reading of the commentary on Zechariah by Didymus the Blind alongside that of Theodore of Mopsuestia suggests that popular categorising of Antiochene and Alexandrian biblical exegesis as 'historical' or 'allegorical' is inadequate and misleading.
2005 / 1-84227-213-6 / approx. 280pp

Andrew Sloane

On Being a Christian in the Academy

Nicholas Wolterstorff and the Practice of Christian Scholarship

An exposition and critical appraisal of Nicholas Wolterstorff's epistemology in the light of the philosophy of science, and an application of his thought to the practice of Christian scholarship.

2003 / 1-84227-058-3 / xvi + 274pp

Damon So

Jesus' Revelation of His Father

A Narrative-Conceptual Study of the Trinity with Special Reference to Karl Barth

This book explores the trinitarian dynamics in the context of Jesus' revelation of his Father in his earthly ministry with references to key passages in Matthew's Gospel. It develops from the exegeses of these passages a non-linear concept of revelation which links Jesus' communion with his Father to his revelatory words and actions through a nuanced understanding of the Holy Spirit, with references to K. Barth, G.W.H. Lampe, J.D.G. Dunn and E. Irving.

2005 / 1-84227-323-X / approx. 380pp

Daniel Strange

The Possibility of Salvation Among the Unevangelised

An Analysis of Inclusivism in Recent Evangelical Theology

For evangelical theologians the 'fate of the unevangelised' impinges upon fundamental tenets of evangelical identity. The position known as 'inclusivism', defined by the belief that the unevangelised can be ontologically saved by Christ whilst being epistemologically unaware of him, has been defended most vigorously by the Canadian evangelical Clark H. Pinnock. Through a detailed analysis and critique of Pinnock's work, this book examines a cluster of issues surrounding the unevangelised and its implications for christology, soteriology and the doctrine of revelation.

2002 / 1-84227-047-8 / xviii + 362pp

Scott Swain

God according to the Gospel

Biblical Narrative and the Identity of God in the Theology of Robert W. Jenson

Robert W. Jenson is one of the leading voices in contemporary Trinitarian theology. His boldest contribution in this area concerns his use of biblical narrative both to ground and explicate the Christian doctrine of God. *God according to the Gospel* critically examines Jenson's proposal and suggests an alternative way of reading the biblical portrayal of the triune God.

2006 / 1-84227-258-7 / approx. 180pp

Graham Tomlin
The Power of the Cross
Theology and the Death of Christ in Paul, Luther and Pascal
This book explores the theology of the cross in St Paul, Luther and Pascal. It offers new perspectives on the theology of each, and some implications for the nature of power, apologetics, theology and church life in a postmodern context.

1999 / 0-85364-984-7 / xiv + 344pp

Graham J. Watts
Revelation and the Spirit
A Comparative Study of the Relationship between the Doctrine of Revelation and Pneumatology in the Theology of Eberhard Jüngel and of Wolfhart Pannenberg
The relationship between Revelation and pneumatology is relatively unexplored. This approach offers a fresh angle on two important twentieth century theologians and raises pneumatological questions which are theologically crucial and relevant to mission in a postmodern culture.

2005 / 1-84227-104-0 / xxii + 232pp

Nigel G. Wright
Disavowing Constantine
Mission, Church and the Social Order in the Theologies of John Howard Yoder and Jürgen Moltmann
This book is a timely restatement of a radical theology of church and state in the Anabaptist and Baptist tradition. Dr Wright constructs his argument in dialogue and debate with Yoder and Moltmann, major contributors to a free church perspective.

2000 / 0-85364-978-2 / xvi + 252pp

Paternoster
9 Holdom Avenue
Bletchley
Milton Keynes MK1 1QR
United Kingdom

Web: www.authenticmedia.co.uk/paternoster

November 2004